Effectiveness Research in Marriage and Family Therapy

Edited by Douglas H. Sprenkle, Ph.D.

Published by
the American Association for Marriage and Family Therapy

Alexandria, VA

The American Association for Marriage and Family Therapy
promotes and advances the common professional interests of
Marriage and Family Therapists.

This document is published by:

The American Association for Marriage and Family Therapy
112 S. Alfred Street
Alexandria, VA 22314
703-838-9808
www.aamft.org

Table of Contents

About the Editor

Douglas H. Sprenkle, Ph.D., is Professor of Marriage and Family Therapy within the Department of Child Development and Family Studies at Purdue University. He received his Ph.D. from the marriage and family therapy program at the University of Minnesota in 1975. As part of his doctoral dissertation, he was one of the co-developers, with David Olson and Candyce Russell, of the Circumplex Model of Marital and Family Systems. Healthy and dysfunctional couple and family functioning remains one of his ongoing areas of research interest.

For 9 years Doug was the Director of the Doctoral Program in Marriage and Family Therapy (MFT) at Purdue. He won the Osborne Award, given biannually by the National Council on Family Relations to the outstanding teacher in family studies. He is a past Editor (1990–1997) of the *Journal of Marital and Family Therapy,* and is the author of over 100 scholarly articles and six books, including *Family Therapy Research: A Handbook of Methods* (with Sidney Moon) and the *Family Therapy Sourcebook, 2nd Edition* (with Fred Piercy and Joseph Wetchler). He also served two terms on the Commission on Accreditation for Marriage and Family Therapy Education.

Doug has received three major career achievement awards in the areas of research, teaching, and service to the profession from the American Association for Marriage and Family Therapy (AAMFT): the Cumulative Career Contribution to Marriage and Family Therapy Research, the Training Award, and the Significant Contribution to Family Therapy Award. In 2001, he was a plenary speaker at the Annual Meeting of AAMFT on the subject of the research-practice gap in MFT and what to do about it.

Doug's current areas of research include isolating common mechanisms of change across MFT theories, researching the practitioner/scientist gap in the field, and studying the relationship between family and business variables in family business families.

5

About the Contributors

C. Everett Bailey, Ph.D., Psychological Counseling Services, Ltd., Scottsdale, Arizona.

Scott A. Baldwin, B.S., Department of Psychology, The University of Memphis, Memphis, Tennessee.

Steven Beach, Ph.D., Institute for Behavioral Research, University of Georgia, Athens, Georgia.

Thomas L. Campbell, M.D., Departments of Family Medicine and Psychiatry, University of Rochester School of Medicine & Dentistry, Rochester, New York.

Lisa Dixon, M.D., School of Medicine, University of Maryland, Baltimore, Maryland.

William Fals-Stewart, Ph.D., Research Institute on Addictions, University at Buffalo, The State University of New York, Buffalo, New York.

W. Kim Halford, Ph.D., Department of Psychology, Griffith University, Queensland, Australia.

Scott W. Henggeler, Ph.D., Family Services Research Center, Department of Psychiatry and Behavioral Sciences, Medical University of South Carolina, Charleston, South Carolina.

Susan M. Johnson, Ed.D., Department of Psychology, University of Ottawa, Ottawa, Ontario, Canada.

Galena H. Kline, M.A., Department of Psychology, University of Denver, Denver, Colorado.

Howard A. Liddle, Ph.D., Center for Treatment Research on Adolescent Drug Abuse, Department of Psychiatry and Behavioral Sciences, University of Miami, Miami, Florida.

Alicia Lucksted, Ph.D., School of Medicine, University of Maryland, Baltimore, Maryland.

Ellen Lukens, D. Phil., School of Social Work, Columbia University, New York, New York.

Howard J. Markman, Ph.D., Department of Psychology, University of Denver, Denver, Colorado.

Eric E. McCollum, Ph.D., Virginia Polytechnic Institute and State University, Falls Church, Virginia.

William R. McFarlane, M.D., Department of Psychiatry, University of Vermont and Maine Medical Center, Portland, Maine.

William F. Northey, Jr., Ph.D., American Association for Marriage and Family Therapy, Alexandria, Virginia.

Timothy J. O'Farrell, Ph.D., Harvard Families and Addiction Program, Harvard Medical School Department of Psychiatry at the VA Boston Healthcare System, Brockton, Massachusetts.

Karen H. Rosen, Ed.D., Virginia Polytechnic Institute and State University Falls Church, Virginia.

Cynthia L. Rowe, Ph.D., Center for Treatment Research on Adolescent Drug Abuse, Department of Psychiatry and Behavioral Sciences, University of Miami, Miami, Florida.

William R. Shadish, Ph.D., Department of Psychology, The University of Memphis, Memphis Tennessee.

Ashli J. Sheidow, Ph.D., Family Services Research Center, Department of Psychiatry and Behavioral Sciences, Medical University of South Carolina, Charleston, South Carolina.

Wendy K. Silverman, Ph.D., Department of Psychology, Child and Family Psychosocial Research Center, Florida International University, Miami, Florida.

Douglas H. Sprenkle, Ph.D., Department of Child Development and Family Studies, Purdue University, West Lafayette, Indiana.

Scott Stanley, Ph.D., Department of Psychology, University of Denver, Denver, Colorado.

Sandra M. Stith, Ph.D., Virginia Polytechnic Institute and State University, Falls Church, Virginia.

Karen C. Wells, Ph.D., Department of Psychiatry and Behavioral Sciences, Division of Medical Psychology, Duke University Medical Center, Durham, North Carolina.

Acknowledgments

The editor and publisher would like to thank the participants of the 2002 AAMFT Research Conference and other reviewers for providing feedback on early drafts of the chapters.

Mary Ann Adams, Sheila M. Addison, James F. Alexander, Jared R. Anderson, C. Everett Bailey, Steven Beach, Richard J. Bischoff, Josephine Bonomo, Michael Bowers, Gayle Boyd, Kay P. Bradford, Brent A. Bradley, Kathleen Briggs, Gregory W. Brock, Penny S. Brucker, Thomas L. Campbell, Jason S. Carroll, Andrew Christensen, Jennifer J. Connor, Thomas A. Cornille, Darci B. Cramer-Benjamin, D. Russell Crane, Becky R. Davenport, Wayne Holt Denton, Megan L. Dolbin-MacNab, Jason H. Edwards, Todd M. Edwards, Scott A. Edwards, Rhonda A. Faulkner, Jerry E. Gale, Karen Gautney, Harold Goldsmith, William A. Griffin, Suzanne Hanna, Jennifer L. Harkness, Steven M. Harris, Scott Henggeler, Jennifer R. Hill, Kristen E. Holm, Mary E. Hotvedt, Douglas W. Huenergardt, David C. Ivey, Susan M. Johnson, Lee N. Johnson, Margaret K. Keiley, Scott A. Ketring, Thomas G. Kimball, Carmen Knudson-Martin, Steven M. Kogan, Judith Landau, Christopher R. Latty, Jeffry H. Larson, Jay Lebow, Janie Long, David P. Mackinnon, Howard Markman, Nina Martin, Eric E. McCollum, William McFarlane, Marcia L. Michaels, Richard B. Miller, James P. Morris, Rajeswari Natrajan, Thorana S. Nelson, Briana S. Nelson, William F. Northey, Mark Odell, Timothy O'Farrell, Michael M. Olson, F. Ryan Peterson, Colleen M. Peterson, Shruti S. Poulsen, Melissa Racioppo, Belinda Richardson, W. David Robinson, Karen H. Rosen, Cynthia Rowe, Robert G. Ryder, Jonathan G. Sandberg, Thomas L. Sexton, William Shadish, Sterling T. Shumway, Patricia L. Sims, Justin M. Smith, Angela L. Smith, Craig W. Smith, Douglas H. Sprenkle, Sandra M. Stith, Volker K. Thomas, Stephanie R. Walsh, Karen S. Wampler, Richard S. Wampler, Linna Wang, Darwin R. West, Mark B. White, Jason B. Whiting, Elizabeth A. Wieling, Amanda S. Willert, Darren A. Wozny, Christine MiYoung Yoon, and Chunhong Zhang.

Chapter 1   *Editor's Introduction*

Douglas H. Sprenkle, Ph.D., Department of Child Development and Family
Studies, Purdue University, West Lafayette, Indiana.

This volume offers compelling evidence that marriage and family therapy
(MFT) has made major strides in becoming a more evidence-based discipline.
This progress is quite remarkable given that as recently as the late 1980s, the
field could be characterized as a coterie of competing religions. As A. J.
Werry wrote as recently as 1989:

> Sadly, at the moment, family therapy has many of the hallmarks of a
> religion with several competing sects led by feuding charismatic
> prophets each claiming to have a premium on the truth, but with few of
> the attributes of a profession rooted in ethics and skepticism. (p. 381)

Although many family therapists, in my judgment, are still too influenced by
charismatic model developers and unsubstantiated claims, the papers here give
me the confidence to say that Werry's blanket indictment of the field is no longer
valid.

My confidence in the *science* of MFT has been greatly increased by the
recent developments in the field, which are emphasized in this volume. In 1995,
when I was Editor of the *Journal of Marital and Family Therapy,* the American
Association for Marriage and Family Therapy (AAMFT) published its first major
review of research as a special issue of the Journal, guest edited by William
Pinsof and Lyman Wynne (1995). Although that volume offered fairly robust evidence for the efficacy of MFT interventions, there has been a dramatic increase
in the number and quality of investigations across almost all the areas of
research. Many conclusions that were tentative then, now appear to be more
definitive. Many interventions that appeared promising then, now are backed by
credible outcome data.

To be sure, the evidence across all the areas reviewed here is uneven and certain topics/approaches remain empirically underdeveloped. Nonetheless, the
overall picture regarding the science of MFT has, in my judgment, improved
quite dramatically. I believe even the most hard-nosed MFT skeptic, after reading (especially) the chapters here on family-based treatment related to drug
abuse, conduct disorder and delinquency, alcoholism, and family management of
schizophrenia (not coincidentally the areas in which there has been the most
high-quality, accretive, programmatic research) will no longer question the legit-
imacy of at least these models. In terms of what the disbelieving outside world
wants of us, then, MFT is clearly showing signs of coming of age.

Purpose, Scope, and Intended Audience of This Volume

The purpose of this volume is to present a state-of-the-art assessment of research in MFT—what we know, don't know, and what we need to know and do—both substantively and methodologically. The subtopics covered include family interventions for conduct disorder and delinquency (chapter 2), substance abuse (3), childhood behavior disorders (4), alcohol abuse (5), marital problems (6), relationship enhancement (7), domestic violence (8), severe mental illness (9), affective disorders (10), physical disorders (11), and meta-analysis of MFT interventions (12). There were no chapters on relationship enhancement or domestic violence in the 1995 volume. We included them both to reflect research being carried out in these areas and to encourage more investigations on these important topics. The areas covered are far from comprehensive, however, since we tried to emphasize themes for which there have been clinical trials (in which treatment subjects are assigned randomly to experimental and control groups under carefully monitored conditions). Although there are limitations to clinical trials research, some of which are noted below, they remain the "gold standard" for recognition by the scientific community and by external audiences. This emphasis also means that other important types of research, like qualitative investigations, are unfortunately not given much attention.

To give a historical perspective, authors were specifically asked to make connections between the previous research reviews, especially Pinsof and Wynne (1995), and the conclusions they would make in the current volume. We wanted you, the reader, to gain a better sense of how research in these areas has evolved over time and where progress has been most rapid or restrained. The authors also wrote good summaries, so you can profitably skim the volume for major ideas before reading it in detail.

We also wanted this series of papers to have broad appeal. Family therapy research has many stakeholders (Doherty, 1997). Although we expected other researchers to be interested in this volume, other important stakeholders of MFT research include:

- Clinicians, who seek guidance for best practices.
- Teachers and trainers, who are the purveyors of knowledge for the next generation of MFTs.
- Governance structures within MFT professional organizations, like AAMFT, which represent the field to a variety of constituencies.
- The mass media, who tell vastly more people about MFT than do members of the profession.
- Policymakers, whose decisions are informed by research.
- Insurers and provider organizations, which are increasingly demanding evidence-based treatments.

Without compromising sound scholarship and integrity (these papers are, first and foremost, scientific research reviews), we tried to make them at least somewhat relevant to this diverse group of stakeholders. We were most deliberate about wanting to help clinicians to see connections between these research findings and the world of practice. Specifically, all authors were challenged to spell out implications of these findings for clinical decision making and the practice of MFT. These were the sections of these papers that were most often edited and re-written, as I tried to take this mission quite seriously. In addition, authors were asked to note with asterisks (**) in their reference lists, books and treatment manuals that were specifically written for clinicians, or chapters or papers that are particularly rich with clinical illustrations or details. I hope that this will help make the related materials more accessible, and will also encourage clinicians to read more about the models described in the studies.

These efforts were done in recognition of the fact that over 80% of the members of AAMFT work in settings that can be considered predominantly clinical (Sprenkle, Bailey, Lyness, Ball, & Mills, 1997). I wanted this volume to speak to this constituency. Another reason for this thrust is my ongoing belief that a major gap exists between research and practice in MFT, and that the consequences of this gap are highly deleterious for the field.

The Research-Practice Gap in MFT and the False Dichotomy Between Clinical Judgment and the Scientific Method

The researcher-practice gap, which plagues all clinical fields, may be particularly prevalent in MFT:

> The culture [of MFT] does not support research. Ours remains a field where it is still possible for a highly charismatic individual to create a model of family therapy, become successful on the workshop circuit, and get lucrative book contracts to promulgate the model without offering evidence for its efficacy beyond personal testimony. In many ways, rock-star status is accorded the clinical model developers and the "master therapists." Researchers, when contrasted with the "stars," are at best warm-up acts, and at worst bit players. (Crane, Wampler, Sprenkle, Sandberg, & Hovestadt, 2002, p.76)

On the other side, ours also remains a field in which researchers sometimes disdain clinicians, fail to listen to the wisdom of good clinicians, and typically do not work very hard at making their work clinically accessible.

Only a few of the disastrous consequences of this split will be highlighted here. *In the first place*, since research is often inaccessible or appears unrelated to the concerns of clinicians, research often gets dismissed as irrelevant, incomprehensible, or both. Practice is not research informed, and errors are perpetuated (Heppner, Kivlighan, & Wampold, 1999).

In the second place, the gap perpetuates a false dichotomy between clinical judgment and the scientific method. Larry Beutler and his colleagues have written:

Art and science are not enemies. The painter operates within the bounds of physical laws—blue and yellow make green; when two objects occur in close juxtaposition, they appear related, and so on. The effective artist works within these laws to apply novel contexts and interpretations. In the same way, the effective [evidenced based] therapist is more than a technician who applies sterile technologies to solve problems. (Beutler, Bongar, & Shurkin, 1998, p. 75)

As Goodyear and Benton (1986) put it: "The best scientists overlap with the best artists in their capacity for alternative ways of perceiving, in their creativity, and in their openness to new experiences" (p.290). Even if family therapy were to become much more informed by science, it will never become the equivalent of "paint by the numbers." Even if we were to discover the most potent change mechanisms for particular clients under particular sets of circumstances (the dream of some researchers), it will always require clinical artistry to *implement* these change mechanisms.

Clinical judgment and the scientific method are two overlapping ways of knowing, both to be valued and both to be questioned. The primary contribution of the science of therapy is that it forces us to use certain *rules of evidence* in the same way that the court system requires certain rules of evidence—for example, no "hearsay" evidence is allowed in court. I once heard someone say, perhaps cynically, that, "science is a set of rules to minimize our lying to each other." Perhaps this is another way of saying that science recognizes that people promoting a clinical model/technique look at their own work through their own filters and lenses. Many of the rules of science are organized common sense, like: "to be claimed effective, therapy models must be replicated in neutral settings by investigators not so personally invested in proving the model." Or, "to be claimed effective, therapy models must be compared with credible alternatives," since clients will almost always report that treatments are helpful. To the best of my knowledge, no psychotherapy theory has ever been abandoned on the basis of informal client feedback!

What is the alternative to having these rules? As W. M. Pinsof (personal communication, July 20, 2001) has said, the alternative is the *jungle,* where whoever is the most charismatic, and persuasive, and powerful predominates. Is that what we really want for our field?

Is science ever wrong? Certainly! The science of the day led medics to bleed people, led nutritionists to reject foods as worthless that contained few vitamins, which we now know are rich in antioxidants. In MFT, early studies led the founders of behavioral marital therapy to think it more effective than it was. In sex therapy, Masters and Johnson's early research created the impression that sex therapy techniques were miracle cures.

But the strength of science is that it is *correctable.* Good scientists know the limits of samples and probability theory. They hedge their conclusions and suggest alternative explanations for their findings. I give enormous credit, for example, to the late Neil Jacobson, one of the founders/leaders of Behavioral Marital Therapy (BMT). He had the fortitude to apply more rigorous outcome criteria as his research progressed, and to expose his own model as *less successful* than he had originally thought. What did Jacobson do then? He modified the model in response to research feedback, not once but at least twice. First, he took a primarily behavioral model and added a cognitive emphasis. Later, when this change proved insufficient, his data led him and his colleagues to add components of "affect" and "acceptance" to the model (Jacobsen & Christensen, 1996).

In the third place, the research-practice gap challenges our status as an ethical profession. The AAMFT Code of Ethics clearly requires us to advance the welfare of client. But, how can we do that if most practitioners have insufficient information regarding which of our treatments are effective, which do little good, and which may cause harm? Can we be a responsible profession without greater attention to what has been called the "ethics of evidence?" (Mike, 1999). While I have great respect for clinical wisdom as one avenue of truth, as with science, it can sometimes not only be wrong, but also harmful. If there were ever to be a family therapy "Hall of Shame," it would have to include, for example, MFTs blaming families, and especially mothers, for their schizophrenic offspring.

In the fourth place, since the gap has led to the devaluing of research in MFT, it has contributed to the field's "outsourcing" most of our research to those whose primary professional discipline is something other than MFT. Only 1 of the 21 authors in the 1995 research review (Pinsof & Wynne, 1995) was a graduate of an MFT program and none was currently affiliated with an MFT program (Crane et al., 2002). In the current volume, the situation has improved but not dramatically. Of the 27 authors, 6 (including myself) are graduates of the Commission on Accreditation for Marriage and Family Therapy Education (COAMFTE) accredited programs and 4 are currently affiliated with such programs. While I am grateful to the (primarily) psychologists and psychiatrists who have done the work, I also have major concerns about the "outsourcing" of our research. Those who are primarily marriage and family therapists ought to be taking key roles in determining the treatments tested, the variables examined, and the outcomes measured. As Crane et al. (2002) put it:

> We have to take responsibility for setting the research agenda and training the requisite MFT researchers and stop depending on other disciplines to do it for us...No one else will do research on MFT training. No one else will do research on matters that are uniquely important to MFTs. (p. 78)

Furthermore, a fair percentage of the research in the 1995 volume was not about the MFT that most of us practice. In the current volume many of the interventions tested, while significant and important "family" interventions (like parent training, or family education and support, or family psychoeducation), are not interventions conducted by a family therapist using systems theories or models. Although this can be positively reframed as evidence for the multidisciplinary nature of MFT (Pinsof & Wynne, 1995), to the extent that it represents the failure of MFTs to research their distinctive models, it is not a virtue.

What Are Empirically Supported Treatments?

Ever since Hans Esynck delivered a potentially devastating critique of psychotherapy in the 1950s, researchers have been concerned with how to demonstrate that treatments have credible empirical support. In the 1960s, '70s, and '80s they developed increasingly tight methodologies. More formal criteria were adapted in the 1990s by both the American Psychiatric Association and Division 12 of the American Psychological Association. Psychologists Chambless and Hollon (1998) offered criteria for what has taken on the formal name of "empirically supported treatments" or ESTs. This designation requires that clinical subjects be randomly assigned to a specified treatment, a no-treatment control, and an alternative treatment or a placebo control. The therapy has to demonstrate that it is significantly better than a no-treatment group or placebo, and at least equally as good as a previously established alternative. Furthermore, the studies should require treatment manuals, well-specified criteria for including or excluding subjects, reliable and valid outcome measures, and appropriate statistical analysis. To meet the criteria of "efficacious," there should be at least two independent investigations that meet these standards. To meet the criteria of "possibly efficacious," only one study is required. To be considered both "efficacious and specific," the approach needs to be demonstrated as superior to alternative treatments in at least two independent demonstrations meeting the standards noted above (Beach, 2002).

Criticisms of the EST Movement

While strongly supporting the value of evidence-informed practice, there have been critical voices both outside (Wampold, 2001) and inside family therapy (Duncan & Miller, 2000) concerning the EST movement. These authors raise serious questions about what being an EST means. For one thing, they note that certain treatments have been "privileged" to have been researched far more than others, and the EST movement erroneously sends a subtle message that little-researched models are inferior or worthless. ESTs also promote a kind of homogeneity of treatment for problems that are themselves not homogeneous (e.g. depression is multicausal). Therefore, ESTs are believed to reduce treatment options, client choice, and do not pay sufficient attention to client "fit" with a particular treatment approach or the unique nature of the client's problems. They create the erroneous assumption that therapy is something "done" by a therapist, using a standardized procedure, to a "passive" client; and that the reason for success has much more to do with the method than the client's own efforts. Finally, these authors question whether the kind of highly controlled trials, necessary to establish an EST, have much to do with the real world of clinical practice.

In chapter 12 of the current volume, Shadish and Baldwin raise some additional concerns about ESTs that are less philosophical. Shadish is a leading proponent of meta-analysis. For those not familiar with this procedure, it is a quantitative method of combining results from multiple studies, typically by creating a common metric called an "effect size." A common metric is necessary because studies typically use different outcome measures, and therefore comparing their results is like comparing apples and oranges. The most common effect size is the standardized difference between group means. If an approach achieves an effect size of 1.0 across studies, this means, on average, that the mean of the experimental group on the outcome measure is one standard deviation unit higher than the mean of the control group.

Shadish and Baldwin (chapter 12, this volume) argue that the label of EST implies a too narrow understanding of what has been evaluated empirically. They assert that 25 years of accumulated meta-analytic research is marginalized since there is significant empirical support for a large number of therapies that are not on the official EST list. They believe that ESTs are really only one type of empirically supported treatment and might, more accurately, be called "effective, manualized, population-specific treatments." A variety of procedures have achieved considerable recognition from scholarly and governmental bodies based on meta-analytic summaries, even though these procedures do not have manuals or meet other criteria for ESTs. Furthermore, the EST criteria place too much emphasis on statistical significance and thereby marginalize studies in which there is insufficient statistical power.

Shadish and Baldwin (chapter 12) propose what they call "meta-analytically supported treatments" or MASTs. They then go on to specify a fairly rigorous set of criteria for an approach to be considered a MAST. For example, all the studies contributing to the meta-analysis of the approach must be randomized trials comparing the treatment to a control group. Whereas only about 5 MFT approaches meet the criteria for ESTs, 24 meet the criteria for MASTs, including broad categories like family therapy in general, and more narrow treatments such as emotion focused therapy for couples (which is also an EST).

I personally welcome Shadish and Baldwin's recasting of what can be considered a rigorously empirically supported treatment, because this broadening can be done without compromising scientific integrity. I also agree with these authors that the term EST relates to a specific kind of empirically supported treatment. I also concur with the aforementioned critics that we should be cautious about the conclusions we draw from the knowledge that an approach is an EST. Certainly we can't leap to conclusions like "other approaches are worthless," or that an EST will necessarily be the best approach (fit) for this particular client (or therapist).

At the same time, if the conclusions we draw about what it means to be an EST are held in check, I think we can and should support this movement. Demonstrating that approaches are effective under these carefully controlled conditions is an important step because, if an approach is not effective under these circumstances, it is probably not worth pursuing. Then, further research can demonstrate the extent to which the method also works when the method is applied more flexibly across a broader range of clients and problems. In chapter 6 of this volume, for example, Sue Johnson, one of the founders of emotion focused therapy (EFT), which also has earned the designation as an EST, marshals evidence that this model works effectively in real world settings, with typical clients, and with therapists who use the treatment manual flexibly.

Earlier I mentioned that without credible empirical support, the MFT field would not have credibility in the outside world. Although an internal debate about the limits of these methods is helpful, and prevents us from drawing erroneous or overstated conclusions, we cannot divorce ourselves from the scientific method as one avenue of truth, without marginalizing the discipline. As Carol Anderson (1986) put it so eloquently, and presciently, over a decade and a half ago:

> As a field, we must address the issue of what constitutes acceptable evidence of efficacy and how we go about obtaining it. It is absolutely vital that the field of family therapy develop a respect for research, knowledge of basic research methods, and the requirements of scientific inquiry. Without this knowledge and respect, the field of family therapy will not continue to develop and will not receive the support it requires from academic institutions, governmental policies or funding agencies. This does not mean that we must all do research, nor that we need to use empirical methods that do not reflect systems thinking. It does mean, however, that we must be able to evaluate research and that we must hold to its basic tenets. We must evaluate ourselves and our colleagues, using strict research criteria, or we will be no different from psychoanalysts whose work has become increasingly discounted rather than accepted. In the world of increased emphasis on cost-effectiveness and decreased resources, unless we can offer proof of efficacy, acceptable to the scientific community, we will eventually cease to exist. (p. 353)

Methodological Strengths of the Research Reported in This Volume

Recognizing, then, that science and the scientific method are avenues of truth, which, despite their limitations, should be honored, what are the strengths of the research reported in this volume?

- Almost all the research is based on randomized clinical trials.
- The majority of the chapters report on methods that have been manualized.
- The majority of chapters report on methods that have been replicated by

independent investigators.

- The majority of the chapters report on interventions for which there was close supervision and training of the therapists.
- In about half the chapters evidence is offered for adherence to treatment protocols, and treatment fidelity is also linked to outcome.
- The majority of chapters report the use of multiple outcome measures including nonreactive dependent variables like incarceration, hospitalization, etc.
- The majority of chapters report on special efforts to recruit/retain subjects, and many family treatments have demonstrated great success in recruiting/retaining difficult subjects.
- Most of the chapters report attention to comorbidity and research being done with multiproblem subjects and families.
- The majority of chapters pay attention to the issue of the transportability of the results to practice settings.
- In most of the areas reported, there is long-term follow-up data of several years or more.
- In almost all the areas, there are systematic, accretive research programs, so that one study can build on another.
- In almost half of the areas, there have been efforts to identify the mechanisms of change (why and how the interventions seem to work) through process research.
- The theoretical rationale for many of the interventions is grounded in basic (nonintervention) social science research linking family dynamics and problematic behavior, e.g., the link between poor parent-adolescent relationships and teenage drug abuse. Therefore many of the family approaches have a strong empirically based theoretical rationale in literatures related to child development and family studies.

These strengths are not distributed equally. Furthermore, some of the methodological concerns raised by Pinsof and Wynne in 1995 remain. For example, there is still no set of core common outcome measures to facilitate comparisons across studies. Only three of the chapters offer evidence regarding the economic evaluation of the methods described (cost effectiveness/cost benefit research), in spite of the great importance of these evaluations to the field.

The Challenges Facing MFT Research

Because of these strengths, marriage and family therapy research has earned a place at the table of credibility. However, this is hardly a time for complacency because the tasks that lie ahead are quite daunting. In the remainder of this chapter, I will describe some of the challenges facing MFT research in the coming decades.

The Challenge of Transportability

Perhaps one of the ironies of the current volume is that some of most impressive results are achieved with the most difficult treatment populations (e.g., with families of drug abusers, delinquents, alcoholics, and schizophrenics). Yet, the authors of these chapters also spend the most time talking about the challenges of transporting their models to real world settings. O'Farrell and Fals-Stewart (chapter 5), for example, note that none of the alcohol research has been done in office settings. McFarlane, Dixon, Lukens, and Lucksted (chapter 9) bemoan that family approaches to schizophrenia are rarely offered outside of research settings and that its "… use in clinical practice is alarmingly limited." Perhaps this is not surprising, because achieving success with these difficult treatment groups often requires developing comprehensive programs that impact the larger ecology in which the problems are embedded. For teenage drug abuse and conduct disorders, for example, therapy is not your typical 1 hour per week outpatient psychotherapy. Therapists must be extensively trained and supervised. They often have small caseloads because they are sometimes required to be available 24 hours per day and must network with peers, schools, and other community resources. In the case of Multisystemic Therapy for conduct disordered youth (described by Henggeler and Sheidow in chapter 2), the therapists are also unusually well-paid in order to recruit and retain the most talented personnel. These programs get the results they do, in part, because of a large upfront investment. They are cost-effective because the things they prevent (arrests, incarceration, hospitalization) are even more expensive.

Transporting these programs to typical clinical settings also requires an enormous upfront investment. These models certainly cannot be learned effectively in brief trainings, let alone a weekend workshop. The authors also offer evidence that there is a marked deterioration of results without adequate training and supervision. (The evidence these programs offer for the value of supervision may be helpful to MFT because the field has always stressed the value of supervision, and MFT is one of the few professions that mandate special training for supervisors.)

Furthermore, the process of transporting these programs to existing agencies, with established methods and entrenched bureaucracies, is highly political. In chapter 9, William McFarlane and colleagues recount in great detail some of the barriers erected by patients, clinicians, administrators, and mental health authorities. McFarlane et al. offer a fascinating account of a success as well as a failure in transporting family programs for schizophrenics, and MFTs would do well to study their reflections on the process. It is not surprising that Henggeler and Sheidow (chapter 2) concluded that transportability requires a very different set of skills than developing and evaluating a treatment model. Nonetheless, they also believe that the field is primed for transportability research and that this will be one of the most important research agendas in the future.

Problems in transportability relate, of course, to the issues of the generalizability and external validity of our findings. These problems are also the basis for one of the aforementioned criticisms of ESTs. For this reason the case could be made that most of our research remains what has technically been called "efficacy" research; or research that determines whether a treatment works under more ideal "research-therapy" conditions, as opposed to "effectiveness" research, or research that works under "normal therapy" field conditions (Pinsof & Wynne, 1995, p. 342). There is much more attention given in the current volume to the issue of transportability than in 1995, but the number of actual studies done in real world conditions still remains limited. Research on emotion focused couples therapy (chapter 6) may be a welcome exception. It is also encouraging that the National Institute of Mental Health has recognized the problem and is encouraging and funding more field research.

The Challenge of Cultural Adaptation and Individual/Family Difference
A tour through the "suggestions for future research" sections of the various chapters highlights the need for more research regarding cultural adaptation of these treatment models as well as adaptations for individual and family differences. Examples include: the need to adapt the conduct disorder programs for youth with serious mental disturbances, more research on the alcohol programs with women and minorities, how to adapt family schizophrenia models for Asian families, and more research on the use of couples therapy with gay partners. The demands of a more diverse culture will necessitate such effort. Perhaps this research thrust will also address the criticism that ESTs assume a homogeneous population that rarely exists. The challenge of cultural adaptation is one example of the larger concern, raised by Pinsof and Wynne in 1995, that MFT research needs to be guided by a differentiated clinical theory that specifies the interaction among treatments, disorder/problems, and patient/system moderating variables (Pinsof & Wynne, 1995).

The Challenge of the Common Factors Movement
The next two challenges are rooted in the concern that we know much more about what treatments work than why they work. The chief advocates for the common factors approach in MFT have been Hubbell, Duncan, and Miller (1999). They assert that we give too much importance to our sacred models and techniques when we try to explain why change occurs. Rather, according to the common factors scholars, change occurs because treatment activates a series of common change mechanisms that are believed to operate in all effective psychotherapies. These authors draw heavily on research reviews in the individual psychotherapy literature by such notables as Michael Lambert (1992) and, more recently, Bruce Wampold (2001). However, their ideas have empirical support in the MFT research literature in the meta-analysis chapters in both the 1995 *Journal of Marital and Family Therapy* special issue (Shadish, Ragsdale, Glaser, & Montgomery, 1995), as well as in the Shadish and Baldwin chapter (chapter

12) in the current volume. Specifically, Shadish et al.'s data support the assertion that while MFT approaches offer clear evidence of effectiveness, there is little evidence that they are *differentially* effective (relative to each other). In 1995, Shadish et al. put it this way: "Despite some superficial evidence apparently favoring some orientations over others, no orientation is yet demonstrably superior to any other. This finding parallels the psychotherapy literature generally" (p. 348). These authors then went on to assert that what modest theoretical orientation differences do show up may be the result of confounds with other variables like client characteristics, the use of different and/or reactive measures, and so forth. When these authors entered potential methodological confounds into a regression analysis, all orientation differences disappeared. In the current volume, Shadish and Baldwin conclude that "... there is little evidence for differential efficacy among the various approaches to marriage and family interventions, particularly if mediating and moderating variables are controlled." They demonstrate, for example, how some therapies look better simply because they use measures that are more reactive to change. It is the choice of a particular measure, not the intervention itself, that leads to a greater effect size. Therefore, although differences between treatments do show up in individual studies, they tend to disappear in meta-analyses when these confounds are controlled across large numbers of studies.

The common factors scholars do not suggest that models are worthless, but rather that they work mainly for reasons that are not unique or specific to the models (Blow & Sprenkle, 2001). Rather, all successful methods activate common change mechanisms that are thought to be primarily responsible for change. Examples include a strong working alliance with the client (including an emotional bond, shared goals, and a set of therapeutic tasks that seem credible to the client), the therapist's belief that the therapy is efficacious, the client's confidence in the therapist, and the client's involvement/participation/commitment to change. Furthermore, many interventions that have different names in diverse models are conceptually and practically quite similar (Sprenkle, Blow, & Dickey, 1999). Based on his comprehensive meta-analysis of individual psychotherapy, Wampold (2001) estimates that only about eight percent of psychotherapeutic variance is due to specific effects (linked with particular therapeutic models). Although this result is hardly the last word on the subject (and the analysis was not primarily performed on MFT data), it is very provocative for our field, which has placed such a strong emphasis on differences among models.

The common factors argument is a challenge to our field in at least two ways. First, whatever one thinks of the common factors argument, the major meta-analyses in the MFT research literature appear to support the argument. Either there are, in fact, no meaningful differences among our models; or, alternatively there are differences but they are too "fine grained" to be teased out by extant research methods or the research questions we are asking. Certainly, the burden of proof rests on the proponents of specificity, and this constitutes a challenge to the proponents of model uniqueness. A very positive outcome of addressing this challenge would be more process research that examines the mechanism of change (why change occurs) within our models. Although the current chapters offer some evidence that this research is happening, this task is still in its infancy.

Second, the common factors argument challenges us to look for more commonalities among our methods. For example, as one reads about the three powerful and effective models described in chapter 2 of this volume on the treatment of conduct disorders, one gets the clear impression that there are significant areas of overlap among them. In fact, the authors, Henggeler and Sheidow clearly state: "Although each of the aforementioned evidence-based treatments were developed independently, they share several commonalities in their conceptualization, delivery, and procedures." They note that particularly as the models are moved into real life community settings, the reasons for their success and the parallels among the programs take on heightened interest. In chapter 9 of this volume on schizophrenia, the authors write that the World Schizophrenia Fellowship spurred the major treatment model developers to develop a consensus, based first on empirical evidence, regarding the key components that cut across models. The authors note that, "...this process led to convergence of concept rather than the usual process of the field splitting into competing schools." Subsequent research has demonstrated that, when these core ingredients are present, disparate methods work about equally well. This search for commonalities seems to have been very fruitful. I have written elsewhere that the history of family therapy has been a history of accentuating differences (Sprenkle et al., 1999). Perhaps it is time to place more emphasis on the search for common mechanisms of change.

The Challenge To Help Clinicians "Make Their Next Move"

Although the research in this volume will hopefully help reduce the researcher-clinician gap, it will not close it. While the volume offers helpful guidance about treatments that work, and even some about approaches that apparently don't (e.g., the famous Johnson Institute intervention to get alcoholics to accept treatment), clinicians want information, *during* treatment, regarding their "next move."

This is essentially the argument set forth by William Pinsof and Lyman Wynne (2000) in their very influential article on what they called "progress research." The process of medicine became truly scientific (and the research and practice gap was reduced markedly) when physicians gained tools (e.g., blood pressure gauges, electrocardiographs) that enabled them to rely on feedback in the course of treatment to make decisions about their next move. Pinsof and Wynne argued that therapists need means for obtaining information about client change systems *during* therapy, what Howard, Moras, Brill, Martinovich, and

Lutz (1996) called "client-focused" research. Pinsof and Wynne argued further, as do the common factors critics, that both efficacy and effectiveness research suffer from a uniformity myth, and that most good therapy is "disciplined improvisation." They argued that a major research emphasis should be on how clients learn and how therapists can facilitate this process. This would reduce the attention to "uniform" treatment models and increase attention to client change processes (Helmeke & Sprenkle, 2000). This would also require more attention to proximal outcomes, rather than just final outcomes at the end of therapy. In my judgment this research agenda could keep the field busy for at least the next 50 years!

The Challenge of Research "Where the Money Isn't"

I was struck in reading these chapters how the most impressive research is clearly linked to the areas where major research dollars are at work. All of the authors, and many of the investigators (but not all—e.g., Functional Family Therapy) described in the chapters on drug abuse, conduct disorder, alcoholism, and schizophrenia, run full-time, well-funded research teams that are housed in medical schools. (As an aside, it will be very challenging for teaching faculty in MFT programs to compete for these dollars.) It is also clear that these problems are characterized by highly florid symptoms that are very disruptive (and costly) to society. While I am impressed by, and value this research, I am also concerned that less "disruptive" behavior may not get the attention it deserves. For example, there appears to be much more research money for "externalizing" problems of youth than for "internalizing" disorders like anxiety and depression. Because the depressed child, seated in the classroom, is much less disruptive (unless, unfortunately he or she commits suicide) than his or her conduct disorder counterpart, the former apparently gets much less research attention.

Therefore, a lot of the more generic and less "disruptive" (at least in the eyes of society) problems that clinicians face daily are, relatively speaking, researched less. For example, there is nothing in the current volume on research related to eating disorders, or on common couple problems like infidelity.

The challenge of doing research "where the money isn't" is formidable but not impossible. Sue Johnson, for example, the author of chapter 6 on Marital Therapy, has run a consistent, productive research program without major funding. It is quite remarkable that this "shoestring" operation has produced a research record worthy of her model (EFT) being designated an EST. Along with the "big grants persons," she can also be a role model for the next generation of MFT researchers.

Implications for Training

If MFT is to continue to grow as an evidence-based discipline, this will also have major implications for how MFTs are trained. Although most of our COAMFTE accredited programs are excellent models for clinical training, they are mostly grossly deficient as models for research training, both on the masters and doctoral levels (Crane et al., 2002). Sadly, this probably reflects the culture of family therapy generally, which has heretofore not valued research. Family therapy training often remains focused on learning the classic models of family therapy, as though they are primarily responsible for therapeutic change—an assumption that is dubious at best, and borders on professional scandal, at worst (Sprenkle et al., 1999). Many family therapy faculty were themselves not trained in evidenced-based models and methodologies, and research training is largely outsourced to members of other professions. Given these training issues, it is hardly surprising that few graduates of the MFT programs are the leading researchers who are publishing in volumes like this one.

Fortunately, the AAMFT Board of Directors has recognized this serious problem and in 1998 made the promotion of the scientist-practitioner model in its training programs one of the six major goals of the Association. Perhaps publishing this volume only 7 years after the first AAMFT sponsored review, publishing research reports in the *Family Therapy Magazine,* making the theme of the 2001 Annual Meeting of AAMFT "Evidenced-Based Therapy," sponsoring a series of three special Research Conferences, and now requiring that "empirical" models be taught in accredited programs, are all indications that the culture of MFT is beginning to change. The reader is referred to Crane et al. (2002) for a very comprehensive list of specific suggestions regarding improving research training in our academic programs. Among other things these authors recommend are: requiring empirical master's theses, creating research practica and internships, and making postdoctoral research training normative.

Conclusion

This editor's introduction began with a fairly positive assessment of the "state of the art" of MFT research that appears in this volume. At least in comparison with the state of the field even a decade and a half ago, the quantity and quality of research has improved dramatically. I tempered this conclusion, however, with a number of major challenges that the field will need to address in ensuing decades, especially if we are serious about bridging the disastrous gap between researchers and clinicians that continues to plague the field.

I hope that you will enjoy these papers and that they will enrich both your thinking and, if relevant, your practice. I would like to conclude with the thought that the best and most sensitive clinicians and researchers have taught us that MFT is an extraordinarily complex operation that defies simple description. We need the wisdom of both art and science to grasp it. It is this very complexity that enables me to stay excited about what I do as an MFT clinician/researcher, even in the seventh decade of my life.

References

Anderson, C. M. (1986). The all-too-short trip from positive to negative connotation. *Journal of Marital and Family Therapy, 12*, 351–354.

Beach, S. (2002, July). *Marital and family therapy for depression.* Paper presented at the American Association for Marriage and Family Therapy Research Conference, Reno, NV.

Blow, A. J., & Sprenkle, D. H. (2001). Common factors across theories of marriage and family therapy: A modified Delphi study. *Journal of Marital and Family Therapy, 27*, 385–402.

Beutler, L. E., Bongar, B., & Shurkin, J. N. (1998). *A consumer's guide to psychotherapy.* New York: Oxford University Press.

Chambless, D. L., & Hollon, S. D. (1998). Defining empirically supported therapies. *Journal of Consulting and Clinical Psychology, 66*, 7–18.

Crane, D. R., Wampler, K. S., Sprenkle, D. H., Sandberg, J. G., & Hovestadt, A. J. (2002). The scientist-practitioner model in marriage and family therapy doctoral programs. *Journal of Marital and Family Therapy, 28*, 75–83.

Doherty, W. J. (1997, July). *Stakeholders in marriage and family therapy research.* Paper presented at the American Association for Marriage and Family Therapy Research Conference, Santa Fe, NM.

Duncan, B. L., & Miller, S. D. (2000). *The heroic client: Doing client directed, outcome-informed therapy.* San Francisco: Jossey-Bass.

Goodyear, R. K., & Benton, S. (1986). The rules of science and research in the counselor's work. In A. J. Palmo & W. J. Weikel (Eds.), *Foundations of mental health counseling* (pp. 287–308). Springfield, IL: Charles C. Thomas.

Helmeke, K. B., & Sprenkle, D. H. (2000). Clients' perceptions of pivotal moments in couple's therapy: A qualitative study of change in therapy. *Journal of Marital and Family Therapy, 26*, 469–484.

Heppner, P. P., Kivlighan, D. M., & Wampold, B. E. (1999). *Research design in counseling, 2nd ed.* Belmont, CA: Wadsworth.

Hubbell, M. A., Duncan, B. L., & Miller, S. (1999). *The heart and soul of change: What works in therapy.* Washington, DC: The American Psychological Association.

Howard, K. I., Moras, K., Brill, P. L., Martinovich, Z., & Lutz, W. (1996). The evaluation of psychotherapy: Efficacy, effectiveness, patient progress. *American Psychologist, 51*, 1059–1064.

Jacobson, N. S., & Christensen, A. (1996). *Integrative couple therapy: Promoting acceptance and change.* New York: W.W. Norton.

Lambert, M. J. (1992). Psychotherapy outcome research: Implications for integrative and eclectic therapists. In J. C. Norcross & M. R. Goldfried (Eds.), *Handbook of psychotherapy integration* (pp. 94–129). New York: Basic Books.

Mike, V. (1999). Outcome research and the quality of healthcare. *Evaluation and the Health Professions, 22*, 3–22.

Pinsof, W. M., & Wynne, L. C. (Eds.). (1995). *Family therapy effectiveness: Current research and theory.* Washington, DC: American Association for Marriage and Family Therapy. (Also published as a special issue of the *Journal of Marital and Family Therapy, 21*, no. 4).

Pinsof, W. M., & Wynne, L. C. (2000). Toward progress research: Closing the gap between family therapy practice and research. *Journal of Marital and Family Therapy, 26*, 1–8.

Shadish, W. R., Ragsdale, K., Glaser, R. R., & Mongomery, L. M. (1995). The efficacy and effectiveness of marital and family therapy: A perspective from meta-analysis. *Journal of Marital and Family Therapy, 21*, 345–360.

Sprenkle, D. H., Bailey, C. E., Lyness, K., Ball, D., & Mills, S. (1997). Submission patterns to the archival journal of the profession of MFT. *Journal of Marital and Family Therapy, 23*, 371–380.

Sprenkle, D. H., Blow, A. J., & Dickey, M. (1999). Common factors and other non-technique variables in marriage and family therapy. In M. A. Hubble, B. L. Duncan, & S. Miller (Eds.), *The heart and soul of change: What works in therapy* (pp. 329–360). Washington, DC: American Psychological Association.

Wampold, B. E. (2001). *The great psychotherapy debate: Models, methods, and findings.* Mahwah, NJ: Erlbaum.

Werry, J. S. (1989). Family therapy: Professional endeavor or successful religion? *Journal of Family Therapy, 11,* 377–382.

Chapter 2   *Conduct Disorder and Delinquency*

Scott W. Henggeler, Ph.D., Family Services Research Center, Department of Psychiatry and Behavioral Sciences, Medical University of South Carolina, Charleston, South Carolina.

Ashli J. Sheidow, Ph.D., Family Services Research Center, Department of Psychiatry and Behavioral Sciences, Medical University of South Carolina, Charleston, South Carolina.

T he purpose of this chapter is to review those family-based treatments of conduct disorder and delinquency in adolescents that have been identified by federal entities and leading reviewers as efficacious, and to suggest implications for clinical practice and future research. Treatment research regarding adolescent substance abuse and conduct disorder in children is examined in other chapters in this volume (chapteers 3 and 4 respectively).

Overview of Epidemiology, Determinants, and Costs

Epidemiology

Among mental health problems that occur during youth, conduct problems are the most common referral reason for treatment services (Frick, 1998; Kazdin, 1995). The prevalence of conduct disorder in the general population has been estimated at 1% to 6%, although rates vary greatly depending on the sample studied and the diagnostic criteria used (see Loeber, Burke, Lahey, Winters, & Zera, 2000, for a review). For instance, a recent assessment of rural American youth that used DSM-IV criteria observed a rate of 2.6% (Angold & Costello, 2000). Rates found in impoverished urban communities, however, have been more than twice those found for other urban and suburban communities (Loeber, Farrington, Stouthamer-Loeber, & Van Kammen, 1998; Tolan & Henry, 1996). In addition, males have a substantially higher incidence rate than females, with observed rates of conduct disorder ranging from 1% to 9% for studies of girls and observed rates ranging from 2% to 16% for studies of boys (see Loeber et al., 2000 review).

Minor offenses, such as those observed in conduct disordered children, often escalate over time to more serious forms of criminal behavior. Longitudinal studies of adolescents have revealed trajectories of antisocial behavior that begin with minor delinquent acts and end in serious criminal activity (Gorman-Smith, Tolan, Loeber, & Henry, 1998; Kelley, Loeber, Keenan, & DeLamatre, 1997; Nagin & Tremblay, 1999). Indeed, the most chronic and serious of adolescent offenders typically initiate violent offending during childhood rather than adolescence

(Loeber, Farrington, & Waschbusch, 1998; Tolan & Gorman-Smith, 1998). However, the majority of individuals who engage in violence did not commit their first violent offense until adolescence, with an average age for first serious offense of 16 years (Elliott, 1994; Elliott, Huizinga, & Morse, 1986; Kelley et al., 1997; Nagin & Tremblay, 1999). Regarding more prevalence of nonviolent criminal behavior, a recent normative study found an arrest rate of 8% among youth between the ages of 12 and 16 years, with 3% (40% of those who had ever been arrested) reporting two or more arrests (Snyder & Sickmund, 1999). The Office of Juvenile Justice and Delinquency Prevention (Stahl, 2001) reported that U.S. juvenile courts handled over 1.7 million cases in 1998, up 44% from 1989. Three-quarters of the cases were male adolescents, down from 81% in 1989. Of the 1 million cases in 1998 that were brought before a judge, 63% were adjudicated, and 26% of adjudicated cases resulted in a residential placement.

Correlates and Determinants

Clear evidence exists for a multidetermined ecological conceptualization of adolescent conduct disorder and delinquency. Associations between deviant behavior and individual, family, peer, school, and community constructs have been identified across numerous longitudinal and cross-sectional samples, and have been summarized in several recent reviews (e.g., Hann & Borek, 2001; Hawkins et al., 1998; Lipsey & Derzon, 1998). For instance, individual factors that have been linked to antisocial behavior include biological processes (e.g., adrenal hormones, serotonin levels, teratogenic effects) and cognitive functioning (e.g., social information processing, problem solving, and verbal ability). Family factors associated with conduct problems include caregiver characteristics (e.g., drug use, maternal age, caregiver psychopathology) and family-level characteristics (e.g., conflict management, monitoring and supervision). Peer influences include association with deviant peers, lack of association with prosocial peers, and poor socialization skills. School related predictors of conduct problems include low academic achievement, dropout, low commitment to education, and poor structure within the school. Finally, community constructs, such as violence exposure, neighborhood criminal activity, neighborhood supports and mobility have been predictive of conduct problems.

Personal and Societal Costs

Behavior problems such as conduct disorder and delinquency are linked to the development of later, more severe antisocial problems. As noted previously, longitudinal studies of deviant adolescent behavior have found escalating trajectories of offending (Gorman-Smith et al., 1998; Kelley et al., 1997; Nagin & Tremblay, 1999). Further, conduct problems are clearly associated with an increased risk for other types of mental health problems (Feehan, McGee, Raja, & Williams, 1994; Loeber & Keenan, 1994; Offord, Boyle, Racine, & Fleming,

1992). Epidemiological initiatives evaluating the occurrence of psychopathology within the juvenile delinquency population are finding rates of anxiety and depression that critically exceed rates found within the general adolescent population. In some cases, prevalence rates are more than twice as high as in the general population (L. A. Teplin, personal communication, March, 2002; Wasserman, McReynolds, Lucas, Fisher, & Santos, 2002).

On a societal level, victim costs, criminal justice system costs (e.g., incarceration costs, costs of an arrest to juvenile justice authorities and juvenile court), and productivity loss (due to incarceration) have been estimated as high as 1.3 to 1.5 million dollars for an average career criminal (Snyder & Sickmund, 1999). Specific monetary costs for the victim and the system level costs were recently evaluated by researchers at the Washington State Institute for Public Policy (Aos, Phipps, Barnoski, & Lieb, 2001). For instance, victim monetary costs were estimated at over 1 million dollars for a single murder, with close to an additional 2 million dollar cost for quality of life. Total costs (i.e., victim costs, victim quality of life costs, and system costs) for other crimes were estimated at $180,236 for a single sex offense, $100,966 for a robbery, and $66,273 for an aggravated assault. Similarly, Aos et al. estimated total costs for a 15-year-old offender from offense until age 22 years to be $120,235, based on reoffense rates in Washington of 45.8%, an average number of 2.44 reconvictions during this timeframe, and an adjustment for the probability of specific crimes occurring (e.g., murder 1.3%, rape 1.3%, aggravated assault 16.7%). Effective treatments, therefore, hold the potential of both reducing crime and providing cost savings.

Recent Evaluations of Family-Based Treatments by Reviewers and Federal Stakeholders

Family-based treatments for adolescent conduct problems and delinquency have undergone more rigorous testing in recent years than other types of treatments. The 1993 review of family and marital psychotherapies by Shadish et al. reported on 18 studies treating conduct disorder, and found an overall effect size of .53. The 3 studies that specifically treated delinquency generated a more moderate overall effect size of .34. In a more recent review, Chamberlain and Rosicky (1995) highlighted the emergence of family-based ecological treatments for adolescent conduct problems. Such approaches are individualized for multiproblem families of adolescents with conduct problems, and conceptualize problems and interventions from an ecological perspective. Thus, treatment may occur in multiple systems within the youth's environment (e.g., family, peers, school, neighborhood), and treatment foci may include emphases on improving family interactions and caregiver functioning, developing the family's social support system, increasing youth's prosocial peer relationships, minimizing youth contact with antisocial peers, and enhancing school supports and interactions. Importantly, these emphases are consistent with the aforementioned literature on the multidetermined nature of antisocial behavior in adolescents.

As the swell of evidence for multisystemic causes and correlates of conduct problems has become available, family-based ecological treatment approaches have garnered increasing support among reviewers and policy makers. For instance, in the highly respected Blueprints for Violence Prevention report, Mihalic, Irwin, Elliott, Fagan, and Hansen (2001) reviewed more than 500 programs designed to treat and prevent youth conduct problems and found only 3 that met modestly stringent criteria for effectiveness in reducing criminal behavior in adolescents. These model programs had multiple replications of significant and sustained positive effects within strong research designs. The 3 programs identified for juvenile offenders were all family-based ecological models: Functional Family Therapy, Multisystemic Therapy, and Oregon Treatment Foster Care.

Family-based ecological treatments have also been identified as model approaches in reviews by the U.S. Surgeon General (U.S. Public Health Service, 1999, 2001) and the National Advisory Mental Health Council of National Institute of Mental Health (NIMH, 2001), and researchers continue to highlight such treatments of serious antisocial behavior in adolescents as "best practice" and exemplary treatments (e.g., Kazdin & Weisz, 1998). Using criteria suggested by Chambless and Hollon (1998) for identifying empirically supported therapies, Kazdin and Weisz, for example, highlighted Multisystemic Therapy as an exemplary model for treating youth externalizing disorders. Their criteria were: (a) multiple randomized control trials; (b) well-described, replicable treatment procedures; (c) uniform therapist training and monitoring of treatment fidelity; (d) use of clinical samples; (e) broad-based assessment of outcomes (e.g., evidence of clinical significance and of "real world" functioning); and (f) evidence of long-term outcomes. As discussed by the authors, these criteria are currently our best method for evaluating effectiveness across treatment models, and are achieved through a systematic program of clinical research informed by clients, researchers, clinicians, and others involved in the provision and utilization of services.

In sum, three family-based treatments that focus on addressing known risk factors for antisocial behavior in adolescents across their social ecology have been widely cited by reviewers and federal entities such as the Surgeon General as having considerable promise or established effectiveness. As described later in this chapter, these three treatment approaches include key similarities that, together, have important implications for clinical practice.

Empirically Supported Family-Based Treatments

This chapter focuses on the three family-based treatments for adolescent conduct problems that have been identified as having empirical support: Functional Family Therapy, Multisystemic Therapy, and Oregon Treatment

Foster Care. These treatment models are systemic approaches that are individualized and comprehensive to address the multiple problems among youth with serious conduct problems and their families. A brief introduction to the clinical procedures and quality assurance mechanisms of each approach is provided, and more detailed information can be obtained through the respective treatment manuals highlighted in the references section. In addition, controlled outcome and process research and cost analyses are presented for each model.

Functional Family Therapy (FFT)

FFT has been used for nearly 30 years in the treatment of youth conduct problems. The treatment is described in an earlier clinical volume (Alexander & Parsons, 1982) and a recent treatment manual (Alexander et al., 1998) published as part of the Blueprint for Violence Prevention series. Treatment is provided by a single part-time or full-time therapist (FFT therapists have been student trainees, paraprofessionals, and professionals), and therapists are responsible for 12 to 16 active cases. FFT averages 12 sessions over 3 months, with more difficult cases requiring 26 to 30 hours of direct service, and often occurs in the home.

Clinical procedures. FFT includes three sequential phases of treatment, with different intervention techniques used to achieve the goals of each phase (Alexander et al., 1998; Alexander & Sexton, 2002; Sexton & Alexander, 2002).

Phase 1. Engagement and motivation. One goal of this phase is to enhance the family members' perceptions of therapist responsivity and credibility. Therapists accomplish this goal by behaving responsively and respectfully toward the family and making family members feel as comfortable as possible through dress, attitude, affect, and availability. A second goal is to create a therapist-family context that is conducive to desired change. For example, FFT emphasizes the importance of creating a balanced alliance with each family member. To achieve this goal, the practitioner works to reduce anger, blaming, hopelessness, and other negative behaviors and emotions among family members using techniques such as reframing.

Phase 2. Behavior change. This stage focuses primarily on changing family interactions through building interpersonal and problem solving skills. As Alexander et al. (1998) noted, FFT change techniques fall under two categories: parent training and communication training. Parent training is usually emphasized with families of younger children and follows relatively well-specified protocols developed in the behavioral parent training literature. Communication skills training is also based primarily on the behavioral literature and emphasizes elements such as brevity, directness, and active listening. During this phase, relationship skills remain important, but therapist interactions primarily focus on restructuring family relations in ways that will facilitate desired behavior change (Alexander & Sexton, 2002).

Phase 3. Generalization. The goal of this final phase is to extend positive intrafamily change by incorporating relations with community systems such as mental health and juvenile justice authorities. Here, the therapist acts largely as a case manager or collaborates with a case manager in attempting to anchor the family in a supportive community context. To accomplish this goal, therapists must possess extensive knowledge of community resources and have positive relations with community social service agencies.

Quality assurance. The FFT model maintains quality assurance through standardized training of therapists and supervisors, therapist reports from each session, supervision of therapists, and consultation with FFT experts (Alexander et al., 1998). Specifically, quality assurance includes: (a) an initial 2–3 day training workshop; (b) an on-site consultation visit each year, including group and individual meetings; (c) individual telephone consultations with each intervention staff once or more per year; (d) a process summary measure completed by the therapist following each client session; (e) a counseling process questionnaire completed by family members after every other treatment session; and (f) weekly supervision by an FFT supervisor with at least a Master's degree, including review of process measures and occasional review of audiotaped client sessions. Importantly, an innovative Internet-based system for tracking therapist performance and clinical progress from multiple perspectives (i.e., client, therapist, supervisor) across FFT dissemination sites has recently become operational. Such systems have the clear potential to promote program fidelity and corresponding youth and family outcomes.

Controlled outcome research. Research of FFT has spanned 3 decades, and primarily has used matched comparison designs. As summarized in Table 1, FFT has been evaluated in one randomized and two quasi-experimental studies. The initial study (Alexander & Parsons, 1973) was a randomized trial of male and female offenders, aged 13 to 16 years, who were referred by the Salt Lake County Juvenile Court for primarily status offenses. Forty-six families received FFT through the University of Utah, while 40 comparison families received client-centered family group therapy, psychodynamic family therapy, or no treatment. The recidivism rate for status offenses of those youth receiving FFT was less than the three other groups by 50% or more.

In a replication (Gordon, Arbuthnot, Gustafson, & McGreen, 1988) including 54 rural Ohio youth who were more disadvantaged and had committed more serious offenses than youth in the initial trial, FFT was conducted in-home (versus the clinic-based treatment previously utilized) and averaged 16 sessions. Youth referred for FFT as a condition of probation were matched to control youth randomly selected from those not referred for family treatment based on schools attended. FFT resulted in a recidivism rate of 11% compared to 67% for the no-treatment controls, a reduction in recidivism of over 80%. Within the treatment group, none of the 12 females recidivated compared to 3 of the 4 control females. Three of the 15 males in the treatment group recidivated, with a group total of three offenses, compared to 15 of the 23 untreated males, who committed a group total of 24 offenses. In another study, Barton, Alexander, Waldron, Turner, and

Warburton (1985) reported three quasi-experimental evaluations of FFT that included therapists with different levels of training (e.g., undergraduates, probation officers) treating youths presenting different levels of problems severity (e.g., status offenders, youths returning from placement) and their families. Results were generally favorable, though few methodological details were provided for these studies.

The most recent investigation of FFT, yet to be submitted for peer review, was an urban, community-based trial for the treatment of violent, drug abusing youth (Sexton, Ostrom, Bonomo, & Alexander, 2000, as reported in Sexton & Alexander, 2002). Results of this matched trial for youth receiving FFT indicate a reoffense rate of 20% versus 36% for the matched controls receiving usual services. Furthermore, youth receiving FFT committed fewer crimes and engaged in less severe criminal acts. Overall, FFT research has found a significant reduction in recidivism compared to treated and untreated controls (Alexander et al., 1998), and outcomes have been stable for as long as 5 years (Gordon et al., 1988) posttreatment.

Cost analyses. In the most comprehensive cost analysis of offender treatment to date, Aos et al. (2001) reported that studies of FFT, some of which had been carried out by researchers independent of the treatment developers, were reasonably strong in their research design (i.e., produced a rating of 3–4 on a 5-point scale of confidence in study findings). After controlling for confidence ratings of research designs, FFT had an effect size of -.25 for basic recidivism (proportion of offenders to nonoffenders). At an average cost of $2,161 per participant, FFT produced an average of $14,149 in placement and juvenile justice savings for each treated youth compared to the standard juvenile justice program. When crime victim costs were included in the formula, the savings reached $59,067 per participant.

Process research. Taken as a whole, FFT aims to reduce adolescent antisocial behavior by changing the "self-defeating cycles and malevolent emotional reactions [with which] families enter therapy" (Sexton & Alexander, 2002, p. 21). The developers suggest that the meaning of deviant youth behavior is found within the family's relational pattern, a complex network of relations among beliefs, emotions, and behavior patterns. Thus, they propose that FFT therapists bring about improved functioning through delineation and alteration of the family relational system. Research of FFT has included in-session process evaluation, with results indicating that FFT results in improved family functioning (e.g., less silence, more equality of speech, more positive interactions; Alexander & Parsons, 1973; Barton et al., 1985). FFT researchers, however, have not related such outcomes directly to deviant behavior outcomes.

Multisystemic Therapy (MST)

MST has been in development for more than 25 years. A clinical volume (Henggeler, Schoenwald, Borduin, Rowland, & Cunningham, 1998) describes

Table 1
Treatment Outcomes Presented in Peer-Reviewed Publications

Reference	Population	Sample size	Follow-up (in years)	Design
Functional Family Therapy				
Alexander & Parsons (1973)	JSO	86	1.0	Randomized
Klein, Alexander, &	SIB	56	2.9	
Parsons (1977)				
Barton et al. (1985)	SJO	74	1.3	Matched
Gordon et al. (1988)	SJO	54	2.5	Matched
Gordon, Graves, &		45	5.0	
Arbuthnot (1995)				
Multisystemic Therapy				
Henggeler et al. (1986)	JO	57	0	Matched
Borduin et al. (1990)	ASO	16	3.0	Randomized
Henggeler et al. (1992);	SJO	84	1.1	Randomized
Henggeler et al. (1993)				
Borduin et al. (1995)	SJO	176	4.0	Randomized
Henggeler et al. (1997)	SJO	155	1.7	Randomized
Henggeler, Pickrel, et al. (1999)	SUD	118	1.0	Randomized
Schoenwald et al. (1996)		118	1.0	
Brown et al. (1999)		118	0.5	
Henggeler et al. (in press)		80	4.0	
Oregon Treatment Foster Care				
Chamberlain (1990)	SUD	32	1.0	Matched
Chamberlain & Reid (1998)	SUD	79	1.0	Randomized

JSO = Juvenile status offenders   JO = Juvenile offenders
SIB = Siblings of status offenders   ASO = Adolescent sexual offenders
SJO = Serious juvenile offenders   SUD = Substance using delinquents

MST interventions for adolescent antisocial behavior in detail, and a recent volume describes MST adaptations to treat youths with serious emotional disturbance and their families (Henggeler, Schoenwald, Rowland, & Cunningham, 2002). In general, the interventions described in these volumes focus on the individual, family, peer, school, and social network variables that are linked with identified problems, as well as on the interface of these systems. MST programs target youths with serious antisocial behavior that are at imminent risk of a costly out-of-home placement. Treatment is provided by full-time Master's level therapists that carry caseloads of 4–6 families. Three to four therapists work within a team, supervised by an advanced Master's level or doctoral level supervisor to provide 24-hour/7 day a week availability. Treatment entails an average of approximately 60 hours of direct service over 3 to 6 months. MST strictly follows a home-based (e.g., home, school, community) model of service delivery, with treatment provided at times that are convenient to the families. This model is extremely effective at engaging families in treatment and removing barriers to service access (e.g., Henggeler, Pickrel, Brondino, & Crouch, 1996).

Clinical procedures. In designing particular intervention strategies, MST adapts empirically-based interventions from pragmatic, problem-focused treatments that have at least some empirical support. These include strategic family therapy (Haley, 1987), structural family therapy (Minuchin, 1974), behavioral parent training (Munger, 1993), and cognitive behavior therapies (Kendall & Braswell, 1993). In addition and as appropriate, biological contributors to identified problems are identified and psychopharmacological treatment is integrated with psychosocial treatment.

A frequent goal of treatment at the family level, for example, is to enhance caregivers' capacity to effectively monitor adolescent behavior and whereabouts, and to provide positive consequences for responsible youth behavior and sanctions for irresponsible behavior. Hence, the therapist will often help the caregivers develop increased family structure, operationalize desired youth behavior, and identify natural reinforcers to be linked with desired behavior. Importantly, the therapist also identifies barriers to the effective implementation of these new rules and consequences. Such barriers might include caregiver substance abuse, caregiver mental health difficulties, high levels of family stress, and so forth. The therapist then helps to design interventions to overcome these barriers, understanding that new family rules and contingencies cannot be implemented effectively or consistently until barriers are removed.

Similarly, at the peer level a frequent goal of treatment is to decrease the youth's involvement with delinquent and drug using peers and to increase his or her association with prosocial peers. Interventions for this purpose are optimally conducted by the youth's caregivers, with the guidance of the therapist, and might consist of active support and encouragement of associations with nonproblem peers (e.g., providing transportation and increased privileges) and substantive discouragement of associations with deviant peers (e.g., applying significant sanctions). Caregivers are encouraged to use indigenous opportunities for youths to develop relations with prosocial peers under adult supervision. Such opportunities include church youth groups, after school activities, and community recreational resources.

Likewise, under the guidance of the therapist, the caregivers develop strategies to monitor and promote the youth's school performance and/or vocational functioning. Typically included in this domain are strategies for opening and maintaining positive communication lines with teachers and for restructuring after school hours to promote academic efforts. Emphasis is placed on developing a collaborative relationship between the parents and school personnel. Hence, the MST model views the caregivers as key to achieving desired outcomes, and interventions typically focus on the family and the family's interface with key social systems.

Quality assurance. The MST model includes a comprehensive quality assurance system. The overriding purpose of this system is to help therapists and supervisors achieve desired clinical outcomes for youths and families by supporting treatment fidelity. Indeed, several recent empirical studies have demonstrated linkages between therapist adherence to MST treatment principles, based on caregiver reports on a standardized adherence measure, and short- and long-term clinical outcomes (Henggeler, Melton, Brondino, Scherer, & Hanley, 1997; Henggeler, Pickrel, & Brondino, 1999; Huey, Henggeler, Brondino, & Pickrel, 2000; Schoenwald, Henggeler, Brondino, & Rowland, 2000). These findings support the view that therapists should be provided with strong clinical support to optimize clinical outcomes. Hence, MST programs, operating in 27 states and 7 nations, include multiple layers of clinical and programmatic support. Specifically, provider organizations receive extensive organizational consultation to assure the provision of necessary resources (e.g., funding, low caseloads, and interagency collaboration) prior to and following the development of MST programs. The assessment, intervention, supervision, and consultation processes are all manualized and focused on the nine guiding principles of MST. Treatment integrity is sustained through initial didactic and experiential training, followed by regular booster sessions by MST experts, weekly supervision within the MST treatment team (consisting of therapists and MST supervisor), and weekly consultation with an MST expert. Supervision and consultation includes feedback from measures of treatment integrity, including monthly caregiver-reported ratings of therapist adherence (Henggeler & Borduin, 1992) and, in the case of research trials, expert ratings of therapy tapes. Thus, therapist adherence to the treatment model is monitored continuously.

Controlled outcome research. Compared with the other treatment models discussed here, MST has been the focus of a greater number of clinical trials. The majority of these trials have focused on treating youths presenting serious antisocial behavior and at imminent risk of out-of-home placement. As presented in Table 1, three published randomized trials with violent and chronic offenders, one published randomized trial with sexual offenders, one published randomized trial with substance using offenders, and one quasi-experimental trial with inner-city delinquents (Borduin, Henggeler, Blaske, & Stein, 1990; Borduin et al., 1995; Brown, Henggeler, Schoenwald, Brondino, & Pickrel, 1999; Henggeler, Clingempeel, Brondino, & Pickrel, in press; Henggeler et al., 1997; Henggeler, Melton, & Smith, 1992; Henggeler, Melton, Smith, Schoenwald, & Hanley, 1993; Henggeler, Pickrel, et al., 1999; Henggeler et al., 1986; Schoenwald, Ward, Henggeler, Pickrel, & Patel, 1996) have supported the efficacy of MST. All but one of the MST studies have been randomized controlled trials. Further, studies have typically been completed in field settings and maintained few exclusion criteria, features that strengthen support for treatment effectiveness. In addition, juveniles in the comparison condition for all trials have received treatment (typically services usually available in the community for juvenile offenders), lending further validity to MST treatment effects.

Outcomes have consistently favored MST in comparison with control conditions. For example, MST treatment effects have included improved family relations and functioning, increased school attendance, decreased adolescent psychiatric symptoms, and reduced substance use. Reductions in rates of recidivism have ranged between 25% to 70% across studies for youth treated with MST compared to treated control groups. Moreover, MST has produced decreased rates of days in out-of-home placement ranging from 47% to 64% compared to usual services. Group differences have been observed as much as 5 years posttreatment.

MST clinical trials have also been conducted with youth that are not currently offenders, but are at imminent risk for out-of-home placement in psychiatric or foster-care settings. Successful MST outcomes have been observed for youths presenting psychiatric emergencies (i.e., suicidal, homicidal, psychotic; Henggeler, Rowland, et al., 1999; Schoenwald, Ward, Henggeler, & Rowland, 2000) and for children in maltreating families (Brunk, Henggeler, & Whelan, 1987).

Cost analyses. In their cost analysis, Aos et al. (2001) placed the highest level of confidence in the findings of MST studies, noting that some studies had been carried out by researchers other than the developers and were conducted in real world community settings (in comparison with efficacy studies conducted in university settings). At an average cost of $4,743 per family, MST had an average effect size of -.31, and produced $31,661 in reduced placement and juvenile justice costs. Further savings from costs to victims increased this figure to $131,918 per participant.

Process research. MST aims to effect change in deviant youth behavior through altering the individual, family, peer, school, and social network variables that have been linked with delinquent behavior. In one of only two efforts to relate family-based treatment outcomes directly to the mechanisms hypothesized to bring about those outcomes, Huey et al. (2000) used data from two separate randomized trials (Henggeler et al., 1997; Henggeler, Pickrel, et al., 1999) to demonstrate the mediation of treatment outcomes by family functioning and peer relationship variables. Results showed that the observed treatment group differences on antisocial behavior were mediated by improved family cohesion and monitoring and by decreased affiliation with deviant peers. Thus, the theoretical foundations of the MST model have been supported by the observed data.

Oregon Treatment Foster Care (OTFC)

Developed in the early 1980s, OTFC is based on principles of social learning theory and is specified in a treatment manual (Chamberlain & Mihalic, 1998) entitled "Multidimensional Treatment Foster Care," published as part of the Blueprint for Violence Prevention series. Youth receiving OTFC are placed with trained foster parent(s) in lieu of restrictive residential placement, with an ultimate goal of the youth transitioning home to the biological or adoptive family. Typically, only one youth is placed with each foster family at a time. Treatment is provided by a team, consisting of trained foster parents, a full-time case manager, individual and family therapists, and other resource staff. Treatment is intensive, with each team responsible for 10 active cases and the case manager providing 24-hour/7 day a week availability over a 6 to 12 month period. Foster parents are contacted daily by the case manager to review the youth's behavior and modify the treatment plan. Treatment teams also meet weekly, and family therapy is provided to prepare the biological/adoptive family for the youth's return.

Clinical procedures. The main objectives of OTFC are to provide: (a) close supervision, (b) fair and consistent limits, (c) predictable consequences for rule breaking, (d) a supportive relationship with mentoring adult(s), and (e) reduced exposure to delinquent peers while encouraging prosocial youth relationships. Thus, specific interventions occur in a variety of environmental contexts. As in the case of MST, a range of treatment modalities is integrated to achieve change in youth with severe problems.

For instance, behavioral parent training is employed for teaching both foster parents and biological parents to manage the youth's behavior in a consistent and noncoercive manner. Here, an individualized behavioral program is tailored for each youth through collaboration of the OTFC treatment team. This program includes a comprehensive point system that rewards normative behaviors each day (e.g., school attendance, completion of chores, completing activities on time, having a cooperative attitude). The youth's compliance with the behavioral program is related to a three-level system of privileges. In the first level, points from one day are exchanged for privileges on the succeeding day. The overall accumulation of these points determines advancement to level two, where points can be accumulated throughout the week to be exchanged for an expanded list of privileges. Level three offers a further expansion of privileges, as well as the freedom to participate in approved activities that are not directly supervised by adults. A loss of points results in loss of privileges, demotion to a lower level, or addition of chores (prespecified in behavioral plan). Other family-level interventions include intensive supervision of the youth's activities and monitoring of his or her interactions with peers. Family therapy sessions with the biological family (or other aftercare resource) are also conducted throughout placement in foster care. These sessions emphasize supervision, encouragement, discipline, and problem solving. Youth have home visits that begin with short (e.g., 1- to 2-hour) stays, increasing to overnight visits as treatment progresses.

OTFC also incorporates school-based behavioral interventions and academic supports. For instance, the individualized behavioral program includes daily tracking of school behavior, with teachers signing off on attendance, completion of work, and attitude. The OTFC treatment team offers full collaboration with school counselors and teachers, including provision of support if the youth becomes disruptive while in school. In addition, OTFC includes individual therapy for the youth that is integrated into treatment. This may include psychiatric consultation and medication management that is coordinated by the case manager. In particular, individual therapy includes skills training for youth to develop skills for having positive relationships with adults and for generating relationships with prosocial peers. Such treatment is behaviorally oriented and may include development of problem solving skills, social perspective taking, and nonaggressive methods of self-expression.

Quality assurance. Similar to FFT and MST, OTFC maintains quality assurance through standardized training and close supervision of treatment providers (Chamberlain & Mihalic, 1998). Foster care parents are trained during a 20-hour didactic and experiential program. Upon successful completion of this program, which includes screening of the foster home and parents, daily contact between case managers and OTFC parents and weekly supervision meetings of OTFC teams provide further instruction that maintains treatment integrity. The daily contact between case managers and foster parents is also used to review the youth's progress on the behavioral treatment plan and to coordinate other services (e.g., psychiatric consultation, school supports). This daily contact is structured, with data collected on the Parent Daily Report Checklist (see Chamberlain & Mihalic, 1998), and the daily point cards are collected at weekly supervision meetings. These data are reviewed periodically by the program director, who is responsible for treatment integrity and provides weekly supervision to the OTFC case managers and therapists. Other than the Parent Daily Report Checklist, there are currently no quantifiable measures of adherence to the OTFC model for ongoing treatment programs. However, as part of a research investigation of OTFC, staff in the comparison conditions (group homes) and OTFC foster parents have been interviewed to assess treatment integrity (Chamberlain, Ray, & Moore, 1996). Significant differences were observed for types of additional services, adult mentoring, peer involvement, and perceived mechanisms of change.

Controlled outcome research. Of the three treatment models discussed in this chapter, OTFC is the most recently developed and, as noted in Table 1, only two studies have been conducted to test the effectiveness of OTFC for treating juvenile offenders (Chamberlain, 1990; Chamberlain & Reid, 1998). Because OTFC is intended for treating youth that have exhausted less restrictive methods of treatment, youth in these two trials were severe and chronic offenders. The initial investigation of OTFC compared sixteen 13- to 18-year-olds, matched by age, sex, and date of commitment to 16 youth in other community residential treatment settings. Youth receiving OTFC were less likely to run away from the treatment setting, more likely to complete treatment, and experienced fewer days of incarceration during the 2 years posttreatment.

The second investigation was a randomized trial of 79 male 12- to 17-year-olds receiving either OTFC or standard group care (Chamberlain & Reid, 1998). Youth treated with OTFC were again less likely to run away and more likely to complete treatment. Notably, during the year after commitment to OTFC or group care, youth in the OTFC condition spent an average of 59 days residing with biological parents or relatives in contrast to 31 days for youth in the group care condition. Youth in OTFC spent an average of 53 days in detention facilities, compared to an average of 129 days for youth in group care. Further, youth who received OTFC engaged in fewer offenses at 1 year posttreatment, as measured by both official arrests and self-report of criminal offenses.

In two other randomized trials, OTFC was modified to treat youth leaving psychiatric hospitalization (Chamberlain & Reid, 1991), and to treat children being placed in foster care following parental abuse or neglect (Chamberlain, Moreland, & Reid, 1992). Both of these trials found positive effects for OTFC, with fewer youth problems during treatment and in the months following treatment. In the study comparing OTFC methods and "regular" foster care for abused or neglected children, the aim was to measure the effect of OTFC, controlling for the effect of increased payment included with OTFC treatment. OTFC methods resulted in fewer disruptions to placement and less foster parent dropout, compared with foster families receiving the increased fee without OTFC training and support, and foster families receiving neither.

Cost analyses. The cost analysis by Aos et al. (2001) included the one study of OTFC using random assignment and the one study using matched controls, with a cost estimate of approximately $2,052 per youth in addition to the cost of the foster placement. With reasonable to sound confidence in conclusions about treatment differences, Aos et al. concluded that OTFC had an average effect size of -.37 for basic recidivism, generating $21,836 in reduced placement and juvenile justice costs compared to placement in group homes. Adding costs to victims produced savings of $87,622 per participant.

Process research. Like the other models described here, OTFC proposes that the reduction in delinquency observed among treated youth occurs through alteration of the structure of the youth's environment and the relations within that environment. In only the second effort within family-based treatment research to directly relate youth outcome to hypothesized mechanisms of change, Eddy and Chamberlain (2000) found that modifying behavior management within the family and youth association with deviant peers mediated the treatment effects of OTFC. That is, like Huey et al. (2000), they found evidence that the observed treatment group differences on youth deviant behavior were, in part, explained by improved supervision, discipline, and positive adult-youth relations, and by decreased affiliation with deviant peers. Such analyses support the ecological framework underlying the OTFC model as well as the theoretical underpinnings of the other models described here.

Similarities Between Models

Although each of the aforementioned evidence-based treatments was developed independently, they share several commonalities in their conceptualization, delivery, and procedures. Most importantly, they succeed in meeting the recommendations for adolescent treatment development set forth by the U.S. Surgeon General and the NIMH task force (National Advisory Mental Health Council Workgroup on Child and Adolescent Mental Health Intervention Development and Deployment, 2001; U.S. Public Health Service, 1999, 2001). That is, these family-based approaches (a) use the science base of known risk factors for the development and maintenance of conduct problems, (b) provide an effective alternative to costly and largely ineffective restrictive placements for youth offenders, and (c) use respectable scientific methods (e.g., matched comparison or randomized clinical trials) to evaluate effectiveness. Moreover, these programs accomplish effectiveness at a substantial cost savings. As the developers of these approaches have begun to disseminate their models to community settings detached from research investigations, the bases of their success and the parallels among the approaches become of heightened interest.

Evidence-Based Development and Integration

FFT, MST, and OTFC use the existing knowledge base in child psychopathology and treatment in the conceptualization, design, and implementation of interventions. Treatment planning is informed by evidence of known risk factors across the youth and family's social ecology (Atkins & McKay, 2001). For instance, recognition of involvement with antisocial peers is a vital element across the three models, and specific interventions are aimed at reducing this negative influence on youth conduct problems. Family structure and monitoring of youth are also identified as critical areas of intervention across the models. In addition, the evidence base on psychotherapy research is incorporated into these treatment models. For example, behavioral techniques are used across these approaches to provide structure within home and school settings.

Commitment to Rigorous Evaluation

FFT, MST, and OTFC have each developed an evidence base through multiple clinical trials that aimed to systematically evaluate treatment effectiveness. Matched group and randomized trials of FFT have evaluated a wide array of clinical outcomes. Randomized control trials, the "gold standard" for clinical research, have frequently been used to test the effectiveness of MST. The effectiveness of OTFC has been examined using both matched and randomized trials. Most important to establishing effectiveness in this multiproblem population, outcome studies of these treatment models have typically included "real world" youth in community settings. That is, treatment was provided in a manner consistent with what could be provided by a community agency, rather than within a university setting. Further, youth research participants have been clinically impaired and accurately represent the population of youth with conduct problems.

Treatment Specification

As noted previously, FFT, MST, and OTFC intervention guidelines have been specified in manuals and texts that focus on similar sets of issues. For example, strategies to promote treatment engagement and reduce barriers to service access are emphasized in each approach. MST and OTFC provide clinician availability 24 hours a day/7 days a week. MST clinicians provide all services within the youth's ecology, and FFT devotes the initial phase of treatment to obtaining adequate engagement. These procedures have resulted in extraordinarily high rates of treatment engagement and completion. Youth treated with OTFC completed treatment programs at a rate of 73% compared to 36% for the control group. FFT research reports a treatment completion rate of 80%, while recent MST studies have achieved 97% and 98% treatment completion rates, respectively.

Similarly, all three models maintain a specific focus on generalization of treatment progress. Although the treatments are time-limited, substantial portions of time are devoted to establishing supports and resources that will help maintain changes made during treatment. For instance, FFT devotes an entire phase of treatment to this focus, while OTFC continues to provide individual and family therapy as the youth transitions back to the home. MST focuses on generalization throughout treatment, utilizing and enhancing resources and supports already present within the youth's surroundings to maintain treatment change. The clear ecological concentration on generalization that these evidence-based models maintain is instrumental in producing long-term change, and makes them somewhat unique among treatments for adolescent conduct problems.

Quality Assurance Systems

Quality assurance systems have been used to support the replication of each model at independent sites with supervisors other than the treatment developers. Consistent with an emphasis on quality assurance, the importance of treatment adherence for promoting favorable treatment outcomes for violent youth was highlighted by the U.S. Surgeon General (U.S. Public Health Service, 2001). Hence, close monitoring of treatment providers to enhance treatment fidelity is a clear and consistent focus of each of the evidence-based approaches. For instance, OTFC foster parents discuss youth behavior on a daily basis with case managers, reporting on progress and planning for the following day. Besides monitoring clinical interventions, this contact can be used to maintain adherence to the treatment model. Within MST, fidelity is overtly specified through structured supervisory and consultation protocols used to monitor and support treatment integrity. Indeed, several recent empirical studies of MST have demonstrated linkages between therapist adherence to MST treatment principles and short- and long-term clinical outcomes (Henggeler et al., 1997; Henggeler, Pickrel, et al., 1999; Huey et al., 2000; Schoenwald, Henggeler, et al., 2000).

Current Demand for Transport and Dissemination

The success of these family-based models in combination with significant national need for effective services for youths with serious antisocial behavior has created considerable demand for the transport of FFT, MST, and OTFC into daily practice. The transport of a complex evidence-based practice to field settings, however, requires a different set of skills than needed in the development and evaluation of these models. Although the developers of FFT have maintained a very hands-on approach to their transport of this model to providers in more than 20 different states and other nations, the developers of MST and, more recently, OTFC have pursued strategies that emphasize the creation of new organizations that are explicitly committed to effective transport and dissemination. The emphases of these organizations on ongoing fidelity monitoring and quality assurance by teams of experts is very different than the "workshop" model of dissemination that has dominated the field of family therapy historically. It remains to be seen, however, which dissemination strategies are more effective at promoting youth and family outcomes.

Future Research

Suggestions for future research pertain primarily to the evidence-based models reviewed in this chapter. In general, these suggestions assume that reasonable evidence of efficacy and effectiveness has been demonstrated in well-designed clinical trials. Until a treatment model has demonstrated efficacy, the conduct of transportability, process, and adaptation research, as discussed subsequently, is probably not warranted.

Transportability

As Schoenwald and Hoagwood (2001) have described, little is known about the parameters of the successful transport of evidence-based treatments to community settings. FFT, MST, and OTFC are in the unique position of having evoked considerable demand for transport from funders and stakeholder groups. Several states and at least two foreign nations have funded the development of organizations dedicated to the effective transport of MST to provider organizations within their boundaries. Hence, in contrast with the vast majority of treatment models and the majority of evidence-based treatments, the treatments of adolescent conduct problems reviewed in this chapter are primed for transportability research.

Transportability research can examine numerous processes and variables associated with the effective transport of an evidence-based treatment. For example, what are the characteristics of the intervention, provider organizations, community stakeholders, and funding structure that are associated with the adoption of a treatment model? As Schoenwald and Hoagwood (2001) noted, in the same way that multiple, interrelated factors and processes within and between social systems influence the development of antisocial behavior in adolescents, multiple characteristics of stakeholders (e.g., affinity for innovation) and broader social systems (e.g., state level initiatives, funding structures) likely influence the adoption of a treatment model.

Many questions also can be asked regarding the implementation of evidence-based practices in community settings. For example, what are the determinants of treatment fidelity in community-based settings? How do therapist training background, experience, gender, and theoretical orientation influence fidelity? What types of quality assurance protocols are most efficient at promoting therapist adherence? Can incentives be used to increase adherence and improve outcomes? Does organizational culture and climate influence therapist behavior, and, if so, how? Similarly, an important area of research that is virtually untouched pertains to the sustainability of evidence-based practices. Again, conceptualized from a multidetermined ecological framework, what factors from the level of the provider through the funding structures are associated with program sustainability, and how are these factors linked with program drift over time?

Therapy Process

Some progress has been achieved in examining the mechanisms of the effective treatments of antisocial behavior in adolescents. For example, MST (Huey et al., 2000) and OTFC (Eddy & Chamberlain, 2000) studies have shown that improved family relations leads to decreased youth association with deviant peers, which, in turn, is associated with decreased criminal activity. In addition, several studies cited previously have demonstrated that therapist adherence to MST protocols was associated with improved clinical outcomes. Although these studies begin to depict the processes by which these evidence-based practices work, they are only initial steps. Little is known about how specific therapist in-session behaviors are associated with family behaviors and clinical outcomes (Clingempeel & Henggeler, in press). Similarly, pretreatment characteristics of adolescents and caregivers might interact with treatment process in varied ways that alter the course of treatment. In trials in which pertinent data are available, mediational analyses could inform theories of change. Further, constructive or dismantling designs in new research could be used to investigate process theories (see Clingempeel & Henggeler, in press).

Adaptations for Other Clinical Populations

The current treatment specifications for FFT, MST, and OTFC have produced favorable outcomes for youths presenting serious antisocial behavior. Such protocols, however, will not necessarily be effective in treating other types of serious clinical problems. Thus, for example, several substantive changes to standard MST were required (see Henggeler, Schoenwald, et al., 2002) in its adaptation for treating youths with serious emotional disturbance (e.g., decreased case loads, increased psychiatric involvement, integration of evidence-based pharmacological treatment). Similarly, other adaptations are being made to enhance the effectiveness of MST in treating adolescent substance abuse (e.g., Randall, Henggeler, Cunningham, Rowland, & Swenson, 2001).

Major research opportunities exist, therefore, in adapting the treatment and quality assurance protocols of the evidence-based treatments described in this chapter to serve the needs of youths presenting a wide range of other serious clinical problems. In a very real sense, these intervention models are ahead of the pack in many ways (e.g., manualization, established efficacy, quality assurance protocols, and dissemination). Hence, they are in prime positions to provide the clinical, supervisory, and organizational infrastructure needed to support the development of effective services for clinical problems that do not have corresponding effective treatments. Needed are additional specification of the refinements and corresponding validation studies (i.e., well implemented randomized trials). These complex needs can provide the grist for many years of research.

Clinical Implications

The development, validation, and dissemination activities of FFT, MST, and OTFC have important, and possibly unsettling, implications for typical modes of clinical practice. In general, these evidence-based treatment models, and a wealth of services research (Weisz & Jensen, 1999) suggest that current practice methods are probably not effective. Importantly, they suggest several directions in the establishment of more effective practice.

Address Known Risk Factors

Many family therapy approaches have not necessarily focused on known risk factors. Yet, a wealth of knowledge has emerged during the past several decades regarding the determinants of antisocial behavior in adolescents. FFT, MST, and OTFC are clear in their focus on these factors. As someone recovering from a heart attack should address known risk factors (e.g., exercise, smoking, drug use, hypertension, cholesterol, obesity) if he or she desires to reduce the probability of a second attack, it only makes sense for therapists to focus on known risk factors when treating adolescents with antisocial behavior.

Follow Treatment Protocols

FFT, MST, and OTFC are operationalized with flexible, yet structured, protocols. Therapists are provided guidelines in which certain types of interventions are appropriate for certain types of situations, and other types of interventions are proscribed. For example, each of these treatments integrates behavioral interventions within ecological conceptual frameworks. Similarly, at least two of the models proscribe certain interventions (e.g., group treatment) that are used widely in practice.

Embrace Quality Assurance Systems

Serious antisocial behavior in adolescents can be extremely difficult to treat, and such youths are often embedded in families with many other challenging problems (e.g., caregiver mental illness and drug abuse, poverty, high stress, low social support). To expect a lone clinician to treat this array of problems effectively on a consistent basis is unrealistic. Clinicians should be surrounded with strong clinical support from peers, supervisors, and possibly even other experts in the field. This support should endeavor to optimize clinical outcomes by helping therapists adhere to validated treatment protocols and to develop and implement strategies for overcoming barriers to desired clinical outcomes.

Reward Accountability and Effectiveness

As indicated in the cost effectiveness analyses for FFT, MST, and OTFC, effective clinicians can save service systems considerable costs, most immediately and directly by preventing expensive out-of-home services. It seems only fair that a proportion of those savings should be passed onto the treatment program and effective clinician. Although the intrinsic rewards remain, such extrinsic rewards for clinical success are rare, and require structures in which outcomes are tracked and accountability is high. Almost everyone can win in an effective accountability system (e.g., performance contracts); youth and family functioning are improved, clinicians and their program benefit from their success, funders save money from reduced placements, and fewer community members are victimized.

Conclusion

Since Chamberlain and Rosicky's (1995) review, evidence for the effectiveness of certain family-based treatments (i.e., FFT, MST, OTFC) of conduct problems in adolescents has advanced to the point that major federal entities such as the Surgeon General have identified highly promising or effective treatments, and stakeholders across the nation have requested that these treatments be transported to their communities. Chamberlain and Rosicky foresaw the potential of ecologically oriented family treatments to successfully address the multiple needs of youths with severe conduct problems. In the years following their review, several well implemented randomized trials have supported the efficacy of such ecological treatment models.

This chapter identified several similar features among FFT, MST, and OTFC that most likely account for their success. Future treatment developers should consider these features in the design and specification of new treatment models. In addition, the validation and initial transport of FFT, MST, and OTFC to community-based programs across the nation have opened up new lines of research that are on the cutting edge of the National Institutes of Health agenda—research examining the transport of evidence-based practices to community settings. Such research as well as studies adapting these models to other clinical populations hold the potential to significantly improve the nation's outcomes for youths with serious clinical problems and their families.

References

References marked with a double asterisk are recommended for clinicians.

**Alexander, J., Barton, C., Gordon, D., Grotpeter, J., Hansson, K., Harrison, R., et al. (1998). *Blueprints for violence prevention, book three: Functional Family Therapy.* Boulder, CO: Center for the Study and Prevention of Violence.

Alexander, J. F., & Parsons, B. V. (1973). Short-term behavioral intervention with delinquent families: Impact on family process and recidivism. *Journal of Abnormal Psychology, 81,* 219–225.

Alexander, J. F., & Parsons, B. V. (1982). *Functional Family Therapy: Principles and procedures.* Carmel, CA: Brooks & Cole.

Alexander, J. F., & Sexton, T. L. (2002). Functional Family Therapy (FFT) as an integrative, mature clinical model for treating high risk, acting out youth. In J. Lebow (Ed.), *Comprehensive handbook of psychotherapy, volume IV: Integrative/Eclectic* (pp. 111–132). New York: John Wiley.

Angold, A., & Costello, E. J. (2000). The Child and Adolescent Psychiatric Assessment (CAPA). *Journal of the American Academy of Child & Adolescent Psychiatry, 39,* 39–48.

Aos, S., Phipps, P., Barnoski, R., & Lieb, R. (2001). *The comparative costs and benefits of programs to reduce crime* (Document 01-05-1201). Olympia: Washington State Institute for Public Policy.

Atkins, M. S., & McKay, M. M. (2001). Conduct disorder. In M. Hersen & V. B. Van Hasselt (Eds.), *Advanced abnormal psychology* (2nd ed., pp. 209–222). New York: Kluwer Academic/Plenum.

Barton, C., Alexander, J. F., Waldron, H., Turner, C. W., & Warburton, J. (1985). Generalizing treatment effects of Functional Family Therapy: Three replications. *American Journal of Family Therapy, 13,* 16–26.

Borduin, C. M., Henggeler, S. W., Blaske, D. M., & Stein, R. J. (1990). Multisystemic treatment of adolescent sexual offenders. *International Journal of Offender Therapy & Comparative Criminology, 34,* 105–113.

Borduin, C. M., Mann, B. J., Cone, L. T., Henggeler, S. W., Fucci, B. R., Blaske, D. M., et al. (1995). Multisystemic treatment of serious juvenile offenders: Long-term prevention of criminality and violence. *Journal of Consulting and Clinical Psychology, 63,* 569–578.

Brown, T. L., Henggeler, S. W., Schoenwald, S. K., Brondino, M. J., & Pickrel, S. G. (1999). Multisystemic treatment of substance abusing and dependent juvenile delinquents: Effects on school attendance at posttreatment and 6-month follow-up. *Children's Services: Social Policy, Research, & Practice, 2,* 81–93.

Brunk, M. A., Henggeler, S. W., & Whelan, J. P. (1987). Comparison of multisystemic therapy and parent training in the brief treatment of child abuse and neglect. *Journal of Consulting and Clinical Psychology, 55,* 171–178.

Chamberlain, P. (1990). Comparative evaluation of specialized foster care for seriously delinquent youths: A first step. Community Alternatives: *International Journal of Family Care, 2,* 21–36.

**Chamberlain, P., & Mihalic, S. (1998). *Blueprints for violence prevention, book eight: Multidimensional treatment foster care.* Boulder, CO: Center for the Study and Prevention of Violence.

Chamberlain, P., Moreland, S., & Reid, K. (1992). Enhanced services and stipends for foster parents: Effects on retention rates and outcomes for children. *Child Welfare, 71,* 387–401.

Chamberlain, P., Ray, J., & Moore, K. J. (1996). Characteristics of residential care for adolescent offenders: A comparison of assumptions and practices in two models. *Journal of Child & Family Studies, 5,* 285–297.

Chamberlain, P., & Reid, J. B. (1991). Using a specialized foster care community treatment model for children and adolescents leaving the state mental hospital. *Journal of Community Psychology, 19,* 266–276.

Chamberlain, P., & Reid, J. B. (1998). Comparison of two community alternatives to incarceration for chronic juvenile offenders. *Journal of Consulting and Clinical Psychology, 66,* 624–633.

Chamberlain, P., & Rosicky, J. G. (1995). The effectiveness of family therapy in the treatment of adolescents with conduct disorders and delinquency. *Journal of Marital & Family Therapy, 21,* 441–459.

Chambless, D. L., & Hollon, S. D. (1998). Defining empirically supported therapies. *Journal of Consulting and Clinical Psychology, 66,* 7–18.

Clingempeel, W. G., & Henggeler, S. W. (in press). Randomized clinical trials (RCTs), developmental theory, and antisocial youth: Guidelines for research. *Development and Psychopathology.*

Eddy, J. M., & Chamberlain, P. (2000). Family management and deviant peer association as mediators of the impact of treatment condition on youth antisocial behavior. *Journal of Consulting and Clinical Psychology, 68,* 857–863.

Elliott, D. S. (1994). Serious violent offenders: Onset, developmental course, and termination. The American Society of Criminology 1993 presidential address. *Criminology, 32,* 1–21.

Elliott, D. S., Huizinga, D., & Morse, B. (1986). Self-reported violent offending: A descriptive analysis of juvenile violent offenders and their offending careers. *Journal of Interpersonal Violence, 1,* 472–514.

Feehan, M., McGee, R., Raja, S. N., & Williams, S. M. (1994). DSM-III-R disorders in New Zealand 18-year-olds. *Australian & New Zealand Journal of Psychiatry, 28,* 87–99.

Frick, P. J. (1998). *Conduct disorders and severe antisocial behavior.* New York: Plenum Press.

Gordon, D. A., Arbuthnot, J., Gustafson, K. E., & McGreen, P. (1988). Home-based behavioral-systems family therapy with disadvantaged juvenile delinquents. *American Journal of Family Therapy, 16,* 243–255.

Gordon, D. A., Graves, K., & Arbuthnot, J. (1995). The effect of functional family therapy for delinquents on adult criminal behavior. *Criminal Justice & Behavior, 22,* 60–73.

Gorman-Smith, D., Tolan, P. H., Loeber, R., & Henry, D. B. (1998). Relation of family problems to patterns of delinquent involvement among urban youth. *Journal of Abnormal Child Psychology, 26,* 319–333.

Haley, J. (1987). *Problem-solving therapy* (2nd ed.). San Francisco: Jossey-Bass.

Hann, D. M., & Borek, N. (2001). *Taking stock of risk factors for child/youth externalizing behavior problems* (NIH Publication No. 02-4938). Washington, DC: Department of Health and Human Services, Public Health Service, National Institutes of Health, National Institute of Mental Health.

Hawkins, J. D., Herrenkohl, T., Farrington, D. P., Brewer, D., Catalano, R. F., & Harachi, T. W. (1998). A review of predictors of youth violence. In R. Loeber & D. P. Farrington (Eds.), *Serious & violent juvenile offenders: Risk factors and successful interventions* (pp. 106–146). Thousand Oaks, CA: Sage.

Henggeler, S. W., & Borduin, C. M. (1992). *Multisystemic therapy adherence scales.* Charleston, SC: Medical University of South Carolina, Department of Psychiatry and Behavioral Science.

Henggeler, S. W., Clingempeel, W. G., Brondino, M. J., & Pickrel, S. G. (in press). Four-year follow-up of multisystemic therapy with substance abusing and dependent juvenile offenders. *Journal of the American Academy of Child & Adolescent Psychiatry.*

Henggeler, S. W., Melton, G. B., Brondino, M. J., Scherer, D. G., & Hanley, J. H. (1997). Multisystemic therapy with violent and chronic juvenile offenders and their families: The role of treatment fidelity in successful dissemination. *Journal of Consulting and Clinical Psychology, 65,* 821–833.

Henggeler, S. W., Melton, G. B., & Smith, L. A. (1992). Family preservation using multisystemic therapy: An effective alternative to incarcerating serious juvenile offenders. *Journal of Consulting and Clinical Psychology, 60,* 953–961.

Henggeler, S. W., Melton, G. B., Smith, L. A., Schoenwald, S. K., & Hanley, J. H. (1993). Family preservation using multisystemic treatment: Long-term follow-up to a clinical trial with serious juvenile offenders. *Journal of Child & Family Studies, 2,* 283–293.

Henggeler, S. W., Pickrel, S. G., & Brondino, M. J. (1999). Multisystemic treatment of substance abusing and dependent delinquents: Outcomes, treatment fidelity, and transportability. *Mental Health Services Research, 1,* 171–184.

Henggeler, S. W., Pickrel, S. G., Brondino, M. J., & Crouch, J. L. (1996). Eliminating (almost) treatment dropout of substance abusing or dependent delinquents through home-based multisystemic therapy. *American Journal of Psychiatry, 153,* 427–428.

Henggeler, S. W., Rodick, J. D., Borduin, C. M., Hanson, C. L., Watson, S. M., & Urey, J. R. (1986). Multisystemic treatment of juvenile offenders: Effects on adolescent behavior and family interaction. *Developmental Psychology, 22,* 132–141.

Henggeler, S. W., Rowland, M. D., Randall, J., Ward, D. M., Pickrel, S. G., Cunningham, P. B., et al. (1999). Home-based multisystemic therapy as an alternative to the hospitalization of youths in psychiatric crisis: Clinical outcomes. *Journal of the American Academy of Child & Adolescent Psychiatry, 38,* 1331–1339.

**Henggeler, S. W., Schoenwald, S. K., Borduin, C. M., Rowland, M. D., & Cunningham, P. B. (1998). *Multisystemic treatment of antisocial behavior in children and adolescents.* New York: Guilford Press.

Henggeler, S. W., Schoenwald, S. K., Rowland, M. D., & Cunningham, P. B. (2002). *Serious emotional disturbance in children and adolescents: Multisystemic therapy.* New York: Guilford Press.

Huey, S. J., Jr., Henggeler, S. W., Brondino, M. J., & Pickrel, S. G. (2000). Mechanisms of change in multisystemic therapy: Reducing delinquent behavior through therapist adherence and improved family and peer functioning. *Journal of Consulting and Clinical Psychology, 68,* 451–467.

Kazdin, A. E. (1995). *Conduct disorders in childhood and adolescence* (2nd ed.). Thousand Oaks, CA: Sage.

Kazdin, A. E., & Weisz, J. R. (1998). Identifying and developing empirically supported child and adolescent treatments. *Journal of Consulting and Clinical Psychology, 66,* 19–36.

Kelley, B. T., Loeber, R., Keenan, K., & DeLamatre, M. (1997). *Developmental pathways in boys' disruptive and delinquent behavior* (NCJ 165692). Washington, DC: U.S. Department of Justice, Office of Justice Programs, Office of Juvenile Justice and Delinquency Prevention.

Kendall, P. C., & Braswell, L. (1993). *Cognitive-behavioral therapy for impulsive children, 2nd Edition.* New York: Guilford Press.

Klein, N. C., Alexander, J. F., & Parsons, B. V. (1977). Impact of family systems intervention on recidivism and sibling delinquency: A model of primary prevention and program evaluation. *Journal of Consulting and Clinical Psychology, 45,* 469–474.

Lipsey, M. W., & Derzon, J. H. (1998). Predictors of violent or serious delinquency in adolescence and early adulthood: A synthesis of longitudinal research. In R. Loeber & D. P. Farrington (Eds.), *Serious & violent juvenile offenders: Risk factors and successful interventions* (pp. 86–105).

Thousand Oaks, CA: Sage.

Loeber, R., Burke, J. D., Lahey, B. B., Winters, A., & Zera, M. (2000). Oppositional defiant and conduct disorder: A review of the past 10 years, Part I. *Journal of the American Academy of Child & Adolescent Psychiatry, 39*, 1468–1484.

Loeber, R., Farrington, D. P., Stouthamer-Loeber, M., & Van Kammen, W. B. (1998). *Antisocial behavior and mental health problems: Explanatory factors in childhood and adolescence.* Mahwah, NJ: Erlbaum.

Loeber, R., Farrington, D. P., & Waschbusch, D. A. (1998). Serious and violent juvenile offenders. In R. Loeber & D. P. Farrington (Eds.), *Serious & violent juvenile offenders: Risk factors and successful interventions* (pp. 13–29). Thousand Oaks, CA: Sage.

Loeber, R., & Keenan, K. (1994). Interaction between conduct disorder and its comorbid conditions: Effects of age and gender. *Clinical Psychology Review, 14*, 497–523.

Mihalic, S., Irwin, K., Elliott, D., Fagan, A., & Hansen, D. (2001). *Blueprints for violence prevention.* Boulder, CO: Center for the Study of Violence Prevention.

Minuchin, S. (1974). *Families & family therapy.* Cambridge, MA: Harvard University Press.

Munger, R. L. (1993). *Changing children's behavior quickly.* Lanham, MD: Madison.

Nagin, D., & Tremblay, R. E. (1999). Trajectories of boys' physical aggression, opposition, and hyperactivity on the path to physically violent and nonviolent juvenile delinquency. *Child Development, 70*, 1181–1196.

National Advisory Mental Health Council Workgroup on Child and Adolescent Mental Health Intervention Development and Deployment. (2001). *Blueprint for change: Research on child and adolescent mental health.* Washington, DC: National Institute of Mental Health.

Offord, D. R., Boyle, M. H., Racine, Y. A., & Fleming, J. E. (1992). Outcome, prognosis, and risk in a longitudinal follow-up study. *Journal of the American Academy of Child & Adolescent Psychiatry, 31*, 916–923.

Randall, J., Henggeler, S. W., Cunningham, P. B., Rowland, M. D., & Swenson, C. C. (2001). Adapting multisystemic therapy to treat adolescent substance abuse more effectively. *Cognitive & Behavioral Practice, 8*, 359–366.

Schoenwald, S. K., Henggeler, S. W., Brondino, M. J., & Rowland, M. D. (2000). Multisystemic therapy: Monitoring treatment fidelity. *Family Process, 39*, 83–103.

Schoenwald, S. K., & Hoagwood, K. (2001). Effectiveness, transportability, and dissemination of interventions: What matters when. *Psychiatric Services, 52*, 1190–1197.

Schoenwald, S. K., Ward, D. M., Henggeler, S. W., Pickrel, S. G., & Patel, H. (1996). Multisystemic therapy treatment of substance abusing or dependent adolescent offenders: Costs of reducing incarceration, inpatient, and residential placement. *Journal of Child & Family Studies, 5*, 431–444.

Schoenwald, S. K., Ward, D. M., Henggeler, S. W., & Rowland, M. D. (2000). Multisystemic therapy versus hospitalization for crisis stabilization of youth: Placement outcomes 4 months postreferral. *Mental Health Services Research, 2*, 3–12.

Sexton, T. L., & Alexander, J. F. (2002). Functional Family Therapy: An empirically supported, family-based intervention model for at-risk adolescents and their families. In T. Patterson (Ed.), *Comprehensive handbook of psychotherapy, volume II: Cognitive, behavioral, and functional approaches* (pp. 117–140). New York: John Wiley.

Shadish, W. R., Montgomery, L. M., Wilson, P., Wilson, M. R., Bright, I., & Okwumabua, T. (1993). Effects of family and marital psychotherapies: A meta-analysis. *Journal of Consulting and Clinical Psychology, 61*, 992–1002.

Snyder, H. N., & Sickmund, M. (1999). *Juvenile offenders and victims: 1999 national report* (NCJ 178257). Pittsburgh, PA: U.S. Department of Justice, Office of Justice Programs, Office of Juvenile Justice and Delinquency Prevention, National Center for Juvenile Justice.

Stahl, A. L. (2001). *Delinquency cases in juvenile courts, 1998* (FS–200131). Washington, DC: U.S. Department of Justice, Office of Justice Programs, Office of Juvenile Justice and Delinquency Prevention.

Tolan, P. H., & Gorman-Smith, D. (1998). Development of serious and violent offending careers. In R. Loeber & D. P. Farrington (Eds.), *Serious & violent juvenile offenders: Risk factors and successful interventions* (pp. 68–85). Thousand Oaks, CA: Sage.

Tolan, P. H., & Henry, D. (1996). Patterns of psychopathology among urban poor children: Comorbidity and aggression effects. *Journal of Consulting and Clinical Psychology, 64,* 1094–1099.

U.S. Public Health Service. (1999). *Mental health: A report of the Surgeon General.* Rockville, MD: U.S. Department of Health and Human Services, National Institutes of Health, National Institute of Mental Health.

U.S. Public Health Service. (2001). *Youth violence: A report of the Surgeon General.* Washington, DC: Author.

Wasserman, G. A., McReynolds, L. S., Lucas, C. P., Fisher, P., & Santos, L. (2002). The voice DISC-IV with incarcerated male youths: Prevalence of disorder. *Journal of the American Academy of Child & Adolescent Psychiatry, 41,* 314–321.

Weisz, J. R., & Jensen, P. S. (1999). Efficacy and effectiveness of child and adolescent psychotherapy and pharmacotherapy. *Mental Health Services Research, 1,* 125–157.

Chapter 3   *Substance Abuse*

Cynthia L. Rowe, Ph.D., Center for Treatment Research on Adolescent Drug Abuse, Department of Psychiatry and Behavioral Sciences, University of Miami, Miami, Florida

Howard A. Liddle, Ph.D., Center for Treatment Research on Adolescent Drug Abuse, Department of Psychiatry and Behavioral Sciences, University of Miami, Miami, Florida.

D eveloping and disseminating effective treatments for drug abusers represents one of the nation's most urgent public health priorities (Leshner, 1997). In the United States, 14 million individuals (6.3% of the population) age 12 and over report current use of an illicit drug, with almost 10% of youth aged 12 to 17 reporting illicit drug use in the past 30 days (Substance Abuse and Mental Health Services Administration [SAMHSA], 2001). Not only does drug abuse devastate the lives of youth and adults alike, but it costs the United States over 100 billion dollars each year in health and crime costs, an estimated 50% increase since 1985 (National Institute on Drug Abuse [NIDA], 1998). Although less than 5% (only about 4 billion dollars) of this figure is accounted for by treatment costs (NIDA, 1998), the need for services continues to increase for marijuana, heroin, and amphetamine abusers (SAMHSA, 1999). Trends also indicate that the need for treatment will continue to increase for older adults as the baby boomer generation ages (SAMHSA, 1999). Among youth, surveys indicate that perceived harmfulness of regular marijuana and LSD use and disapproval of heroin use are decreasing, and availability of club drugs such as ecstasy is on the rise (Johnston, O'Malley, & Bachman, 2001). Further, the fact that 60% of treatment admissions for drug abuse represent repeat treatment episodes suggests that treatments delivered in standard community practice are having little long-term impact (SAMHSA, 1999). Young substance abusers not only fail to receive empirically supported treatments, but the majority who need help never receive services of any kind (Dennis, 2002). Thus, the quest to develop and disseminate more effective treatments for this significant public health problem continues to be a top priority for practitioners, researchers, policy makers, and federal funding agencies (e.g., Crits-Cristoph & Siqueland, 1996; NIDA, 2002).

Specific aspects of family life and family relationships have strong and consistent connections to the initiation, exacerbation, and relapse of drug problems. Relationship factors such as poor parent-adolescent relationships consistently predict adolescent drug use across cultures and time (Brook, Brook, Arencibia-Mireles, Richter, & Whiteman, 2001) even more so than salient factors such as family structure (Friedman, Terras, & Glassman, 2000). Parenting practices including low monitoring, ineffective discipline, and poor communication are also important factors in the initiation and maintenance of drug abuse problems among youth (Liddle, Rowe, Dakof, & Lyke, 1998; McGillicuddy, Rychtarik, Duquette, & Morsheimer, 2001), although parenting clearly interacts with a host of other social and emotional factors in predicting the onset of drug abuse and related problems (Dishion & Kavanagh, 2000). Other family variables have been shown to exert a strong protective influence against drug problems (Morojele & Brook, 2001). For instance, youth whose parents strongly disapprove of drug use are significantly less likely to report current use of an illicit drug (SAMHSA, 2001). Drug abuse in adulthood is also influenced by family factors, and family members can provide critical leverage in helping addicts initiate and maintain abstinence (Stanton & Todd, 1982). Studies show that couple and marital factors, such as the partner's poor coping strategies for dealing with their partner's drug problem (Barber, 1995), and generally negative communication patterns within the marriage (Fals-Stewart & Birchler, 1998) are associated with the substance abuser's more frequent use. Further, research shows that maintaining close relationships within healthy families-of-origin may buffer adult drug abusers from relapse (Lavee & Altus, 2001).

Because of the family's important role in drug abuse initiation, escalation, and recovery, family-based interventions have been of interest to drug abuse treatment researchers for over 20 years (Stanton & Todd, 1982). Recent federal funding initiatives reflect the importance of involving families in the process of deterring and curtailing substance abuse (e.g., Center for Substance Abuse Treatment's "Strengthening Families" substance abuse prevention program). Further, national standards for drug abuse practice in various mental health specialties reflect this increased attention to the role of the family in drug abuse assessment, prevention, and intervention (American Psychiatric Association, 1995; Bukstein & the Work Group on Quality Issues, 1997). These practice guidelines prescribe family involvement as a central feature of substance abuse interventions for both adolescents and adults (Crits-Christoph & Siqueland, 1996; Heath & Stanton, 1998; McCrady & Ziedonis, 2001; O'Farrell & Fals-Stewart, 1999; Platt, Widman, Lidz, Rubenstein, & Thompson, 1998). In reviewing the theoretical and historical bases of family-based drug treatment, McCrady and Epstein (1996) concluded that, "the mental health field has made the second half of the 20th century the era of the family" (p. 117). Berscheid (1999) further noted that psychology's increasing focus on "relationship science," which looks to contextual, interactional, and social environment factors to explain and intervene to change human behavior, has the potential to unite researchers and practitioners as well as to impact policy makers to address public health issues by implementing strategies to strengthen families.

In their 1995 review of the evidence for family therapy's efficacy in treating drug abuse, Liddle and Dakof concluded that family-based approaches demonstrated "promising, but not definitive" empirical support. The authors summarized their review by stating that, "considering the adolescent and adult areas together, there is promising but not definitive efficacy evidence—the number of studies is not large, the target populations are not inclusive, and conclusions are drawn from studies with a variety of methodological limitations" (p. 522).

Although their review of the adult literature revealed few advances since Stanton and Todd's (1979) original work, Liddle and Dakof concluded that the subspecialty area of family therapy for adolescent drug abusers was poised for major breakthroughs. Several manualized family-based approaches designed specifically for drug abusing teens had been subjected to rigorous investigation, and were found to successfully engage and retain teens and family members in treatment (e.g., Szapocznik et al., 1989) and reduce adolescents' drug use and related emotional and behavioral problems (e.g., Friedman, 1989; Henggeler et al., 1991; Liddle, 2002a), as well as improve their school performance and family functioning (e.g., Brown, Henggeler, Schoenwald, Brondino, & Pickrel, 1999; Liddle et al., 2001). Indeed, in the years since this review, the potential of family-based treatment for adolescent drug abuse has been realized in many ways. Important developments are also apparent in the adult area, building on empirically established family-based interventions with alcoholics and their families (e.g., Fals-Stewart et al., 2000).

This chapter is an update on the progress of family-based treatment for drug abuse in the years since Liddle and Dakof's 1995 review. Many advances are evident, particularly in the adolescent area, and favorable developments in the adult specialty are apparent as well.

Progress in Family-Based Treatment for Adolescent Drug Abuse

Family-based treatments have been heralded in a number of recent reviews as among the most promising approaches for the treatment of adolescent drug problems (Stanton & Shadish, 1997; Waldron, 1997; Weinberg, Rahdert, Colliver, & Glantz, 1998; Williams & Chang, 2000; Winters, Latimer, & Stinchfield, 1999). The first wave of randomized controlled trials of family-based interventions for adolescent drug abuse established the significant promise of family-based treatments in ameliorating adolescent drug abuse and related problems (Friedman, 1989; Joanning, Quinn, Thomas, & Mullen, 1992; Lewis, Piercy, Sprenkle, & Trepper, 1990; Liddle & Dakof, 1995; Szapocznik, Kurtines, Foote, Perez-Vidal, & Hervis, 1983, 1986; Szapocznik et al., 1988). Yet before the mid 1990s, appropriately so, given the available data at the time, conclusions about the potential of family-based interventions for adolescent drug abuse were cautious and tentative. Recent statements regarding its superiority are much more definitive. For example, in their comprehensive review of drug abuse treatment for adolescents, Williams and Chang (2000) concluded that, "there is evidence that treatment is superior to no treatment, but insufficient evidence to compare the effectiveness of treatment types. The exception to this is that outpatient family therapy appears superior to other forms of outpatient treatment" (p. 159). In another review of adolescent drug abuse treatment, Waldron (1997) concluded that, "when compared to alternative, nonfamily interventions, family therapy appears to emerge as the superior treatment" (p. 229).

These conclusions are based on the accumulation of evidence from these early studies as well as findings from a second wave of family-based intervention studies, which built on the foundations set by the first generation of research and adhered to more rigorous standards of clinical research now held in the fields of psychotherapy and drug abuse treatment research. The creation and use of therapy manuals has facilitated the dissemination and replication of family-based therapies in various adolescent treatment and research settings. Greater attention to methodological challenges such as accurate assessment of family processes and the conceptualization of these interactional processes vis-à-vis individual level variables (Liddle & Rowe, 1998), evaluation of therapist adherence to treatment protocols (Henggeler, Melton, Brondino, Scherer, & Hanley, 1997; Hogue et al., 1998), investigation of therapeutic process and its relationship to in-session outcomes (Diamond & Diamond, 2001), and the application of sophisticated analytical methods for measuring change over time are evident as well. Although significant challenges remain, the past decade has seen major advances in family-based treatments for adolescent drug abusers. These research results are reviewed below.

Engagement and Retention in Family-Based Treatment

Teenage drug abusers can be difficult to engage and retain in drug treatment, and the family dysfunction that is linked to a range of adolescent problem behaviors also creates serious obstacles to providing adequate services to these youth. Family-based approaches have the advantage of addressing some of the very barriers, such as parental resistance to change (Stoolmiller, Duncan, Bank, & Patterson, 1993), family adversity (Prinz & Miller, 1994), and perceived challenges of therapy itself and a disconnected relationship with the therapist (Kazdin, Holland, & Crowley, 1997) that keep troubled youth from getting the help they need (Coatsworth, Santisteban, McBride, & Szapocznik, 2001; Fishman, Andes, & Knowlton, 2001; Miller & Prinz, 1990; Spoth & Redmond, 1995). In fact, one of family therapy's stellar contributions to the treatment of adolescent drug abuse is the development of strategies and specialized methods for engaging difficult youth and their families into treatment (e.g., Henggeler, Pickrel, Brondino, & Crouch, 1996). For instance, in early studies using strategic-structural engagement strategies with troubled Hispanic boys and their families, Szapocznik et al. (1988, 1989) demonstrated that their intervention was more successful in retaining families than alternative treatments. These researchers continued to refine these engagement techniques within the Brief Strategic Family Therapy clinical research program (BSFT; see Szapocznik & Williams, 2000), using three core structural family therapy (Minuchin, 1974) strategies of "joining" (creating an alliance with each family member and assuming leadership to facilitate change), "family pattern diagnosis" (identifying family interactions linked to poor engagement and other presenting problems), and "restructuring" (using reframing, de-triangulation, and other interventions to alter family interactions that keep the youth and family from getting help). These studies have shown that BSFT engagement strategies successfully retain families and produce effects among severe cases, and have explored cultural factors that influence engagement (Coatsworth et al., 2001; Santisteban et al., 1996). Miller and Prinz (1990) suggested that these types of multisystemic, broad-based engagement-focused enhancements to existing family-based interventions are promising and warrant further investigation.

Well defined, intensive family-based interventions more effectively engage youth in treatment as compared to standard engagement practices (e.g., an initial phone contact to schedule the first session). Santisteban et al. (1996) replicated Szapocznik et al.'s (1988) engagement study, documenting that family therapy plus a specialized engagement intervention resulted in an 81% rate of engagement into treatment compared to a rate of 57% for family-based therapy only, and 62% for adolescent group therapy. Donohue et al. (1998) found that 89% of cases receiving family-based engagement attended the first session compared to 60% of cases receiving standard parent-only engagement procedures. Overall session attendance was also higher for the family-based treatment (83% vs. 57%). Promising family-based engagement interventions are also being developed for particularly resistant and severe adolescent drug abusing populations, including homeless runaway youth (Slesnick, Meyers, Meade, & Segelken, 2000) and juvenile offenders (Dembo, Cervenka, Hunter, & Wang, 1998; Donohue et al., 1998).

Family-based treatment also retains teenage drug abusers in therapy as successfully as other state-of-the-art drug treatments and more effectively than standard drug treatment as usual. For instance, Multisystemic Therapy (MST; Henggeler & Borduin, 1990), a social ecological approach to altering the multiple risk factors that create and maintain adolescent substance abuse and delinquency, has demonstrated impressive retention rates for very difficult youth and families. For example, Henggeler et al. (1996) reported a 98% treatment completion rate for substance abusing, delinquent teens in MST (130 days of treatment on average). Further, retention in certain intensive forms of family-based therapy is dramatically higher than "treatment as usual" (TAU) provided within the juvenile justice system (Henggeler et al., 1991, 1996). Finally, results of a meta-analysis revealed that retention in family-based therapy is generally better than in other well-established adolescent drug treatments (Stanton & Shadish, 1997). Thus, the ability of family-based interventions to engage and retain drug abusing youth and their families, among the most difficult populations to maintain in therapy, has been very well established.

Drug Use

The results of the newest generation of rigorously controlled studies leave little doubt about the ability of family-based treatment approaches to significantly reduce adolescent drug use (Stanton & Shadish, 1997; Waldron, 1997). Significant drug use reductions over the course of therapy have been demonstrated in all controlled trials of family-based therapy, with effects on alcohol and marijuana use as well as hard drugs including cocaine, heroin, and other narcotics (Henggeler, Pickrel, & Brondino, 1999; Liddle et al., 2001). In many controlled studies, family-based therapy has also shown greater reductions in adolescent drug use over the course of therapy compared to alternative treatments, including individual therapy (Liddle, 2002a; Waldron, Slesnick, Brody, Turner, & Peterson, 2001), adolescent group therapy (Liddle et al., 2001), and family psychoeducational drug counseling (Liddle et al., 2001). For example, both family-based approaches tested in the Cannabis Youth Treatment (CYT) study, a multi-site randomized clinical trial of five state-of-the-art approaches for adolescent marijuana dependence effectively reduced adolescent drug use (Dennis et al., in press). The first approach, Multidimensional Family Therapy (MDFT; Liddle, 2002b), is a developmentally and ecologically oriented approach to reducing adolescent drug use and related problems by intervening in the multiple systems that maintain these symptoms. MDFT reduced adolescents' substance use by 27% from intake to discharge in the CYT study. A second family-based approach tested in the CYT study, the Family Support Network (FSN), combined individual cognitive behavior therapy (CBT) sessions and Motivational Enhancement Therapy (MET) for the adolescent with parent psychoeducational groups, home visits, and case management services. FSN reduced past month symptoms related to substance abuse by 44% between intake and the end of treatment. At the 3-month assessment (treatment discharge), 65% of MDFT and 64% of FSN adolescents had no past month substance abuse disorder symptoms. FSN was also more effective in reducing drug use with higher drug use severity adolescents than the comparison individual and group therapy conditions (Dennis et al., in press).

Waldron et al. (2001) recently examined the efficacy of a combination Functional Family Therapy (FFT; Alexander & Parsons, 1982) plus individual CBT approach in comparison to FFT-only, individual CBT-only, and peer group therapy for substance abusing adolescents. FFT is a behaviorally based, systems oriented family therapy approach that aims to alter the maladaptive family patterns maintaining the adolescent's problems. Treatment targets change in these destructive interactional patterns and uses behavioral interventions to reinforce positive ways of responding and to establish more effective problem-solving approaches within the family. Early research on FFT, among the first well-controlled trials of family therapy for adolescent behavior problems (Alexander & Parsons, 1973; Barton, Alexander, Waldron, Turner, & Warburton, 1985), established that FFT improved family functioning and reduced recidivism among delinquent teens to a greater extent than juvenile court based group therapy, group home therapy, psychodynamic therapy, or no treatment. Results of the more recent study by Waldron et al. (2001) revealed that teens in combination FFT+CBT and in the FFT-only conditions had fewer days of drug use at 4-month follow-up than youth in CBT-only and group treatment. Combination FFT+CBT also demonstrated significant reductions in drug use between intake to treatment and the 7-month follow-up assessment.

Teens in family-based therapy not only reduce their drug use during therapy, but studies convincingly demonstrate that they can maintain these treatment gains up to 12 months postdischarge. For example, in the CYT study described earlier, teens in MDFT continued to reduce their substance use problems between the 3- and 12-month follow-up assessments (Dennis et al., in press). In another controlled trial, teens in MDFT had less substance use at the 12-month postdischarge follow-up than youth in either group treatment or multifamily education therapy (Liddle et al., 2001). Even more promising are results suggesting that adolescent drug use continues to decline from discharge to 12-months posttreatment among adolescents in MDFT whereas decreases in drug involvement leveled off among adolescents in the comparison CBT treatment, a state of the science, manualized individual adolescent intervention (Liddle, 2002a). Preliminary results of an ongoing randomized clinical trial comparing intensive MDFT with residential treatment for severe drug abusing comorbid teens show that MDFT more effectively reduces drug use from intake to 12 months postintake (Liddle, Dakof, & Henderson, 2002). The longest drug use outcomes in family-based treatment to date have been measured by Henggeler, Clingempeel, Brondino, and Pickrel (2002), who recently published 4-year outcomes of a clinical trial comparing MST and community services as usual. Results of urine samples indicated higher percentages of marijuana abstinence at the 4-year follow-up among young adults who had received MST (55%) as teenagers than those who had received services as usual (28%). Further, Stanton and Shadish's (1997) meta-analysis found that whereas the family based therapy intake to discharge effect sizes are superior to alternative approaches for substance abuse, their superiority is even more pronounced when effect sizes are examined for longer follow-up assessments.

In sum, the evidence for family-based therapy's ability to reduce teen drug use and sustain these treatment gains in the year following treatment is unequivocal. Several studies also suggest that certain family therapy approaches can more significantly impact drug use than alternative state-of-the-art nonfamily treatments. More long-term outcome data are needed, however, to determine the trajectories of drug use for youth who have had family-based treatments as they enter young adulthood. One ongoing clinical trial is currently examining the long-term (4 year) comparative effects of MDFT versus residential treatment for dually diagnosed severe drug abusing teens (Liddle et al., 2002).

Behavioral and Emotional Problems Associated With Drug Use

We now know that psychiatric comorbidity is "the usual, rather than the unusual, state of affairs" in treating drug abusers, including adolescents (Leshner, 1997, p. 692). The majority of teenage drug abusers present both internalizing and externalizing symptoms in addition to their drug problems (Rowe, Liddle, & Dakof, 2001). Research consistently demonstrates that adolescent substance abuse in combination with psychiatric disorders is a more complex and challenging clinical phenomenon than either substance abuse or psychiatric problems alone (Bukstein, Brent, & Kaminer, 1989; Kaminer, 1999; Riggs, 1998). Adolescent substance abusers with comorbid psychiatric disorders have earlier onset of substance use, greater frequency of use, and more chronic substance use than those without comorbid disorders (Clark & Neighbors, 1996; Greenbaum, Prange, Friedman, & Silver, 1991; Horner & Scheibe, 1997; Rohde, Lewinsohn, & Seeley, 1996). Because of the reality of comorbidity among adolescent drug abusers, interventions for these youth must actively target and successfully impact these associated problems. Failure to do so results in compromised treatment and poor outcomes (Grella, Hser, Joshi, & Rounds-Bryant, 2001). Family-based approaches, which target change in the multiple systems implicated in the development and maintenance of both drug use and psychiatric problems, are among the most effective treatments for adolescent substance abusers with comorbid disorders (Clark & Bukstein, 1998; Henggeler et al., 1991; Liddle, 2002a).

Controlled trials of family therapy indicate that state-of-the-art, multiple systems focused, family-based approaches for adolescent drug abuse also effectively reduce associated behavioral problems, such as aggression and delinquency. For example, teens in MDFT demonstrated significant reductions in externalizing problems between intake and 12 months postdischarge (Liddle et al., 2001). Some studies suggest that family therapy has an advantage over other approaches in ameliorating conduct problems among adolescent drug abusers. For instance, Henggeler et al. (1999) found that between intake and the 6-month follow-up, adolescents in MST had 46% fewer incarceration days and 50% fewer days in restrictive out-of-home placements than youth in the treatment as usual condition. In the first controlled trial of adolescent drug treatment following teens for more than 1 year, Henggeler et al. (1991) demonstrated that adolescents in MST had fewer drug-related arrests than adolescents who had been treated in individual therapy 4 years later. These long-term effects were recently replicated by Henggeler et al. (2002), who reported fewer convictions for aggressive crimes among young adults who had received MST 4 years earlier than those who had been referred for services as usual (0.15 vs. 0.57 on average). Finally, Liddle (2002a) found that parents' reports of youths' aggression and delinquency and adolescents' reports of their own depression and anxiety improved significantly between the beginning of treatment and the 12-month follow-up among adolescents in MDFT. However, for teens in CBT, initial gains in these symptoms leveled off from treatment termination to the 12-month follow-up. These studies provide solid support for the efficacy of family-based therapy in reducing problem behaviors associated with adolescent drug abuse, as well as preliminary evidence that family-based therapy may be more effective than other types of treatments in ameliorating comorbid symptoms.

Overall, the findings indicate that certain types of family-oriented interventions for adolescent drug abusers can reduce their comorbid symptoms, particularly externalizing problems such as aggression and delinquency. Few studies of family-based treatment for adolescent drug abuse have examined or demonstrated their impact on comorbid internalizing symptoms, however. Studies of the newest generation of intensive, multisystemic family therapy models are examining the benefits of incorporating psychiatric evaluation and medication services as adjuncts to family-based therapy for adolescent drug abuse (e.g., Rowe, Liddle, McClintic, & Quille, 2002).

School Attendance and Performance

Adolescents with drug abuse and associated behavioral problems typically experience limited academic success and tend to have low commitment and bonding to school (Chatlos, 1997; Hawkins, Catalano, & Miller, 1992). School outcomes profoundly impact the long-term trajectories of problem teens. For instance, a parent's endorsement of the importance of academic success has been shown to be a strong predictor of positive outcome in family therapy (Dakof, Tejeda, & Liddle, 2001). School success and reconnection are thus among the most important outcomes in adolescent drug treatment because they are critical components in the process of creating a prosocial, productive trajectory for the teen. In reviewing clinical trials of family-based approaches, however, very few of these studies examine changes over time in school performance. Yet in every study reporting outcomes in the domain of academic functioning, adolescents in family therapy improved significantly in school, and in two studies showed more impressive gains than in other treatments. For example, Liddle et al. (2001) found that adolescents in MDFT exhibited significantly higher increases in grade point average from intake to 1 year posttreatment (improving one grade level on average) than teens in group drug treatment or multifamily psychoeducational treatment. Brown et al. (1999) reported that the percentage of youth who were regularly attending school increased more significantly among youth in MST compared to those in treatment as usual from intake to 6 months posttermination. Finally, Azrin et al. (2001) reported significant pre–posttreatment improvements in school performance and satisfaction for adolescent drug abusers in behavioral family therapy that were maintained up to 6 months posttreatment. Overall, these findings provide encouraging evidence of the efficacy of family-based therapy in improving drug abusing adolescents' involvement in school, yet the interface between families and schools in the context of family-based interventions is an area that is wide open for further empirical investigation. Specifically, nothing is known about the processes by which school performance improves over the course of family therapy, or the most effective therapeutic interventions for intervening in the academic domain.

Family Functioning

Family-based treatments for adolescent drug abuse are based on the fundamental premise that certain parent and family factors that contribute to the initiation and exacerbation of the teen's substance use must be changed in order to assist the adolescent in maintaining a drug-free lifestyle (Liddle, 1999). A range of family problems have been consistently associated with adolescent substance abuse and related problems, including poor parenting practices, high conflict, and parent-adolescent disengagement (Liddle et al., 1998). Studies of adolescent drug treatment have shown that broadly defined and measured family factors have been linked to adolescents' outcomes. For instance, parental participation in standard adolescent drug abuse treatment predicts a teen's more favorable drug use outcomes at both 6- and 12-month follow-ups (Hsieh, Hoffman, & Hollister, 1998). Shoemaker and Sherry (1991) established that posttreatment family functioning was one of the most important predictors of adolescents' drug use in the 3 months following residential treatment. Although these broad level associations between family functioning and adolescent drug treatment outcomes can be made, surprisingly little evidence directly links family change in treatment to decreases in adolescent substance use over time (Waldron, 1997). Studies of family-based treatments have thus focused increasing attention on accurately measuring and evaluating the extent to which families change over the course of family therapy.

There is growing evidence that family-based treatment improves family functioning, including family-level variables such as conflict and cohesion and specific parenting deficits, as well as or better than alternative treatment approaches. For instance, Waldron et al. (2001) reported significant improvements in family conflict between intake and the 7-month follow-up for teens treated in combination FFT+CBT as well as those receiving group treatment. Liddle et al. (2001) also found family-based therapy to be superior to alternative treatments in improving family functioning. These investigators used observational ratings of global family health (positive, developmentally adaptive family interactions) to demonstrate that MDFT more positively impacted family functioning from pretreatment to 12 months postdischarge than adolescent group therapy or multifamily drug education. Finally, Schmidt, Liddle, and Dakof (1996) demonstrated that parents of youth treated in MDFT significantly improved their parenting skills over the course of therapy, and that these changes were related to decrease in the drug use and problem behavior of the teens.

Much more research is needed in this area to illuminate the ways in which families change in treatment and critically, how therapists facilitate these positive shifts (see Diamond & Liddle, 1996; Diamond, Liddle, Hogue, & Dakof, 1999). One avenue for more accurately measuring family-level change in treatment is the use of observational methods. In addition, studies linking specific changes in family functioning to adolescent drug use outcomes will be critical in advancing this specialty (see Treatment Process Studies section below for preliminary work in this area). In sum, an issue with methodological and substantive aspects, the matter of how best to determine if families change (behavioral ratings of video-tapes, for instance vs. self report of changes in families) remains an unsolved, and for that matter, underaddressed, research issue.

Economic Evaluation of Family-Based Interventions for Adolescent Drug Abuse
One area of notable progress in family-based treatment for adolescent drug abuse in the past decade is an increased focus on cost considerations and out-comes. We now know that the costs to society of drug abuse are significant and that these costs have increased dramatically in the past two decades (Harwood, Fountain, Carothers, Gerstein, & Johnson, 1998). Societal costs of substance abuse include tangible costs such as health costs, legal costs, and treatment costs, as well as intangible costs to individuals, families, and communities such as anx-iety, distress, and family disruption (French, Rachal, & Hubbard, 1991). The costs of treating chronic substance abuse, when considered in terms of multiple placements and "treatment careers" frequently initiated during adolescence, are astounding (Hubbard & French, 1991). In the current era of decreased funding for drug abuse services and increased accountability for outcomes, examination of relative costs and benefits of family-based treatment is an essential area of investigation.

In the first investigation of the cost-effectiveness of family-based treatment for adolescent drug abuse, Schoenwald, Ward, Henggeler, Pickrel, and Patel (1996) demonstrated that MST, an intensive community- and home-based approach to treating drug abuse and delinquency, was more cost-effective than standard outpatient treatment. Costs of treatment were compared to reductions in days of incarceration, hospitalization, and residential treatment over a 1-year period following treatment. MST significantly reduced the youth's involvement with the legal system after treatment, and this decrease was not offset by an increase in the use of other out-of-home placements. In fact, during the year fol-lowing treatment, youth who received family-based therapy experienced 46% fewer days of incarceration and 64% fewer days of inpatient psychiatric or resi-dential treatment than those in treatment as usual.

As part of the Cannabis Youth Treatment (CYT; Dennis et al., in press) study described below, French et al. (2002) conducted the most extensive and method-ologically sound economic evaluation of adolescent drug treatment to date. In the first phase of the economic evaluation, French and his team used the well stan-dardized and structured Drug Abuse Treatment Cost Analysis Program (DAT-CAP; French, Dunlap, Zarkin, McGeary, & McLellan, 1997) interview to com-pare the costs of the experimental interventions against data from the National Treatment Improvement Study (NTIES; Gerstein & Johnson, 1999), which provides formal cost estimates of adolescent outpatient drug treatment. The average weekly cost of MDFT (Liddle, 2002b) and FSN (Hamilton, Brantley, Tims, Angelovich, & McDougall, 2000) was less than the lower or upper weekly estimates of standard outpatient drug treatment. The weekly cost of FSN per adolescent was $244 and the average weekly cost of MDFT per adolescent was $164, in comparison to an average weekly cost of outpatient adolescent drug treatment in the NTIES study of $365. Thus, MDFT and FSN are both clearly sustainable under current funding levels. Moreover, cost benefit analyses indicate that MDFT had statistically significant baseline to follow-up reductions in drug use consequences as well as the lowest comparative dollar cost of drug use consequences at the 1-year follow-up assessment (French et al., 2002).

Although family-based interventions for adolescent drug abuse have demonstrated cost-effectiveness in comparison to standard outpatient treatment, a critical question remains regarding the comparative costs and benefits of intensive family-based approaches in relation to residential treatment. One such investigation is currently underway to compare the total and net monetary benefits of MDFT versus residential treatment for adolescent drug abuse. Preliminary cost analyses conducted by French et al. (in press) suggest that an integrative, intensive home-based version of MDFT for dually diagnosed severe drug abusing youth designed as an alternative to residential treatment is significantly less expensive than standard residential treatment in the community (Liddle et al., 2002). Results of the cost analysis using the DATCAP indicate that there is a substantial difference in expense (nearly a 3:1 difference) to deliver the two treatments in this trial. The residential treatment condition has a weekly cost per client of $1,138 while intensive MDFT's weekly cost per client is $384. Further, preliminary comparative efficacy data indicate that MDFT produces better outcomes in addition to its significantly lower cost. Systematic benefit-cost analyses are currently underway to examine the relative costs of each treatment in relation to their benefits in terms of reduced substance use and delinquency, and improvements in school behavior.

In the current political and social climate of accountability, treatment researchers and providers need to inquire about a treatment's clinical impact in the context of the intervention's costs. These economic evaluation studies have offered encouraging results; the findings have the potential to increase providers' and policy makers' incentives to use these cost-effective approaches in the community, given that these models may produce better outcomes at lower costs.

Treatment Process Studies of Family-Based Approaches for Adolescent Drug Abuse

Therapy process research helps treatment developers make sense of complex family-based treatments, providing important information about why certain interventions are effective, what specific techniques lead to what types of client change, and the timing and sequences of successful interventions (Diamond &

Diamond, 2001). By outlining the mechanisms of change in family therapy, investigators can pinpoint which interventions are most important during specific stages of treatment. Thus, process research has the potential to lead to the development of more effective treatments and to bridge the gap between science and practice by increasing the relevance of empirical findings to practitioners (Pinsof & Wynne, 2000).

Considerable progress has been made in examining the process of family-based therapies of adolescent drug abuse and identifying mechanisms of change in these models since Liddle and Dakof's (1995) review of the field. For instance, investigators have examined the impact of adolescent engagement interventions on improving initially poor therapist-adolescent alliances over the first three sessions of MDFT (Diamond et al., 1999). Significant gains in working alliance were evident when therapists emphasized the following alliance-building interventions: attending to the adolescent's experience, formulating personally meaningful goals, and presenting one's self as the adolescent's ally. Lack of improvement or deterioration in alliance was associated with the therapist continually socializing the adolescent to the nature of therapy, thus waiting too long to discuss how the therapy could be personally meaningful for the teenager. A second examination of the alliance-building process in MDFT attended to the role of culturally important theme development. Jackson-Gilfort, Liddle, Tejeda, and Dakof (2001) investigated whether therapeutic discussion of culturally specific themes enhanced treatment engagement of African American male substance abusing youths. Exploration of particular themes—anger and rage, alienation, and the journey from boyhood to manhood (i.e., what it means to become an African American man) were associated with both increased participation and decreased negativity by adolescents in the very next treatment session. These and other studies of the alliance in family therapy have yielded clinically important findings; however, future research needs to examine the links between the therapeutic relationship and outcomes in family therapy.

Process research also focuses on the nature and sequences that determine important change events in family therapy, or those interventions that lead to successful resolution of problems or relational shifts within the family. Diamond and Liddle (1996) used task analysis to identify the combination of clinical interventions and family interactions necessary to resolve in-session impasses in MDFT (clinical situations characterized by negative exchanges, emotional disengagement, and poor problem-solving between parents and adolescents). Therapist behaviors that contributed to defusing these negative interactions included: (a) actively blocking, diverting, or addressing and working through negative affect; (b) implanting, evoking, and amplifying thoughts and feelings that promote constructive dialogue; and (c) creating emotional treaties among family members by alternately working in session with parents alone and adolescents alone—a kind of shuttle diplomacy. In cases with successful resolution of the impasse, the therapist transformed the nature and tone of the conversation in the session, shifting the parent's blaming to a focus on their feelings of regret and loss, and eliciting the adolescent's thoughts and feelings about relationship roadblocks with the parent and others. The most conflicted and pessimistic families were least likely to move to a new conversational level. The study broke down in behavioral terms the components of the impasse, defining the unfolding sequential contributions of both parent and adolescent and specifying the relation of different therapist actions to the impasse.

Finally, process research in this specialty has illuminated the links between parent and adolescent change in therapy. For example, Schmidt et al. (1996) investigated the nature and extent of change in parenting behaviors in MDFT, as well as the link between parental subsystem change and reduction in adolescent drug abuse and other symptomatology. Parents showed significant decreases in negative parenting behaviors (e.g., negative affect, verbal aggression) and increases in positive parenting (e.g., monitoring and limit-setting, positive affect and commitment) over the course of therapy. In addition, these changes in parenting behaviors were associated with reductions in adolescent drug use and problem behaviors (59% of families showed improvement in both parenting practices and adolescent symptomatology). These results support an elemental tenet of family-based treatments: Change in a fundamental aspect of the family system (parenting practices) is related to change at the critical level of interest—reduction of adolescent symptoms, including drug abuse. Furthermore, these data suggest that parenting risk and protective factors for drug use are accessible to intervention within a therapeutic environment. These process studies have contributed to the development and testing of new versions of the MDFT approach (Liddle, 2002a; Rowe et al., 2002).

Several studies have investigated mechanisms of change in MST. In an early study, Mann, Borduin, Henggeler, and Blaske (1990) found that families with delinquent adolescents had more cross-generational coalitions (unhealthy alignments between mother and son and disengagement between father and son) and marital conflict than healthy control adolescents. Further, over the course of MST, decreases in adolescents' and fathers' symptoms were linked to improvements in the marital relationship (increased support and communication between husband and wife). Although the results did not support the link between reductions in adolescents' symptoms and improved parent-adolescent relationships, these findings provide critical support for fundamental assumptions of the negative impact of unhealthy, unbalanced coalitions in family therapy. However, subsequent research by MST investigators revealed a clear association between improved family functioning (increased parental monitoring and cohesion) and reduced delinquency among adolescents, mediated by decreased affiliation with delinquent peers (Huey, Henggeler, Brondino, & Pickrel, 2000). This study was important and unique in that it investigated the extent to which MST "dosage," or the extent of fidelity to the prescribed MST model, impacted the improvements of family functioning and adolescent symptoms. In fact, therapists' adherence to MST determined the extent of family change, which was associated with reduced affiliation with negative peers, and subsequently with decreased delinquency. Finally, Cunningham, Henggeler, Brondino, and Pickrel (1999) tested a fundamental assumption of family based therapies; namely, that empowering parents in treatment would be associated with improved youth and family functioning. This presumed mechanism of change was only partially supported as evidenced by a direct link from increased parental empowerment to improved family functioning but not to decreased behavior problems among youth. These process studies shed light on the essential ingredients and mechanisms of change in MST specifically and in family-based treatment more generally.

Finally, FFT researchers have investigated the sequences of therapist and family behavior that lead to positive behavior from delinquent adolescents and their parents in session. Robbins, Alexander, Newell, and Turner (1996) found that therapist reframes were the only interventions that were met with positive responses from delinquent adolescents in first sessions of functional family therapy, suggesting that the reframe may have a particularly important role in engaging resistant adolescents during the early stage of therapy. Robbins, Alexander, and Turner (2000) subsequently studied the processes by which therapists were able to disrupt defensive interactions among delinquent adolescents and their parents in session. Similar to the first study, therapist reframes were the only interventions that effectively reduced family members' defensive statements. These studies have been instrumental in outlining specific in-session therapist behaviors that lead to changes in family members' behavior needed to shape longer-term positive outcomes.

These studies illuminate some of the important processes of family therapy's interior, yet significant work remains to link in-session interactions to adolescent and family outcomes (Waldron, 1997). One important ongoing study by Alexander and colleagues investigates core mechanisms of change in three empirically supported family-based models for problem youth (MDFT, FFT, and BSFT). Preliminary findings suggest that the processes by which models achieve their effects are distinct and that these differences are clinically meaningful. This important area of investigation has the potential to reduce the research-practice gap. For instance, process research linking specific aspects of family-based interventions to reductions in adolescents' drug use and improvements in family functioning will advance dissemination efforts by identifying the most essential ingredients of these models—those intervention components that are most critical to implement in existing programs.

Evaluating Therapist Adherence and Linking It to Outcome

Treatment adherence research is another area of significant growth in the past decade in the specialty of family-based treatment for adolescent drug abuse. Treatment adherence refers to the degree to which a given therapy is implemented in accordance with essential theoretical and procedural aspects of the model

(Waltz, Addis, Koerner, & Jacobson, 1993). Treatment adherence evaluation is aimed at identifying which ingredients of a given treatment have been practiced by therapists as prescribed in theory and in its manual. Thus, it can provide valuable insight on successes and failures in model delivery, as well as on the pragmatics of implementing treatments with various client populations. In this regard, adherence evaluation represents an essential step in the development and refinement of effective treatments (Kazdin, 1994). Several adherence studies have been conducted on family therapy models for adolescent drug abuse in recent years (Henggeler et al., 1997; Hogue et al., 1998; Huey et al., 2000), demonstrating that these complex, manualized treatments can be implemented with a high degree of adherence.

Four recent studies have focused on treatment adherence with adolescents with substance abuse and related behavioral problems. Hogue et al. (1998) used the Therapist Behavior Rating Scale (TBRS), a 26-item process coding instrument, to rate therapist adherence to treatment protocols in MDFT and CBT. The TBRS is based on intensive review of the MDFT manual and pilot coding of more than 50 hours of clinical videotape material (Hogue, Liddle, & Rowe, 1996). Hogue et al. (1998) found that, in accordance with their respective models, therapists practicing MDFT emphasized interactional and affect-focused interventions, whereas therapists practicing CBT used behavioral and addictions-focused techniques. Three adherence studies of MST (Henggeler et al., 1999; Huey et al., 2000; Schoenwald, Henggeler, Brondino, & Rowland, 2000) investigated levels of therapist adherence and the impact of adherence on treatment outcomes. These studies showed that acceptable adherence can be achieved given intensive adherence monitoring procedures (i.e., training and supervision of cases by model experts), and that therapist adherence predicted improvements in family relations and reductions in delinquent peer associations, which in turn predicted reductions in delinquent behavior.

These adherence studies have important practical implications for the field of family-based treatment of adolescent drug abuse. Findings that therapists can implement these models with high levels of fidelity to their respective manuals are encouraging in the context of new research focused on transporting and disseminating these interventions into practice.

Transporting Effective Family-Based Treatment Into Practice

Because of their ecological perspective on adolescent problems and the intuitive appeal of this perspective (Liddle, 1995), their accumulating efficacy evidence (Stanton & Shadish, 1997), and their systemic approach to creating change, family-based models hold considerable promise for transfer into community settings. Yet despite the significant recent advances in this subspecialty establishing the superiority of family-based treatment over other state-of-the-art treatments as well as standard drug treatment as delivered in the community, major obstacles remain in the successful transportation of these models into everyday clinic practice. The issue of transporting these therapies to office based private practice settings remains a virtually unexplored area in the field. Although major initiatives are now supporting the dissemination of family-based models such as MST, FFT, BSFT, and MDFT into the community, and these model developers have focused increasing efforts on transporting these models into practice (see Alexander, Sexton, & Robbins, 2001), there is only limited empirical support for these efforts. As in the drug treatment and mental health fields generally, there is virtually no evidence of the feasibility, acceptability, or effectiveness of empirically supported treatments as performed by front-line drug abuse providers (Tims, Inciardi, Fletcher, & Horton, 1997).

For instance, when Henggeler et al. (1999) studied the implementation of MST in community-based clinics without direct supervision from the developers of MST, their dissemination efforts resulted in significantly weaker drug use and delinquency outcomes than in previous studies by Henggeler and colleagues (see Henggeler et al., 1997). In this study, adolescents in MST treated by community therapists trained by clinic supervisors rather than MST experts demonstrated comparable drug use and delinquency outcomes to adolescents in treatment as usual. Not only was therapist adherence lower in the current study than in previous studies of MST, but levels of therapist adherence were associated with disappointing drug use outcomes. The results of this study support the conclusions of many reports from the literature on the unappreciated complexity of technology transfer efforts (Institute of Medicine, 1998).

A current study by Liddle, Rowe, et al. (2002) is examining the process of transporting an empirically based family therapy approach into the drug treatment community. This study represents the first systematic attempt, in an experimental study, to refine, adapt, and implement the MDFT model into an existing community-based drug treatment program for adolescent drug abusers. This 4-phase study evaluates the feasibility and durability of integrating MDFT interventions into a day drug treatment program for teens. During the Baseline phase, assessment of the existing day treatment organizational climate and client outcomes were assessed. The Training phase involved intensive training of day treatment program staff by expert MDFT supervisors. During the current phase, Implementation, MDFT supervisors continue to provide supervision, yet this guidance will be withdrawn during the final phase of the study to test the durability of the implementation. Preliminary data indicate some encouraging results of the technology transfer effort. The number of family sessions held by social workers in the day treatment program increased from the Baseline phase to the first 3 months of the Implementation phase, indicating that day treatment staff members are implementing the MDFT model in practice. Further, indicators of staff acceptance of the model and satisfaction with their work using MDFT interventions are promising. Yet the most important finding of this study to date is the knowledge gained about this process of model transportation. The authors conclude that rather than being a linear, unidirectional process in which researchers teach therapists to implement a certain therapy, successful dissemination must be an active, collaborative, flexible, and evolving process in which researchers adapt and refine a given model for integration within an existing setting or treatment program. This study represents only a beginning in the study of the transportation process in adolescent drug abuse treatment research.

The dissemination of empirically based family interventions into community practice may represent the most important area of study of contemporary adolescent drug treatment research. Regardless of the presenting problem, type of intervention, or population targeted, researchers have a long way to go in successfully adapting and transporting empirically based therapies into community settings. Continued efforts in this arena represent the potential breakthroughs of the next generation of adolescent drug treatment research.

Summary of family intervention science for adolescent drug problems. There is clear evidence of great progress in adolescent family-based drug treatment research in recent years. New studies, addressing some of the concerns of earlier reviews and adhering to higher standards of science, have unequivocally established the ability of adolescent specific family-based models to reduce drug use during therapy and maintain these reductions up to 1 year posttreatment. In some studies, family-based treatments have established superiority in comparison to other well-established models, such as individual CBT and peer group therapy, in reducing drug use and related symptoms. These same studies also demonstrate evidence of family therapy's positive effects on comorbid externalizing symptoms, school problems, and family functioning. Studies of treatment process have furthered treatment development efforts aimed at increasing the effectiveness of these approaches. The cost-effectiveness of intensive, multisystems, integrative family treatment approaches in comparison to drug treatment as delivered in standard community-based programs has been established. Therapists can be trained to deliver these models with excellent levels of adherence to manual prescribed protocols.

Despite all of these reasons for excitement in the field, these treatment models are utilized by only a very small minority of community treatment providers, and the treatments that are delivered in the vast majority of drug treatment clinics have never been empirically tested (O'Farrell & Fals-Stewart, 1999). The quest to transport empirically supported family-based treatment models into the community settings where they are needed most with the same level of therapist adherence and positive outcomes as has been demonstrated in research trials is far from being realized.

Progress in Family-Based Treatment for Adult Drug Abuse

In 1995, Liddle and Dakof reported that the development of the subspecialty of family-based treatment for adult drug abuse was unfortunately limited. In their review of this area, they concluded that "potential routes of investigation have been neglected (e.g., marital therapy approaches, although present in the alcoholism area, are virtually absent in the drug abuse field); promising lines of work have not been expanded or sustained (e.g., the work of Stanton & Todd, 1982); and the very definition of family therapy for adult addicts has not gone beyond initial conceptualizations" (p. 518). The most encouraging support for family therapy with adult addicts at that time was the program of research of Stanton and colleagues. Stanton and Todd (1982) reported that an innovative and integrative structural-strategic family therapy model reduced drug use more effectively than a family movie condition and standard drug counseling, although no differences were found on vocational or educational functioning. In a subsequent study, this research group showed that a home detoxification program was more effective than standard detoxification for substance abusers (Stanton, 1985). However, limitations of these and other studies of family-based treatment for adult drug abusers and the lack of replication and follow up by investigators dampened enthusiasm for these results.

A more optimistic review of family-based treatment for adult drug abuse was included as part of Stanton and Shadish's (1997) meta-analysis of family therapy for drug abuse problems. These authors concluded that family therapy works equally well for both adults and adolescents, and that family therapy studies with adults (6 studies) as well as adolescents (9 studies) tend to be of good design quality, show better results for family than nonfamily approaches, and, with adult narcotic addicts, is a cost-effective component of methadone maintenance. Yet reviewers agree that the subspecialty of family-based treatment for adult drug problems has lagged behind the field of family-based adult alcoholism treatment (McCrady & Epstein, 1996; O'Farrell & Fals-Stewart, 1999). Several authors have suggested that the application of effective family-based models for alcoholics hold promise for the treatment of adult drug abusers (Liddle & Dakof, 1995; Epstein & McCrady, 1998). In fact, recent years have seen great progress in the refinement and evaluation of family-based approaches originally designed for alcoholic patients with drug abusing adults and their families. Two areas in particular have benefited from this type of empirical attention: (a) working with significant family members to facilitate engagement of the drug abuser into treatment, and (b) the application of behavioral marital/couples therapy that previously demonstrated efficacy with alcoholic populations (Moyers & Hester, 1999), to drug abusers and their spouses/partners.

Mobilizing Family Members To Increase Treatment Engagement
   Family factors have been shown to significantly influence the engagement of drug abusers into treatment. For instance, Hser, Maglione, Polinsky, and Anglin (1998) reported that significant family problems may undermine drug abusers' motivation to follow through on treatment referrals. DeCivita, Dobkin, and Robertson (2000) concluded that significant family members' willingness to become involved in treatment depends both on the patients' openness to receiv-

ing their support as well as the therapists' active recruitment and invitation of them into the treatment process.

Because of the leverage provided by family members and concerned significant others, and the promise of such approaches with alcoholics and their significant others (e.g., Meyers, Miller, & Smith, 2001), several treatment research groups are developing and testing interventions designed to increase engagement of drug abusers into treatment by mobilizing these family supports (e.g., Landau et al., 2000). For instance, Dakof et al. (in press) provided a randomized, experimental test of the efficacy of a manualized, in-home drug abuse treatment enrollment and retention intervention that intervenes at the level of the individual and family. This program has roots in (a) the relational model of women's development (Dakof, 2000); (b) family therapy models of treating drug abuse (Liddle, Dakof, & Diamond, 1991); and (c) family preservation models of service delivery (Wells, 1995). The sample included 103 black mothers of substance exposed infants. Results demonstrated that significantly more women assigned to the enrollment and retention intervention ("Engaging Moms Program") enrolled into drug abuse treatment than did women assigned to the community engagement as usual (control) condition (88% vs. 46%). Although 67% in the Engaging Moms Program received at least 4 weeks of drug abuse treatment compared to 38% of the control women, only 39% of Engaging Moms clients and 35% of control clients stayed in treatment for at least 90 days. Thus, the Engaging Moms Program has considerable promise in facilitating treatment entry and initial engagement but did not influence retention.

Kirby, Marlowe, Festinger, Garvey, and LaMonaca (1999) randomized 32 family members and significant others (FSOs) of drug abusers to either a "Community Reinforcement Training" (CRT) intervention, adapted from Sisson and Azrin's (1986) approach with alcoholics and their wives, or a 12-step self-help group. The study was designed to examine differences in the interventions' acceptability to and benefits for FSOs, as well as impact on treatment entry of the drug abuser. The behaviorally oriented CRT approach uses community reinforcement strategies in the following areas: increasing FSO motivation for change, communication training, increasing positive interactions, nonreinforcement of drug use, suggesting and initiating counseling, handling dangerous situations, and developing outside activities. Follow-up assessments conducted 10 weeks later revealed significantly greater retention of the FSOs in treatment as well as higher rates of treatment engagement among drug abusers whose FSOs were assigned to CRT. However, results revealed no significant differences in the improvements of the FSOs' social or emotional functioning from baseline to the 10-week follow-up. Thus, the CRT approach, previously shown to be effective with alcoholics and their significant others (Meyers et al., 2001), shows promise with drug abusers and their FSOs as well.

In sum, preliminary evidence for the success of engagement interventions with family members and significant others suggests that these specialized interventions may hold promise for enlisting these natural supports to motivate drug abusers into treatment. However, neither intervention linked this initial success in engagement to retention of the drug abuser in treatment or other treatment outcomes. In fact, Dakof et al. (in press) were unable to demonstrate enhanced retention in treatment, although engagement was significantly better in the Engaging Moms intervention. Longer follow up of the CRT intervention would increase enthusiasm for its efficacy with drug abusing populations.

Behavioral Couples Therapy for Drug Abusers and Their Spouses

Couples' interactional patterns have been implicated in drug abusers' level of use and relapse after treatment (e.g., Fals-Stewart & Birchler, 1998). In the alcoholism field, the success of behavioral marital/couples therapy in helping alcoholics reduce their drinking, reducing incidents of domestic violence, and showing significant cost-savings in reduced hospitalizations and jail costs (O'Farrell & Fals-Stewart, 1999) has ignited considerable interest in its potential to help substance abusers initiate and maintain recovery (McCrady & Epstein, 1996). Epstein and McCrady (1998) suggested that the application of behavioral couples therapy (BCT) to treating drug abusers offers one of the most promising areas of family-based treatment research with substance abusers. The impressive research program of William Fals-Stewart and colleagues described below reveals that the application of BCT to the treatment of drug abuse is one of the most exciting developments in the field in the last decade.

Recent studies suggest that BCT may in fact have considerable promise in the treatment of drug abusers as well as alcoholic patients. In their first trial of BCT's efficacy with drug abusers, Fals-Stewart, Birchler, and O'Farrell (1996) examined the efficacy of BCT in comparison to individual-based therapy for 80 male drug abusers and their partners. The BCT approach involves an initial agreement for the drug abuser to commit to sobriety and the partner to reinforce this commitment daily, as well as strategies to help the drug abuser cope with cravings and for the couple to deal with crises concerning relapse, communicate more effectively, and increase enjoyable activities that do not involve substance use. Couples who received BCT (individual, group, and couples sessions) had better relationship outcomes and husbands had fewer days of drug use, longer periods of abstinence, and fewer drug-related arrests and hospitalizations up to 1-year follow-up than those in individual therapy (involving cognitive and behavioral coping skills training). Further, these authors established greater cost-effectiveness as well as relative benefit-cost of BCT than individual therapy (Fals-Stewart, O'Farrell, & Birchler, 1997). An extension of this study examining the clinical significance of these results, which involved subsequent analyses of these data using growth curve modeling analyses, found that a larger proportion of drug abusers in BCT significantly reduced their drug use and improved their relational functioning than those in individual behavior therapy (Fals-Stewart et al., 2000). Finally, investigators demonstrated greater effects of BCT on partner violence in this clinical trial (Fals-Stewart, Kashdan, O'Farrell, & Birchler, 2002).

These initial results, which established preliminary efficacy evidence for BCT in terms of drug use, relationships outcomes, and reduced partner violence, as well as better cost outcomes, have subsequently been replicated and expanded with other populations and outcomes. Winters, Fals-Stewart, O'Farrell, Birchler, and Kelley (2002) replicated these results with 75 female drug abusers, showing longer periods of continuous abstinence and lower levels of drug, alcohol, and family problems up to 1-year follow-up among female drug abusers who received BCT than those who participated in individual behavior therapy only. In another replication study, Kelley and Fals-Stewart (2002) also demonstrated that children's behavioral functioning improved more dramatically from intake to 12 months follow-up when their drug abusing fathers participated in BCT than when they received individual behavioral therapy or a psychoeducational attention control treatment. As in the first trial of BCT, father's drug use and couples' relationship quality also improved most significantly in BCT from intake to 12 months in this study. BCT has also demonstrated greater efficacy as a component of methadone maintenance than individual drug counseling plus methadone maintenance treatment (Fals-Stewart, O'Farrell, & Birchler, 2001). BCT demonstrates greater abstinence and compliance with naltrexone medication treatment and fewer legal and family problems at 12 months posttreatment than individual therapy for opiate addicts (Fals-Stewart & O'Farrell, in press). Finally, a new study establishes BCT's promise for increasing medication compliance among HIV-positive drug abusers (Fals-Stewart, O'Farrell, & Martin, 2002). Taken together, this very impressive series of studies conducted during the last several years suggests that BCT impacts both male and female drug abusers' substance use, medication compliance, their relationships with their partners and overall family functioning, as well as their children's adjustment more significantly than alternative treatment up to 1 year posttreatment.

Summary of Family Intervention Science With Adult Drug Abusers

New lines of research investigating family-based engagement and behavioral couples interventions for adult drug abusers are very promising. Family-based strategies for motivating drug abusers into treatment appear to positively impact engagement rates, although further treatment development efforts are needed to extend these interventions past the early phase of treatment engagement. Studies of behavioral couples therapy with a range of drug abusing populations have established impressive effects on drug use, medication compliance, relationship adjustment, and the functioning of children of drug abusing couples in therapy, with encouraging cost-effectiveness findings emerging. These two lines of research represent significant advances, yet as Liddle and Dakof (1995) indicated, the potential of family interventions for adult drug abusers has yet to be fully realized. The initial success of Stanton and Todd (1982) in applying structural-strategic interventions with this population has not been further explored. Couples interventions incorporating other marital approaches and techniques have not been applied with drug abusers. Process research examining the mechanisms by which family-based engagement strategies and BCT exert their effects and could be refined and improved has not been conducted. Thus, although significant progress on several fronts can be noted and these developments are extremely exciting, the subspecialty of family-based interventions for adult drug abusers has work ahead.

Clinical Implications

This section offers some suggestions about how these many studies can inform clinical practice. The present volume is intended for those professionals who earn a living doing therapy as well as for researchers. Hence we consider the previously summarized research from the point of view of a sampling of the most important clinical lessons learned from these years of research.

The field is in a new developmental stage and these advances can benefit one's practice in many areas. We know more now about substance abuse and its etiology, concomitants, and treatment than ever before. In the adolescent specialty, for instance, there are several treatments with demonstrated efficacy, manuals, training/supervision, and dissemination protocols. There is also increasing experience and an empirical base that outlines the issues and best procedures to adopt, adapt, and implement these therapies into a variety of everyday clinical settings. In the adult area, several family-based interventions demonstrate significant promise for implementation into community practice settings.

One implication of this new landscape for practicing clinicians is the question of how clinicians will learn about, and not just in superficial ways, the family-based substance abuse treatments that work. Professional associations have a role in sponsoring practitioner development along these lines, but individual responsibility to learn new clinical methods will never disappear. In fact, the more one expects to learn about these new therapies at a level of actually being able to do them, the more individual responsibility and one's immediate work environment determine the degree of proficiency and skill that can be achieved. The predicted information and knowledge explosion has come to pass. Today, even more so than scientific and professional journals, the Internet gives access to a bounty of sources that can teach therapists about everything from the names, trends, and incidence and prevalence and use patterns of the newest illegal drugs, treatment articles, practice guidelines, and treatment manuals that have been used in controlled studies (e.g., http://www.health.org). Thus, the extent to which research findings such as those discussed above can truly impact everyday clinical practice depends both on the researcher's ability to make results clinically relevant, meaningful, and accessible, as well as the clinician's motivation and efforts to incorporate these resources into their work.

Defining Core Clinical Certainties

Family therapy emphasized relativism, teaching therapists to be careful of univariate, simple truths. The family therapy tradition stressed the importance of accessing multiple, and perhaps necessarily different and sometimes contradictory, perspectives. Our development as a field, however, has also hinged on the accumulation of scientific findings in improving clinical effectiveness. As these values and their concomitant activities become more present on the contemporary family therapy scene, and we can retain the skepticism that ought to go with the pursuit of ultimate Truths, research-derived or otherwise, we have found certain conclusions about clinical work in the substance abuse area to be consistent over time and across studies. We find them robust in terms of our data and experience, and capable of offering practical clinical rules that can influence practice in positive ways.

Let Development Rule

A developmental perspective about human problems and their resolution has been fundamental to treatment development and research with adolescents and their families. Developmental knowledge about teens, parents, and families during the second decade of a child's life provides a foundation for much of the clinical work described below. The tremendous increase in knowledge about drug abuse and delinquency etiology, including the variety of personal and contextual circumstances that elevate risk for dysfunction, as well as those factors that produce adaptive developmental outcomes and protect individuals from problems, has transformed intervention and prevention efforts. Specific knowledge, and not just vague, broad-based sensibilities about the importance of developmental thinking, is required to perform optimal clinical work with teenagers and their families. We have found that acquiring developmental knowledge informs every aspect of one's work with a case.

Expanded Focus of Family-Based Interventions

Family therapy, as a clinical orientation and method, was meant to provide a better, more effective alternative to narrow, individualistic thinking and therapy. But expanding the focus from individuals to families, although an improvement, can be limiting as well. Gradually, family therapy has become able to focus not only on families as one locale of development and solutions, but also it focused on individuals and broader systems outside the immediate family. We came to understand how important it is to be able to focus on multiple systems of individuals' lives, and to understand how these systems interact in the service of good or poor development. The bottom-line clinical implication here is the need to work with different units and levels, and to work on different issues and content foci at the same time. One manifestation of this clinical rule is immediately apparent in the realm of engagement. What motivates a parent to participate in therapy may not motivate a teen. Thus, engagement strategies for a teen and his or her parent are quite different, although certain themes are consistent, such as presenting one's self as an ally and instilling hope that their lives can be better given a coordinated, focused approach.

Conclusions and Future Directions

There is certainly cause for great excitement in the growing field of family-based interventions for drug abuse problems. Since Liddle and Dakof's (1995) review, new strides have been made in both the adolescent and adult areas. Any number of contemporary reviews of state-of-the-art adolescent drug treatment cite family-based treatment as one of the most promising approaches, if not the treatment of choice, for adolescent drug abuse (e.g., Weinberg et al., 1998). Further, practice guidelines for adolescent drug abuse now prescribe family intervention as an essential component of treatment (Bukstein et al., 1997), and even with adult drug abusers, Joint Commission on the Accreditation of Healthcare Organizations standards include family involvement as a critical aspect of the assessment process (McCrady & Ziedonis, 2001). There is little doubt given the existing empirical base that the family-based treatment field is at the cutting edge of drug abuse intervention science.

Despite the significant advances reviewed below and the mounting evidence for family therapy's efficacy in treating drug abuse problems, great challenges still lie ahead. In the adult subspecialty, major breakthroughs that build on evolving work on family-based engagement techniques and couples therapy are possible. The work of Fals-Stewart and colleagues in behavioral couples therapy is particularly exciting, and process studies of this approach could illuminate possible mechanisms of action that may lead to the development of more effective family-based interventions for adult drug abusers. Family-based engagement strategies might be further explored and developed to determine their possible impact on treatment retention and longer-term drug use and related outcomes. The potential of other approaches, such as structural-strategic family interventions and insight-oriented and other couples therapy approaches have yet to be realized with drug abusing clients. The subspecialty of family-based treatment for adult drug abuse remains an evolving area of investigation with a number of possible avenues to pursue.

New directions in the adolescent specialty area offer a number of potential breakthroughs. The assessment of longer-term outcomes following family-based treatment, especially as youth enter young adulthood and meet increasing demands for maturity and responsibility, will provide a new lens through which to view the treatment of adolescent drug abuse. More sophisticated statistical models, such as growth mixture modeling and hierarchical linear models, now allow investigators to track individual change over time and to examine treatment responses at a finer level of detail. Support for the "treatment career" perspective of drug abuse may be provided by longer-term follow-up studies, supporting new policies in the funding of drug treatment and systems-level changes that incorporate aftercare models. However these funding and policy level changes will only occur with increased evidence of the cost-effectiveness and relative benefit-cost of family-based interventions. Treatment development efforts will continually seek to improve the outcomes of these very difficult to treat, frequently chronic individuals. Further specification of mechanisms of action through process research and linking therapeutic interventions to outcomes will guide these efforts.

Yet the greatest challenge for family intervention science in the drug abuse field is quite possibly the puzzle of how to effectively transport these models into community-based practice where they are needed most. With very few exceptions, the technological advances cited here remain completely removed from the realities of day-to-day, front-line drug abuse clinical practice. Although researchers in the adolescent area have begun to explore process and outcomes of family intervention transportation, the major conclusion of these initial studies may be that this work is more complex and difficult than originally anticipated. The concept of taking a certain model and placing it into an existing clinical setting with all of its complexities, systems-level and individual-level obstacles to implementation, and limits on time and resources, is probably unrealistic. Contemporary visions of dissemination research, some of which build on technology transportation failures, tend to emphasize the need for flexibility and adaptation by researchers, as well as the use of interventions up front designed to create foundations and readiness to accept and integrate the new treatments among clinicians (Simpson, 2002). Further research specifying the essential ingredients of family-based interventions incorporating components analysis and dismantling strategies will be crucial in such efforts to adapt and refine these models for a variety of practice settings. Thus, new models of what these dissemination studies might look like are still evolving, and family-based intervention scientists, with their appreciation of the complexity of systems and their systemic perspective on change, have much to offer in this realm.

Practitioners are discovering as they attempt to incorporate empirically supported therapies that for many reasons, these therapy approaches are more difficult to adopt than either researchers or clinicians anticipated. An all or nothing strategy has prevailed in dissemination and technology transfer discussions and activities. Yet it is possible to look at the models for what the clinician can use, rather than using the approach in its entirety. Dissemination has been guided by a mindset of influencing practice by replacing current practice models with empirically supported therapies. Perhaps this approach of exporting entire treatment protocols will succeed and change practice. At the same time, as anyone who has been around the movement knows, there is much that has to change in a particular environment or practice setting for such major dissemination efforts to succeed. An intermediate stage of transformation might involve the incorporation of aspects or pieces of models to influence current practice. This middle ground might allow incorporation of certain procedures or modules into existing practices.

The case of engagement comes to mind. Santisteban et al.'s (1996) studies have demonstrated the strong potential of family systems based engagement methods that could be integrated at the front end of an existing therapy. These manualized, specialized engagement strategies would be easier to train therapists in than some of the multicomponent empirically supported therapies and furthermore, they would cause less systemic reverberation, and require less systemic commitment to sustain in everyday practice. Recent findings show lackluster retention of teens in standard outpatient drug therapy (e.g., in one study, only 27% of adolescents in outpatient drug treatment remained in the program for 90 days or more; Hser et al., 2001). Given these findings, and the contrasting and strikingly superior engagement rates in the family-based treatment literature, the urgency to transport available, manual-guided, effective engagement techniques into standard drug treatment practice would seem to be profound. Retaining a "change everything or change nothing" strategy prohibits experimentation in potentially valuable areas of thought and work. Exploring the addition of different components of models into existing practices and systems of care might reveal interesting clinical surprises.

The responsibility for bridging the research-practice gap lies not only with the research community but also with policy makers, community practitioners, and therapy educators and trainers. In the drug abuse field, funders and treatment providers are increasingly seeking out opportunities for transporting these models into practice settings. Providers and clinical administrators across the country are expressing interest in integrating models such as BSFT, FFT, MDFT, and MST into their treatment programs, and policy makers are creating new avenues to facilitate such efforts. Yet as noted above, these dissemination projects require significantly more time, resources, and collaboration than many anticipated. Most practicing family therapists do not receive training in empirically supported models and are thus not prepared to implement the most efficacious approaches in practice. Marriage and family therapy trainers therefore have an important role to play in decreasing the research-practice disconnect. Family therapy organizations such as American Family Therapy Academy and American Association for Marriage and Family Therapists have devoted resources to research-based conferences and have increased focus on empirically supported therapies in recent years, making a significant statement about the importance of these approaches to the future of family therapy. Marriage and family therapy training programs are essential in this process. Family therapy training associations and accreditation bodies must address the role of empirically supported family and couple therapies in their mission and training endeavors to have any substantial impact on the implementation of these models into practice.

References

References marked with a double asterisk are recommended for clinicians.

Alexander, J. F., & Parsons, B. V. (1973). Short-term behavioral intervention with delinquent families: Impact on family process and recidivism. *Journal of Abnormal Psychology, 81,* 219–225.

**Alexander, J. F., & Parsons, B. V. (1982). *Functional family therapy.* Monterey, CA: Brooks/Cole.

Alexander, J. F., Sexton, T. L., & Robbins, M. S. (2001). The developmental status of family therapy in family psychology intervention science. In H. A. Liddle, D. A. Santisteban, R. F. Levant, & J. H. Bray (Eds.), *Family psychology: Science-based interventions* (pp. 17–40). Washington, DC: American Psychological Association.

American Psychiatric Association. (1995). *Practice guidelines for treatment of patients with substance use disorders: Alcohol, cocaine, opioids.* Washington, DC: Author.

Azrin, N. H., Donohue, B., Teichner, G. A., Crum, T., Howell, J., & DeCato, L. A. (2001). A controlled evaluation and description of individual-cognitive problem solving and family-behavior therapies in dually-diagnosed conduct-disordered and substance-dependent youth. *Journal of Child and Adolescent Substance Abuse, 11*(1), 1–43.

Barber, J. G. (1995). Working with resistant drug abusers. *Social Work, 40*(1), 17–23.

Barton, C., Alexander, J. F., Waldron, H., Turner, C. W., & Warburton, J. (1985). Generalizing treatment effects of Functional Family Therapy: Three replications. *American Journal of Family Therapy, 13,* 16–26.

Berscheid, E. (1999). The greening of relationship science. *American Psychologist, 54*(4), 260–266.

Brook, J. S., Brook, D. W., Arencibia-Mireles, O., Richter, L., & Whiteman, M. (2001). Risk factors for adolescent marijuana use across cultures and time. *Journal of Genetic Psychology, 162*(3), 357–374.

Brown, T. L., Henggeler, S. W., Schoenwald, S. K., Brondino, M. J., & Pickrel, S. G. (1999). Multisystemic treatment of substance abusing and dependent juvenile offenders: Effects on school attendance at posttreatment and 6-month follow-up. *Children's Services: Social Policy, Research, and Practice, 2,* 81–93.

Bukstein, O. G., Brent, D. A., & Kaminer, Y. (1989). Comorbidity of substance abuse and other psychiatric disorders in adolescents. *American Journal of Psychiatry, 146,* 1131–1141.

**Bukstein, O. G., & the Work Group on Quality Issues (1997). Practice parameters for the assessment and treatment of children and adolescents with substance use disorders. *Journal of the American Academy of Child and Adolescent Psychiatry, 36*(Suppl. 10), 140S–156S.

Chatlos, J. C. (1997). Substance use and abuse and the impact on academic difficulties. *Child and Adolescent Psychiatric Clinics of North America, 6,* 545–568.

Clark, D. B., & Bukstein, O. G. (1998). Psychopathology in adolescent alcohol abuse and dependence. *Alcohol Health and Research World, 22,* 117–121.

Clark, D. B., & Neighbors, B. (1996). Adolescent substance abuse and internalizing disorders. *Adolescent Substance Abuse and Dual Disorders, 5,* 45–57.

Coatsworth, J. D., Santisteban, D. A., McBride, C. K., & Szapocznik, J. (2001). Brief Strategic Family Therapy versus community control: Engagement, retention, and an exploration of the moderating role of adolescent symptom severity. *Family Process, 40*(3), 313–332.

Crits-Cristoph, P., & Siqueland, L. (1996). Psychosocial treatment for drug abuse: Selected review and recommendations for national health care. *Archives of General Psychiatry, 53,* 749–756.

Cunningham, P. B., Henggeler, S. W., Brondino, M. J., & Pickrel, S. G. (1999). Testing underlying assumptions of the family empowerment perspective. *Journal of Child and Family Studies, 8*(4), 437–449.

Dakof, G. A. (2000). Understanding gender differences in adolescent drug abuse: Issues of comorbidity and family functioning. *Journal of Psychoactive Drugs, 32*, 25–32.

Dakof, G. A., Quille, T. J., Tejeda, M. J., Alberga, L. R., Bandstra, E., & Szapocznik, J. (in press). Enrolling and retaining cocaine abusing mothers into drug abuse treatment. *Journal of Consulting and Clinical Psychology.*

Dakof, G. A., Tejeda M., & Liddle, H. A. (2001). Predictors of engagement into adolescent drug abuse treatment. *Journal of the American Academy of Child and Adolescent Psychiatry, 40*(3), 274–281.

DeCivita, M., Dobkin, P. L., & Robertson, R. N. (2000). A study of barriers to the engagement of significant others in adult addiction treatment. *Journal of Substance Abuse Treatment, 19*, 135–144.

Dembo, R., Cervenka, K. A., Hunter, B., & Wang, W. (1998). Engaging high risk families in community based intervention services. *Aggression and Violent Behavior, 4*(1), 41–58.

Dennis, M. L. (2002, May). Treatment research on adolescent drug and alcohol abuse: Despite progress, many challenges remain. *Connection* (pp. 1-2, 7). Washington, DC: Academy for Health Services Research and Health Policy.

Dennis, M. L., Titus, J. C., Diamond, G., Babor, T., Donaldson, J., Godley, S. H., et al. (in press). The Cannabis Youth Treatment (CYT) experiment: A multi-site study of five approaches to outpatient treatment for adolescents. *Addiction.*

Diamond, G. S., & Diamond, G. M. (2001). Studying a matrix of change mechanisms: An agenda for family-based process research. In H. A. Liddle, D. A. Santisteban, R. F. Levant, & J. H. Bray (Eds.), *Family psychology: Science-based interventions* (pp. 41–66). Washington, DC: American Psychological Association.

Diamond, G. S., & Liddle, H. A. (1996). Resolving a therapeutic impasse between parents and adolescents in Multidimensional Family Therapy. *Journal of Consulting and Clinical Psychology, 64*, 481–488.

Diamond, G. M., Liddle, H. A., Hogue, A., & Dakof, G. A. (1999). Alliance building interventions with adolescents in family therapy: A process study. *Psychotherapy, 36*, 355–368.

Dishion, T. J., & Kavanagh, K. (2000). A multilevel approach to family-centered prevention in schools: Process and outcome. *Addictive Behaviors, 25*(6), 899–911.

Donohue, B., Azrin, N., Lawson, H., Friedlander, J., Teicher, G., & Rindsberg, J. (1998). Improving initial session attendance of substance abusing and conduct disordered adolescents: A controlled study. *Journal of Child and Adolescent Substance Abuse 8*(1), 1–13.

Epstein, E. E., & McCrady, B. S. (1998). Behavioral couples treatment of alcohol and drug use disorders: Current status and innovations. *Clinical Psychology Review, 18*(6), 689–711.

Fals-Stewart, W., & Birchler, G. R. (1998). Marital interactions of drug-abusing patients and their partners: Comparisons with distressed couples and relationship to drug-using behavior. *Psychology of Addictive Behaviors, 12*(1), 28–38.

Fals-Stewart, W., Birchler, G. R., & O'Farrell, T. J. (1996). Behavioral couples therapy for male substance-abusing patients: Effects on relationship adjustment and drug-using behavior. *Journal of Consulting and Clinical Psychology, 64*(5), 959–972.

Fals-Stewart, W., Kashdan, T. B., O'Farrell, T. J., & Birchler, G. R. (2002). Behavioral couples therapy for male drug abusing patients and their partners: The effect on interpartner violence. *Journal of Substance Abuse Treatment, 22*, 1–10.

Fals-Stewart, W., & O'Farrell, T. J. (in press). Behavioral family counseling and naltrexone for male opioid dependent patients. *Journal of Consulting and Clinical Psychology.*

Fals-Stewart, W., O'Farrell, T. J., & Birchler, G. R. (1997). Behavioral couples therapy for male methadone maintenance patients: Effects on drug-using behavior and relationship adjustment. *Behavior Therapy, 32*, 391–411.

Fals-Stewart, W., O'Farrell, T. J., & Birchler, G. R. (2001). Behavioral couples therapy for male substance abusing patients: A cost outcomes analysis. *Journal of Consulting and Clinical Psychology, 65*, 789–802.

Fals-Stewart, W., O'Farrell, T. J., Feehan, M., Birchler, G. R., Tiller, S., & McFarlin, S. K. (2000). Behavioral couples therapy versus individual-based treatment for male substance-abusing patients: An evaluation of significant individual change and comparison of improvement rates. *Journal of Substance Abuse Treatment, 18*, 249–254.

Fals-Stewart, W., O'Farrell, T. J., & Martin, J. (2002, March). Using behavioral family counseling to enhance HIV-medication compliance among HIV-infected male drug abusing patients. Paper presented at "Treating Addictions in Special Populations" Conference, Binghamton, NY.

Fishman, H. C., Andes, F., & Knowlton, R. (2001). Enhancing family therapy: The addition of a community resource specialist. *Journal of Marital and Family Therapy, 27*(1), 111–116.

French, M. T., Dunlap, L. J., Zarkin, G. A., McGeary, K. A., & McLellan, A. T. (1997). A structured instrument for estimating the economic cost of drug abuse treatment. The Drug Abuse Treatment Cost Analysis Program (DATCAP). *Journal of Substance Abuse Treatment, 14*, 1–11.

French, M. T., Rachal, J. V., & Hubbard, R. L. (1991). Conceptual framework for estimating the social cost of drug abuse. *Journal of Health and Social Psychology, 2*, 1–22.

French, M. T., Roebuck, C., Dennis, M., Babor, T., Diamond, G., Godley, S., et al. (in press). The economic cost of outpatient marijuana treatment for adolescents: Findings from a multi-site experiment. *Addiction.*

Friedman, A. S. (1989). Family therapy vs. parent groups: Effects on adolescent drug abusers. *The American Journal of Family Therapy, 17*, 335–347.

Friedman, A. S., Terras, A., & Glassman, K. (2000). Family structure versus family relationships for predicting to substance use/abuse and illegal behavior. *Journal of Child and Adolescent Substance Abuse, 10*(1), 1–16.

Gerstein, D. R., & Johnson, R. A. (1999). *Adolescent and young adults in the national treatment improvement evaluation study* (National Evaluation Data Services Report). Rockville, MD: Center for Substance Abuse Treatment.

Greenbaum, P. E., Prange, M. E., Friedman, R. M., & Silver, S. E. (1991). Substance abuse prevalence and comorbidity with other psychiatric disorders among adolescents with severe emotional disturbances. *Journal of the American Academy of Child and Adolescent Psychiatry, 30*, 575–583.

Grella, C. E., Hser, Y. I., Joshi, V., & Rounds-Bryant, J. (2001). Drug treatment outcomes for adolescents with comorbid mental and substance use disorders. *Journal of Nervous and Mental Disease, 189*(6), 384–392.

Hamilton, N., Brantley, L., Tims, F., Angelovich, N., & McDougall, B. (2000). *Family Support Network (FSN) for adolescent cannabis users.* (Volume 3 of the Cannabis Youth Treatment [CYT] manual series). Rockville, MD: Substance Abuse and Mental Health Services Administration, Center for Substance Abuse Treatment (http://www.samhsa.gov/csat/csat.htm).

Harwood, H., Fountain, D., Carothers, S., Gerstein, D., & Johnson, R. (1998). Gender differences in the economic impacts of clients before, during and after substance abuse treatment. *Drugs and Society, 13*(1-2), 251–269.

Hawkins, J. D., Catalano, R. F., & Miller, J. Y. (1992). Risk and protective factors for alcohol and other drug problems in adolescence and early adulthood: Implications for substance abuse prevention. *Psychological Bulletin, 112*, 64–105.

Heath, A. W., & Stanton, M. D. (1998). Family-based treatment: Stages and outcomes. In R. J. Frances & S. I. Miller (Eds.), *Clinical textbook of addictive disorders* (2nd ed., pp. 496–520). New York: Guilford.

Henggeler, S. W., & Borduin, C. M. (1990). *Family therapy and beyond: A multisystemic approach to treating the behavior problems of children and adolescents.* Pacific Grove, CA: Brooks/Cole.

Henggeler, S. W., Borduin, C. M., Melton, G. B., Mann, B. J., Smith, L. A., Hall, J. A., et al. (1991). Effects of multisystemic therapy on drug use and abuse in serious juvenile offenders: A progress report from two outcome studies. *Family Dynamics of Addiction Quarterly, 1,* 40–51.

Henggeler, S. W., Clingempeel, W. G., Brondino, M. J., & Pickrel, S. G. (2002). Four-year follow-up of multisystemic therapy with substance-abusing and substance-dependent juvenile offenders. *Journal of the American Academy of Child and Adolescent Psychiatry, 41*(7), 868–874.

Henggeler, S. W., Melton, G. B., Brondino, M. J., Scherer, D. G., & Hanley, J. H. (1997). Multisystemic therapy with violent and chronic juvenile offenders and their families: The role of treatment fidelity in successful dissemination. *Journal of Consulting and Clinical Psychology, 65,* 821–833.

Henggeler, S. W., Pickrel, S. G., & Brondino, M. J. (1999). Multisystemic treatment of substance abusing and dependent delinquents: Outcomes, treatment fidelity, and transportability. *Mental Health Services Research, 1,* 171–184.

Henggeler, S. W., Pickrel, S. G., Brondino, M. J., & Crouch, J. L. (1996). Eliminating (almost) treatment dropout of substance abusing or dependent delinquents through home-based multisystemic therapy. *American Journal of Psychiatry, 153,* 427–428.

Hogue, A., Liddle, H. A., & Rowe, C. (1996). Treatment adherence process research in family therapy: A rationale and some practical guidelines. *Psychotherapy: Theory, Research, Practice, & Training, 33,* 332–345.

Hogue, A., Liddle, H. A., Rowe, C., Turner, R. M., Dakof, G., & LaPann, K. (1998). Treatment adherence and differentiation in individual versus family therapy for adolescent substance abuse. *Journal of Counseling Psychology, 45,* 104–114.

Horner, B. R., & Scheibe, K. E. (1997). Prevalence and implications of attention-deficit hyperactivity disorder among adolescents in treatment for substance abuse. *Journal of the American Academy of Child and Adolescent Psychiatry, 36,* 30–36.

Hser, Y. I., Grella, C. E., Hubbard, R. L., Hsieh, S. C., Fletcher, B. W., Brown, B. S., et al. (2001). An evaluation of drug treatments for adolescents in 4 US cities. *Archives of General Psychiatry, 58*(7), 689–695.

Hser, Y., Maglione, M., Polinsky, M. L., & Anglin, M. D. (1998). Predicting drug treatment entry among treatment-seeking individuals. *Journal of Substance Abuse Treatment, 15,* 213–220.

Hsieh, S., Hoffman, N. G., & Hollister, C. D. (1998). The relationship between pre-, during, and post-treatment factors and adolescent substance abuse behaviors. *Addictive Behaviors, 23,* 477–488.

Hubbard, R. L., & French, M. T. (1991). New perspectives on the benefit-cost and cost-effectiveness of drug abuse treatment. In W. S. Cartwright & J. M. Kaple (Eds.), *Economic costs, cost-effectiveness, financing, and community-based drug treatment* (NIDA Research Monograph No. 113, DHHS Publication No. ADM 91-1823, pp. 94–113). Washington, DC: U.S. Government Printing Office.

Huey, S. J., Henggeler, S. W., Brondino, M. J., & Pickrel, S. G. (2000). Mechanisms of change in multisystemic therapy: Reducing delinquent behavior through therapist adherence and improved family and peer functioning. *Journal of Consulting and Clinical Psychology, 68,* 451–467.

Institute of Medicine. (1998). *Bridging the gap between practice and research: Forging partnerships with community-based drug and alcohol treatment.* Washington, DC: National Academy Press.

Jackson-Gilfort, A., Liddle, H. A., Tejeda, M. J., & Dakof, G. A. (2001). Facilitating engagement of African American male adolescents in family therapy: A cultural theme process study. *Journal of Black Psychology, 27*(3), 321–340.

Joanning, H., Quinn, Q., Thomas, F., & Mullen, R. (1992). Treating adolescent drug abuse: A comparison of family systems therapy, group therapy, and family drug education. *Journal of Marital and Family Therapy, 18,* 345–356.

Johnston, L. D., O'Malley, P., & Bachman, J. (2001). *National survey results on drug use from the Monitoring the Future study.* Rockville, MD: National Institute on Drug Abuse.

Kaminer, Y. (1999). Addictive disorders in adolescents. *The Psychiatric Clinics of North America, 22*, 275–288.

Kazdin, A. E. (1994). Methodology, design, and evaluation in psychotherapy research. In A. E. Bergin & S. L. Garfield (Eds.), *Handbook of psychotherapy and behavior change* (4th ed., pp. 19–71). New York: John Wiley & Sons.

Kazdin, A. E., Holland, L., & Crowley, M. (1997). Family experience of barriers to treatment and premature termination from child therapy. *Journal of Consulting and Clinical Psychology, 65*(3), 453–463.

Kelley, M. L., & Fals-Stewart, W. (2002). Couples- versus individual-based therapy for alcohol and drug abuse: Effects on children's psychosocial functioning. *Journal of Consulting and Clinical Psychology, 70*(2), 417–427.

Kirby, K. C., Marlowe, D. B., Festinger, D. S., Garvey, K. A., & LaMonaca, V. (1999). Community reinforcement training for family and significant others of drug abusers: A unilateral intervention to increase treatment entry of drug users. *Drug and Alcohol Dependence, 56*, 85–96.

Landau, J., Garrett, J., Shea, R. R., Stanton, M. D., Brinkman-Sull, D., & Baciewicz, G. (2000). Strength in numbers: The ARISE method for mobilizing family and network to engage substance abusers in treatment. *American Journal of Drug and Alcohol Abuse, 26*(3), 379–398.

Lavee, Y., & Altus, D. (2001). Family relationships as a predictor of post-treatment drug abuse relapse: A follow-up study of drug addicts and their spouses. *Contemporary Family Therapy: An International Journal, 23*(4), 513–530.

Leshner, A. I. (1997). Drug abuse and addiction treatment research: The next generation. *Archives of General Psychiatry, 54*, 691–694.

Lewis, R. A., Piercy, F. P., Sprenkle, D. H., & Trepper, T. S. (1990). Family-based interventions for helping drug-abusing adolescents. *Journal of Adolescent Research, 5*, 82–95.

Liddle, H. A. (1995). Conceptual and clinical dimensions of a multidimensional, multisystems engagement strategy in family-based adolescent treatment. *Psychotherapy: Theory, Research, and Practice, 32*, 39–58.

Liddle, H. A. (1999). Theory development in a family-based therapy for adolescent drug abuse. *Journal of Clinical Child Psychology, 28*, 521–532.

Liddle, H. A. (2002a). Advances in family-based therapy for adolescent substance abuse: Findings from the Multidimensional Family Therapy research program. In L. S. Harris (Ed.), *Problems of Drug Dependence 2001: Proceedings of the 63rd Annual Scientific Meeting* (NIDA Research Monograph No. 182, NIH Publication No. 02-5097, pp. 113–115). Bethesda, MD: National Institute on Drug Abuse.

**Liddle, H. A. (2002b). *Multidimensional family therapy for adolescent cannabis users, Cannabis Youth Treatment (CYT) series* (Volume 5). Rockville, MD: Center for Substance Abuse Treatment.

Liddle, H. A., & Dakof, G. A. (1995). Efficacy of family therapy for drug abuse: Promising but not definitive. *Journal of Marital and Family Therapy, 21*, 511–544.

Liddle, H. A., Dakof, G. A., & Diamond, G. (1991). Adolescent substance abuse: Multidimensional family therapy in action. In E. Kaufman & P. Kaufman (Eds.), *Family therapy of drug and alcohol abuse* (pp. 120–171). Boston: Allyn and Bacon.

Liddle, H. A., Dakof, G. A., & Henderson, C. E. (2002, June). *Controlled trial of a family-based alternative to residential drug treatment for co-morbid adolescent substance abusers: Preliminary findings.* Poster presented at the annual conference of the College on Problems of Drug Dependence. Quebec City, Quebec, Canada.

Liddle, H. A., Dakof, G. A., Parker, K., Diamond, G. S., Barrett, K., & Tejeda, M. (2001). Multidimensional family therapy for adolescent drug abuse: Results of a randomized clinical trial. *American Journal of Drug and Alcohol Abuse, 27*(4), 651–688.

Liddle, H. A., & Rowe, C. L. (1998). Family measures in drug abuse prevention research. In R. Ashery (Ed.), *Drug abuse prevention through family interventions* (NIDA Research Monograph 177, pp. 324–372). Rockville, MD: National Institute on Drug Abuse.

Liddle, H. A., Rowe, C. L., Dakof, G., & Lyke, J. (1998). Translating parenting research into clinical interventions for families of adolescents. *Clinical Child Psychology and Psychiatry, 3*, 419–443.

**Liddle, H. A., Rowe, C. L., Quille, T., Dakof, G., Mills, D. S., Sakran, E., et al. (2002). Transporting a research-based adolescent drug treatment into practice. *Journal of Substance Abuse Treatment* (Special Issue on Transferring Research into Practice, D. Simpson, Ed.), 22, 1–13.

Mann, B. J., Borduin, C. M., Henggeler, S. W., & Blaske, D. M. (1990). An investigation of systemic conceptualizations of parent-child coalitions and symptom change. *Journal of Consulting and Clinical Psychology, 58,* 336–344.

McCrady, B. S., & Epstein, E. E. (1996). Theoretical bases of family approaches to substance abuse treatment. In F. Rotgers & D. S. Keller (Eds.), *Treating substance abuse: Theory and technique. The Guilford Substance Abuse Series* (pp. 117–142). New York: Guilford.

**McCrady, B. S., & Ziedonis, D. (2001). American Psychiatric Association practice guideline for substance use disorders. *Behavior Therapy, 32,* 309–336.

McGillicuddy, N. B., Rychtarik, R. G., Duquette, J. A., & Morsheimer, E. T. (2001). Development of a skill training program for parents of substance-abusing adolescents. *Journal of Substance Abuse Treatment, 20,* 59–68.

**Meyers, R. J., Miller, W., & Smith, J. E. (2001). Community reinforcement and family training (CRAFT). In R. J. Meyers & W. R. Miller (Eds.), *A community reinforcement approach to addiction treatment. International Research Monographs in the Addictions* (pp. 147–160). New York: Cambridge University Press.

Miller, G. E., & Prinz, R. J. (1990). Enhancement of social learning interventions for childhood conduct disorder. *Psychological Bulletin, 108,* 291–307.

Minuchin, S. (1974). *Families & family therapy.* Oxford, England: Harvard University Press.

Morojele, N. K., & Brook, J. S. (2001). Adolescent precursors of intensity of marijuana and other illicit drug use among adult initiators. *Journal of Genetic Psychology, 162*(4), 430–450.

Moyers, T. B., & Hester, R. K. (1999). Credentialing, documentation, and evaluation. In B. S. McCrady & E. E. Epstein (Eds.), *Addictions: A comprehensive guidebook* (pp. 414–420). New York: Oxford University Press.

National Institute on Drug Abuse. (1998). Drug abuse cost to society set at $97.7 billion, continuing steady increase since 1975. *NIDA Notes, 13*(4), 1–5.

National Institute on Drug Abuse. (2002). *Modifying and testing efficacious behavioral therapies to make them more community friendly.* Request for Applications RFA-DA-02-006. Rockville, MD: Author (http://www.nida.nih.gov).

**O'Farrell, T. J., & Fals-Stewart, W. (1999). Treatment models and methods: Family models. In B. S. McCrady & E. E. Epstein (Eds.), *Addictions: A comprehensive guidebook* (pp. 287–305). New York: Oxford University Press.

**Pinsof, W. M., & Wynne, L. C. (2000). Toward progress research: Closing the gap between family therapy practice and research. *Journal of Marital and Family Therapy, 26*(1), 1–8.

Platt, J. J., Widman, M., Lidz, V., Rubenstein, D., & Thompson, R. (1998). The case for support services in substance abuse treatment. *American Behavioral Scientist, 41*(8), 1050–1062.

Prinz, R. J., & Miller, G. E. (1994). Family-based treatment for childhood antisocial behavior: Experimental influences on dropout and engagement. *Journal of Consulting and Clinical Psychology, 62*(3), 645–650.

Riggs, P. D. (1998). Clinical approach to treatment of ADHD in adolescents with substance use disorders and conduct disorder. *Journal of the American Academy of Child and Adolescent Psychiatry, 37,* 331–332.

Robbins, M. S., Alexander, J. F., Newell, R. M., & Turner, C. W. (1996). The immediate effect of reframing on client attitude in family therapy. *Journal of Family Psychology, 10*(1), 28–34.

Robbins, M. S., Alexander, J. F., & Turner, C. W. (2000). Disrupting defensive family interactions in family therapy with delinquent adolescents. *Journal of Family Psychology, 14*(4), 688–701.

Rohde, P., Lewinsohn, P. M., & Seeley, J. R. (1996). Psychiatric comorbidity with problematic alcohol use in high school students. *Journal of the American Academy of Child and Adolescent Psychiatry, 35,* 101–109.

Rowe, C. L., Liddle, H. A., & Dakof, G. A. (2001). Classifying clinically referred adolescent substance abusers by level of externalizing and internalizing symptoms. *Journal of Child and Adolescent Substance Abuse, 11*(2), 41–65.

**Rowe, C., Liddle, H. A., McClintic, K., & Quille, T. J. (2002). Integrative treatment development: Multidimensional family therapy for adolescent substance abuse. In F. W. Kaslow & J. Lebow (Eds.), *Comprehensive handbook of psychotherapy: Integrative/eclectic* (Vol. 4, pp. 133–161). New York: John Wiley & Sons.

Santisteban, D. A., Szapocznik, J., Perez-Vidal, A., Kurtines, W. M., Murray, E. J., & LaPerriere, A. (1996). Efficacy of intervention for engaging youth and families into treatment and some variables that may contribute to differential effectiveness. *Journal of Family Psychology, 10,* 35–44.

Schmidt, S. E., Liddle, H. A., & Dakof, G. A. (1996). Changes in parental practices and adolescent drug abuse during Multidimensional Family Therapy. *Journal of Family Psychology, 10,* 12–27.

Schoenwald, S. K., Henggeler, S. W., Brondino, M. J., & Rowland, M. D. (2000). Multisystemic therapy: Monitoring treatment fidelity. *Family Process, 39,* 83–103.

Schoenwald, S. K., Ward, D. M., Henggeler, S. W., Pickrel, S. G., & Patel, H. (1996). MST treatment of substance abusing or dependent adolescent offenders: Costs of reducing incarceration, inpatient, and residential placement. *Journal of Child and Family Studies, 5,* 431–444.

Shoemaker, R. H., & Sherry, P. (1991). Posttreatment factors influencing outcome of adolescent chemical dependency treatment. *Journal of Adolescent Chemical Dependency, 2,* 89–105.

Simpson, D. D. (2002). A conceptual framework for transferring research to practice. Introduction to the Special issue. *Journal of Substance Abuse Treatment, 22*(4), 171–182.

Sisson, R. W., & Azrin, N. H. (1986). Family-member involvement to initiate and promote treatment of problem drinkers. *Behavior Therapy and Experimental Psychiatry, 17,* 15–21.

Slesnick, N., Meyers, R. J., Meade, M., & Segelken, D. H. (2000). Bleak and hopeless no more: Engagement of reluctant substance-abusing runaway youth and their families. *Journal of Substance Abuse Treatment, 19,* 215–222.

Spoth, R., & Redmond, C. (1995). Parent motivation to enroll in parenting skills programs: A model of family context and health belief predictors. *Journal of Family Psychology, 9,* 294–310.

Stanton, M. D. (1985). The family and drug abuse. In T. Bratter & G. Forrest (Eds.), *Alcoholism and substance abuse: Strategies for clinical intervention* (pp. 398–430). New York: Free Press.

Stanton, M. D., & Shadish, W. R. (1997). Outcome, attrition, and family-couples treatment for drug abuse: A meta-analysis and review of the controlled, comparative studies. *Psychological Bulletin, 122*(2), 170–191.

Stanton, M. D., & Todd, T. C. (1979). Structural therapy with drug addicts. In E. Kaufman & P. Kaufman (Eds.), *Family therapy of drug and alcohol abuse* (pp. 55–59). New York: Gardner Press.

**Stanton, M. D., & Todd, T. C. (1982). *Family therapy for drug abuse and addiction.* New York: Guilford Press.

Substance Abuse and Mental Health Services Administration. (1999). *SAMHSA Treatment Episode Data Set* (TEDS). Rockville, MD: Author.

Substance Abuse and Mental Health Services Administration. (2001). *Summary of findings from the 2000 National Household Survey on Drug Abuse.* Rockville, MD: Author.

Stoolmiller, M., Duncan, T., Bank, L., & Patterson, G. R. (1993). Some problems and solutions in the study of change: Significant patterns in client resistance. *Journal of Consulting and Clinical Psychology, 61*(6), 920–928.

Szapocznik, J., Kurtines, W. M., Foote, F. H., Perez-Vidal, A., & Hervis, O. (1983). Conjoint versus one-person family therapy: Some evidence for the effectiveness of conducting family therapy through one person. *Journal of Consulting and Clinical Psychology, 51,* 889–899.

Szapocznik, J., Kurtines, W. M., Foote, F., Perez-Vidal, A., & Hervis, O. (1986). Conjoint versus one-person family therapy: Further evidence for the effectiveness of conducting family therapy through one person with drug-abusing adolescents. *Journal of Consulting and Clinical Psychology, 54,* 395–397.

Szapocznik, J., Perez-Vidal, A., Brickman, A. L., Foote, F. H., Santisteban, D., Hervis, O., et al. (1988). Engaging adolescent drug abusers and their families in treatment: A strategic structural systems approach. *Journal of Consulting and Clinical Psychology, 56,* 552–557.

Szapocznik, J., Rio, A. T., Murray, E., Cohen, R., Scopetta, M. A., Rivas-Vasquez, A., et al. (1989). Structural family versus psychodynamic child therapy for problematic Hispanic boys. *Journal of Consulting and Clinical Psychology, 57,* 571–578.

**Szapocznik, J., & Williams, R. A. (2000). Brief strategic family therapy: Twenty-five years of interplay among theory, research and practice in adolescent behavior problems and drug abuse. *Clinical Child and Family Psychology Review, 3*(2), 117–134.

Tims, F., Inciardi, J. A., Fletcher, B. W., & Horton, A. M. (Eds.). (1997). *The effectiveness of innovative strategies in the treatment of drug abuse.* Westport, CT: Greenwood Press.

Waldron, H. B. (1997). Adolescent substance abuse and family therapy outcome: A review of randomized trials. In T. H. Ollendick & R. J. Prinz (Eds.), *Advances in clinical child psychology* (Vol. 19, pp. 199–234). New York: Plenum Press.

Waldron, H. B., Slesnick, N., Brody, J. L., Turner, C. W., & Peterson, T. R. (2001). Treatment outcomes for adolescent substance abuse at 4- and 7-month assessments. *Journal of Consulting and Clinical Psychology, 69*(5), 802–813.

Waltz, J., Addis, M., Koerner, K., & Jacobson, N. (1993). Testing the integrity of a psychotherapy protocol: Assessment of adherence and competence. *Journal of Consulting and Clinical Psychology, 61,* 620–630.

Weinberg, N. Z., Rahdert, E., Colliver, J. D., & Glantz, M. D. (1998). Adolescent substance abuse: A review of the past 10 years. *Journal of the American Academy of Child and Adolescent Psychiatry, 37,* 252–261.

Wells, K. (1995). Family preservation services in context: Origins, practices, and current issues. In I. M. Schwartz and P. AuClair (Eds.), *Home-based services for troubled children* (pp. 1–28). Lincoln, NE: University of Nebraska Press.

Williams, R. J., & Chang, S. Y. (2000). A comprehensive and comparative review of adolescent substance abuse treatment outcome. *Clinical Psychology: Science and Practice, 7,* 138–166.

Winters, J., Fals-Stewart, W., O'Farrell, T. J., Birchler, G. R., & Kelley, M. L. (2002). Behavioral couples therapy for female substance-abusing patients: Effects on substance use and relationship adjustment. *Journal of Consulting and Clinical Psychology, 70*(2), 344–355.

Winters, K., Latimer, W., & Stinchfield, R. (1999). Adolescent treatment. In P. J. Ott, R. E. Tarter, & R. T. Ammerman (Eds.), *Sourcebook on substance abuse: Etiology, epidemiology, assessment, and treatment* (pp. 350–361). Boston: Allyn and Bacon.

Chapter 4   *Childhood Behavioral and Emotional Disorders*

William F. Northey, Jr., Ph.D., American Association for Marriage and Family Therapy, Alexandria, Virginia.

Karen C. Wells, Ph.D., Department of Psychiatry and Behavioral Sciences, Division of Medical Psychology, Duke University Medical Center, Durham, North Carolina.

Wendy K. Silverman, Ph.D., Department of Psychology, Child and Family Psychosocial Research Center, Florida International University, Miami, Florida.

C. Everett Bailey, Ph.D., Psychological Counseling Services, Ltd, Scottsdale, Arizona.

According to the Surgeon General of the United States (U.S. Department of Health and Human Services, 1999), 1 in 5 children in the U.S. exhibits signs and symptoms of a DSM-IV disorder during the course of a year, and 5% of children suffer from a mental disorder that causes "extreme functional impairment." Further, the identification of children with behavioral problems has doubled in the last 2 decades (Kelleher, McInerny, Gardner, Childs, & Wasserman, 2000) and children are being identified with behavioral problems at an earlier age (Keenan & Wakschlad, 2000). This chapter will review clinical studies of family-based interventions conducted primarily since the review of childhood behavioral and emotional disorders by Estrada and Pinsof (1995). However, this review will be narrower in its focus by summarizing the randomized clinical trials.

In 1995 Estrada and Pinsof concluded that there was "a stunning lack of research on what has classically been defined as family therapy in regard to childhood disorders" (p. 433). The research on childhood behavioral and emotional disorders reviewed by Estrada and Pinsof focused almost exclusively on the effectiveness of parent management training (PMT). Further, despite the fact that they set out to review the literature on family therapy for childhood schizophrenia, depression, suicide, and learning disabilities, they could not find any research on those particular childhood problems and instead focused on conduct disorder (CD), attention deficit/hyperactivity disorder (ADHD), fears and anxiety disorders, and autistic disorders.

In many ways things have not changed substantially since 1995 in regards to classically defined family therapy models. Most of the research conducted on childhood behavioral and emotional disorders have either been parent training, the inclusion of parents in primarily individually focused treatment, or family group therapy. The one exception was the research on adolescent depression conducted by Brent et al. (1997) who developed a systemic behavior family therapy, which borrowed from Functional Family Therapy.

There have been some changes since the 1995 review, however. First, the types of interventions studied have changed slightly in that parents' emotional needs have been considered (Cobham, Dadds, & Spence, 1998) and family group therapy has been studied (e.g., Barrett, 1998; Lewinsohn, Clarke, Hops, & Andrews, 1990; Silverman et al., 1999; Spence, Donovan, & Brechman-Toussaint, 2000). Further, there has also been an increase in the treatment literature for the types of childhood disorders studied. In addition to CD, ADHD, and anxiety disorder, the current volume covers more research on depression and gives more specific attention to oppositional defiant disorder (ODD). The number of studies on depression and anxiety disorders, however, remains seriously limited.

Notwithstanding the paucity of research in general and on specific disorders in particular, Estrada and Pinsof (1995) concluded that the inclusion of parents led to better outcomes for children and parents for some of the disorders. For example, PMT improved child management skills, but seemed to have little effect on the core ADHD symptoms (i.e., inattention, impulsivity, and overactivity), and for fear and anxiety disorders, only tentative support was garnered at the time. In contrast, in the current chapter we have more evidence that family-based interventions are effective in alleviating core ADHD and CD symptoms, there is stronger evidence for the efficacy of family-based interventions for anxiety disorders, and several recent studies suggest family interventions may be effective in alleviating depression in children.

The number and quality of studies focusing on family interventions for childhood behavioral and emotional disorders varies significantly by diagnosis and age group. There are many more studies that have assessed the effectiveness of family interventions on externalizing disorders than on internalizing disorders. In fact, there are certain disorders, such as bipolar depression and obsessive-compulsive disorder, for which there has been very little research on the impact that family therapy might have on the amelioration of those disorders. Additionally, there are more studies focusing on older children than younger ones. It is also noteworthy that most of the family-based treatments are either skill building or cognitive behavioral interventions with parent training the most commonly studied family intervention. For the most part, the inclusion of parents in the treatment of children with emotional and behavioral problems provides at least comparable results in most cases, and in some cases improves the outcomes for some children.

Definitions

As mentioned previously, the majority of outcome research conducted on childhood behavioral and emotional disorders is "family-based" rather than family therapy. This was also the case in 1995, so Estrada and Pinsof used a very broad definition of family therapy that included family-based interventions. The primary difference between family-based and family therapy is the focus of the treatment. For the most part, family-based interventions utilize parents as "cotherapists" to continue the therapeutic gains made in session to the home. The degree to which parents are involved varies and ranges from presession meetings with the therapist to conjoint meetings with the child and therapist. Family therapy differs in that: parents and children are generally seen conjointly, it focuses on the needs of the parents (and other family members), and it considers the family processes that may contribute to the child's problematic behaviors. Further, while the primary focus of treatment may be with the child initially identified with the problem, any and all family members may also become the focus of treatment if necessary to resolve the presenting problem or other problems that arise during the treatment process.

Internalizing behaviors refers to behaviors such as anxiety, inhibition, shyness, immaturity, sadness, and social withdrawal. According to the DSM-IV (American Psychiatric Association, 1994), internalizing behavior problems are equated with anxiety and mood disorders. DSM-IV anxiety disorders include separation anxiety disorder (the only anxiety disorder specific to childhood), social phobia, specific phobia, generalized anxiety disorder, agoraphobia, panic disorder with and without agoraphobia, obsessive-compulsive disorder, posttraumatic stress disorder, acute stress disorder, anxiety disorder due to a general medical condition, substance-induced anxiety disorder, and anxiety disorder not otherwise specified. DSM-IV mood disorders include major depressive episode, dysthymic disorder, depressive disorder not otherwise specified, bipolar disorders, cyclothymic disorder, mood disorder due to a general medical condition, and substance-induced mood disorder. Externalizing disorders include ODD, ADHD, CD, and substance abuse disorders. ODD is a recurrent pattern of negativistic interpersonal behavior characterized by disobedience and defiance toward benevolent authority figures. CD is a more serious behavior disorder characterized by aggressive and antisocial behavior and major community rules violations. CD and substance abuse disorders affect adolescents more generally and will be covered in other chapters (see chapters 2 & 3), with ODD and ADHD being the primary focus of the second section of this chapter.

Prevalence Estimates

Estimated prevalence rates of "any anxiety disorder" appear to range between 5.78% and 17.7%, with overanxious/generalized anxiety disorder, separation anxiety disorder, and specific phobia being most prevalent. Several studies have found that, with the exception of separation anxiety disorder, the prevalence of anxiety disorders generally increases with age. Inconsistencies have been reported, however, and appear to depend on the specific disorder (e.g., Anderson, Williams, McGee, & Silva, 1987; Cohen, Cohen, & Brook, 1993; McGee, Feehan, Williams, & Anderson, 1992). The range of remission for an initial anxiety disorder diagnosis in youth is 34% to 54% (or, 46% to 66% do not remit) (Woodward & Fergusson, 2001). Even when there is remission, however, oftentimes other disorders develop, particularly another anxiety disorder, a new depressive disorder, or a new externalizing behavior disorder. For example, Last, Hansen, and Franco (1998) found that 15.5% of the original sample (of 5- to 18-year-olds) developed another anxiety disorder, 13.1% a depressive disorder, and 7.1% an externalizing behavior disorder. One explanation for such findings is that the expression of anxiety disorders changes in accordance with the level of socioemotional development. Another explanation, not incompatible with the aforementioned, is that the presence of an anxiety disorder creates a risk for the development of other disorders (Kovacs & Devlin, 1998; Woodward & Fergusson, 2001).

Recent prevalence estimate rates for depressive disorders have been found to range from 1.8% to 18% (Anderson et al., 1987; Feehan, McGee, Raja, & Williams, 1994; Kessler et al., 1994; McGee et al., 1990; Newman et al., 1996), with rates increasing with age. The high risk of recurrent depression in depressed children and adolescents appears to persist into young adulthood (Kovacs & Devlin, 1998). In three separate clinical samples of children and adolescents with major depression, remission rates ranged from 31% to 46% (McCauley, Myers, Mitchell, & Calderon, 1993; Rao, Ryan, Birmaher, & Dahl, 1995). Interestingly, remission rates of depression do not appear to be influenced by whether the youth had a comorbid anxiety disorder in the index depressive episode (Kovacs, Gatsonis, Paulauskas, & Richards, 1989; McCauley et al., 1993; Rao et al., 1995), though new episodes of anxiety disorders do appear to be influenced by the presence of comorbid anxiety during major depression (e.g., Rao et al., 1995). The upshot of the available information regarding the course of anxiety and depressive disorders is that children and adolescents do not necessarily "outgrow" these disorders, thereby rendering it urgent that effective treatments be developed.

In a recent review of 14 studies of various samples, Lahey, Miller, Gordon, and Riley (1999) reported prevalence estimates for ODD ranging from 0.3% to 22.5% with a median of all estimates being about 3.2%. The studies included in this review were population-based studies and included birth cohort samples, household samples, and school-based samples. Evidence from longitudinal studies on large clinical samples indicates that the incidence of ODD increases with age and there is a developmental progression from ODD to CD. In the Pittsburgh Youth Survey, the weighted prevalence of a DSM diagnosis of ODD was 2.2 at age 7, 4.8 at age 10, and 5.0 at age 13 (Loeber, Farrington, Stouthamer-Loeber, & Van Kammen, 1998) and in the first waves of the Developmental Trends Study (Lahey, Loeber, Quay, Frick, & Grimm, 1992; Loeber, Green, Lahey, Frick, & McBurnett, 2000; Loeber, Keenan, Lahey, Green, & Thomas, 1993), newly developing cases of CD were very frequently (80% of cases) preceded by ODD patterns. In addition, older children with CD typically retained the behaviors of ODD that they displayed earlier in development. About one-fourth of all boys with ODD progressed to CD and about one-half retained the ODD diagnosis but did not progress to CD 3 years later. In subsequent waves, as the boys got older, those who met criteria for ODD in the first wave were even more likely to meet criteria for CD (Loeber et al., 2000). Therefore, a substantial majority of clinic referred 7- to 12-year-old boys with ODD appear to retain this pattern of behavior or progress to the even more serious symptoms of CD later in development.

ADHD is one of the most common and impairing of the childhood psychological disorders. Recent epidemiological studies using independently administered, structured diagnostic interviews indicate that between 3% to 5% of youth meet criteria for ADHD (Angold, Erkanli, Egger, & Costello, 2000; Jensen et al., 1999), which means that at least one child in almost every classroom in America is affected by this disorder. Recent studies indicate that ADHD is both underdiagnosed and overdiagnosed in practice. In two of these studies, only 12% to 25% of independently assessed children who met criteria for diagnosis of ADHD received treatment (Jensen et al., 1999; Wolraich, Hannah, Baumgaertel, & Feurer, 1998), whereas in another recent study, the rate of stimulant treatment was almost twice the rate of parent reported ADHD and the majority of stimulant treated children did not meet diagnostic criteria for ADHD (Angold et al., 2000).

In addition to its central features, ADHD is usually associated with one or more comorbid conditions, associated features or functional deficits, or combination of these, which add to the impairment picture. Chief among the complicating comorbid conditions are ODD (35% to 60% of ADHD cases in clinical and epidemiological samples); CD (30% to 50% of ADHD cases); specific learning disabilities (10% to 26% of ADHD cases when conservative estimates are employed); and anxiety (25% to 40% of ADHD cases) (Barkley, 1996; Biederman, Faraone, & Lapey, 1992; Conners & Erhardt, 1998; Hinshaw, 1992). Among the complicating functional impairments are: difficulties in the school domain with academic achievement and disruptive classroom behavior, difficulties in the peer domain, and most relevant to our topic, difficulties in the family domain (for reviews, see Wells, in press; Wells et al., 2000).

Furthermore, despite the early prevailing view that ADHD was a time-limited disorder of prepuberty, prospective studies on psychiatric clinic samples have revealed ADHD to be a chronic disorder in a substantial majority of children who receive the diagnosis, with antisocial outcomes, substance abuse, and continued attentional, family, interpersonal, and occupational difficulties persisting into adolescence and adulthood (Klein & Manuzza, 1991; Weiss & Hechtman, 1993).

Efficacy of Family-Based Interventions

Anxiety Disorders

In the first clinical trials focused on the effectiveness of psychotherapy for children with anxiety disorders, Kendall and colleagues (1994, 1997) found individual child-focused cognitive behavioral treatment ($n = 27$) was more efficacious in reducing DSM-III-R anxiety disorders (separation anxiety disorder, overanxious/generalized anxiety disorder, and social phobia) in children (aged 9 to 13 years) relative to a waitlist control condition ($n = 20$). The results from these two trials were viewed as very promising and important first steps in developing efficacious treatments for anxiety disorders in children. Although promising, not all children benefited from individual therapy: The percentage of children who continued to meet diagnosis for their targeted anxiety disorder ranged from approximately 28% to 36% (Kendall, 1994; Kendall et al., 1997). In an attempt to improve the efficacy of treatment for anxious children, attention shifted to interventions that included the parents and family.

Most of the treatment research studies that have evaluated the efficacy of family-focused interventions in reducing anxiety disorders in children have been grounded primarily in the concepts and procedures of cognitive behavior therapy. As pointed out by Herbert (1998), despite epistemological differences between behavioral and systems approaches to family therapy, there are similarities. The similarities include: (a) an emphasis on interactional, not intrapsychic causes; (b) discovering repetitive sequences in interpersonal processes; (c) an emphasis on observable behaviors; (d) viewing a child's presenting problem as representing broader classes of interactional patterns; and (e) using behavioral interventions to change dysfunctional patterns of interpersonal behavior. Thus, these behavioral family-based child anxiety treatment programs involve not only graded child exposures to fearful or anxiety provoking situations and training children in using cognitive and behavioral strategies, but also promote parents' reinforcement/support for their child's successful handling of his or her fear/avoidant behaviors and improving parenting skills and the parent-child relationship (e.g., Barrett, 1998; Barrett, Dadds, & Rapee, 1996).

For this review, the literature summarized in this section focuses exclusively on randomized clinical trials that have been conducted during the past decade for mood and anxiety disorders in children (see also Silverman & Berman, 2001). First, the clinical trials that evaluated the efficacy of using a family-based cognitive behavioral treatment approach in which the children and parents (not the entire family) are seen together by the therapist are summarized. The second part of this section summarizes the clinical trials that evaluated the efficacy of using a family-based cognitive behavioral treatment approach in which the children and parents are seen together with other children and parents in a group treatment approach. It is worth noting that in addition to these clinical trials, a literature consisting of single case study designs in which family/parents were incorporated also has accumulated (e.g., Albano, Marten, Holt, Heimberg, & Barlow, 1995; Dadds, Heard, & Rapee, 1991; Heard, Dadds, & Conrad, 1992; Howard & Kendall, 1996; Kearney & Silverman, 1990, 1999; Knox, Albano, & Barlow, 1996), forming an impressive series of clinical replications (Hayes, Barlow, & Nelson-Gray, 1999).

Efficacy for Family-Based Cognitive Behavior Therapy
    A clinical trial conducted in Brisbane, Australia by Barrett et al. (1996) compared the relative efficacy of family-based cognitive behavior therapy (FCBT; n = 25) to individual child-focused cognitive behavioral treatment (ICBT; n = 28 [i.e., the program found to be efficacious in Kendall, 1994, and Kendall et al., 1997]), relative to a waitlist control condition (n = 26) in reducing anxiety disorders in youth (ages 7 to 14 years) with primary diagnoses of overanxious disorder, separation anxiety disorder, and social phobia. Treatment sessions for the ICBT condition were 60 to 80 minutes in length and lasted for 12 weeks. The waitlist condition was similarly 12 weeks in length. In FCBT, the child was seen for ICBT for 30 minutes and 40 minutes were then spent with the child and his or her parents together. In these 40 minutes, emphasis was placed not only on providing child-focused cognitive behavioral treatment but also on how parents interact with their children during displays of child anxiety, parental management of child emotional upsets, and communication and problem-solving skills.
    Results indicated that across the individual and family-based intervention conditions, diagnostic recovery rates were significantly higher for youth in these two conditions (i.e., 69.8% of cases no longer met diagnostic criteria for an anxiety disorder) than for youth in the waitlist control condition (i.e., 26% of cases no longer met diagnostic criteria for an anxiety disorder). In addition, on all the child and parent rating scales, youth in the two treatment conditions showed significant improvement relative to the youth in the waitlist control condition. The only exception to this was on a child self-rating anxiety scale, on which the control group also showed improvement.
    Most interesting was the finding that youth who received the family-based cognitive behavioral intervention, FCBT, had significantly higher diagnostic recovery rates (84%) than youth who received ICBT (57.1%). Improvement also was evident on child and parent rating scales, though statistically significant differences between the treatment conditions (i.e., ICBT vs. FCBT) were not as apparent on these measures. An interesting age by treatment interaction was observed in that younger children showed more improvement in FCBT than older children in ICBT. In addition to diagnostic recovery and self-rating scales, children's perceived threat interpretations and response plans to ambiguous hypothetical situations were assessed at pre- and posttreatment (and postwait). Interestingly, youth in *both* ICBT and FCBT displayed reductions in threat interpretation and avoidant responses; youth in the waitlist condition remained the same from pre- to postwait.

Follow-up assessment in Barrett et al. (1996) indicated that treatment recovery was maintained at 12 months. For example, 70.3% of youth in ICBT no longer met criteria for diagnostic status for an anxiety disorder. Youth in FCBT showed greater improvement in diagnostic recovery (i.e., 95.6% of cases no longer met criteria for an anxiety diagnosis), though differences between the ICBT and FCBT conditions were not as pronounced on most of the child and parent rating scales.

Barrett, Duffy, Dadds, and Rapee (2001) reported long-term (5 to 7 years posttreatment) maintenance of treatment gains from the Barrett et al. (1996) study. For both the ICBT and FCBT conditions, treatment gains were maintained for this period as evidenced by continued absence of the targeted anxiety disorder diagnosis as reported by the youth, and on all the child and parent rating scales. Most interesting was the absence of any differences between the two intervention conditions. The only exception was levels of self-rated fear: Children who received FCBT rated significantly less fear at long-term follow-up in comparison to children who received ICBT.

Another study conducted recently in Australia provides additional evidence for the efficacy of a family-based cognitive behavioral intervention (Cobham et al., 1998). In this study, however, parental involvement included not only parental management of the child's anxiety, but also parental management of their own anxiety. The potential utility of such an approach had been suggested by other investigators (Ginsburg, Silverman, & Kurtines, 1995; Silverman & Kurtines, 1996a, 1996b, in press) and is under investigation by Silverman and her research group, in a National Institute of Mental Health funded project. In the Cobham et al. (1998) study, 67 children and adolescents aged 7 to 14 years with anxiety disorders (separation anxiety disorder, overanxious disorder, generalized anxiety disorder, simple phobia, social phobia, or agoraphobia) were assigned to conditions according to parental anxiety level. Participants were then classified into groups based on one or both parent(s) scoring as anxious ($n = 35$), or neither parent scoring as anxious (i.e., nonanxious; $n = 32$). Within these two groups, participants were then randomly assigned to ICBT or FCBT, which included parental management of child *and* parental anxiety (referred to hereafter as FCBT+). Total client contact time was about the same in the two treatment conditions, though FCBT+ involved a greater number of sessions than the ICBT condition (ten 1-hour child sessions and four 1-hour parent sessions for FCBT+ vs. ten 1.5-hour sessions for ICBT).

In terms of the main findings, for youth whose parents were in the nonanxious condition, 82% in the ICBT condition no longer met criteria for an anxiety disorder at posttreatment as compared to 80% in the FCBT+ condition. However, for those youth whose parents were anxious, only 39% in the ICBT condition no longer met criteria for an anxiety disorder. This compared to a 77% diagnostic recovery rate for those youth with anxious parents in the FCBT+ condition. In other words, ICBT was found to be highly efficacious for youth with nonanxious parents. However, the addition of a parent anxiety management component in FCBT+ was important for diagnostic recovery for those youth whose parents were anxious. In terms of follow-up, the above noted patterns were generally maintained at 6 and 12 months across most of the outcome measures.

With respect to family-based interventions for obsessive-compulsive disorder (OCD), there is an absence of randomized controlled clinical trials. However, March, Mulle, and Herbel (1994) conducted an open trial that evaluated a family-based cognitive behavioral treatment program for 15 children and adolescents (ages 8 to 18 years). The program emphasized: helping youth and parents view OCD as a medical illness separate from the child's core identity; graded child exposures in situations that elicited obsessions and led to compulsions; and training parents in providing support and reward for their children's exposures. Specifically, parents received a "self-help" instruction booklet that included strategies on how to manage themselves with respect to their child's OCD and the weekly "homework" assignments. Parents also were encouraged to comment on the progress of their children's treatment at the beginning of each session. Of the 15 participants, all but 1 also received some form of medication, 2 received adjunctive family therapy, and 2 received supportive psychotherapy. The mean number of sessions of the family-based cognitive behavioral treatment program was 10.44; the mean length of treatment was 8.0 months; the mean length of follow-up was 7.3 months. Despite the methodological limitations of this study (e.g., differing adjunctive treatments received by patients, differing number of sessions, not all patients received all measures), the findings may be viewed as promising in that 9 cases experienced at least a 50% reduction in symptoms at posttreatment; 6 were asymptomatic. No cases relapsed at follow-up.

Efficacy for Family-Based Group Cognitive Behavior Therapy

Providing evidence for the efficacy of a group modality in reducing anxiety disorders in children and adolescents has considerable practical significance. It has, for example, practical significance for practitioners in the current context of the growth of HMOs, problems with third party payments, and other such issues. In this context, there has been pressure mounting on practitioners to offer services that are not only efficacious, but also cost and time efficient (Kazdin, Siegel, & Bass, 1990). Demonstrating that anxiety disorders in children and adolescents can be reduced in a group format (with or without a family/parental component) thus has important practical implications in that it serves to provide empirical evidence that practitioners can elect to work with this population via this cost and time efficient format. In addition, in the search for cost and time efficient interventions, demonstrating the efficacy of family-based group cognitive behavior therapy (FGCBT) takes on further practical significance as children and their parents expend considerable time and energy in the treatment process at high financial cost.

In a randomized clinical trial, Barrett (1998) demonstrated that two group treatment modalities, one that was family-based (i.e., FGCBT; $n = 17$) and one that was not family-based (i.e., GCBT; $n = 23$) were both more efficacious than a waitlist control condition ($n = 20$) in reducing children's anxiety disorders (i.e., overanxious disorder, separation anxiety disorder, and social phobia in children aged 7 to 14 years). Although results indicated that the family-based group approach (FGCBT) did not create a significant difference in recovery rate relative to GCBT at posttreatment, youth in FGCBT showed somewhat better improvement than youth in the GCBT condition as evidenced by: (a) less family disruption, (b) greater parental perception of ability to deal with child's behaviors, and (c) lower child's reports of fear. At 1-year follow-up, youth in FGCBT maintained lower scores for internalizing and externalizing behaviors as reported by parents and higher diagnostic recovery rates (84.8% of cases in FGCBT being diagnosis free vs. 64.5% of cases in GCBT being diagnosis free).

Silverman et al. (1999) reported the results of another randomized clinical trial that provided further empirical evidence for the efficacy of GCBT and incorporating family/parents in reducing anxiety disorders in children and adolescents. In this GCBT condition, youth and parents attended separate but concurrent groups (conducted by two separate therapists). Parallel content was presented in the child and parent sessions (see Silverman & Kurtines, 1996a, 1996b for details). To establish the therapeutic efficacy of the intervention in maintaining as well as producing treatment gains, participants were randomly assigned to conditions with an assignment ratio of 2 to 1 (GCBT to control). Thus, of the 56 youth (34 boys, 22 girls; 6 to 16 years old; average age, 9.96 years) and parents who participated in the study, 37 (67%) of the participants were assigned to GCBT and 19 (33%) to the waitlist. Inclusion criteria were primary DSM-III-R diagnosis of either social phobia, overanxious disorder, or generalized anxiety disorder.

Findings indicated that the family-based GCBT condition in this study was more efficacious than the waitlist condition. For example, 64% of the cases in GCBT were recovered at posttreatment; only 12.5% were recovered in the waitlist condition. This pattern of improvement (from pre- to posttest) also was observed for the clinician ratings of severity, as well for the child- and parent-completed anxiety measures, and additional parent ratings. In addition, the pattern for all the child- and parent-completed measures similarly indicated a continued reduction in degree and severity of anxious symptoms from posttreatment to 3-month follow-up, with improvement leveling off at that time but still being maintained at 6- and 12-month follow-up.

Mendlowitz et al. (1999) conducted a clinical trial examining group treatment for anxiety disorders in children ($N = 68$; ages 7 to12 years old; the specific disorders were not indicated). Three conditions were compared: (a) GCBT for children only, (b) GCBT for children and parents, and (c) GCBT for parents only. A waitlist control condition also was included. Improvement was noted for all treatment conditions in terms of reduction in anxiety symptoms; however, children in the GCBT for children and parents condition (i.e., condition "b" above), showed significantly greater improvement in their coping strategies relative to children in the other conditions. Spence et al. (2000) conducted a clinical trial for children and adolescents with social phobia (N = 50; ages 7 to 14 years old) in which GCBT was compared to FGCBT and a waitlist control. In this study, FGCBT consisted mainly of enhanced contingency management techniques taught to parents during therapy sessions. Results indicated that both group treatment conditions showed significant improvements at posttreatment and 12-month follow-up when compared to the waitlist condition. Comparisons between the two treatment conditions did not show statistically significant differences suggesting both conditions (i.e., GCBT and FGCBT) were efficacious in reducing symptoms of social phobia.

The clinical trials conducted to date on family interventions for children with anxiety disorders supports the efficacy of these interventions. The primary theoretical model utilized is cognitive behavioral. The interventions generally involve graded exposures to fearful or anxiety provoking situations, teaching parents to support and reinforce the child's successful handling of the situation, improving parenting skills, and improving the parent-child relationship. Recovery rates for children who received family-based interventions are generally high (better than 60%) and the therapeutic gains are maintained for as many as 7 years. There does seem to be some moderating variables involved in family treatment in that younger children and parents who experience high levels of anxiety seem to benefit more from family involvement than older children and parents who do not suffer from anxiety disorders.

Depression

Relative to treatment research on reducing anxiety disorders in children and adolescents, there is considerably less treatment research on the efficacy of family-focused interventions in reducing mood disorders in children. In recent reviews of the empirically supported treatments for child and adolescent mood disorders (Kaslow & Thompson, 1998), marital (Alexander, Holtzworth-Munroe, & Jameson, 1994) and family (Robbins, Szapocznik, Alexander, & Miller, 2001) treatments, not one marital or family-based study that focused on reducing child depression was published in a peer-refereed scientific journal; and of the seven adolescent studies, only three involved parents or were family-based. These three studies are summarized below. The three existing studies are similar to the child anxiety treatment studies summarized above in their use of rigorous methodological procedures (i.e., structured diagnostic interviews, treatment integrity checks). The authors have not found any additional treatment studies in the literature since these reviews.

Efficacy for Family-Based Group Cognitive Behavior Therapy in the Schools

Lewinsohn et al. (1990) compared the relative efficacy of a school-based group cognitive behavioral treatment program ("Coping with Depression"), a school-based group cognitive behavioral treatment program that involved parental participation, and a waitlist control condition in adolescents (N = 59; ages 14 to 18 years). The course includes 14 to 16 two-hour sessions conducted over a 7- to 8-week period for groups of up to 10 adolescents. All participants met DSM-III or Research Diagnostic Criteria for a depressive disorder. In both GCBT conditions emphasis was placed on (a) providing psychoeducation about the nature of depression; (b) emphasizing skills training to promote self-control over one's mood and coping with problem situations; and (c) using the group in various activities, such as role-plays.

In the condition that involved parental participation (referred to as family-based group cognitive behavior therapy here, or FGCBT), parallel material was provided in that parents met with therapists weekly for 2 hours, during which time the skills being taught to the adolescent were taught to parents. In addition, parents were trained in providing support and positive reinforcement and assistance as their adolescent began using the skills being taught. Parents also received training in the communication and problem-solving skills being taught to the adolescent. Two joint sessions also were held in which the adolescents and parents practiced these skills on issues salient to their family.

Overall, results indicated that although adolescents in both the GCBT and FGCBT conditions showed significant declines in depression and other internalizing symptoms on measures completed by both the youth and parent compared to adolescents in the waitlist condition, both treatment conditions showed these gains and the conditions were not differentially effective. These effects were maintained at 2-year follow-up.

Lewinsohn, Clarke, Rohde, Hops, and Seeley (1996) provided a replication and extension of Lewinsohn et al. (1990) among 96 adolescents (ages 14 to 18 years) who met diagnostic criteria for major depressive disorder or dysthymic disorder. The main "extension" was the additional evaluation of the differential effects of: (a) receiving booster sessions every 4 months for 2 years versus (b) being assessed every 4 months for 2 years but no booster sessions versus (c) being assessed annually with no booster sessions. Once again, both the GCBT and FGCBT conditions showed significant declines in depression and internalizing symptoms as assessed by youth and parent measures, with no significant differences found between the treatment conditions. Interestingly no differences also were found between the three follow-up conditions.

Efficacy for Systemic Behavior Family Therapy
Brent et al. (1997) compared the relative efficacy of systemic behavior family therapy (n = 35), individual cognitive behavior therapy (n = 37), and individual nondirective supportive therapy (n = 35) in a clinic-referred sample of adolescents (ages 13 to 18 years) who met DSM-III-R criteria for major depressive disorder. All treatments ranged from 12 to 16 sessions. The systemic behavior family therapy condition (SBFT) was viewed as a "logical alternative treatment choice for adolescent depression, because it is a commonly used method of treat-

ment for adolescents, and because parental depression, poor perceived support, and parent-child discord are associated with onset, prolonged course, and recurrence of depression and suicidality in youth" (p. 880). SBFT consisted of two phases. The first phase drew from "functional family therapy, in which the therapist clarifies the concerns that brought the family into treatment and provides a series of reframing statements designed to optimize engagement in therapy and identification of dysfunctional behavior patterns" (p. 878). The second phase drew from a problem-solving model that focuses on communication and problem-solving skills and the alteration of family interaction patterns. Worth noting is the fact that all participants received "family psychoeducation" about affective illness and its treatment. Specifically, in the first three sessions all parents received a psychoeducational manual and were invited to discuss questions and concerns about the treatment of depression with up to 1 hour spent on psychoeducational issues.

Results indicated that cognitive behavior therapy was superior to SBFT and nondirective supportive therapy in reducing adolescent depression. This was true in terms of diagnostic recovery rates, rates of symptomatic improvement, and parent ratings of treatment credibility. However, no group differences emerged for effect on suicidality (all conditions showed significant decreases in suicidality) and functional impairment. In explaining the latter set of findings, Brent et al. (1997) suggested that perhaps the processes involved in reducing depression differ from those in reducing suicidality, and that perhaps relief of functional impairment lags behind relief of depressive symptoms. Also, regarding the reason SBFT was not found to be more efficacious in this study than the other individual focused treatments, the authors suggested that perhaps the developmental needs of adolescents necessitate a more individually focused treatment approach.

In a subsequent study, Kolko, Brent, Baugher, Bridge, and Birmaher (2000) reported the results of therapy specificity (e.g., does cognitive therapy produce specific effects on cognitions; does SBFT produce specific effects on family functioning) and mediation effects (e.g., do changes in cognitions lead to or mediate change in cognitive therapy; do changes in family functioning lead to or mediate change in SBFT) at posttreatment and 2-year follow-up. Most relevant to this chapter were the not very encouraging results about SBFT with respect to specific and mediational effects. That is, although SBFT produced a greater effect on general family functioning than individual nondirective supportive therapy, so did cognitive behavior therapy. Moreover, cognitive behavior therapy showed a greater impact on two other family variables (i.e., behavioral control and marital satisfaction) compared with nondirective supportive therapy, whereas SBFT did not. In addition, although at 2-year follow-up SBFT showed a specific effect on family conflict relative to cognitive behavior therapy, so did nondirective supportive therapy. The results further showed that family dysfunction (or improvement thereof) did not mediate treatment outcome, but neither did cognitive distortion (or improvement thereof).

Despite the limited number of clinical trials on depression in children and adolescents, the small number of studies provides preliminary support for family interventions. Two of the three studies conducted have employed a group format and provided the intervention in school settings. All the interventions studied had a strong family psychoeducation component, in addition to skill building and teaching parents how to support their children. The findings from the research on SBFT provided the most equivocal results. The family therapy interventions were found to be inferior to the cognitive behavioral interventions when it came to the reduction of depressive symptomology; however, there were no differences between the conditions in reducing suicidality. These findings coupled with those from the research on anxiety disorders, do support the utility of family-based interventions for internalized disorders. However, the research is still in its infancy. Replicating and extending these findings in future research is needed.

Oppositional Defiant Disorder

Parent Training (PT) is the primary evidence-based family treatment for ODD, and it is considered by many to be the treatment of choice for ODD. PT addresses many of the problematic family interaction patterns theorized to contribute to ODD, including coercive behaviors (e.g., negative commands directed to others, disapproval, humiliating statements, noncompliance, negativity, physical aggression, yelling), problematic parenting (e.g., poorly formulated and poorly delivered commands, scolding, nagging, threatening, criticism, negative and ineffective consequences, lower rates of positive attention and rewards), negatively reinforcing and escalating chains of coercive interaction, and insecure attachment. The most interesting findings from this research are that aversive parent and child behaviors do not occur in isolation from one another, but rather take place in tight, reciprocal control processes during moment-to-moment interactions. Aggressive children and their parents tend to respond to one another in mutually negatively reinforcing and escalating chains of coercive interaction. Aspects of macroscopic family interaction also have been found across studies of the relationship of family variables to child aggression. The most robust of these are (a) low levels of parental involvement in their children's activities, (b) poor supervision and monitoring, and (c) harsh and inconsistent discipline practices (Loeber & Stouthamer-Loeber, 1986).

Among the earliest empirical studies on PT as a treatment modality for ODD were those of Gerald Patterson and his colleagues in the early 1970s. Because of the historical context in which they were developed, these PT studies tended to be based in an operant model in which the child was the client who had target behaviors toward which parents were taught to apply effective consequences utilizing available reinforcers. The relationship of the parent and child was not seen so much as a focus of intervention in these early studies. Rather the parent was taught to become an in situ "therapist" for his or her child.

Later, based largely on the work of Connie Hanf from the Oregon Health

Science Center, a clinician who did not herself publish, a shift began to occur in which PT focused not just on teaching parents to increase and decrease target behaviors in their child, but also on changing the parent-child relationship. Traces of this shift can be seen in the early work of Rex Forehand (Forehand & McMahon, 1981). It reaches its clearest articulation in the work of Sheila Eyberg and her colleagues (Eyberg & Boggs, 1998; Foote, Schuhmann, Jones, & Eyberg, 1998) in what the authors now refer to as Parent-Child Interaction Therapy, which has an explicitly stated goal of targeting the interaction patterns and relationship between the parent and child, and training in nurturance as well as in discipline. However, each of these models (and that of Barkley for ADHD children; see section on ADHD) is anchored in the work of Connie Hanf (Hanf & Kling, 1973), with whom each of these first generation PT researchers trained.

Though varying in details and emphasis, each of the above models of PT shares some core characteristics derived from Hanf's original two-stage model. In the first stage, parents are taught various skills for applying positive social attention to their child in a play context led by the child. Over time positive parent skills are also applied, not just during play, but contingently, when children display prosocial behaviors. There is a heavy emphasis on the prosocial behavior, "compliance to parents' instructions" since oppositional noncompliance is a defining symptom of ODD and is a keystone characteristic of children with all varieties of disruptive behavior disorders. Parents are also taught to ignore instances of minor disruptive behavior, in order to reduce the high rates of nattering, threatening, and ineffective discipline attempts. In stage two of these models, the emphasis shifts to teaching parents to give effective instructions and set effective, age appropriate rules with children, as well as skills for setting effective limits (i.e., effective punishment) on noncompliant and other disruptive behavior. The usual punishment technique taught to parents of young oppositional children is time-out. There is a great deal of emphasis on in vivo role-playing and practice in sessions as well as weekly homework assignments to continue practice at home. There are many details and nuances to the implementation of these models, and the reader is referred to treatment manuals that explicate these details with session outlines and much therapeutic commentary (Forehand & McMahon, 1981; Hembree-Kigin & McNeil, 1995).

PT for oppositional behavior problem children is one of the most well researched treatment modalities in child psychology and there is incontrovertible evidence for its short-term effectiveness, especially with younger oppositional behavior problem children (i.e., ages 6 to 12 years). Reviews of this literature have appeared recently (Brestan & Eyberg, 1998; Kazdin, 1994; Serketich & Dumas, 1996) so we will not exhaustively review it in this chapter. Suffice it to say that in randomized trials, PT has been compared to waitlist controls, to attention placebo control, and to other active family treatment, and it has almost always been found to be superior to these control and comparative conditions, especially on measures of child noncompliance and other disruptive behaviors (e.g., Bernal, Klinnert, & Schultz, 1980; Patterson, Chamberlain, & Reid, 1982; Peed, Roberts, & Forehand, 1977; Schuhmann, Foote, Eyberg, & Boggs, 1998; Walter & Gilmore, 1973; Wells & Egan, 1988; Wiltz & Patterson, 1974). Effect sizes for PT on child outcomes range from .73 to .84, in the moderate range (Serketich & Dumas, 1996). In addition, generalization of treatment effects (maintenance) across short periods of time posttreatment have been demonstrated, and some effects seem to persist even over years for some but not all children and families (i.e., Baum & Forehand, 1981; Eyberg et al., 2001; Forehand & Long, 1988; Forehand, Rogers, McMahon, Wells, & Griest, 1981; Forehand, Steffe, Furey, & Walley, 1983). For example, Forehand and Long (1988) demonstrated that relative to a nonreferred sample, a sample of children who had participated in a parent training program 4.5 to 10.5 years earlier was functioning well. However, not all studies report maintenance of treatment effects (Forehand & Long, 1988) and even for those that do, conclusions are based on group averages. Examination of these studies shows that 30% to 50% of treated families fail to show clinically significant improvements as a function of treatment (Webster-Stratton, 1985).

When maintenance failure occurs, it seems to be related to such variables as family poverty, maternal isolation, and parent psychopathology, especially depression in mothers (Dumas, 1989). These factors seem to interfere with the ability of parents to continue to apply effective parenting skills learned during treatment when the weekly support of the therapist is still available. Setting generalization effects (especially generalization of treatment effects from the home to the school) are more equivocal, with some studies showing no evidence for setting generalization (e.g., Breiner & Forehand, 1981; Forehand, Griest, & Wells, 1979) while other studies do show evidence of such generalization (Funderburk et al., 1998). Finally, when noncompliance is the primary target of treatment, behavioral generalization (i.e., generalization of treatment effects to other "nontarget" behaviors such as overt aggression, tantrums, destructiveness, and inappropriate verbal behavior) has been demonstrated (Wells, Forehand, & Griest, 1980).

Webster-Stratton has developed a variation of parent training programs for youth with oppositional problems. What is unique about this program is its use of a standard package of 10 videotaped presentations of modeled parenting skills shown by a therapist to groups of parents. The 250 vignettes include examples of parents interacting with their children in both appropriate and inappropriate ways. After each vignette the therapist leads a discussion of the relevant interactions. Three major treatment outcome studies have been conducted demonstrating the immediate and long-term salutary effects of this program on both mothers and children's behaviors, mothers' perceptions of their children, and mothers' satisfaction with treatment. Maintenance of effects was largely demonstrated at 1-year follow-up (Webster-Stratton, 1981, 1984; Webster-Stratton, Kolpacoff, & Hollinsworth, 1988).

PT has also been compared to other family treatment models. Baum, Reyna-McGlone, and Ollendick (1986) reported that a group version of PT was more effective at posttreatment and at 6- to 8-month follow-up than a parent discussion group based on the systematic training for effective parenting (STEP) program. Wells and Egan (1988) compared PT to systems family therapy and found superior results on observational measures of parent and child behaviors but not on parent self-report measures.

The social validity of PT has also been demonstrated. Forehand, Wells, and Griest (1980) showed that following PT, oppositional children's inappropriate behaviors improved to within the normal range on both direct observations and on parent perception measures, and parents' ratings indicate high satisfaction with (Baum & Forehand, 1981) and acceptability of the treatment (Cross Calvert & McMahon, 1987).

In spite of the generally very positive short-term results associated with PT for ODD, results have tended to be based on parents and families who stay in therapy and do not drop out. However, attrition from research studies as well as from therapy is a significant problem. In a recent study, 38% of families dropped out of PT treatment prematurely (Eyberg, 1996). Families who drop out may have more comorbid and social problems and may be less likely to profit from therapy had they stayed in (McMahon, Forehand, Griest, & Wells, 1981). Thus, one important area of future inquiry is how to keep families in treatment once they have begun, and how to address the multiple problems presented by these and other families who present for PT.

With regard to the latter point, several research groups have examined the impact of other family and context variables on parenting behavior and child aggression. This work has shown that parents of aggressive children display more anxiety and depression, more marital distress, and more extrafamilial distress (insularity and social isolation) than do parents of nonaggressive children (for a review see Connell & Goodman, 2002; Griest & Wells, 1983; Johnston & Mash, 2001; Jouriles, Murphy, & O'Leary, 1989). These factors predict more limited treatment success and also predict premature termination or attrition from treatment.

Evidence of adverse extrafamilial and contextual effects such as marital distress, social isolation, anxiety, and depression has led to calls for the development and evaluation of enhancement procedures to address these variables while conducting parent training (Griest & Wells, 1983; Miller & Prinz, 1990; Webster-Stratton, 1994) in order to (a) improve treatment outcome, (b) improve maintenance of treatment effects, and (c) reduce attrition from treatment. Several research evaluations of such "adjunctive strategies" added to PT have occurred and indicated that this is a promising line for future effectiveness research. These adjunctive strategies have included teaching parents self-control skills in addition to PT (Wells, Griest, & Forehand, 1980); training parents in the social learning principles that underlie PT (McMahon et al., 1981), including expanded exemplars of common parent-child situations in PT (Powers & Roberts, 1995); and adding a multimodal treatment package, called Parent Enhancement Therapy, to PT. Parent Enhancement Therapy includes modules to address parent stress, parent marital communication, and parent social isolation (Griest et al., 1982). Webster-Stratton (1994) added a treatment component for parents on coping with distress to a basic videotaped PT program. In general all of these studies supported the efficacy of these adjunctive procedures in enhancing the outcome and maintenance of treatment effects over and beyond those obtained with PT alone.

Prinz and Miller (1994) studied dropout of PT and found that families whose treatment focused exclusively on parent training dropped out more often than families who had more opportunities during treatment to discuss broader contextual issues beyond child management. Unfortunately, there is little evidence that inclusion of adjunctive strategies have been incorporated into clinical practice. Since these findings were based on efficacy studies conducted in academic, laboratory settings, services research is sorely needed to ascertain the portability and effectiveness of these strategies into real clinical settings.

The research on the effectiveness of family-based interventions for ODD is well established, but has focused almost exclusive on PT or its variants. PT is efficacious in helping parents better manage their children's behavior and teaches parents to use effective parenting techniques. PT is clearly very effective in the short-term, but longer-term outcomes are mixed. The reasons for this are varied, but family poverty, maternal isolation, and parental psychopathology have all been suggested as factors that mediate the impact of the intervention. Further, the generalization of appropriate behavior to school settings is also problematic. Despite these limitations, the research clearly shows that the behavior of children who receive the intervention move from the clinical to the normal range.

Attention Deficit Hyperactivity Disorders

It must be stated from the outset that stimulant medication is considered by most experts (but not all) in the field to be the first line unimodal treatment of choice for ADHD, and recent research in well-controlled studies bears this out (Klein & Abikoff, 1997; Multimodal Treatment Study of Children with Attention Deficit Hyperactivity Disorder [MTA] Cooperative Group, 1999a). However, the combination of psychosocial treatment and medication is more effective than medication alone on some measures of ADHD children's functioning (Klein & Abikoff, 1997; MTA Cooperative Group, 1999a); is more effective for some comorbid subtypes (MTA Cooperative Group, 1999b); and combination treatment is the only treatment that produces normalization of function in ADHD children (Klein & Abikoff, 1997). Multimodal psychosocial treatment of ADHD includes PT as one of its components and this literature is summarized below.

Since 1980, there have been 15 randomized controlled clinical trials in the published literature that have examined PT as a single treatment or as a component of a clinical behavior therapy package for youth with ADHD. In most of the studies of PT with ADHD youth, PT ran for the usual 8 to 12 sessions described by Barkley (1998) and included many of the same components. In addition, Barkley added an initial presentation on the nature of ADHD and the basis for PT as one component of treatment for this disorder. However, in the most recent and largest evaluation of behavior therapy with ADHD youth (MTA Cooperative Group, 1999a), PT was expanded to address many additional family and school issues and ran for 27 group sessions and 8 individual sessions over 14 months (Wells et al., 1996, 2000).

The first 12 sessions from the PT program in the MTA study were adapted from programs of Barkley (1998) and Forehand and McMahon (1981). Parents were taught skills of positive reinforcement, giving effective commands and establishing home rules, use of effective punishment procedures (time-out and response cost), as well as using skills outside of home. In this version of PT, parents were also taught early in the program how to set up a cooperative, home-school Daily Report Card (DRC) with the child's teacher in the school. This is often done early in behavioral treatment of ADHD youth, especially for those who will not be treated with stimulant medication, due to the serious difficulties that these children have in school and the need to offer some help with these problems early in treatment.

Although most clinical PT programs for ADHD end with these fundamental interventions, expanded PT for ADHD incorporates other interventions to address the multilevel problems often present in families with ADHD youth. Expanded sessions address stress, anger, and mood management in parents, and direct a great deal of attention to teaching, modeling, and role-playing with parents the skills necessary for becoming advocates for their child in the schools. Parents are taught how to contact relevant school personnel, how to ask for and conduct a meeting in school, how to work with the teacher to set up a home-school DRC, and how to set up homework structures and procedures for the child in the home. This work with parents complements and coordinates with what is done in the schools (for details and session-by-session outlines of PT for ADHD see Barkley, 1998, and Wells et al., 1996, 2000).

The randomized clinical trials of parent training with ADHD youth have shown that parent training produces reductions in inattention and overactivity (Anastopoulos, Shelton, DuPaul, & Guevremont, 1993; Dubey, O'Leary, & Kaufman, 1983; Sonuga-Barke, Daley, Thompson, Laver-Bradbury, & Weeks, 2001), in child noncompliance and conduct problems (Pisterman et al., 1989; Pollard, Ward, & Barkley, 1983; Sonuga-Barke et al., 2001), and in child aggression (Anastopoulos et al., 1993). As would be expected, improvements in parenting skills (Pisterman et al., 1989, 1992) also have been found. Notably, some studies also have reported reductions in parent stress, and improvements in parent self-esteem with parent training (Anastopoulos et al., 1993; Pisterman et al., 1992; Sonuga-Barke et al., 2001). Effect sizes for PT for ADHD of 1.2 have been reported on ADHD symptoms (assessed by rating scale; Anastopoulos et al.,

1993; Horn et al., 1991). Anastopoulos et al. reported that 64% of their sample demonstrated clinically significant changes in terms of percentage of children no longer in the clinical range on ADHD Rating Scale (DuPaul, 1991) with PT compared with 27% for a waitlist control group.

Other studies have examined multicomponent behavior therapy programs of which PT is one component. The most typical combination involves PT plus teacher consultation (TC). This is done because the effects of PT are centered on home behavior and generalization of PT effects to the school would not necessarily be expected. The combination of these two interventions has been referred to as clinical behavior therapy, as it fits best in a traditional outpatient, clinical model (Hinshaw et al., 2000; Pelham & Waschbusch, 1999). In TC, the therapist works with the teacher to set up a DRC focusing on classroom behavior and academic performance, and may also consult with the teacher on classroom wide behavior management strategies if indicated and acceptable to the teacher. Several studies have combined PT and TC (Horn, Ialongo, Greenberg, Packard, & Smith-Winberry, 1990; Horn et al., 1991; Pelham et al., 1988) and compared them to medication, with results generally showing that the combination of PT plus TC results in significant improvement in children's home and school behavior. Even greater improvements are noted when PT and TC are also combined with stimulant medication (Pelham et al., 1988).

Only two empirical studies have examined PT or other family-based interventions with adolescents. In the first, three family-based treatments were compared: PT, Family Problem Solving and Communication Training, and Structural Family Therapy. All three treatments produced statistically significant improvements and none was superior to the others. However, only a few subjects showed clinically significant improvements and clinically significant effect sizes, while moderate to large for ADHD symptoms were relatively small for social and academic behavior (Barkley, Anastopoulos, Guevremont, & Fletcher, 1992). In the most recent study with adolescents, Family Problem Solving and Communication training alone was compared to PT followed by Family Problem Solving Training. Both treatments produced significant improvements but did not differ. However, dropout rates were lower with the combination treatment.

Although multimodal treatment that includes medications is generally considered the treatment of choice for ADHD, there is convincing evidence that PT is effective in reducing the inattention and hyperactivity associated with ADHD. The 15 clinical trials that have been conducted since 1980 provide some of the best evidence for the efficacy of family interventions for childhood behavioral and emotional disorders. More recently PT has been expanded to focus on family and school issues that are part and parcel of the ADHD diagnosis. This expanded focus on the other systems in which these children interact illustrates the complexity of the problems experienced by these children and their families and the need to help parents deal with them effectively.

Conclusions

The studies summarized provide empirical evidence for the efficacy of family cognitive behavioral therapy, family group cognitive behavioral therapy, and parenting training for the treatment of behavioral and emotional disorders in children. In some cases the support for family interventions is quite impressive; however, in other cases (e.g., anxiety and depression) the relatively few clinical trials make definitive conclusions difficult. The data support the conclusion that family-based interventions produce results comparable to individually oriented interventions, and in some cases—especially in the treatment of externalizing disorders, younger children, and when parents are also experiencing emotional problems—family-based interventions are superior to individual treatments and should be the treatment of choice. Although no specific type of family intervention has been shown to be superior to any other to date, it is possible that some interventions may be better suited for some families. All the family-based interventions that have been evaluated were primarily behavioral or cognitive behavioral family therapy (though Brent et al., 1997, also had a systemic family treatment). When other family therapy models have been utilized as a comparison group, behavioral and cognitive behavioral family therapy have been found to be equally effective or more effective than the comparison family treatments (Barkley et al., 1992; Wells & Egan, 1988). The fact that only a handful of extant family therapy models have been systematically tested is disconcerting. The field of family therapy has a long history of working with children and the careful evaluations of the models typically used by marriage and family therapists are seriously needed.

Future Directions

There are some obvious marriage and family therapy models that seem deserving of testing, especially those models that have been shown to be highly efficacious with adolescents and children with other types of behavior problems such as Multisystemic Therapy (chapter 2), Multidimensional Family Therapy (chapter 3), and Functional Family Therapy (chapters 2 & 3). In addition, interpersonal family therapy (IFT), which has been outlined by Kaslow and Racusin (1994) for use with depressed children and adolescents, also holds promise. IFT is grounded in family systems theory, cognitive behavioral theory, object relations theory, and developmental psychopathology, and rests on the assumption that reducing children's depressive symptoms can be accomplished by focusing on current problems as they reflect dysfunctional family interactional processes. IFT focuses on reducing depressive symptoms, enhancing the quality of family interactions, and improving children's functioning in cognitive, affective, interpersonal, and adaptive behavior (Kaslow & Racusin, 1994).

As some of the research by Kolko et al. (2000) illustrated, individual thera-

py seems to have a positive impact on family variables. This finding was supported by the work of Kazdin and Wassel (2000) who found that interventions
focused primarily on changing children's problematic behavior led to statistically significant improvements in parent symptoms and family functioning. The
corollary to this finding may be that effective couples interventions may improve
outcomes for children. However, to date there have been no systematic analyses
of the impact of marital or couples therapy on reducing behavioral and emotional disorders in children.

As noted, the child and adolescent mood reduction treatment research literature is very sparse, and the three major clinical trials (two by Lewinsohn's
research group and the other by Brent's research group) generally are supportive
for cognitive behavior therapy, but more mixed for family-based approaches. The
Kolko et al. (2000) findings (as well as the findings of Barrett et al., 1996, who
found improvement in the family interaction task even for children in the individual cognitive behavioral treatment) are particularly important as they raise
serious questions about whether therapies, particularly family therapies that
focus on changing family interactional patterns, have therapy specificity (i.e.,
does family therapy produce a specific effect on family functioning while other
therapeutic approaches do not) and are the actual mediators (i.e., mechanisms) of
change, as theory would predict. There has been surprisingly little research on
whether family/parents interventions (or any intervention for that matter) actually produce specific effects on the targeted domains/variables (i.e., is there treatment specificity) and, more importantly, whether changes on these variables
result in (i.e., mediate) treatment response.

Perhaps, for example, the improvements that are produced in individual
child therapy on child's problems lead to or mediate changes in family functioning (without necessarily directly intervening on family functioning via family
therapy). Indeed, to our knowledge, there have been no studies in the child treatment literature designed to *directly* evaluate specificity and mediational effects
for these targeted variables. Weersing and Weisz (2002) reached a similar conclusion in a recent review of this issue and as they further noted, although the
issue can be examined post-hoc (as in Kolko et al., 2000), a direct and full evaluation of this issue requires a different type of experimental design than the
"usual" randomized clinical trial.

There are several directions for future research in family treatment models
for externalizing disorders. Children and families rarely present for treatment
with "pure" disorders and no contextual stressors. It is the rule rather than the
exception that children and families who present to clinics often have multiple
comorbidities, functional impairments, and contextual stressors that impact on
their presenting clinical picture. It is time that we expanded beyond a simple
Parent Training model into a "Behavioral-Systemic Family Therapy" Model
(Griest & Wells, 1983) to reflect this reality. Such a model would be anchored in
Parent Training as its foundation, because it is a proven treatment model for the

core characteristics of ODD and the associated characteristics of ADHD. However, it would also incorporate other "adjunctive" treatment strategies to address the multiple comorbidities and functional and contextual issues that families present in clinic settings (such as parent depression, marital conflict, and parent insularity and stress). The effectiveness of these multicomponent strategies should be evaluated to ascertain their incremental effectiveness over PT alone for multiproblem families. The work of Griest et al. (1982), Dadds (1992), Hengeller and Sheidow (chapter 2), and Rowe and Liddle (chapter 3) are exemplary of this type of research and more evaluations of multicomponent programs for multiproblem families should be undertaken.

The effects of an expanded Behavioral-Systems Family Therapy model should be measured not just on immediate treatment outcome, but on all aspects of generalization (i.e., across time, settings, behaviors, and siblings). Positive (or negative) effects on other family targets that are related to child aggression (e.g., marital distress, parent depression) should be routinely measured. In addition, treatment dropout should be measured and studied as a phenomenon in its own right. Its predictors should be identified and "treatments" developed and evaluated specifically for their impact on dropout.

Family therapists and family researchers also should not shy away from studies evaluating the interaction of drug therapy and family therapy for ADHD and ODD. This point is probably most acceptable for ADHD, which is clearly a neuropsychologically based disorder (Barkley, 1998) and for which drug treatment is a proven effective treatment (Wells, in press). However, even for ODD there is preliminary evidence that drug treatments may have some usefulness (McMahon & Wells, 1998; Waslick, Werry, & Greenhill, 1999). Studies examining the interaction of drug and family treatments for childhood emotional and behavioral disorders should be considered an important priority for future research in this area because family-based treatments are the psychosocial treatments of choice for this disorder.

Systemically, there is a need to develop treatment models that incorporate the assessment and treatment of the family interactions surrounding the child's behavior. This is the difference between family-based treatment of childhood disorders and family therapy. Family-based treatments do involve both parents and children and are effective in treating childhood disorders, but they do not address the process of family interactions and their effect on children's functioning. From the developmental psychopathology literature (Cummings, Davies, & Campbell, 2000) we know that a variety of different adverse parenting behavior and functioning (parental psychopathology, substance use, neglect, etc.) can lead to negative outcomes for children. In order to address the specific parental responses that inhibit child adjustment and exacerbate symptomatic behavior, treatment needs to go beyond teaching behavioral parenting techniques to include interventions that address family dynamics and parental functioning surrounding the child's disorder.

Implications for Marriage and Family Therapists

It is clear from the clinical research literature on childhood behavioral and emotional disorders that PT models of family intervention should be incorporated routinely into the clinical practices of marriage and family therapists. Several treatment manuals are commercially available (e.g., Barkley & Benton, 1998; Hinshaw, 1994; McMahon & Forehand, in press; Silverman & Kurtines, 1996a) and workshops are routinely given around the country by the developers of these models. Marriage and family therapists should avail themselves of training opportunities and utilize these models as standard treatment for this large group of children and families presenting to clinics.

The availability of a few family-based treatment models notwithstanding, there is a dearth of writing on working with children and families in general. Bailey and Stigen (2000) found that only 7.5% of all the published articles in MFT journals in the 1990s focused on children (age 12 and under) and of those published, a small minority focused on specific disorders. Increasing the training opportunities for MFTs to learn about effective interventions with children and families is needed, in addition to more research in this area.

For those MFTs who do work with children and families, they should assist researchers in the development of new adjunctive treatments as recommended in the previous section. Since clinicians working in real world clinical settings are most likely to see these multiproblem families, they are in a unique position to assist in the identification and development of adjunctive treatment models to address these multiple problems. An optimal approach would be one in which clinicians and clinical researchers work hand in hand in developing and evaluating new and innovative treatment models. In this regard, researchers should honor the work of clinicians who work in the trenches and have a much greater appreciation of the full clinical picture of multiproblem families. Likewise, clinicians should familiarize themselves with the research literature on treatment evaluation, so that they understand what has been done, and can then assist in the development of ideas for continually advancing the field.

Finally, because ODD and ADHD persist into adolescence for a significant percentage of cases, there is a great need for more research expanding these family treatment models into work with adolescents and their families. There are very few studies on family treatment models with ODD and ADHD adolescents and this is a rich area for treatment development and evaluation.

Future Considerations

Although this review focused exclusively on DSM-IV diagnosable disorders, it is clear that this nomenclature may not be ideal for organizing research on childhood behavioral and emotional problems. Children who experience serious psychosocial impairment present themselves in a variety of settings and are often involved with multiple systems, including social and child protective services, juvenile justice, and education. Involvement with each of these systems brings with it a variety of issues that generally complicate the treatment process. Further, these systems often have different labels for the behaviors exhibited by children and different responses to these behaviors. Future research on family therapy should attempt to reconcile the disparate experiences of these families in these different systems of care.

Further, while the primary treatment modality for children with behavioral and emotional disorders is outpatient therapy, with 5% to 10% of children and their families utilizing these services (Burns, Hoagwood, & Mzazek, 1999), there is an assortment of other interventions that have emerged in the last 20 years. These include home-based services, treatment foster care, day treatment, case management, and wrap-around services. Matching children and families to the appropriate level of service is another avenue that must be considered in making therapeutic decisions and should be considered in the development of research protocols that will be studying this population. Due to the diversity of interventions and the costs associated with them, descriptions of these costs and cost-benefit analyses should also be included.

References

References marked with a double asterisk are recommended for clinicians.

Albano, A. M., Marten, P. A., Holt, C. S., Heimberg, R. G., & Barlow, D. H. (1995). Cognitive-behavioral group treatment for social phobia in adolescents: A preliminary study. *Journal of Nervous & Mental Disease, 183,* 649–656.

Alexander, J. F., Holtzworth-Munroe, A., & Jameson, P. B. (1994). The process and outcome of marital and family therapy: Research review and evaluation. In A. E. Bergin & S. L. Garfield (Eds.), *Handbook of psychotherapy and behavior change* (4th ed., pp. 595–630). New York: Wiley.

American Psychiatric Association. (1994). *Diagnostic and statistical manual of mental disorders* (4th ed.). Washington, DC: Author.

Anastopoulos, A. D., Shelton, T., DuPaul, G. J., & Guevremont, D. C. (1993). Parent training for attention deficit hyperactivity disorder: Its impact on parent functioning. *Journal of Abnormal Child Psychology, 21,* 581–595.

Anderson, J. C., Williams, S. M., McGee, R., & Silva, P. A. (1987). DSM-III disorders in preadolescent children: Prevalence in a large sample from the general population. *Archives of General Psychiatry, 44,* 69–76.

Angold, A., Erkanli, A., Egger, H. L., & Costello, E. J. (2000). Stimulant treatment for children: A community perspective. *Journal of the American Academy of Child and Adolescent Psychiatry, 39,* 975–994.

Bailey, C. E., & Stigen, S. L. (2000, November). *Including children in family therapy.* Poster presented at the annual conference of the American Association for Marriage and Family Therapy, Denver, CO.

Barkley, R. A. (1996). Attention-deficit/hyperactivity disorder. In E. J. Mash & R. A. Barkley (Eds.), *Child psychopathology* (pp. 63–112). New York: Guilford Press.

**Barkley, R. A. (1998). *Attention-deficit hyperactivity disorder: A handbook for diagnosis and treatment* (2nd ed.). New York: Guilford Press.

**Barkley, R. A., & Benton, C. M. (1998). *Your defiant child: 8 steps to better behavior.* New York: Guilford Press.

Barkley, R. A., Anastopoulos, A. D., Guevremont, D. G., & Fletcher, K. F. (1992). Adolescents with attention deficit hyperactivity disorder: Mother-adolescent interactions, family beliefs and conflicts, and maternal psychopathology. *Journal of Abnormal Child Psychology, 20,* 263–288.

Barrett, P. M. (1998). Evaluation of cognitive-behavioral group treatments for childhood anxiety disorders. *Journal of Clinical Child Psychology, 27,* 459468.

Barrett, P. M., Dadds, M. R., & Rapee, R. M. (1996). Family treatment of childhood anxiety: A controlled trial. *Journal of Consulting and Clinical Psychology, 64,* 333–342.

Barrett, P. M., Duffy, A. L., Dadds, M. R., & Rapee R. M. (2001). Cognitive-behavioral treatment of anxiety disorders in children: Long-term (6-year) follow-up. *Journal of Consulting and Clinical Psychology, 69,* 135–141.

Baum, C. G., & Forehand, R. (1981). Long term follow-up of parent training by use of multiple outcome measures. *Behavior Therapy, 12,* 643–652.

Baum, C. G., Reyna-McGlone, C. L., & Ollendick, T. H. (1986, November). *The efficacy of behavioral parent training: Behavioral parent training plus clinical self-control training, and a modified STEP program with children referred for noncompliance.* Paper presented at the meeting of the Association for Advancement of Behavior Therapy, Chicago, IL.

Bernal, M. E., Klinnert, M. D., & Schultz, L. A. (1980). Outcome evaluation of behavioral parent training and client centered parent counseling for children with conduct problems. *Journal of Applied Behavior Analysis, 13,* 677–691.

Biederman, J., Faraone, S. V., & Lapey, K. (1992). Comorbidity of diagnosis in attention-deficit hyperactivity disorder. In G. Weiss (Ed.), *Child and adolescent psychiatric clinics of North America: Attention-deficit hyperactivity disorder* (pp. 335–360). Philadelphia: Saunders.

Breiner, J. L., & Forehand, R. (1981). An assessment of the effects of parent training on clinic-referred children's school behavior. *Behavioral Assessment, 3,* 31–42.

Brent, D. A., Holder, D., Kolko, D., Birmaher, B., Baugher, M., Roth, C., et al. (1997). A clinical psychotherapy trial for adolescent depression comparing cognitive, family, and supportive therapy. *Archives of General Psychiatry, 54,* 877–885.

**Brestan, E. V., & Eyberg, S. M. (1998). Effective psychosocial treatments of conduct-disordered children and adolescents: 29 years, 82 studies, and 5,272 kids. *Journal of Clinical Child Psychology, 27,* 180–189.

Burns, B. J., Hoagwood, K., & Mrazek, P. J. (1999). Effective treatment for mental disorders in children and adolescents. *Clinical Child and Family Psychology Review, 2,* 199–254.

Cobham, V. E., Dadds, M. R., & Spence, S. H. (1998). The role of parental anxiety in the treatment of childhood anxiety. *Journal of Consulting and Clinical Psychology, 66,* 893–905.

Cohen, P., Cohen, J., & Brook, J. S. (1993). An epidemiological study of disorders in late childhood and adolescence: II. Persistence of disorders. *Journal of Child Psychology and Psychiatry, 34,* 867–875.

Connell, A. M., & Goodman, S. H. (2002). The associations between psychopathology in fathers versus mothers and children's internalizing and externalizing behavior problems: A meta-analysis. *Psychological Bulletin, 128,* 746–773.

Conners, C. K., & Erhardt, D. (1998). Attention-deficit hyperactivity disorder in children and adolescents. In A. S. Bellack & M. Herse (Eds.), *Comprehensive clinical psychology* (pp. 487–525). New York: Pergamon.

Cross Calvert, S., & McMahon, R. J. (1987). The treatment acceptability of a behavioral parent training. *Behavior Therapy, 18*(2), 165–179.

Cummings, E. M., Davies, P. T., & Campbell, S. B. (2000). *Developmental psychopathology and family process: Theory, research, and clinical implications.* New York: Guilford Press.

Dadds, M. R. (1992). Concurrent treatment of marital and child behaviour problems in behavioural family therapy. *Behaviour Change, 9*(3), 139–148.

Dadds, M. R., Heard, P. M., & Rapee, R. M. (1991). Anxiety disorders in children. *International Review of Psychiatry, 3,* 231–241.

Dubey, D. R., O'Leary, S. G., & Kaufman, K. F. (1983). Training parents of hyperactive children in child management: A comparative outcome study. *Journal of Abnormal Child Psychology, 11,* 229–246.

Dumas, J. E. (1989). Treating antisocial behavior in children: Child and family approaches. *Clinical Psychology Review, 9,* 197–222.

DuPaul, G. J. (1991). Parent and teacher ratings of ADHD symptoms: Psychometric properties in a community based sample. *Journal of Clinical Child Psychology, 20,* 245–253.

Estrada, A. U., & Pinsof, W. M. (1995). The effectiveness of family therapies for selected behavioral disorders of childhood. *Journal of Marital and Family Therapy, 21,* 403–440.

Eyberg, S. M. (1996). Parent-child interaction therapy. In T. Ollendick (Chair), *Developmentally based integrated psychotherapy with children: Emerging models.* Symposium presented at the annual meeting of the American Psychological Association, Toronto, Ontario, Canada.

Eyberg, S. M., & Boggs, S. R. (1998). Parent-child interaction therapy: A psychosocial intervention for the treatment of young conduct-disordered children. In J. M. Briesmeister & C. E. Schaefer (Eds.), *Handbook of parent training: Parents as co-therapists for children's behavior problems* (2nd ed., pp. 61–97). New York: John Wiley & Sons.

Eyberg, S. M., Funderburk, B. W., Hembree-Kigin, T. L., McNeil, C. B., Querido, J. G., & Hood, K. K. (2001). Parent-child interaction therapy with behavior problem children: One and two year maintenance of treatment effects in the family. *Child & Family Behavior Therapy, 23*(4), 1–20.

Feehan, M., McGee, R., Raja, S. N., & Williams, S. M. (1994). DSM-III-R disorders in New Zealand 18-year-olds. *Australian & New Zealand Journal of Psychiatry, 28,* 87–99.

Foote, R. C., Schuhmann, E. M., Jones, M. L., & Eyberg, S. M. (1998). Parent-child interaction therapy: A guide for clinicians. *Clinical Child Psychology & Psychiatry, 3*(3), 361–373.

Forehand, R., Griest, D. L., & Wells, K. C. (1979). Parent behavioral training: An analysis of the relationship among multiple outcome measures. *Journal of Abnormal Child Psychology, 7,* 229–242.

Forehand, R., & Long, N. (1988). Outpatient treatment of the acting out child: Procedures, long term follow-up data, and clinical problems. *Advances in Behaviour Research & Therapy, 10,* 129–177.

**Forehand, R., & McMahon, R. (1981). *Helping the noncompliant child: A clinician's guide to parent training.* New York: Guilford.

Forehand, R., Rogers, T., McMahon, R., Wells, K., & Griest, D. (1981). Teaching parents to modify child behavior problems: An examination of some follow-up data. *Journal of Pediatric Psychology, 6,* 313–322.

Forehand, R., Steffe, M. A., Furey, W. A., & Walley, P. B. (1983). Mothers' evaluation of a parent training program completed three and one-half years earlier. *Journal of Behavior Therapy and Experimental Psychiatry, 14,* 339–342.

Forehand, R., Wells, K. C., & Griest, D. L. (1980). An examination of the social validity of a parent training program. *Behavior Therapy, 11,* 488–502.

Funderburk, B. W., Eyberg, S. M., Newcomb, K., McNeil, C. B., Hembree-Kigin, T., & Capage, L. (1998). Parent-child interaction therapy with behavior problem children: Maintenance of treatment effects in the school setting. *Child & Family Behavior Therapy, 20*(2), 17–38.

Ginsburg, G. S., Silverman, W. K., & Kurtines, W. M. (1995). Family involvement in treating children with anxiety and phobic disorders: A look ahead. *Clinical Psychology Review, 15*, 457–473.

Griest, D. L., Forehand, R., Rogers, T., Breiner, J. L., Furey, W., & Williams, C. A. (1982). Effects of parent enhancement therapy on the treatment outcome and generalization of a parent training program. *Behaviour Research and Therapy, 20*, 429–436.

Griest, D. L., & Wells, K. C. (1983). Behavioral family therapy with conduct disorders in children. *Behavior Therapy, 14*, 37–53.

Hanf, C., & Kling, J. (1973). *Facilitating parent-child interaction: A two-stage model.* Unpublished manuscript, University of Oregon Medical School.

*Hembree-Kigin, T. L., & McNeil, C. B. (1995). *Parent-child interaction therapy.* New York: Plenum Press.

Hayes, S. C., Barlow, D. H., & Nelson-Gray, R. O. (1999). *The scientist practitioner: Research and accountability in the age of managed care.* Needham Heights, MA: Allyn & Bacon.

Heard, P. M., Dadds, M. R., & Conrad, P. (1992). Assessment and treatment of simple phobias in children: Effects on family and marital relationships. *Behaviour Change, 9*, 73–82.

**Herbert, M. (1998). Family treatment. In P. J. Graham (Ed.), *Cognitive-behaviour therapy for children and families.* New York: Cambridge University Press.

Hinshaw, S. P. (1992). Academic underachievement, attention deficits, and aggression: Comorbidity and implications for intervention. *Journal of Consulting and Clinical Psychology, 60*, 893–903.

**Hinshaw, S. P. (1994). *Attention deficits and hyperactivity in children.* Thousand Oaks, CA: Sage.

Hinshaw, S. P., Owens, E. B., Wells, K. C., Kraemer, H. C., Abikoff, H. B., Arnold, L. E., et al. (2000). Family processes and treatment outcome in the MTA: Negative/ineffective parenting practices in relation to multimodal treatment. *Journal of Abnormal Child Psychology, 28*, 555–568.

Horn, W. F., Ialongo, N., Greenberg, G., Packard, T., & Smith-Winberry, C. (1990). Additive effects of behavioral parent training and self-control therapy with attention deficit hyperactivity disordered children. *Journal of Clinical Child Psychology, 19*, 98–110.

Horn, W. F., Ialongo, N. S., Pascoe, J. M., Greenberg, G. A., Packard, T., Lopez, M., et al. (1991). Additive effects of psychostimulants, parent training, and self-control therapy with ADHD children. *Journal of the American Academy of Child and Adolescent Psychiatry, 30*, 233–240.

Howard, B. L., & Kendall, P. C. (1996). Cognitive-behavioral family therapy for anxiety-disordered children: A multiple-baseline evaluation. *Cognitive Therapy and Research, 20*, 423–443.

Jensen, P. S., Kettle, L., Roper, M. T., Sloan, M. T., Dulcan, M. K., Hoven, C., et al. (1999). Are stimulants overprescribed? Treatment of ADHD in four U.S. communities. *Journal of the American Academy of Child and Adolescent Psychiatry, 38*, 797–804.

Johnston, C., & Mash, E. J. (2001). Families of children with attention-deficit/hyperactivity disorder: Review and recommendations for future research. *Clinical Child and Family Psychology Review, 4*, 183–207.

Jouriles, E. N., Murphy, C. M., & O'Leary, K. D. (1989). Interspousal aggression, marital discord, and child problems. *Journal of Consulting and Clinical Psychology, 57*, 453–455.

Kaslow, N. J., & Racusin, G. R. (1994). Family therapy for depression in young people. In W. M. Reynolds & H. F. Johnston (Eds.), *Handbook of depression in children and adolescents* (pp. 345–363). New York: Plenum Press.

Kaslow, N. J., & Thompson, M. P. (1998). Applying the criteria for empirically supported treatments to studies of psychosocial interventions for child and adolescent depression. *Journal of Clinical Child Psychology, 27*, 146–155.

Kazdin, A. E. (1994). Psychotherapy for children and adolescents. In A. E. Bergin & S. L. Garfield (Eds.), *Handbook of psychotherapy and behavior change* (pp. 543–594). New York: Wiley.

Kazdin, A. E., Siegel, T. C., & Bass, D. (1990). Drawing on clinical practice to inform research on child and adolescent psychotherapy: Survey of practitioners. *Professional Psychology: Research and Practice, 21*, 189–198.

Kazdin, A. E., & Wassell, G. (2000). Therapeutic changes in children, parents and families resulting from treatment of children with conduct problems. *Journal of the American Academy of Child and Adolescent Psychiatry, 39,* 414–420.

Kearney, C. A., & Silverman, W. K. (1990). A preliminary analysis of a functional model of assessment and treatment for school refusal behavior. *Behavior Modification, 14,* 340–366.

Kearney, C. A., & Silverman, W. K. (1999). Functionally based prescriptive and nonprescriptive treatment for children and adolescents with school refusal behavior. *Behavior Therapy, 30,* 673–695.

Keenan, K., & Wakschlad, L. S. (2000). More than the terrible twos: The nature and severity of behavior problems in clinic-referred preschool children. *Journal of Abnormal Child Psychology, 28,* 33–46.

Kelleher, K. J., McInerny, T. K., Gardner, W. P., Childs, G. E., & Wasserman, R. C. (2000). Increasing identification of psychosocial problems: 1979–1996. *Pediatrics, 105,* 1313–1321.

Kendall, P. C. (1994). Treating anxiety disorders in children: Results of a randomized clinical trial. *Journal of Consulting and Clinical Psychology, 62,* 100–110.

Kendall, P. C., Flannery-Schroeder, E. C., Panichelli-Mindel, S. M., Southam-Gerow, M., Henin, A., & Warman, M. (1997). Therapy for youths with anxiety disorders: A second randomized clinical trial. *Journal of Consulting and Clinical Psychology, 65,* 366–380.

Kessler, R. C., McGonagle, K. A., Zhao, S., Nelson, C. B., Hughes, M., Eshleman, S., et al. (1994). Lifetime and 12-month prevalence of DSM-III-R psychiatric disorders in the United States. *Archives of General Psychiatry, 51,* 8–19.

Klein, R. G., & Abikoff, H. (1997). Behavior therapy and methylphenidate in the treatment of children with ADHD. *Journal of Attention Disorders, 2,* 89–114.

Klein, R. G., & Manuzza, S. (1991). Long-term outcome of hyperactive children: A review. *Journal of the American Academy of Child and Adolescent Psychiatry, 30,* 383–387.

Knox, L. S., Albano, A. M., & Barlow, D. H. (1996). Parental involvement in the treatment of childhood obsessive compulsive disorder: A multiple-baseline examination incorporating parents. *Behavior Therapy, 27,* 93–115.

Kolko, D. J., Brent, D. A., Baugher, M., Bridge, J., & Birmaher, B. (2000). Cognitive and family therapies for adolescent depression: Treatment specificity, mediation, and moderation. *Journal of Consulting and Clinical Psychology, 68,* 603–614.

Kovacs, M., & Devlin, B. (1998). Internalizing disorders in childhood. *Journal of Child Psychology & Psychiatry & Allied Disciplines, 39,* 47–63.

Kovacs, M., Gatsonis, C., Paulauskas, S., & Richards, C. (1989). Depressive disorders in childhood: IV. A longitudinal study of comorbidity with and risk for anxiety disorders. *Archives of General Psychiatry, 46,* 776–782.

Lahey, B. B., Loeber, R., Quay, H. C., Frick, P. J., & Grimm, S. (1992). Oppositional defiant and conduct disorders: Issues to be resolved for DSM-IV. *Journal of the American Academy of Child and Adolescent Psychiatry, 31,* 539–546.

Lahey, B. B., Miller, T. L., Gordon, R. A., & Riley, A. W. (1999). Developmental epidemiology of the disruptive behavior disorders. In H. C. Quay & A. E. Hogan (Eds.), *Handbook of disruptive behavior disorders* (pp. 23–48). New York: Kluwer Academic.

Last, C. G., Hansen, C., & Franco, C. (1998). Cognitive-behavioral treatment of school phobia. *Journal of the American Academy of Child and Adolescent Psychiatry, 37,* 404–411.

Lewinsohn, P. M., Clarke, G. N., Hops, H., & Andrews, J. (1990). Cognitive-behavioral group treatment of depression in adolescents. *Behavior Therapy, 21,* 385–401.

**Lewinsohn, P. M., Clarke, G. N., Rohde, P., Hops, H., & Seeley, J. R. (1996). A course in coping: A cognitive-behavioral approach to the treatment of adolescent depression. In E. D. Hibbs & P. S. Jensen (Eds.), *Psychosocial treatments for child and adolescent disorders: Empirically based strategies for clinical practice* (pp. 109–135). Washington, DC: American Psychological Association.

Loeber, R., Farrington, D. P., Stouthamer-Loeber, M., & Van Kammen, W. B. (1998). *Antisocial behavior and mental health problems: Explanatory factors in childhood and adolescence.* Mahwah, NJ: Erlbaum.

Loeber, R., Green, S. M., Lahey, B. B., Frick, P. J., & McBurnett, K. (2000). Findings on disruptive behavior disorders from the first decade of the developmental trends study. *Clinical Child & Family Psychology Review, 3*(1), 37–60.

Loeber, R., Keenan, K., Lahey, B. B., Green, S. M., & Thomas, C. (1993). Evidence for developmentally based diagnoses of oppositional defiant disorder and conduct disorder. *Journal of Abnormal Child Psychology, 21,* 377–410.

Loeber, R., & Stouthamer-Loeber, M. (1986). Family factors as correlates and predictors of juvenile conduct problems and delinquency. In N. Morris & M. Tonry (Eds.), *Crime and justice* (vol. 7, pp. 29–149). Chicago: University of Chicago Press.

March, J. S., Mulle, K., & Herbel, B. (1994). Behavioral psychotherapy for children and adolescents with obsessive-compulsive disorder: An open trial of a new protocol-driven treatment package. *Journal of the American Academy of Child and Adolescent Psychiatry, 33,* 333–341.

McCauley, E., Myers, K., Mitchell, J., & Calderon, R. (1993). Depression in young people: Initial presentation and clinical course. *Journal of the American Academy of Child and Adolescent Psychiatry, 32,* 714–722.

McGee, R., Feehan, M., Williams, S., & Anderson, J. (1992). DSM-III disorders from age 11 to age 15 years. *Journal of the American Academy of Child and Adolescent Psychiatry, 31,* 50–59.

McGee, R., Feehan, M., Williams, S., Partridge, F., Silva, P. A., & Kelly, J. (1990). DSM-III disorders in a large sample of adolescents. *Journal of the American Academy of Child and Adolescent Psychiatry, 29,* 611–619.

**McMahon, R., & Forehand, R. (in press). *Helping the noncompliant child: A clinician's guide to parent training. Second edition.* New York: Guilford Press.

McMahon, R. J., Forehand, R., Griest, D. L., & Wells, K. C. (1981). Who drops out of treatment during parent behavioral training? *Behavioral Counseling Quarterly, 1,* 79–85.

**McMahon, R. J., & Wells, K. C. (1998). Conduct problems. In E. J. Mash & R. A. Barkley (Eds.), *Treatment of childhood disorders* (2nd ed., pp. 111–207). New York: Guilford Press.

Mendlowitz, S. L., Manassis, K., Bradley, S., Scapillato, D., Miezitis, S., & Shaw, B. F. (1999). Cognitive-behavioral group treatments in childhood anxiety disorders: The role of parental involvement. *Journal of the American Academy of Child and Adolescent Psychiatry, 38,* 1223–1229.

Miller, G. E., & Prinz, R. J. (1990). Enhancement of social learning family interventions for childhood conduct disorder. *Psychological Bulletin, 108,* 291–307.

Multimodal Treatment Study of Children with Attention Deficit Hyperactivity Disorder (MTA) Cooperative Group. (1999a). A 14-month randomized clinical trial of treatment strategies for Attention Deficit Hyperactivity Disorder (ADHD). *Archives of General Psychiatry, 56,* 1073–1086.

Multimodal Treatment Study of Children with Attention Deficit Hyperactivity Disorder (MTA) Cooperative Group. (1999b). Effects of co-morbid anxiety disorder, family poverty, session attendance, and community medication on treatment outcome for Attention-Deficit Hyperactivity Disorder. *Archives of General Psychiatry, 56,* 1088–1096.

Newman, D. L., Moffit, T. E., Caspi, A., Magdol, L., Silva, P. A., & Stanton, W. R. (1996). Psychiatric disorder in a birth cohort of young adults: Prevalence, comorbidity, clinical significance, and new case incidence from ages 11 to 21. *Journal of Consulting and Clinical Psychology, 64*, 552–562.

Patterson, G. R., Chamberlain, P., & Reid, J. B. (1982). A comparative evaluation of a parent-training program. *Behavior Therapy, 13*, 638–650.

Peed, S., Roberts, M., & Forehand, R. (1977). Evaluation of the effectiveness of a standardized parent training program in altering the interaction of mothers and their noncompliant children. *Behavior Modification, 1*, 323–350.

Pelham, W. E., Schnedler, R. W., Bender, M., Nilsson, D., Miller, J., Budrown, M., et al. (1988). The combination of behavior therapy and methylphenidate in the treatment of attention deficit disorder: A therapy outcome study. In L. M. Bloomingdale (Ed.), *Attention deficit disorder* (vol. 3, pp. 29–48). Oxford, United Kingdom: Pergamon.

**Pelham, W. E., & Waschbusch, D. A. (1999). Behavioral intervention in attention-deficit/hyperactivity disorder. In H. C. Quay and A. E. Hogan (Eds.), *Handbook of disruptive behavior disorders* (pp. 255–278). New York: Kluwer Academic/Plenum.

Pisterman, S., Firestone, P., McGrath, P., Goodman, J. T., Webster, I., Mallory, R., et al. (1992). The role of parent training in treatment of preschoolers with ADHD. *American Journal of Orthopsychiatry, 62*, 397–408.

Pisterman, S., McGrath, P., Firestone, P., Goodman, J. T., Webster, I., & Mallory, R. (1989). Outcome of parent-mediated treatment of preschoolers with attention deficit disorder with hyperactivity. *Journal of Consulting and Clinical Psychology, 57*, 628–635.

Pollard, S., Ward, E., & Barkley, R. A. (1983). The effects of parent training and Ritalin on the parent-child interactions of hyperactive boys. *Child and Family Therapy, 5*, 51–69.

Powers, S. W., & Roberts, M. W. (1995). Simulation training with parents of oppositional children: Preliminary findings. *Journal of Clinical Child Psychology, 24*, 89–97.

Prinz, R. J., & Miller, G. E. (1994). Family-based treatment for childhood antisocial behavior: Experimental influences on dropout and engagement. *Journal of Consulting and Clinical Psychology, 62*, 645–650.

Rao, U., Ryan, N. D., Birmaher, B., & Dahl, R. E. (1995). Unipolar depression in adolescents: Clinical outcome in adulthood. *Journal of the American Academy of Child and Adolescent Psychiatry, 34*, 566–578.

**Robbins, M. S., Szapocznik, J., Alexander, J. F., & Miller, J. (2001). Family systems therapy with children and adolescents. In A. S. Bellack & M. Hersen (Series Eds.), & T. H. Ollendick (Vol. Ed.), *Children & adolescents: Clinical formulation and treatment: Vol. 5. Comprehensive clinical psychology* (pp. 149–183). Amsterdam: Elsevier Science.

Schuhmann, E. M., Foote, R. C., Eyberg, S. M., & Boggs, S. R. (1998). Efficacy of parent-child interaction therapy: Interim report of a randomized trial with short-term maintenance. *Journal of Clinical Child Psychology, 27*, 34–45.

Serketich, W. J., & Dumas, J. E. (1996). The effectiveness of behavioral parent training to modify antisocial behavior in children: A meta-analysis. *Behavior Therapy, 27*, 171–186.

**Silverman, W. K., & Berman, S. L. (2001). Psychosocial interventions for anxiety disorders in children: Status and future directions. In W. K. Silverman & P. D. A. Treffers (Eds.), *Anxiety disorders in children and adolescents: Research, assessment and intervention* (pp. 313–334). Cambridge, United Kingdom: Cambridge University Press.

**Silverman, W. K., & Kurtines, W. M. (1996a). *Childhood anxiety and phobic disorders: A pragmatic approach*. New York: Plenum Press.

Silverman, W. K., & Kurtines, W. M. (1996b). Transfer of control: A psychosocial intervention model for internalizing disorders in youth. In E. D. Hibbs & P. S. Jensen (Eds.), *Psychosocial treatment of child and adolescent disorders: Empirically based strategies for clinical practice* (pp. 63–82). Washington, DC: American Psychological Association.

Silverman, W. K., & Kurtines, W. M. (in press). Progress in developing an exposure-based transfer of control approach in the treatment of anxiety disorders in children. In E. D. Hibbs & P. S. Jensen (Eds.), *Psychosocial treatment of child and adolescent disorders: Empirically based strategies for private practice* (2nd ed.). Washington, DC: American Psychological Association.

Silverman, W. K., Kurtines, W. M., Ginsburg, G. S., Weems, C. F., Lumpkin, P. W., & Hicks-Carmichael, D. (1999). Treating anxiety disorders in children with group cognitive behavior therapy: A randomized clinical trial. *Journal of Consulting and Clinical Psychology, 67,* 995–1003.

Sonuga-Barke, E. J. S., Daley, D., Thompson, M., Laver-Bradbury, C., & Weeks, A. (2001). Parent-based therapies for preschool attention-deficit/hyperactivity disorder: A randomized, controlled trial with a community sample. *Journal of the American Academy of Child and Adolescent Psychiatry, 40,* 402–408.

Spence, S. H., Donovan, C., & Brechman-Toussaint, M. (2000). The treatment of childhood social phobia: The effectiveness of a social skills training-based, cognitive behavioural intervention, with and without parent involvement. *Journal of Child Psychology and Psychiatry and Allied Disciplines, 41,* 713–726.

U.S. Department of Health and Human Services. (1999). *Mental health: A report of the Surgeon General.* Rockville, MD: Author.

Walter, H. I., & Gilmore, S. K. (1973). Placebo versus social learning effects in parent training procedures designed to alter the behaviors of aggressive boys. *Behavior Therapy, 4,* 361–377.

Waslick, B., Werry, J. S., & Greenhill, L. L. (1999). Pharmacotherapy and toxicology of oppositional defiant disorder and conduct disorder. In H. C. Quay & A. E. Hogan (Eds.), *Handbook of disruptive behavior disorders* (pp. 455–474). New York: Kluwer Academic.

Webster-Stratton, C. (1981). Modification of mothers' behaviors and attitudes through a videotape modeling group discussion program. *Behavior Therapy, 12,* 634–642.

Webster-Stratton, C. (1984). Randomized trial of two parent-training programs for families with conduct-disordered children. *Journal of Consulting and Clinical Psychology, 52,* 666–678.

Webster-Stratton, C. (1985). Comparisons of behavior transactions between conduct-disordered children and their mothers in the clinic and at home. *Journal of Abnormal Child Psychology 13,* 169–183.

Webster-Stratton, C. (1994). Advancing videotape parent training: A comparison study. *Journal of Consulting and Clinical Psychology, 62,* 583–593.

Webster-Stratton, C., Kolpacoff, M., & Hollinsworth, T. (1988). Self-administered videotape therapy for families with conduct problem children: Comparison to two other cost effective treatments and a control group. *Journal of Consulting and Clinical Psychology, 56,* 558–566.

Weersing, V. R., & Weisz, J. R. (2002). Mechanisms of action in youth psychotherapy. *Journal of Child Psychology and Psychiatry and Allied Disciplines, 43,* 3–29.

**Weiss, G., & Hechtman, L. T. (1993). *Hyperactive children grown up: ADHD in children, adolescents, and adults.* New York: Guilford.

Wells, K. C. (in press). Treatment of ADHD in children and adolescents. In P. Barrett and T. Ollendick (Eds.), *Handbook of interventions that work with children and adolescents: Prevention and treatment.* West Sussex, England: John Wiley & Sons.

Wells, K. C., Abikoff, H., Abramowitz, A., Courtney, M., Cousins, L., Del Carmen, R., et al. (1996). *Parent training for attention deficit hyperactivity disorder: MTA study.* Unpublished manuscript.

Wells, K. C., & Egan, J. (1988). Social learning and systems family therapy for childhood oppositional disorder: Comparative treatment outcome. *Comprehensive Psychiatry, 29,* 138–146.

Wells, K. C., Forehand, R., & Griest, D. L. (1980). Generality of treatment effects from treated to untreated behaviors resulting from a parent training program. *Journal of Clinical Child Psychology, 9,* 217–219.

Wells, K. C., Griest, D. L., & Forehand, R. (1980). The use of a self-control package to enhance temporal generality of a parent training program. *Behaviour Research and Therapy, 18,* 347–358.

Wells, K. C., Pelham, W. E., Jr., Kotkin, R. A., Hoza, B., Abikoff, H. B., Abramowitz, A., et al. (2000). Psychosocial treatment strategies in the MTA Study: Rationale, methods, and critical issues in design and implementation. *Journal of Abnormal Child Psychology, 28,* 483–505.

Wiltz, N. A., & Patterson, G. R. (1974). An evaluation of parent training procedures designed to alter inappropriate aggressive behavior of boys. *Behavior Therapy, 5,* 215–221.

Wolraich, M. L., Hannah, J. N., Baumgaertel, A., & Feurer, I. D. (1998). Examination of DSM-IV criteria for attention deficit hyperactivity disorder in a county-wide sample. *Journal of Developmental & Behavioral Pediatrics, 19,* 162–168.

Woodward, L. J., & Fergusson, D. M. (2001). Life course outcomes of young people with anxiety disorders in adolescence. *Journal of the American Academy of Child and Adolescent Psychiatry, 40,* 1086–1093.

Chapter 5   *Alcohol Abuse*

Timothy J. O'Farrell, Ph.D., Harvard Families and Addiction Program, Harvard Medical School Department of Psychiatry at the VA Boston Healthcare System, Brockton, Massachusetts.

William Fals-Stewart, Ph.D., Research Institute on Addictions, University at Buffalo, The State University of New York, Buffalo, New York.

Nearly 30 years ago the U.S. National Institute on Alcohol Abuse and Alcoholism (NIAAA) hailed marital and family therapy as "one of the most outstanding current advances in the area of psychotherapy of alcoholism" (Keller, 1974, p. 161). This NIAAA report also called for controlled studies to test these promising methods.

In 1976, Steinglass reviewed family treatment studies reported between 1950 and 1975. He concluded that there were few such studies, very little evidence demonstrating the efficacy of family treatment, and significant methodological shortcomings in most studies.

In 1989, McCrady reviewed studies not included in Steinglass's (1976) earlier review. McCrady evaluated the effectiveness of family treatments derived from a family disease perspective based on Al-Anon and 12-step principles, a family systems perspective based on general systems theory, and a behavioral perspective based on reinforcement principles. McCrady concluded "that despite the widespread popularity of family-involved alcoholism treatment, there is a paucity of well-controlled research in this area, that all of the research has evaluated marital rather than family therapy, and that there are notable discrepancies between the popularity of clinical practices and the empirical bases of practice" (p. 165, emphasis in original). In terms of the gap between research and practice, McCrady noted that clinically popular family disease and family systems approaches have little or no empirical support, and that behavioral approaches, which have relatively more empirical support, are virtually unused in clinical practice.

In 1995, reviewing studies they identified from 1972 to 1993, Edwards and Steinglass examined effectiveness, cost-effectiveness, and factors influencing effectiveness of family-involved alcoholism treatment. The authors concluded that family therapy is effective in motivating alcoholics to enter treatment, marginally more effective than individual alcoholism treatment once the drinker has sought help, and modestly beneficial in supporting aftercare and relapse prevention. They found no data on cost-effectiveness of family treatment. Finally, they suggested that gender of the alcoholic patient, investment in the relationship, and perceived support from the spouse for abstinence may moderate the effectiveness of family-involved alcoholism treatment.

This chapter reviews studies of the effectiveness of family-involved alcoholism treatment. It is intended to be a comprehensive review of studies to date comparing family-involved treatment with one or more comparison conditions, and so it does not just update the earlier reviews. However, much of the work reviewed does represent an update in that 22 of the 38 studies reviewed in this chapter were not included in the earlier reviews.[1]

This chapter presents study results for two main stages of change of family-involved treatment to (a) improve family coping and/or initiate change when the alcoholic individual is unwilling to seek help or (b) aid the alcoholic's recovery once the individual has sought help. We also discuss the current status of issues raised by the earlier reviews and suggest future directions for research. Finally, we consider the implications of outcome research for clinical practice by marriage and family therapists and summarize our final conclusions.

Effectiveness/Efficacy for Marital and Family Therapy in Treating Alcoholism

Potentially relevant studies were identified in several ways: (a) searching bibliographies of prior review articles (Collins, 1990; Edwards & Steinglass, 1995; McCrady, 1989; O'Farrell, 1989, 1995; O'Farrell & Fals-Stewart, 2001; Orford, 1984, 1990; Steinglass, 1976, 1979); (b) performing database searches through June 2002 of PsychINFO, Current Contents, Social Sciences Citation Index, MEDLINE, Project CORK, ETOH, and Dissertation Abstracts Online; (c) searching the bibliographies of all articles identified by the first two steps; and (d) asking researchers known for their work on family treatment for alcoholism to alert us to potentially relevant unpublished studies conducted by them or by their colleagues.

Studies were included in this review if they met the following criteria. First, studies had to evaluate one or more treatment groups, in which spouses and/or other family members of an alcoholic adult were involved in treatment efforts to (a) improve family coping and/or initiate change when the alcoholic individual was unwilling to seek help or (b) aid the alcoholic's recovery once the individual had sought help. Second, studies had to include a comparison group, either a waitlist control group, an individually-based treatment without a family-involved component, or an alternative family treatment method. Third, in most studies, cases were randomly assigned to treatment and comparison conditions, but as with prior reviews, a few quasi-experimental studies without random assignment were included. Finally, we required objective outcome data in one or more of five categories: (a) alcohol consumption or alcohol-related problems by the alcoholic person, (b) alcoholism treatment entry or attendance, (c) couple or family adjustment, (d) individual adjustment for the alcoholic person (i.e., unrelated to alcohol use), and (e) individual adjustment for the spouse or other family member. We obtained 38 studies meeting these criteria.

In describing study results below, outcomes described as favoring a treatment over a comparison group mean that the difference between the treatment and comparison groups reached statistical significance in the original study. Similarly, outcomes described as showing improvement from before to some time point after treatment, mean that the difference between the outcome scores before and after treatment reached statistical significance in the original study.

Helping the Family and Initiating Change
When the Alcoholic Resists Treatment

The 10 studies reviewed in this section evaluated treatment in which spouses or other family members of an alcoholic adult took part in efforts to (a) improve family members' coping and well-being or (b) initiate change when the alcoholic individual was unwilling to seek help.

Helping the Family

Spouses and other family members often experience many stressors and heightened emotional distress caused by the negative consequences of the alcoholic's drinking. Two approaches try to help family members cope with their emotional distress and concentrate on their own motivations for change rather than trying to motivate the drinker to change. These are efforts to teach specific coping skills to deal with alcohol-related situations involving the drinker, or to help the family member use the concepts and resources of Al-Anon.

Coping Skills Therapy

Zetterlind, Hansson, Aberg-Orbeck, and Berglund (1998) randomly assigned 39 spouses of alcoholics who were not in treatment to coping skills therapy, group support, or a one-session information only control group. Results at 1-year followup showed spouses who received coping skills therapy and group support had greater decreases in emotional distress than did the information only control group.

Rychtarik and McGillicuddy (1998) randomly assigned 172 women with male alcoholic partners who were not in treatment to manual-guided coping skills training, a manual-guided Al-Anon facilitation program, or a waiting-list control group. On a role-play observational measure of coping skills, skill training therapy was better than Al-Anon facilitation, and both treatment groups were better than the waitlist control. Spouses in both treatment groups reported less depression and anxiety than those in the waitlist control. Finally, spouses who obtained coping skills therapy received less violence from their male partners in the year after treatment than did women who received Al-Anon facilitation therapy (Rychtarik & McGillicuddy, 2002).

Al-Anon and the 12-Step Family Disease Approach

This 12-step program is the most widely used source of support for family members troubled by a loved one's alcohol problem. Al-Anon advocates that family members detach themselves from the alcoholic's drinking in a loving way, accept that they are powerless to control the alcoholic, and seek support from other Al-Anon members (Al-Anon Family Groups, 1981).

Referral to Al-Anon. This was examined as a control condition in two studies of methods to initiate change in the alcoholic (Barber & Gilbertson, 1996; Sisson & Azrin, 1986). Referral to Al-Anon did not produce treatment entry or changed drinking habits in either study. This is not surprising because changing the alcoholic is not an Al-Anon goal. However, in the study that measured spouse well-being (Barber & Gilbertson, 1996), spouses referred to Al-Anon reported reduced personal problems related to the drinkers' alcohol use compared to the waitlist control.

Al-Anon Facilitation Therapy (AFT). AFT is a manual-guided, therapist-delivered counseling method designed to encourage involvement in this 12-step program for families of alcoholics (Nowinski, 1999). Two well-controlled, randomized studies with adequate sample sizes found positive results for AFT. In the Rychtarik and McGillicuddy (1998) study, AFT reduced emotional distress and increased coping behaviors more than a waitlist control for spouses of treatment resistant alcoholics. In a second study (Miller, Meyers, & Tonigan, 1999), AFT showed significant reductions in emotional distress and family conflict, and improvements in family cohesion and relationship happiness for spouses and parents of treatment resistant alcoholics. These AFT improvements were similar to the improvements observed among spouses and parents who received the other interventions studied.

Group therapy based on Al-Anon concepts for wives of alcoholic men. Dittrich and Trapold (1984) randomly assigned 23 wives of treatment resistant alcoholics to an 8-week group therapy program based on Al-Anon concepts or to a waitlist control condition. Results showed greater reduction in enabling behaviors, anxiety and depression, and greater increases in self-concept at the end of treatment for the experimental group than for the waitlist control. Similar results occurred for those on the waiting list once they had completed treatment. Improvements after treatment were maintained at 2- and 4-month follow-up.

Initiating Change in the Alcoholic

Four methods have been studied with a primary goal of initiating change in the treatment resistant alcoholic in addition to helping the spouse or family member cope better. These include Community Reinforcement and Family Training (CRAFT), the Johnson Institute Intervention, Unilateral Family Therapy, and Pressure to Change.

The Community Reinforcement and Family Training Approach

Community Reinforcement and Family Training (CRAFT) is a program for teaching the nonalcoholic family member how to: (a) reduce the risk of physical abuse and other dangerous situations; (b) encourage sobriety by reinforcing nondrinking, extinguishing drinking, and planning competing nondrinking activities; (c) increase positive relationship communication; (d) engage in outside activities to reduce dependence on the relationship with the alcoholic; and (e) encourage the alcoholic to seek professional treatment (Meyers, Smith, & Miller, 1998).

In an initial CRAFT study, Sisson and Azrin (1986) randomly assigned 12 family members (mostly wives) of treatment resistant alcoholics to either the CRAFT program or to a traditional disease model program consisting of alcohol education, individual supportive counseling, and referral to Al-Anon. Six of seven alcoholics entered treatment after relatives had received CRAFT. After their relative started CRAFT, the alcoholics showed more than a 50% reduction in average consumption prior to treatment entry and nearly total abstinence in the 3 months after entering treatment. None of the five alcoholics whose relatives received the traditional program entered treatment and their drinking was not reduced.

In the second CRAFT study, Miller et al. (1999) used a larger sample, equally intensive treatments, and therapists strongly committed to their respective approaches to overcome the limitations of the earlier Sisson and Azrin (1986) study. Miller et al. randomly assigned 130 concerned significant others (CSOs, i.e., mainly spouses and parents) of treatment resistant alcoholics to (a) CRAFT, (b) a Johnson Institute Intervention to prepare for a confrontational family meeting, or (c) an Al-Anon facilitation therapy designed to encourage involvement in the 12-step program. All treatments were manual guided with 12 hours of contact planned. The CRAFT approach (64% engagement rate) was significantly more effective in engaging initially unmotivated alcohol abusing adults in alcohol treatment as compared with the more commonly used alternative methods of the Johnson Institute Intervention (22%) or Al-Anon (14%). All three approaches were associated with similar significant improvements in CSO functioning and relationship quality. Finally, treatment engagement rates across the three methods were higher for CSOs who were parents than for spouses.

The Johnson Institute Intervention

This method involves three to four educational and rehearsal sessions to prepare family members for a family confrontation meeting with the alcoholic known as an "intervention." Confrontation is done to overcome the denial of the alcoholic and promote treatment entry. During the intervention session itself, family members confront the alcohol abuser about his or her drinking and strongly encourage entry to an alcohol treatment program (Johnson, 1986; Liepman, 1993). Although this method is widely used in treatment centers in the United States, the only randomized study (Miller et al., 1999) of the Johnson Institute Intervention found that only 22% of CSOs treated with this method were successful in getting their alcoholic family member to enter treatment. As just described above, this rate is much lower than CRAFT and not much higher than Al-Anon, which does not try to change the alcoholic's behavior. An earlier uncontrolled study (Liepman, Nirenberg, & Begin, 1989) reported similar results in that only 25% of families given the intervention training succeeded in getting the alcoholic to enter treatment. The reason for these disappointing findings is that a substantial majority of families do not go through with the family confrontation meeting; only 29% in the Liepman et al. study and 30% in the Miller et al. study of families given the intervention training completed the confrontation. When family members completed the confrontation in these two studies, most succeeded in getting their alcoholic into treatment (86% in the Liepman et al. study and 75% in the Miller et al. study). These results are similar to an earlier clinical report (Logan, 1983) that 90% of 60 families who completed the family confrontation intervention meeting got their alcoholic to enter treatment. Adherents of the Johnson Institute Intervention approach have often cited "a 90% success rate" which we now know does not apply for an intent-to-treat basis (which has about a 20% success rate) but only for the minority of families willing and able to use the method.

The Unilateral Family Therapy Approach

Unilateral Family Therapy (UFT) assists the nonalcoholic spouse to strengthen his or her coping capabilities, to enhance family functioning, and to facilitate greater sobriety on the part of the alcohol abuser (Thomas & Ager, 1993). UFT provides a series of graded steps the spouse can use prior to confrontation. These steps may be successful in their own right, or at least pave the way for a positive outcome to a UFT "programmed confrontation" experience, which is similar to the Johnson approach and adapted for use with an individual spouse. In an initial pilot study of 25 spouses (Thomas, Santa, Bronson, & Oyserman, 1987), spouses who received UFT, as compared with those who did not, had lower emotional distress, higher marital satisfaction, and greater likelihood that the alcoholic partner had entered alcohol treatment and/or substantially reduced their drinking. A second study (Thomas, Yoshioka, Ager, & Adams, 1990) randomly assigned spouses to UFT ($n = 23$) or waiting list ($n = 19$). The UFT group, as compared with the waitlist control group, had more alcoholic partners who entered alcohol treatment; lower scores on spouse enabling, psychopathology and life distress; and higher marital satisfaction.

The Pressure To Change Approach

The Pressure to Change approach (PTC; Barber & Crisp, 1995) is also for partners living with heavy drinkers who deny their alcohol problem and refuse treatment. PTC involves 5 to 6 counseling sessions to train the partner how to use five gradually increasing levels of pressure on the drinker to seek help or to moderate his or her drinking. There have been three studies of PTC. The first PTC study (Barber & Crisp) randomly assigned 23 partners living with heavy drinkers who denied their alcohol problem and refused treatment to PTC delivered individually, PTC in a group format, or a waiting list control group. Results showed that almost two-thirds of the drinkers whose partners received PTC made a significant move toward change, compared with none of the drinkers in the waitlist control group. Movement toward change was defined as the drinker either (a) seeking treatment, (b) ceasing drinking, or (c) reducing drinking to a level acceptable to the partner and maintaining this change for at least 2 weeks. If the definition of drinker change was restricted to seeking treatment, PTC still had significantly better results than the control group. Two other studies also found greater movement toward change in the drinker for individual, group, and self-help manual versions of PTC than for a wait list control group (Barber & Gilbertson, 1996, 1998). In two of the three PTC studies, spouses who received PTC had greater reductions in depressive symptoms and personal problems related to the drinker's alcohol use as compared with the waitlist control.

Conclusions About MFT When the Alcoholic is Unwilling to Seek Help
     Considerable progress in research on family-involved treatment when the alcoholic is unwilling to seek help has been made. None of the 10 studies on this stage of change reviewed here were included in McCrady's (1989) earlier reviews and only 3 were included in the review by Edwards and Steinglass (1995). A number of new findings have emerged.
     First, a major development has been the first controlled studies of the 12-step family disease approach showing improvement in CSO individual functioning after Al-Anon Facilitation or referral to Al-Anon that is greater than in a waitlist control group (Rychtarik & McGillicuddy, 1998; Barber & Gilbertson, 1996) and equivalent to other family-involved methods (Rychtarik & McGillicuddy, 1998; Miller et al., 1999) when the alcoholic is unwilling to seek help. The availability of a therapist manual for AFT (Nowinski, 1999) should lead to more studies of AFT.
     Second, all the methods studied (i.e., coping skills training and Al-Anon to help the CSO, and the various methods to initiate change in the alcoholic) resulted in reduced emotional distress in the CSO relative to baseline or a waitlist control group. The durability of the improved CSO functioning is not known given the limited follow-up periods used in most of these studies. Further, as Rychtarik and McGillicuddy (1998) noted, although the different treatment methods lead to similar improvements in CSO functioning, they may do so through different processes of change. For example, in the Rychtarik and McGillicuddy study, both coping skills training and AFT led to reduced CSO depression and improved CSO coping skills; however, the improved coping skills accounted for the reduced depression in those who received coping skills training but not in those who received AFT, suggesting different change processes in the two methods.
     Third, the popular Johnson Institute Intervention family confrontation

method did not fare well in the first randomized, controlled study (Miller et al., 1999) of this popular method. The study was well designed, had a relatively large sample, and used therapists well trained and committed to this approach. Treatment engagement rates were not much higher than for Al-Anon, which does not try to change the alcoholic's behavior. The disappointing results confirmed an earlier uncontrolled study (Liepman et al., 1989). The intervention appears to be effective only for the minority of families willing and able to use the method. Until data show that this confrontational approach is effective in motivating treatment entry, treatment programs should consider discontinuing this approach in favor of more effective alternative methods.

Fourth, the very favorable treatment engagement rates for the CRAFT approach in a small-scale initial study (85%; Sisson & Azrin, 1986) have been confirmed in a large-scale well-controlled study (64%; Miller et al., 1999) with CSOs of alcoholics. CRAFT has been equally effective in motivating drug abusers into treatment, with engagement rates of 74% in an uncontrolled study (Meyers, Miller, Hill, & Tonigan, 1999) and 64% (versus 17% for referral to Naranon) in a controlled study (Kirby, Marlowe, Festinger, Garvey, & LaMonaca, 1999). There are also other reasons to recommend this approach. CRAFT is manualized and relatively brief with treatment entry occurring after an average of five sessions. It is based on a consistent conceptual approach and part of the community reinforcement method for treating adult and adolescent substance abuse (Hunt & Azrin, 1973; Meyers & Miller, 2001). It has been used with both spouses and parents. Studies of CRAFT have included substantial proportions of minority participants, but not many CSOs of female alcoholics. Finally, CRAFT is a more effective alternative to engage alcoholics in treatment than popular confrontational or detachment approaches. Therefore, CRAFT needs replication by another group of investigators, and research to see if it is successful at engaging female alcoholics in treatment. Successful replication should then lead to dissemination of the CRAFT approach to facilitate increased treatment utilization by alcoholic individuals.

Fifth, three studies show that the recently developed PTC approach is better than waitlist control on initiating change in the drinker (Barber & Crisp, 1995; Barber & Gilbertson, 1996, 1998). However, the measure of drinker change is not altogether convincing in that it includes either treatment entry or reduced drinking for the rather brief period of 2 weeks. The rate of treatment entry (31% across the three PTC studies) is less than half of that obtained in the CRAFT studies. Nonetheless PTC appears to be a promising approach. It is brief, and well-specified in a manual for therapists and a self-help manual for CSOs. If it can be shown that PTC produces durable reductions in the drinker's alcohol use and related family dysfunction, it may be of particular use in countries without extensive alcohol treatment systems.

Sixth, UFT is a creative, pioneering approach that has inspired and informed other methods. However, data on its effectiveness consist of a small pilot study

(Thomas et al., 1987) and a modest randomized trial (Thomas et al., 1990), neither of which have a full report of results published. UFT typically involves weekly sessions for 6 months and a therapist's manual is not available. UFT is not ready for replication or widespread use.

MFT To Aid Recovery When the Alcoholic Has Sought Help

The 28 studies reviewed in this section evaluated treatment in which spouses or other family members of an alcoholic adult were involved in treatment efforts to aid the alcoholic's recovery and help the family after the alcoholic had sought treatment.

Behavioral Couples Therapy

Behavioral couples therapy (BCT) sees the alcoholic patient together with the spouse or cohabiting partner to build support for abstinence and to improve relationship functioning. BCT assumes that spouses can reward abstinence, and that alcoholic patients from happier, more cohesive relationships with better communication have a lower risk of relapse. BCT has two main components: alcohol-focused interventions to directly build support for abstinence; and relationship-focused interventions to increase positive feelings, shared activities, and constructive communication. While current work on BCT usually focuses on both drinking and the relationship, some earlier studies included only one type of intervention. BCT alcohol-focused interventions have included behavioral contracting (e.g., to promote disulfiram ingestion, daily statements of intent to stay abstinent, or aftercare attendance) and teaching spouses to decrease behaviors that trigger or enable drinking. The 17 controlled studies of BCT are discussed next.

BCT With a Behavioral Contract To Maintain Disulfiram as the Alcohol-Focused Method

Disulfiram (Antabuse) is a medication that produces unpleasant symptoms (flushing, headache, nausea, vomiting, dizziness, light-headedness, tachycardia) if a person consumes alcohol. The rationale for disulfiram in treating alcoholism is that most alcoholics taking disulfiram will not drink for fear of getting sick. Fuller, Branchey, and Brightwell's (1986) large scale clinical trial found that disulfiram was not effective due to serious problems with patient acceptance and compliance. However, abstinence was observed among patients who took the medication consistently. Further, the low patient acceptance may have been related to the fact that the disulfiram was not an integral part of the alcoholism counseling used. Findings such as these have led to the use of behavioral contracts between the alcoholic and a spouse or significant other to maintain compliance with disulfiram and to make disulfiram an integral part of alcoholism counseling.

Community reinforcement approach studies of disulfiram contracts. Azrin (1976) tried to improve the Community Reinforcement Approach (CRA) by adding a disulfiram contract in which the spouse or family member observed the patient take disulfiram each day. Male alcoholic patients ($N = 18$) were randomly assigned to get the standard state hospital alcoholism program (with little or no family involvement) or the standard program plus CRA with disulfiram contract. CRA patients at 6-month follow-up, compared to standardly treated patients, drank less, worked more, spent more time with their families and out of institutions, and were less likely to get separated or divorced. Follow-up for 2 years of CRA subjects (follow-up for the control group was limited to 6 months) showed that positive outcomes for CRA subjects were maintained with at least 90% days abstinent for each 6-month period during the 2-year follow-up. CRA patients after the intensive counseling period had continuing counseling "at intervals of about every 2 months" (p. 343) for an unstated duration, but presumably through the 2-year follow-up. The high level of abstinence associated with periodic monitoring of patients' use of the disulfiram contract is similar to results in the Project CALM study of relapse prevention sessions described below.

Azrin, Sisson, Meyers, and Godley's (1982) subsequent CRA study more explicitly evaluated the benefits of disulfiram contracts. Outpatients (43 total, 7 women) in a rural community alcoholism clinic were randomly assigned to: (a) a prescription and instructions to take disulfiram, plus traditional individual counseling based on a disease model approach; (b) a disulfiram contract with spouse or family member, plus traditional individual disease model counseling; or (c) disulfiram contract plus CRA. Patients receiving CRA and a disulfiram contract did best. Traditional therapy without disulfiram contract did worst. Outcomes for those in traditional therapy with disulfiram contract were intermediate between the other two groups. During the 6-month follow-up period, the two groups that got the disulfiram contract had better disulfiram compliance and better drinking outcomes (i.e., fewer drinking days, less alcohol consumed, and less intoxication) than the traditional group without the disulfiram contract. At 6-month follow-up, the CRA plus disulfiram contract group was almost fully abstinent, drinking on the average 0.4 days a month. The traditional group without disulfiram contract, in contrast, had stopped disulfiram and was drinking on the average 16.4 days a month. Further, married or cohabiting clients assigned to disulfiram contract and traditional treatment did about as well on the outcome measures as they did with CRA plus disulfiram contract. Single clients, however, did better when the disulfiram contract was accompanied by CRA than traditional therapy.

Project CALM studies of disulfiram contracts. The Counseling for Alcoholics' Marriages (CALM) Project BCT program (Rotunda & O'Farrell, 1997) includes disulfiram contracts along with relationship-focused interventions to increase positive feelings, shared activities, and constructive communication. In the Project CALM disulfiram contract (O'Farrell & Bayog, 1986), each day at a specified time the alcoholic asks the spouse to witness the taking of disulfiram and thanks the spouse for doing so. The spouse, in turn, thanks the alcoholic for taking disulfiram and records the observation on a calendar provided by the therapist. Both partners agree not to discuss past drinking or fears about future drinking at home, but reserve these discussions for the therapy sessions. Thus, the CALM contract seeks to restructure the couple's relationship to reduce conflicts about drinking and to decrease the spouse's anxiety, distrust, and need to control the alcoholic. The CALM contract tries to deal with these relationship dynamics of the early sobriety period in order to increase support for abstinence and reduce risk of relapse.

An initial Project CALM study (O'Farrell, Cutter, Choquette, Floyd, & Bayog, 1992; O'Farrell, Cutter, & Floyd, 1985) randomly assigned 36 couples, in which the husband had recently begun individual alcohol counseling that included a disulfiram prescription, to (a) 10 weekly sessions of a BCT couples group with a disulfiram contract; (b) 10 weeks of an interactional couples group (McCrady, Paolino, Longabaugh, & Rossi, 1979) without a disulfiram contract; or (c) a no-marital-treatment control group without a disulfiram contract. During treatment, BCT was better than interactional or individual counseling at stabilizing abstinence and improving marital relationships. Specifically, at posttreatment all three groups had increased on days abstinent, but BCT had more days abstinent than interactional; and BCT had more patients (BCT = 100%, interactional = 58%, individual = 58%) with positive outcomes of greater than 95% days abstinent and no days separated.[2] On marital functioning, BCT improved on 5 measures (marital adjustment, areas of change, marital stability, positive interaction, days separated), interactional improved on 2 (areas of change, positive interaction), and individual improved on none of the 8 measures studied. BCT improved more than interactional on marital adjustment but BCT and interactional did not differ on the other marital measures.

During the 2-year follow-up period, the three treatments did not differ on days abstinent and BCT had better marital adjustment and fewer drinking-related problems than individual. Specifically, BCT compared to individual showed (a) less time separated through 18-month follow-up; (b) wives' marital adjustment remained improved throughout the 2-year period for BCT with no improvement for individual; (c) better wives' marital adjustment at 2-month and 12-month (p =.06) follow-up and at 24-month follow-up (for wives with pretreatment marital adjustment scores greater than 67); and (d) a trend (p = .056) toward fewer drinking-related negative consequences. This trend probably represents a true effect that was too weak to be detected with the relatively small sample size (Kazdin & Bass, 1989). Fewer negative consequences among BCT cases are consistent with more positive wives' marital adjustment scores and fewer days separated for BCT than control couples despite no differences in days abstinent. In male alcoholics' marriages, negative consequences of drinking that disrupt the lives of the spouse and family are associated with poor marital adjustment

(Zweben, 1986) and separations (O'Farrell, Harrison, & Cutter, 1981) to a greater extent than is the frequency of drinking.

BCT and interactional did not differ on days abstinent during follow-up, but wives' marital adjustment remained improved throughout the 2-year period for BCT without improvement for interactional. Further, as described in detail below, BCT compared to interactional had more favorable cost-benefit and cost-effectiveness results because interactional patients who failed to stay sober during treatment incurred substantial hospital and jail costs during follow-up (O'Farrell et al., 1996b). Relative to individual, interactional showed less time separated and a trend ($p = .09$) toward fewer drinking-related negative consequences during the 2-year follow-up.

In sum, during treatment, BCT was better than interactional or individual counseling at stabilizing abstinence and improving marital relationships. In the 2-year follow-up, BCT compared to individual had fewer drinking-related negative consequences, better marital adjustment, and less time separated; and BCT compared to interactional had better marital adjustment and more favorable cost-benefit and cost-effectiveness results. Interactional had results between BCT and individual because, relative to individual, interactional improved on some aspects of marital adjustment during treatment and had less time separated and fewer alcohol-related problems during follow-up. BCT did not produce less drinking than interactional or individual during follow-up, perhaps because disulfiram contract use decreased quickly after treatment ended.[3]

A second Project CALM study evaluated couples relapse prevention (RP) sessions for maintaining change after BCT (O'Farrell, Choquette, Cutter, Brown, & McCourt, 1993; O'Farrell, Choquette, & Cutter, 1998). Continued use of the disulfiram contract, especially for individuals suffering more severe drinking problems, was a goal of the RP sessions. In this study, 59 male alcoholic patients, after participating in weekly BCT sessions for 5 to 6 months, were randomly assigned to receive or not to receive 15 additional conjoint couples RP sessions over the next 12 months. Outcome measures were collected before and after BCT and at quarterly intervals for the 30 months after the end of BCT.

This study produced three major findings. First, alcoholics who got RP after BCT had more days abstinent, used the disulfiram contract more, and maintained improved marriages longer than those who got BCT alone. Specifically, BCT-plus-RP produced more days abstinent[4] and greater use of the disulfiram contract than BCT-only; and these superior drinking outcomes for BCT-plus-RP lasted through 18 months follow-up (i.e., 6 months after the end of RP). BCT-plus-RP had better wives' marital adjustment than BCT-only throughout the 30-month follow-up, with the superiority of BCT-plus-RP over BCT-only being greatest for wives with poorer pretreatment marital adjustment during the later months of follow-up. BCT-plus-RP also maintained their improved marriages longer (through 24-month follow-up) than BCT-only (through 12-month follow-up). Second, for alcoholics with more severe drinking and marital problems, RP produced better drinking and marital outcomes throughout the 30-month follow-up period. Specifically, alcoholics with more severe alcohol problems at study entry used the disulfiram contract more and showed a less steep decline in use of the disulfiram contract throughout the 30 months after BCT if they received RP than if they did not. Further, alcoholics with more severe marital problems had better marital adjustment and more days abstinent and maintained relatively stable levels of abstinence if they got RP, while those who did not get RP had poorer marital adjustment and fewer abstinent days and showed a steep decline in abstinent days in the 30 months after BCT. Third, greater use of the disulfiram contract and more use of BCT-targeted marital behaviors (e.g., shared recreational activities, constructive communication) were associated with more days abstinent and more positive marital adjustment after BCT for all subjects irrespective of the amount of aftercare received. In sum, for the entire sample, BCT-plus-RP produced better marital outcomes throughout the 30-month follow-up and better drinking outcomes during and for the 6 months following RP sessions, relative to BCT-only outcomes. For alcoholics with more severe marital and drinking problems, BCT-plus-RP produced better drinking outcomes than BCT-only throughout the 30-month follow-up period.

Other studies of disulfiram contracts. Two other studies of disulfiram contracts have been reported. The disulfiram contract in these studies included only daily monitoring of disulfiram with little or no attention to verbal reinforcement or relationship aspects of the contract. Chick et al. (1992) did the largest study of disulfiram contracts to date. Subjects were patients ($N = 126$, 16% women) at seven alcoholism treatment centers in the United Kingdom. In addition to outpatient counseling, patients were randomly assigned to: (a) supervised 200-mg daily dose of disulfiram in which an informant (usually the spouse) supervised daily ingestion of disulfiram by the patient; or (b) supervised use of vitamin C to control for the effects of receiving supervised medication and outpatient counseling (patients were told this rationale). Over the 6-month study period, supervised disulfiram plus counseling produced more abstinence, less drinking, and fewer alcohol-related social and health problems than counseling with supervised vitamin C.

In the only study to find no advantage for the disulfiram contract (Keane, Foy, Nunn, & Rychtarik, 1984), 25 male alcoholics being discharged from a 4-week inpatient alcohol treatment program were randomly assigned for a 3-month period to: (a) disulfiram contract with significant other, usually the wife, to observe daily taking of disulfiram plus instructions for the wife to use positive reinforcement for contract compliance; (b) disulfiram contract without reinforcement; or (c) disulfiram prescription without contract. At 3-month follow-up, 84% of all subjects were still abstinent and taking disulfiram daily by collateral report, with no significant differences among treatment groups. The short duration of follow-up and the small sample size may have precluded emergence of group differences. Motivational and instructional aspects common to all subjects appear to have increased compliance in the noncontract group beyond levels reported by others (Azrin et al., 1982; Fuller et al., 1986; Chick et al., 1992).

BCT With a Behavioral Contract Other Than a Disulfiram Contract

Six BCT studies used a behavioral contract other than a disulfiram contract. All six studies showed positive outcomes for BCT as compared with individual-based treatment.

Early BCT behavioral contract studies. Three early BCT studies used a behavioral contract other than a disulfiram contract as the alcohol-focused method. First, Hunt and Azrin (1973) included BCT as one component in the initial CRA study. This BCT consisted of the couple making written agreements for specific activities each spouse would do to make the relationship rewarding. BCT always included an agreement that the spouse would "discontinue physical and social contact with the client as much as possible" (p. 95) if the alcoholic drank. Sixteen male alcoholic patients were randomly assigned to get the standard state hospital alcoholism program consisting of 25 hours of alcohol education lectures and films (with little or no family involvement) or the standard program plus CRA. CRA patients at 6-month follow-up, compared to standardly treated patients, drank less, worked more, spent more time with their families and out of institutions, and were less likely to get separated or divorced.

Second, Hedberg and Campbell (1974) compared behavioral family counseling (BFC) to three individually-oriented behavioral treatments (systematic desensitization, covert sensitization, and electric shock avoidance conditioning) for 49 alcoholic patients (4 women) at a mental health center. BFC mainly with couples consisted of communication skills training and "Behavioral contracts were also designed for each family. . .to modify certain identified behaviors and help achieve abstinence . . ." (p. 253). At 6-month follow-up, BFC was the most effective treatment for all patients regardless of whether the patients' goal was abstinence or controlled drinking; and BFC was particularly effective for patients with abstinence goals. Specifically, 80% (8 of 10) of BFC clients achieved their goal of abstinence for the 6-month follow-up period as compared to 42% (11 of 26) of alcoholics in the three other individual behavioral treatments $[X^2(1) = 2.74, p < .05]$. Further, when clients with both abstinence and controlled drinking goals were considered, there was a trend for better BFC outcomes in that 73% (11 of 15) of BFC clients as compared to 47% (16 of 34) of those in the other treatments achieved their goal $[X^2(1) = 1.94, p = .08]$.[5]

Third, male alcoholics who had just completed a 4-week inpatient alcohol program were randomly assigned to (a) a behavioral contract with a family member (spouse, parent, or sibling) to reinforce aftercare attendance or (b) standard aftercare arrangements. Nearly twice as many contract patients as standard control patients attended aftercare sessions, and patients in the contract condition had significantly more months abstinent and were more likely to be employed and classified as a treatment success (Ahles, Schlundt, Prue, & Rychtarik, 1983; Ossip-Klein, Vanlandingham, Prue, & Rychtarik, 1984). *The Project CALM "sobriety contract."* The Project CALM BCT program also can be used without disulfiram. The disulfiram contract is replaced with a "sobriety contract" (O'Farrell & Fals-Stewart, 2000) in which each day at a specified time the alcoholic patient initiates a brief discussion and reiterates his or her intention to stay abstinent that day (in the tradition of one day at a time). The couple agrees not to discuss drinking or drug use at other times, to mark that they had the discussion on a calendar provided, and to end it with a statement of appreciation to each other. If the sobriety contract includes 12-step meetings or urine screens, these also are marked on the calendar. Three studies used the Project CALM sobriety contract as part of BCT that also included increasing positive couple and family activities and teaching communication skills. These were the first studies to include an attention placebo control group. All three studies showed BCT had more abstinence and better relationship adjustment in the year after treatment than did the placebo control group or individual treatment.

First, Kelley and Fals-Stewart (2002) randomly assigned 71 married/cohabiting men with a primary alcohol dependence diagnosis for a 20-week period to one of three equally intensive 32-session outpatient treatments: (a) BCT consisting of 12 BCT sessions and 20 individual cognitive behavioral therapy sessions; (b) Individual-Based Treatment (IBT) consisting of 32 individual cognitive behavioral therapy sessions; or (c) couples-based Psychoeducational Attention Control Treatment (PACT) consisting of 12 couple education sessions and 20 individual cognitive behavioral sessions. Results in the year after treatment showed that BCT produced more days abstinent and more positive scores on relationship adjustment measures than did IBT or PACT.

Second, Fals-Stewart, O'Farrell, and Birchler (2001) randomly assigned 80 married or cohabiting male alcoholic patients for a 12-week period to either (a) Brief BCT (12 sessions—6 BCT sessions alternating with 6 individual sessions), (b) BCT (24 sessions—12 BCT sessions alternating with 12 individual counseling sessions), (c) IBT (12 individual sessions), or (d) PACT (12 sessions—6 individual sessions alternating with 6 educational sessions for the couple). Both BCT versions used the sobriety contract. Group comparisons indicated Brief BCT and BCT were significantly more effective than IBT or PACT, with BCT having more days abstinent and more positive relationship adjustment scores during the year after treatment. Furthermore, Brief BCT and BCT produced equivalent posttreatment outcomes.

Third, Fals-Stewart and O'Farrell (2002) added naltrexone observation by the spouse to the sobriety contract in a recent pilot study. Naltrexone is a recovery medication that reduces cravings and desire to drink and improves drinking outcomes (O'Malley et al., 1992). In this study, 80 male alcohol-dependent married or cohabiting men were randomly assigned to one of four equally intensive 12-week treatment conditions. In all conditions, individual counseling sessions consisted of 12-step facilitation, the treatment as usual (TAU) provided by the treatment program. All patients were given a prescription for naltrexone, which they were encouraged to take by the agency physician as part of their treatment regimen. Treatment conditions were: (a) BCT with daily naltrexone contract to observe and reinforce naltrexone ingestion plus individual TAU sessions (BCT-NC); (b) BCT without daily naltrexone contract plus individual TAU sessions (BCT); (c) PACT of couple education about alcoholism plus individual TAU sessions (PACT); and (d) TAU individual sessions only (TAU). Results during the 12-week treatment phase and a 6-month follow-up period showed that the BCT-NC group with the sobriety plus naltrexone contract produced better naltrexone compliance and a trend ($p = .06$) toward more days abstinent than the other three treatment conditions.

BCT With an Alcohol-Focused Method Other Than a Behavioral Contract

Some BCT studies have used an alcohol-focused method other than behavioral contracting. Noel and McCrady (1993) developed a method called "alcohol-focused spouse involvement." It involves teaching the spouse specific skills to deal with alcohol-related situations. The spouse is taught how to reinforce abstinence, decrease behaviors that trigger drinking, decrease behaviors that protect the alcoholic from naturally occurring adverse consequences of drinking, assertively discuss concerns about drinking-related situations, and respond to help the drinker in drink refusal situations.

McCrady et al. (1986) randomly assigned 53 alcoholics (27% women) and their spouses to one of three 15-session outpatient behavioral treatments: (a) minimal spouse involvement (MSI) in which the spouse simply observed the alcohol abuser's individual therapy; (b) alcohol-focused spouse involvement (AFSI) as described above plus the MSI interventions; (c) alcohol behavioral marital therapy (ABMT) in which all skills taught in the MSI and AFSI conditions were included as well as relationship-focused interventions. Results during and in the 6 months after treatment indicated that subjects in all three groups had decreased drinking, increased life satisfaction, and increased marital satisfaction, sexual activity, and job stability. These positive results did not differ for the three treatments tested. Despite this general pattern of improvement for all patients irrespective of treatment condition, some results favored ABMT over the other spouse-involved therapies. Specifically, ABMT couples (a) maintained their marital satisfaction after treatment better and tended to have more stable marriages (i.e., fewer and shorter separations) than the other two groups; and (b) were more compliant with homework assignments, decreased the number of drinking days more during treatment, and their posttreatment drinking increased more slowly than AFSI couples.

Follow-up data through 18 months from this study (McCrady, Stout, Noel, Abrams, & Nelson, 1991) provided more evidence favoring ABMT. Although subjects in all conditions had decreased frequency of any drinking and of heavy drinking and increased life satisfaction, patterns of outcome varied across the three treatment conditions. ABMT subjects showed gradual improvement in proportions of abstinent days and abstinent plus light drinking days over the last 9 months of follow-up, while subjects in the other conditions showed gradual deterioration on these drinking outcomes. ABMT patients also had fewer marital separations and more improvement in marital satisfaction and subjective well-being than their counterparts in the other two conditions.[6]

In a study of methods to maintain change after ABMT, McCrady, Epstein, and Hirsch (1999) randomly assigned 90 male alcoholics and their female partners to fifteen 90-minute weekly sessions of: (a) ABMT without special maintenance interventions; (b) RP/ABMT which had ABMT plus maintenance interventions based on an RP model and 4 to 8 booster sessions in the 12 months following the main treatment; or (c) AA/ABMT which had ABMT plus maintenance interventions based on a 12-step AA and Al-Anon model. In the first 6 months after treatment, patients that completed at least 5 sessions showed increased abstinence, reduced heavy drinking, and overall improvement for all three treatment groups that was similar to other outpatient treatment studies; but there were no group differences. Two outcome variables favored the purely BCT treatment conditions (ABMT and RP/ABMT) over AA/ABMT: time to the first heavy drinking day was longer for ABMT than for AA/ABMT; and RP/ABMT had shorter drinking episodes than AA/ABMT. Patients who complied with post-treatment maintenance plans (i.e., booster sessions in RP/ABMT and AA meetings in AA/ABMT) were more likely to be abstinent than those who did not.

Longabaugh and colleagues (Longabaugh, Beattie, Noel, Stout, & Malloy, 1993; Longabaugh, Wirtz, Beattie, Noel, & Stout, 1995) conducted a study of patient treatment matching to determine the relative effectiveness of different amounts of BCT for different client characteristics. This study randomly assigned 229 alcoholic patients (31% women) to one of three 20-session outpatient cognitive behavioral treatments: (a) extended cognitive behavioral (ECB) that did not involve significant others; (b) extended relationship-enhanced (ERE) that had 8 sessions for the patient with a concerned partner (spouse, relative, or friend) focused on supporting abstinence (using methods closely adapted from McCrady's AFSI procedures) and strengthening the relationship; and (c) brief broad spectrum (BBS) that had 4 sessions of partner involvement with the same goals as the ERE partner sessions. A hierarchical latent growth model was used to analyze the data on percent days abstinent of 188 patients (82%) followed for 18 months. The three treatments did not differ overall, but there were significant interaction effects that followed study predictions. Results showed that ERE was significantly more effective than the other two treatments in increasing abstinence of patients entering treatment with a network unsupportive of abstinence or with a low level of investment in their network, whereas BBS treatment was more effective for patients with either (a) both a social network unsupportive of abstinence and a low level of network investment or (b) high investment in a network supportive of abstinence. ECB outcomes were neither as good as those matched nor as bad as those mismatched to the different amounts of BCT. Longabaugh interpreted these complex results as follows. In the context of 20 planned sessions, for patients with a moderate level of problems in relationship support, 8 sessions of BCT was more effective than 4 or no sessions of BCT. For those with a high level of problems in relationship support, treatments which spent more time strengthening individual coping and little or no time on BCT were more effective, and 8 BCT sessions were not sufficient, suggesting that more BCT sessions were needed to deal effectively with higher levels of relationship problems.

Shoham, Rohrbaugh, Stickle, and Jacob (1998) adapted the AFSI procedure into a more general cognitive behavioral (CB) couples therapy and compared it with couples therapy based on family systems therapy (FST) concepts. As described in more detail under studies of family systems therapy below, CB and FST did not differ overall. However, for couples high on pretreatment measure of demand-withdraw interaction, FST was better than CB at retaining such couples in treatment.

BCT With a Relationship Focus and Without a Specific Alcohol-Focused Method

Two studies examined BCT that focused on the couple's relationship but did not describe a specific alcohol-focused method as part of the BCT. First, Bowers and Al-Redha (1990) randomly assigned 16 alcoholics (2 women) and their spouses to standard individual counseling or to a BCT couples group that focused on rehearsal of communication skills and negotiation of desired changes. BCT had significantly lower alcohol consumption at 6-month follow-up than standard treatment and a trend toward lower consumption at 12-month follow-up.

Second, Monti et al. (1990) randomly assigned 69 male alcoholics in a 28-day inpatient program to: (a) a communication skills training group (CST), (b) a communication skills training group with participation of a family member most often the spouse (CST-F), or (c) a cognitive behavioral mood management training group (CBMMT). Patients who received CST or CST-F drank significantly less alcohol per drinking day in the 6 months after treatment than those in CBMMT, but groups did not differ in abstinence rates or time to relapse. Although all groups improved in alcohol-specific coping skills, CST improved most in skill in alcohol-specific high-risk role-plays. Monti suggested that failure to find an advantage for adding family members to CST might have occurred for two reasons. First, the standard inpatient program was based on a family systems model and required family members to be involved in family therapy, education and Al-Anon and Alateen. Second, including family in CST nearly doubled the therapy group size and may have reduced opportunities for clients to practice new skills in CST-F sessions.

Expanded Outcome Domains in BCT—Social Costs,
Partner Violence, and Child Adjustment
Studies of the Project CALM BCT program have extended the outcome domains examined. Expanded outcome domains for which BCT has shown favorable results have included social costs, partner violence, and child adjustment.
Cost-benefit and cost-effectiveness of BCT. Holder, Longabaugh, Miller, and Rubonis (1991) reviewed cost-effectiveness of treatments for alcoholism using efficacy data from clinical trials and average costs of various treatments as reported by providers, insurance carriers, and experts in the field. The authors concluded that BCT had evidence of both effectiveness and cost-effectiveness based on seven controlled studies showing BCT superior to comparison groups. They also recommended that future studies should carefully measure both cost and effectiveness in order to move beyond the rather general estimates used in their review. Heeding this recommendation, O'Farrell et al. (1992, 1993) conducted cost analyses for the two Project CALM studies of disulfiram contracts already described above. Two approaches were used: cost-benefit analysis and cost-effectiveness analysis (Yates, 1994, 1999). *Cost-benefit analysis,* which addresses the question of whether an intervention is economically justified usually from society's perspective, compares the cost of delivering the intervention with the economic benefits of the intervention, with both costs and benefits expressed in dollars. Benefits typically include reductions in costs due to reduced use of health care and other services after the intervention. *Cost-effectiveness analysis,* which seeks to identify the least costly method of achieving a desired treatment outcome, compares alternative interventions on the cost per unit of clinical effect (e.g., cost per unit of improvement in days abstinent).

O'Farrell et al. (1996b) presented cost outcomes for the first study comparing BCT plus individual, interactional couples therapy plus individual, and individual counseling alone (O'Farrell et al., 1985, 1992). The *cost-benefit analysis* of BCT plus individual alcoholism counseling showed: (a) average costs per case for alcohol-related hospital treatments and jail stays decreased from about $7,800 in the year before treatment to about $1,100 in the 2 years after BCT, with cost savings averaging about $6,700 per case; and (b) a benefit-to-cost ratio of $8.64 in cost savings for every dollar spent to deliver BCT. None of the positive cost-benefit results observed for BCT were true for subjects given interactional couples therapy plus individual alcoholism counseling, for which posttreatment utilization costs increased. Interactional therapy had fewer days abstinent during treatment than BCT (O'Farrell et al., 1992, p. 539), and interactional cases of patients who failed to stay sober during treatment incurred substantial hospital and jail costs during follow-up. Thus, adding BCT to individual alcoholism counseling produced a positive cost-benefit while the addition of interactional couples therapy did not. Individual counseling alone had a significantly more positive benefit-to-cost ratio than BCT plus individual counseling because the cost of delivering individual counseling was about half the cost of delivering BCT plus individual counseling. *Cost-effectiveness analyses* indicated that BCT plus individual counseling was less cost-effective than individual counseling alone and modestly more cost-effective than interactional therapy in producing abstinence from drinking. When marital adjustment outcomes were considered, the three treatments were equally cost-effective except during the active treatment phase when BCT was more cost-effective than interactional couples therapy.

O'Farrell et al. (1996a) presented cost outcomes for the second study in which BCT with added couples RP sessions was compared with BCT alone (O'Farrell et al., 1993). Costs of treatment delivery and health and legal service utilization were measured for the 12 months before and 12 months after BCT. *Cost-benefit analysis* results for both standard BCT and for the longer and more costly form of BCT with additional RP sessions showed decreases in health care and legal costs after treatment as compared to before treatment, with average cost savings per case of $5,053 for BCT-only and $3,365 for BCT-plus-RP. The benefit-to-cost ratios showed $5.97 for BCT-only and $1.89 for BCT-plus-RP in cost savings for every dollar spent to deliver the respective treatment. Although adding RP to BCT led to less drinking and better marital adjustment (O'Farrell et al., 1993) as described above, it did not lead to greater cost savings in health and legal service utilization or a more favorable benefit-to-cost ratio than BCT-only. Adding RP to BCT nearly doubled the cost of delivering the basic BCT program. *Cost-effectiveness analyses* indicated that BCT-only was more cost-effective than BCT-plus-RP in producing abstinence from drinking, but the two treatments were equally cost-effective when marital adjustment outcomes were considered. Since BCT-only was less effective clinically than BCT-plus-RP in producing abstinent days, it was the lower cost of BCT-only that produced its greater cost-effectiveness in relation to abstinence.

What can we conclude from these two studies of cost outcomes after BCT? First, the benefit-to-cost ratios show $8.64 in the first study and $5.97 in the second study in cost savings for every dollar spent to deliver BCT. Taken together, the data from these two studies show that reduced hospital and jail days after BCT save more than 5 times the cost of delivering the standard Project CALM BCT program for alcoholism. Second, neither study showed superior cost-effectiveness for BCT or for BCT-plus-RP when compared to a less costly, less intensive treatment even though BCT was clinically more effective. The greater cost of the BCT dictated the results in both studies. Interestingly, Fals-Stewart, O'Farrell, and Birchler (1997) found BCT was clinically more effective and had greater cost-benefit and cost-effectiveness when compared with equally intensive, equally costly to deliver individual-based treatment for male primary drug abuse patients.

Partner violence reductions after BCT. Two naturalistic studies have examined partner violence before and after BCT (with a Project CALM disulfiram contract) in comparison with a nonalcoholic comparison sample. O'Farrell, Murphy, Hoover, Fals-Stewart, and Murphy (2002) replicated with a larger, more varied, intent-to-treat sample their initial study findings of dramatically reduced violence associated with abstinence after BCT (O'Farrell & Murphy, 1995; O'Farrell, Van Hutton, & Murphy, 1999). This study examined partner violence before and in the 2 years after BCT for 303 married or cohabiting male alcoholic patients, and used a demographically matched nonalcoholic comparison sample. In the year before BCT, 60% of alcoholic patients had been violent toward their female partner, times the comparison sample rate of 12%. In the year after BCT, violence decreased significantly to 24% of the alcoholic sample but remained higher than the comparison group. Among remitted alcoholics after BCT, violence prevalence of 12% was identical to the comparison sample and less than half the rate among relapsed patients (30%). Results in the second year after BCT were similar to the first year. Thus, partner violence decreased after BCT, and clinically significant violence reductions occurred for patients whose alcoholism was remitted after BCT. Attending more scheduled BCT sessions and using BCT-targeted behaviors (e.g., disulfiram contract, positive activities) during and after treatment were related to less drinking and less violence after BCT, suggesting that skills couples learn in BCT may promote both sobriety and reduced violence.

Birchler and Fals-Stewart (2001) studied whether couples in BCT (with a Project CALM sobriety contract) learn to deal nonviolently with conflicts. They examined changes during treatment in frequency of couple conflicts (e.g., yelling, name-calling, threatening to hit, hitting) among male alcoholic patients ($N = 99$) randomly assigned to one of three equally intensive treatments: (a) BCT, (b) IBT, or (c) a PACT. Consistent with study hypotheses, male and female partners who participated in BCT reported less frequent conflicts during treatment than those couples assigned to IBT or PACT. These results suggest that in BCT, couples do learn to handle their conflicts with less hostility and aggression. The next step would be to show that these improved conflict management skills actually lead to less violence after BCT.

Impact of BCT on the children of couples undergoing BCT. In the first report on this topic, Kelley and Fals-Stewart (2002) randomly assigned 71 married/cohabiting men with a primary alcohol dependence diagnosis to one of three equally intensive outpatient treatments: (a) BCT with a Project CALM sobriety contract, (b) IBT, or (c) couples-based PACT. As described above, results in the year after treatment showed that BCT produced more days abstinent and more positive relationship adjustment scores than did IBT or PACT. Most important, BCT improved psychosocial functioning of the couples' children more than IBT or PACT. Children of fathers in all three treatments showed improved functioning in the year after treatment, but children of fathers who got BCT improved more than did children in the other two treatments. Further, only when fathers were treated in BCT was there a significant reduction in the percentage of children with clinically significant levels of impaired psychosocial functioning. Thus, BCT improved children's functioning in the year after treatment more than did individual-based treatment or couple psychoeducation; and of these three treatments, only BCT showed reduction in the number of children with clinically significant impairment.

Family Systems Therapy

Family Systems Therapy (FST) has incorporated many core concepts of family systems theory into models of the alcoholic family system (Rohrbaugh, Shoham, Spungen, & Steinglass, 1995; Steinglass, Bennett, Wolin, & Reiss, 1987). Therapy focuses on the interactional rather than the individual level. FST uses a variety of techniques to affect interactions within the family. Greatest emphasis is put on identifying and altering family interaction patterns that are associated with problematic alcohol use. FST can be applied to couples therapy or whole family therapy.

McCrady et al. (1979) evaluated the relative effectiveness of adding joint hospitalization and couples therapy based on a systems perspective to individual treatment for alcohol problems. Married alcoholics ($N = 33$, 40% women) were randomly assigned to (a) individual involvement in which only the drinker attended group therapy; (b) couples involvement in which the drinker and spouse participated in an outpatient interactional couples therapy group in addition to concurrent individual treatment groups for each spouse; or (c) joint admission in which both partners were initially hospitalized and then participated in both the couples group therapy and individual therapy groups following discharge. At 6-month follow-up, findings indicated significant decreases in the quantity of alcohol consumed for both the couples involvement and joint admission treatment groups but not for the individual treatment group. All groups showed significant decreases in marital problems, depression and other psychological symptoms, and alcohol-related problems.

Orchen (1983) randomly assigned 48 heavy drinkers at an outpatient community mental health center to: (a) brief, strategic family systems therapy; (b) biofeedback; (c) relaxation training; or (d) a waitlist control group. Treatments had six sessions. For the family therapy sessions, "significant people in the individual's network are included in the treatment" (p. 48), suggesting that children and other family members beyond spouses were included. Family therapy improved more than waitlist control on a global clinician rating described as "overall condition," and showed a greater reduction in drinking than the other three groups in the 6 weeks from pre- to posttest. Groups did not differ on anxiety and depression at posttest.

Grigg (1994) randomly assigned 114 male alcoholics and their spouses to 15 sessions of (a) experiential systemic couples therapy, (b) experiential systemic individual therapy, or (c) individual supportive treatment. Results showed groups did not differ; and all groups improved from baseline to posttreatment and 15-week follow-up on the husbands' alcohol dependence symptoms, couple and family relationships, and symptoms of emotional distress.

Kearney (1984) randomly assigned 10 married alcoholics (2 women) at an outpatient alcohol treatment program to 10 weeks of twice weekly sessions of either multiple family group therapy or individual conjoint family therapy. Children in the family were included in both treatments. Data collected before and after treatment showed no differences between the treatments on couple or family functioning. Drinking outcomes were not assessed.

Bennun (1988) randomly assigned 12 married alcoholic patients (4 women) in an outpatient alcohol program to an average of 8 to 9 sessions of family problem solving therapy or family systems therapy based on the Milan school. Outcome data were collected before and after treatment and at 6-month followup. Results showed groups did not differ; and both groups improved from baseline to posttreatment and follow-up on the alcoholics' alcohol dependence symptoms, and on husbands' and wives' satisfaction with couple and family relationships, and on children's satisfaction with family relationships.

Zweben, Pearlman and Li (1988) randomly assigned 218 alcohol abusers to either (a) eight sessions of conjoint therapy based on a systemic perspective in which alcohol abuse was viewed as having adaptive consequences for the couple (Steinglass et al., 1987) or (b) a single session of advice counseling which also involved the spouse. Results for 116 (17% women) alcohol abusers with completed follow-up interviews over an 18-month period showed that couples in both treatments had significant improvement on all marital adjustment and drinking-related outcome measures; but there were no significant between-group differences on any measure.

Shoham et al. (1998) studied retention in treatment for 63 couples with a male alcoholic partner who had been randomly assigned to 20 scheduled sessions of either cognitive behavioral therapy (CBT) or family systems therapy (FST). Although the authors did not find main effect differences in retention between the two treatments, they did find an interesting moderator effect. Couples high on pretreatment measures of demand-withdraw interaction (a pattern in which the wife demands and the husband withdraws) attended fewer sessions and more often failed to complete CBT, whereas demand-withdraw interaction made little difference in FST. Shoham et al. suggested that the alcoholic husband in such couples withdrew from a high-demand CBT therapy in the same way he tended to withdraw from a demanding wife. CBT in this study was "a high demand cognitive behavioral therapy that focused primarily on the partners as individuals" and FST was "a low demand systemic treatment focused on the partners as a couple" (p. 572). CBT required that patients become abstinent by session 12, and used breathalyzer tests at each session to check compliance, whereas in FST "the therapist remained neutral about change until the clients as a couple explicitly chose to pursue a change goal related to drinking" (p. 561). The authors acknowledged that the CBT used might not represent less demanding behavioral approaches such as motivational interviewing (Miller & Rollnick, 1991) or other BCT methods (e.g., Project CALM; Rotunda & O'Farrell, 1997). These intriguing findings merit further study. If replicated and extended to outcomes beyond retention in treatment, these results could have important implications for matching couples to treatments.

Other MFT Approaches

Four studies examined family methods that do not follow a behavioral, systems, or 12-step family disease approach. The first two are early eclectic studies that used sequential rather than random assignment to conditions and developed pragmatic and effective methods to involve the spouse.[7] The remaining studies had more equivocal findings.

Corder, Corder, and Laidlaw (1972) added a 4-day intensive residential couples group workshop to a standard 4-week inpatient alcohol rehabilitation program. The workshop involved 20 patients and wives in aftercare planning, improving their communication, doing and planning shared recreational activities, AA and Al-Anon meetings, and alcohol education lectures. The control group of 20 patients received equally intensive treatment in the standard individual inpatient rehab program only without spouse involvement. At 6-month follow-up the couples workshop group had significantly better outcomes of higher sobriety rates, better aftercare participation, more recreational activities together, and less unemployment.

Cadogan (1973) assigned 40 (5 women) inpatient alcoholics and their spouses to outpatient couples group therapy after the drinkers' hospital discharge or a waiting list control condition. At 6 months after hospital discharge, the 20 alcohol abusers who received the couples therapy for a 3- to 6-month period had significantly more abstinence and less drinking than the 20 control patients who did not. Thus, these favorable outcomes are for the time period when the patients were receiving couples therapy.

Fichter and Frick (1993) studied 100 German alcoholic patients (42% women) living with a relative (over 90% spouses) and receiving a 6-week inpatient program followed by a recommended 6-week outpatient program. Patients were randomized during the inpatient program to: (a) a weekly group for relatives plus family sessions on communication, or (b) a weekly group to encourage self-help initiatives. Outcome data on whether or not the patient had remained continuously abstinent were collected after treatment and at 6- and 18-month follow-up. Relatives' group had a higher abstinence rate (95.9%) than self-help (80.4%) at discharge from inpatient care but the two groups did not differ at later time periods. Relatives group, compared with self-help patients more often sought additional outpatient counseling in the 6 months after inpatient discharge, and in the entire 18-month period had fewer and shorter inpatient treatments for alcohol problems. Fichter and Frick suggested that greater aftercare use by relatives group patients may have prevented more severe relapses and rehospitalization. The authors also considered why the relatives group did not have better abstinence. First, the additional treatments studied were only a small part of the total treatment received (9 of 126 hours total), and may not have been sufficiently intensive to make a difference. Second, many relatives were resistant to being in the relatives group and their participation was less than desired. Other explanations also should be considered. The outcome measure of continuous abstinence is relatively insensitive because it counts infrequent, low level drinking the same as frequent, heavy, problem drinking. Less use of further inpatient treatment by the family-involved group suggests that a more sensitive drinking measure might well have favored the relatives group patients. Finally, the relatives group did not involve the patient and relative together but rather provided separate concurrent treatment for relatives, not the most effective way to involve family members in treatment.

Chapman and Huygens (1988) randomly assigned 113 alcoholic patients (20% women) after a 2-week inpatient detoxification to (a) a 6-week inpatient program in which "families were involved as much as possible in family therapy"; (b) a 6-week outpatient evening program of twice weekly sessions with the patient's spouse or friend also invited to attend; or (c) a single 1- to 2-hour confrontational interview in the presence of the patient's spouse, relative, or friend whenever possible. "On a variety of outcome measures, that included both levels of drinking and general functioning taken 6 and 18 months after baseline, no treatment appeared to be consistently more effective than another" (p. 67). The major problem with this generally well-executed study is that no information is provided on the extent to which family or significant others were actually involved in the three treatments. Only 40% of the sample were married, and no other information is provided on family or significant others, so most patients may have had little or no family involvement. Interestingly, irrespective of treatment received, patients who had been coerced by someone else to enter treatment had less drinking and more abstinence at 18-month follow-up.

Conclusions About MFT To Aid Recovery When the Alcoholic Has Sought Help

Considerable progress in research on family-involved treatment to aid recovery when the alcoholic has sought help has been made. A number of findings merit consideration.

First, evidence has accumulated for the effectiveness of behavioral couples therapy (BCT). BCT produces more abstinence and fewer alcohol-related problems, happier relationships, fewer couple separations, and lower risk of divorce than does standard or individual-based treatment (Ahles et al., 1983; Azrin, 1976; Azrin et al., 1982; Bowers & Al-Rehda, 1990; Chick et al., 1992; Fals-Stewart & O'Farrell, 2002; Fals-Stewart et al., 2001; Hedberg & Campbell, 1974; Hunt & Azrin, 1973; Kelley & Fals-Stewart, 2002; McCrady et al., 1991; O'Farrell et al., 1992). In 12 of the 15 studies that compared BCT with a standard or individual-based treatment, positive results favored BCT. BCT was better than individual treatment for some patients in one (Longabaugh et al., 1995) of the 3 remaining studies but not in the other 2 (i.e., Keane et al., 1984; Monti et al., 1990). The 3 remaining studies of BCT used alternative treatment comparison groups. Results showed that family systems therapy was better than a variant of BCT at retaining couples with more seriously disturbed communication patterns (Shoham et al., 1998), and that BCT with an added focus on relapse prevention had better outcomes than standard BCT (McCrady et al., 1999; O'Farrell et al., 1998).

BCT with alcoholic patients also positively affects other domains in addition to drinking and relationship adjustment. BCT shows substantial reductions in domestic violence (e.g., O'Farrell & Murphy, 1995) and in hospital and jail stays after BCT that save over 5 times the cost of delivering BCT (O'Farrell et al., 1996a, 1996b). BCT also improves psychosocial functioning of the couples' children more than does individual-based treatment (Kelley & Fals-Stewart, 2002). Finally, BCT has shown greater abstinence and more positive relationship functioning in 6 of 6 studies with primary drug abuse patients (for reviews, see O'Farrell & Fals-Stewart, 2000, 2002; and chapter 3 of this volume).

Second, the BCT alcohol-focused method with the strongest support is a behavioral contract to promote abstinence and behaviors directly associated with abstinence. Such a behavioral contract has positive support in 11 of 12 studies (Ahles et al., 1983; Azrin, 1976; Azrin et al., 1982; Chick et al., 1992; Fals-Stewart & O'Farrell, 2002; Fals-Stewart et al., 2001; Hedberg & Campbell, 1974; Hunt & Azrin, 1973; Kelley & Fals-Stewart, 2002; O'Farrell, et al., 1992, 1998). The disulfiram contract is the specific type of contract with the greatest support, showing favorable outcomes in 5 of 6 studies (Azrin, 1976; Azrin et al., 1982; Chick et al., 1992; O'Farrell, et al., 1992, 1998), but not in the Keane et al. (1984) study. The evidence for the effectiveness of disulfiram contracts suggests that this method should be disseminated to the treatment community as part of a BCT treatment package that includes relationship-focused methods.

Limited disulfiram use by U.S. alcohol treatment programs (O'Farrell, Allen, & Litten, 1995) may pose barriers for adoption of BCT with a disulfiram contract. Further, some alcoholic patients will not be medically cleared to take disulfiram and others will refuse. The Project CALM "sobriety contract" in which the spouse verbally reinforces the alcoholic patient's statement of intent to stay abstinent and other behaviors (e.g., AA attendance, clean urine screens) leading to abstinence may be better positioned for adoption by treatment programs. It showed positive results in 3 well-controlled studies (Fals-Stewart et al., 2001; Fals-Stewart & O'Farrell, 2002; Kelley & Fals-Stewart, 2002). It is a flexible method to which recovery medications can be added quite easily. It fits well with 12-step meetings or individual counseling.

Third, family systems therapy (FST) in alcoholism treatment was the focus of 7 studies. Two studies found better drinking outcomes for FST than individual treatment (McCrady et al., 1979; Orchen, 1983) or a waitlist control (Orchen, 1983), while one did not (Grigg, 1994). Three of four studies comparing FST to other types of family treatment (Bennun, 1988; Kearney, 1984; Zweben et al., 1988) found no differences, while one study (Shoham et al., 1998) found FST was superior to BCT (without a behavioral contract) for couples with more seriously disturbed communication patterns. Important FST contributions were initial controlled studies that included whole families in treatment (Bennun, 1988; Orchen, 1983) and examined children's ratings of outcome (Bennun, 1988; Grigg, 1994; Kearney, 1984).

Fourth, an initial study of a family disease approach (McCrady et al., 1999) found that adding to BCT an emphasis on AA and Al-Anon as a maintenance intervention did not improve outcomes, probably because most clients did not attend 12-step meetings regularly. As study authors noted ". . .higher rates of sustained AA involvement might have been achieved using therapists specifically trained in and committed to a Twelve-Step model of treatment" (p. 1392).

Future Research Directions

This section considers the current status of issues raised by earlier reviews (i.e., Edwards & Steinglass, 1995; McCrady, 1989). It also suggests directions for future research.

Edwards and Steinglass (1995) concluded that MFT is effective in motivating alcoholics to enter treatment. Considerable work has strengthened this conclusion since the earlier review. Seven controlled studies, 4 of which were done after the earlier reviews, support this conclusion. New approaches have shown positive results in controlled studies (e.g., Barber & Crisp's [1995] Pressure to Change Approach) and others have shown promise in initial large scale pilot testing (e.g., A Relational Intervention Sequence for Engagement [ARISE]; Landau et al., 2000). A large scale controlled study added further support for the efficacy of the Community Reinforcement and Family Training (CRAFT) approach and questioned the efficacy of the Johnson Intervention approach. Finally, Al-Anon facilitation was developed to formalize therapists' use of a family disease model approach to help families cope better. We now have 4 controlled studies supporting the 12-step family disease approach to helping families when, as McCrady (1989) noted, we had none at the time of earlier reviews. The present review's updated conclusion is that MFT is effective in motivating alcoholics to enter treatment and in helping spouses and other family members cope better even if the alcoholic does not enter treatment.

Edwards and Steinglass (1995) concluded that, once the alcoholic enters treatment, MFT was marginally more effective than individual-based treatment. The present review described 22 studies comparing MFT with individual treatment. Twelve of these 22 studies were not included in the earlier review. Sixteen of the 22 studies showed better outcomes for MFT than for individual treatment: 12 of 15 BCT studies, 2 of 3 family systems studies, and 2 of 4 studies of other approaches. The present review's updated conclusion is that MFT, particularly using a behavioral approach, is clearly more effective than individual-based treatment at increasing abstinence and improving relationship functioning for alcoholics.

In terms of MFT to maintain treatment gains and prevent relapse, the evidence base supporting MFT is smaller for this stage of change as noted in the earlier review. The number of studies is limited and can be summarized quite readily. First, behavioral contracts between patient and family member increased aftercare attendance and abstinence after an alcohol rehabilitation program (Ahles et al., 1983). Second, adding a relapse prevention component to BCT led to shorter drinking episodes among patients who drank (McCrady et al., 1999). Finally, two BCT studies (Azrin, 1976; O'Farrell et al., 1998) suggested that continued therapist contact over relatively long periods of 1 to 2 years after the end of the intensive phase of treatment to reinforce continued use of treatment-targeted behaviors (e.g., disulfiram) can improve abstinence outcomes. The advantage of such prolonged treatment may be most apparent among patients with more severe drinking and relationship problems (O'Farrell et al., 1998). An important practical issue in applying these results will be the need to develop funding models to pay for such low intensity treatment over extended periods.

Cost-effectiveness of MFT was an area for which prior reviews found no evidence. Edwards and Steinglass (1995) suggested that MFT would reduce costs to society for treatment services, legal involvement, and so forth, and called for research on this topic. As described earlier, two studies have shown a positive cost-benefit for BCT, indicating that reductions in hospital and jail stays after BCT save over 5 times the cost of delivering BCT (O'Farrell et al., 1996a, 1996b). However, when BCT plus individual therapy was compared with individual treatment alone on cost-effectiveness (e.g., how much each treatment costs to produce an abstinent patient), BCT was not more cost-effective even though it was clinically more effective (O'Farrell et al., 1996b), because BCT plus individual therapy costs more to deliver than individual counseling alone. When BCT was compared with equally intensive, equally costly to deliver individual treatment for male primary drug abuse patients, BCT was clinically more effective and had greater cost-benefit and cost-effectiveness (Fals-Stewart et al., 1997). More research on cost outcomes of MFT is needed.

Gender of the alcoholic patient was posited by Edwards and Steinglass (1995) as a moderating variable for MFT, with the suggestion that MFT may be less effective for women than for men alcoholic patients. Because no study has specifically examined gender, we simply do not know if MFT is effective with female patients. Therefore, an important priority for future research is that studies should include women patients in sufficient numbers so that the effectiveness of MFT specifically for women alcoholics can be determined. The same recommendation is made for patients from ethnic minority groups. Understanding whether MFT is effective with women and minority patients is a high priority because, despite some notable exceptions, studies reviewed in this chapter included mostly white male patients.

Related to the need for studies of MFT for the female alcoholic patient is the need for research on MFT for couples in which both the male and female member have a current alcohol or other substance use problem. Efforts to treat women alcoholic patients with MFT will encounter this type of couple frequently because women alcoholic patients are considerably more likely to have a male heavy drinking partner than male alcoholic patients are to have a heavy drinking female partner (Jacob & Bremer, 1986; Wilsnack & Beckman, 1984). However, MFT studies have not addressed this difficult clinical challenge, so there is no evidence base to support using MFT with such couples. In our clinical experience, such "dual problem couples" may benefit from MFT under certain circumstances. If both members want to stop drinking when they first see the therapist, or if this mutual decision to seek abstinence can be attained in the first few sessions, then MFT may be workable. When only one member of the couple wants to change, it may be better for this person to get individual counseling and MFT may not be advisable.

Research is needed to determine whether MFT improves outcomes for treatment of problem drinkers as it does for alcoholism. A large number of individuals who do not meet diagnostic criteria for alcoholism are, nonetheless, heavy problem drinkers (Institute of Medicine, 1990). Only two studies have examined MFT with problem drinkers, one with positive results and one without. Sobell, Sobell, and Leo (1993) did not find an advantage for adding spouse involvement to a guided self-change intervention. Walitzer and Dermen (2001) found that involving the spouse in treatment led to improved drinking outcome relative to individual-based drinking moderation training for male problem drinkers.

The mechanisms and processes through which MFT produces favorable outcomes need to be examined in future research. For example, greater use by patients and spouses of treatment-targeted behaviors in BCT (e.g., daily behavioral contract, recreational activities) is associated with more abstinence after treatment (O'Farrell et al., 1993, 1998). Studies have only begun to examine this issue and there is much work to be done.

The present review also provides an update on some key conclusions of McCrady's (1989) review. First, she noted that all of the research had evaluated marital rather than family therapy. While the preponderance of studies continues to focus on couples and spouses, studies of family systems therapy involving the whole family (Bennun, 1988; Kearney, 1984; Orchen, 1983) have appeared in the literature. In addition, parents and other family members have been included in some approaches to motivate treatment entry by the reluctant alcoholic (e.g., CRAFT; Miller et al., 1999) and in some behavioral approaches (e.g., Chick et al., 1992). Second, her observation that clinically popular family disease and family systems approaches have little or no empirical support is no longer true. Now there is evidence that the Al-Anon family disease approach meets its goal of improving family members' coping regardless of whether the alcoholic changes his or her behavior (e.g., Nowinski, 1999; Rychtarik & McGillicuddy, 1998). In terms of family systems therapy, the present review found 7 studies, 3 of which showed better results for family systems therapy than for the comparison groups examined. Finally, McCrady's comments about behavioral approaches continue to be true today, namely that behavioral approaches have more empirical support than other MFT methods, but they remain virtually unused in clinical practice (as described next).

Technology transfer research is an important priority to determine whether the effectiveness of MFT in treatment of alcoholism observed in research studies generalizes to community-based clinics and practitioners. Some initial work on this problem has been conducted for BCT. A national survey of substance abuse treatment programs showed that only 27% of the programs used couple-based treatment, 5% used a behavioral approach to couples therapy, and none used the type of BCT shown effective with alcoholics in research (Fals-Stewart & Birchler, 2001). The survey also revealed some barriers to adoption of BCT. Among barriers mentioned were the number of BCT sessions typically delivered, and the need for specially trained staff to deliver BCT. Recent studies have addressed both of these issues. As described earlier, a brief version of BCT produced equivalent outcomes to a more typical extended version of BCT, and both versions of BCT had better abstinence and relationship outcomes than individually-based treatment (Fals-Stewart et al., 2001). In a second study, Fals-Stewart and Birchler (2002) found equivalent outcomes for bachelor's and master's level counselors in delivering BCT when counselors received very close monitoring by expert BCT supervisors. Clearly, work on transportability of evidence-based MFT methods to clinical practice settings is in its infancy, and there is much work to be done.

Implications For Marriage And Family Therapists

MFT clinicians who wish to use evidence-based approaches in their work with alcoholic patients and their families will find some promising methods in this review. These approaches include Al-Anon facilitation to help families cope better, CRAFT to encourage alcoholics to enter treatment, and BCT to support abstinence and repair relationships for alcoholics who have sought help. None of these approaches is currently in widespread use. To assist MFT practitioners with gaining further information, titles in the reference list that may be especially useful in describing these clinical methods have been marked with a double asterisk (e.g., O'Farrell, 1993). For more information on BCT via the internet: go to www.bhrm.org and click on "clinical guidelines," then click on "addiction guidelines" to select BCT information.

Training in evidence-based approaches for MFT students and clinicians is needed. One obstacle is that the most appropriate venue for such training is not entirely clear. Should this training be done in MFT master's or doctoral programs that already have a full curriculum, or in specialized institutes or continuing education programs? Another obstacle is that two of the three evidence-based approaches (CRAFT, BCT) are behavioral approaches while the vast majority of MFT clinicians have strong training and allegiance to a family systems approach. Unfortunately, a family systems approach to treating alcoholism, while influential on a conceptual level, has not been formalized in a manualized treatment and shown in repeated empirical tests to be effective. Perhaps this obstacle could be overcome if leading MFT educators taught their students how to integrate systemic thinking with behavioral methods in clinical practice.

This chapter has documented effective MFT approaches for use with alcoholics and their families. Studies of MFT to help the family and encourage the alcoholic to enter treatment may generalize well to MFT office practice. However, most studies of MFT to aid the alcoholic who has sought treatment were conducted in alcoholism treatment settings or in university-affiliated research clinics. None of the studies were done in MFT office practice settings, so we do not know if the results of the studies reviewed here would generalize to the typical practice of marriage and family therapists. In alcoholism treatment settings and in research projects focused on alcoholism, participants are aware that alcoholism will be addressed in the therapy. In such settings, participants have at least some recognition of the alcohol problem and at least tacit readiness to address the problem. In MFT practice, clients often do not recognize and may not be ready to address the alcohol problem. Therefore, the MFT approaches described in this chapter may work in the MFT office practice setting only if clients have some readiness for changing the alcohol problem or if the MFT practitioner is able to help clients develop such problem recognition and readiness for change.

Overall Conclusions

We reviewed studies of MFT in alcoholism treatment to (a) improve family coping and/or initiate change when the alcoholic individual is unwilling to seek help or (b) aid the alcoholic's recovery and relationships once the individual has sought help.

Studies of MFT when the alcoholic is unwilling to seek help provide a number of findings: (a) 12-step Al-Anon facilitation and referral help family members as intended and believed by its many adherents; (b) the popular Johnson intervention apparently does not work very well to promote treatment entry because most families do not actually perform the confrontation; (c) a variety of methods reduce the emotional distress of family members living with an alcoholic; and (d) the Community Reinforcement and Family Training approach promotes treatment entry effectively and should be disseminated if replicated successfully by another group of investigators.

Studies of MFT to aid recovery when the alcoholic has sought help also provide a number of findings:

1. Evidence supporting behavioral couples therapy (BCT) has grown—

studies show better drinking and relationship outcomes for BCT than for individual treatment, and recent studies show BCT has additional beneficial outcomes (e.g., reduced domestic violence, cost-benefit ratio of 5:1; improved functioning of the couples' children).

2. The disulfiram contract procedure, the type of BCT alcohol-focused behavioral contract with the greatest research support, should be disseminated to the treatment community as part of a BCT treatment package.

3. The Project CALM "sobriety contract" also should be considered for dissemination.

4. Family systems therapy (a) had less drinking than individual treatment or a waitlist control in 2 studies, (b) retained couples with more troubled relationships in treatment better than BCT, and (c) had the first studies to treat the entire family and examine children's ratings of outcome.

5. The first controlled study of a family disease approach did not find an advantage for adding an emphasis on AA and Al-Anon to BCT.

References

References marked with a double asterisk are recommended for clinicians.

Ahles, T. A., Schlundt, D. C., Prue, D. M., & Rychtarik, R. C. (1983). Impact of aftercare arrangements on maintenance of treatment success in abusive drinkers. *Addictive Behaviors, 8*, 53–58.

**Al-Anon Family Groups. (1981). *This is Al-Anon*. New York: Author.

Azrin, N. H. (1976). Improvements in the community-reinforcement approach to alcoholism. *Behaviour Research and Therapy, 14*, 339–348.

Azrin, N. H., Sisson, R. W., Meyers, R., & Godley, M. (1982). Alcoholism treatment by disulfiram and community reinforcement therapy. *Journal of Behavior Therapy and Experimental Psychiatry, 13*, 105–112.

Barber, J. G., & Crisp, B. R. (1995). The "pressure to change" approach to working with the partners of heavy drinkers. *Addiction, 90*, 269–276.

Barber, J. G., & Gilbertson, R. (1996). An experimental study of brief unilateral intervention for the partners of heavy drinkers. *Research on Social Work Practice, 6*, 325–336.

Barber, J. G., & Gilbertson, R. (1998). Evaluation of a self-help manual for the female partners of heavy drinkers. *Research on Social Work Practice, 8*, 141–151.

Bennun, I. (1988). Treating the system or symptom: Investigating family therapy for alcohol problems. *Behavioural Psychotherapy, 16*, 165–176.

Birchler, G. R. & Fals-Stewart, W. (2001). *Use of behavioral couples therapy with alcoholic couples: Effects on maladaptive responses to conflict during treatment*. Poster presented at the 35th Annual Convention of the Association for the Advancement of Behavior Therapy, Philadelphia, PA.

Bowers, T. G., & Al-Redha, M. R. (1990). A comparison of outcome with group/marital and standard/individual therapies with alcoholics. *Journal of Studies on Alcohol, 51*, 301–309.

Cadogan, D. A. (1973). Marital therapy in the treatment of alcoholism. *Quarterly Journal of Studies on Alcohol, 34*, 1187–1194.

Chapman, P. L. H. & Huygens, I. (1988). An evaluation of three treatment programs for alcoholism: An experimental study with 6- and 18-month follow-ups. *British Journal of Addiction, 83*, 67–81.

Chick, J., Gough, K., Falkowski, W., Kershaw, P., Hore, B., Mehta, B., et al. (1992). Disulfiram treatment of alcoholism. *British Journal of Psychiatry, 161*, 84–89.

Collins, R. L. (1990). Family treatment of alcohol abuse: Behavioral and systems perspectives. In. R. L. Collins, K. E. Leonard, & J. S. Searles (Eds.), *Alcohol and the family: Research and clinical perspectives* (pp. 285–308). New York: Guilford.

Corder, B. F., Corder, R. F., & Laidlaw, N. D. (1972). An intensive treatment program for alcoholics and their wives. *Quarterly Journal of Studies on Alcohol, 33*, 1144–1146.

Dittrich, J. E., & Trapold, M. A. (1984). Wives of alcoholics: A treatment program and outcome study. *Bulletin of the Society of Psychologists in Addictive Behaviors, 3*, 91–102.

Edwards, M., & Steinglass, P. (1995). Family therapy treatment outcomes for alcoholism. *Journal of Marital and Family Therapy, 21*, 475–509.

Fals-Stewart, W., & Birchler, G. R. (2001). A national survey of the use of couples therapy in substance abuse treatment. *Journal of Substance Abuse Treatment, 20*, 277–283.

Fals-Stewart, W., & Birchler, G. R. (2002). Behavioral couples therapy with alcoholic men and their intimate partners: The comparative effectiveness of bachelor's and master's level counselors. *Behavior Therapy, 33*, 123–147.

Fals-Stewart, W., & O'Farrell, T. J. (2002). [Behavioral couples therapy increases compliance with naltrexone among male alcoholic patients]. Unpublished data. Research Institute on Addiction, Buffalo, NY.

Fals-Stewart, W., O'Farrell, T. J., & Birchler, G. R. (1997). Behavioral couples therapy for male substance abusing patients: A cost outcomes analysis. *Journal of Consulting and Clinical Psychology, 65*, 789–802.

Fals-Stewart, W., O'Farrell, T. J., & Birchler, G. R. (2001). Use of abbreviated couples therapy in substance abuse. In J. V. Cordova (Chair), *Approaches to brief couples therapy: application and efficiency.* Symposium conducted at the World Congress of Behavioral and Cognitive Therapies, Vancouver, British Columbia, Canada.

Fichter, M. M., & Frick, U. (1993). The key relative's impact on treatment and course of alcoholism. *Psychiatry and Clinical Neuroscience 243*, 87–94.

Fuller, R. K., Branchey, L., & Brightwell, D. R., et al. (1986). Disulfiram treatment of alcoholism: A Veterans Administration Cooperative Study. *Journal of the American Medical Association, 256*, 1449–1455.

Grigg, D. N. (1994). *An ecological assessment of the efficacy of individual and couples treatment formats of experiential systemic therapy for alcohol dependency.* Unpublished doctoral dissertation, University of British Columbia, Canada.

Hedberg, A. G., & Campbell, L. (1974). A comparison of four behavioral treatments of alcoholism. *Journal of Behavior Therapy and Experimental Psychiatry, 5*, 251–256.

Holder, H., Longabaugh, R., Miller, W. R., & Rubonis, A. V. (1991). The cost effectiveness of treatment for alcohol problems: A first approximation. *Journal of Studies on Alcohol, 52*, 517–540.

Hunt, G. M., & Azrin, N. H. (1973). A community-reinforcement approach to alcoholism. *Behaviour Research and Therapy, 11*, 91–114.

Institute of Medicine (1990). *Broadening the base of treatment for alcohol problems.* Washington, DC: National Academy of Science Press.

Jacob, T., & Bremer, D. A. (1986). Assortative mating among men and women alcoholics. *Journal of Studies on Alcohol, 47*, 219–222.

**Johnson, V. E. (1986). *Intervention: How to help someone who doesn't want help.* Minneapolis, MN: Johnson Institute Books.

Kaufman, E. (1985). Family systems and family therapy of substance abuse: An overview of two decades of research and clinical experience. *The International Journal of the Addictions, 20,* 897–916.

Kazdin, A. E., & Bass, D. (1989). Power to detect differences between alternative treatments in comparative outcome research. *Journal of Consulting and Clinical Psychology, 57,* 138–147.

Keane, T. M., Foy, D. W., Nunn, B., & Rychtarik, R. G. (1984). Spouse contracting to increase Antabuse compliance in alcoholic veterans. *Journal of Clinical Psychology, 40,* 340–344.

Kearney, M. S. (1984). A comparative study of multiple family group therapy and individual conjoint family therapy within an outpatient community chemical dependency treatment program. Unpublished doctoral dissertation, University of Minnesota.

Keller, M. (Ed.). (1974). Trends in treatment of alcoholism. In *Second special report to the U.S. Congress on alcohol and health* (pp. 145–167). Washington, DC: Department of Health, Education, and Welfare.

Kelley, M. L., & Fals-Stewart, W. (2002). Couples versus individual-based therapy for alcoholism and drug abuse: Effects on children's psychosocial functioning. *Journal of Consulting and Clinical Psychology, 70,* 417–427.

Kirby, K. C., Marlowe, D. B., Festinger, D. S., Garvey, K. A., & LaMonaca, V. (1999). Community reinforcement training for family and significant others of drug abusers: A unilateral intervention to increase treatment entry of drug users. *Drug and Alcohol Dependence, 56,* 85–96.

Landau, J., Garrett, J., Shea, R. R., Stanton, M. D., Brinkman-Sull, D., & Baciewicz, G. (2000). Strength in numbers: The ARISE method for mobilizing family and network to engage substance abusers in treatment. *American Journal of Drug and Alcohol Abuse, 26,* 379–398.

Liepman, M. R. (1993). Using family member influence to motivate alcoholics to enter treatment: The Johnson Institute Intervention approach. In T. J. O'Farrell (Ed.), *Treating alcohol problems: Marital and family interventions* (pp. 54–77). New York: Guilford Press.

Liepman, M. R., Nirenberg, T. D., & Begin, A. M. (1989). Evaluation of a program designed to help family and significant others to motivate resistant alcoholics into recovery. *American Journal of Drug and Alcohol Abuse, 15,* 209–221.

Logan, D. G. (1983). Getting alcoholics to treatment by social network intervention. *Hospital and Community Psychiatry, 34,* 360–361.

Longabaugh, R., Beattie, M., Noel, N., Stout, R., & Malloy, P. (1993). The effect of social investment on treatment outcome. *Journal of Studies on Alcohol, 54,* 465–478.

Longabaugh, R., Wirtz, P. W., Beattie, M., Noel, N., & Stout, R. (1995). Matching treatment focus to patient social investment and support: 18-month follow-up results. *Journal of Consulting and Clinical Psychology, 63,* 296–307.

McCrady, B. S. (1989). Outcomes of family-involved alcoholism treatment. In M. Galanter (Ed.), *Recent developments in alcoholism: Vol. 7. Treatment research* (pp. 165–182). New York: Plenum.

McCrady, B. S., Epstein, E., & Hirsch, L. (1999). Maintaining change after conjoint behavioral alcohol treatment for men: Outcomes at 6 months. *Addiction, 94,* 1381–1396.

McCrady, B. S., Noel N. E., Abrams, D. B., Stout, R. L., Nelson, H. F., & Hay, W. N. (1986). Comparative effectiveness of three types of spouse involvement in outpatient behavioral alcoholism treatment. *Journal of Studies on Alcohol, 47,* 459–467.

McCrady, B. S., Paolino, T. J., Jr., Longabaugh, R., & Rossi, J. (1979). Effects of joint hospital admission and couples treatment for hospitalized alcoholics: A pilot study. *Addictive Behaviors, 4,* 155–165.

McCrady, B., Stout, R., Noel, N., Abrams, D., & Nelson, H. (1991). Comparative effectiveness of three types of spouse involved alcohol treatment: Outcomes 18 months after treatment. *British Journal of Addiction, 86,* 1415–1424.

Meyers, R. J., & Miller, W. R. (Eds.). (2001). *A community reinforcement approach to addiction treatment.* New York: Cambridge University Press.

Meyers, R. J., Miller, W. R., Hill, D. E., & Tonigan, J. S. (1999). Community reinforcement and family training (CRAFT): Engaging unmotivated drug users in treatment. *Journal of Substance Abuse, 10*(3), 291–308.

**Meyers, R. J., Smith, J. E., & Miller E. J. (1998). Working through the concerned significant other: Community reinforcement and family training. In W. R. Miller & N. Heather (Eds.). *Treating addictive behaviors: Processes of change* (2nd edition). New York: Plenum Press.

Miller, W. R., Meyers, R. J., & Tonigan, J. S. (1999). Engaging the unmotivated in treatment for alcohol problems: A comparison of three strategies for intervention through family members. *Journal of Consulting and Clinical Psychology, 67,* 688–697.

Miller, W. R., & Rollnick, S. (1991). *Motivational interviewing: Preparing people to change addictive behavior.* New York: Guilford Press.

Monti, P. M., Abrams, D. B., Binkoff, J. A., Zwick, W. R., Liepman, M. R., Nirenberg, T. D., et al. (1990). Communication skills training, communication skills training with family, and cognitive behavioral mood management training for alcoholics. *Journal of Studies on Alcohol, 51,* 263–270.

Noel, N. E., & McCrady, B. S. (1993). Alcohol-focused spouse involvement with behavioral marital therapy. In T. J. O'Farrell (Ed.), *Treating alcohol problems: Marital and family interventions* (pp. 210–235). New York: Guilford Press.

**Nowinski, J. K. (1999). *Family recovery and substance abuse: A twelve-step guide for treatment.* Thousand Oaks, CA: Sage.

O'Farrell, T. J. (1989). Marital and family therapy in alcoholism treatment. *Journal of Substance Abuse Treatment, 6,* 23–29.

**O'Farrell, T. J. (Ed.). (1993). *Treating alcohol problems: Marital and family interventions.* New York: Guilford Press.

O'Farrell, T. J. (1995). Marital and family therapy. In R. Hester & W. R. Miller (Eds.), *Handbook of alcoholism treatment approaches* (2nd ed.). (pp. 195–220). Boston: Allyn and Bacon.

O'Farrell, T. J., Allen, J. P., & Litten, R. Z. (1995). Disulfiram (Antabuse) contracts in treatment of alcoholism. In J. D. Blaine & L. Onken (Eds.), *Integrating behavior therapies with medications in the treatment of drug dependence* (NIDA Research Monograph 150, pp. 65–91). Washington, DC: National Institute on Drug Abuse.

**O'Farrell, T. J., & Bayog, R. D. (1986). Antabuse contracts for married alcoholics and their spouses: A method to maintain Antabuse ingestion and decrease conflict about drinking. *Journal of Substance Abuse Treatment, 3,* 1–8.

O'Farrell, T. J., Choquette, K. A., & Cutter, H. S. G. (1998). Couples relapse prevention sessions after behavioral marital therapy for alcoholics and their wives: Outcomes during three years after starting treatment. *Journal of Studies on Alcohol, 59,* 357–370.

O'Farrell, T. J., Choquette, K. A., Cutter, H. S. G., Brown, E. D., Bayog, R., McCourt, W., et al. (1996a). Cost-benefit and cost-effectiveness analyses of behavioral marital therapy with and without relapse prevention sessions for alcoholics and their spouses. *Behavior Therapy, 27,* 7–24.

O'Farrell, T. J., Choquette, K. A., Cutter, H. S. G., Brown, E. D., & McCourt, W. F. (1993). Behavioral marital therapy with and without additional couples relapse prevention sessions for alcoholics and their wives. *Journal of Studies on Alcohol, 54,* 652–666.

O'Farrell, T. J., Choquette, K. A., Cutter, H. S. G., Floyd, F. J., Bayog, R. D., Brown, E. D., et al. (1996b). Cost-benefit and cost-effectiveness analyses of behavioral marital therapy as an addition to outpatient alcoholism treatment. *Journal of Substance Abuse, 8,* 145–166.

O'Farrell, T. J., Cutter, H. S. G., Choquette, K. A., Floyd, F. J., & Bayog, R. D. (1992). Behavioral marital therapy for male alcoholics: Marital and drinking adjustment during the two years after treatment. *Behavior Therapy, 23,* 529–549.

O'Farrell, T. J., Cutter, H. S. G., & Floyd, F. J. (1985). Evaluating behavioral marital therapy for male alcoholics: Effects on marital adjustment and communication from before to after therapy. *Behavior Therapy, 16,* 147–167.

O'Farrell, T. J., & Fals-Stewart, W. (2000). Behavioral couples therapy for alcoholism and drug abuse. *Journal of Substance Abuse Treatment, 18,* 51–54.

O'Farrell, T. J., & Fals-Stewart, W. (2001). Family-involved alcoholism treatment: An update. In M. Galanter (Ed.), *Recent developments in alcoholism, volume 15: Services research in the era of managed care* (pp. 329–356). New York: Plenum.

**O'Farrell, T. J., & Fals-Stewart, W. (2002). Marital and family therapy. In R. Hester & W. R. Miller (Eds.), *Handbook of alcoholism treatment approaches* (3rd edition). Boston: Allyn and Bacon.

O'Farrell, T. J., Harrison, R. H., & Cutter, H. S. G. (1981). Marital stability among wives of alcoholics: An evaluation of three explanations. *British Journal of Addiction, 76,* 175–189.

O'Farrell, T. J., & Murphy, C. M. (1995). Marital violence before and after alcoholism treatment. *Journal of Consulting and Clinical Psychology, 63,* 256–262.

**O'Farrell, T. J., & Murphy, C. M. (2002). Behavioral couples therapy for alcoholism and drug abuse: Encountering the problem of domestic violence. In C. Wekerle & A. M. Wall (Eds.), *The violence and addiction equation: Theoretical and clinical issues in substance abuse and relationship violence* (pp. 293–303). New York: Brunner-Routledge.

O'Farrell, T. J., Murphy, C. M., Hoover, S., Fals-Stewart, W., & Murphy, M. (2002). Domestic violence before and after couples-based alcoholism treatment: The role of treatment involvement and abstinence. Manuscript submitted for publication.

O'Farrell, T. J., Van Hutton, V., & Murphy, C. M. (1999). Domestic violence before and after alcoholism treatment: A two-year longitudinal study. *Journal of Studies on Alcohol, 60,* 317–321.

O'Malley, S. S., Jaffe, A. J., Chang, G., Schottenfeld, R. S., Meyer, R. E., & Rounsaville, B. (1992). Naltrexone and coping skills therapy for alcohol dependence: A controlled study. *Archives of General Psychiatry, 49,* 881–887.

Orchen, M. D. (1983). A treatment efficacy study comparing relaxation training, EMG biofeedback, and family therapy among heavy drinkers. Unpublished doctoral dissertation, Long Island University.

Orford, J., (1984). The prevention and management of alcohol problems in the family setting: A review of work carried out in English-speaking countries. *Alcohol and Alcoholism, 19,* 109–122.

Orford, J., (1990). Alcohol and the family: An international review of the literature with implications for research and practice. In L. T. Kozlowski, H. M. Annis, H. D. Cappell, F. B. Glaser, M. S. Goodstadt, Y. Israel, H. Kalant, E. M. Sellers, & E. R. Vingilis (Eds.), *Research advances in alcohol and drug problems* (Vol. 10, pp. 81–155). New York: Plenum.

Orford, J., & Harwin, J. (Eds.). (1982). *Alcohol and the family.* London: Croom Helm.

Ossip-Klein, D. J., Vanlandingham, W., Prue, D. M., & Rychtarik, R. G. (1984). Increasing attendance at alcohol aftercare using calendar prompts and home based contracting. *Addictive Behaviors, 9,* 85–89.

**Rohrbaugh, M., Shoham, V., Spungen, C., & Steinglass, P. (1995). Family systems therapy in practice: A systemic couples therapy for problem drinking. In B. M. Bongar & L. E. Beutler (Eds.), *Comprehensive textbook of psychotherapy: Theory and practice. Oxford textbooks in clinical psychology, Vol. 1* (pp. 228–253). New York: Oxford University Press.

Rotunda, R., & O'Farrell, T. J. (1997). Marital and family therapy of alcohol use disorders: Bridging the gap between research and practice. *Professional Psychology, 28,* 246–252.

Rychtarik, R. G., & McGillicuddy, N. B. (1998). *Effects of skill training and twelve-step facilitation on posttreatment coping skills in women with alcoholic partners.* Poster presented at the International Conference on the Treatment of Addictive Behaviors, Santa Fe, NM.

Rychtarik, R. G., & McGillicuddy, N. B. (2002). *Reducing violence against women with alcoholic partners.* Poster presented at the Research Society on Alcoholism meeting, San Francisco, CA.

Shoham, V., Rohrbaugh, M. J., Stickle, T. R., & Jacob, T. (1998). Demand-withdraw couple interaction moderates retention in cognitive behavioral versus family-systems treatments for alcoholism. *Journal of Family Psychology, 12,* 557–577.

Siegel, S. (1956). *Nonparametric statistics for the behavioral sciences.* New York: McGraw-Hill.

Sisson, R. W., & Azrin, H. H. (1986). Family-member involvement to initiate and promote treatment of problem drinkers. *Journal of Behavior Therapy and Experimental Psychiatry, 17,* 15–21.

Sobell, L. C., Sobell, M. B., & Leo G. I. (1993). *Spousal support as a motivational intervention for problem drinkers.* Paper presented at the 27th Annual meeting of the Association for the Advancement of Behavior Therapy, Atlanta, GA.

Steinglass, P. (1976). Experimenting with family treatment approaches to alcoholism, 1950–1975: A review. *Family Process, 15,* 97–123.

Steinglass, P. (1977). Family therapy in alcoholism. In B. Kissin & H. Begleiter (Eds.), *The biology of alcoholism* (Vol. 5, pp. 259–299). New York: Plenum.

Steinglass, P. (1979). Family therapy with alcoholics: Review. In E. Kaufman & P. Kaufman (Eds.), *Family therapy of drug and alcohol abuse* (pp. 147–186). New York: Gardner Press.

Steinglass, P., Bennett, L., Wolin, S., & Reiss, D. (1987). *The alcoholic family.* New York: Basic Books.

Thomas E. J., & Ager, R. D. (1993). Unilateral family therapy with spouses of uncooperative alcohol abusers. In T. J. O'Farrell (Ed.), *Treating alcohol problems: Marital and family interventions* (pp. 3–33). New York: Guilford Press.

Thomas, E. J., Santa, C. A., Bronson, D., & Oyserman, D. (1987). Unilateral family therapy with spouses of alcoholics. *Journal of Social Service Research, 10,* 145–162.

Thomas, E. J., Yoshioka, M., Ager, R., & Adams, K. B. (1990). *Reaching the uncooperative alcohol abuser through a cooperative spouse.* Paper presented at the Fifth Congress of the International Society for Bio-Medical Research on Alcoholism, Toronto, Ontario, Canada.

Walitzer, K., & Dermen, K. (2001). Spouse-involvement and behavioral couples therapy produce better drinking outcomes for heavily-drinking men than does individual treatment. In T. J. O'Farrell (Chair), *Behavioral couples therapy for alcohol and drug problems.* Symposium conducted at the 24th Annual Research Society on Alcoholism Scientific Meeting, Montreal, Quebec, Canada.

Wilsnack, S. C., & Beckman, L. J. (1984). *Alcohol problems in women.* New York: Guilford Press.

Yates, B. T. (1994). Toward the incorporation of costs, cost-effectiveness analysis, and cost-benefit analysis into clinical research. *Journal of Consulting and Clinical Psychology, 62,* 729–736.

Yates, B. T. (1999). *Measuring and improving cost, cost-effectiveness, and cost-benefit for substance abuse treatment programs: A manual* (NIH Publication Number 99-4518). Rockville, MD: National Institute on Drug Abuse.

Zetterlind, U., Hansson, H., Aberg-Orbeck, K., & Berglund, M. (1998). *Coping skill therapy, group support and information for spouses of alcoholics: A controlled randomized study.* Poster presented at the International Conference on the Treatment of Addictive Behaviors, Santa Fe, NM.

Zweben, A. (1986). Problem drinking and marital adjustment. *Journal of Studies on Alcohol 47,* 167–172.

Zweben, A., Pearlman, S., & Li, S. (1988). A comparison of brief advice and conjoint therapy in the treatment of alcohol abuse: The results of the Marital Systems study. *British Journal of Addiction, 83,* 899–916.

Author Note

Preparation of this chapter was supported by grants from the National Institute on Alcohol Abuse and Alcoholism (K02AA00234), the National Institute on Drug Abuse (R01DA12189), and by the Department of Veterans Affairs.

Correspondence about this chapter should be sent to Timothy O'Farrell, Ph.D., Harvard Families and Addiction Program (116B1), Harvard Medical School Department of Psychiatry at the VA Boston Healthcare System (116B1), 940 Belmont St., Brockton, MA 02301 or via email to timothy_ofarrell@hms.harvard.edu.

End Notes

1   The following 22 studies were not included in the earlier reviews: Barber & Crisp (1995); Barber & Gilbertson (1996); Barber & Gilbertson (1998); Bennun (1988); Bowers & Al-Redha (1990); Chapman & Huygens (1988); Chick et al. (1992); Dittrich & Trapold (1984); Fals-Stewart & O'Farrell (2002); Fals-Stewart, O'Farrell, & Birchler (2001); Fichter & Frick (1993); Grigg (1994); Keane, Foy, Nunn, & Rychtarik (1984); Kearney (1984); Kelley & Fals-Stewart (2002); McCrady, Epstein, & Hirsch (1999); Miller, Meyers, & Tonigan (1999); Monti et al. (1990); Orchen (1983); Rychtarik & McGillicuddy (1998); Shoham, Rohrbaugh, Stickle, & Jacob (1998); Zetterlind, Hansson, Aberg-Orbeck, & Berglund (1998).

2   In O'Farrell et al. (1985, p. 163), this better positive outcomes finding was described as showing a trend ($p < .10$) toward a significant difference based on inspection of Table I in Siegel (1956, p. 261). For this review, we used SPSS to calculate Fisher's exact probability test and found the result was significant ($p = .040$, two-tailed).

3   We present a more positive interpretation of BCT results than Edwards and Steinglass (1995) did. Their review did not have access to the cost-benefit results favoring BCT over interactional (O'Farrell et al., 1996b). Their review also did not consider (a) overall more positive outcomes (i.e., >95% days abstinent and no separations) for BCT than the other 2 groups during treatment; (b) fewer abstinent days for BCT than interactional during treatment, an important result because patients who did not stay abstinent during treatment had high follow-up costs for rehospitalization and legal system use; (c) findings of less time separated and fewer alcohol-related negative consequences that favored BCT over individual therapy during the 2-year follow-up.

4   In reviewing O'Farrell et al. (1993), Edwards and Steinglass (1995, p. 499) said: "At the end of the RP program, the BCTRP subjects had achieved more abstinent days (94%) than the BCT group (82%), but these differences were not significant." This interpretation was incorrect. As indicated by O'Farrell et al. (1993, p. 658), following a significant Treatment by Time Interaction [$F(3, 171) = 2.76$, $p = .044$], "one way ANOVAs run at each of the four follow-up periods (i.e., post, 3-, 6-, and 12-month follow-up) showed that the BCT-plus-RP group had significantly more days abstinent than the BCT-only control group at 6 month follow-up [$F(1, 57) = 5.16$, $p = .027$] and at 12-month follow-up [$F(1, 57) = 5.07$, $p = .028$]. This result means that, during months 4 to 6 and months 7 to 12 after BCT, alcoholics who received the additional RP had more days abstinent than those who did not receive the additional RP sessions." O'Farrell et al. (1998) provided outcomes from extended follow-ups that showed BCT also had more days abstinent during months 13 to 18 after BCT.

5   Hedberg and Campbell (1974) did not provide statistical analyses of their results. We conduct-ed the analysis presented based on data they provided. Edwards and Steinglass (1995) calculat-ed the chi-square analysis differently and concluded that BFC had significantly better outcomes for all patients and only showed a trend toward better outcomes for those with abstinent goals.

6   Edwards and Steinglass (1995) in their review described the lack of differences among treat-ments on abstinence at 6-month follow-up, but they did not report the other 6-month follow-up results that favored the ABMT group or the 18-month follow-up results reported by McCrady et al. (1991).

7   Edwards and Steinglass (1995) cited Corder et al. (1972) and Cadogan (1973) as showing pos-itive outcomes for family systems therapy. However, the original articles do not mention fami-ly systems concepts. In earlier reviews Steinglass (1976, 1977) described these studies as mul-tiple-couples group therapy and not as family systems studies. Steinglass (1976) specifically noted that the therapy was not carried out by trained family therapists and did not follow fam-ily therapy principles, but rather that the therapy "was carried out by alcohol specialists, firmly grounded in group therapy techniques who were extending their approaches to include family members" (p. 117). Other reviews (e.g., Kaufman, 1985; O'Farrell, 1995; Orford, 1990; Orford & Harwin, 1982) also described this as a couples group study not as a family systems study.

Chapter 6   *Marital Problems*

Susan M. Johnson Ed.D., Department of Psychology, University of Ottawa, Ottawa, Ontario, Canada.

There is a new focus on marriage in North America and therefore a new context for couples therapy. The divorce rate appears to be declining. Present data tell us that 43% of U.S. couples and 37% of Canadian couples who married in 1996 will divorce. This appears to be more positive than a few years ago; however, the negative impact of chronic distress in close relationships, which may not end in formal divorce, is also becoming more explicit, as is the impact of divorce and separation. Since 1960 the proportion of children who do not live with their own two parents has more than doubled, and although there is controversy over the impact of divorce on children, there is no controversy on the negative impact of marital conflict on children (Cummings & Davies, 1994; Tresch Owen & Cox, 1997) and its impact on children's sense of security (Frosch, Mangelsdorf, & McHale, 2000). Social scientists point out that we also have an epidemic of depression and anxiety in our society, linking this epidemic to the loss of "social capital"—that is, a sense of community and belonging (Twenge, 2000). Research has specifically linked relationship distress to clinical depression, especially in women, and to anxiety disorders, such as posttraumatic stress disorder (Whisman, 1999). Research has also confirmed the danger in the lack of positive close relationships; for example, loneliness has been linked to heart disease and reduced immune system responsiveness. Conversely, the positive effects of marriage on health, especially for men, are clear (Kiecolt-Glasser & Newton, 2001). While the divorce rate has diminished then, the price of relationship distress, for individuals and for society as a whole, is clearer and more compelling.

In light of these facts, it is perhaps not so surprising that government, at least in the U.S., is beginning to consider how to actively promote stronger, more stable adult partnerships. It is as if, having considered the limitations and negatives of marriage in the 1960s and 1970s, we are again realizing the long-term benefits of close, long-term relationships and the institution of marriage. The general public also appears to be moving rapidly away from the idea of adult love as a mysterious passion that simply comes and goes. The number of self-help books on relationships disappearing from the bookstore shelves testifies to a new thirst for knowledge about how to actively shape and maintain long-term partnerships. Also, in the academic world, adult love and bonding, which was virtually ignored until very recently, is now a topic of serious study.

In spite of this new climate, if we just consider the number of new outcome studies on different models of couples therapy, one could argue that not much that is new and important has happened since the series of comprehensive reviews were published in the late 1990s (Baucom, Shoham, Mueser, Daiuto, & Stickle, 1998; Bray & Jouriles, 1995; Christensen & Heavey, 1999). However, this review will suggest that, in spite of the relatively small numbers of new outcome studies, a revolution is occurring in the field of couples therapy; a revolution that is addressing, on many different levels, the core issue of research in psychotherapy; namely, the significance of such research to the practicing clinician. The central issue with regard to research in couples therapy is quite simply that we, as researchers, have not made research clinically accessible and relevant enough, and we, as clinicians, have not seen research as an aid and so have not used it. This review then, is written from the standpoint of a clinician who does therapy and also conducts and uses research; that is, from the perspective of a practitioner-scientist (to reverse the usual phrase), rather than from the standpoint of a scientific researcher whose main task is to list studies and evidence in a particular area. Part of this latter stance is an air of complete objectivity. This review is written more from the standpoint that complete objectivity is impossible, that evidence arises in a personal and political context and every way of seeing is also a way of not seeing.

The Effectiveness of Couples Therapy: What Is New?

There have been only a few recent changes in the realm of empirically validated treatments. If we consider that more than one study is necessary for validation and that there must be a study by researchers other than the main proponents of a particular model, only two formally designated empirically supported treatments exist as of yet: behavioral approaches (BMT; Dunn & Schwebel, 1995; Jacobson & Addis, 1993) and emotionally focused couples therapy (EFT; Johnson, Hunsley, Greenberg, & Schindler, 1999). The behavioral approach is based on an exchange/negotiation model of adult intimacy and focuses on negotiating pleasing behaviors and teaching problem solving and communication skills. Cognitive components, such as the restructuring of attributions, have been added to these interventions (Baucom & Epstein, 1990), but do not seem to have enhanced effectiveness (Jacobson & Addis, 1993). The emotionally focused approach is based on an attachment model of adult intimacy and focuses on restructuring key emotional responses and interactions to create a more secure bond between partners (Johnson, 1996).

In addition to these two designated empirically supported treatments, there has been one additional study using insight-oriented couples therapy (IOCT; Snyder & Wills, 1989) and one preliminary trial of integrative behavioral couples therapy, which adds elements such as the promotion of acceptance to traditional behavioral interventions (IBCT; Jacobson, Christensen, Prince, Cordova, & Eldridge, 2000). In this trial IBCT did seem to show superior results to traditional BMT with 70% of IBCT couples reaching recovery at the end of treatment, whereas only 55% of couples receiving BMT reached recovery. In a larger ongoing study, after 26 sessions, 71% of IBCT clients appear to be showing steady significant improvement while only 59% of BMT clients show such improvement and appear to then begin a downward trajectory (Christensen, personal communication).

Given preliminary findings that IBCT was more effective in reducing blaming and promoting softer emotional expression in sessions than BMT (Cordova, Jacobson, & Christensen, 1998), it is expected that the long-term results of the above study will favor IBCT. In general, the linking of in-session, specific results with more distal results at the end of treatment and at follow-up seem to hold promise for outcome research and its relevance to clinicians.

The formulation of IBCT was fostered by the recognition of the somewhat disappointing results that have emerged for BMT over the years (although Behavioral Couples Therapy, BCT, for alcoholism, as described in chapter 5 of this volume, appears to be quite effective). There has also been a need to begin to integrate a focus on affect in behavioral couples therapy. It was also perhaps spurred on by the fact that a central problem in the field of couples therapy has been that the researchers have most often identified themselves as behaviorists while the majority of clinicians identify themselves as integrative, eclectic, or systemic. A central question for this chapter is then: Is there anything new in this field that has not been captured and summarized by the previous reviews mentioned above? And if there is new evidence, does it call into question or help us reconsider our perspective on outcome research, or on the connection between research and clinical practice in couples therapy?

First, we must note that, in terms of outcome research, the field of couple and family therapy (C&FT) has been influenced by generalizations and conclusions based on research in individual psychotherapy. The cliche used to summarize, or even dismiss outcome research is the so-called "Dodo" concept. Some researchers, often those who have collapsed numerous studies into large meta-analyses, believe that, like the Dodo bird, the idea of some models of intervention being more effective than others is extinct and there are no discernable differences in outcome for different kinds of intervention (Shadish, Ragsdale, Glaser, & Montgomery, 1995). Chambless (1996, 2002) pointed out that this concept was based originally on research conducted without carefully defined treatments or subject populations, and overgeneralizations from one large recent study on the individual treatment of depression. Differences among competently conducted therapies may also be small for some problems but striking for others (such as agoraphobia). If treatments are in fact very similar, it is also to be expected that results will also tend to be similar. Others have pointed out that even when different treatments result in similar mean effects, there is good evidence that hidden within these effects are widely disparate outcomes (Howard, Krause, Saunders, & Kopta, 1997). Even in research on individual therapy however, the Dodo cliche now appears to be outdated (although Wampold, 2001, takes a different position). Differences between treatments are found; for example, Foa, Rothbaum, Riggs, and Murdock (1991) and others have demonstrated that prolonged exposure interventions are more effective than interventions such as supportive counseling for trauma survivors.

As the nature of various problems becomes clearer, and as some treatments become more focused and "on target" for the problems they address, it is perhaps easier to find differences in interventions. Couples therapy, as a modality, also has demonstrated differential outcomes. For example, couple interventions have demonstrated better outcomes than medication in the treatment of depression both at the end of treatment and at follow-up (Leff et al., 2000). In a comparative outcome study, EFT was found to be more effective than behavioral problem and communication training interventions (Johnson & Greenberg, 1985), and IOMT was found to be considerably more effective than behavioral interventions at 4-year follow-up (Snyder, Wills, & Grady-Fletcher, 1991) because only 3% of IOMT couples versus 38% of BMT couples were found to have divorced. Differential effects have also been found in family therapy research. Szapocznik, Robbins, Mitrani, Santisteban, and Hervis (in press) found that a particular model of family therapy achieved better outcomes than group therapy with drug abusing adolescents.

Whether we can find differences between treatments may depend on the power, the effect size[1] in statistical terms, of the treatment. For clinicians, considering estimates of the power of treatments across studies and statistics, such as the percentage of recoveries a treatment generates, may help capture in a pragmatic way the usefulness of specific interventions and differences in effectiveness between interventions. In general, the present criteria for classifying treatments as empirically validated make the mistake of not taking sufficiently into account the power of the treatment to address specific problems (Christensen & Heavey, 1999). The power of EFT has been confirmed in a recent meta-analysis of the four most rigorous EFT outcome studies. This analysis found that EFT was associated with a 70% to 73% recovery rate for relationship distress (90% significant improvement over controls) and an effect size of 1.3. This result is considerably better than the 35% recovery rate calculated for couples receiving behavioral interventions (Jacobson et al., 1984), and the 42% recovery rate found for couples receiving a combined cognitive and behavioral treatment (Baucom et al., 1998). It is also superior to the general effect size across past studies of couples therapy, which is estimated at 0.60 (Shadish et al., 1993), and the 0.95 effect size found in a meta-analysis of BMT (Hahlweg & Markman, 1988), as well as the 0.79 effect size found for BMT by Dunn and Schwebel (1995). At the moment, EFT, which integrates a systemic focus on interactional pattern with a constructivist focus on how partners organize their emotional experience and communication, appears to give initial evidence for the best outcome results of the empirically supported couple interventions. However, since effect sizes are strongly influenced by mediators like the choice of instruments employed, the allegiance of the investigators, and the talent of the therapists, one must be cautious about drawing firm conclusions based on comparisons of effect sizes from disparate studies.

Issues With Relating Outcome Research To Practice

Even if interventions can be differentiated in terms of effectiveness, there have been questions as to the purity or rigor of the research setting as it relates to the pragmatism of practice. Some have argued that the couples seen in research are not the same as couples seen in everyday practice, that is, couples with multiple problems. The experience of this researcher is that there is very little difference between the couples in research projects and couples in clinical practice (even if I would like them to be and give them more intake questionnaires). As Chambless (1996) states, "pure cases are not numerous" (p. 233). Many efficacy studies do not exclude clients with multiple problems, and many include clients with severe comorbidity and histories of previous failed treatments (Jacobson & Christensen, 1996; Wilson, 1998b). There is the necessity, in studies and in practice, to make clinical decisions about the sequencing and integration of treatments. For example, do you send a client for individual therapy for posttraumatic stress disorder (PTSD) before or after using couples therapy to create safety in her marriage? (Johnson, 2002). Well, it depends on the client.

A more relevant issue, which is not emphasized in the literature, and is perhaps more pertinent, is that in research projects therapists are usually well supervised. This then colors intervention and, it can be argued, optimizes results. We should consider then that research may offer us a "best case" scenario as regards outcome, rather than an everyday scenario. This is particularly true in areas in which training is limited and therapists are forced to learn using only written materials: To learn therapy relying only on a book is like learning ballet from a book—extremely difficult. These kinds of issues have resulted in a call for effectiveness research rather than efficacy studies. However, Christensen and Heavey (1999) pointed out that in fact effectiveness research is usually of poor quality, uses retrospective data and select samples, and that it may be better to conduct more clinical efficacy trials in more naturalistic settings.

Another issue addressed in the literature is the use of treatment manuals in research studies and how such manuals translate into clinical practice. The controversy over treatment manuals seems to minimize the clinical realities of the research context. In fact, unless interventions are one-dimensional and narrowly focused on one symptom and so can be truly formulaic, manuals simply offer a prototype and a guide to the focus and structure of therapy. All cooks use basic recipes and also think of a meal as a unique work of art. Manuals offer a way of seeing and a map for intervention; they do not reduce the multidimensional drama of conducting therapy to a "paint by numbers" task. They are also more self-correcting and flexible than is often assumed (Wilson, 1998a), while clinical practice is somewhat less self-correcting (Kendall, Kipnis, & Otto-Salaj, 1992). The focus promoted by the use of a manual also facilitates clients' active engagement. Controlled outcome studies using manuals typically report very high levels of therapeutic alliance. If treatment is to become more collaborative it is important to be able to share with clients what the therapist is doing and the rationale behind interventions. In fact, manual based therapy does not impair the practice of the skilled practitioner, but it does tend to improve training (Moras 1993) and raise the level of performance of less expert practitioners (Craighead & Craighead, 1998). A recent study in which beginning therapists implemented a manual-based EFT intervention in only eight sessions still found EFT to be effective (Denton, Burleson, Clark, Rodriguez, & Hobbs, 2000), albeit with a higher dropout rate than usual. Perhaps most importantly, manual-based treatments do not, as has been suggested, impede the development of innovative clinical strategies. On the contrary, knowing what it is you do tends to help you question, study nonresponders, and add to and reshape interventions, as happened in the case of the delineation of the attachment injuries that can block recovery in EFT (Johnson, Makinen, & Millikin, 2001). Accountability spurs on innovation. However, there does seem to be a need to ensure that manuals are "therapist friendly," that they attend to nonspecifics, such as how to engage the client in therapy, and above all, that manuals specify the critical components of change and how to shape them. For example, a recent study on EFT (Bradley & Furrow, in press) found that specific EFT interventions, such as heightening affect, were associated with clients completing a key change event in EFT. This information is now being used to improve the training of EFT therapists.

The Stability of Treatment Effects

Do we have any new data on the stability of treatment effects? Relapse has been identified as a particular issue of concern for couples therapy as a modality for over a decade (Jacobson & Addis, 1993). Dunn and Schwebel (1995) in their meta-analysis found that IOMT was more effective at follow-up than BMT or cognitive behavioral marital therapy (CBT); however, they grouped results from EFT studies with the IOMT study in this analysis, even though these interventions differ. A follow-up study on the effects of EFT with the maritally distressed parents of chronically ill children, who are under recurring stress and at particular risk for distress and divorce (Quittner & DiGirolamo, 1998), found treatment results on marital satisfaction and intimacy level to be stable or even enhanced after 2 years (Clothier, Manion, Walker, & Johnson, in press). It is interesting to speculate as to why results may be more stable for couples treated with EFT, even in a stressed population. Attachment needs for comfort and reassuring connection are particularly salient during times of stress. Facing such stress tends to pull couples apart, unless partners can respond with secure bonding interactions that mitigate stress. This bonding is the focus of EFT interventions. Each stress event may then be an occasion for the creation of greater trust and security and continue to enhance satisfaction. The addressing of "latent affective components" of distress in IOMT and EFT may also enhance their long-term effectiveness (Snyder et al., 1991).

Who Benefits From Therapy—Or How Can We Predict Success?

In terms of general contrasts between predictors of success in EFT and BMT, the best predictor of success in BMT appears to be initial level of distress; this variable is estimated to account for up to 46% of outcome variance. The more distressed couples are at the beginning of BMT, the more distressed they are at the end. The best predictor of success in EFT appears to be the female partner's belief that her partner still cares for her, and initial distress was not found to be a powerful predictor of outcome variance. Studies found that it is harder to treat older couples and traditional couples using BMT, whereas EFT seems to work better for couples over 35 and traditionality was not found to impact outcome (Jacobson & Addis, 1993; Johnson & Talitman, 1997; Whisman & Jacobson, 1990). EFT has also been found to work well for low income and low education level couples (Denton et al., 2000), and for couples when husbands were rated as "inexpressive" by their spouse (Johnson & Talitman, 1997). Snyder et al. (1991) found that problem solving during a conflict resolution exercise in IOMT predicted higher marital instability. This may imply that superficial, instrumental, report-oriented conversations may impede the emotional engagement necessary for relationship repair. This fits with research on the active ingredients of EFT in which depth of emotional experiencing in key sessions was associated with the completion of change events (Johnson & Greenberg, 1988).

For most forms of couple intervention, the basic contraindication is violence in the relationship. In general, risk factors and treatment feasibility issues regarding violence in close relationships are beginning to be addressed (Bograd & Mederos, 1999). Different forms of violent behavior are becoming delineated, for example "hot" violence versus a "cold" more calculated form of violence, to assess which are more amenable to treatment (Jacobson & Gottman, 1998), and violent behavior is being placed in the context of general relationship theories, such as attachment theory (Holtzworth-Munroe, Stuart, & Hutchinson, 1997). Violent men have been found to be more insecure, more dependent on and preoccupied with their wives, and less trusting and comfortable with closeness. The link between abusive family relationships and various forms of serious dysfunction is also becoming more delineated (Allen, 2001).

Do clients in better therapeutic relationships achieve better outcomes? The impact of general therapist factors on outcome in individual therapy has been studied extensively. For example, in an exhaustive review, Orlinsky, Grawe, and Parks (1994) identified factors such as therapist credibility, skill, collaborativeness, empathic understanding, affirmation of the client, and attention to the client's affective experience as associated with outcome. The quality of the therapeutic alliance is generally considered to be a key factor in successful intervention; generally, it appears to account for about 9% to 10% of the variance in outcome (Beutler, 2002; Horvath & Symonds, 1991). In an EFT study, the alliance was differentiated into three elements: bond, task relevance, and engagement and goal agreement. The best predictor of success was the task element of the alliance. This implies that EFT works best when the couple finds working with emotions and patterns of attachment responses relevant and engaging (Johnson & Talitman, 1997). In this study, the quality of the alliance accounted for 22% of the variance in satisfaction at the end of therapy. However, the alliance may be more important and more subject to change at different times in therapy and with different kinds of clients. Research on individual therapy has found that when therapists do not correct problems in the alliance and instead become focused on techniques, such as focusing on distorted cognitions, the alliance worsens and negatively impacts outcome (Castonguay, Goldfried, Wiser, Rue, & Hayes, 1996).

In this area, there is a need for research on predictors of success in more diverse populations, and on how to maximize the effectiveness of therapy for these populations. For example, there is still very limited clinical literature on gay couples (Igartua, 1998; Mohr, 1999), and no clinical studies have been conducted with this population. The little research that exists indicates that similarities between opposite-sex and same-sex couples far outweigh differences, but that where differences exist, they may favor gay relationships. Green, Bettinger, and Zacks (1996) reported that lesbian couples are on the whole closer, happier, and more flexible in their relationships. Gay relationships tend to be more egalitarian and, rather than being "fused," tend to foster self-actualization. There is also very little data on the difficulties of interracial couples (Crohn, 1998) or on how immigrants, many of whom began their partnerships as arranged marriages, fare in couples therapy and how we can tailor interventions to their needs (Sluzki, 1998).

Four Areas of Growth

Although there are many debates about the role of outcome oriented research in our field, there appears to be a growing general agreement that we have no choice but to become more research based. Those who fund our profession and the credibility and ethics of our profession demand it. As Sprenkle noted in his 2001 address at the American Association for Marriage and Family Therapy (AAMFT) conference in Nashville, research enables us to grow as a discipline, and not be characterized by "competing sects led by feuding charismatic prophets." However, outcome research is only one form of inquiry and there have been many developments, perhaps revolutionary developments, in other areas in the last few years.

Specifically, there have been great strides in four areas. The first of these areas is the continuing research into the nature of clinical problems that has continued to refine our understanding of the nature of relationship distress. Mapping the territory of distress offers us the chance to be more "on target" and so intervene with maximum effectiveness. The second area is research into the process of change in therapy. This kind of research does much to bridge the gap between clinician and researcher. Beutler, Williams, and Wakefield (1993) found that the most strongly endorsed clinician request was for research studies that focus on therapist and/or client behaviors leading to important moments of change during therapy. The third developing area is the application of couples therapy as an effective treatment for individual disorders. The essence of the systemic perspective is the belief that people and their problems are best understood and best treated in their interpersonal context, so this kind of research makes ultimate sense to couple and family therapists. More than this however, there is a growing recognition that couples therapy, linking self and family system as it does, has enormous potential to create positive shifts on multiple levels, in individuals, in adult partnerships, and in key family interactions. The fourth area of growth here is that couple and family therapy is becoming less isolationist, and is beginning to integrate general research from clinical psychology, human development, and social psychology to inform, guide, and evaluate interventions. Such research can help couple therapists understand the processes that perpetuate dysfunctional coping, offer a conceptual map of key elements in a relationship, and understand the nature of change. For example, there is more and more focus in the couple and family field on the negative impacts of emotional disconnection, between adolescents and parents and between adult partners, and the potential for change when fears about rejection and abandonment are shared (Liddle et al., 2000). This kind of research appears to be fueling a shift from an overriding concern with issues such as differentiation and enmeshment in C&FT into a focus on elements such as nurturance, often neglected in our field (Mackay, 1996), and the quality of emotional engagement and attachment. These four areas, which we will now examine in more detail, together with the outcome research outlined above, constitute an active revolution in couples therapy.

Research Into the Nature of Relationship Distress

Part of a modality coming of age is being able to clearly delineate that nature of the problems it addresses and use this understanding as a basis for intervention (Johnson & Lebow, 2000). The seminal work on the nature of marital distress conducted by researchers such as Gottman (1994) has continued in the last few years, although the validity of his powerful predictions of divorce has also been questioned (Heyman & Smith Slep, 2001). Recent research has emphasized that support and emotional engagement are key elements of a marital relationship and that these elements can have more power to predict the future of the relationship than conflict behaviors. Pasch and Bradbury (1998) found that wives' negativity when soliciting or providing support predicted relationship outcomes 2 years later. The pattern in this research is clear: Affective tone is more important than the content of dialogue or whether couples can problem solve particular issues. Soothing and support are key factors in successful marriages, and marriages work best when partners can de-escalate the other's negative emotion and when wives, in particular, tend to use "softened start-up" when bringing up issues. The amount of anger expressed or the number of conflicts does not necessarily create relationship distress; however, contempt and defensive distance tend to be more problematic (Gottman, Coan, Carrere, & Swanson, 1998). Research is also helping to delineate when problems will occur, to grasp the critical periods and events in the life of a marriage. Many problems, for example, begin with the transition to parenthood (Cox, Paley, Burchinal, & Payne, 1999) when companionate activities decrease and conflict and marital distress increase. Research can also help us understand what happens to couple relationships after traumatic events such as the death of a child (Oliver, 1999) and how we can best intervene.

A field of scientific enquiry has three levels: description, prediction, and explanation. One of the problems in couples therapy is that without a theory of love to help make sense of the above descriptive research results, the labels we give to phenomena may be arbitrary. Stanley, Bradbury, and Markman (2000) suggested that it is not the husband's refusing his wife's "influence" (as Gottman suggests) that is the key factor in predicting marital satisfaction; it is whether husbands are able to tolerate and respond to their wives' expressions of negative affect, which are often also bids for support. This interpretation and indeed much of these data seems to this practitioner-scientist to fit elegantly with, and is best understood and explained by, an attachment perspective on love. This perspective focuses precisely on emotional engagement and responsiveness as the foundation for stable connection, and views many complaints as attachment "protest" aimed at engaging the spouse. From an attachment point of view, the "positive sentiment override" effect, which is stressed in the research on marital distress and which enables partners to filter negative or neutral behaviors and repair rifts, refers to the confidence a partner has that the other will be responsive when needed and stay close, that is to the level of attachment security in a relationship (Johnson & Best, in press).

As Gottman et al. (1998) suggested, a clear understanding of the nature of marital distress and happiness must be the basis for intervention in couples therapy, rather than models of individual functioning taken from the individual psychotherapy field. As a result of this research, recent models of intervention such as IBCT pay more attention to emotion and to the creation of supportive interactions, such as acceptance. Gottman et al. identified EFT as consonant with his team's research results on the nature of distress in close relationships.

Process Research Into the Nature of Change

In the field of couples therapy, we need to consider not just what to change but how change occurs (Goldfried & Wolfe, 1996). This can be done in many different ways. We can examine how clients see change, or how specific common interventions seem to impact the change process, or how specific change events occur in key sessions in a particular model, and how clients complete key change tasks.

Client perceptions of change. Research incorporating the client's perceptions of the change process is only just beginning. Recent research into clients' perceptions of specific pivotal moments of change in eclectic sessions of couples therapy using videotapes, transcripts, and interviews suggest that such moments are highly personal and idiosyncratic for each spouse, and that repetition is important. This research (Helmeke & Sprenkle, 2000) suggests more specifically that, "focusing and refocusing on subject matter that is emotionally important to the client seems to be the key factor related to the occurrence of pivotal moments" (p. 480). Christensen, Russell, Miller, and Peterson (1998) found that clients were able to identify changes in affect and how it influenced communication, as well as changes in cognition, and general communication patterns. Clients spoke about how important talking about needs was and how new affective experience created new meanings. It would be interesting to use methods applied in individual therapy such as interpersonal process recall (Elliott, 1984) with couples to ascertain in more detail how they perceive change events in therapy. Couples therapists, under the influence of postmodern ideas, appear to be moving into a more collaborative stance with clients, rather than a neutral or expert stance. This kind of process research makes clients collaborative partners in the development of interventions.

Common interventions. Is it possible to identify and research common core interventions that cut across models? On a general level, involvement in therapy and collaboration in assignments was found to be the most robust predictor of improvement in BMT (Holtzworth-Munroe, Jacobson, Deklyen, & Whisman, 1989). Tabbi (1996) also suggested that active experiencing and involvement should precede explanation in effective couple and family therapy sessions. In this vein, Nichols and Fellenberg (2000) examined enactments in family therapy and found that successful enactments (that created positive shifts) were structured by the therapist. In these enactments, the therapist was specific about the topic and how the conversation should go, and the most frequent observed productive way to close an enactment was to describe the problem dynamic that had occurred in the conversation. These authors commented that the process worked best when therapists resisted the urge to preach and teach, and helped clients speak for and about themselves and go deeper into their feelings. Butler and Wampler (1999) also found that couples preferred enactment-based interactions and struggled less in therapy than if the therapist channeled all interactions through him or herself. The above research is more relevant to some models of therapy than others in that some models do not attempt to delve deeper into feelings or to structure engagement in enactments.

Softenings, key change events in EFT, are specific kinds of enactments in which the therapist structures new kinds of interactions that have been found in past research to promote affiliative emotional engagement and positive outcome (Johnson & Greenberg, 1988). Successful softenings are characterized by deepening levels of emotional experience and a movement towards affiliative interactions. As noted previously, recent research (Bradley & Furrow, in press) has examined these softening events in EFT, where critical blaming partners risk and reach for closeness, and identified the most frequent therapist interventions associated with them. These interventions were: heightening key emotional responses; reframing responses, often in terms of attachment fears and needs; and evocative responding to deepen emotional experience. The use of these specific interventions is predicted by the EFT model. However, in the events examined, researchers found that therapists also tended to give a brief image of attachment responses that were just out of the partner's reach, using phrases like, "So you could never. . . ." This has now been consciously incorporated into EFT training. On a concrete level this is an example of how process research can lead into a delineation of therapist behaviors in change events and can then result in the refinement of interventions.

Task performance. If we consider specific tasks in therapy and how they are successfully completed it is possible to formulate key change elements and a change sequence for each task. For example, in family therapy the tasks of resolving conflict (Diamond & Liddle, 1999), or mitigating blame (Melidonis & Bry, 1995), or reframing presenting problems (Coulehan, Friedlander, & Heatherington, 1998) have been examined. In the task of sustaining engagement in family therapy, Friedlander, Heatherington, Johnson, and Skowron (1994) found that acknowledging one's contribution to an impasse, exploring and confiding underlying emotions, validating the other's feelings, and recognizing the benefits of engagement led to new attributions about the other person and new responses. An interesting example of this kind of research in EFT is current investigations into resolving impasses in the change process. This research involves delineating the steps in recovery from traumatic relational experience—termed an attachment injury (Johnson et al., 2001). This research is also an example of a new development in the field towards understanding the critical elements in the general task of forgiveness and reconciliation in couples therapy (Gordon, Baucom, & Snyder, 2000; Worthington & Drinkard, 2000). It is also an example of "progress" research advocated by Pinsof and Wynne (2000), who suggested that we study how change occurs naturalistically—then test and refine to see what processes facilitate such change and how therapists can potentiate this change. Process research that develops and tests theories of change is a clear and direct route to the modification and/or refinement of models of therapy.

In the research on attachment injuries, a task analytic strategy was followed (Greenberg, 1991). First, a marker or cue that a specific task was arising in therapy was identified. In this case, in the second stage of EFT when a partner is about to take a significant risk and re-engage the other partner, a past abandonment or wound arises vividly in the session and blocks risk-taking. The wounded partner draws back from emotional engagement and states some version of "never again." Case examples of clients who managed to work through these impasses were then examined and a sequence of steps associated with success was formulated. These steps were then verified and refined in new cases and are now being tested in a larger study to see if, in key sessions, their presence distinguishes those who resolve these injuries and reach reconciliation from those who do not. Once the sequence of steps of competent performance in this change event is verified, we can then examine the specific interventions that facilitate these steps. Already the preliminary case studies suggest that the resolution of these injuries is associated with factors such as the wounded partner being able to express deep hurts and losses and the other partner staying emotionally engaged and actively responding to these emotions with compassion and comfort.

Studies that link within-session behaviors with different kinds of change processes, such as the creation of pivotal moments and completion of key tasks, have the potential to bridge the gap between research and practice, helping clinicians make decisions about what to do with particular clients at particular points in therapy (Persons & Silberschatz, 1998; Pinsof & Wynne, 2000).

Couples Therapy for Individual Disorders

Individual and relationship problems often occur together and reciprocally impact each other (Halford, Bouma, Kelley, & Young, 1999), and the quality of an individual's relationships clearly plays a pivotal role in many disorders (Fincham & Beach, 1999). Couples therapy can address individual disorders on many levels (Baucom et al., 1998). First, the partner can be used as a coach in treatment focused on the individual; second, the couple relationship as it impacts an individual disorder can be addressed; or third, couples therapy can be used to improve the functioning of the individual and the relationship. There may also be certain disorders that are extremely difficult to significantly improve without the creation of a supportive close family relationship, such as posttraumatic stress disorder (Johnson 2002).

An example of the first level is the use of the spouse as a coach in the treatment of anxiety disorders. Barlow, O'Brien, and Last (1984) found that inclusion of the spouse boosted treatment effectiveness in agoraphobia from 46% to 68%. An example of the second level is the use of a form of conjoint treatment that focuses on violent behavior in male partners. Brannen and Rubin (1996) have used couple interventions that focus on modifying violent behavior, and have been able to demonstrate a reduction of violence in some couples, without putting women at greater risk than if the offenders were in gender-specific treatment.

If we consider the third level, improving couples communication can enhance the treatment of anxiety problems such as agoraphobia and may help prevent relapse (Daiuto, Baucom, Epstein, & Dutton, 1998). At present, couples therapy appears to be generally used as the sole treatment for only one disorder, depression, the so-called common cold of mental illness. The role of relationship distress in the generation, promotion, and maintenance of depression has become more clear and has been linked to an attachment perspective on close relationships (Anderson, Beach, & Kaslow, 1999; Davila, 2001; Whiffen & Johnson, 1998). From this perspective depression is a natural result of the inability to create a secure connection with a primary attachment figure on whom we depend.

This inability evokes loss and a sense of vulnerability and powerlessness, as well as doubts about the innate worth of the self. It is not surprising then that as Weissman (1987) stated, depression is 25 times more likely to occur in those who are maritally distressed. A lack of supportive relationships can also potentiate other stressors or undermine a client's response to individual therapy. There have been several studies that support the use of behavioral couples therapy to reduce depression (Beach, Whisman, & O'Leary, 1994; Jacobson, Dobson, Fruzzetti, Schmaling, & Salusky, 1991), and one study on a couples version of interpersonal psychotherapy (Foley, Rounsaville, Weissman, Sholomaskas, & Chevron, 1989). In general, these studies found that couples therapy is as effective as individual therapy for depression if marital distress is present, and has the added advantage of improving the depressed person's relationship. There is some evidence that EFT also impacts depression (Johnson et al., 1999), and the previously mentioned Leff et al. (2000) study also found couples therapy to be a compelling treatment for depression. Couples therapy can also be separate but integrated into individual therapies for depression (Whisman & Uebelacker, 1999). There is strong evidence that not addressing the marital distress with depressed partners can undermine the effects of individual therapy. If depressed partners are maritally distressed at the end of their treatment for depression, they are at risk for recurrence of depression and negative long-term outcome (Whisman, 2001).

The use of couples therapy to address depression has progressed further than many other areas in which couples therapy is just beginning to be used as a treatment for individual problems or as a key element in this treatment. Research with clinical and community samples demonstrates a clear association between marital functioning and anxiety disorders even when controlling for the effects of comorbidity (McLeod, 1994). The creation of a safe and supportive couple relationship has obvious implications for the treatment of anxiety disorders such as posttraumatic stress disorder (PTSD; Lebow & Gurman, 1995). Research is also helping us understand the systemic implications of individual disorders such as PTSD and depression and how a spouse can become secondarily traumatized as a result of living with a trauma survivor or feel burdened by a depressed partner (Benezon & Coyne, 2000; Nelson & Wampler, 2000). In a multidimensional problem like chronic PTSD, different treatment elements and modalities (such as couple and individual therapy) are best coordinated into an integrated whole (Johnson, 2002). It helps then to have a coherent theoretical map (such as attachment theory) of problems and change processes to facilitate this integration.

As the impact of close relationships on coping with distress and illness becomes more articulated (Manne, Taylor, Dougherty, & Kemeny, 1997), couples therapy is also being seen as a way to help partners cope with physical illness, such as cancer and heart disease (Bultz, Speca, Brasher, Geggie, & Page, in press; Carlson, Bultz, Speca, & St-Pierre, 2000; Schmaling & Goldman Sher, 2000). New research, for example, found that actively processing and expressing emotions enhances the adjustment and health status of breast cancer patients significantly, but only if their social contexts, often a partner, were perceived as highly receptive (Stanton et al., 2000). There is evidence that women with better spouse relationships whose husbands show specific supportive behaviors are protected from exacerbations in rheumatoid arthritis (Zautra et al., 1998), and the impact of marriage on men's health is also clear; for example, men who disclose to their wives after heart attacks were less likely to die, even after controlling for a biomedical index that is highly predictive of prognosis (Helgeson, 1991). The treatment of sexual dysfunction with couples interventions has been addressed in other recent reviews (Baucom et al., 1998). However, one study seemed particularly interesting in that it took a most difficult and complex problem, low sexual desire, and addressed it on many levels. Hurlbert, White, Powell, and Apt (1993) compared a package of partner assisted sexual skills training, a general couples intervention, and orgasm consistency training with a women only counseling group. The combined treatment package was superior to both waitlist group and the women only group on measures of sexual compatibility, desire, and satisfaction. A brief EFT intervention for low sexual desire has been tested, but failed to find significant results (MacPhee, Johnson, & van der Veer, 1995).

Couples therapy is also used as a key ingredient in the treatment of addictions such as alcoholism (see chapter 5), but, as previous reviews have made clear (Baucom et al., 1998), there are only two programs that have been systematically evaluated: Azrin's (1976) Community Reinforcement Approach, and the Counseling for Alcoholics' Marriages (CALM) Project (O'Farrell, 1993). The latter, which has empirical support, focuses on relationship skills, the creation of disulfiram contracts with the spouse, and relapse prevention. Problem drinking couples are characterized by high rates of negative affect expression, few supportive behaviors, and frequent withdrawal in conflict situations. Problem drinking and marital distress then reciprocally reinforce each other (Halford et al., 1999). The CALM program has been found to promote sobriety and influence other key factors such as the prevalence of marital violence in these couples (O'Farrell & Murphy, 1995). These researchers found that the addition of couples interventions to a course of individual therapy reduced substance abuse more, as well as improved marital satisfaction, and prevented relapse (Fals-Stewart et al., 2000; O'Farrell, Choquette, & Cutter, 1998). Of course, some alcoholics will not agree to such treatment programs and/or to couples therapy. There is little research on the necessary or sufficient components of alcohol oriented behavioral couples therapy or tests on mediators of change (Epstein & McCrady, 1998). Interestingly, all of these studies tested behavioral interventions; however, a survey showed that although 27% of programs addressing alcoholism in the U.S. used some form of couples therapy, none used behavioral interventions specifically and only 5% used them at all (Fals-Stewart & Birchler, 2001). Couples therapy has also begun to be used as part of the treatment of drug abusing women, showing promising initial results (Trepper, McCollum, Dankoski, Davis, & LaFazia, 2000), and with drug-abusing men, resulting in longer abstinence and less drug use (Fals-Stewart, Birchler, & O'Farrell, 1996).

As Pinsof and Wynne (1995) pointed out, involving family members in treatment seems to potentiate most other forms of individual intervention. Also for change to endure, it would seem essential that it occur in and be supported in the natural environment (Gurman, 2001).

The Integration of Research From Other Areas

C&FT has tended in the past to be more than a little isolationist. However, as a discipline comes of age it usually becomes more integrative and incorporates research from other disciplines to broaden and deepen its own vision.

One area that has expanded the scope of couples therapy is recent research and writing on gender and feminist perspectives. Research has confirmed that gender-stereotyped roles are bad for relationship stability and satisfaction (Heavey, Layne, & Christensen, 1993), and that in negative marital interactions men tend to withdraw while women demand. Other research has found that gender differences, for example, in conceptions of love, are often less than expected (Fehr & Broughton, 2001). Both men and women seem to hold companionate views of love. Studies have also not found large differences between men and women on key aspects of communication, such as levels of self-disclosure (Dindia & Allen, 1992). What seems to matter for marital satisfaction is not absolute levels of skillfulness, but the similarity in skills between male and female partners (Burleson & Denton, 1992). However, fundamental differences in the content and structure of men and women's self-representations have been found (Cross & Madson, 1997). Women incorporate representations of significant others, while men's construals are less relational. Women are then more attuned to the emotional quality of marital functioning and more sensitive to relational events. This may account for their heightened risk for depression in unhappy relationships. Men and women may also respond differently in therapy. In a gender-based comparison, wives responded more positively to therapist reflections, and husbands responded more positively to reframing (Brown-Standridge & Piercy, 1988). New research also suggests that women handle stress differently than men. Oxytocin, the cuddle hormone (Carter, 1998; Hazan & Zeifman, 1994) released at orgasm and at breast-feeding, seems to also calm women under stress. Rather than fight or flight, oxytocin seems to create a "tend and befriend" response that lowers blood pressure and so promotes health and longevity, as well as resilience through closer relationships. As we understand gender better, we can understand how men and women's responses differ and how we can tune our interventions to their specific needs and sensitivities. Observation of key therapy sessions in EFT suggests that when expressing vulnerability, men speak in terms of performance, failure, and rejection, whereas women speak of being alone and abandoned. This kind of clinical observation could cue more systematic study and consider how different models of intervention deal with this phenomenon. Feminist writers have formulated a gender neutral set of criteria

(Haddock, Schindler Zimmerman, & MacPhee, 2000) to increase personal agency, develop egalitarian relationships and examine gender constraints in therapy, and have addressed whether models of couples therapy are generally consonant with feminist values. Exchange theory, which is the theoretical base of BMT, has been viewed as dissonant with feminist ideas (Wood, 1995), whereas EFT and attachment theory has been viewed as generally echoing feminist values (Vatcher & Bogo, 2001).

Perhaps the very best example of how other areas such as developmental and social psychology can contribute to the field of couples therapy is the recent explosion of research on adult attachment (Cassidy & Shaver, 1999; Johnson & Whiffen, in press). As Anderson (2000) pointed out in her plenary speech at a recent AAMFT conference, we have set out on the vast and troubled ocean of improving distressed primary relationships in a very small theoretical boat. Attachment theory offers to couple therapists a clear comprehensive theory of relatedness that is supported by creative empirical research, is consonant with systems theory (Johnson & Best, in press), has considerable cross-cultural validity (van Ijzedoorn & Sagi, 1999), and has clear, specific implications for clinical intervention. Attachment security—that is, how confident a person is that his or her key attachment figure, such as a spouse, will be accessible and responsive when needed—has been clearly linked to the quality of love relationships (Collins & Read, 1990) and specific factors such as support seeking (Simpson & Rholes, 1994) and conflict behaviors (Simpson, Rholes, & Phillips, 1996). For example, partners who display an avoidant style in close relationships are not generally cool or distant; they are this way in specific contexts, exactly when they or the other partner are anxious and vulnerable. This theory links habitual ways of regulating emotion and models of self to habitual ways of engaging others; it links self and system. Secure attachment promotes resilience and autonomy, and is associated with key relational responses, such as the ability to process ambiguous information effectively, consider alternative perspectives, empathize with others, monitor patterns in interactions, self-disclose openly, and collaborate in problem solving (summarized in Johnson & Whiffen, 1999). There is nothing so practical as a good theory, and attachment theory helps the therapist understand distressed clients' responses; for example, it predicts that when attachment security is uncertain, a partner will pursue, fight, and even bully a spouse into responding to attachment cues, even if this has a negative general impact on the relationship. A good theory can help clinicians understand very specific responses. For example, a recent study found that attachment insecurity is linked to spouses being reactive to more recent events when evaluating a relationship (Feeney, 2002) and that those who use avoidant strategies in close relationships use these strategies particularly when they or the other partner is vulnerable, whereas at other times they may appear as very sociable. A good theory also helps the therapist form general treatment goals and pinpoint which specific responses can transform a relationship. Research into attachment also challenges pathologizing concepts of dependence that have long been part of the C&FT field. Attachment theory implies, in a way that coalesces with empirical data on the nature of marital distress, that for many distressed partners the problem is not one of enmeshment or lack of differentiation, but lack of secure emotional connection.

Conclusions and New Directions in Couples Therapy

If we consider the conclusions of the last major review of couples therapy in the *Journal of Marital and Family Therapy* (Bray & Jouriles, 1995), some of the issues raised are still very pertinent. For example, research still needs to help delineate the special needs of diverse groups of couples from different cultures. Remarriages, in particular, seem to be an important focus for study so we can hone interventions that particularly address special issues in these relationships. The previous review also addressed the issue of relapse prevention, and suggested interventions such as booster sessions in the event that one round of therapy does not last a lifetime. The issue of relapse prevention would seem to be an excellent focus for future research and clinical innovation. It is perhaps an area in which marriage education, enrichment, and therapy can be integrated. This review suggested that, since the previous review was written, the field of couples therapy has grown and become more coherent as a discipline. If, as some commentators have noted, we appear to be heading into a golden era for family therapy, this may be even more true of couples therapy. What must we do to ensure that this occurs?

Liddle et al. (2000) noted that we must keep moving away from a bag of tricks mentality. First, we need coherent theoretical networks that are substantive and empirically tested but not so abstract that they do not generate specific interventions. Such relational theories have been hard to come by. Some behavioral interventions are based on quid pro quo exchange theories. However, research suggests that these kinds of interactions are found only in very distressed couple relationships. Some models of couple interventions are based on theories of enmeshment and fusion that have very little empirical basis. Second, we need more descriptive and process research that attempts to close the gap between clinicians and researchers. In order to close this gap, we must also write research studies in a more accessible manner oriented toward clinicians rather than other researchers (Goldfried & Wolfe, 1996). We can also use different research designs using replicated case studies (Jones, 1993) conducted by clinicians with and for clients to generate hypotheses for larger studies. We must examine the process of change and the successful completion of specific tasks in therapy.

Perhaps we also need to change our mind set regarding research. Research is defined in the dictionary as systematic investigation. Surely, the passion of clinicians to understand problems and shape more powerful interventions can be at least as generative as large research grants and complex statistical analysis. We can then use "bottom up" rather than "top down" research based on observation in therapy sessions to track, examine, and analyze the phenomena of how clients experience their problems and key moments of change. Research focused on key tasks and the steps in the change process can improve manuals (Goldfried, 2000) and specify which therapist interventions facilitate specific steps in change. Teaching clinicians the methods of intensive case study in graduate school and giving such studies a special place in journals would help considerably. The scientist-practitioner model was set out in 1950 at the Bolder conference (Raimy, 1950). Perhaps this model needs to be revised, and more emphasis given to the wisdom of clinicians rather than the rigors and requirements of complex statistical methods that were originally formulated to study samples of seeds, samples of thousands. We do not need to use the model of abstract science as the only guide. We do not need to indulge in "physics envy." We can put the needs of the practitioner first and still be scientists. In a practitioner-scientist model, practice is the beginning and end of the process of investigation. We begin by examining relational processes or in-session phenomena, placing these in the context of theories of relationship and theories of change, analyzing the data and forming conclusions, finally returning to the significance of this analysis for the moment-to-moment process of therapy, the fostering of powerful interventions and healthy functioning.

It is worth considering for a moment why clinicians often do not pour over research journals. The couple and family interventions themselves have sometimes been accused of being too technical, abstract, and detached from the real lives and experience of ordinary people (Merkel & Searight, 1992), and ignoring factors such as emotion, which is also a way of knowing. If this is occasionally true of interventions, it is certainly even more true of many of the descriptions of research methods, analyses, and conclusions in the literature. Also much effort and technical analysis seems to go into telling clinicians what they already know—what they routinely observe in sessions. An example might be the recent arguments about analyses between Gottman and Levenson (2002) and other researchers in *Family Process,* the significance of which turns out to be that some marriages are volatile and may end before other distressed marriages that are more disengaged. On the other hand, some research is crucial and tells us practice oriented corrective and enlightening information. It is useful to realize that until recently nearly all research on marital interaction and many of our interventions were focused entirely on conflict and conflict reduction (Flora & Segrin, 2000; Karney & Bradbury, 1995). However, conflict is by no means the whole story with regards to intimate relationships, so the ending of conflict is no longer the all-encompassing goal for couples therapy.

It is also true that research results can specifically redirect and refine in-session practice. On the macro level, recent research has brought emotion and how it shapes interactions more into focus in C&FT. Again and again, relationship distress is associated with a spouse displaying emotion and the other spouse not responding to this affect (Johnson & Bradbury, 1999). Research on the expression of emotion suggests that simple attention to and expression of emotion can exacerbate distress, unless emotion is recast and restructured (Littrell, 1998). Specifically, this research suggests that a client must remain focused on emotional stimuli long enough for a new response to occur. Such studies confirm the need for a slower pace and repetition in couple sessions in which strong affect is being processed. Other research tells us that using imagery elicits physiological responses that abstract words do not and so promotes engagement with emotional experience (Borkovec, Roemer, & Kinyon, 1995). On a micro level, even general research that is not specifically about therapy can suggest refinements in intervention. Husbands' gaze in positive interactions predicts both spouses' satisfaction (Flora & Segrin, 2000). Reading this study confirmed my inclination to insist that partners turn and look directly at each other to enhance emotional engagement in change events.

What then are some of the key implications of this review for the practicing clinician? First, couple interventions are continuing to be refined and tested and outcomes are becoming more and more promising. Missing elements, such as emotion, are becoming integrated into interventions, although some models remain opposed to such integration (Miller & de Shazer, 2000). There is evidence that we can find differences in how different interventions impact relationships, and I believe that clinicians, who spend much time and effort learning specific models and interventions, will resonate with these findings (Rounsaville & Carroll, 2002). We are beginning to delineate the key differences between research studies and clinical practice and struggle more fruitfully with key issues such as how to help couples create lasting change in their relationships and how to deal with difficult issues such as violence and abuse. We know more about the basic nature of relationship distress and couple interventions are now being used to address "individual" problems, such as depression and anxiety disorders that occur in, and are influenced by, relational realities. Our understanding of gender and the part it plays in defining relationships is expanding, as is our knowledge of the nature of adult love. In general, there is more focus on nurturance, support, and connection, and less on issues such as boundaries and enmeshment. Studies of the change process in couples therapy sessions are increasing and beginning to provide direct guidance for the therapist in his or her efforts to initiate specific change procedures and events. The outlining of pivotal moments of change and key tasks focused on the defining elements of a close relationship are invaluable to a therapist facing a complex interpersonal drama and seeking to renew and restore it.

Given all of the above, this chapter suggests that a revolution is occurring in the field of couples therapy. A new science of relationships is evolving and supporting a renewal of the discipline of couples therapy (Bersheid, 1999). This revolution is much more earth shaking than the "quiet" revolution noted by Lebow (1997), when he spoke of the increasing integration of interventions across different models. The field of couples therapy appears to be in the process of integrating description, prediction, and explanation. Theory, practice, and systematic investigation are beginning to create a coherent whole. If this is to continue and flower, clinicians and researchers need each other; clinical experience is often too unsystematic and idiosyncratic to add to the reliable body of knowledge, but clinicians can engage in systematic observation and so germinate the seeds of further knowledge and research endeavors. Researchers need the "white heat of relevance," the significance and ecological validity of clinical realities (Soldz & McCullough, 2000) to keep them on track and tell them what matters. The final stage in this revolution will be when systematic investigation moves closer to the moment-to-moment magic that is therapy and when practitioners see research as a powerful resource and are inspired by research investigations to do more efficient and effective therapy.

References

References marked with a double asterisk are recommended for clinicians.

**Allen, J. G. (2001). *Traumatic relationships and serious mental disorders*. New York: Wiley.

Anderson, C. M. (2000, October). *The ones we left behind: Family therapy and the treatment of mental illness*. Paper presented at the annual meeting of the American Association for Marriage and Family Therapy, Denver, CO.

Anderson, P., Beach, S. R., & Kaslow, N. J. (1999). Marital discord and depression: The potential of attachment theory to guide integrative clinical intervention. In T. Joiner & J. C. Coyne (Eds.), *The interactional nature of depression*. Washington, DC: American Psychological Association Press.

Azrin, N. H. (1976). Improvements in the community reinforcement approach to alcoholism. *Behavior Research and Therapy, 14*, 339–348.

Barlow, D. H., O'Brien, G. T., & Last, C. G. (1984). Couples treatment of agoraphobia. *Behavior Therapy, 15*, 51–58.

**Baucom, D. H., & Epstein, N. (1990). *Cognitive-behavioral marital therapy*. New York: Brunner/Mazel.

Baucom, D., Shoham, V., Mueser, K., Daiuto, A., & Stickle, T. (1998). Empirically supported couple and family interventions for marital distress and mental health problems. *Journal of Consulting and Clinical Psychology, 66*, 53–88.

**Beach, S. R. H., Whisman, M., & O'Leary, K. D. (1994). Marital therapy for depression: Theoretical foundations, current status and future directions. *Behavior Therapy, 25*, 345–371.

Benezon, N. R., & Coyne, J. (2000). Living with a depressed spouse. *Journal of Family Psychology, 14*, 71–79.

Berscheid, E. (1999). The greening of relationship science. *American Psychologist, 54*, 260–266.

Beutler, L. E. (2002). The dodo bird is extinct. *Clinical Psychology: Science & Practice, 9*, 30–34.

Beutler, L. E., Williams, R. E., & Wakefield, P. J. (1993). Obstacles to disseminating applied psychological science. *Applied and Preventative Psychology, 2*, 53–58.

**Bograd, M., & Mederos, F. (1999). Battering and couples therapy: Universal screening and selection of treatment modality. *Journal of Marital and Family Therapy, 25*, 291–312.

Borkovec, T., Roemer, L., & Kinyon, J. (1995). Disclosure and worry: Opposite sides of the emotional processing coin. In J. Pennebaker (Ed.), *Emotion, disclosure and health* (pp. 47–70). Washington, DC: American Psychiatric Press.

**Bradley, B., & Furrow, J. (in press). Toward a mini-theory of EFT therapist behaviors facilitating a softening. *Journal of Marital and Family Therapy*.

Brannen, S. J., & Rubin, A. (1996). Comparing the effectiveness of gender-specific and couples groups in a court mandated spouse abuse treatment program. *Research on Social Work Practice, 6,* 405–424.

Bray, J. H., & Jouriles, E. H. (1995). Treatment of marital divorce and prevention of divorce. *Journal of Marital and Family Therapy, 21,* 461–473.

**Brown-Standridge, M. D., & Piercy, F. P. (1988). Reality creation versus reality confirmation: A process study in marital therapy. *American Journal of Family Therapy, 16,* 252–260.

Bultz, B. D., Speca, M., Brasher, P., Geggie, P., & Page, S. (in press). A randomized control trial of a brief psychoeducational support group for partners of early stage breast cancer patients. *Psycho-oncology.*

Burleson, B. R., & Denton, W. H. (1992). A new look at similarity and attraction in marriage. *Communication Monographs, 59,* 268–287.

Butler, M. H., & Wampler, K. S. (1999). Couple responsible therapy process: Positive proximal outcomes. *Family Process, 38,* 27–54.

**Carlson, L. E., Bultz, B. D., Speca, M., & St-Pierre, M. (2000). Partners of cancer patients: Current psychosocial interventions and suggestions for improvement. *Journal of Psychosocial Oncology, 18,* 33–42.

Carter, C. S. (1998). Neuroendocrine perspectives on social attachment and love. *Psychoendocrinology, 23,* 779–818.

**Cassidy, J., & Shaver, P. (1999). *Clinical handbook of attachment: Theory, research and clinical applications.* New York: Guilford Press.

Castonguay, L. G., Goldfried, M. R., Wiser, S., Rue, P., & Hayes, A. M. (1996). Predicting the effect of cognitive therapy for depression: A study of unique and common factors. *Journal of Consulting and Clinical Psychology, 64,* 497–504.

Chambless, D. L. (1996). In defense of dissemination of empirically supported psychological interventions. *Clinical Psychology: Science & Practice, 3,* 230–235.

Chambless, D. L. (2002). Beware the Dodo bird: The dangers of overgeneralization. *Clinical Psychology: Science & Practice, 9,* 13–16.

Christensen, A., & Heavey, C. L. (1999). Interventions for couples. *Annual Review of Psychology, 50,* 165–190.

**Christensen, L. L., Russell, C. S., Miller, R. B., & Peterson, C. M. (1998). The process of change in couples therapy: A qualitative investigation. *Journal of Marital and Family Therapy, 24,* 177–188.

Cox, M. J., Paley, B., Burchinal, M., & Payne, C. C. (1999). Marital perceptions and interactions across the transition to parenthood. *Journal of Marriage and the Family, 61,* 611–625.

Clothier, P. F., Manion, I. G., Walker, J. G., & Johnson, S. M. (in press). Emotionally focused interventions for couples with chronically ill children: A two year follow-up. *Journal of Marital and Family Therapy.*

Collins, N., & Read, S. (1990). Adult attachment, working models and relationship quality in dating couples. *Journal of Personality and Social Psychology, 58,* 644–663.

**Cordova, J., Jacobson, N., & Christensen, A. (1998). Acceptance versus change interventions in behavioral couples therapy: Impact on couples in-session communication. *Journal of Marital and Family Therapy, 24,* 437–455.

**Coulehan, R., Friedlander, M. L., & Heatherington, L. (1998). Transforming narratives: A change event in constructivist family therapy. *Family Process, 37,* 465–481.

Craighead, W. E., & Craighead, L. W. (1998). Manual based treatments: Suggestions for improving their clinical utility and acceptance. *Clinical Psychology: Science & Practice, 5,* 403–407.

Crohn, J. (1998). Interracial couples. In M. McGoldrick (Ed.), *Revisioning family therapy: Race, culture and gender in clinical practice* (pp. 295–308). New York: Guilford.

Cross, S. E., & Madson, L. (1997). Models of self: Self-construals and gender. *Psychological Bulletin, 122,* 5–37.

**Cummings, E. M., & Davies, P. (1994). Children and marital conflict. New York: Guilford Press.

Daiuto, A. D., Baucom, D., Epstein, N., & Dutton, S. S. (1998). The application of behavioral couples therapy to the assessment and treatment of agoraphobia: Implications of clinical research. *Clinical Psychology Review, 18,* 663–687.

Davila, J. (2001). Paths to unhappiness: The overlapping courses of depression and romantic dysfunction. In S. R. H. Beach (Ed.), *Marital and family processes in depression: A scientific foundation for clinical practice* (pp. 71–87). Washington, DC: American Psychological Association Press.

Denton, W. H., Burleson, B. R., Clark, T. E., Rodriguez, C. R., & Hobbs, B. V. (2000). A randomized trial of emotionally focused therapy for couples in a training clinic. *Journal of Marital and Family Therapy, 26,* 65–78.

**Diamond, G. S., & Liddle, H. A. (1999). Transforming negative parent-adolescent interactions: From impasse to dialogue. *Family Process, 38,* 5–26.

Dindia, K., & Allen, M. (1992). Sex differences in self-disclosure: A meta-analysis. *Psychological Bulletin, 112,* 106–124.

Dunn, R., & Schwebel, A. (1995). Meta-analytic review of marital therapy outcome research. *Journal of Family Psychology, 9,* 58–68.

Elliott, R. (1984). A discovery oriented approach to significant events in psychotherapy: Interpersonal process recall. In L. Rice & L. S. Greenberg (Eds.), *Patterns of change* (pp. 249–286). New York. Guilford Press.

Epstein, E. E., & McCrady, B. S. (1998). Behavioral couples treatment of alcohol and drug use disorders: Current status and observations. *Clinical Psychology Review, 18,* 689–711.

Fals-Stewart, W., & Birchler, G. R. (2001). A national survey of the use of couples therapy in substance abuse treatment. *Journal of Substance Abuse Treatment, 20,* 277–283.

Fals-Stewart, W., Birchler, G. R., & O'Farrell, T. (1996). Behavioral couples therapy for male substance abusing patients: Effects on relationship adjustment and drug-abusing behavior. *Journal of Consulting and Clinical Psychology, 64,* 959–972.

Fals-Stewart, W., O'Farrell, T. J., Feehan, M., Birchler, G. R., Tiller, S., & McFarlin, S. K. (2000). Behavioral couples therapy versus individual-based treatment for male substance abusing patients: An evaluation of significant individual change and comparison of improvement rates. *Journal of Substance Abuse Treatment, 18,* 249–254.

Feeney, J. A. (2002). Attachment, marital interaction, and relationship satisfaction: A diary study. *Personal Relationships, 9,* 39–55.

Fehr, B., & Broughton, R. (2001). Gender and personality differences in conceptions of love: An interpersonal analysis. *Personal Relationships, 8,* 115–136.

Fincham, F., & Beach, S. (1999). Conflict in marriage. *Annual Review of Psychology, 50,* 47–78.

Flora, J., & Segrin, C. (2000). Affect and behavioral involvement in spousal complaints and compliments. *Journal of Family Psychology, 14,* 641–657.

Foa, E. B., Rothbaum, B. O., Riggs, D. S., & Murdock, T. B. (1991). Treatment of post-traumatic stress disorder in rape victims. *Journal of Consulting and Clinical Psychology, 59,* 715–723.

Foley, S. H., Rounsaville, B. J., Weissman, M. M., Sholomaskas, D., & Chevron, E. (1989). Individual versus conjoint interpersonal therapy for depressed patients with marital disputes. *International Journal of Family Psychiatry, 10,* 29–42.

**Friedlander, M. L., Heatherington, L., Johnson, B., & Skowron, E. A. (1994). Sustaining engagement: A change event in family therapy. *Journal of Counseling Psychology, 41,* 438–448.

Frosch, C. A., Mangelsdorf, S. C., & McHale, J. L. (2000). Marital behavior and the security of preschooler-parent attachment relationships. *Journal of Family Psychology, 14,* 144–161.

Goldfried, M. (2000). Reflections of a scientist practitioner. In S. Soldz & L. McCullough (Eds.), *Reconciling empirical and clinical knowledge* (pp. 17–32). Washington, DC: American Psychological Association Press.

Goldfried, M. R., & Wolfe, B. E. (1996). Psychotherapy practice and research: Repairing a strained alliance. *American Psychologist, 51,* 1007–1016.

**Gordon, K. C., Baucom, D. H., & Snyder, D. K. (2000). The use of forgiveness in marital therapy. In M. E. McCullough, K. I. Paragament, & C. E. Thoresen (Eds.), *Forgiveness: Theory, research and practice* (pp. 203–227). New York: Guilford Press.

**Gottman, J. (1994). *What predicts divorce?* Hillsdale, NJ: Erlbaum.

**Gottman, J., Coan, J., Carrere, S., & Swanson, C. (1998). Predicting marital happiness and stability from newlywed interactions. *Journal of Marriage and the Family, 60,* 5–22.

Gottman, J., & Levenson, R. (2002). A two factor model for predicting when a couple will divorce: Exploratory analyses using 14 year longitudinal data. *Family Process, 41,* 83–96.

Green, R. J., Bettinger, M., & Zacks, E. (1996). Are lesbian couples fused and gay couples disengaged? In J. Laird & R. Green (Eds.), *Lesbians and gays in couples and families: A handbook for therapists* (pp. 185–229). San Francisco: Jossey-Bass.

Greenberg, L. S. (1991). Research on the process of change. *Psychotherapy Research, 1,* 14–24.

Gurman, A. (2001). Brief therapy and family and couples therapy: An essential redundancy. *Clinical Psychology: Science & Practice, 8,* 51–65.

**Haddock, S., Schindler Zimmerman, T., & MacPhee, D. (2000). The power equity guide: Attending to gender in family therapy. *Journal of Marital and Family Therapy, 26,* 153–170.

Hahlweg, K., & Markman, H. J. (1988). Effectiveness of behavioral marital therapy: Empirical status of behavioral techniques in preventing and alleviating marital distress. *Journal of Consulting and Clinical Psychology, 56,* 440–477.

**Halford, K. W., Bouma, R., Kelley, A., & Young, R. (1999). Individual psychopathology and marital distress: Analysing the association and implications for therapy. *Behavior Modification, 23,* 179–216.

Hazan, C., & Zeifman, D. (1994). Sex and the psychological tether. In K. Bartholomew & D. Perlman (Eds.), *Attachment processes in adulthood: Advances in personal relationships, vol. 5* (pp. 151–177). London, PA: Jessica Kingsley.

Heavey, C., Layne, C., & Christensen, A. (1993). Gender and conflict structure in marital interaction. *Journal of Consulting and Clinical Psychology, 61,* 16–27.

Helgeson, V. S. (1991). The effects of masculinity and social support on recovery from myocardial infarction. *Psychosomatic Medicine, 53,* 621–633.

Helmeke, K. B., & Sprenkle, D. H. (2000). Client's perceptions of pivotal moments in couples therapy: A qualitative study of change in therapy. *Journal of Marital and Family Therapy, 26,* 469–483.

Heyman, R. E., & Smith Slep, A. M. (2001). The hazards of predicting divorce without cross-validation. *Journal of Marriage and Family, 63,* 473–479.

**Holtzworth-Munroe, A., Jacobson, N. S., Deklyen, M., & Whisman, M. A. (1989). Relationship between behavioral marital therapy outcome and process variables. *Journal of Consulting and Clinical Psychology, 57,* 658–662.

Holtzworth-Munroe, A., Stuart, G. L., & Hutchinson, G. (1997). Violent versus non-violent husbands: Differences in attachment patterns, dependency and jealousy. *Journal of Family Psychology, 11,* 314–331.

Horvath, A. O., & Symonds, D. B. (1991). Relationship between working alliance and outcome in psychotherapy: A meta-analysis. *Journal of Counseling Psychology, 38,* 139–149.

Howard, K. I., Krause, M. S., Saunders, S. M., & Kopta, S. M. (1997). Trials and tribulations in the meta-analyses of treatment differences. *Psychological Bulletin, 122,* 221–225.

Hurlbert, D. F., White, L. C., Powell, R. D., & Apt, C. (1993). Orgasm consistency training in the treatment of women reporting low sexual desire: An outcome comparison of women only groups and couple only groups. *Journal of Behavior Therapy and Experimental Psychiatry, 24,* 3–13.

Igartua, K. (1998). Therapy with lesbian couples: Issues and interventions. *Canadian Journal of Psychiatry, 43,* 391–396.

Jacobson, N., & Addis, M. (1993). Research on couples and couples therapy: What do we know? *Journal of Consulting and Clinical Psychology, 61,* 85–93.

Jacobson, N. S., & Christensen, A. (1996). Studying the effectiveness of psychotherapy: How well can clinical trials do the job? *American Psychologist, 51,* 1031–1039.

Jacobson, N. S., Christensen, A., Prince, S. E., Cordova, J., & Eldridge, K. (2000). Integrative behavioral couple therapy: An acceptance based, promising new treatment for couple discord. *Journal of Consulting and Clinical Psychology, 68,* 351–355.

Jacobson, N. S., Dobson, K., Fruzzetti, A. E., Schmaling, D. B., & Salusky, S. (1991). Marital therapy as a treatment for depression. *Journal of Consulting and Clinical Psychology, 59,* 547–557.

Jacobson, N. S., Follette, W. C., Revenstorf, D., Baucom, D. H., Hahlweg, K., & Margolin, G. (1984). Variability in outcome and clinical significance of behavioral marital therapy: A reanalysis of outcome data. *Journal of Consulting and Clinical Psychology, 52,* 497–504.

Jacobson, N. S., & Gottman, J. (1998). *When men batter women.* New York: Guilford Press.

Johnson, M. D., & Bradbury, T. N. (1999). Marital satisfaction and topographical assessment of marital interaction: A longitudinal analysis of newlywed couples. *Personal Relationships, 6,* 19–40.

**Johnson, S. M. (1996). *Creating connection: The practice of emotionally focused marital therapy.* New York: Brunner/Mazel (now Taylor/Routledge).

**Johnson, S. M. (2002). *Emotionally focused couple therapy with trauma survivors: Strengthening attachment bonds.* New York: Guilford Press.

**Johnson, S. M., & Best, M. (in press). A systematic approach to restructuring adult attachment: The EFT model of couples therapy. In P. Erdman & T. Caffery (Eds.), *Attachment and family systems: Conceptual, empirical and therapeutic relatedness.* New York: Brunner-Routledge.

Johnson, S. M., & Greenberg, L. S. (1985). The differential effects of experiential and problem solving interventions in resolving marital conflicts. *Journal of Consulting and Clinical Psychology, 53,* 175–184.

Johnson, S. M., & Greenberg, L. S. (1988). Relating process to outcome in marital therapy. *Journal of Marital and Family Therapy, 14*(2), 175–183.

Johnson, S. M., Hunsley, J., Greenberg, L., & Schindler, D. (1999). Emotionally focused couples therapy: Status & challenges. *Clinical Psychology: Science & Practice, 6,* 67–79.

Johnson, S. M., & Lebow, J. (2000). The coming of age of couple therapy: A decade review. *Journal of Marital and Family Therapy, 26,* 9–24.

**Johnson, S. M., Makinen, J., & Millikin, J. (2001). Attachment injuries in couple relationships: A new perspective on impasses in couples therapy. *Journal of Marital and Family Therapy, 27,* 145–155.

Johnson, S. M., & Talitman, E. (1997). Predictors of success in emotionally focused marital therapy. *Journal of Marital and Family Therapy, 23,* 135–152.

Johnson, S. M., & Whiffen, V. (1999). Made to measure: Attachment styles in couples therapy. *Clinical Psychology: Science & Practice, Special Edition on Individual Differences and Couples Therapy, 6,* 366–381.

**Johnson, S. M., & Whiffen, V. (Eds.). (in press). *Attachment theory: A perspective for couple and family therapy.* New York: Guilford Press.

Jones, E. E. (1993). Introduction to special section: Single case research in psychotherapy. *Journal of Consulting and Clinical Psychology, 61,* 371–372.

Karney, B. R., & Bradbury, T. N. (1995). The longitudinal course of marital quality and stability: A review of theory, method and research. *Psychological Bulletin, 118,* 3–34.

Kendall, P. C., Kipnis, D., & Otto-Salaj, L. (1992). When clients don't progress: Influence on and explanations for lack of therapeutic progress. *Cognitive Therapy and Research, 16,* 269–282.

Kiecolt-Glasser, J. K., & Newton, T. L. (2001). Marriage and health: His and hers. *Psychological Bulletin, 127,* 472–503.

Lebow, J. (1997). The integrative revolution in couple and family therapy. *Family Process, 36,* 1–17.

Lebow, J., & Gurman, A. (1995). Research assessing couple and family therapy. In J. Spence, J. Darley, & D. Foss (Eds.), *Annual Review of Psychology, 46,* 27–57.

Leff, J., Vearnals, C. R., Brewin, C. R., Wolff, G., Alexander, B., Asen, E., et al. (2000). The London Depression Intervention Trial: Randomized controlled trial of antidepressants v. couple therapy in the treatment and maintenance of people with depression living with a partner: Clinical outcome and costs. *British Journal of Psychiatry, 177,* 95–100.

**Liddle, H. A., Rowe, C., Diamond, G. M., Sessa, F. M., Schmidt, S., & Ettinger, D. (2000). Towards a developmental family therapy: The clinical utility of research on adolescence. *Journal of Marital and Family Therapy, 26,* 485–500.

Littrell, J. (1998). Is the re-experiencing of painful emotion therapeutic? *Clinical Psychology Review, 18,* 71–102.

**Mackay, S. K. (1996). Nurturance: A neglected dimension of family therapy with adolescents. *Journal of Marital and Family Therapy, 22,* 489–508.

MacPhee, D., Johnson, S. M., & van der Veer, J. (1995). Marital therapy for women with low sexual desire. *Journal of Sex and Marital Therapy, 21,* 159–182.

Manne, S. L., Taylor, K. L., Dougherty, J., & Kemeny, N. (1997). Supportive and negative responses in the partner relationship: Their association with psychological adjustment among individuals with cancer. *Journal of Behavioral Medicine, 20,* 101–125.

Merkel, W. T., & Searight, H. R. (1992). Why families are not like swamps, solar systems or thermostats: Some of the limits of systems theory as applied to family therapy. *Contemporary Family Therapy, 14,* 33–51.

McLeod, J. D. (1994). Anxiety disorders and marital quality. *Journal of Abnormal Psychology, 103,* 767–776.

**Melidonis, G. G., & Bry, B. H. (1995). Effects of therapist exceptions questions on blaming and positive statements in families with adolescent behavior problems. *Journal of Family Psychology, 9,* 451–457.

Miller, G., & de Shazer, S. (2000). Emotions in solution-focused therapy: A re-examination. *Family Process, 39,* 5–24.

**Mohr, J. J. (1999). Same-sex attachment. In J. Cassidy & P. Shaver (Eds.), *Handbook of Attachment: Theory, research and clinical applications* (pp. 378–394). New York: Guilford Press.

Moras, K. (1993). The use of treatment manuals to train psychotherapists. *Psychotherapy, 51,* 8–19.

Nelson, B. S., & Wampler, K. S. (2000). Systemic effects of trauma in clinic couples: An exploratory study of secondary trauma resulting from childhood abuse. *Journal of Marital and Family Therapy, 26,* 171–184.

**Nichols, M. P., & Fellenberg, S. (2000). The effective use of enactments in family therapy: A discovery-oriented process study. *Journal of Marital and Family Therapy, 26,* 143–152.

O'Farrell, T. J. (Ed.). (1993). A behavioral marital therapy couples group program for alcoholics and their spouses. *Treating alcoholic problems: Marital and family interventions* (pp. 170–209). New York: Guilford Press.

O'Farrell, T. J., Choquette, K. A., & Cutter, H. S. (1998). *Journal of Studies on Alcohol, 59,* 357–370.

O'Farrell, T. J., & Murphy, C. M. (1995). Marital violence before and after alcoholism treatment. *Journal of Consulting and Clinical Psychology, 63,* 256–262.

Oliver, L. E. (1999). Effects of a child's death on the marital relationship: A review. Omega. *Journal of Death and Dying, 39,* 197–227.

Orlinsky, D. E., Grawe, K., & Parks, B. K. (1994). Process and outcome in psychotherapy—noch einmal. In A. E. Bergin & S. L. Garfield (Eds.), *Handbook of psychotherapy and behavior change* (pp. 257–310). New York: Wiley.

**Pasch, L. A., & Bradbury, T. N. (1998). Social support, conflict and the development of marital dysfunction. *Journal of Consulting and Clinical Psychology, 66,* 219–230.

Persons, J. B., & Silberschatz, G. (1998). Are the results of randomized controlled trials useful for psychotherapists? *Journal of Consulting and Clinical Psychology, 66,* 126–135.

Pinsof, W., & Wynne, L. (1995). The efficacy of marital and family therapy: An empirical overview, conclusions, and recommendations. *Journal of Marital and Family Therapy, 21,* 585–613.

Pinsof, W. M., & Wynne, L. C. (2000). Toward progress research: Closing the gap between family therapy practice and research. *Journal of Marital and Family Therapy, 26,* 1–8.

Quittner, A. L., & DiGirolamo, A. M. (1998). Family adaptation to childhood disability and illness. In R. T. Ammerman & J. V. Campo (Eds.), *Handbook of pediatric psychology & psychiatry, vol. 2: Disease, injury and illness* (pp. 70–102). Boston: Allyn & Bacon.

Raimy, V. (1950). *Training in clinical psychology.* New York: Prentice Hall.

Rounsaville, B. J., & Carroll, K. M. (2002). Commentary on dodo bird revisited: Why aren't we dodos yet. *Clinical Psychology: Science & Practice, 9,* 17–20.

**Schmaling, K. B., & Goldman Sher, T. (2000). *The psychology of couples and illness: Theory research and practice.* Washington, DC: American Psychological Association Press.

Shadish, W. R., Montgomery, L. M., Wilson, P., Wilson, M. R., Bright, I., & Okwumabua, T. (1993). Effects of family and marital psychotherapies: A meta-analysis. *Journal of Consulting and Clinical Psychology, 61,* 992–1002.

Shadish, W. R., Ragsdale, K., Glaser, R. R., & Montomery, L. M. (1995). The efficacy and effectiveness of marital and family therapy: A perspective from meta-analysis. *Journal of Marital and Family Therapy, 21,* 345–360.

**Simpson, J., & Rholes, W. (1994). Stress and secure base relationships in adulthood. In K. Bartholomew & D. Perlman (Eds.), *Attachment processes in adulthood* (pp. 181–204). London, PA: Jessica Kingsley.

Simpson, J., Rholes, W. S., & Phillips, D. (1996). Conflict in close relationships: An attachment perspective. *Journal of Personality and Social Psychology, 71,* 899–914.

Sluzki, C. E. (1998). Migration and the disruption of the social network. In M. McGoldrick (Ed.), *Revisioning family therapy: Race, culture and gender in clinical practice* (pp. 360–369). New York: Guilford Press.

Snyder, D., & Wills, R. (1989). Behavioral versus insight oriented marital therapy: Effects on individual and interspousal functioning. *Journal of Consulting and Clinical Psychology, 57,* 39–46.

Snyder, D. K., Wills, R. M., & Grady-Fletcher, A. (1991). Long-term effectiveness of behavioral versus insight-oriented marital therapy: A 4 year follow-up. *Journal of Consulting and Clinical Psychology, 59,* 138–141.

Soldz, S., & McCullough, L. (2000). *Reconciling empirical knowledge and clinical experience: The art and science of psychotherapy.* Washington, DC: American Psychological Association Press.

Stanley, S., Bradbury, T., & Markman, H. (2000). Structural flaws on the bridge from basic research on marriage to intervention for couples. *Journal of Marriage and the Family, 62,* 256–264.

Stanton, A. L., Danoff-Burg, S., Cameron, C. L., Bishop, M., Collins, C., Kirk, S., et al. (2000). Emotionally expressive coping predicts psychological and physical adjustment to breast cancer. *Journal of Consulting and Clinical Psychology, 68,* 875–882.

**Szapocznik, J., Robbins, M., Mitrani, V., Santisteban, D., & Hervis, O. (in press). Brief strategic family therapy with behavior problem hispanic youth. In F. Kaslow (Ed.), *Comprehensive handbook of psychotherapy*. New York: Wiley & Sons.

Tabbi, R. (1996). *Doing family therapy: Craft and creativity in clinical practice*. New York: Guilford.

Trepper, T. S., McCollum, E. E., Dankoski, M. E., Davis, S. K., & LaFazia, M. A. (2000). Couples therapy for drug abusing women in an inpatient setting: A pilot study. *Contemporary Family Therapy, 22,* 201–221.

Tresch Owen, M. T., & Cox, M. J. (1997). Marital conflict and the development of infant-parent attachment relationships. *Journal of Family Psychology, 11,* 152–164.

Twenge, J. M. (2000). The age of anxiety? Birth cohort change in anxiety and neuroticism. *Journal of Personality and Social Psychology, 79,* 1007–1021.

van Ijzendoorn, M. H., & Sagi, A. (1999). Cross cultural patterns of attachment: Universal and contextual dimensions. In J. Cassidy & P. Shaver (Eds.), *Handbook of attachment: Theory, research and clinical applications* (pp. 713–734). New York: Guilford.

**Vatcher, C. A., & Bogo, M. (2001). The feminist/emotionally focused therapy practice model: An integrated approach for couple therapy. *Journal of Marital and Family Therapy, 27,* 69–84.

Wampold, B. E. (2001). *The great psychotherapy debate: Models, methods, and findings*. Mahwah, NJ: Erlbaum.

Weissman, M. M. (1987). Advances in psychiatric epidemiology: Rates and risk for major depression. *Archives of General Psychiatry, 135,* 459–462.

**Whiffen, V., & Johnson, S. M. (1998). An attachment theory framework for the treatment of childbearing depression. *Clinical Psychology: Science & Practice, 5,* 478–492.

Whisman, M. A. (1999). Marital dissatisfaction and psychiatric disorders: Results from the National Co-morbidity Study. *Journal of Abnormal Psychology, 108,* 701–706.

Whisman, M. A. (2001). Marital adjustment and outcome following treatments for depression. *Journal of Consulting and Clinical Psychology, 69,* 125–129.

Whisman, M. A., & Jacobson, N. S. (1990). Power, marital satisfaction and response to marital therapy. *Journal of Family Psychology, 4,* 202–212.

Whisman, M., & Uebelacker, L. A. (1999). Integrating couple therapy with individual therapies and antidepressant medications in the treatment of depression. *Clinical Psychology: Science & Practice, 6,* 415–429.

Wilson, G. T. (1998a). The clinical utility of randomized controlled trials. *International Journal of Eating Disorders, 24,* 13–30.

Wilson, G. T. (1998b). Manual based treatment and clinical practice. *Clinical Psychology: Science & Practice, 5,* 363–375.

Wood, J. (1995). Feminist scholarship and the study of relationships. *Journal of Social and Personal Relationships, 12,* 103–120.

Worthington, E. L., & Drinkard, D. T. (2000). Promoting reconciliation through psychoeducational and therapeutic interventions. *Journal of Marital and Family Therapy, 26,* 93–101.

Zautra, A. J., Hoffman, J. M., Matt, K. S., Yocum, D., Potter, P. T., Castro, W. L., et al. (1998). An examination of individual differences in the relationship between interpersonal stress and disease activity among women with rheumatoid arthritis. *Arthritis Care and Research, 11,* 271–279.

End Note

[1]   An effect size allows us to say that average treated couples satisfaction scores will be better than a percentage of those untreated. An effect size of 0.60 means that 65% of treated couples improved. It is essentially the difference between two means when divided by the measurement error in the system.

Chapter 7   *Relationship Enhancement*

W. Kim Halford, Ph.D., Department of Psychology Griffith University, Queensland, Australia.

Howard J. Markman, Ph.D., Department of Psychology, University of Denver, Denver, Colorado.

Scott Stanley, Ph.D., Department of Psychology, University of Denver, Denver, Colorado.

Galena H. Kline, M.A., Department of Psychology, University of Denver, Denver, Colorado.

"Marriage is one of the most nearly universal of human institutions. No other touches so intimately the life of practically every member of the earth's population." (Terman, 1938, p. 1).

I think a man and woman should choose each other for life, for the simple reason that a long life with all its accidents is barely enough for a man and a woman to understand each other; and in this case to understand is to love. (John Butler Yeats)

C ouple relationship education[1] developed from the work of religious marriage celebrants such as priests, rabbis, and ministers who offered brief counsel to marrying couples in the hope of strengthening those marriages (Hunt, Hof, & DeMaria, 1998). In the early 1950s, religious organizations, and in particular the Catholic Church, began to offer structured relationship education programs in a group format for marrying couples (Hunt et al., 1998). In the mid-1950s in the United States (Hunt et al., 1998), Australia (Harris, Simons, Willis, & Barrie, 1992), and other Western countries, secular organizations also began to offer programs. By the late 1990s, between one quarter and one third of marrying couples in the United States, Australia, and Britain were attending some form of relationship education (Halford, 1999; Simons, Harris, & Willis, 1994; Stanley, 2001; Sullivan & Bradbury, 1997).

Most relationship education programs offered in Western countries, with some notable exceptions, have not been systematically evaluated (Halford, 1999; Stanley, 2001). When it comes to the great problems faced by Western countries as the result of marital distress and divorce, there is a legitimate tension between the desire to know more about effective couple relationship education and the desire to act now (Stanley, Markman, & Jenkins, 2002). In this chapter, we examine relationship education as a means of promoting positive couple relationships based on current knowledge, even though our knowledge has major limitations.

Evidence-based couple relationship education is an emerging field. In 1995, the American Association for Marriage and Family Therapy sponsored the last review of the couple intervention literature. In that review, research on relationship education and the prevention of marital problems was mentioned in several articles; however, there was no article specifically devoted to reviewing research on relationship education. The invitation to write the current chapter devoted solely to relationship education symbolizes the creation of a critical mass of research on couple relationship education.

We view couple relationship education as a set of evidence-based tools and principles that complements couple therapy. As a field, marriage and family therapy is faced with challenges in reaching people who need our services. Several of the other articles in this series document how much high-quality couple therapy can help distressed couples. However, we know that in the United States and Australia the majority of divorcing couples (between 80% and 90%) have not consulted a mental health professional (Glenn et al., 2002; Wolcott & Glezer, 1989). In general, people with marital problems were more likely to see a member of clergy for help than a mental health professional (Glenn et al., 2002). Relationship education offers a complementary approach to couple therapy whereby marriage and family therapists' (MFT) expertise can be shared with couples. Furthermore, we suggest that an important way MFTs can broaden their reach to couples is by collaborating with clergy in offering relationship education.

In this chapter we begin by examining what is known about the influences on sustaining positive couple relationships. Approaches to couple relationship education and evidence for their effectiveness are considered. In conclusion, suggestions are offered as guidelines for best practice of relationship education to promote positive couple relationships.

Influences on Couple Relationships

The vast majority of partners entering committed couple relationships report high initial relationship satisfaction (Bradbury, 1998; Glenn, 1998; Markman, Stanley, & Blumberg, 2001), and hope that relationship will be life-long (Millward, 1990). However, on average, relationship satisfaction declines across the first 10 years of marriage, and a substantial proportion of couples endure relationship distress before ending their marriage (Glenn, 1998; Holman, 2001). The divorce rate for first marriages is about 40% to 45% in the United States, the United Kingdom, and Australia, and about 35% in Germany (Australian Bureau of Statistics, 2001; McDonald, 1995; United States Census Bureau, 2002). Data on cohabiting couple relationships are much more limited than for married couples, but suggest that the rates of relationship problems and breakdown are substantially higher for cohabiting couples than for married couples (McDonald, 1995).

Despite the high divorce rates in many Western countries, the majority of married couples remain together all their lives. Furthermore, at any given time in the

United States and Australia, approximately 85% to 90% of currently married people report high to very high relationship satisfaction (Beach, Arias, & O'Leary, 1986; Stanley & Markman, 1997). Most experts agree that a happy marriage affords numerous benefits for individuals (Glenn et al., 2002; Halford & Markman, 1997; Waite & Gallagher, 2000), and that marital distress is a generic risk factor for a variety of child and adult mental health problems (Coie et al., 1993).

Given that almost all couples commence their marriages with satisfying relationships, what enables some couples to sustain continuing high relationship satisfaction, while satisfaction erodes for others? There are over 200 published longitudinal studies attempting to predict couple relationship satisfaction and stability from psychological and sociodemographic variables (for reviews see Bradbury, 1998; Glenn, 1998; Holman, 2001; Karney & Bradbury, 1995; Larson & Holman, 1994). Halford (1999) extended a model proposed by Karney and Bradbury (1995) and suggested that there are four broad classes of variables that impact the trajectory of relationship satisfaction over time: couple interaction, life events impinging upon the couple, enduring individual characteristics of the partners, and contextual variables. Contextual variables refer to the cultural and social circumstances within which couple relationships exist.

The variables described below can be thought of as risk and protective factors that influence the chances of a couple sustaining a happy relationship over time or of heading down the path towards distress and/or divorce. We consider some of these factors to be static, in the sense that they are not likely to change as a function of intervention, and some are dynamic, in the sense that they can be changed in preventive interventions involving relationship education (Stanley & Markman, 1998).

Couple Interaction

Couple interaction refers to the cognitive, behavioral, and affective processes that occur when partners are together. Couple communication has been the most extensively studied aspect of couple interaction. Effective communication predicts relationship satisfaction (Karney & Bradbury, 1995; Markman & Hahlweg, 1993), and observed effective communication in engaged couples predicts stable, highly satisfying relationships, at least over the first 5 to 10 years of marriage (Clements, Cordova, Markman, & Laurenceau, 1997; Gottman, Coan, Carrere, & Swanson, 1998; Markman, 1981; Markman & Hahlweg, 1993; Pasch & Bradbury, 1998). However, there are two caveats to the research on couple communication and relationship satisfaction. First, some aspects of couple communication are predicted by relationship satisfaction, and it seems likely that satisfaction and communication reciprocally influence each other (Noller & Feeney, 1998). Second, the specific communication deficits that predict deterioration in relationship satisfaction are somewhat inconsistent across studies, and there is controversy over what communication behaviors may promote sustained relationship satisfaction (Gottman et al., 1998; Stanley, Bradbury, & Markman, 2000).

It is noteworthy that the communication observed in engaged couples does not correlate with their reported relationship satisfaction at the time (Markman & Hahlweg, 1993; Sanders, Halford, & Behrens, 1999). It seems that communication difficulties do not stop couples from falling in love or forming committed relationships, but sustaining relationship satisfaction is more likely when there is good communication and conflict management (Markman, 1981; Pasch & Bradbury, 1998). For couples that have been married for some time, these same communication assets predict sustained relationship satisfaction and decreased risk of relationship breakup (Clements et al., 1997; Gottman, 1993, 1994; Markman et al., 2001; Notarius & Markman, 1993).

There are a number of other aspects of couple interaction found to predict a satisfying relationship. Holding realistic and flexible relationship expectations about the importance of communication, appropriate methods of conflict resolution, family and friends, and gender roles is correlated with relationship satisfaction (Eidelson & Epstein, 1982) and also predicts satisfaction (Larsen & Olson, 1989; Olson & Fowers, 1986). Attribution of the cause of any relationship difficulties to stable characteristics of the spouse predicts deteriorating relationship satisfaction (Fincham, Bradbury, Arias, Byrne, & Karney, 1997; Fincham, Harold, & Gano-Phillips, 2000). Reporting relationship history with a shared view of events (labeled as a sense of "we-ness"), and emphasizing working jointly to overcome adversity (labeled as "glorifying the struggle"), predicts sustained relationship satisfaction (Carrere, Buehlman, Gottman, Coan, & Ruckstuhl, 2000; Stanley, Whitton, & Markman, in press). Furthermore, the extent to which partners make individual effort to sustain their relationships, which is referred to as relationship self-regulation (Halford, Wilson, Lizzio, & Moore, in press), also is associated with relationship satisfaction. Relationship self-regulation includes attending to and monitoring the relationship, being able to describe influences on the relationship, having goals for the relationship, and taking self-initiated action to enhance the relationship (Halford et al., in press).

An important minority of engaged and marrying couples shows continuing or even escalating verbal and physical aggression in the early years of their relationship (Murphy & O'Leary, 1989; O'Leary et al., 1989). The occurrence of even low severity violence (the most common forms involve pushing, slapping, or shoving) is a predictor of relationship breakup in the early years of marriage (Lawrence & Bradbury, 2001; Rogge & Bradbury, 1999). This less severe couple violence seems to be associated with problems in conflict management within the couple (Holtzworth-Munroe, Meehan, Herron, Rehman, & Stuart, 2000), and the aggression most often is reciprocal (O'Leary et al., 1989; Straus & Gelles, 1986). Such aggression can be the target of relationship education programs (Holtzworth-Munroe, Markman, & O'Leary, 1995). In contrast, more severe acts of violence such as beating up, kicking, punching, and attacking with a weapon most often are perpetrated unilaterally by men (Holtzworth-Munroe et al., 2000). The perpetration of such severe aggression often is associated with risk of injury or even death for women (Browne & Williams, 1993). Even without physical injuries, women repeatedly assaulted by their partners have a high risk of depression, alcohol abuse, psychosomatic disorders, and are high users of the health care system (Cascardi, Langhinrichsen, & Vivian, 1992; Stets & Straus, 1990). Severe violence by men often involves high levels of coercive control, and the men who perpetrate such violence often have strong antisocial or dysphoric personality traits (Holtzworth-Munroe et al., 2000).

Life Events

Life events refer to developmental transitions, and acute and chronic circumstances that impinge upon a couple or individual partners. Relationship problems often are argued to be more likely to develop during periods of high rates of change and stress (Karney & Bradbury, 1995). For example, the transition to parenthood often is associated with a decline in couple relationship satisfaction (Cowan & Cowan, 1992). However, some couples report that transition to parenthood enhances relationship satisfaction and commitment (Belsky & Rovine, 1990; Shapiro, Gottman, & Carrere, 2000).

Couples with more positive couple interaction are believed to be particularly resilient to the negative effects of stressful life events (Markman, Halford, & Cordova, 1997). In fact, successfully supporting each other through stressful events predicts sustained relationship satisfaction (Shapiro et al., 2000). Mutual support through traumatic events, such as severe illness in one partner, is reported by many couples to bring them closer together (Halford, Scott, & Smythe, 2000). Couples who have good communication skills, who have flexible, realistic expectations of relationships, and who view major stress as a shared challenge, are likely to find it easier to negotiate the changes required to adapt to major life events (Freedman, Low, Markman, & Stanley, 2002). For example, newlywed couples that show good communication of mutual support are resilient to negative effects of stressful life events (Pasch & Bradbury, 1998). Thus, similar life events may be associated with increased or decreased relationship satisfaction in different couples, depending upon the couple's capacity to jointly support and cope with those events.

Individual Characteristics

Individual characteristics refer to stable historical, personal, and experiential factors that each partner brings to a relationship (Bradbury, 1995). Many normal personality variations do not contribute much variance to prediction of relationship satisfaction (Gottman, 1994; Karney & Bradbury, 1995; Markman et al., 2001). However, high ability to regulate negative affect (low neuroticism) consistently has been found to predict high relationship satisfaction (Karney & Bradbury, 1997). Moreover, a secure attachment style reflecting low anxiety over abandonment and comfort with emotional closeness also predicts sustained relationship satisfaction (Davila & Bradbury, 2001).

A major risk for relationship distress is psychological disorder. High rates of relationship problems consistently have been reported in populations with severe psychiatric disorder (Halford, 1995), and in people with depression, alcohol abuse, and some anxiety disorders, especially panic disorder and general anxiety disorder (Emmelkamp, De Haan, & Hoogduin, 1990; Halford, Bouma, Kelly, & Young, 1999; Halford & Osgarby, 1993; Whisman, 1999). Relationship problems and individual problems can exacerbate each other (Halford et al., 1999). In addition, certain personal vulnerabilities may dispose people to both psychological disorders and relationship problems. For example, deficits in interpersonal communication and negative affect regulation are risk factors that predict the onset of both alcohol abuse (Block, Block, & Keyes, 1988) and relationship problems (Arellano & Markman, 1995; Clements et al., 1997; Lindahl & Markman, 1990; Markman & Hahlweg, 1993). This common risk factor might be part of the reason for the correlation between marriage and alcohol problems.

Relationship history predicts relationship satisfaction. In the family of origin, having parents who stayed together in a mutually satisfying relationship (DeGraaf, 1991; Glenn & Kramer, 1987; Glenn & Shelton, 1983; Pope & Mueller, 1976) and used nonviolent conflict management (e.g., Burgess, Hartman, & McCormack, 1987; Mihalic & Elliot, 1997; Widom, 1989) predicts relationship satisfaction and stability. A strong couple relationship between one's parents is associated with more positive expectations of marriage (Black & Sprenkle, 1991; Gibardi & Rosen, 1991), and with observable assets in communication and conflict management in couples prior to marriage (Halford, Sanders, & Behrens, 2000; Sanders et al., 1999). Positive expectations and effective communication are likely learned from parents' relationships and subsequently mediate positive adult relationships of the offspring.

In a couple's own relationship history, the longer and better couples know each other before marriage (Birchnell & Kennard, 1984; Grover, Russel, Schumm, & Paff-Bergen, 1985; Kurdek, 1991, 1993), and choosing not to cohabit before marriage (Janus & Janus, 1993; Kline et al., 2002; Trussel & Rao, 1987) are associated with greater reported relationship satisfaction after marriage. In many Western countries (Sweden, France, Switzerland, West Germany, East Germany, the United States, and Canada), premarital cohabitation is associated with high rates of divorce (DeMaris & Rao, 1992; Hall & Zhao, 1995; Kieran, 2002). Premarital cohabitation is also associated with low marital satisfaction (Stanley et al., in press), poor perceived and observed communication (DeMaris & Leslie, 1984), high marital conflict (Thomson & Colella, 1992), higher rates of wife infidelity (Forste & Tanfer, 1996), and high perceived likelihood of divorce (Thomson & Colella, 1992).

It is unclear what causal connections, if any, exist between premarital cohabitation and poor marital outcomes. It could be that the association is an artefact in that individuals who choose to cohabit have certain personal characteristics that make them more likely to divorce (Clarksberg, Stolzenberg, & Waite, 1995).

Alternatively, cohabitation may have a causal impact by pressuring couples who would have otherwise broken up to marry, putting them at risk for later marital dissolution. A third possibility is that some characteristics of the couple relationship itself, such as limited commitment by the partners, might result in cohabitation before marriage. This limited commitment might mediate increased risk of relationship problems. Consistent with this last possibility, recent research suggests couples who cohabit prior to engagement may be more at risk for marital dissatisfaction than those who live together only after making the commitment of engagement (Kline et al., 2002). Decisions about duration of the relationship prior to marriage, and whether to cohabit, are influenced by a wide range of factors including individual characteristics, the views of family and friends, religiosity, and relationship commitment. Any of these variables might explain the observed association between cohabitation and elevated risk of relationship problems.

Context

Couple relationships occur within a cultural context that defines how couple relationships are supposed to be. While there are general assumptions about relationship standards shared across Western cultures, there also are important variations both within and between those cultures. For example, German couples without relationship problems engage in similar levels of verbal negativity as Australian distressed couples (Halford, Hahlweg, & Dunne, 1990), suggesting that greater levels of negativity are more acceptable and less dysfunctional in the German cultural context than in Australia. Partners who differ in their ethnic, racial, or cultural background often differ in their expectations and beliefs about relationships (Jones & Chao, 1997). This diversity in partner assumptions and beliefs can be a source of great strength for a relationship when the partners are able to draw on the wisdom and strengths of different cultural traditions. At the same time, substantial differences in expectations can be a significant source of conflict between the partners (Jones & Chao, 1997). Marriages in which partners have very different cultural backgrounds break down at somewhat higher rates than other marriages (Birchnell & Kennard, 1984; Kurdek, 1991), though the magnitude of this effect is small (White, 1990).

A related issue is the relationship between religiosity and marital satisfaction. Research suggests when both partners attend church regularly they have a slightly lower risk for marital dissolution and report higher marital satisfaction (Call & Heaton, 1997; Mahoney, Pargament, Tarakeshwar, & Swank, 2001). In addition, having similar religious beliefs and activities contributes to marital success (Heaton & Pratt, 1990). Taken with the research presented above on cultural differences and similarity, it seems that couples fare best when they have similar core values and beliefs.

While the partner role is central to most adults in couple relationships, other roles of each partner are part of the context in which couple interaction occurs, and these other roles can impact in a positive or negative manner on the couple relationship. Work often provides extra stimulation and ideas to enrich the relationship, but excessive work demands also can compete for time with the partner (Thompson, 1997). There are consistent findings that approval of one's spouse and relationship by friends and extended family are predictive of better relationship satisfaction and stability (Booth & Johnson, 1988; Kurdek, 1991). At the same time, excessive intrusion by family on selection of dating partners and subsequent mate selection may predict relationship problems (Benson, Larson, Wilson, & Demo, 1993).

Conclusions

A wide range of variables predicts the trajectory of relationship satisfaction and stability. It is known some of these variables interact. For example, poor communication and support has a large negative impact on relationship satisfaction mainly when couples confront high rates of negative life stresses (Pasch & Bradbury, 1998). However, we have little knowledge of how most variables predicting relationship outcomes interact with each other (Bradbury, Cohan, & Karney, 1998). Despite these limitations in our knowledge of prediction of risk for relationship problems, we still can identify couples that are at relatively high risk of future relationship deterioration. Given that a substantial proportion of couples will sustain high relationship satisfaction without relationship education (Halford, 1999), it would seem useful to target couples at high risk of problems in order to maximize the potential benefits of relationship education.

Couple Relationship Education

Approaches to Couple Relationship Education

There is a wide diversity of currently available couple relationship education programs (Berger & Hannah, 1998). Usually these programs are made up from a mixture of four components: awareness, feedback, cognitive change, and skills training. Awareness focuses on the transmission of information, clarification of expectations, and increasing couples' awareness of key relationship processes that influence relationship outcomes. Feedback consists of individualized assessment and feedback to the couple about their current relationship functioning. Frequently the feedback is provided via an inventory. The most widely used inventories are PREPARE (Olson, Fournier, & Druckman, 1996), the Facilitating Open Couple Communication Understanding and Study (FOCCUS; Markey & Micheletto, 1997), and Relationship Evaluation (RELATE; Larson, Newell, Topham, & Nichols, 2002). In these programs, each partner completes a self-report inventory that assesses a broad range of couple functioning dimensions, and the couple is provided with systematic feedback about the results of that assessment. Cognitive change attempts to encourage cognitions believed to promote positive couple relationships. For example, Markman et al. (2001) advocate discussion that promotes commitment to the relationship and benign (nonblaming) attribution of the causes of negative partner behavior.

In skills training, couples receive a mixture of lectures, demonstrations, and audio-visual presentations about key relationship skills, plus opportunities to practice these skills and receive feedback from educators. There are a number of examples of such programs including Guerney and colleagues' Relationship Enhancement Program (RE; Guerney, 1977, 1987; Guerney & Maxson, 1990), Markman and colleagues' Premarital Relationship Enhancement Program (PREP; Markman et al., 2001), the Minnesota Couples Communication Program (MCCP; Miller, Nunnally, & Wackman, 1975), and Practical Application of Intimate Relationship Skills (PAIRS; DeMaria & Hannah, 2002).

The various skills-training programs have a number of content areas in common. For example, positive communication, conflict management, and positive expressions of affection are included in Relationship Enhancement, PREP, and MCCP (Guerney, 1977; Markman et al., 2001; Miller et al., 1975). There also are significant variations. For example, in PREP there are multiple foci of intervention, but a substantial emphasis early in the curriculum is the prevention and remediation of destructive conflict, as this is argued to be central to the prevention of relationship problems (Markman et al., 2001). In Relationship Enhancement, the development of partner empathy receives very strong emphasis (Guerney, 1977), while this has less emphasis in PREP. In the Couple CARE program (Halford & Moore, in press), self-regulation of communication, rather than training specific communication skills, is emphasized. Moreover, programs have changed as research has shed light on what predicts relationship outcomes. For example, MCCP and RE have devoted more emphasis to conflict management while PREP focuses more attention now to commitment, respect, love, and friendship (Markman et al., 2001).

The Effects of Relationship Education

There are many research studies that have evaluated relationship education and enrichment, and there have been numerous reviews and meta-analyses of that evidence (e.g., Bagarozzi & Rauen 1981; Bradbury & Fincham, 1990; Christensen & Heavey, 1999; Dyer & Halford, 1998; Giblin, Sprenkle, & Sheehan, 1985; Guerney & Maxson, 1990; Hahlweg & Markman, 1988; Sayers, Kohn, & Heavey, 1998; van Widenfelt, Markman, Guerney, Behrens, & Hosman, 1997). There is a general finding that most couples that complete competently run pre-marriage education programs report high satisfaction with the programs (Harris et al., 1992). This high satisfaction is evident across programs that include various mixes of awareness, feedback, cognitive change, and skills training (Halford, 1999). When given comprehensive programs with all these components, participants rate the skill training in communication as the most helpful (Stanley et al., 2001). Although high consumer satisfaction is desirable and participant perceptions of the value of various components are informative about face validity, neither of these outcomes demonstrates an effect of relationship education on relationship outcomes.

Only relationship education with a strong skill-based focus has been evaluated in controlled trial evaluations. The pioneering studies of Guerney and colleagues, and Miller, Wampler, and associates, established by the mid-1980s that skill-based relationship education produces large improvements in relationship skills immediately after programs (Giblin et al., 1985; Hahlweg & Markman, 1988). Some immediate, modest improvements in relationship satisfaction also were reported, though many studies found little or no immediate impact on relationship satisfaction (Giblin et al., 1985; Hahlweg & Markman, 1988). Building on these very important early studies, subsequent research from the mid-1980s to the mid-1990s showed that changes in how couples communicate and handle conflict persist over time (see van Widenfeldt, et al., 1997; Silliman & Shumm, 2000; or Silliman, Stanley, Coffin, Markman, & Jordan, 2002, for reviews).

The primary goal of relationship education is to promote long-term relationship satisfaction. However, we have been able to locate 12 controlled trials evaluating relationship education programs for currently satisfied couples that include follow-up assessments of 6 months or more. All these programs have targeted engaged, dating, or recently married or cohabiting couples, and have consisted of four to eight face-to-face group sessions of 2 to 3 hours duration. All of these studies were of skills-based programs, and the studies are summarized in Table 1.

Relationship skills acquired through relationship education are maintained over a period of some years (Hahlweg, Markman, Thurmair, Engel, & Eckert, 1998; Halford, Sanders, & Behrens, 2001; Markman, Renick, Floyd, Stanley, & Clements, 1993), though attenuation of training effects may occur over a 5- to 10-year period (Stanley, Markman, St. Peters, & Leber, 1995). Only five published studies have follow-ups of more than 12 months, and all of these studies have focused on PREP or a variant of PREP. Markman and colleagues found in two studies that skills-based relationship education was associated with enhanced relationship satisfaction or functioning 2 and 5 years after marriage (Hahlweg et al., 1998; Markman et al., 1993). The Markman et al. study also found that across the 3-, 4-, and 5-year follow-ups, the intervention couples reported significantly fewer instances of spousal physical violence than control couples. However, in a third study using a Dutch version of PREP, no intervention effects were evident at 2-year follow-up (van Widenfelt, Hosman, Schaap, & Van der Staak, 1996).

In the Hahlweg et al. (1998) and Markman et al. (1993) studies that showed long-term benefits of PREP, some of these effects (on satisfaction and divorce rates) became evident only after 4 to 5 years. The 2-year follow-up in the van Widenfelt et al. (1996) study might be insufficient to allow enough erosion of satisfaction to occur in the control group such that a prevention effect was

Table 1
Promotion of Relationship Satisfaction and Communication Skills—Summary of Controlled Trials

Authors/Year	Couples (n)	Intervention	Measures	Key Findings
Ridley & Bain, 1983; Avery, Ridley, Leslie, & Milholland, 1980; Ridley, Jorgensen, Morgan, & Avery, 1982	54	Guerney RE	SR of relationship satisfaction & quality. OBS—for 37 couples only—audiotape of couple "request for change" interaction.	RE couples improved in communication and relationship adjustment from pre- to posttest. Increases in communication skills maintained at 6-month follow-up. No follow-up data reported on perceived relationship adjustment.
Halford et al., 2001	83[a]	Couple CARE[b]	SR of relationship satisfaction. OBS—couple communication.	High-risk couples showed sustained gains in communication to 1-year follow-up. High-risk couples receiving Couple CARE showed higher satisfaction at 4-year follow-up than high-risk control couples. Low-risk couples did not benefit from Couple CARE.
Hahlweg et al., 1998	81	EPL[c]	SR of relationship satisfaction. OBS—videotape of couple problem-solving interaction.	EPL couples improved in communication skills and non-verbal positivity from pre- to posttraining, and maintained gains at 1.5-, 3-, and 5-year follow-ups. No differences between groups on relationship satisfaction at posttraining, but EPL couples demonstrate significantly higher relationship satisfaction at 3- and 5-year follow-up.

(continued on next page)

Table 1
Promotion of Relationship Satisfaction and Communication Skills—Summary of Controlled Trials (continued)

Authors/Year	Couples (n)	Intervention	Measures	Key Findings
Markman et al., 1988; Markman et al., 1993	114	PREP	SR of relationship satisfaction. OBS—videotape of couple problem-solving interaction.	PREP couples showed significant gains in communication at posttraining, these maintained to 1.5- and 3-year follow-up.
Miller et al., 1975	32	MCCP	OBS—audiotape of couple interaction over planning task.	PREP couples relationship satisfaction greater at 1.5- and 3-year follow-up. Males maintained higher relationship satisfaction through 4- and 5-year follow-ups.
Renick, Blumberg, & Markman, 1992[d]	24	PREP	SR of relationship satisfaction. OBS—videotape of couple problem-solving interaction.	Compared to controls, MCCP couples significantly improved in communication skills.
Stanley et al., 2001	138	PREP	SR of relationship satisfaction and communication. OBS—videotape of couple problem-solving interaction.	Compared to Engaged Encounter controls, PREP couples increased in communication skills from pre to posttraining. PREP couples showed trend towards increase in relationship satisfaction at 2-month follow-up.

Table 1

Promotion of Relationship Satisfaction and Communication Skills—Summary of Controlled Trials (continued)

Authors/Year	Couples (n)	Intervention	Measures	Key Findings
van Widenfelt et al., 1996	67[e]	"Dutch PREP"[f]	SR of problem intensity, problem solving efficacy, and relationship satisfaction.	From pre- to posttraining, couples who completed PREP delivered by clergy and lay leaders showed increases in positive patterns of communication and decreases in negative patterns when compared to those receiving naturally occurring premarital training. As expected, there were no differences on relationship satisfaction. All couples deteriorated over time on all measures, no evidence of effect of PREP.
Wampler & Sprenkle, 1980	52	MCCP	SR of relationship quality. OBS—audiotape of couple problem-solving interaction.	MCCP couples improved in communication skills significantly more than attention-only and control couples and increased in perceived relationship quality. Increases in perceived relationship quality maintained at 6-month follow-up, but improvements in communication skills were not maintained.

Note. MCCP = Minnesota Couples Communication Project; OBS = observational data; PREP = Premarital and Relationship Enhancement Program; RE = Relationship Enhancement Program; SR = self-report. [a]Stratified into high- and low-risk based on parental divorce or violence. [b]Six-session group program compared to an awareness control condition. [c]"German PREP" plus segment on Christian marriage. [d]Not from original source. Most detailed published report. [e]With history of parental divorce. [f]Plus family-of-origin session detectable from PREP. Also, the couples in the van Widenfelt et al. study were more distressed, older, and had been together for much longer than the couples in the Markman et al. or Hahlweg et al. studies. Perhaps the versions of PREP used in these studies worked best for couples early in their relationship to assist them to avoid negative interaction patterns, and to establish positive couple interaction patterns, but was less successful in helping couples who had been together longer to change ingrained interaction patterns. Unfortunately, as the van Widenfelt et al. study did not report data on changes in observed couple communication, we do not know if PREP changed the Dutch couples' conflict management skills.

Neither the Markman et al. (1993) nor Hahlweg et al. (1998) studies were true, randomized controlled trials. Markman and colleagues randomly assigned couples to either be offered or not offered the relationship education program. Only about one third of couples offered the program agreed to participate. In the Hahlweg et al. study, couples could choose whether to undertake the skills-based relationship education program or a standard church-provided program. Thus, there was self-selection into PREP in both studies.

The fourth study was a randomized controlled trial of a skills-based relationship education program, with collection of relationship satisfaction and stability data at 4-year follow-up (Halford et al., 2001). The relationship education program evaluated was Self-PREP which is similar in content to PREP, but has a self-regulation focus. A unique aspect of this study was that couples were stratified into high- and low-risk for relationship problems on the basis of negative family-of-origin experiences (parental divorce or interparental violence). Couples completing Self-PREP were found to have significantly higher relationship satisfaction at 4-year follow-up than couples in a control condition, but this effect was only evident for couples at high risk of relationship problems. The possibility that relationship education may have differential effects for low- and high-risk couples needs further exploration.

The fifth study is, to our knowledge, the largest trial of any couple intervention, and is an ongoing, randomized controlled trial of PREP delivered in religious settings, settings where most couples who marry are already receiving services (Stanley et al., 2001). To date, 105 religious organizations have been randomly assigned to one of three conditions: (a) PREP delivered by trained clergy (RO PREP), (b) PREP delivered by University of Denver trained psychologists (DU PREP), or (c) naturally occurring premarital relationship education (NO). Early results are that the NO condition couples deteriorate from pre- to postintervention on observed couple communication, while the two PREP groups improve. These data suggest that we can successfully train trainers to use evidence-based programs in community settings and set the stage for widely disseminating relationship education programs (e.g., Johnson et al., 2002).

In summary, there is strong evidence that skill-based relationship education helps couples acquire and maintain relationship skills. There are three studies (two quasi-experimental and one randomized controlled trial) that suggest PREP promotes sustained relationship satisfaction and stability. This is not to say that skill-based relationship education in general, or PREP in particular, is the only effective form of couple relationship education. But PREP and its variants currently is the only form of couple relationship education that has been evaluated in controlled trials for its long-term effects.

The negative findings in one study evaluating PREP suggest that at least the version of PREP used by van Widenfelt et al. (1996) might not be effective for couples with long-established relationships. However, PREP and programs like it are regularly updated based on ongoing basic and outcome research (Stanley, Markman, & Whitton, 2002), and newer variants of PREP might meet the needs for such couples. Alternatively, couple relationship education for couples in longer established relationships may need different emphases than relationship education for couples in the early stages of committed relationships.

The consistent positive findings for the effects of PREP with premarital couples are striking given that there are complex problems associated with longitudinal outcome research. Notably, there often are higher dropout rates from studies for the most distressed couples (usually in control conditions), which suggest that current findings may underestimate true effect sizes (Stanley et al., 2001). In one study the benefit of Self-PREP, an Australian variant of PREP, in sustaining relationship satisfaction was restricted to high-risk couples (Halford et al., 2001). Prevention of relationship distress and breakup is likely to be detected more in high- than low-risk couples, as by definition high-risk are those couples who in the absence of intervention have a high future prevalence of relationship distress. However, even low-risk couples have some risk of future distress, and larger scale trials with greater power than the Halford et al. study may detect benefits in maintenance of relationship satisfaction for low-risk couples. Moreover, there may be positive benefits of relationship education for low- and high-risk couples that have not been assessed adequately because the measures of relationship satisfaction used in existing evaluations have a heavy emphasis upon problems. Specifically, the Dyadic Adjustment Scale (DAS; Spanier, 1976) has been used in most evaluations of skill-based relationship education and it includes a large number of items on conflict. The sensitivity of relationship satisfaction measures like the DAS to positive aspects of couple relationships has been questioned (Fincham, Beach, & Kemp-Fincham, 1997). Consequently, when evaluating relationship education given to couples early in relationships there may well be ceiling effects when utilizing such measures (Dyer & Halford, 1998).

Beyond the effects on skills and maintenance of relationship satisfaction, there are a number of potential benefits that have been articulated for relationship education. Stanley (2001) has suggested that relationship education might promote increased commitment to work on the relationship and facilitate early presentation for couple therapy should relationship problems develop. While these actions are often encouraged in relationship education, studies are needed to test the hypothesis that relationship education enhances these outcomes.

Mediators of Relationship Education Effects
The mediators of the effects of skill-based relationship education have not been evaluated. Markman et al. (2001) argued that negative communication and ineffective conflict management erode relationship satisfaction, and that PREP has an effect, at least in part, by promoting positive communication through teaching skills such as active listening. Gottman, Carrere, Swanson, and Coan (2000) disputed the value of teaching of such communication skills, arguing that the presence of such skills does not predict the trajectory of relationship satisfaction. However, Stanley et al. (2000) suggested that active listening skills can inhibit the use of negative, destructive communication.

Halford et al. (in press) suggest that increases in relationship self-regulation mediate the effects of relationship education. Within this framework, maintaining self-directed appraisal, goal setting, and self-implemented change to promote the relationship mediate the long-term maintenance of relationship satisfaction. While relationship self-regulation has been shown to predict relationship satisfaction (Wilson, Halford, Lizzio, Kimlin, & Islen, 2002), and relationship education to increase self-regulation, it has not been shown that increases in relationship self-regulation mediate enhanced maintenance of relationship satisfaction or stability (Halford & Moore, in press). Progress in providing effective relationship education is likely to be assisted by future research elucidating the mediators of the effects of relationship education.

Guidelines for Best Practice in Relationship Education

Assess the Risk Profile of Couples
As noted earlier, research has identified a number of predictors of the trajectory of relationship satisfaction and stability. This range of variables usefully can be conceptualized as falling into two categories of *static indicators* and *dynamic factors*. Static indicators cannot be changed at the time of intervention. For example, age and family-of-origin experiences are static variables that predict the chance of relationship stability and sustained relationship satisfaction. In contrast, dynamic factors can be changed. For example, realistic relationship expectations and effective couple communication predict relationship satisfaction, and these factors can be changed by relationship education (Markman et al., 2001; Stanley & Markman, 1997).

Many risk indicators can be measured relatively easily. For example, parental divorce, age, previous marriages, length of time the partners have known each other, cohabitation history, and the presence of stepchildren can be assessed by simple questions. Assessment of these indicators can help couples or educators to assess the relative risk level for future relationship problems. Protective factors, such as good couple communication and relationship expectations, often are more time consuming to assess than risk indicators. For example, observed communication is a reliable predictor of relationship satisfaction, but requires sophisticated audiovisual recording equipment and highly trained observers to conduct the assessment. However, some dynamic protective factors are reliably associated with certain protective indicators. For example, parental relationship stability and nonaggressive conflict management in the family of origin are associated with positive communication in engaged couples (Halford et al., 2000; Sanders et al., 1999). Thus, it is possible to evaluate couples on easily assessed protective indicators like parental stability and nonaggressive conflict management, and these protective indicators are markers of likely positive communication. In couples without these protective indicators, promotion of positive communication can be targeted in relationship education. When communication improves in couples who are low in protective indicators (i.e., couples at high risk of relationship problems), this helps couples sustain relationship satisfaction (Halford et al., 2001).

The widely used PREPARE, RELATE, and FOCCUS inventories have established validity in predicting the course of relationship satisfaction in the early years of marriage (Fowers & Olson, 1986; Larsen & Olson, 1989; Williams & Jurich, 1995). It has not been shown that simply completing and receiving feedback based on these measures assists couples sustain satisfying relationships, though it might. Even if research ultimately shows that assessment and feedback by themselves are ineffective, it could be that these assessments can guide couples and relationship educators on the educational needs of couples.

Encourage High-Risk Couples to Attend Relationship Education

In most Western countries 50% or more of couples who marry remain together for the rest of their lives (McDonald, 1995) and the vast majority of these couples report being satisfied in their relationship at least most of the time (Stanley & Markman, 1997). Relationship education provided to low-risk couples may make little difference to relationship satisfaction or stability, as many of these couples would have stable, mutually satisfying relationships without relationship education. On the other hand, relationship education is likely to be of particular benefit to high-risk couples (Halford, 1999; Sullivan & Bradbury, 1997). Yet, relationship education almost always is offered universally to couples entering committed relationships, irrespective of risk level (Halford, 1999). This might not matter if high-risk couples self-select to attend relationship education. Unfortunately, there is little evidence that high-risk couples are particularly likely to attend relationship education; in fact, there is some evidence that high-risk couples may be less likely to attend than low-risk couples (Sullivan & Bradbury, 1997).

There has not been systematic research evaluating strategies to encourage high-risk couples to attend relationship education. However, Karney et al. (1995)

reported that mass media outreach encourages high-risk couples to present for research studies on couples. In conducting a study targeting high-risk couples (Halford et al., 2001), we found that newspaper articles describing factors that put couples at high risk, combined with descriptions of relationship education programs that might reduce that risk, yielded high proportions of high-risk couples. In Australia, it has been suggested that government-funded relationship education programs should monitor the risk profiles of couples attending their programs and describe their strategies for encouraging high-risk couples to attend (Halford, 1999).

One underserved higher-risk population includes couples and individuals who face economic disadvantage. We are currently involved in several large-scale dissemination projects in which we are training trainers to teach PREP to couples who are poor and often from minority backgrounds. To date, we have found that there is widespread interest in relationship education in these communities. By training people who couples already know and who are trained to contextualize relationship education skills and principals to meet the needs of the couples they work with, we can reach out to diverse and traditionally underserved populations (Stanley, Markman, & Jenkins, 2002).

Assess and Educate About Relationship Aggression

As noted earlier, physical and verbal aggression occurs at high rates early in couple relationships, even less severe physical aggression is a strong predictor of relationship breakdown (Lawrence & Bradbury, 2001; Rogge & Bradbury, 1999). Yet, reports from relationship educators suggest that relationship aggression is rarely assessed or discussed in relationship education programs (Halford, 1999). Many individuals in the early stages of their relationships have idealized and unrealistic perceptions of their partners, relationships, and their relationship futures (Fowers, Applegate, Olson, & Pomerantz, 1994; Fowers, Lyons, & Montel, 1996). In this phase, realistic assessment of negative behaviors needs to be presented sensitively to avoid alienating people with positive relationship illusions. But, helping couples to appreciate the dangers of resorting to aggression as a means of managing conflict and helping partners to develop more effective conflict management should be emphasized in relationship education. Less severe couple aggression is reduced by skill-based relationship education that enhances conflict management (Markman et al., 1993).

Offer Relationship Education At Change Points

Traditionally relationship education primarily has been offered to couples entering committed relationships, often coinciding with marriage (Hunt et al., 1998). Entry to marriage is a good time for relationship education since couples often face significant challenges in developing committed relationships. Most couples find that initial overwhelming attraction to their partner moderates, that new relationship roles and routines need to be developed, and means of negotiating conflict need to evolve (Huston, McHale, & Crouter, 1986; Veroff, Douvan, & Hatchett, 1995). Between 10% to 15% of couples separate within the first 3 to 4 years of marriage (McDonald, 1995) and 33% of couples divorce within 10 years of marriage (Australian Bureau of Statistics, 2001).

In addition to the time of entry to a committed relationship, there are a number of other life events and developmental processes that couples experience that can be associated with increased risk of relationship problems. For example, the transition to parenthood, relocation, major illness, and unemployment are all associated with increased risk of relationship problems (Belsky & Kelly, 1994; Gagnon, Hersen, Kabacoff, & van Hasselt, 1999; Jordan, Stanley, & Markman, 1999; Larson & Holman, 1994). Relationship education that assists couples to make these challenging life transitions may help couples sustain relationship satisfaction and commitment.

Promote Early Presentation of Relationship Problems

In couples that have deteriorating relationship satisfaction, satisfaction often progressively deteriorates and leads to contemplation of dissolution of the relationship (Gottman, 1993). In couples with long-standing, severe relationship distress, motivation to change the relationship can be low and long-term success rates for couple therapy are modest (Halford, 2001). Low levels of presenting relationship satisfaction, greater length of time of distress experience (Jacobson, Follette, & Pagel, 1986; Johnson & Talitman, 1997; Whisman & Jacobson, 1990), and severe problems in managing conflict (Snyder, Mangrum, & Wills, 1993) are associated with poor response to intensive couple therapy. Negative patterns of couple interaction typically become entrenched over time and resistant to change (Markman, Floyd, Stanley, & Storaasli, 1988). Erosion of positive feelings between the partners and relationship disengagement often follow from prolonged distress. Low levels of emotional affection, such as little tenderness or low frequency of sex, predict poor response to couple therapy (Jacobson & Addis, 1993; Snyder et al., 1993).

Given that long-established distress predicts poor response to couple therapy, early presentation for brief relationship education when distress is mild might produce better results. Kaiser, Hahlweg, Fehm-Wolfsdorf, and Groth (1998) showed that a PREP-style program helped mildly distressed couples improve their communication and relationship satisfaction and that these benefits persisted for a period of years. Couples with mild to moderate distress provided with two to four couple sessions focusing on assessment, feedback, and brief suggestions increased their relationship satisfaction substantially (Cordova, Warren, & Gee, 2001; Halford, Osgarby, & Kelly, 1996; Worthington et al., 1995). Thus, within relationship education programs for currently satisfied couples, encouragement to present early if problems develop should be emphasized.

Match Content to Couples With Special Needs

Some couples have special needs in relationship education. An example is when a partner has a psychological disorder that impacts the relationship, such as alcohol abuse or depression (Halford et al., 1999). In such couples, helping the partner with the disorder to change his or her behavior is likely an important element of promoting a mutually satisfying relationship. For example, encouraging heavy drinkers to moderate drinking using a brief intervention can enhance relationship satisfaction (Kelly, Halford, & Young, 2000). An effective brief alcohol-focused intervention consists of motivational interviewing, goal setting, and training in how to cope in settings in which there is a high risk of problem drinking (e.g., going to a party where alcohol is being served, going out to dinner at a restaurant where a couple has shared drinks before). When such a brief alcohol-focused intervention is combined with enhancement of couple communication, this improves the couple's relationship stability (Bouma, Halford, & Young, 2002).

An important example of couples with special needs is couples forming stepfamilies. Negotiating parenting arrangements in stepfamilies is often reported to be difficult (Cissna, Cox, & Bochner, 1990), particularly with respect to the role of stepparents in major decisions and discipline of children (Visher & Visher, 1991). Furthermore, the role an ex-partner and biological parent plays in decision-making can be a source of disagreement between both the ex-partners and the current partners (Brown, Eichenberger, Portes, & Christensen, 1991; Wallerstein & Johnston, 1990). Many couples report that stepparent-child relationships and parenting roles are major sources of conflict (Bray, 1988). Effective interventions to promote satisfying stepfamily couple relationships probably need to address the challenges of co-parenting with an ex-partner and helping to develop the relationships of stepparents with children (Lawton & Sanders, 1994).

Enhance Accessibility of Evidence-Based Relationship Education Programs

The evidence-based skill training approaches to relationship education initially were developed and offered through university departments (e.g., Markman et al., 2001). In recent years, projects have been designed to disseminate evidence-based relationship education. The PREP program has been evaluated when offered through religious organizations in the United States and Germany and found to be effective (Hahlweg et al., 1998; Stanley et al., 2001). For example, as reviewed earlier, clergy and lay leaders trained in PREP in a randomized dissemination trial were taught to deliver the program as effectively as psychologists and other marriage and family professionals (Stanley et al., 2001). Moreover, the clergy continue to use significant aspects of the program in their practice with couples up to 3 years later (Markman et al., 2002). PREP and similar skill-based relationship education programs have been offered in weekly group sessions, weekends, and most recently in a flexile delivery mode via videotapes, self-directed learning guides, and telephone-based consultation (Halford & Moore, in press). The increasing diversity of methods of accessing evidence-based relationship education should enhance its accessibility to couples. Marriage and family therapists (MFTs) can lead dissemination of couple relationship education through strategies like collaboration with clergy, as it is to clergy whom most couples first turn for relationship education and help with relationship problems (Halford, 1999; Johnson et al., 2002).

It is possible the perceived expertise about relationships, and social influence thereby accorded to clergy and other leaders in faith-based organizations might enhance the effects of couple relationship education for religious couples. The collaboration between MFTs and clergy might take various forms. One option is for MFTs to be consultants and provide training and support to clergy in their relationship education efforts, such as Hahlweg et al. (1998) and Stanley et al. (2001) have done. Moreover, once known to clergy, MFTs might establish referral networks, as most clergy we know would be glad to refer couples to low-cost, culturally sensitive services, especially those featuring educationally- and research-based interventions.

Clinical Implications

Each of the current authors follows the scientist-practitioner model in our careers. The best practice approaches to couple relationship education translate scientific findings to easy to use but powerful principals for both practitioners and clients to follow (Stanley & Markman, 1997). Here we focus on three big-picture research-based principals that inform action and seem to work, that we believe should be in any best practice relationship education program, and are in our own programs (PREP, Couple CARE).

Tolstoy was wrong! Tolstoy (1961) wrote "All happy families are like one another; each unhappy family is unhappy in its own way" (p. 17). Decades of research have proven him to be wrong—in fact, the opposite is true (Notarius & Markman, 1993). Marital happiness comes in many shapes and forms, whereas marital distress is linked to a small number of negative patterns, which are often called "danger signs" (Markman et al., 2001). The good news here is that we don't have to give advice about how to have a great relationship, but to educate people about how to avoid the pitfalls that lead to distress and divorce. Thus, we can respect the vast diversity of cultural, ethnic, and religious traditions and differences between and among couples and focus on educating all partners about the importance of handling differences constructively—to talk without fighting about the inevitable conflicts and sensitive issues that all couples face (Markman et al., 2001).

Protect and preserve positive connections. Despite the importance of handling negative emotions, there is clearly more to having a stable, satisfying relationship than just dealing well with conflict. People get married for many reasons: in order to be friends, have fun, be a team, share everyday tasks, and raise a family, and to share love, romance, and sensuality. Couples need to ensure there is sufficient time in their lives for these great things to happen. Best practice relationship education programs inform couples of the natural tendency to take relationships for granted, and help couples develop strategies for making and keeping their relationship the top priority in their lives (Stanley, 1998).

Do your own part. Halford and colleagues (Halford, 2001; Halford, Sanders & Behrens, 1994, 2001) have focused their relationship enhancement efforts on promoting relationship self-regulation, getting each person to do his or her own part to have a great relationship. This work has translated the theory and research on the importance of regulating negative affect in intimate relationships that is shared by social learning (Lindahl & Markman, 1990) and attachment perspectives (Furman & Flanagan, 1997) to action. Too often people who are getting divorced explain what happened by saying "I made the wrong choice, I married the wrong person" (Levine & Markman, 2001). We often tell couples that having a great relationship is much more than finding a suitable partner; a great relationship is made *after* you make the choice to marry and is about being the best partner you can be (Markman et al., 2001).

In recent work on what is being called *safety theory* (Markman, Stanley, & Whitton, 2002; Stanley, Whitton, & Markman, in press), we let couples know that research and theory strongly suggest that there are two types of safety: (a) safety in interaction, which is being able to talk openly and well (enough) about key issues; and (b) safety in commitment, which is security of support and a sense of a clear future. In sum, if we had one session with a couple or one opportunity to educate a group of couples, based on research and clinical experience, we would help partners to take personal action to do two things: (a) help them stop (or avoid the tendency towards) fighting destructively and to talk without fighting about important issues, and (b) help them protect and preserve a lasting love through nurturing positive connections and being committed to one another. This will help couples be "Safe at Home!"

Conclusion

The huge costs and suffering associated with marital distress and divorce have focused attention on relationship education as a means of helping couples sustain mutually satisfying relationships. While there is much we do not know, there is a substantial body of evidence that guides us in this enterprise. In another decade, we will know substantially more about the key dynamics contributing to relationship happiness as well as more about helping couples have better relationships. We will also have more evidence on which couples respond best to different types of intervention strategies. Yet, the societal need and desire for couples to strengthen their marriages is so high, we need to act on what we know as well as to know we need more knowledge (Stanley, Markman, & Jenkins, 2002). Existing research allows identification of couples at high risk of relationship problems. Skill-based relationship education shows considerable promise as an intervention to enhance relationship outcomes. The implementation of the best practice guidelines proposed in this chapter is intended as a step toward realizing the benefits of relationship education.

References

References marked with a single asterisk indicate resources to recommend to couples, and references marked with a double asterisk are recommended for clinicians.

Arellano, C., & Markman, H. (1995). The Managing Affect and Differences Scale (MAPS): A self-report measure assessing conflict management in couples. *Journal of Family Psychology, 9,* 319–334.

Australian Bureau of Statistics. (2001). *Marriage and divorces, Australia.* Canberra, Australia: Author.

Avery, A. W., Ridley, C. A., Leslie, L. A., & Milholland, T. (1980). Relationship enhancement with premarital dyads: A six-month follow-up. *American Journal of Family Therapy, 8*(3), 23–30.

Bagarozzi, D. A., & Rauen, P. I. (1981). Premarital counseling: Appraisal and status. *The American Journal of Family Therapy, 9,* 13–27.

Beach, S. R. H., Arias, I., & O'Leary, K. D. (1986). The relationship of marital satisfaction and social support to depressive symptomatology. *Journal of Psychopathology and Behavioural Assessment, 8,* 305–316.

*Belsky, J., & Kelly, J. (1994). *Transition to parenthood.* New York: Delacorte Press.

Belsky, J., & Rovine, M. (1990). Patterns of marital change across the transition to parenthood: Pregnancy to three years postpartum. *Journal of Marriage and the Family, 52,* 5–19.

Benson, M. J., Larson, J., Wilson, S. M., & Demo, D. H. (1993). Family of origin influences on late adolescent romantic relationships. *Journal of Marriage and the Family, 55,* 663–672.

**Berger, R., & Hannah, M. T. (Eds.). (1998). *Preventative approaches in couple therapy.* New York: Brunner-Mazel.

Birchnell, J., & Kennard, J. (1984). Early and current factors associated with poor quality marriages. *Social Psychiatry, 19,* 31–40.

Black, L. E., & Sprenkle, D. H. (1991). Gender differences in college students' attitudes toward divorce and their willingness to marry. *Journal of Divorce and Remarriage, 15,* 47–60.

Block, J., Block, J. H., & Keyes, S. (1988). Longitudinally foretelling drug usage in adolescence: Early childhood personality and environmental precursors. *Child Development, 59,* 336–355.

Booth, A., & Johnson, D. (1988). Premarital cohabitation and marital success. *Journal of Family Issues, 9,* 255–272.

Bouma, R. O., Halford, W. K., & Young, R. (2002). *Evaluation of the Controlling Alcohol and Relationship Enhancement (CARE) program with hazardous drinkers.* Manuscript submitted for publication.

Bradbury, T. N. (1995). Assessing the four fundamental domains of marriage. *Family Relations, 44,* 459–468.

Bradbury, T. N. (Ed.). (1998). *The developmental course of marital dysfunction.* New York: Cambridge University Press.

Bradbury, T. N., Cohan, C. L., & Karney, B. R. (1998). Optimizing longitudinal research for understanding and preventing marital dysfunction. In T. N. Bradbury (Ed.), *The developmental course of marital dysfunction* (pp. 279–311). New York: Cambridge University Press.

Bradbury, T. N., & Fincham, F. D. (1990). Preventing marital dysfunction: Review and analysis. In F. D. Fincham & T. N. Bradbury (Eds.), *The psychology of marriage: Basic issues and applications* (pp. 375–401). New York: Guilford.

Bray, J. H. (1988). Children's development during early remarriage. In E. M. Hetherington & J. D. Arasteh (Eds.), *Impact of divorce, single parenting and stepparenting on children* (pp. 279–298). Hillsdale, NJ: Erlbaum.

Brown, J. H., Eichenberger, S. A., Portes, P. R., & Christensen, D. N. (1991). Family functioning factors associated with the adjustment of children of divorce. *Journal of Divorce and Remarriage, 17,* 81–96.

Browne, A., & Williams, K. R. (1993). Gender, intimacy and lethal violence: Trends from 1976 through 1987. *Gender and Society, 7,* 78–98.

Burgess, A. W., Hartman, C. R., & McCormack, A. (1987). Abused to abuser: Antecedents of socially deviant behaviors. *American Journal of Psychiatry, 144,* 1431–1436.

Call, V. R. A., & Heaton, T. B. (1997). Religious influence on marital stability. *Journal for the Scientific Study of Religion, 36,* 382–392.

Carrere, S., Buehlman, K. T., Gottman, J. M., Coan, J. A., & Ruckstuhl, L. (2000). Predicting marital stability and divorce in newlywed couples. *Journal of Family Psychology, 14,* 42–58.

Cascardi, M., Langhinrichsen, J., & Vivian, D. (1992). Marital aggression, impact, injury and health correlates for husbands and wives. *Archives of Internal Medicine, 152,* 1178–1184.

Christensen, A., & Heavey, C. L. (1999). Interventions for couples. *Annual Review of Psychology, 50,* 165–190.

Cissna, K. N., Cox, D. E., & Bochner, A. P. (1990). The dialectic of marital and parental relationships within the stepfamily. *Communication Monographs, 57,* 44–61.

Clarksberg, M., Stolzenberg, R. M., & Waite, L. J. (1995). Attitudes, values, and entrance into cohabitational versus marital unions. *Social Forces, 74,* 609–634.

Clements, M. L., Cordova, A. D., Markman, H. J., & Laurenceau, J. (1997). The erosion of satisfaction over time and how to prevent it. In R. J. Sternberg & M. Hojjat (Eds.), *Satisfaction in close relationships.* New York: Guilford.

Coie, J. D., Watt, N. F., West, S. G., Hawkins, J. D., Asarnow, J. R., Markman, H. J., et al. (1993). The science of prevention: A conceptual framework and some directions for a national research program. *American Psychologist, 48,* 1013–1022.

Cordova, J. V., Warren, L. Z., & Gee, C. B. (2001). Motivational interviewing as an intervention for at-risk couples. *Journal of Marital and Family Therapy, 27,* 315–326.

*Cowan, C. P., & Cowan, P. A. (1992). *When partners become parents.* New York: Basic Books.

Davila, J., & Bradbury, T. (2001). Attachment insecurity and the distinction between unhappy spouses who do and do not divorce. *Journal of Family Psychology, 15*(3), 371–393.

DeGraaf, A. (1991). De invloed van echtscheiding van de ouders op demografisch gedrag van de vrouw [The impact of divorced parents on women's demographic behavior]. *Maandststistiek van de Bevolking, 39,* 30–38.

DeMaria, R., & Hannah, M. (2002). *Building intimate relationships: Bridging treatment, education and enrichment through the PAIRS Program.* New York: Brunner-Routledge.

DeMaris, A., & Leslie, G. R. (1984). Cohabitation with future spouse: Its influence upon marital satisfaction and communication. *Journal of Marriage and the Family, 46,* 77–84.

DeMaris, A., & Rao, V. (1992). Premarital cohabitation and subsequent marital stability in the United States: A reassessment. *Journal of Marriage and the Family, 54,* 178–190.

Dyer, C., & Halford, W. K. (1998). Prevention of relationship problems: Retrospect and prospect. *Behaviour Change, 15,* 107–125.

Eidelson, R. J., & Epstein, N. (1982). Cognition and relationship maladjustment: Development of a measure of dysfunctional relationship beliefs. *Journal of Consulting and Clinical Psychology, 50,* 715–720.

Emmelkamp, P. M. G., De Haan, E., & Hoogduin, C. A. I. (1990). Marital adjustment and obsessive-compulsive disorder. *British Journal of Psychiatry, 156,* 55–60.

Fincham, F. D., Beach, S. R. H., & Kemp-Fincham, S. I. (1997). Marital quality: A new theoretical perspective. In R. J. Sternberg & M. Hojjat (Eds.), *Satisfaction in close relationships* (pp. 275–304). New York: Guilford.

Fincham, F. D., Bradbury, T. N., Arias, I., Byrne, C. A., & Karney, B. R. (1997). Marital violence, marital distress, and attributions. *Journal of Family Psychology, 11*(3), 367–372.

Fincham, F. D., Harold, G. T., & Gano-Phillips, S. (2000). The longitudinal association between attributions and marital satisfaction: Direction of effects and role of efficacy expectations. *Journal of Marriage and the Family, 14*(2), 267–285.

Forste, R., & Tanfer, K. (1996). Sexual exclusivity among dating, cohabiting, and married women. *Journal of Marriage and the Family, 58*, 33–47.

Fowers, B. J., Applegate, B., Olson, D. H., & Pomerantz, B. (1994). Marital conventionalization as a measure of marital satisfaction: A confirmatory factor analysis. *Journal of Family Psychology, 8*, 98–103.

Fowers, B. J., Lyons, E. M., & Montel, K. H. (1996). Positive marital illusions: Self-enhancement or relationship enhancement? *Journal of Family Psychology, 10*, 192–208.

Fowers, B. J., & Olson, D. H. (1986). Predicting marital success with PREPARE: A predictive validity study. *Journal of Marital and Family Therapy, 12*, 403–413.

Freedman, C. M., Low, S. M., Markman, H. J., & Stanley, S. M. (2002). Equipping couples with the tools to cope with predictable and unpredictable crisis events: The PREP program. *International Journal of Emergency Mental Health, 4*(1), 49–56.

Furman, W., & Flanagan, A. S. (1997). The influence of earlier relationships on marriage: An attachment perspective. In W. K. Halford & H. J. Markman (Eds.), *Clinical handbook of marriage and couples intervention* (pp. 179–202). Chichester, England: Wiley.

Gagnon, M. D., Hersen, M., Kabacoff, R. I., & van Hasselt, V. B. (1999). Interpersonal and psychological correlates of marital dissatisfaction in late life: A review. *Clinical Psychology Review, 19*, 359–378.

Gibardi, L., & Rosen, L. A. (1991). Differences between college students from divorced and intact families. *Journal of Divorce and Remarriage, 15*, 175–191.

Giblin, P., Sprenkle, D. H., & Sheehan, R. (1985). Enrichment outcome research: A meta-analysis of premarital, marital and family interventions. *Journal of Marital and Family Therapy, 11*, 257–271.

Glenn, N. D. (1998). The course of marital success and failure in five American 10-year cohorts. *Journal of Marriage and the Family, 60*, 269–282.

Glenn, N. D., & Kramer, K. B. (1987). The marriages and divorces of the children of divorce. *Journal of Marriage and the Family, 49*, 811–825.

Glenn, N. D., & Shelton, B. A. (1983). Pre-adult background variables and divorce: A note of caution about over-reliance on variance. *Journal of Marriage and the Family, 45*, 405–410.

Glenn, N. D., Nock, S., Waite, L., Doherty, W., Gottman, J., Makey, B., et al. (2002). Why marriage matters: Twenty-one conclusions from the social sciences. *American Experiment Quarterly, 5*, 34–44.

Gottman, J. M. (1993). The role of conflict engagement, escalation, and avoidance in marital interaction: A longitudinal view of five types of couples. *Journal of Consulting and Clinical Psychology, 61*, 6–15.

Gottman, J. M. (1994). *What predicts divorce? The relationship between marital processes and marital outcomes.* Hillsdale, NJ: Erlbaum.

Gottman, J. M., Carrere, S., Swanson, C., & Coan, J. (2000). Reply to 'From basic research to interventions.' *Journal of Marriage and the Family, 62*, 265–273.

Gottman, J. M., Coan, J., Carrere, S., & Swanson, C. (1998). Predicting marital happiness and stability from newlywed interactions. *Journal of Marriage and the Family, 60*, 5–22.

Grover, K. J., Russel, C. S., Schumm, W. R., & Paff-Bergen, L. A. (1985). Mate selection processes and marital satisfaction. *Family Relations, 34,* 383–386.

Guerney, B. G. (1977). *Relationship enhancement.* San Francisco: Jossey-Bass.

**Guerney, B. G. (Ed.). (1987). *Relationship enhancement manual.* Bethesda, MD: Ideal.

Guerney, B. G., & Maxson, P. (1990). Marital and family enrichment research: A decade review and a look ahead. *Journal of Marriage and the Family, 52,* 1127–1135.

Hahlweg, K., & Markman, H. J. (1988). Effectiveness of behavioral marital therapy: Empirical status of behavioral techniques in preventing and alleviating marital distress. *Journal of Consulting and Clinical Psychology, 56,* 440–447.

Hahlweg, K., Markman, H. J., Thurmair, F., Engel, J., & Eckert, J. (1998). Prevention of marital distress: Results of a German prospective longitudinal study. *Journal of Family Psychology, 12,* 543–556.

Halford, W. K. (1995). Marriage and the prevention of psychiatric disorder. In B. Raphael & G. D. Burrows (Eds.), *Handbook of preventive psychiatry* (pp. 121–138). Amsterdam: Elsevier.

Halford, W. K. (1999). *Australian couples in Millenium three: A research and development agenda for marriage and relationship education.* Report to the National Family Strategy Task Force, Australian Department of Family and Community Services. Brisbane, Australia: Australian Academic Press.

**Halford, W. K. (2001). *Brief couple therapy: Helping partners help themselves.* New York: Guilford.

Halford, W. K., Bouma, R., Kelly, A., & Young, R. (1999). The interaction of individual psychopathology and marital problems: Current findings and clinical implications. *Behavior Modification, 23,* 179–216.

Halford, W. K., Hahlweg, K., & Dunne, M. (1990). The cross-cultural consistency of marital communication associated with marital distress. *Journal of Marriage and the Family, 52,* 109–122.

*Halford, W. K., & Markman, H. J. (Eds.). (1997). *Clinical handbook of marriage and couples interventions.* New York: Wiley.

**Halford, W. K., & Moore, E. (in press). Relationship education and the prevention of couple relationship problems. In A. S. Gurman & N. Jacobson (Eds.), *Clinical handbook of couple therapy* (3rd ed.). New York: Guilford.

Halford, W. K., & Osgarby, S. (1993). Alcohol abuse in individuals presenting for marital therapy. *Journal of Family Psychology, 11,* 1–13.

Halford, W. K., Osgarby, S. M., & Kelly, A. B. (1996). Brief behavioural couples therapy: A preliminary evaluation. *Behavioural and Cognitive Psychotherapy, 24,* 263–273.

Halford, W. K., Sanders, M. R., & Behrens, B. C. (1994). Self-regulation in behavioral couples therapy. *Behavior Therapy, 25,* 431–452.

Halford, W. K., Sanders, M. R., & Behrens, B. C. (2000). Repeating the errors of our parents? Family of origin spouse violence and observed conflict management in engaged couples. *Family Process, 39,* 219–236.

Halford, W. K., Sanders, M. R., & Behrens, B. C. (2001). Can skills training prevent relationship problems in at-risk couples? Four-year effects of a behavioral relationship education program. *Journal of Family Psychology, 21,* 750–768.

Halford, W. K., Scott, J., & Smythe, J. (2000). Couples and cancer. In K. Schmaling & T. Sher (Eds.), *Couples and illness* (pp. 135–170). Washington, DC: American Psychological Association.

Halford, W. K., Wilson, K. L., Lizzio, A., & Moore, E. M. (in press). Does working at your relationship work? Relationship self-regulation and relationship outcomes. In J. Feeney & P. Noller (Eds.), *Marriage.* Cambridge, MA: Cambridge University Press.

Hall, D. R., & Zhao, J. Z. (1995). Cohabitation and divorce in Canada: Testing the selectivity hypothesis. *Journal of Marriage and the Family, 57,* 421–427.

Harris, R., Simons, M., Willis, P., & Barrie, A. (1992). *Love, sex and water skiing: The experience of pre-marriage education in Australia.* Adelaide: University of South Australia, Center for Human Resource Studies.

Heaton, B., & Pratt, E. (1990). The effects of religious homogamy on marital satisfaction and stability. *Journal of Family Issues, 11*, 191–207.

Holman, T. B. (2001). *Premarital prediction of marital quality or break up: Research, theory and practice.* New York: Kluwer.

Holtzworth-Munroe, A., Markman, H., & O'Leary, D. (1995). The need for marital violence prevention efforts: A behavioral-cognitive secondary prevention program for engaged and newly married couples. *Applied and Preventive Psychology: Current Scientific Perspectives, 4*, 77–88.

Holtzworth-Munroe, A., Meehan, J. C., Herron, K., Rehman, U., & Stuart, G. L. (2000). Testing the Holtzworth-Munroe and Stuart batterer typology. *Journal of Consulting and Clinical Psychology, 68*, 1000–1019.

Hunt, R., Hof, L., & DeMaria, R. (1998). *Marriage enrichment: Preparation, mentoring, and outreach.* Philadelphia: Brunner/Mazel.

Huston, T. L., McHale, S., & Crouter, A. (1986). When the honeymoon's over: Changes in the marital relationship over the first year. In R. L. Gilmour & S. W. Duck (Eds.), *The emerging field of personal relationships* (pp. 109–132). Hillsdale, NJ: Erlbaum.

Jacobson, N. S., & Addis, M. E. (1993). Research on couples and couple therapy: What do we know? Where are we going? *Journal of Consulting and Clinical Psychology, 61*, 85–93.

Jacobson, N. S., Follette, W. C., & Pagel, M. (1986). Predicting who will benefit from behavioral marital therapy. *Journal of Consulting and Clinical Psychology, 54*, 518–522.

Janus, S. S., & Janus, C. C. (1993). *The Janus report on human sexuality.* New York: Riley.

Johnson, C. A., Stanley, S. M., Glenn, N. D., Amato, P. A., Nock, S. L., Markman, H. J., et al. (2002). *Marriage in Oklahoma: 2001 baseline statewide survey on marriage and divorce.* Stillwater, OK: Oklahoma State University, Bureau for Social Research.

Johnson, S. M., & Talitman, E. (1997). Predictors of success in emotionally focused couples therapy. *Journal of Marital and Family Therapy, 23*, 135–152.

Jones, A. C., & Chao, C. M. (1997). Racial, ethnic and cultural issues in couples therapy. In W. K. Halford & H. J. Markman (Eds.), *Clinical handbook of marriage and couples intervention* (pp. 157–178). Chichester, England: Wiley.

Jordan, P., Stanley, S., & Markman, H. (1999). *Becoming parents: How to strengthen your marriage as your family grows.* San Francisco: Jossey-Bass.

Kaiser, A., Hahlweg, K., Fehm-Wolfsdorf, G., & Groth, T. (1998). The efficacy of a compact psychoeducational group training program for married couples. *Journal of Consulting and Clinical Psychology, 66*, 753–760.

Karney, B. R., & Bradbury, T. N. (1995). The longitudinal course of marital quality and stability: A review of theory, method and research. *Psychological Bulletin, 118*, 3–34.

Karney, B. R., & Bradbury, T. N. (1997). Neuroticism, marital interaction, and the trajectory of marital satisfaction. *Journal of Personality and Social Psychology, 66*, 413–424.

Karney, B. R., Davila, J., Cohan, C. L., Sullivan, K. T., Johnson, M. D., & Bradbury, T. N., (1995). An empirical investigation of sampling strategies in marital research. *Journal of Marriage and the Family, 57*, 909–920.

Kelly, A., Halford, W. K., & Young, R. (2000). Brief alcohol treatment for women with marital problems. *Addiction, 57*, 1032–1037.

Kieran, K. (2002). Cohabitation in Western Europe: Trends, issues, and implications. In A. Booth & A. Crouter (Eds.), *Just living together: Implications of cohabitation on families, children, and social policy.* Mahwah, NJ: Erlbaum.

Kline, G. H., Stanley, S. M., Markman, H. J., Olmos-Gallo, P. A., St. Peters, M., Whitton, S. W., et al. (2002). *Timing in everything: Pre-engagement cohabitation and increased risk for poor marital outcomes.* Manuscript submitted for publication.

Kurdek, L. A. (1991). Marital stability and changes in marital quality in newlywed couples: A test of the contextual model. *Journal of Social and Personal Relationships, 8,* 27–48.

Kurdek, L. A. (1993). Predicting marital dissolution: A 5-year prospective longitudinal study of newlywed couples. *Journal of Personality and Social Psychology, 64,* 221–242.

Larsen, A. S., & Olson, D. H. (1989). Predicting marital satisfaction using PREPARE: A replication study. *Journal of Marital and Family Therapy, 15,* 311–322.

Larson, J. H., & Holman, T. B. (1994). Premarital predictors of marital quality and stability. *Family Relations, 43,* 228–237.

Larson, J. H., Newell, K., Topham, G., & Nichols, S. (2002). A review of three comprehensive premarital assessment questionnaires. *Journal of Marital and Family Therapy, 28,* 233–239.

Lawrence, E., & Bradbury, T. N. (2001). Physical aggression and marital dysfunction: A longitudinal analysis. *Journal of Family Psychology, 15,* 135–154.

Lawton, J. M., & Sanders, M. R. (1994). Designing effective behavioral family interventions for stepfamilies. *Clinical Psychology Review, 14,* 463–496.

Levine, J., & Markman, H. (Eds.). (2001). *Why do fools fall in love? Understanding the magic, mystery and meaning of successful relationships.* San Francisco: Jossey-Bass.

Lindahl, K., & Markman, H. J. (1990). Communication and negative affect regulation in the family. In E. Blechman (Ed.), *Emotions and families* (pp. 99–116). New York: Plenum Press.

Mahoney, A., Pargament, K. I., Tarakeshwar, N., & Swank, A. B. (2001). Religion in the home in the 1980s and 1990s: A meta-analytic review and conceptual analysis of links between religion, marriage, and parenting. *Journal of Family Psychology, 15,* 559–596.

**Markey, B., & Micheletto, M. (1997). *Instructor manual for FOCCUS.* Omaha, NE: Archdiocese of Omaha.

Markman, H. J. (1981). The prediction of marital distress: A five-year follow-up. *Journal of Consulting and Clinical Psychology, 49,* 760–762.

Markman, H. J., Floyd, F. J., Stanley, S. M., & Storaasli, R. D. (1988). Prevention of marital distress: A longitudinal investigation. *Journal of Consulting and Clinical Psychology, 56,* 210–217.

Markman, H. J., & Hahlweg, K. (1993). The prediction and prevention of marital distress: An international perspective. *Clinical Psychology Review, 13,* 29–43.

Markman, H. J., Halford, W. K., & Cordova, A. D. (1997). In W. K. Halford & H. J. Markman (Eds.), *Clinical handbook of marriage and couples intervention* (pp. 695–716). Chichester, England: Wiley.

Markman, H. J., Renick, M. J., Floyd, F., Stanley, S., & Clements, M. (1993). Preventing marital distress through communication and conflict management training: A four and five year follow-up. *Journal of Consulting and Clinical Psychology, 61,* 70–77.

*Markman, H. J., Stanley, S. M., & Blumberg, S. L. (2001). *Fighting for your marriage: New and revised version.* San Francisco: Jossey-Bass.

Markman, H. J., Stanley, S. M., & Whitton, S. (2002, April). *Safe at home: The role of communication, conflict, and commitment in the fundamental desire for emotional safety.* Paper presented at the meeting of American Psychological Association Division 43, Family Psychology: the Art of Science, Chicago, IL.

Markman, H. J., Whitton, S., Thompson, H., St. Peters, M., Stanley, S. M., & Leber, D. (2002). *Use of an empirically based marriage education program by religious organizations: Results of a dissemination trial.* Manuscript in preparation.

McDonald, P. (1995). *Families in Australia: A sociodemographic perspective.* Melbourne: Australian Institute of Family Studies.

Mihalic, S. W., & Elliot, D. (1997). A social learning theory model of marital violence. *Journal of Family Violence, 12,* 21–47.

**Miller, S., Nunnally, E., & Wackman, D. (1975). Minnesota Couples Communication Program (MCCP): Premarital and marital groups. In D. H. Olson (Ed.), *Treating relationships* (pp. 21–40). Lake Mills, IA: Graphic.

Millward, C. (1990). Expectations of marriage of young people. *Family Matters, 28,* 1–12.

Murphy, C. M., & O'Leary, K. A. (1989). Psychological aggression predicts physical aggression in early marriage. *Journal of Consulting and Clinical Psychology, 57,* 579–582.

Noller, P., & Feeney, J. A. (1998). Communication in early marriage: Responses to conflict, nonverbal accuracy, and conversational patterns. In T. N. Bradbury (Ed.), *The developmental course of marital dysfunction* (pp. 11–43). New York: Cambridge University Press.

Notarius, C., & Markman, H. J. (1993). *We can work it out: Making sense of marital conflict.* New York: G. P. Putnam's Sons.

O'Leary, K. D., Barling, J., Arias, I., Rosenbaum, A., Malone, J., & Tyree, A. (1989). Prevalence and stability of physical aggression between spouses: A longitudinal analysis. *Journal of Consulting and Clinical Psychology, 57,* 263–268.

**Olson, D. H., Fournier, D. G., & Druckman, J. M. (1996). PREPARE. Minneapolis, MN: Life Innovations.

Olson, D. H., & Fowers, B. J. (1986). Predicting marital success with PREPARE: A predictive validity study. *Journal of Marital and Family Therapy, 12,* 403–413.

Pasch, L. A., & Bradbury, T. N. (1998). Social support, conflict, and the development of marital dysfunction. *Journal of Consulting and Clinical Psychology, 66,* 219–230.

Pope, H., & Mueller, C. W. (1976). The intergenerational transmission of marital instability: Comparisons by race and sex. *Journal of Social Issues, 32,* 49–66.

Renick, M. J., Blumberg, S., & Markman, H. J. (1992). The Prevention and Relationship Enhancement Program (PREP): An empirically-based preventive intervention program for couples. *Family Relations, 41,* 141–147.

Ridley, C. A., & Bain, A. B. (1983). The effects of a premarital relationship enhancement program on self-disclosure. *Family Therapy, 10*(1), 13–24.

Ridley, C. A., Jorgensen, S. R., Morgan, A. G., & Avery, A. W. (1982). Relationship enhancement with premarital couples: An assessment of effects on relationship quality. *American Journal of Family Therapy, 10*(3), 41–48.

Rogge, R. D., & Bradbury, T. N. (1999). Till violence does us part: The differing roles of communication and aggression in predicting adverse marital outcomes. *Journal of Consulting and Clinical Psychology, 67,* 340–351.

Sanders, M. R., Halford, W. K., & Behrens, B. C. (1999). Parental divorce and premarital couple communication. *Journal of Family Psychology, 13,* 60–74.

Sayers, S. L., Kohn, C. S., & Heavey, C. (1998). Prevention of marital dysfunction: Behavioral approaches and beyond. *Clinical Psychology Review, 18,* 713–744.

Shapiro, A. F., Gottman, J. M., & Carrere, S. (2000). The baby and the marriage: Identifying factors that buffer against decline in marital satisfaction after the first baby arrives. *Journal of Family Psychology, 14,* 59–70.

Silliman, B., & Schumm, W. R. (2000). Marriage preparation programs: A literature review. *Family Journal-Counseling & Therapy for Couples & Families, 8*(2), 133–142.

Silliman, B., Stanley, S. M., Coffin, W., Markman, H. J., & Jordan, P. L. (2002). Preventive interventions for couples. In H. Liddle, D. Santisteban, R. Levant, & J. Bray (Eds.), *Family psychology: Science-based interventions* (pp. 123–146). Washington, DC: American Psychological Association.

Simons, M., Harris, R., & Willis, P. (1994). *Pathways to marriage: Learning for married life in Australia.* Adelaide: University of South Australia, Centre for Research in Education and Work.

Snyder, D. K., Mangrum, L. F., & Wills, R. M. (1993). Predicting couples' response to marital therapy: A comparison of short- and long-term predictors. *Journal of Consulting and Clinical Psychology, 61,* 61–69.

Spanier, G. B. (1976). Measuring dyadic adjustment: New scales for assessing the quality of marriage and similar dyads. *Journal of Marriage and the Family, 38,* 15–28.

*Stanley, S. M. (1998). *The heart of commitment: Compelling research that reveals the success of a lifelong, intimate marriage.* Nashville, TN: Nelson.

Stanley, S. M. (2001). Making the case for premarital training. *Family Relations, 50,* 272–280.

Stanley, S. M., Bradbury, T. N., & Markman, H. J. (2000). Structural flaws in the bridge from basic research on marriage to interventions for couples: Illustrations from Gottman, Coan, Carrere, and Swanson (1998). *Journal of Marriage and the Family, 62*(1), 256–264.

Stanley, S. M., & Markman, H. J. (1997). *Marriage in the 90s: A nationwide random phone survey.* Denver, CO: PREP.

Stanley, S. M., & Markman, H. J. (1998). Acting on what we know: The hope of prevention. In *Strategies to strengthen marriage: What we know, what we need to know.* Washington DC: The Family Impact Seminar.

Stanley, S. M., Markman, H. J., & Jenkins, N. (2002). *Marriage educations and government policy: Helping couples who choose marriage achieve success.* Denver, CO: PREP.

Stanley, S. M., Markman, H. J., St. Peters, M., & Leber, B. D. (1995). Strengthening marriages and preventing divorce: New directions in prevention research. *Family Relations, 44,* 392–401.

Stanley, S. M., Markman, H. J., & Whitton, S. (2002). *Communication, conflict, and commitment: Insights on the foundations of relationship success from a national survey.* Manuscript submitted for publication.

Stanley, S. M., Whitton, S. W., & Markman, H. J. (in press). Maybe I do: Interpersonal commitment and premarital or non-marital cohabitation. *Journal of Family Issues.*

Stanley, S. M., Markman, H. J., Prado, L. M., Olmos-Gallo, P. A., Tonelli, L., St. Peters, M., et al. (2001). Community based premarital prevention: Clergy and lay leaders on the front lines. *Family Relations, 50,* 67–76.

Stets, J. E., & Straus, M. A. (1990). The marriage license as a hitting license: A comparison of dating, cohabiting and married couples. In M. A. Straus & R. J. Gelles (Eds.), *Physical violence in American families: Risk factors and adaptation to violence in 8415 families* (pp. 131–164). New Brunswick, NJ: Transaction.

Straus, M. A., & Gelles, R. (1986). Societal change and change in family violence from 1975 to 1985 as revealed by two national surveys. *Journal of Marriage and the Family, 48,* 465–479.

Sullivan, K. T., & Bradbury, T. N. (1997). Are premarital prevention programs reaching couples at risk for marital dysfunction? *Journal of Consulting and Clinical Psychology, 65,* 24–30.

Terman, L. M. (1938). *Psychological factors in marital happiness.* New York: Dryden Press.

Thompson, B. M. (1997). Couples and the work-family interface. In W. K. Halford & H. J. Markman (Eds.), *Clinical handbook of marriage and couples intervention* (pp. 273–290). Chichester, England: Wiley.

Thomson, E., & Colella, U. (1992). Cohabitation and marital stability: Quality or commitment? *Journal of Marriage and the Family, 54,* 259–267.

Tolstoy, L. (1961). *Anna Karenina* (D. Magarshack, Trans.). New York: New American Library.

Trussel, J., & Rao, K. U. (1987). Premarital cohabitation and marital stability: A reassessment of the Canadian evidence. *Journal of Marriage and the Family, 51,* 535–544.

United States Census Bureau. (2002). *Number, timing and duration of marriages and divorces:* 1996. Washington, DC: Author.

van Widenfelt, B., Hosman, C., Schaap, C., & Van der Staak, C. (1996). The prevention of relationship distress for couples at risk: A controlled evaluation with nine-month and two-year follow-ups. *Family Relations, 45,* 156–165.

van Widenfelt, B., Markman, H. J., Guerney, B., Behrens, B. C., & Hosman, C. (1997). Prevention of relationship problems. In W. K. Halford & H. J. Markman (Eds.), *Clinical handbook of marriage and couples intervention* (pp. 651–677). Chichester, England: Wiley.

Veroff, J., Douvan, E., & Hatchett, S. J. (1995). *Marital instability: A social and behavioral study of the early years.* Westport, CT: Praeger.

Visher, E. B., & Visher, J. S. (1991). Therapy with stepfamily couples. *Psychiatric Annals, 21,* 462–465.

Wallerstein, J. S., & Johnston, J. R. (1990). Children of divorce: Recent findings regarding the long-term effects and recent studies of joint and sole custody. *Pediatric Reviews, 11,* 197–204.

Waite, L., & Gallagher, M. (2000). *The case for marriage.* New York: Doubleday.

Wampler, K. S., & Sprenkle, D. (1980). The Minnesota Couple Communication Program: A follow-up study. *Journal of Marriage and the Family, 42,* 577–585.

Whisman, M. A. (1999). Marital dissatisfaction and psychiatric disorders: Results from the National Comorbidity Survey. *Journal of Abnormal Psychology, 108,* 701–706.

Whisman, M. A., & Jacobson, N. S. (1990). Power, marital satisfaction, and response to marital therapy. *Journal of Family Psychology, 4,* 202–212.

White, L. K. (1990). Determinants of divorce. A review of research in the eighties. *Journal of Marriage and the Family, 52,* 904–912.

Widom, C. S. (1989). Does violence beget violence? A critical examination of the literature. *Psychological Bulletin, 106,* 3–28.

Williams, L., & Jurich, J. (1995). Predicting marital success after five years: Assessing the predictive validity of FOCCUS. *Journal of Marital and Family Therapy, 21,* 141–153.

Wilson, K. L., Halford, W. K., Lizzio, A., Kimlin, S., & Islen, G. (2002). *How much do couples work at their relationships? Development of the self-regulation for effective relationships scale.* Manuscript submitted for publication.

Wolcott, I., & Glezer, H. (1989). *Marriage counselling in Australia: An evaluation.* Melbourne: Australian Institute of Family Studies.

Worthington, E. L., McCullough, M. E., Shortz, J. L., Mindes, E. J., Sandage, S. J., & Chartrand, J. M. (1995). Can couples assessment and feedback improve relationships? Assessment as a brief relationship enrichment procedure. *Journal of Counseling Psychology, 42,* 466–475.

Author Notes

Preparation of this paper was supported by an Australian Research Council Grant entitled "Evaluation of a flexible delivery relationship education program" to W. Kim Halford and Keithia L. Wilson and from the National Institute of Mental Health: Division of Services and Intervention Research, Adult and Geriatric Treatment and Prevention Branch, Grant 5-RO1-MH35525-12, "The Long-term Effects of Premarital Intervention" (awarded to Howard Markman, Scott Stanley, and Lydia Prado).

Endnotes

1   In this chapter we use the term "couple relationship education" to denote any educational process that is intended to assist couples in committed relationships who are currently satisfied in their relationship to sustain that high mutual satisfaction. Often relationship education is provided to marrying or married couples and the term used is "marriage education," but we prefer the somewhat more inclusve term of couple relationship education.

Chapter 8   *Domestic Violence*

Sandra M. Stith, Ph.D., Virginia Polytechnic Institute and State University,
Falls Church, Virginia.

Karen H. Rosen, Ed.D., Virginia Polytechnic Institute and State University
Falls Church, Virginia.

Eric E. McCollum, Ph.D., Virginia Polytechnic Institute and State University
Falls Church, Virginia.

S pouse abuse remains a pervasive problem in American society despite 20 years of widespread efforts to improve prevention, detection, and treatment as well as community and legal response. Spouse abuse has tremendous personal and social costs. According to a national survey, about 16% of married couples reported experiencing an incident of physical assault sometime during the year (Straus & Gelles, 1990). A consideration of cost must include medical, mental health, police, legal, and social services to victims and perpetrators. In 1994, females accounted for 39% of the hospital emergency room visits for all violence-related injuries but accounted for 84% of the persons treated for injuries inflicted by intimates (Bureau of Justice Statistics, 1998). American women are 4 times more likely to be injured by an intimate partner than in a motor vehicle accident (American Medical Association, 1992). Naturally, abusive relationships are related to significant distress, which decreases individual and family quality of life. Survey findings suggest that wife beating has significant adverse effects on women's mental and physical health. One study indicated that severely assaulted women have twice as many headaches, 4 times the rate of depression, nearly 6 times more suicide attempts, and twice as many days in bed due to illness as women who were not abused (Gelles & Straus, 1988).

Undetected violence can also have significant effects for other members of the family not directly involved in abuse. Partner abuse has been linked to profound and long-lasting negative emotional and behavioral effects on children who witness assaultive behavior (Jaffe & Sudderman, 1995). Children who have observed violence between their parents have been found to assault their siblings and their parents, to commit violent crimes outside the family, and to assault their own intimate partners more often than children who have not witnessed violence between their parents (Straus & Gelles, 1990; O'Leary, 1988). Furthermore, children in families in which there is partner abuse are also more likely to be hit themselves (Jaffe, Wolfe, & Wilson, 1990).

Although historically spouse abuse has been viewed as a private family matter, it is now viewed as a societal problem as well as a crime subject to legal punishment. This paradigmatic shift in perspective has brought a great deal of change in how spouse abuse is handled in our communities. Whereas legal authorities were once reluctant to intervene in violence that was thought to be a private matter between partners, perpetrators now are often faced with jail time or mandatory treatment. Two clear messages emerge: the aggressor must be held accountable, and the victim must be protected. Beyond these two primary concerns, spouse abuse treatment goals vary according to the theoretical perspective of the treatment program. Currently most programs for offenders and all treatment programs that have been formally evaluated are designed for male offenders. Most treatment is administered to men in groups, while concurrent support services and treatment for women victims and their children are offered. This model of "parallel track" treatment is based on the belief that conjoint treatment will increase the danger to victims of abuse by forcing them to confront their abusers directly, will increase the emotional intensity of the couple relationship which may also lead to violence, and will suggest that the victim is at least partially responsible for her abuse because she is being asked to make changes in relationship patterns along with the perpetrator. Although a number of investigators have begun to explore ways to work with couples safely and productively, couples treatment remains controversial.

The primary purpose of this chapter is to review the research that has been conducted to determine the effectiveness of conjoint models of spouse abuse treatment. We will review the research on couples approaches to domestic violence treatment that has included some type of outcome assessment, and discuss some of the methodological concerns with the research that has been conducted to date. Because no programs addressing female violence have been assessed, this review will address only treatment programs focusing on male violence. Also, although the research on couples treatment is quite sparse, family therapists have been writing about their approaches for treating violent couples for some time; therefore we will also discuss several couples treatment programs that have not been empirically evaluated. First, however, because batterer group treatment remains the most widely used and most accepted treatment for domestic violence, we will begin by presenting a brief synopsis of the various kinds of batterers group treatment approaches, and what is known about the effectiveness of this approach.

Batterers' Group Treatment Approaches

Most programs for offenders treat men in psychoeducational, gender-specific groups. Practice guidelines vary but most are based on an underlying conviction about what causes and maintains abuse. Thus, cognitive behavioral approaches are based on the belief that abuse-supporting beliefs, lack of behavioral self-control, and poor relationship skills result in abuse; feminist approaches are based on the belief that male socialization in the context of societally-sanctioned oppression of women results in abuse; and attachment-based approaches are based on the belief that abuse arises from the abusers' attachment injuries from childhood being reactivated in contemporary relationships. In practice, most batterers' treatment programs incorporate different theoretical approaches and interventions. However, although batterers' treatment appears to produce a moderate reduction in recidivism of domestic violence when compared to control groups, no intervention has been shown to be differentially more effective than the other within the same sample (Babcock & La Taillade, 2000).

Batterer program evaluations suggest that from 50% to 80% of program completers are nonviolent at follow-up (see Table 1). However, this body of research is plagued with a variety of problems. Measures of effectiveness vary from study to study. Some studies consider reduction in violence as the measure of success whereas others use complete cessation of violent behavior as the criterion of success (Edleson & Tolman, 1992). Although simple re-assault rate does not reflect the severity or impact of physical abuse, nor whether emotional abuse is occurring, it does offer a gross indicator of behavior. Studies also vary in whose report is used to measure outcome. Some studies depend on male self-report, whereas others use the abused partner's report, or police reports of re-arrest. Because men tend to report less violence than their partners, and only a small percentage of violence is reported to the police (Edleson & Brygger, 1986), partner report is considered the gold standard. Thus, the success rates reported in Table 1 are based on partner report and the measure of success is cessation of all physically violent acts, unless otherwise noted by an asterisk. It should also be noted that even when partners' reports are the measure, only a small percent of the partners are located, especially at follow-up. Therefore, it should be taken into consideration that reported recidivism rates are based on the reports of female partners who were located and willing to respond.

Another issue that has been a factor in evaluating batterers' group treatment approaches is problems with the methodological designs used. Studies that have no comparison group, or no pretest data, are limited in terms of what they tell us about effectiveness. Quasi-experimental designs, in which treatment completers are compared to some sort of control or contrast group, and true experimental designs, in which clients are randomly assigned to treatments and control groups, provide more robust evidence of what works. Table 1 separates quasi-experimental studies from true experimental designs.

Still another issue to consider when interpreting batterers' treatment outcomes is dropout rate. Although treatment seems to be successful for approximately half of those men who complete treatment, many studies report that only about one-third of batterers initially assigned to treatment, in fact, complete the program (Babcock & La Taillade, 2000). Men who choose to complete treatment tend to be more educated, more often employed, and less likely to have a criminal record than men who drop out (Babcock & Steiner, 1999). We know very little about what works for the dropout subpopulation. More rigorous studies must examine not only the outcome for those who complete treatment, but also must be clear about the dropout rate and compute at least some estimates of success

Table 1: Evaluations of Male Batterer Group Treatments

Quasi-Experimental Designs

Author/Year	Treatment Approach	Dropout Rate	Tx Grp Recidivism Rate/(n)	Comparison Group Recidivism Rate/Group Type/n	Follow-up Period
Babcock & Steiner, 1999	Psycho-ed	63%	8%/(106)[a]	23%/dropouts/178[a]	2 yr
Chen, Bersani, Myers, & Denton, 1989	Psycho-ed	37%	5%/(120)[a]	10%/untreated/101[a]	14 mo
Dobash, Dobash, Cavanagh, & Lewis, 1996	Psycho-ed	unknown	30%/(40)	62%/untreated/80	1 yr
Dutton, 1986	Cogn-beh	unknown	16%/(50)	40%/untreated/50	6 mo–3 yr
Dutton, Bodnarchuk, Kropp, Hart, & Ogloff, 1997	Cogn-beh	52%	23%/(156)[a]	50%/dropouts/167[a]	4 mo–11 yr
Edleson & Grusznski, 1988	Cogn-beh/Fem	31%	41%/(84)	48%/dropouts/37	6 mo
Edleson & Syers, 1991	32 session 12 session Education Combined	54%	23%/(30) 40%/(40) 36%/(22) 40%/(29)	21%/self help/19	18 mo 18 mo 18 mo 18 mo
Gondolf, 2002	Cogn-beh (multi-site)	32%	40%/(560)	67%/dropouts/280	30 mo
Hamberger & Hastings, 1988	Cogn-beh	51%	28%/(32)	47%/dropouts/36	12 mo
Harrell, 1991	Integrated	unknown	43%/(8)	12%/untreated/112	4 mo
Newell, 1994	Psycho-ed	43%	23%/(155)[a]	36%/dropouts/118[a]	2 yr

Author/Year	Treatment Approach	Dropout Rate	Tx Grp Recidivism Rate/(n)	Comparison Group Recidivism Rate/ Group Type/n	Follow-up Period
Experimental Designs (cont'd)					
Davis, 1998	Psycho-ed:Tx 1 Tx 2	33%	14%/(129) 18%/(61)	22%/control/186	1 yr
Feder, 1999	Psycho-ed/Fem	31%	48%/(149) [a]	45%/control/188[a]	1 yr
Ford & Regoli, 1993	Varied: Tx 1 Tx 2	unknown	29%/(127) 34%/(114)	35%/control/106 35%/control/106	6 mo 6 mo
Palmer, Brown, & Berrera, 1992	Psycho-ed	50%	10%/(30)[a]	31%/control/28[a]	1 yr
Saunders, 1996	Cogn-beh Psychodynamic	31%	42%/(83) 38%/(53)	compares two treatment groups	12–24 mo
Stosny, 1995	Attachment	38%	13%/(31)[a]	59%/control/32[a]	1 yr

Note. Cogn-beh = cognitive behavioral; Fem = feminism; Psycho-ed = psychoeducational; TX = treatment.

[a]Success not measured by cessation of all physically violent acts or not based solely on partner reports.

rate based on the completers and noncompleters combined—a strategy becoming increasingly common in substance abuse treatment studies in which treatment attrition is also a significant problem (Liddle & Dakof, 1995). Table 1 shows the dropout rate for each study in which that information was provided.

Finally, the time period in which outcome is measured varies widely from study to study. Although more than 50% of the men who complete batterers' treatment stop physically abusive behavior for some period of time following intervention (Tolman & Edleson, 1995), it is not clear how durable these changes are. Treatment providers and victims need to know if this behavior change lasts, and over what time period. In Table 1, the follow-up period of each study is reported.

Although group treatment programs for male offenders appear to be effective in eliminating physical violence for some men, there is no single approach that has been demonstrated to be the treatment of choice for all men under all circumstances. In fact, there may be negative effects for some men who participate in men's groups (Edleson & Tolman, 1992). For example, group members may support each other's negative attitudes about women or implicitly or explicitly support abusive behavior. Additionally, men may come home from group feeling like their wives have no reason to complain because they are not as abusive as other men in the group (Tolman, 1990). In one study, 10%–15% of female partners reported that their lives had worsened since their male partner began attending a batterer's program (Gondolf, 2002). In another study a significant proportion of female partners reported an increase in verbal abuse since their partners attended the treatment program (Dutton, 1986). Given the lack of convincing evidence that traditional men's treatment programs are widely effective, there is room to test other approaches, including conjoint treatment.

Conjoint Treatment for Domestic Violence

Although controversy exists about the appropriateness of treating violent couples together, a variety of reasons can be offered for providing couples therapy for domestic violence. First, a consistent research finding is that male batterers are a heterogeneous group (Gondolf, 1988; Saunders, 1992; Stuart & Holtzworth-Munroe, 1995). Holtzworth-Munroe and Stuart (1994) reviewed the batterer typology literature and reported that three descriptive dimensions (i.e., severity of marital violence, generality of violence [toward the wife or toward others], and presence of psychopathology/personality disorders) have consistently been found to distinguish subtypes of batterers. They suggest that three subtypes of batterers exist (i.e., family only, dysphoric/borderline, and generally violent/antisocial) and that tailoring treatment to each subtype of violent men might improve treatment outcome. From the growing domestic violence typology literature, it has become increasingly clear that all batterers do not need the same type of treatment. Most clinicians and researchers that advocate the use of conjoint approaches suggest that it should be limited to one subtype of batterer—the family-only batterer without apparent psychopathy, who is most likely to benefit from couple therapy (Stuart & Holtzworth-Munroe, 1995).

In addition to treating subgroups of batterers differently, there is also reason to include female partners in treatment. Both men and women are often violent in relationships. In fact, most research has found that women initiate and carry out physical assaults on their partners as often as do men (Stith & Straus, 1995). Despite the much lower probability of physical injury resulting from attacks by women, assaults by women are serious, just as it would be serious if men "only" slapped their wives or "only" slapped female fellow employees (Straus, 1993). If reciprocal violence is taking place in relationships, treating men without treating women is not likely to stop the violence. In fact, cessation of partner violence by one partner is highly dependent on whether the other partner also stops hitting (Feld & Straus, 1989; Gelles & Straus, 1988). Most importantly, when women use violence in relationships, they are at greater risk of being severely assaulted by their partners (Feld & Straus, 1989; Gondolf, 1998). Moreover, although men's treatment groups address men's role in intimate partner violence, they do not address any underlying relationship dynamics that may impact each partner's decision to remain in the violent relationship despite the violence, or may play a part in maintaining the violence. Because 50% to 70% of battered wives remain with their abusive partners or return to them after leaving a women's shelter or otherwise separating from them (Feazelle, Mayers, & Deschner, 1984), failing to provide services to both parties in an ongoing relationship may inadvertently disadvantage the female partner who chooses to stay. In a study involving the prediction of mild and severe husband-to-wife physical aggression with 11,870 randomly selected military personnel, Pan, Neidig, and O'Leary (1994) found that marital discord was the most accurate predictor of physical aggression against a partner. For every 20% increase in marital discord, the odds of mild spouse abuse increased by 102%, and the odds of severe spouse abuse increased by 183%. Because marital discord is a strong predictor of physical aggression toward a partner, it would seem that failure to address marital problems at some point in the treatment of men and/or women would make it likely that physical abuse would recur.

Review of Literature on Conjoint Treatment for Domestic Violence

Studies of typical family therapy client populations—those who come for regular outpatient marital therapy, not domestic violence treatment—show marital violence rates as high as 67% (O'Leary, Vivian, & Malone, 1992). Despite this staggering figure, only a few published studies have examined the effectiveness of couples treatment for husband-to-wife physical aggression. A number of issues limit the usefulness of this body of research in understanding the impact of couples counseling on treating domestic violence. Most of these studies are based on various types of cognitive behavioral treatment, leaving recent innovations in couples treatment such as Emotionally Focused Couples Therapy (Johnson, 1996) untested with domestic violence. Also, the therapeutic modality differs across studies with some studies testing individual couple therapy (one therapist working with one couple) while others examine multi-couple group therapy. Finally, as with studies of batterer treatment described above, methodological problems plague the study of conjoint treatment for domestic violence. We could find only six studies, for instance, that can be considered experimental. In this section we will review the existing outcome literature on couples treatment of domestic violence. The studies are summarized in Table 2.

Experimental Design

Only six studies can be conceptualized as being experimental (i.e., couples are randomly assigned to two or more treatment conditions). One study compared individual treatment, multi-couple treatment, rigorous monitoring, and no treatment within a military setting (Dunford, 2000). Two studies compared individual couple therapy with multi-couple therapy for domestic violence (Harris, Savage, Jones, & Brooke, 1988; Stith, McCollum, Rosen, & Locke, 2002). Stith et al. (2002) also included a nonrandom comparison group in their analyses. Two studies compared a cognitive behavioral men's group with a cognitive behavioral couples group (Brannen & Rubin, 1996; O'Leary, Heyman, & Neidig, 1999). Finally, one study compared individual treatment for substance abusers with a combination of individual treatment and behavioral couples therapy for substance abusers and looked at the impact of each treatment program on domestic violence (Fals-Stewart, Kashdan, O'Farrell, & Birchler, 2002).

Dunford (2000) conducted the only experimental study that included a conjoint treatment condition and a "no treatment" control group. He randomly assigned 861 Navy couples to one of four interventions: a 26-week cognitive behavioral therapy (CBT) men's group followed by six monthly sessions, a 26-week CBT multi-couple group followed by six monthly sessions, a "rigorously monitored" group, and a control group. The control group did not receive any formal intervention. Victimized wives in the control group were contacted by the military agency responsible for preventing and responding to domestic violence—the Family Advocacy Center (FAC)—as soon as possible after the presenting incident to ensure that the women were not in immediate danger of continued abuse. Once their safety was assured, FAC provided wives with safety planning information. No other formal intervention was offered.

In the rigorously monitored group, a case manager at the FAC saw perpetrators monthly for 12 months and provided individual counseling. Every 6 weeks a record search was completed to determine if perpetrators had been arrested or referred to court anywhere in San Diego County. Wives were called monthly and asked about repeat abuse. They were told that they did not have to reveal anything about their husband's behavior if doing so would place them in jeopardy. At the end of each treatment session, case managers sent progress reports to per-

Table 2: Evaluations of Couples Treatment for Domestic Violence

Experimental Design

Author/Year	Treatment Approach	Dropout Rate	Recidivism Rate	Measure of Recidivism	Follow-up Period
Dunford, 2000 Navy Study	CBT men's (164 men) (32 sessions) CBT couples group (158 men) (32 sessions) Monitoring (155 men) No treatment control (145 men)	29% Overall	Men's=29% Couples=30% Monitor=27% Control=35% No significant diff	Wives report of being "pushed or hit"	12 mo
Harris, Savage, Jones, & Brooke, 1988	Couples group (23 couples) (12 sessions) Individual couples (35 couples) (open-ended)	16% 67%	50% response; 18% recidivism No significant diff	Wives report of any violence	6–12 mo
Stith, McCollum, Rosen, & Locke, 2002	Individual couples (n=20) (18 sessions) Couples group (n=22) (18 sessions) No-treatment comparison group (n=9)	30% 27%	100% response rate 43% recidivism 25% recidivism 66% recidivism No significant diff	Wives report of any violence	6 mo
Brannen & Rubin, 1996	Men's/women CBT groups (26 couples) (12 sessions) Couples group CBT (26 couples) (12 sessions)	27% 4%	62% response rate 8.3% recidivism 7.1% recidivism No significant diff	Wives report of any violence	6 mo

Table 2: Evaluations of Couples Treatment for Domestic Violence (cont'd)

Author/Year	Treatment Approach Rate	Dropout	Recidivism Rate Recidivism	Measure of Period	Follow-up
O'Leary, Heyman, & Neidig, 1999	Men's/women CBT groups (30 couples) Couples group CBT (44 couples) (14 sessions)	50% 45%	84% response rate 74% recidivism No significant diff	Wives report of acts on MCTS	12 mo
Fals-Stewart, Kashdan, O'Farrell, & Birchler, 2002	Individual substance treatment (n=43 individuals) (56 sessions) BCT couples treatment (n=43 couples) (56 sessions/ 12 conjoint)	14.33% 14.33%	Before treatment 50% violence After treatment Ind= 43% recidivism BCT=18% recidivism	Wives report of any violence	12 mo
Quasi-Experimental Design					
Author/Year	Treatment Approach	Dropout Rate	Response/ Recidivism Rate	Measure of Recidivism	Follow-up Period
O'Farrell, Van Hutton, & Murphy, 1999	BCT for alcoholism (n=88) Matched community sample	No report	Before treatment 61.3% violent; 1 yr=22.7% 2 yrs=18.7% 9.1%	Wives report of acts on CTS	1 and 2 yr
Pre–Post Design					
Author/Year	Treatment Approach	Dropout Rate	Response/ Recidivism Rate	Measure of Recidivism	Follow-up Period
Lindquist, Telch & Taylor, 1983	CBT couples group (n=8 couples) (9 week group)	40%	50% response 100% recidivism	Man's self-report	6–8 mo

Table 2: Evaluations of Couples Treatment for Domestic Violence (cont'd)

Author/Year	Treatment Approach Rate	Dropout	Recidivism Rate Recidivism	Measure of Period	Follow-up
Riza, Stacey & Shupe, 1985	Individual couple treatment and multi-couple group treatment	Unclear	78% reduction or cessation of violence	Unclear	12 mo
Shupe, Stacey, & Hazelwood, 1987	18-week men's (194) Open-ended couples (27) 12-week couples (20)	41% aggregate	33% response 25% recidivism across programs	Wives report of any violence	1–3 yr
Taylor, 1984	Individual couples treatment (n=50)	No report	45% recidivism	Unclear	6 mo
Deschner & McNeil, 1986	6 week gender-specific group followed by 6 week couples group (n=134 individuals)	39%	54% response rate 15% recidivism	Self-report	8 mo
Harris, 1986	Individual sessions interspersed with couple sessions (n=40)	No report	Authors report "73% success rate"	Not clear	Unclear
Perez & Rasmussen, 1997	Bowen couple therapy (n=118) (open-ended)	No report	62% improving or improved 27% little or no improvement 11% in crisis	Therapists' assessment	Unclear
Johannson & Tutty, 1998	Couples group after 24-wk separate gender groups (n=15 couples) (12-week group)	13%	85% response 7 still together 43% recidivism	Wives report of any violence	12 mo

petrators and their commanding officers, specifying the presence or absence of instances of abuse. This process of rigorous monitoring was an attempt to create a "fishbowl" for perpetrators in which they felt that any instance of repeat abuse would be identified and dealt with by the military authorities.

The men's group, which used a cognitive behavioral treatment approach, met weekly for 6 months and then monthly for another 6 months, for a total 1-year treatment period. Treatment was based on a curriculum developed by Saunders (1996) and Wexler (1999). Each session had a series of tasks that the group leader was obliged to complete including both didactic and process activities.

The multi-couple group was organized in much the same way as the men's group, with 26 weekly sessions that included both didactic and process activities followed by six monthly sessions. As in the men's group, the six monthly sessions that followed consisted of content review and process activities. The multi-couple group curriculum was also based on the cognitive behavioral model and was developed by Geffner and Mantooth (2000). The interventions were similar to those used in the men's group, with the addition of wives to observe their partners being confronted about their abuse and to learn constructive ways of dealing with conflict (Dunford, 2000).

FAC records indicated that 71% of the cases were judged as having successfully completed treatment. Fifteen percent of the men were discharged from the Navy and therefore did not complete treatment. The remainder of the cases (14%) were considered as not having completed treatment. Thus, a conservative estimate of the dropout rate would be 29% if those leaving the Navy were defined as dropouts along with those labeled "not completing treatment." Analysis of the data revealed that 83% of the men completing treatment (men's, conjoint, and rigorous monitoring) did not re-injure their wives during a 1-year follow-up period. Because 79% of the men in the control group also did not re-injure their wives, there were no significant differences between groups on rate of re-injury. Findings also revealed no significant differences between groups on a variety of other outcome measures including "being pushed or hit," sexual abuse, and control abuse. Thus, in the military setting, the no-treatment group seemed to do as well as the treatment groups.

Two issues limit the usefulness of this for understanding the effectiveness of conjoint treatment in the general population. First, this study was conducted with active duty military members. When repeat violence occurs with this group, commanders are notified and the recidivism can impact the individual's career. Thus, findings from this study may not be generalizable to the civilian population. Also, a major problem with this study's ability to compare conjoint couples treatment with the other interventions is that the average number of wives actually attending the conjoint group sessions was relatively low. The ratio of attendance of women to men was 2 women for every 5 men. Thus, although some review articles (e.g., Babcock & La Taillade, 2000) include Dunford's (2000) study as a test of couples' therapy for domestic violence, in actuality, very few couples participated in the conjoint treatment modality. Although couples were randomly assigned to groups, wives were not asked about their willingness to participate in treatment before the random assignment was made, nor were they required to attend, as were their active duty husbands.

In addition, the multi-couple group was not conceptualized as a systemic intervention, but rather as an intervention that added wives to a men's treatment program so that wives could "witness authority figures confronting the offensive and oppressive nature of spouse abuse" (Dunford, p. 469).

Although Dunford's (2000) findings have limited usefulness in evaluating couples treatment, they did demonstrate that adding wives to a males' treatment group did not increase the risk to the wives. Wives participating in the conjoint groups were no more likely to be assaulted or injured than wives whose husbands participated only in men's treatment.

One early study (Harris et al., 1988) randomly assigned 81 couples that had contacted a family-service agency requesting relationship counseling to a multi-couple group treatment program or to couples counseling. Although the authors indicate that they also had a waiting-list control group, they do not compare the outcome of the treatment groups to the outcome of the control group. To be eligible for the program, a man had to use physical and/or sexual violence toward his partner or property and frighten or control her. The woman (when interviewed individually) had to indicate that she wished to remain in the relationship and report that she did not feel endangered. Furthermore, the man had to exhibit no psychotic symptoms, no evidence of serious brain injury, and no pervasive substance abuse that was not being treated concurrently.

The multi-couple group program consisted of 10 weekly 3-hour sessions. During the first 90 minutes of each session, the men and women met separately in same-sex peer groups. The women's group focused on the process of ending victimization, and the men's group concentrated on confronting violent behaviors and understanding attitudes that contribute to controlling behavior. Afterwards, the men and women met together with both group leaders for 1-hour teaching sessions on topics that included time-out procedures and the cycle of violence. Two review sessions were held at 1 month and 4 months after the program ended.

The individual couples counseling program was a "family systems-based form of treatment modified so that the therapist explicitly addressed the violence against the woman as the primary problem in the relationship using concepts developed in the group program" (Harris et al., 1988, p. 149). Treatment in this condition continued until the couple and therapist mutually agreed that all goals had been accomplished.

Sixty-seven percent of the 35 couples assigned to individual couples counseling dropped out before completing treatment, whereas only 16% of the 23 couples assigned to the multi-couple group dropped out. Only a small number of the initial couples completed all pre and post measures (5 couples who had completed couples counseling; 16 couples who participated in the multi-couple group). Repeated-measures analysis of variance indicated that scores on all aspects of psychological well-being assessed (i.e., levels of violence, mood states, self-confidence, and social support) did not vary by treatment group or by sex, but that participants' mean pre- and posttests scores for all the measures were significantly different; that is, participants showed positive changes over time, regardless of sex or treatment group. Follow-up results revealed that the goal of stopping the physical violence was achieved for over 80% of the couples based on reports by women who participated in the follow-up interview, and that these results did not differ by treatment group. However, because couples in the individual couples treatment program were much less likely to complete treatment, "all couple counseling for this population has ceased in this setting" (Harris et al., 1988, p. 154). Despite this apparent condemnation of couples therapy, the group intervention included a strong couples component.

Stith et al. (2002) conducted another study comparing individual couples treatment for domestic violence with multi-couple group treatment. The program they developed uses an integrated family therapy approach that incorporates aspects of Solution-Focused Therapy to treat domestic violence. The authors added individual couples therapy or multi-couple group therapy to a gender-specific treatment approach. Couples were excluded from the treatment if there was ongoing substance abuse, if the wife reported a previous serious injury as a result of domestic violence, or if the husband had a general pattern of violence against others. Both partners, in individual sessions, had to report that they wanted conjoint treatment and that they felt comfortable expressing their concerns with their partner present.

Because their primary objective was to develop a treatment manual, Stith et al. (2002) gathered qualitative data throughout the project and made revisions to the protocol during the 4-year project based on the qualitative data. In the early stages of the program, the men completed a 12-week cognitive behavioral group intervention before beginning the conjoint program. However, women that had not participated in the gender-specific group reported that they felt disadvantaged when the conjoint treatment began because the men had a shared language about abuse and many had met each other before beginning the multi-couple group. Therefore, in the later stages of the project, and in their current work, both partners completed a 6-week gender-specific psychoeducational group before beginning conjoint therapy. After completing the men's group or the gender-specific groups, couples were randomly assigned to either a 12-week multi-couple group intervention (22 couples) or to a 12-week individual couple intervention (20 couples). Results from these groups were compared to a comparison group consisting of couples in which the men completed the men's group and the couples completed pretests and follow-up tests, but the couples were not able to participate in the couples intervention for a variety of reasons, primarily because of scheduling conflicts (9 couples). Thirty percent of the couples assigned to the individual couple treatment and 27% of the couples assigned to multi-couple treatment dropped out before completing treatment.

Six months after treatment, every female partner in each group was contacted. Those in the individual couple treatment condition reported a 43% recidivism rate whereas those in the multi-couple group treatment condition reported a 25% recidivism rate. Women in the comparison group reported a 66% recidivism rate (Stith et al., 2002). Probably because of the small sample size, the differences between groups were not statistically significant.

Two years after treatment ended, 19 of the 30 wives completing treatment were contacted (Stith, McCollum, & Rosen, unpublished manuscript). Only 1 female partner reported a subsequent violent incident (i.e., 6.25% recidivism). Four of the 9 wives in the comparison group were contacted and 2 reported a subsequent violent incident (i.e., 50% recidivism). Seventy percent of the couples who completed treatment and were able to be contacted (23 couples) were still together. In contrast, only 20% of the comparison couples who were able to be contacted (5 couples) were still together. Several wives who reported that they had gotten divorced indicated that the couples counseling program gave them the courage to end the marriage. One wife reported that there was no reoccurrence of violence because the counseling enabled her to get the courage she needed to clearly state that she would not tolerate any further violence. As soon as old patterns resurfaced that traditionally led to her partner being violent she activated her safety plan before he could escalate. They are currently divorced. One wife reported that the couples counseling program made it possible for her to share custody with her husband after their divorce without ongoing violence. Another couple who successfully completed the multi-couple group came in with pretty low expectations. When contacted at 2-year follow-up the wife said, "I was very surprised that he was able to stop being violent—I had always heard that once a man is violent he is always violent. So I am surprised and pleased that he could stop. Now he walks away when he feels himself becoming angry—he hasn't put a hand on me! We are really happy and our relationship is so much better."

Two experimental studies have been conducted comparing Peter Neidig's (Neidig, Friedman, & Collins, 1985) multi-couple group treatment program with a gender-specific cognitive behavioral men's group. In the largest test of Neidig's (O'Leary, Heyman, & Neidig, 1999) model, 75 intact, volunteer couples were assigned to either a gender-specific therapy (GST) or a conjoint 14-week treatment for psychological and physical aggression. Both types of treatment were based on a cognitive behavioral model with the conjoint nature of treatment being the primary difference between the two treatment models.

Physical Aggression Couples Treatment (PACT), the conjoint treatment model tested in this study, is based on Neidig's (Neidig & Friedman, 1984) earlier work and is described in Heyman and Neidig (1997). PACT is not standard marital therapy. The purpose of the treatment is to eliminate violence in the home. The first half of PACT focuses on taking responsibility for one's own violence and on anger control skills. The second half focuses on issues such as improving communication, decreasing jealousy, and renegotiating more equitable marriage contracts. The purpose of working on these issues is to increase alternatives to violence and to decrease conflicts that may lead to violence. Group facilitators used a workbook developed by Neidig (1992) to guide each session of PACT.

To be eligible to participate in this research, the wife, in a separate interview, had to report that she felt comfortable with conjoint treatment, that she was not fearful of speaking her mind in front of her husband, and that she had not needed to seek medical attention for injuries from her husband's violence. Couples were also screened out if the husband met the DSM criteria for alcohol abuse or dependence, if the wife reported that the husband had a drinking problem, if the couple was not married or was married but separated, and if group treatment for aggression was contraindicated by normal practice guidelines (e.g., psychotic or bipolar disorder not being medically treated, a violent criminal past, or if the screening clinician was concerned for the wife's safety).

O'Leary et al. (1999) indicated that the overall dropout rate for their study was 47%. Forty couples were assigned to PACT. Twenty-two (55%) completed 10 out of 14 two-hour sessions and were considered treatment completers. Thirty couples were assigned to GST; 15 (50%) completed at least 10 sessions. The results of this study indicated that both male and female participants significantly reduced their levels of psychological and physical aggression at 1-year follow-up. Two-thirds of husbands did not engage in severe violence in the year following treatment; however, only 26% ceased their violent behaviors completely. No differences were found across treatments in wives' reports of their own safety and in wives' ability to resist taking blame for their husband's violent behavior. The only differential effect for treatment type was that husbands who participated in conjoint treatment reported higher marital satisfaction ratings compared to husbands in GST.

In discussing their findings, O'Leary et al. (1999) also addressed some of the concerns about conjoint treatment. The authors indicated that, "compared to wives in the GST, wives in the conjoint treatment were not fearful of participating with their husbands; were not fearful during the sessions; did not blame themselves for the violence; and were not put at an increased risk for violence during the program" (p. 494). The authors further suggested that, "at this point, both conjoint treatment and GSTs for wife abuse appear to be equally viable modes of intervention. There were significant reductions in men's psychological aggression (i.e., approximately a 50% reduction) that were associated with reductions in physical aggression" (p. 501).

In an earlier test of the same model, Brannen and Rubin (1996) randomly assigned 49 couples to either Neidig's multi-couple group intervention or to gender-specific groups with men and women in separate groups. Participants in this study were intact couples who had a desire to remain in their current relationship and who were court referred. Forty couples completed the treatment program. Seven spouses dropped out (6 were women assigned to the gender-specific group intervention). Thus, the dropout rate was 27% for the gender-specific group and 4% for the couples group.

Whereas the couples group used Neidig's (Neidig & Friedman, 1984) treatment model, the gender-specific men's group intervention was based on a model developed by the Minneapolis-based Domestic Abuse Project (DAP), described in their *Men's Treatment Handbook* (Rusinoff, 1990). The model focuses on establishing accountability for men who batter. The women's intervention focused on empowering and improving victims' ability to protect themselves. Both the gender-specific and the couples intervention consisted of 12 weekly sessions lasting 90 minutes.

Results from this study indicated that for the majority of abusers it did not matter which treatment was used. However, for those with a history of alcohol abuse, the multi-couple approach was superior. Analysis of victim reports 6 months after treatment indicated that neither approach was more effective in sustaining gains. Approximately 92% of the respondents who were able to be located (62% of the participants) indicated that there had been no further incidents of violence after treatment.

In the final study that we were able to identify, which used experimental methods to assess the impact of couples treatment on domestic violence, Fals-Stewart et al. (2002) compared individual treatment for substance abusers with behavioral couples therapy (BCT). In BCT the spouse is included in treatment with the substance-abusing patient to build support for sobriety. Behavioral techniques such as communication training and "Caring Day" assignments are used to reduce risk of relapse. In this study, 80 married or cohabiting male patients with a primary drug abuse diagnosis (with the primary drug of abuse not being alcohol) in a substance abuse outpatient clinic were randomly assigned to one of two treatments. The individual treatment was a behavioral coping skills program. BCT was the other treatment. Both treatments comprised 56 therapy sessions over a 6-month period. Individual treatment had all sessions with the patient alone; BCT had 12 of the sessions with the patient and female partner together. In addition to having fewer substance abuse relapses, couples in BCT also reported more positive relationship adjustment on multiple measures (Fals-Stewart, Birchler, & O'Farrell, 1996). In addition, Fals-Stewart et al. (2002) reported that although nearly half of the couples in both groups reported male-to-female violence in the year before treatment, the number reporting violence in the year after treatment was significantly lower for BCT (18%) than for individual treatment (43%). Thus, although BCT did not specifically focus on domestic violence, conjoint treatment for drug abuse had a significant impact on reducing domestic violence recidivism, while individual treatment did not seem to impact domestic violence recidivism.

Results from each of the experimental studies indicate that violent men who are treated with their female partners (either in individual couple therapy or as part of a multi-couple group) reduced their violence. The study by Fals-Stewart et al. (2002) found that couples therapy for substance abuse was more effective than individual therapy for substance abuse in reducing domestic violence. The study by Brannen and Rubin (1996) found that the multi-couple therapy was more effective than gender-specific therapy in reducing domestic violence for male abusers with a history of alcohol problems. Significant differences were not found between individual couple treatment and multi-couple treatment or between gender-specific treatment and multi-couple treatment in reducing or eliminating violence in the other four studies. There is no evidence from the six experimental studies reviewed here that women are more likely to be endangered in these carefully screened, domestic violence-focused conjoint treatment programs than they are in programs that treat men individually. In addition, adding conjoint treatment sessions to individual treatment for substance abuse appears to reduce domestic violence recidivism more than does treating male substance abusers individually.

Quasi-Experimental Design

In an interesting study of the natural history of domestic violence before and after alcoholism treatment, O'Farrell, Van Hutton, and Murphy (1999) followed couples receiving behavioral marital therapy (BMT) for two years. Comparison rates of domestic violence for a demographically matched nonalcoholic sample were derived from a nationally representative survey of violence in American families (Straus & Gelles, 1990). In the year before BMT, the alcoholics had a significantly higher prevalence of violence and frequency of violent acts (4 to 6 times more prevalent and substantially more frequent) than did their counterparts in the nonalcoholic comparison sample. Of the original 88 couples completing treatment and 1-year follow-up assessments, 75 provided 2-year follow-up data on violence. The percentage of couples experiencing any violent act decreased from 61.3% in the year before BMT to 22.7% in the first year after BMT and to 18.7% in the second year after BMT. The frequency of violent behaviors also decreased significantly. Additionally, during both the first and the second year after BMT the prevalence and frequency of violence by alcoholics were no longer significantly higher than among their counterparts in the nonalcoholic comparison sample. However, violence prevalence and frequency remained at least 1.5 times higher than in the comparison sample.

Another interesting finding from this study was that the extent of violence after BMT was associated with the extent of the alcoholics' drinking. Overall, relapsed alcoholics had a greater level of violence than did remitted alcoholics. Remitted alcoholics no longer had elevated domestic violence levels compared with matched controls whereas relapsed alcoholics did, and the frequency of violence was correlated with the number of days the alcoholic drank. The authors emphasized that "reduced violence among the remitted alcoholics and persistent violence among the relapsed alcoholics does not permit unequivocal interpretation that the continuing drinking caused the continued violence, since other variables may account for the variations in both drinking and violence" (O'Farrell et al., 1999, p. 321). They also emphasized that, like the other nonexperimental studies reviewed here, we cannot conclude that the changes in violence were caused by BMT, because a control group without BMT was not included.

Pre–Posttest Designs
    Outcome has been reported for a number of other programs developed to treat couples in battering relationships. Eight studies are reported in Table 2 and two other studies are briefly described in this section. However, studies regarding the effectiveness of these programs are plagued by substantial methodological shortcomings including limited sample sizes, lack of standardized assessment instruments, outcome reported by only one partner, and one-sample designs. Although these studies do not help us understand how conjoint treatment compares with no treatment or with individual treatment, they do help us understand whether offenders receiving these types of treatment reduce their level of violence. Of course we cannot conclude that the treatment is responsible for the change, because a variety of other factors including time, threats by the partner to divorce, arrest, and so forth, may be responsible for noted changes.
    Only one study found that violence continued for all couples treated in a conjoint treatment program. Lindquist, Telch, and Taylor (1983) pilot tested a 9-week, 2-hour per week multi-couple group with 8 couples. The program focused on positive communication skills, stress management, anger control, and problem solving. Of the 10 individuals who responded at the 6-week follow up, all indicated that the group continued to be of some benefit, and 50% reported no recidivism. However, at the 6-month follow up, all of the 4 couples responding reported between one and four violent incidents.
    All of the other studies reported that couples treatment had some positive impact on domestic violence. For example, Geffner, Mantooth, Franks, and Rao (1989) developed a psychoeducational conjoint therapy based on Rational Emotive Therapy principles. This program includes both individual couple treatment and couple group treatments. Riza, Stacey, and Shupe (1985) evaluated the program and reported that one year after counseling, 78% of treated couples reported a reduction or cessation of violence and 79% remained together. All of the couples surveyed recommended the program to others.
    Taylor (1984) described an eight-stage individual couples treatment program based on a cognitive behavioral approach. His stages included observing stressful cues, changing internal cognitive dialogues, learning to express one's self more assertively, and more effectively resolving conflicts. He reported that at 6-month follow-up 65% of the 50 couples he treated were violence-free. He did not report how these data were gathered nor on whose report they were based.
    Deschner, McNeil, and Moore (1986) reported on a 10-session anger control

group for violence-prone spouses and parents. In their groups, they treated both child and spouse abusers. The first few weeks were gender specific and addressed anger management skills and a commitment to nonviolence; the remaining weeks were conjoint and addressed anger management skills interactionally. Research on the program (Deschner et al., 1986) found that 8 of the 15 couples were violence free at 8-month follow-up. In a further study of this approach, Deschner and McNeil (1986) reported on 134 persons that had come to at least one session of treatment. Of these, 45 had been involved with child abuse alone, 7 with both child and spouse abuse, and the rest with partner abuse only. All had experienced at least two episodes of violence in their family. Eighty-two attended at least four sessions, a dropout rate of 39%. During the follow-up survey 8 months after treatment ended, researchers were able to contact 54% of the group members. According to their self-reports, only 15% had reverted to physical violence at any time since leaving treatment. Most were still with the same partner and were managing to avoid violence.

Harris (1986) conducted a study of 40 couples randomly selected from over 200 couples seen between 1978 and 1983 using Walker's (1979) model of conjoint counseling for battering couples. The model was an early version of cognitive behavioral treatment in which both partners were taught anger management skills. Initially, individual sessions were held with each partner and then conjoint sessions were interspersed with individual sessions. Although the authors reported a 73% success rate, they did not explain how they defined success.

Perez and Rasmussen (1997) described a program that targeted couples at risk for battering. The prevention model is based on a Bowenian approach that focuses on partner differentiation, reducing emotionality, and promoting rational thinking. Couples in the program had experienced one or more episodes of the man using highly coercive behavior, "mild" violence to control the woman, and/or both partners had used coercive behavior. Couples typically participated in weekly, 1 hour-and-15 minute sessions. The number of sessions ranged from 1 to as high as 50, although the average was 8 to 10. Outcome was measured by therapist reports. Of the 118 couples that participated in the program between 1992 and 1995, according to therapist reports, 62% were improving or improved, 27% had little improvement or no improvement, and the remaining 11% were in crisis or referred. The authors did not report rates of violence after treatment or exactly how therapists arrived at improvement rates.

Johannson and Tutty (1998) reported results from exploratory research that evaluated two 12-week groups for couples who had previously completed 24-week separate gender family violence groups. Eligibility criteria for the group included no ongoing severe violence and willingness of both partners to sign a no violence contract. The main focus of the couples group was to help couples integrate the communication, problem solving, and conflict resolution skills learned in the gender-specific groups. Each week the facilitators introduced a theme, such as the effects of childhood abuse or personal values, and the couples practiced communicating their personal experiences with respect to the themes while other couples and the facilitators observed and intervened if communication became difficult. Fifteen couples began the group, but 2 dropped out. Overall, posttest scores on psychological and physical abuse declined. However, because participants were asked to report on violence during the past 12-months each time, considerable overlap occurred in the time period assessed. During treatment, no violence was reported by either partner at the weekly group check-ins or the monthly private screenings. One year after the group had ended, the group facilitators contacted 11 of the 13 couples. Seven remained in their relationship with 4 reporting no further incidents of abuse. Two of the 3 couples who experienced reccurence of violence came back to the agency seeking further relationship counseling.

What Have We Learned From Research on Conjoint Approaches to Domestic Violence?

As indicated earlier, results from the experimental and quasi-experimental studies reviewed here indicate that domestic violence-focused conjoint approaches with carefully screened couples appear to be at least as effective as gender-specific treatment approaches. All but one of the 1-sample studies indicates that after completing conjoint treatment, some couples are able to end the violence in their relationships. No studies have demonstrated that conjoint treatment is more dangerous than gender-specific treatment.

Empirically Untested Approaches to Couples Treatment of Domestic Violence

Several models of couples therapy for domestic violence are being used clinically but have not been empirically tested. We have chosen to discuss three of these because we believe they address important issues in treatment and are rich ground for future research. These models are the Ackerman Institute Model, the Cultural Context Model, and Solution-Focused Brief Therapy.

The Ackerman Institute Model

The work of Goldner, Penn, Sheinberg, and Walker (1990) at the Ackerman Institute for the Family represents an effort to escape the polarization of feminist and systemic ideas in the treatment of domestic violence. The model that has arisen from this work is grounded in the belief that neither the feminist nor the psychological/systemic perspectives by themselves are adequate to explain the complexity of violence in attached relationships. The feminist perspective's focus on power inequity and the culturally sanctioned domination of women by men does not leave room for the ambivalence felt by both men and women in attached relationships who experience both conflict and love for one another. Similarly, exclusive reliance on the psychological/systemic perspective runs the risk of holding victims and perpetrators equally accountable for the violence in the relationship and ignoring the social forces that support violence against women.

The treatment model (Greenspun, 2000) that has grown from this attempt to combine the feminist and psychological/systemic views conceptualizes violence as multiply-determined, the outgrowth of male power and control, couple relational dynamics, and individual factors (e.g., past histories of abuse and trauma, and neurobiological predispositions to violence). Treatment is provided on an outpatient basis by one or two therapists working directly with the clients while a team observes. Greenspun reports that most couples treated with this model so far are self-referred for general marital therapy and violence is identified as a problem during agency intake. A small percentage is court-ordered.

Treatment progresses through three stages—evaluation, individual couple work, and group therapy. During the evaluation stage, the treatment team determines whether or not the couple is appropriate for conjoint work. Some factors are clearly exclusionary (e.g., a history of sociopathy) whereas others may require additional treatment before couples therapy begins (substance abuse, neurobiological factors such as attention deficit disorder, or neurological impairment affecting impulse control, for instance). The primary criteria for inclusion, however, are: "the man's ability to take full responsibility for his use of violence, his capacity to tolerate hearing the woman's description of being victimized by him, and his willingness to work toward stopping his abusive behavior" (Greenspun, 2000, p. 160).

The individual couple therapy stage is brief—five sessions—and aims at addressing the violence directly and helping the perpetrator stop it. Interventions during this phase include helping the perpetrator identify exceptions to his use of violence, connecting impulse toward violence to past abusive experiences, acknowledging and validating the woman's experience of the man's violence, and addressing safety.

The last stage of treatment—group therapy—is used to augment the changes that have begun in the individual couple stage and to generalize treatment into a wider community dedicated to nonviolence. Both multi-couple and gender-specific groups are used. Goals of this phase of treatment include reducing the social isolation of couples, and providing peer support for nonviolence along with peer confrontation of abusive acts or attitudes.

To date, no outcome data are available for this model.

The Cultural Context Model

Almeida and Durkin (1999) described a couples treatment model for domestic violence—the Cultural Context Model—that has grown from over 15 years of clinical experience. This model is based in a feminist analysis of the important part that culture plays in determining many levels of behavior including violence in attached relationships. Culture in this model is a broad category that can serve as both a source of significant strength and connection as well as the medium for attitudes and beliefs that serve to oppress women and children and cede power to men. Thus, any change effort must raise consciousness about the power of men and the role of women and place these issues in their cultural, historical, and sociopolitical contexts.

Domestic violence treatment in the Cultural Context Model is conceptualized in three phases. In the first phase, male perpetrators are seen in male-only groups. The three goals of this phase are to help men become accountable for their violence; help them understand the interplay of gender, race, class, culture, sexual orientation, and domestic violence; and expose them to nonviolent male sponsors. As individuals, sponsors serve a variety of functions in treatment—models, mentors, and confronters—while collectively they bring the voice of the community into the treatment setting and challenge the patriarchal view that violence inside the family is a private matter, of no concern to "outsiders."

Phase 2 of therapy involves group treatment for men and women in gender-specific groups. The goals of these groups are to build on the work of phase 1 and to begin to address relationship issues. Men and women still meet separately in this phase because the emphasis of treatment is different for each. For men, the focus is on learning to value personal accountability to others over concern with self while the focus in women's treatment is on empowerment and stepping out of the role of bearing sole responsibility for the well-being of their families.

Phases 1 and 2 of therapy last for at least 9 months. Throughout this time, therapists look for evidence that men are working to change patterns of dominance. Both men's reports of their own actions and attitudes and, more importantly, women's reports concerning their partners are used to judge whether or not change is occurring. Only when the therapists are convinced that significant change has occurred do the couples begin conjoint therapy.

In phase 3, both men and women remain connected to their gender-specific groups but begin to meet together for couples counseling as well. Almeida and Durkin (1999) did not describe specific goals of couples treatment but did note that groups remain a primary focus of treatment during this phase. Information gained by therapists in couples sessions may be taken back to group to preserve the emphasis on community as the arena for accountability. Thus, a man who reverts to abusive or domineering actions will be challenged in his gender-specific group as well as, presumably, during the couple session.

Almeida and Durkin (1999) reported that in 15 years of using the treatment format described above, "no woman participating in our program has ever been physically hurt" (p. 321). No data on dropout or other outcome data are reported for this model.

Solution-Focused Domestic Violence Couples Treatment

Lipchik and Kubicki (1996), a family therapist and a batterer intervention specialist respectively, described an approach to couples treatment based on the Solution-Focused Brief Therapy model (see, for example de Shazer, 1982, 1985,

1988). This model most resembles typical couples therapy. Couples are seen in an outpatient setting by two therapists, one of who conducts the session while the other observes from behind a one-way mirror. Following an initial conjoint session, partners are seen individually to further assess violence and to formulate safety plans for both the man and woman. Ongoing couples treatment is undertaken only if the following conditions are met:

1. The man says he really wants to stop being abusive in any way his partner experiences it.
2. The man takes responsibility for the abuse.
3. The man takes responsibility for contributing to the quality of the relationship.
4. [The woman] expresses the desire for emotional and physical violence to cease.
5. [The woman] takes responsibility for contributing to the quality of the relationship (Lipchik & Kubicki, 1996, p. 70).

If these conditions are not met, couples therapy is not indicated and one or both partners are referred to whichever noncouples treatments appear to be appropriate—individual therapy, batterer's intervention, shelters, and so forth. Furthermore, couples are evaluated for substance abuse, psychiatric impairment, and the presence of some positive feeling about the relationship before couples treatment begins.

Couples treatment consists of applying the solution-focused model to the issue of violence and whatever other concerns the couples present. Lipchik and Kubicki (1996) made clear that this approach represents a radical departure from more traditional approaches to domestic violence treatment. They eschewed the stance of separating the couple, advocating for the victim, and confronting and resocializing the man in favor of taking a collaborative stance with both partners, motivating the man to take responsibility for his violent acts by not increasing his resistance through confrontation, identifying positive aspects of the relationship and amplifying them, and helping the couple set mutually satisfying goals for treatment. The authors addressed issues of safety in treatment by careful selection of appropriate couples and discontinuing couples treatment if there was a recurrence of abuse. Although Gingerich and Eisengart's (2000) review of outcome studies of Solution-Focused Brief Therapy provides some support for the efficacy of this approach with a variety of types of problems, and Stith et al. (2002) reported on the effectiveness of an integrated version of this model, no studies have tested its usefulness as presented by Lipchik and Kubicki for couples treatment of domestic violence.

Priorities for Future Research

As is clear from the foregoing review, much work remains to be done to fully evaluate the efficacy of couples treatment for domestic violence and to specify with which couples it is appropriate. Both small- and large-scale studies can be useful in this regard. At present, cognitive behavioral approaches are the most common models that have been tested. Other models, including the three we have described in this chapter, are being used clinically with violent couples and should be tested empirically. In addition, recent innovations in marital therapy, including the work of Johnson (1996) and Gottman (1999) may lead to even more useful models for working with couples between whom there has been violence. The development and testing of such models is a further step in the process of carefully evaluating couples therapy for domestic violence.

In addition to simply doing more outcome research in this area, the literature could be strengthened by attention to some of the methodological problems in existing studies. As noted earlier, few studies to date meet the criteria for sound outcome research. It is also important for researchers to use sound and clearly specified outcome criteria. Issues to consider include whose report of outcome (victim, abuser, or a third party like police reports) should be used, what criteria for outcome (e.g., absence of violence, reduction in violence, increase in couple satisfaction, or decrease in patriarchal values) will be measured, and what measurement tool will be used.

Quantitatively measured outcome is important to the evaluation process for couples treatment, but qualitative methods also have a place. Although there is no empirical support for the notion that women who participate in conjoint domestic violence-focused therapy are in more danger of being abused than women who are left out of the treatment process, little is known about how women *experience* domestic violence-focused couples therapy. It is important to know what conditions help them feel safe to participate fully in couples sessions and what conditions lead them to hold back. In addition, philosophical concerns must mesh with empirical ones. If couples treatment decreases violence and improves relationships but leaves women *feeling* more to blame and in danger, it would clearly be a mistake to judge such a treatment successful. Qualitative methods can certainly make a contribution in understanding women's experience.

Treatment dropout is a major problem in both domestic violence treatment and in domestic violence outcome research. Most studies report that 30% or more of the participants who begin treatment do not complete it. However, little is known about what differentiates those who drop out from those who complete treatment. Perhaps completers are a clear subpopulation of those who are referred for domestic violence treatment and outcomes are therefore only generalizable to that specific group. A better understanding of why clients drop out of treatment would set the stage for adjusting our treatment models to better meet clients' needs and therefore reduce dropout rates. In addition to understanding what leads men to drop out of treatment, it is important to also understand more about the experience of women whose partners drop out compared with women whose partners complete. If partners of dropouts are at more risk, outreach services might be made available to them. Answering such questions about both men and couples who drop out of treatment will give the most complete view of the efficacy of using couples treatment for domestic violence, and its differential effectiveness over other intervention modalities. Process and qualitative research designs could help us begin to understand the factors that lead clients to leave treatment without completing it and the experiences of those who drop out.

Other Research Directions
Unfortunately, we could find no studies that have examined the cost effectiveness of couples treatment nor any that examine who is best able to deliver it and what "dose" of treatment is most effective. Also, no one has conducted research examining the effectiveness of any of these conjoint models with diverse populations. Each of these issues deserves further investigation.

Domestic violence research has increasingly shown a strong link with various other mental health disorders, especially substance abuse and depression. Conjoint treatment models that target individuals with dual diagnoses of both domestic violence and substance abuse or domestic violence and depression could be developed and compared with conjoint treatment models developed to treat these issues in isolation.

We also need research efforts to develop and test programs that treat the entire family, including witnessing children. We know that domestic violence has a profound impact on children living in violent families, and family therapists are especially appropriate mental health providers to develop and test these models. Finally, with communities increasingly mandating treatment for female domestic violence offenders, we need to develop and test treatment programs that specifically address the needs of aggressive female partners.

Implications for Therapists

Domestic violence is common in couples that come for general marital counseling. As noted earlier, O'Leary et al. (1992) found violence rates as high as 67% for couples in a regular outpatient population. Thus, family therapists are already working with violent couples. Unfortunately, they are often not aware that they are doing so. One major implication from the existing body of literature is that family therapists need to become more aware of domestic violence as an issue and make assessment for violence a routine part of treatment regardless of the presenting problem.

Assessment for domestic violence should include both a written assessment instrument and a thorough interview conducted independently with each partner. The most widely used assessment measure is the Conflict Tactics Scale (CTS; Straus, 1979). This is an 18-item self-report inventory of conflict resolution tactics. Both partners indicate whether they or their partner engaged in any of a number of physically aggressive behaviors in the year prior to the assessment.

In addition to a written assessment, each partner should be interviewed separately. The therapists should ask questions in a nonjudgmental, routine way.

Because many couples do not label the slapping, hitting, or shoving that takes place in their relationship as violence, it is important to ask about specific acts and behaviors rather than ask general questions about "violence." When assessment reveals that there has been violence between client partners, regular couples treatment protocols need to be modified. Although much that family therapists do in couples treatment of nonviolent couples is also useful when there has been violence, all of the couples treatment approaches reviewed in this chapter—tested and untested—have made substantial changes from regular outpatient couples treatment practice. The common core ingredients that appear in most of the successful programs include:

1. Clients are carefully screened into the program.
   * Clients who have seriously injured their partners are excluded.
   * Both clients (in separate interviews) must report that they want to participate in couples treatment and that they are not afraid to express their concerns to their partners.
2. The primary focus of treatment is on eliminating all forms of partner abuse (physical, emotional, verbal), not on saving marriages.
3. Most programs emphasize taking responsibility for one's own violence and include a skill-building component including teaching such skills as recognizing when anger is escalating, de-escalating, and taking time-outs.
4. Effectiveness in all the successful programs reviewed here is measured by reduction or elimination of violence.

The therapist's primary responsibility when working with violent couples is to assure the safety of all family members, and this issue must remain at the forefront of treatment until safety is assured. At times, assuring safety means not agreeing to work conjointly with a couple if the risk of repeated violence is too high, if the perpetrator is not motivated to change his violent behavior, or if the victim is being coerced to come to couples therapy as another controlling tactic by the perpetrator. When couples are judged appropriate for conjoint work, specific modifications that therapists should make include having regular individual meetings with partners—especially victims—to develop safety plans, assess for recurrences of violence, and ascertain whether or not the victim feels safe to continue to conjoint treatment. During the assessment phase, individual meetings allow the therapist to determine whether or not the victim is a willing participant in treatment or is being coerced to come. Finally, family therapists must be familiar with, and use, the safety net of community resources for victims and perpetrators of domestic violence including police and judicial resources, women's shelters, and group treatments available through batterers' programs. It is unlikely that couples treatment alone will be sufficient for any but the mildest cases of domestic violence.

As family therapists become more knowledgeable about domestic violence and couples treatment, it is also important that they become more active in the growing regulation of the field. As of 1996, coalitions from more than half of the states and the District of Columbia had adopted standards governing programs or individuals that provide batterer intervention, and 13 other states were developing standards (Healey & Smith, 1998). Although most experts would agree that not enough is known about the effectiveness of current interventions, couples counseling is expressly prohibited in 20 state standards for batterer interventions. Family therapists must educate other domestic violence treatment providers and regulatory bodies about the potential benefits of careful couples treatment in some cases of domestic violence.

Conclusion

Violence between partners in intimate relationships is a complex and troubling phenomenon, one that challenges our conceptions of love and intimate relationships and exacts an immense toll in human suffering and social costs. In order to bring domestic violence out from behind the wall of "private family matters," advocates for battered women some 30 years ago took a strong and uncompromising stance that all violence against women is best dealt with as a crime, that it reflects the patriarchal nature of society, and that any attempt to examine couple dynamics in domestic violence adds to battered women's victimization. At the same time, some aspects of domestic violence were, of necessity, left out of the advocacy movement's analysis. In order to advance an important social change agenda, advocates downplayed the prevalence of female assaults on male partners; the wish many victims have to stay with abusive partners, albeit without continued violence; the different subgroups of batterers, each of which might need a different intervention approach; and the possibility that conjoint treatment could help end violence and empower women in their relationship without suggesting they are responsible for being abused. Over the past 10 years, researchers and treatment professionals have begun to consider these issues in more depth, with a growing interest in conjoint couples therapy being one result.

It is important to note that all of the experimental and quasi-experimental studies reported in this chapter have been published since 1995. The topic of marital therapy for domestic violence was not reviewed in the 1995 Special Issue of the *Journal of Marital and Family Therapy* because no one was conducting experimental studies on this topic at that time. Because domestic violence is such a common occurrence in couples, it is interesting that relative to other issues in this volume, family approaches to domestic violence are not as advanced methodologically. One reason for the underdevelopment of research in this area is that historically, prejudices have existed against conjoint work with couples when violence has occurred.

However, at present, clinical use of couples treatment for domestic violence is increasingly common although the outcome research on this approach remains underdeveloped. It appears as though carefully conceptualized and delivered couples treatment is at least as effective as gender-specific treatment and that couples treatment does not place women at greater risk for injury. However, the body of research on which these conclusions rest is sparse and often unsophisticated. Only six experimental studies have been done and they use different eligibility criteria, outcome measures, and treatment approaches. On balance then, couples treatment certainly appears to hold promise as an effective approach to selected cases of domestic violence, and merits further study. Marriage and family therapists have an important part to play in continuing to develop and test innovative ways of helping couples end violence and improve the quality of their relationships—an endeavor that promises not only to improve the quality of their own lives but also to improve the lives of their children and society as well.

References

References marked with a double asterisk are recommended for clinicians.

**Almeida, R. V., & Durkin, T. (1999). The cultural context model: Therapy for couples with domestic violence. *Journal of Marital & Family Therapy, 25*(3), 313–324.

American Medical Association. (1992). Violence against women. *Journal of The American Medical Association, 267*(23), 107–112.

**Babcock, J. C., & La Taillade, J. J. (2000). Evaluating interventions for men who batter. In J. P. Vincent & E. N. Jouriles (Eds.), *Domestic violence: Guidelines for research-informed practice* (pp. 37–77). London: Jessica Kingsley.

Babcock, J. C., & Steiner, R. (1999). The relationship between treatment, incarceration, and recidivism of battering: A program evaluation of Seattle's coordinated community response to domestic violence. *Journal of Family Psychology, 13*(1), 46–59.

Brannen, S. J., & Rubin, A. (1996). Comparing the effectiveness of gender-specific and couples groups in a court-mandated spouse abuse treatment program. *Research on Social Work Practice, 6*(4), 405–424.

Bureau of Justice Statistics. (1998). *Violence by intimates: Analysis of data on crimes by current or former spouses, boyfriends, and girlfriends.* Retrieved June 3, 2002, from http://www.ojp.usdoj.gov/bjs/abstract/vi.htm

Chen, H., Bersani, C., Myers, S. C., & Denton, R. (1989). Evaluating the effectiveness of a court sponsored abuser treatment program. *Journal of Family Violence, 4,* 309–322.

Davis, R. L. (1998). *Domestic violence: Facts and fallacies.* Westport, CT: Praeger.

de Shazer, S. (1982). *Patterns of brief family therapy.* New York: Guilford.

de Shazer, S. (1985). *Keys to solution in brief therapy.* New York: W. W. Norton.

de Shazer, S. (1988). *Clues: Investigating solutions in brief therapy.* New York: W. W. Norton.

Deschner, J. P., & McNeil, J. (1986). Results of anger control training for battering couples. *Journal of Family Violence, 1*(2), 111–120.

Deschner, J. P., McNeil, J., & Moore, M. (1986). A treatment model for batterers. *Social Casework, 67,* 55–60.

Dobash, R., Dobash, R. E., Cavanagh, K., & Lewis, R. (1996). Re-education programs for violent men—an evaluation. *Research Findings, 46,* 1–4.

Dunford, F. W. (2000). The San Diego Navy experiment: An assessment of interventions for men who assault their wives. *Journal of Consulting and Clinical Psychology, 68*(3), 468–476.

Dutton, D. G. (1986). The outcome of court-mandated treatment of wife assault: A quasi-experimental evaluation. *Violence & Victims, 1*(3), 163–175.

Dutton, G. D., Bodnarchuk, M., Kropp, R., Hart, S. D., & Ogloff, J. R. P. (1997). Wife assault treatment and criminal recidivism: An 11-year follow-up. *International Journal of Offender Therapy and Comparative Criminology, 41*(1), 9–23.

Edleson, J. L., & Brygger, M. P. (1986). Gender differences in reporting of battering incidences. *Family Relations: Journal of Applied Family & Child Studies, 35*(3), 377–382.

Edleson, J. L., & Grusznski, R. J. (1988). Treating men who batter: Four years of outcome data from the Domestic Abuse Project. *Journal of Social Service Research, 12*, 3–22.

Edleson, J. L., & Syers, M. (1991). The effects of group treatment for men who batter: An 18-month follow-up study. *Research on Social Work Practice, 1*, 227–243.

Edleson, J. L., & Tolman, R. M. (1992). *Intervention for men who batter: An ecological approach.* Thousand Oaks, CA: Sage.

Fals-Stewart, W., Birchler, G. R., & O'Farrell, T. J. (1996). Behavioral couples therapy for male substance-abusing patients: Effects on relationship adjustment and drug-using behavior. *Journal of Consulting and Clinical Psychology, 64,* 959–972.

Fals-Stewart, W., Kashdan, M., O'Farrell, T. J., & Birchler, G. R. (2002). Behavioral couples therapy for drug-abusing patients: Effects on partner violence. *Journal of Substance Abuse Treatment, 22,* 87–96.

Feazelle, C. S., Mayers, R. S., & Deschner, J. P. (1984). Services for men who batter: Implications for programs and policies. *Family Relations, 33*(April), 217–223.

Feder (1999). *Women and domestic violence: An interdisciplinary approach.* Binghampton, NY: Haworth Press.

Feld, S. L., & Straus, M. A. (1989). Escalation and desistance of wife assault in marriage. *Criminology, 27,* 141–161.

Ford, D. A., & Regoli, M. J. (1993). The criminal prosecution of wife batterers: Process, problems, and effects. In N. Z. Hilton (Ed.), *Legal responses to wife assault.* Newbury Park, CA: Sage.

Geffner, R., & Mantooth, C. (2000). *Ending spouse/partner abuse: A psychoeducational approach for individuals and couples.* New York: Springer.

Geffner, R., Mantooth, C., Franks, D., & Rao, L. (1989). A psychoeducational conjoint therapy approach to reducing family violence. In P. Caesar & L. Hamberger (Eds.), *Treating men who batter: Theory, practice and programs* (pp. 103–133). New York: Springer.

Gelles, R. J., & Straus, M. A. (1988). *Intimate violence.* New York: Simon & Schuster.

Gingerich, W. J., & Eisengart, S. (2000). Solution-focused brief therapy: A review of the outcome research. *Family Process, 39,* 477–498.

**Goldner, V., Penn, P., Sheinberg, M., & Walker, G. (1990). Love and violence: Gender paradoxes in volatile attachments. *Family Process, 29*(4), 343–364.

Gondolf, E. W. (1988). Who are those guys? Toward a behavioral typology of batterers. *Violence and Victims, 3*(3), 187–203.

Gondolf, E. W. (1998). The victims of court-ordered batterers: Their victimization, helpseeking, and perceptions. *Violence Against Women, 4*(6), 659–676.

Gondolf, E. W. (2002). *Batterer intervention systems: Issues, outcomes, and recommendations.* Thousand Oaks, CA: Sage.

Gottman, J. M. (1999). *The marriage clinic: A scientifically-based marital therapy.* New York: Norton.

**Greenspun, W. (2000). Embracing the controversy: A metasystemic approach to the treatment of domestic violence. In P. Papp (Ed.), *Couples on the fault line: New directions for therapists* (pp. 152–177). New York: Guilford Press.

Hamberger, L. K., & Hastings, J. E. (1988). Skills training for treatment of spouse abusers: An outcome study. *Journal of Family Violence, 3,* 121–130.

Harrell, A. (1991). *Evaluation of court-ordered treatment for domestic violence offenders. Final report to the State Justice Institute.* Washington, DC: The Urban Institute.

Harris, J. (1986). Counseling violent couples using Walker's model. *Psychotherapy, 23*(4), 613–621.

Harris, R., Savage, S., Jones, T., & Brooke, W. (1988). A comparison of treatments for abusive men and their partners within a family-service agency. *Canadian Journal of Community Mental Health, 7*(2), 147–155.

Healey, K. M., & Smith, C. (1998). *Batterer programs: What criminal justice agencies need to know.* Washington, DC: National Institute of Justice.

**Heyman, R. E., & Neidig, P. H. (1997). Physical aggression couples treatment. In W. K. Halford & H. J. Markman (Eds.), *Clinical handbook of marriage and couples interventions* (pp. 589–617). Chichester, England: John Wiley & Sons.

Holtzworth-Munroe, A., & Stuart, G. L. (1994). Typologies of male batterers: Three subtypes and the differences among them. *Psychological Bulletin, 116*(3), 476–497.

Jaffe, J. H., & Sudderman, M. (1995). Child witnesses of woman abuse: Research and community responses. In S. Stith & M. Straus (Eds.), *Understanding partner violence: Prevalence, causes, consequences and solutions.* Minneapolis, MN: National Council on Family Relations.

Jaffe, P. G., Wolfe, D., & Wilson, S. (1990). *Children of battered women.* Newbury Park, CA: Sage.

Johannson, M. A., & Tutty, L. M. (1998). An evaluation of after-treatment couples' groups for wife abuse. *Family Relations, 47*(1), 27–35.

Johnson, S. M. (1996). *The practice of emotionally focused marital therapy: Creating connection.* Brighton, NY: Brunner-Routledge.

Liddle, H. A., & Dakof, G. A. (1995). Efficacy of family therapy for drug abuse: Promising but not definitive. *Journal of Marital & Family Therapy, 21,* 511–543.

Lindquist, C. U., Telch, C. F., & Taylor, J. (1983). Evaluation of a conjugal violence treatment program: A pilot study. *Behavioral Counschild management problemseling & Community Interventions, 3*(1), 76–90.

**Lipchik, E., & Kubicki, A. (1996). Solution-focused domestic violence views: Bridges toward a new reality in couples therapy. In S. D. Miller, M. A. Hubble, & B. L. Duncan (Eds.), *Handbook of solution-focused brief therapy* (pp. 65–97). San Francisco: Josey-Bass.

Neidig, P. H. (1992). *Participants' workbook for PACT.* State University of New York at Stony Brook.

**Neidig, P., & Friedman, D. (1984). *Spouse abuse: A treatment program for couples.* Champlain, IL: Research Press.

Neidig, P. H., Friedman, D. H., & Collins, B. S. (1985). Domestic conflict containment: A spouse abuse treatment program. *Social Casework, 66*(4), 195–204.

Newell, R. G. (1994). The effectiveness of court-mandated counseling for domestic violence: An outcome study. *Dissertation Abstracts International, A. The Humanities and Social Sciences, 55*(5-A), 1193.

O'Farrell, T. J., Van Hutton, V., & Murphy, C. (1999). Domestic violence before and after alcoholism treatment: A two-year longitudinal study. *Journal of Studies on Alcohol, 60,* 317–321.

O'Leary, K. D. (1988). Physical aggression between spouses: A social learning theory perspective. In V. B. Van Hasselt & R. L. Morrison (Eds.), *Handbook of family violence* (pp. 31–55). New York: Plenum Press.

O'Leary, K. D., Heyman, R. E., & Neidig, P. H. (1999). Treatment of wife abuse: A comparison of gender-specific and conjoint approaches. *Behavior Therapy, 30,* 475–505.

O'Leary, K. D., Vivian, D., & Malone, J. (1992). Assessment of physical aggression against women in marriage: The need for multimodal assessment. *Behavioral Assessment, 14*(1), 5–14.

Palmer, S. E., Brown, R. A., & Berrera, M. E. (1992). Group treatment program for abusive husbands: Long-term evaluation. *American Journal of Orthopsychiatry, 62*(2), 276–283.

Pan, H. S., Neidig, P. H., & O'Leary, K. D. (1994). Predicting mild and severe husband-to-wife physical aggression. *Journal of Consulting and Clinical Psychology, 62*(5), 975–981.

Perez, P. J., & Rasmussen, K. (1997). An ounce of prevention: A model for working with couples at-risk for battering. *Contemporary Family Therapy, 19*(2), 229–251.

Riza, W. R., Stacey, W. A., & Shupe, A. (1985). *An evaluation of the effect of the Family Preservation Program in Tyler, Texas* (Vol. 35). Arlington, TX: University of Texas at Arlington, Department of Sociology, Anthropology, and Social Work, Center for Social Research.

Rusinoff, J. S. (1990). *Men's treatment handbook* (2nd ed.). Minneapolis, MN: Domestic Abuse Project.

Saunders, D. G. (1992). A typology of men who batter: Three types derived from cluster analysis. *American Journal of Orthopsychiatry, 62,* 264–275.

Saunders, D. (1996). Feminist-cognitive behavioral and process-psychodynamic treatments for men who batter: Interactions of abuser traits and treatment models. *Violence and Victims, 11*(4), 393–414.

Shupe, A., Stacey, W. A., & Hazelwood, L. R. (1987). *Violent men, violent couples.* Lexington, MA: Lexington Books.

Stith, S. M., McCollum, E. E., & Rosen, K. H. (Unpublished). *The effectiveness of an integrated solution-focused couples treatment program for domestic violence.*

**Stith, S. M., McCollum, E. E., Rosen, K. H., & Locke, L. D. (2002). Multicouple group treatment for domestic violence. In F. Kaslow (Ed.), *Comprehensive textbook of psychotherapy* (Vol. 4). New York: John Wiley & Sons.

Stith, S. M., & Straus, M. A. (1995). Introduction. In S. M. Stith & M. A. Straus (Eds.), *Understanding partner violence: Prevalence, causes, consequences, and solutions* (pp. 1–11). Minneapolis, MN: National Council on Family Relations.

Stosny, S. (1995). *Treating attachment abuse: A compassionate approach.* New York: Springer.

Straus, M. A. (1979). Measuring intrafamily conflict and violence: The conflict tactics (CT) scales. *Journal of Marriage & the Family, 41*(1), 75–88.

Straus, M. A. (1993). Physical assaults by wives: A major social problem. In R. J. Gelles (Ed.), *Current controversies on family violence* (pp. 67–87). Newbury Park, CA: Sage.

Straus, M. A., & Gelles, R. J. (1990). *Physical violence in American families: Risk factors and adaptations to violence in 8,145 families.* New Brunswick, NJ: Transaction.

**Stuart, G. L., & Holtzworth-Munroe, A. (1995). Identifying subtypes of maritally violent men: Descriptive dimensions, correlates and causes of violence, and treatment implications. In S. M. Stith & M. A. Straus (Eds.), *Understanding partner violence: Prevalence, causes, consequences, and solutions* (pp. 162–172). Minneapolis, MN: National Council on Family Relations.

Taylor, J. (1984). Structured conjoint therapy for spouse abuse cases. *Social Casework: The Journal of Contemporary Social Work, 65,* 11–18.

Tolman, R. (1990). *The impact of group process on outcome of groups for men who batter.* Paper presented at the European Congress on the Advancement of Behavior Therapy, Paris, France.

Tolman, R. M., & Edleson, J. L. (1995). Intervention for men who batter: A review of research. In S. M. Stith & M. A. Straus (Eds.), *Understanding partner violence: Prevalence, causes, consequences, and solutions* (pp. 262–272). Minneapolis, MN: National Council on Family Relations.

Walker, L. E. (1979). *The battered woman.* New York: Harper and Row.

Wexler, D. (1999). *Domestic Violence 2000: An integrated skills program for men.* New York: Norton.

Chapter 9   *Severe Mental Illness*

William R. McFarlane, M.D., Department of Psychiatry, University of Vermont and
Maine Medical Center, Portland, Maine.

Lisa Dixon, M.D., School of Medicine, University of Maryland,
Baltimore, Maryland.

Ellen Lukens, D. Phil., School of Social Work, Columbia University,
New York, New York.

Alicia Lucksted, Ph.D., School of Medicine, University of Maryland,
Baltimore, Maryland.

Our purpose here, as part of the series commissioned by the American Association for Marriage and Family Therapy (AAMFT) on family interventions and therapies and the evidence for their effectiveness, is to describe family psychoeducation, the basis for its status as an evidence-based practice (EBP), and barriers to implementation. Proposed strategies for overcoming those barriers are also described. Although the focus is on results and developments since the last such review in the *Journal of Marital and Family Therapy* (Goldstein & Miklowitz, 1995), we start with a brief overview of this work for those who are new to it.

Family psychoeducation originated from several sources in the late 1970s. Perhaps the leading influence was the growing realization that conventional family therapy, in which family dysfunction is assumed and becomes the target of intervention for the alleviation of symptoms, proved to be at least ineffective and perhaps damaging to patient and family well-being. As efforts to develop and apply family therapy to schizophrenia and other psychotic disorders waned, awareness grew, especially among family members themselves and their rapidly growing advocacy organizations, that living with an illness such as schizophrenia is difficult and confusing for patients and families alike.

It became increasingly clear that, under these circumstances, a well-functioning family has to possess the available knowledge about the illness itself and coping skills specific to a particular disorder, skills that are counterintuitive and only nascent in most families. Given that perspective, the most adaptive family was increasingly seen to be the one that has access to information, with the implication that the treatment system is a crucial source of that information. As to coping skills, many families develop methods of dealing with positive (psychotic) and negative (functional and cognitive deficits, such as flattened affect, loss of energy and apathy) symptoms, functional disabilities, and the desperation of their ill relatives through painful trial and error. These successes, however, are rare. A critical need is for families to have access to each other to learn of other families' successes and failures, and to establish a repertoire of coping strategies that are closely tailored to the disorder. Further, family members and significant others involved in the lives and care of adults with serious mental illnesses often provide emotional and instrumental support, case management functions, financial assistance, advocacy, and housing to their relative with mental illness. Doing so can be rewarding but poses considerable burdens (Adamec, 1996; Cochrane, Goering, & Rogers, 1997; Leff, 1994; McFarlane, Lukens, et al., 1995). Family members often find that access to needed resources and information is lacking (Adamec, 1996; Marsh, 1992; Marsh & Johnson, 1997).

Even with this new perspective, it took over 10 years for interest and effort in involving families in the treatment of persons with severe mental illness to be revived, and then it emerged with an entirely different ideology. Investigators began to recognize the crucial role families played in outcome after an acute episode of schizophrenia had occurred and endeavored to engage families collaboratively, sharing illness information, suggesting behaviors that promote recuperation, and teaching coping strategies that reduce the families' sense of burden (Anderson, Hogarty, & Reiss, 1980; Falloon, Boyd, & McGill, 1984; Goldstein, Rodnick, Evans, May, & Steinberg, 1978; Leff, Kuipers, Berkowitz, Eberlein-Vries, & Sturgeon, 1982). The group of interventions that emerged became known as family psychoeducation.

The psychoeducational approach recognizes that schizophrenia is a brain disorder that is usually only partially remediable by medication, and that families can have a significant effect on their relative's recovery. Thus, the psychoeducational approach shifted away from attempting to get families to change their "disturbed" communication patterns towards educating and persuading families that how they behave toward the patient can facilitate or impede recovery by compensating for deficits and sensitivities specific to the various psychotic disorders. For example, a family might interfere with recuperation if, in their natural enthusiasm to promote and support progress, they create unreasonable demands and expectations, but the same family could have a dramatically positive effect on recovery by gradually increasing expectations and supporting an incremental return of functioning.

Research conducted over the last decade has supported the development of evidence-based practice guidelines for addressing family-members' needs for information, clinical guidance, and ongoing support. This research has demonstrated that meeting the needs of family members also dramatically improves patient outcomes, while improving family well-being. Several models have evolved to address the needs of family members: individual family consultation; professionally-led family psychoeducation (Anderson et al., 1980; Falloon et al., 1984), in single-family and multifamily group formats (McFarlane, 2002); various forms of more traditional family therapies (see Marsh, 2001); and a range of professionally-led models of short-term family education—sometimes referred to as therapeutic education (Amenson, 1998; Marsh, 2001). There are also family-led information and support classes or groups such as those of the National Alliance for the Mentally Ill (NAMI; Burland, 1998; Pickett-Schenk, Cook, & Laris, 2000). Of these models, family psychoeducation has a deep enough research and dissemination base to be considered an evidence-based practice. The descriptor "psychoeducation" can be misleading; family psychoeducation includes many cognitive, behavioral, and supportive therapeutic elements, often utilizes a consultative framework, and shares key characteristics with other types of family interventions.

What Is Family Psychoeducation?

A variety of family psychoeducation programs have been developed over the past two decades (Anderson, Reiss, & Hogarty, 1986; Falloon et al., 1984). These programs are professionally created and led, offered as part of a treatment plan for the consumer, and are usually diagnosis-specific. The models differ significantly in format (multiple-family, single-family, relatives only, combined), structure (involvement or exclusion of consumer), duration and intensity of treatment, and setting (hospital or clinic, home). They place variable emphasis on didactic, emotional, cognitive behavioral, clinical, rehabilitative, and systemic techniques. Most have focused first on consumer outcomes, although family understanding and well-being are assumed necessary to achieve those outcomes. All focus on family resiliency and strengths.

Although the existing models of family intervention may appear to have substantial differences, a significant consensus about critical elements of this kind of treatment emerged in 1999, under the encouragement of the leaders of the World Schizophrenia Fellowship (1998). Leff, Falloon, and McFarlane (World Schizophrenia Fellowship, 1998) developed the original consensus, which was then refined and ratified by many recognized clinical researchers working in this field. The process involved selection of the key components, developing a consensus based first on empirical evidence and then on a consensus as to what each component actually represented. The final step was further refinement based on feedback from, and iterative reworking with, nearly all of the principal psychoeducation researchers in the world. Parenthetically, this process led to convergence of concept rather than the usual process of the field splitting into competing schools. The resulting consensus regarding goals, principles and methods, i.e., elements of family intervention that are critical to achieving the empirically validated outcomes reported, was summarized as follows.

Goals For Working With Families
- To achieve the best possible outcome for the individual with mental illness through treatment and management that involves collaboration among professionals, families and patients.

- To alleviate suffering among the members of the family by supporting them in their efforts to foster their loved one's recovery.

Principles For Working With Families

The models of treatment supported with demonstrated effectiveness required clinicians working with families to:

- Coordinate all elements of treatment and rehabilitation to ensure that everyone is working towards the same goals in a collaborative, supportive relationship.
- Pay attention to the social as well as the clinical needs of the patient.
- Provide optimum medication management.
- Listen to families and treat them as equal partners in treatment planning and delivery.
- Explore family members' expectations of the treatment program and for the patient.
- Assess the family's strengths and limitations in their ability to support the patient.
- Help resolve family conflict through sensitive response to emotional distress.
- Address feelings of loss.
- Provide relevant information for patient and family at appropriate times.
- Provide an explicit crisis plan and professional response.
- Help improve communication among family members.
- Provide training for the family in structured problem-solving techniques.
- Encourage the family to expand their social support networks, e.g., participation in multifamily groups and/or family support organizations such as the National Alliance for the Mentally Ill.
- Be flexible in meeting the needs of the family.
- Provide the family with easy access to a professional in case of need if the work with the family ceases.

Evidence-Based Family Intervention Models

Several models have been developed to address the needs and concerns of families of persons with mental illness, including:

- Behavioral family management
- Family psychoeducation
- Psychoeducational multifamily groups
- Relatives groups
- Family consultation
- Professionally-led models of short-term family education (therapeutic education)

Because each model has introduced critical components of treatment that have contributed to the development of family psychoeducational models, they will be described briefly here.

Behavioral family management. The behavioral family management approach, developed by Falloon et al. (1984), is the most behavioral among the models influencing psychoeducation. It follows a sequential framework of assessment, intervention, and ongoing review, and includes a behavioral analysis of the strengths and needs of each family member and the family unit as a whole, followed by single-family treatment sessions in the home. These sessions focus on education about schizophrenia, strategies for improved communication, and the development and rehearsal of problem-solving techniques, all designed to focus on the psychosocial rehabilitation of patients and the needs of family members. The model starts from a strengths perspective, with clinicians assuming that each family member is functioning at his or her best, given the circumstances, contradictions, and challenges involved in contending with a family member with mental illness. This approach has been found effective in one major study in Los Angeles (Falloon et al., 1984) and replicated in a subsequent controlled clinical trial (Randolph et al., 1994).

Family psychoeducation. Developed by Anderson et al. (1980) almost simultaneously with family behavioral management and relatives groups, family psychoeducation is a specific, empirically-based model that includes an intensive engagement effort with family and patient, extended education about the disease and its treatment, and guidelines for recovery based on research and best clinical practice. It pursues a careful, gradual treatment process that promotes a strong stable symptomatic recovery and relapse prevention, followed by an equally careful social and vocational rehabilitation effort, and problem solving based on the needs of both family and patient. Anderson translated her long experience working with families of patients with schizophrenia into a standardized approach that emphasizes partnering with family members, extended joining effort, incorporating family and patient desires and ambitions as the core of the treatment plan, and empathic acceptance of the family's suffering, burdens, and frustrations in caretaking. A key feature is its strong commitment to solve problems raised by family members that are properly the province of the mental health system and/or professional intervention. Much of the approach was derived from structural family therapy—an emphasis on joining the therapist's style and agenda to that of the family and enhancing boundaries within the family. This last point had a rationale different from Minuchin's (1974) original conception. Here, boundaries are necessary to create "barriers to stimulation"; i.e., they are helpful because of the sensitivity to stimulation and cognitive disabilities that are biological substrates of schizophrenia, not because the family is categorically enmeshed.

This approach was also heavily influenced by Hogarty and Ulrich's (1977) finding that relapse is a major impediment to longer-term clinical and functional improvement, but that after roughly a year of remission, most patients can make significant functional gains, are more resistant to stress, and can tolerate increasing mental and physical demands. This translated into working closely with the family, making coordinated efforts to take the next steps toward improved community participation carefully, using clinical condition as the guide to what a given patient might be able to handle. A hallmark is that a considerable period of time is allowed for recovery from the last episode of psychosis—as much as a year, much as is done for heart attacks. The assumption is that psychosis is traumatic for the brain, the person having the episode, and the immediate social support system, and that it requires recuperation to allow functional recovery.

Finally, the approach uses clinical approaches in training families to assist in creating an optimal psychosocial environment for recovery, especially one that is somewhat quieter, less intense, less complex, and moves a bit slower than the world in general. This is perhaps the point on which there is the greatest contrast with family therapy: Here the family is assumed to be functional until proven otherwise, e.g., by resisting or failing to use the treatment. Its members need to adopt a special interactional style and create an unusual social environment to adapt to, and compensate for, the specific sensory and cognitive characteristics of a given disorder. This model was found to be effective in a large clinical trial in which the combination of family psychoeducation and social skills training was found to be even more effective over a 1-year (Hogarty et al., 1986), but not 2-year, course of treatment (Hogarty et al., 1991).

Psychoeducational multifamily groups. The psychoeducational multiple family group (PMFG) brings together aspects of family psychoeducation, family behavioral management, and multiple-family approaches. As such, it is a second-generation treatment model that incorporates the advantages of each of its sources, diminishes their negative features, and leads to a number of synergistic effects that appear to enhance efficacy. Building on the psychoeducational family approach and the family behavioral management approach, the model attempts to reflect contemporary understanding of schizophrenia and other severe mental illnesses from biological, psychological, and social perspectives. Unlike the recent origins of psychoeducation, however, multiple family group work arose nearly 3 decades ago in attempts by Laqueur, LaBurt, and Morong (1964), and Detre, Sayer, Norton, and Lewis (1961), and others to develop psychosocial treatments for hospitalized consumers. The emphasis was more pragmatic than theoretical. Indeed, the first reported successful experience with the modality emerged serendipitously from a need to solve ward management problems. In the process, Laqueur et al. noted improved ward social functioning in inpatients who insisted on attending a group organized for visiting relatives. Detre et al. started a multiple family group to encourage cooperation between resident psychiatrists and social workers on an acute inpatient service. They found a high level of interest in the group among patients and family members alike, as well as improvements in social functioning among patients and in family communication and morale.

Many practitioners have observed that specific characteristics of the multiple family group have remarkable effects on a number of social and clinical management problems commonly encountered in schizophrenia and other severe mental illnesses. Further, the PMFG approach is based on research showing that families attempting to cope with mental illness inevitably experience a variety of stresses that secondarily put them at risk of manifesting exasperation and discouragement as natural reactions. These responses often take the form of high expressed emotion, in which relatives are highly critical or overinvolved, a factor empirically shown to predict and, most likely, cause relapse (Hooley, Rosen, & Richters, 1995). Multifamily groups address social isolation, stigmatization, and increased financial and psychological burden directly. They achieve these by increasing the size and richness of the social support network, connecting the family to other families like themselves, providing a forum for mutual aid, providing an opportunity to hear the experiences of others who have had similar experiences and have found workable solutions, and building hope through mutual example and experience.

The general character of the approach can be summarized as consisting of three components that roughly correspond to the phases of the group. In the first phase, the content of the model follows that developed by Anderson (1983), with its emphasis on joining with each family in a single-family format, conducting a multifamily educational workshop, focusing on preventing relapse, and fostering social and vocational rehabilitation. Unlike the single-family psychoeducational approach, the format for treatment after the workshop is a multifamily group. The second phase involves moving beyond stability to gradual increases in consumers' community functioning, a process that uses PMFG-based problem solving, as in the family behavioral management model, as the primary means for accomplishing social and vocational rehabilitation. This usually occurs during the second year of the PMFG. The third phase consists of deliberate efforts to mold the group into a social network that can persist for an extended period and satisfy family and consumer needs for social contact, support, and ongoing clinical monitoring. This format is also an efficient context in which to continue psychopharmacologic treatment and routine case management. Expansion of the families' social networks occurs through problem solving, direct emotional support, and out-of-group socializing, all involving members of different families in the group. In two different studies at seven simultaneously replicating sites, multifamily groups were shown to be more effective than a single-family version of a combination of family psychoeducation and behavioral family management (McFarlane, Link, Dushay, Marchal, & Crilly, 1995; McFarlane, Lukens, et al., 1995).

Relatives groups. This model, developed by Julian Leff and his associates in the U.K. (Leff et al., 1989; Leff, Kuipers, Berkowitz, & Sturgeon, 1985), involves helping families to enhance coping skills through a combination of in-home individual family sessions in which brief educational material is presented to the families with time allowed for questions and discussion. This is followed by a series of biweekly group interventions conducted by two professionals and designed for parents and other family members, excluding the patient. The particular goal is to structure groups that include family members designated as both high and low in expressed emotion, as a means of encouraging cross-family education and modeling. In addition, the group model targets isolation and creates a forum for focused discussion among family members. Leff and his colleagues eventually devised two different studies to assess the effectiveness of their model. In the first study, they compared patients receiving standard treatment, which involved little or no family intervention, with a family program that combined educational sessions, a relatives group, and family sessions in the home including the patient (Leff et al., 1985). In the second study, Leff et al. (1990) tested the components of the first intervention, so families were invited to attend either ongoing relatives groups, excluding the patient, or individual family sessions at home. When the data from the first and second studies were combined, the relapse rate at 2 years was 75% for those consumers who received standard treatment as compared to 40% for those whose families received any form of intervention, providing strong endorsement for the value of a family support model regardless of format.

Family consultation. Another approach that has been shown to be effective for some types of conditions and families is the family consultation approach, developed by Wynne and colleagues (Weber, McDaniel, & Wynne, 1987; Wynne, 1994; Wynne, McDaniel, & Weber, 1988). In this approach, individual families meet periodically with a professional consultant, often the consumer's psychiatrist or primary practitioner. The goal is to provide information and guidance on an individual basis to address the specific concerns and problems identified by the family, without a pre-specified agenda. The sessions are scheduled as needed. Again, the model is strengths-based with an emphasis on reinforcing the natural resiliency of the family. This approach appears to be especially useful when scheduling meetings involves great inconvenience, in cases in which there are few ongoing problems or acute crises, the family is coping well with the situation or, in contrast, the family faces a crisis or emergency situation. It is a flexible model and may be particularly practical in situations in which the mental health system is fragmented or not highly professionalized. It is often the de facto approach for long-term follow-up, after the family has participated in the more structured models.

Short-term models. In work that focused particularly on family rather than patient outcomes, Solomon, Draine, Mannion, and Meisel (1996, 1997) compared two short-term models of family intervention, either family group education or individualized family consultation, with a waitlist control group. About half of the participants were members of family support groups such as NAMI. For the active treatments, patients were invited. The group education model was well defined and included 10 weekly sessions focusing on education and development of coping skills. To facilitate collaboration between professionals and families, the groups were co-led by a professional and a peer consultant. The families were involved in designing the psychoeducational and problem-solving agenda and could obtain as-needed professional consultation following the conclusion of the group. In contrast, the consultation sessions were individualized, conducted in person or by telephone. Improved self-efficacy, defined as confidence in one's ability to understand and cope with the mental illness of a relative, was the only significantly improved outcome at the conclusion of the interventions. Among those who received individual consultation, self-efficacy improved regardless of prior membership in a self-help group. For those attending the family groups, participants showed significantly increased self-efficacy only if they had never participated in a self-help group. A more recent study assessed the efficacy of the Family-to-Family Education Program, a structured 12-week program developed by the National Alliance for the Mentally Ill (Dixon, Stewart, et al., 2001). After completing the program, the participants demonstrated significantly greater family, community, and service system empowerment, and reduced displeasure and worry about the family member who had a mental illness. These benefits were sustained at 6 months. It is noteworthy that these interventions were short-term in nature and that effects on patients were not assessed. Given recent practice guidelines that emphasize duration of at least 6 months and that the core elements of coping skill training and problem solving were lacking, an extension of these models may or may not have produced improved patient outcomes.

Research Overview

In the preceding *Journal of Marital and Family Therapy* research review in 1995, Goldstein and Miklowitz concluded that family psychoeducation for people afflicted with schizophrenia was highly effective when compared to standard care or medication alone. Going beyond basic efficacy, they described a number of studies in progress or very recently published that addressed the question as to whether there were technical variants that were more or less effective and/or specific subpopulations of patients with schizophrenia for which a given approach was superior. They went on to note that in the U.S., where the bulk of the research had been done, there was little application in routine clinical practice. In the U.K., by contrast, there was at least one national and one major large urban initiative to implement the approach. Finally, they noted that the approach had begun to be tested in other disorders, beginning with bipolar disorder. Each of those themes is reflected in the research reviewed here, although one of them, dissemination and implementation, is in nearly the same discouraging state that it was in 1995.

However, there are newer developments that enrich the field and raise further possibilities for research. We will attempt to review those as well. In particular, there is now some initial research available and underway that attempts to determine if self-help is as effective as professionally conducted family psychoeducation, and if it is not, whether there are aspects of self-help that are superior and should be incorporated in the existing evidence-based approaches.

There is some research suggesting that expanding social networks and providing social support to families and patients is another therapeutic strategy with its own margin of efficacy, especially when families, patients, and clinicians work on common issues together. Further, there is a suggestion of evidence that it is better if the patients are direct participants in the treatment, and stronger evidence that all of these approaches require 9 to 12 months to achieve the level of efficacy reported in the literature. Finally, we review studies here that demonstrate a remarkable cross-cultural and cross-national efficacy. This body of research argues that the therapeutic impact of well-organized family support for those with schizophrenia is as universal as the disorder itself.

A large number of controlled and comparative clinical trials have demonstrated markedly decreased relapse and rehospitalization rates among patients whose families received psychoeducation compared to those who received standard individual services—20% to 50% over 2 years. At least eight literature reviews have been published in the past decade, all finding a large and significant effect for this model of intervention (Baucom, Shoham, Mueser, Daiuto, & Stickle, 1998; Dixon, Adams, & Lucksted, 2000; Dixon & Lehman, 1995; Dixon, McFarlane, et al., 2001; Falloon, Held, Coverdale, Roncone, & Laidlaw, 1999; Goldstein & Miklowitz, 1995; Lam, 1991; McFarlane & Lukens, 1998; Penn & Mueser, 1996; Pitschel-Walz, Leucht, Bauml, Kissling, & Engel, 2001). Since 1978, with the publication of Goldstein et al.'s study showing dramatic short-term effects of educational and coping skills training intervention, there has been a steady stream of rigorous validations of the positive effects of this approach on relapse in schizophrenic disorders. Overall, the relapse rate for patients provided family psychoeducation has hovered around 15% per year, compared to a consistent 30% to 40% for individual therapy and medication or medication alone (Baucom et al., 1998). Table 1 presents the major studies and relapse outcomes, divided by the format of the treatment model tested.

It is important to note that medication is not a variable in these studies: The design of family psychoeducational approaches has medication adherence and its value in promoting recovery as a central element. Therefore, medication is provided in both the experimental and control conditions in every instance.

As a result of the compelling evidence, the Schizophrenia Patient Outcomes Research Team (PORT) project included family psychoeducation in its set of treatment recommendations. The PORT recommended that all families in contact with their relative who has mental illness be offered a family psychosocial intervention spanning at least 9 months and including education about mental illness, family support, crisis intervention, and problem-solving skills training (Lehman et al., 1998). Other best practice standards (American Psychiatric Association, 1997; Frances, Hoffman, Pass, & Andrews, 1987; Frances & Kahn, 1996) have also recommended that families receive education and support programs. In addition, an expert panel that included clinicians from various disciplines, families, patients, and researchers emphasized the importance of engaging families in the treatment and rehabilitation process (Coursey, Curtis, & Marsh, 2000a, 2000b).

Reviewing studies in which there has been no effect found for family psychoeducation is simpler than reviewing studies in which a positive effect has been demonstrated: 3 studies to date out of nearly 30 (Kottgen, Sonnichsen, Mollenhauer, & Jurth, 1984; Linszen et al., 1996; Telles et al., 1995). In the Kottgen study, the ongoing sessions were oriented toward exploring psychodynamic and dysfunctional aspects within the families participating, now considered contraindicated for nearly all families of patients with schizophrenia. In the Telles study, conducted in a Spanish-speaking immigrant sample, there was a reversed effect for family behavioral management among those from a less acculturated subgroup, and no effect for those from the more acculturated subgroup. Other recent studies in Spain have demonstrated the same robust effects as the prior studies in English-speaking countries, suggesting that it was the sample's immigrant status that may have negated the effects of family intervention, not a difference between languages or cultures. In the Linszen et al. study, the control group received individual therapy that was well designed and also achieved low relapse rates comparable to those in the family intervention sample (15% to 16%

Table 1
Relapse in Major Outcome Trials of Family Psychoeducation

| | | | % Relapsed during study | | | |
| | | Duration of treatment (mos.) | SF | SF + MF | FM | Standard treatment |
	n					
Falloon et al. (1984)	36	24	17			83
Leff et al. (1985)	19	24		14		78
Tarrier et al. (1989)	44	9	33			59
Leff et al. (1990)	23	24	33		36	
Hogarty et al. (1991)	67	24	32			67
Xiong et al. (1994)	63	18		44		64
Zhang et al. (1994)	83	18		15		54
Randolph et al. (1994)	41	12	10			40
McFarlane, Link, et al. (1995)	34	48	83		50	
McFarlane, Lukens, et al. (1995)	172	24	44		25	
Schooler et al. (1997)	313	12/24		29	35	
N and means	895	19.7 mos.	29.0	25.5	28.0	63

Note. MF = multifamily format; SF = single family format.

in both conditions). This study also utilized family intervention only during an inpatient admission and not during outpatient treatment. Finally, a study of personal therapy by Hogarty et al. (1997) produced mixed results. In patients living with family, personal therapy had lower relapse rates than family or supportive therapy, but personal adjustment was better in family psychoeducation.

Thus, the nonconfirming studies tend to validate the effectiveness of the studies in which an effect was found—by suggesting that the core elements in fact make a difference, that some patients and families may require cultural and/or contextually specific adaptations of the approach, that longer-term participation by families is required to achieve outcomes, and that other methods may also achieve comparable short-term effects. The Linszen et al. (1996) study illustrates a key finding: Programs lasting longer than 3 months had more robust effects. In fact, consistent efficacy has been demonstrated only in those studies in which intervention was provided on an ongoing basis, lasted at least 6 months, and incorporated problem solving, coping skills training, expanded social support, and communication skills training. As will be explored further in the section on differences in models, it has become clear that education alone has at least short-term salutary effects for family members (Dixon, Stewart, et al., 2001), but other studies have found that there is no lasting effect on patient clinical or functional outcomes (Abramowitz & Coursey, 1989). Further, given the long-term course of illness of schizophrenia, it has appeared to many observers that even the shorter-term positive effects for family members of the education-only models will erode under the influence of the persisting deficits, symptoms, and burdens. Thus, the critical elements include those that involve changes in behavior and ongoing training in diagnosis-specific and clinically oriented coping skills training. Increasingly, as the focus of intervention has shifted to functional aspects, especially employment, the patient has been included in these skills training and behavioral interventions. In the multifamily group approaches, there is another element added—ongoing social support and social network expansion for family members and the patient.

The consensus of previous reviews is that the various approaches, if they include the key elements and continue for a minimum duration, are equally effective. Although not a rigorous criterion, there is nevertheless a remarkable consistency of effects on relapse rates, with minimum reductions of about 50% of the control groups' rates. The differences simply increase with time, so that at 24 months the family-based conditions are well below 50% of the relapse rates in the control groups, approaching 75% in some studies. Baucom et al. (1998) found that in 11 of the most rigorously designed and conducted studies, with an average study duration of 19.7 months, the overall average relapse rate for family intervention was about 27% and for the control groups it was 64%, a reduction of about 58% of the standard or routine treatment rate. These differences in outcome are some of the most substantial and consistent empirical effects achieved by any treatment in the mental health domain.

Three studies have directly compared single- and multifamily formats or approaches, one small sample trial in the U.K. (Leff et al., 1989) and two community-based studies in the U.S. (McFarlane, Link, et al., 1995; McFarlane, Lukens, et al., 1995). Across the three studies, relapse rates for 24 months were 40.3% in the single-family conditions and 24.8% in the multifamily conditions. Table 2 provides the comparison of actual relapse rates and a mean rate for each format.

One of the U.S. studies was a large, multisite effectiveness study conducted in state- or city-operated clinics and hospitals, in which multifamily groups had lower relapse rates in five of the six sites (McFarlane, Lukens, et al., 1995). Given the reduced cost of MFGs, there is a strong bias in the literature and in fiscally hard-pressed mental health centers to adopt the MFG format as the more cost-effective alternative. This study also identified a subgroup for which the single-family format was more effective—families with low expressed emotion and patients with unusually good response to medication during the index hospitalization (McFarlane, 2002). In addition, first-episode cases did substantially *better* in the MFGs than in the single-family format (McFarlane, 2002).

Recent reports have only added to the strong validation of the effects on relapse, particularly because these later studies have been conducted in a variety of international and cultural contexts. Reductions in relapse for family intervention, compared to the control conditions, have been demonstrated in China (Ling et al., 1999; Zhang, Wang, Li, & Phillips, 1994; Zhao, Shen, & Shi, 1999; Zhao et al., 2000), Spain (Montero, Gomez Beneyto, Ruiz, Puche, & Adam, 1992; Muela Martinez & Godoy Garcia, 2001; Tomaras et al., 2000), Scandinavia (Rund et al., 1994), and Britain (Barrowclough et al., 2001). That these effects are additive to, but not substitutive for, antipsychotic medication was illustrated in a recent German study (Wiedemann et al., 2001). The investigators found that behavioral family management did not compensate for the increased risk of relapse posed by targeted drug treatment, in which the patient did not use medication unless experiencing prodromal signs or symptoms of relapse. However, the universality of this approach seems to have been demonstrated in contexts different enough that further generalization in other cultures and countries appears to be likely to succeed, especially if the necessary adaptations are made. For instance, a new model is being developed specifically for Asian Americans, designed to fit this population's different value orientations and cultural characteristics (Bae & Kung, 2000). Another variant is being tested that integrates ethnic minority families with a member with mental illness into the larger community (Connery & Brekke).

In addition, these and other studies, many reported in the past 3 years, have demonstrated significant effects on other areas of functioning. These studies and findings address a frequent criticism of the clinical trials: that relapse is only one dimension of outcome and course of illness. Many consumers and their family

Table 2
Relapse Outcomes in Single- and Multifamily Formats

	n	Duration of treatment (mos.)	% Relapsed during study SF	MF
Leff et al. (1990)	23	24	33	36
McFarlane, Link, et al. (1995)	34	48	83	50
McFarlane, Lukens, et al. (1995)	172	24	44	25
N and means	229	27.6 mos.	48.7	29.8

Note. MF = multifamily format; SF = single family format.

members are more concerned about the functional aspects of the illness, especially housing, employment, social relationships, dating and marriage, and general morale than about remission, which tends to be somewhat abstract as a goal. Several of the previously mentioned models, particularly the American versions—those of Falloon et al. (1984), Anderson et al. (1986), and McFarlane (2002)—have used remission (the absence of relapse) as both a primary target of intervention but also as a necessary first step toward rehabilitative goals and recovery. In addition, these models all include major components designed to achieve functional recovery, and the studies have documented progress in those same domains. More recently, several investigators, including our research team, have shifted focus to targeting these more human aspects of illness and life. Other effects have been shown for:

- Improved family-member well-being (Cuijpers, 1999; Falloon & Pederson, 1985; McFarlane, Dushay, Stastny, Deakins, & Link, 1996; Shi, Zhao, Xu, & Sen, 2000; Solomon, Draine, & Mannion, 1996; Wang et al., 1999; Zhao et al., 1999)
- Increased patient participation in vocational rehabilitation (Falloon et al., 1985)
- Substantially increased employment rates (McFarlane et al., 1996; McFarlane et al., 2000; McFarlane, Lukens, et al., 1995)
- Decreased psychiatric symptoms, including deficit syndrome (Dyck et al., 2000; Falloon et al., 1985; McFarlane, Lukens, et al., 1995; Zhao et al., 2000)
- Improved social functioning (Montero et al., 2001)
- Decreased family medical illnesses and medical care utilization (Dyck et al., 2002)
- Reduced costs of care (Cardin, McGill, & Falloon, 1985; McFarlane, Lukens, et al., 1995; Rund et al., 1994; Tarrier, Lowson, & Barrowclough, 1991).

Mediating Effects

From a theoretical standpoint, this broad spectrum of effects is mediated either by (a) a broad spectrum of numerous intervention components, or (b) a smaller number of nodal alterations whose secondary effects ramify throughout the family system and biological levels. The second option is strongly supported by the findings that all the efficacious family psychoeducational models reduce family expressed emotion and that doing so is directly associated with the reduction in relapse found in clinical trials. This linearity of effects is reassuring, because the intent of the early models, those developed by Leff, Kuipers, and Berkowitz (1983) particularly, was to reduce expressed emotion.

However, the better-known variants—family psychoeducation, family behavioral management, and PMFGs—have deliberately added important new dimensions of intervention, tending to support the first theoretical possibility, that these models have several different domains of effect. These include good general clinical management strategies and empathic engagement of patient and family members in Anderson's (1983) model, problem solving, communication skills training, and in-home sessions in Falloon et al.'s (1984) model, and multi-family participation in problem solving and expanded social networks and support in the PMFG format. Each of these components is designed to impact specific and somewhat separate aspects of the illness and the family system, other than expressed emotion. Falloon et al. (1985) demonstrated that successful mastery of problem solving by family members was more directly associated with relapse prevention than reductions in expressed emotion. McFarlane and colleagues (McFarlane, Link, et al., 1995; McFarlane, Lukens, et al., 1995) have consistently shown that when a very similar version of family psychoeducation is incorporated, multifamily groups lead to lower relapse rates and higher employment than single-family sessions. The simplest explanation is that enhanced social support, inherent only in the multifamily format, reduces vulnerability to relapse, probably by reducing anxiety and general distress (Dyck et al., 2002). Both of these empirical results strongly suggest a multidimensional effect as the explanation for improved clinical outcomes. That argument is strengthened further by recent studies showing dramatic improvements in employment among people with schizophrenia, especially when combined with other interventions, such as supported employment, that are designed to achieve functional goals (McFarlane et al., 1996, 2000). Therefore, both theoretical possibilities are supported by present evidence. Many of the effects of these models are mediated by reductions in expressed emotion, but that effect is enhanced by elements that focus on general empathic support for families and patients, coping and communication skills training, and enhanced social networks and support.

Delivery of the *appropriate components* of family psychoeducation to patients and families appears important in determining outcomes of families and patients. Several studies (Greenberg, Greenley, & Kim, 1995) have demonstrated that programs fail to reduce relapse rates if they present information without also providing family members with skills training, ongoing guidance regarding illness management, and emotional support. Information-only interventions also tend to be quite brief; a meta-analysis of 16 studies found that family interventions of fewer than 10 sessions had no important effects on relatives' burden (Cuijpers, 1999). However, the number of sessions could not explain completely the differential outcomes; length of total time, allowing for refinement of coping skills and strategies by the family and patient, rather than number of sessions may be a factor, as may be the therapists' styles of dealing with the emotional reactions of patients and relatives to the educational material. One study, using a multiple regression analysis of the variables measured, found that coping skill improvement was the best predictor of outcome for the patient, surpassing expressed emotion and other variables to explain patient clinical outcomes (Falloon et al., 1985). The behaviors and disruptions of schizophrenia, in particular, may require more than education to ameliorate family burden and enhance patient outcomes.

It is important to note that most studies evaluated family psychoeducation for schizophrenia or schizoaffective disorder only. However, several controlled studies do support the effects of family interventions for other psychiatric disorders, including dual diagnosis of schizophrenia and substance abuse (Barrowclough et al., 2001; McFarlane, Lukens, et al., 1995), bipolar disorder (Clarkin, Carpenter, Hull, Wilner, & Glick, 1998; Miklowitz & Goldstein, 1997; Miklowitz et al., 2000; Moltz, 1993; Parikh et al., 1997; Simoneau, Miklowitz, Richards, Saleem, & George, 1999; Tompson, Rea, Goldstein, Miklowitz, & Weisman, 2000), major depression (Emanuels-Zuurveen, 1997; Emanuels-Zuurveen & Emmelkamp, 1996; Leff et al., 2000), depression in mothers with disruptive children (Sanders & McFarland, 2000), mood disorders in children (Fristad, Gavazzi, & Soldano, 1998), obsessive-compulsive disorder (Van Noppen, 1999), anorexia (Geist, Heinmaa, Stephens, Davis, & Katzman, 2000) and alcohol abuse (Loveland-Cherry, Ross, & Kaufman, 1999) in adolescents, posttraumatic stress disorder (PTSD) in veterans (Saldanha, 2002), Alzheimer's disease (Marriott, Donaldson, Tarrier, & Burns, 2000), disruptive behavior disorders (Bustamante, 2000; Nicholson & Sanders, 1999), suicidal children (Harrington et al., 1998), congenital abnormalities (Pelchat, Bisson, Ricard, Perreault, & Bouchard, 1999), intellectual impairment (Russell, John, & Lakshmanan, 1999), child molesters (Walker, 2000), and borderline personality disorder (Gunderson, Berkowitz, & Ruizsancho, 1997), including single- and multifamily approaches. Gonzalez and Steinglass (Gonzalez, Steinglass, & Reiss, 1989; Steinglass, 1998) have extended this work to deal with the secondary effects of chronic medical illness.

The best-studied and developed versions of family psychoeducation beyond those for schizophrenia have focused on bipolar disorder. The single-family approach developed by Miklowitz and his colleagues (Miklowitz & Goldstein, 1997; Miklowitz et al., 2000) has been validated in clinical trials and described in a recent volume. The psychoeducational multifamily group model has been described by Moltz and Newmark (2002). The approach must be significantly modified for bipolar disorder. The symptoms, course, and family responses have been shown to be different than in schizophrenia, and recent biological research has highlighted major differences in brain function between the disorders. A key finding is that family expressed emotion affects relapse, but there is a greater biological contribution to relapse than in schizophrenia. For instance, Miklowitz and his colleagues found that family psychoeducation, in the form of single-family behavioral management, reduced relapses markedly, but from nearly 90% to about 50%, as opposed to the 40% to 15% reduction observed for schizophrenia. Thus, biological and psychosocial factors seem to be more evenly weighted in determining course of illness; nevertheless, family psychoeducation remains a powerful treatment in preventing relapse and improving longer-term outcomes in bipolar disorder.

For instance, the multifamily group model, developed by Moltz and Newmark (2002), was first implemented at a public mental health center in the South Bronx of New York City and later at a community mental health center in coastal Maine. It has been effective in both settings. The key elements of this model are the same as in the approach for schizophrenia. Each is modified in important ways to match the clinical and psychosocial problems encountered in bipolar disorder. During joining, sessions are held separately for the individual and the family, although individual and family sessions have similar structure, since the individual with bipolar illness is usually able to participate fully. Meetings with the consumer and the other family members are often carried out separately during the acute phase of illness, but usually together if joining occurs after the manic phase is over and family meetings with the consumer are less likely to be emotionally intense. The content of the joining sessions is modified to reflect the specific impact of bipolar illness on the family. Among several foci, it includes extensive discussion of the history of symptoms and course of illness and discussion of inter-episode functioning. The structure and format of the bipolar workshop are similar to the schizophrenia workshop except that the consumer is included. Content is determined by the specific characteristics of the illness and includes symptoms of manic and depressive episodes, differences from normal highs and lows, the issue of willpower and the question of the "real" personality, among several key topics. The structure of the multifamily group meetings is essentially the same as the schizophrenia model. The patients have reported that, after varying lengths of treatment, they were less angry over time, had less debilitating episodes when they did occur, were better able to manage symptoms and episodes, experienced fewer hospitalizations, and were more able to appreciate their family's experience. Family members reported increased confidence in their ability to cope with the illness, increased confidence in their ill relative's ability to manage the illness, and benefits from the program even if the consumer did not attend.

Future Directions for Research

Family psychoeducation has a solid research base and a consensus among leaders in the field regarding its marked efficacy, essential components and techniques; it should continue to be recommended for application in routine practice. However, there continues to be a number of important gaps in the knowledge needed to make comprehensive evidence-based practice recommendations and to implement them with a wide variety of families:

- More needs to be described, both quantitatively and qualitatively, about the patient/consumer's outcomes and experiences. Most patients have been increasingly enthusiastic about family psychoeducation, but would often not view it as useful or even tolerable at the outset. Also, the benefits that do occur for the primary participants in the treatment need to be linked to the benefits sought by them. This most often occurs around employment, less around relapse. The author's research team, for instance, has focused on employment and other outcomes desired by patients in its last three outcome studies, seeing relapse prevention as a means to more consumer-based outcomes. In the American approaches—family psychoeducation, family behavioral management, and multifamily groups—the patient's perspectives, feelings, hopes, and pains are central to the effort, although this aspect is not emphasized in the respective research reports. It is important to include the descriptions in the treatment manuals as the basis for developing further research on patient/consumer experiences and outcomes. For instance, it is not uncommon in PMFGs that the patients recover to the point that they are doing most of the talking, joking and relating to one another, often remarkable outcomes given where they usually start. These observations need to be quantified and described, though that is not easily done.

- Although the World Schizophrenia Fellowship and others have delineated the core components of a successful family intervention, the minimal ingredients are still uncertain. This was highlighted by the Treatment Strategies in Schizophrenia study (Schooler et al., 1997). The investigators found no significant difference in relapse rates between families receiving the more intensive program that consisted of a simplified version of cognitive behavioral family intervention plus a multiple family group and those receiving a less intensive psychoeducational (supportive) multifamily group program. However, both conditions provided support and education to families far beyond that found in usual services, including most of the key elements of the psychoeducational multifamily groups approach described previously (Schooler et al., 1997). More studies that are *designed* to identify the least intensive and smallest "dose" of family psychoeducation are necessary to increase the cost-effectiveness of the model and to decrease the burden on families.

- Increasing the sophistication, variety, and scope of measurement and outcomes used to evaluate "benefit" is essential. Commonly used benchmarks are subject to complicated intervening variables and need to be correlated with other results. For example, increased hospitalizations for an ill relative could be a good sign in the year after family psychoeducation if it indicates that the patient is getting previously neglected care and that the family is more able to identify prodromal symptoms indicating an impending relapse (McFarlane, Lukens, et al., 1995). In addition, family well-being and health should be routinely measured.

- Since the development of family psychoeducation, other psychosocial programs have also developed a substantial evidentiary base including supported employment and assertive community treatment (ACT; Bond et al., 2001). For instance, ACT in combination with family psychoeducation (FACT) led to better noncompetitive employment outcomes than ACT alone (McFarlane et al., 1996) and the combination of ACT, family psychoeducation, and supported employment led to better competitive employment outcomes than conventional vocational rehabilitation (McFarlane et al., 2000). A more recent study, yet to be published, demonstrated unusually high employment rates for persons with schizophrenia, about 67% at 2 years, using the family-aided ACT approach. In this study, the FACT package incorporated supported employment and cognitive assessments to provide employment opportunities, adaptation of the job to the patient and vice versa, with family involvement in the entire process. The opportunities for family psychoeducation to be combined and/or compared with these new psychosocial models have not been fully explored.

- Research is needed to refine the interventions so they better address different types of families, in different situations, and at different points in course of illness. For example, there is some evidence that individualized consultation may have more benefit (than group psychoeducation) for families who already have ample natural supports or are part of a support group (Solomon, 1996; Solomon, Draine, & Mannion, 1996; Solomon et al., 1997). Multifamily groups are specifically more effective than single-family format for patients who respond only partially to medication, families with high expressed emotion, and first episode cases (McFarlane, 2002).

- Although family psychoeducation has been tested in a wide range of national and global settings, there remains a need to assess modifications in content and outcome among particular American subcultures as well as internationally. As noted previously, in the United States, the one study involving Latino family members reached mixed conclusions, whereas several studies in Spain have found the expected robust results (Canive et al., 1995; Telles et al., 1995). However, studies completed in

China and underway with Vietnamese refugees in Australia have found comparable effects to those conducted with Anglo populations (Xiang, Ran, & Li, 1994; Xiong et al., 1994; Zhang et al., 1994). Single-family format may be more effective in low-expressed emotion African-American families than multifamily groups (McFarlane, 2002).

• What happens after a family has completed a family psychoeducation program? Families of patients with long-term problems and disability may need ongoing support and problem-solving skills to deal with the vicissitudes of illnesses. Lefley (2001) has described ad hoc psychoeducation in informal settings such as an ongoing medical center family support group. McFarlane's (2002) multifamily group structure is usually open-ended for families in need. The Family-to-Family program of the National Alliance for the Mentally Ill (NAMI) in the U.S. is limited to 12 sessions of formal education but offers continuity in the NAMI support and educational group structure (Burland, 1998).

Barriers to Implementation of Family Psychoeducation

Despite the research gaps, the extensive documentation of family psychoeducation's basic benefits prompts questions of why it is rarely offered. In general, low levels of any contact between programs/staff and family members in public and community-based settings may preclude the more substantial educational or support interventions. In addition, the availability of any intervention is limited by the availability of people to provide it and the training necessary to equip them. Such staffing requires willing clinicians, resources, time, and financial reimbursement that have not been forthcoming for family psychoeducation. These imply the existence of larger attitudinal, knowledge, practical, and systemic implementation obstacles.

Patients/Family Members

Implementation of family psychoeducation may be hindered by realities in the lives of potential participants. Practical issues like transportation, time commitment, and competing demands for time and energy are common (Solomon, 1996). If family members perceive that "training" through family psychoeducation includes expectations they will take on yet more care-giving responsibilities, they may stay away (World Schizophrenia Fellowship, 1998). Sessions must be scheduled when facilitators are available, but doing so may not mesh with potential participants' needs. Family members report significant burdens that may pose barriers to attendance though attendance may lighten these burdens (Gallagher & Mechanic, 1996; Mueser, Webb, Pfeiffer, Gladis, & Levinson, 1996).

Stigma, too, is common—family members may not want to be identified with psychiatric facilities. They may feel uncomfortable revealing to others the psychiatric illness in their families and airing their family problems in a public setting.

Family members may also have had negative experiences in the past and be hesitant to open themselves to that possibility again. Most have not had access to information documenting the value of family programs and so may not appreciate their potential (World Schizophrenia Fellowship, 1998). Indeed, hopelessness can be a barrier in that family members may believe that nothing will help. Patients may experience some of the same hesitations as their family members about participating in family psychoeducation. In addition, they may worry about losing the confidential relationship with their treatment teams and about losing autonomy.

Clinicians/Program Administrators

The lack of family psychoeducation availability may reflect mental health providers' under-appreciation and lack of knowledge about its utility and importance (Dixon & Lehman, 1995; Greenberg et al., 1995; Solomon, 1996). Clinicians and administrators may not appreciate the impact of mental illness on families, or may not know about the effectiveness of family psychoeducation (World Schizophrenia Fellowship, 1998). They may focus on medication over psychosocial interventions, and the individualistic orientation of medicine may make family involvement seem superfluous. Additionally, some may still follow theories that blame family dynamics for causing schizophrenia. Bergmark (1994) noted the persistence of psychodynamic theories as a potential barrier since many families perceive them as blaming. The findings regarding expressed emotion that were the original basis for family psychoeducation are often perceived similarly, despite attempts by expressed emotion researchers to avoid any implication of blame.

Important though they are, individuals' knowledge and underlying assumptions are only part of the picture. Wright, Takei, Rifkin, and Murray (1995) found that job and organizational factors were much more predictive of the frequency of mental health professionals' involvement with families than were professionals' attitudes. Clinician work schedule and professional discipline were the strongest predictors, but other organizational factors have posed barriers as well. Dissemination of McFarlane and Deakin's (2002) multiple-family psychoeducation group model has been hindered by a paucity of programmatic leadership supporting implementation, conflicts between the model's philosophy and typical agency practices, insufficient resources supporting practice change, and inadequate attention to human dynamics on a systems level (Dixon, McFarlane, Hornby, & McNary, 1999; McFarlane et al., 1993). For example, reasonable concerns about confidentiality issues may be seen as roadblocks to family involvement rather than as opportunities to create useful innovations that respect everyone's right to privacy (Boise, Heagery, & Eskenazi, 1996). Almost identical barriers to implementation of family treatments were found in Italian health services (Falloon, Casacchia, et al., 1999).

Mental health professionals have also expressed concern about the cost and length of structured family psychoeducation programs (Dixon, Lyles, et al.,

1999), although medication and case management services for clients usually have to be continued for much longer periods. The lack of reimbursement for sessions with families in the absence of the patient, a component of many family psychoeducation programs, is a significant disincentive to provide such services. Caseloads are universally very high, and staff time is stretched thin. Therefore, devoting substantial staff resources to training, organizing, leading, and sustaining family psychoeducation is seen as a luxury (World Schizophrenia Fellowship, 1998). In such an atmosphere, horizons tend to be short. The long-term investment and payoff in reduced crises, hospitalizations, and total treatment costs of family psychoeducation are overshadowed by immediate organizational crises or short-term goals.

Mental Health Authorities

At the level of health care systems, pressures to focus on outcomes, cost effectiveness, and "customer" satisfaction would seem in principle to favor widespread adoption of family information/support interventions. However, other tenets of the current health care environment—such as emphasis on short-term cost savings, technical (as contrasted with human–process-oriented) remedies, and individual pathology—encourage little attention to such services, which may be viewed as ancillary. At this level, also, it seems the evidence and mindset in favor of family psychoeducation has not been accepted. Many of the impediments mentioned above as patient- and program-level issues have their parallels in larger administrative systems: lack of awareness of evidence, ingrained assumptions about how care "should" be structured, and inadequate resources.

Strategies for Overcoming Barriers to Implementing Family Psychoeducation

Research on technology transfer has identified four fundamental conditions that must be met in order for individual or system change to occur: dissemination of knowledge; evaluation of programmatic impact; availability of resources; efforts to address the human dynamics of resisting change (Backer, 1991). Implementation strategies must include clear, widespread communication of the models and of their benefits to all stakeholders. This must be done through channels accessible and acceptable to the various stakeholders—including families, patients, providers, administrators, and policy-makers. It must be accompanied by advocacy, training, and supervision/consultation initiatives to raise awareness and support at all organizational levels (McFarlane, 1994).

Patient/Family Members

On the individual family member and patient level, effective family psychoeducation models include strategies for overcoming barriers to participation such as the family's sense of hopelessness and stigma. For example, offering sessions at home, helping family members understand that the intervention is designed to improve the lives of everyone in the family (not just the patient), being flexible about scheduling family meetings, and providing education during the engagement process destigmatize mental illness and engender hope (Mueser & Glynn, 1999; Tarrier, 1991).

Recent efforts to disseminate family psychoeducation in New York State, Los Angeles, Maine, and Illinois have illustrated clearly the importance of including representatives of the recipients—patients and their families, practitioners—of these services in their planning, adaptation, and eventual implementation. In the New York example, the dissemination was initiated and sponsored by the state's AMI (now NAMI New York) chapter (McFarlane et al., 1993). In comparing dramatic differences in the outcome of dissemination in Maine and Illinois, one key difference is the strong, formal support from NAMI Maine for the effort there, versus occasional resistance by local chapters and the absence of involvement of the state NAMI in Illinois (McFarlane, McNary, Dixon, Hornby, & Cimett, 2001). Experience and now some empirical data illustrate the need to include patients and families in efforts to disseminate. The often-encountered tension between some patient advocacy groups and family advocacy organizations can be bridged by emphasizing the complementarity of the outcomes in family work. As patients' symptoms are reduced and functioning improves, relatives become more engaged in and satisfied with community life, and family burden and medical illness decrease (Dyck et al., 2000; Falloon, Falloon, & Lussetti, 1997; McFarlane et al., 1996).

Clinicians/Program Administrators

Among professionals working in community mental health services, awareness and evidence, although necessary, are often not sufficient for adoption of new programs. Although interventions must maintain high fidelity to their model to obtain client and family outcomes, they also have to be responsive to local organizational and community cultures. Engagement and implementation strategies, as well as the interventions themselves, must be tailored for local and cultural characteristics, workload, and other stresses facing clinicians and agencies, particular diagnoses, relationships, duration of disorder and disability, and whether the ill person is in medical treatment (Guarnaccia & Parra, 1996; Jordan, Lewellen, & Vandiver, 1995). Perhaps even more critical to adoption is matching administrative support and expectations for evidence-based practice with a rationale and explication of advantages that are meaningful to clinicians. Advantages can include avoidance of crises, more efficient case management, gratitude from families and patients, and more interesting, invigorating work-lives for the clinicians. Recent studies demonstrate that on whole, knowledge about empirical advantages of family psychoeducation, such as reduced relapse and rehospitalization rates, carry almost no weight in convincing most working clinicians to change attitudes toward families and adopt a new clinical practice (McFarlane et al., 2001).

Consensus building among agency staff and directors, including a wide range of concerned parties in a bottom-up planning process, is critical but must be tailored to address local operational barriers and contrary beliefs. Successful implementations have also required ongoing supervision, operational consultation, and general support to achieve high levels of adoption. In a sense, these provide ongoing consensus building. For instance, the PORT dissemination found that it was possible to change practice with a high level of technical assistance and a supportive environment reflected in staff agreement with the principles and philosophy of the new program (Dixon, Lyles, et al., 1999). A recent dissemination of a family psychoeducation program in Los Angeles County succeeded due to the persistent advocacy of the local NAMI group, the support of top management, the 9-month duration of training, the high quality and commitment of trainees, and the skill of the trainer (Amenson & Liberman, 2001).

Mental Health Authorities/Government

Although it is tempting to assume that state mental health authorities could mandate adoption of family psychoeducation centrally, experience suggests that a more complex approach is required. New York partially succeeded in dissemination by partnering with the NAMI affiliate and an academic center; unfortunately, the mental health authority there also abruptly terminated their large dissemination program prior to achieving a widespread impact. Maine's recent success was initiated by the trade association of mental health centers/services, with support but little involvement by the state authority, which has recently begun exploring a formal partnership to continue and deepen this largely successful effort. A simultaneous effort in Illinois, initiated by the state authority but distinctly lacking consensus by center directors or the state NAMI chapter, has had much less success. One exception is New Jersey that succeeded in dissemination by setting expectations and requirements for family psychoeducation at the central level.

New Jersey aside, the most likely strategy based on experience to date is one in which provider organizations take the initiative while being supported in implementation by patient and family organizations, the state mental health authority, and the key insurance payers as a consensus-driven partnership. Appropriate reimbursement for the service will follow from this collaboration. Experience also suggests that this process requires several years of consistent effort and ongoing monitoring to succeed. Happily, it is not necessarily a fiscally expensive process: Maine achieved 90+% agency implementation for about $.25 per capita over 4 years, including evaluation costs. The principal costs are in human effort, especially the effort required to overcome resistance to change.

There also must be accountability and tracking of delivery of services to families. Although many states encourage the delivery of services to families, few monitor or make funding contingent on such services being delivered (Dixon, Goldman, Hirad, Adams, & Lucksted, 1999). One systems level option is for mental health centers to create the role of adult family intervention coordinator, who serves as the point-person for such intervention, running interference, supervising clinicians, and monitoring fidelity (Mueser & Fox, 2000).

Family-To-Family Programs
In the absence of professionally-led family psychoeducation programs, voluntary peer-led family education programs have developed, epitomized by Burland's Family-to-Family Education Program (FFEP) provided through NAMI (Burland, 1998; Solomon, 2000; Solomon, Draine, & Mannion, 1996; Solomon, Draine, Mannion, & Meisel, 1996). FFEP is currently available in 41 states, often with wait lists. FFEP and other mutual-assistance family programs are organized and led by trained volunteer family members. They are offered in the community regardless of the ill relative's treatment status, tend to be brief (e.g., 12 weeks for FFEP), and mix families of persons with various diagnoses but focus on schizophrenia and bipolar disorder. Based on a trauma and recovery model of the family experience of coping with mental illness, FFEP merges education with specific supports to help families through stages of apprehending and coping with a relative's mental illness (Burland, 1998). The FFEP focuses first on family member outcomes and well-being, although benefits to the patient are also considered important.

Uncontrolled research on FFEP and its NAMI predecessor program, Journey of Hope, suggest that program participation increased the participants' knowledge of the causes and treatment of mental illness, their understanding of the mental health service system, and their well-being (Pickett-Schenk et al., 2000). A prospective naturalistic study showed that FFEP participants reported significantly less displeasure and worry about their ill family member and significantly more family, community, and service-system empowerment at program completion (Dixon, Stewart, et al., 2001). This finding has now been replicated in a study with a waiting list control design. Benefits observed at the end of the program were sustained at 6-months postintervention (Dixon, Stewart, et al., 2001). Although FFEP currently lacks rigorous scientific evidence of its efficacy in improving clinical or functional outcomes for the patient with mental illness, it shows considerable promise for improving family well-being, at least over short periods. The most recent research and practice has attempted to optimize the clinical opportunities provided by family psychoeducation and peer-based programs such as FFEP by developing partnerships between the two strategies. For example, family psychoeducation programs have utilized FFEP teachers as leaders, and participation in FFEP has facilitated eventual participation in family psychoeducation.

Conclusions

Family psychoeducation has established its efficacy and effectiveness as an evidenced-based practice. To date, its use into routine clinical practice is alarmingly limited. This is particularly unfortunate, because nearly all practitioners, of many disciplines, who use the approach report marked increases in their sense of professional satisfaction, gratification, and enjoyment of their work, and gratitude and appreciation from families and patients, often rarities in work with severe mental illness. Recent research has begun to develop dissemination interventions targeted at programmatic and organizational levels with some success. Ongoing research must continue to develop practical and low-cost strategies to introduce and sustain family psychoeducation in typical practice settings. More research is also needed on identifying the barriers to implementing family psychoeducation in various clinical settings (i.e., the impact of clinicians' attitudes, geographic factors, funding, disconnection of patients from family members, stigma), as well as the extent to which modifications in these factors mediate the outcomes of educational interventions. Dissemination could also be facilitated by further exploration of integration of family psychoeducation with psychosocial interventions such as assertive community treatment, supported work and social skills training, and other evidence-based cognitive behavioral strategies to improve patient treatment outcomes.

However, the first step toward dissemination is awareness among practitioners that new approaches are not only available, they are much more effective than previous models, particularly those that are oriented toward the individual patient alone and those that target family dysfunction. This new approach builds on the fundamental strength of family loyalty and altruism to achieve results that to date have been more cost-effective than any model previously developed for this serious type of disorder.

Perhaps the most immediate implication for family therapists is that these approaches are not difficult to learn or practice, if training and supervision are available, if it is reasonably competent, and if it is applied in practice. Further, using the key elements of the models as described earlier in this chapter, an office practice with a patient with schizophrenia is likely to achieve nearly the same results as a more formalized implementation in an organized practice setting. Family therapists primarily need to see the family as a resource for, not the source of, the disorder, as being equally the victim of a neurological disorder in a loved one as is the patient. The technical aspects could be less important to outcome than simply having the right attitude and an empathic approach to both patient and family. Families themselves are usually appreciative of, and have profound need for, the support of professionals. Focus group feedback has shown repeatedly that it is the basics of family psychoeducation—support, guidance, sharing the burden, information—that families most value. The more technical aspects seem to be effective in achieving outcomes, but are not noticed as much by the recipients. In short, it is far more effective to apply the key elements in whatever way seems to be feasible in one's practice than to not include the family in treatment at all. It is important for clinicians to remember that the first study of the modality, Goldstein et al.'s (1978) crisis family therapy, did not include some of the complements developed later, but was nevertheless dramatically effective and started the process of empirically-based family treatment for schizophrenia.

Hopefully, readers of the *Journal of Marital and Family Therapy* will agree that this is a new frontier for work by family therapists, since they are inherently more familiar with working with families and comfortable with this more complex form of treatment than those with individual therapy as their only background. The question remaining is whether family therapists will be able to adopt the necessary empathic, educational, and supportive approaches that have been proven effective. The authors urge the reader to make the effort, because the rewards are not only great, they tend to be mutual for all concerned.

References

References marked with a double asterisk are recommended for clinicians.

Abramowitz, I. A., & Coursey, R. D. (1989). Impact of an educational support group on family participants who take care of their schizophrenic relatives. *Journal of Consulting and Clinical Psychology, 57*(2), 232–236.

**Adamec, C. (1996). *How to live with a mentally ill person.* New York: John Wiley & Sons.

**Amenson, C. (1998). *Schizophrenia: A family education curriculum.* Pasadena, CA: Pacific Clinics Institute.

Amenson, C. S., & Liberman, R. P. (2001). Dissemination of educational classes for families of adults with schizophrenia. *Psychiatric Services, 52*(5), 589–592.

American Psychiatric Association. (1997). *Practice guidelines for the treatment of schizophrenia.* Washington, DC: Author

Anderson, C. M. (1983). A psychoeducational program for families of patients with schizophrenia. In W. R. McFarlane (Ed.), *Family therapy in schizophrenia* (pp. 99–116). New York: Guilford Press.

Anderson, C., Hogarty, G., & Reiss, D. (1980). Family treatment of adult schizophrenic patients: A psychoeducational approach. *Schizophrenia Bulletin, 6,* 490–505.

**Anderson, C., Reiss, D., & Hogarty, G. (1986). *Schizophrenia and the family: A practitioner's guide to psychoeducation and management.* New York: Guilford Press.

Backer, T. D. (1991). *Drug abuse technology transfer.* Rockville, MD: National Institute on Drug Abuse.

Bae, S.-W., & Kung, W. W.-M. (2000). Family intervention for Asian Americans with a schizophrenic patient in the family. *American Journal of Orthopsychiatry, 70*(4), 532–541.

Barrowclough, C., Haddock, G., Tarrier, N., Lewis, S. W., Moring, J., O'Brien, R., et al. (2001). Randomized controlled trial of motivational interviewing, cognitive behavior therapy, and family intervention for patients with comorbid schizophrenia and substance use disorders. *American Journal of Psychiatry, 158*(10), 1706–1713.

Baucom, D. H., Shoham, V., Mueser, K. T., Daiuto, A. D., & Stickle, T. R. (1998). Empirically supported couple and family interventions for marital distress and adult mental health problems. *Journal of Consulting and Clinical Psychology, 66,* 53–88.

Bergmark, T. (1994). Models of family support in Sweden: From mistreatment to understanding. *New Directions in Mental Health Services, 62,* 71–77.

Boise, L., Heagery, B., & Eskenazi, L. (1996). Facing chronic illness: The family support model and its benefits. *Patient Education and Counseling, 27,* 75–84.

Bond, G., Becker, D., Drake, R., Rapp, C., Meisler, N., Lehman, A., et al. (2001). Implementing supported employment as an evidenced-based practice. *Psychiatric Services, 52*(3), 313–322.

Burland, J. (1998). Family-to-Family: A trauma-and-recovery model of family education. *New Directions for Mental Health Services, 77*, 33–44.

Bustamante, A. M. (2000). Outcome of a standardized strategic family intervention for disruptive behavior disorders: A multisite randomized trial. (Doctoral dissertation, Adelphi University, 2000). *Dissertation Abstracts International: Section B: the Sciences & Engineering, 60*(10-B), 5220.

Canive, J. M., Sanz Fuentenebro, J., Vazquez, C., Qualls, C., Fuentenebro, F., & Tuason, V. B. (1995). Family environment predictors of outcome in schizophrenic patients in Spain: a nine-month follow-up study. *Acta Psychiatrica Scandinavica, 92*, 371–377.

Cardin, V. A., McGill, C. W., & Falloon, I. R. H. (1985). An economic analysis: Costs, benefits, and effectiveness. In I. R. H. Falloon (Ed.), *Family management of schizophrenia: A study of clinical, social, family, and economic benefits* (pp. 115–123). Baltimore: Johns Hopkins University Press.

Clarkin, J. F., Carpenter, D., Hull, D., Wilner, P., & Glick, I. (1998). Effects of psychoeducational intervention for married patients with bipolar disorder and their spouses. *Psychiatric Services, 49*, 531–533.

Cochrane, J., Goering, P., & Rogers, J. (1997). The mental health of informal caregivers in Ontario: An epidemiological survey. *American Journal of Public Health, 87*(12), 2002–2008.

Connery, L., & Brekke, J. (1999). A home-based family intervention for ethnic minorities with a mentally ill member. *Alcoholism Treatment Quarterly, 17*(1-2), 149–167.

Coursey, R., Curtis, L., & Marsh, D. (2000a). Competencies for direct service staff members who work with adults with severe mental illness in outpatient public mental health managed care systems. *Psychiatric Rehabilitation Journal, 23*(4), 370–377.

Coursey, R., Curtis, L., & Marsh, D. (2000b). Competencies for direct service staff members who work with adults with severe mental illness: Specific knowledge, attitudes, skills and bibliography. *Psychiatric Rehabilitation Journal, 23*(4), 378–392.

Cuijpers, P. (1999). The effects of family interventions on relatives' burden: A meta-analysis. *Journal of Mental Health, 8*, 275–285.

Detre, T., Sayer, J., Norton, A., & Lewis, H. (1961). An experimental approach to the treatment of the acutely ill psychiatric patient in the general hospital. *Connecticut Medicine, 25*, 613–619.

Dixon, L., Adams, C., & Lucksted, A. (2000). Update on family psychoeducation for schizophrenia. *Schizophrenia Bulletin, 26*(1), 5–20.

Dixon, L., Goldman, H., Hirad, A., Adams, C., & Lucksted, A. (1999). State policy and funding of services to families of adults with serious and persistent mental illness. *Psychiatric Services, 50*(4), 551–553.

Dixon, L. B., & Lehman, A. F. (1995). Family interventions for schizophrenia. *Schizophrenia Bulletin, 21*(4), 631–644.

Dixon, L., Lyles, A., Scott, J., Lehman, A., Postrado, L., Goldman, H., et al. (1999). Services to families of adults with schizophrenia: From treatment recommendations to dissemination. *Psychiatric Services, 50*(2), 233–238.

Dixon, L., McFarlane, W., Hornby, H., & McNary, S. (1999). Dissemination of family psychoeducation: The importance of consensus building. *Schizophrenia Research, 36*, 339.

Dixon, L., McFarlane, W. R., Lefley, H., Lucksted, A., Cohen, M., Falloon, I., et al. (2001). Evidence-based practices for services to families of people with psychiatric disabilities. *Psychiatric Services, 52*(7), 903–910.

Dixon, L., Stewart, B., Burland, J., Delahanty, J., Lucksted, A., & Hoffman, M. (2001). Pilot study of the effectiveness of the Family-to-Family Education Program. *Psychiatric Services, 52*(7), 965–967.

Dyck, D. G., Short, R. A., Hendryx, M. S., Norell, D., Myers, M., Patterson, T., et al. (2000). Management of negative symptoms among patients with schizophrenia attending multiple-family groups. *Psychiatric Services, 51*(4), 513–519.

Dyck, D., Short, R. A., Voss, W., Hendryx, M. S., Hanken, M., Vitaliano, P., et al. (2002). Service use among patients with schizophrenia in psychoeducational multifamily-group treatment. *Psychiatric Services, 53*(6), 749–754.

Emanuels-Zuurveen, L. (1997). Spouse-aided therapy with depressed patients. *Behavior Modification, 21*(1), 62–77.

Emanuels-Zuurveen, L., & Emmelkamp, P. (1996). Individual behavioural-cognitive therapy v marital therapy for depression in maritally distressed couples. *British Journal of Psychiatry, 169*(2), 181–188.

**Falloon, I., Boyd, J., & McGill, C. (1984). *Family care of schizophrenia*. New York: Guilford.

Falloon, I., Boyd, J., McGill, C., Williamson, M., Razani, J., Moss, H., et al. (1985). Family management in the prevention of morbidity of schizophrenia. *Archives of General Psychiatry, 42*, 887–896.

Falloon, I., Casacchia, M., Lussetti, M., Magliano, L., Morosini, P., Piani, F., et al. (1999). The development of cognitive-behavioural therapies within Italian mental health services. *International Journal of Mental Health, 28*, 60–67.

Falloon, I., Falloon, N., & Lussetti, M. (1997). *Integrated mental health care: A guidebook for patients*. Perugia, Italy: Optimal Treatment Project.

Falloon, I., Held, T., Coverdale, J., Roncone, R., & Laidlaw, T. (1999). Psychosocial interventions for schizophrenia: A review of long-term benefits of international studies. *Psychiatric Rehabilitation Skills, 3*, 268–290.

Falloon, I. R. H., & Pederson, J. (1985). Family management in the prevention of morbidity of schizophrenia: The adjustment of the family unit. *British Journal of Psychiatry, 147*, 156–163.

Frances, A., Hoffman, B., Pass, T., & Andrews, S. (1987). A schizophrenic woman in a high expressed emotion family. *Hospital and Community Psychiatry, 38*(7), 707–708, 717.

Frances, A. D. J., & Kahn, D. A. (1996). Expert consensus guideline series: Treatment of schizophrenia. *The Journal of Clinical Psychiatry, 57*(50, Suppl. 12B), 5–58.

Fristad, M. A., Gavazzi, S. M., & Soldano, K. W. (1998). Multi-family psychoeducation groups for childhood mood disorders: A program description and preliminary efficacy data. *Contemporary Family Therapy, 20*(3), 385–402.

Gallagher, S., & Mechanic, D. (1996). Living with the mentally ill: Effects on the health and functioning of other household members. *Social Science & Medicine, 42*(12), 1691–1701.

Geist, R., Heinmaa, M., Stephens, D., Davis, R., & Katzman, D. K. (2000). Comparison of family therapy and family group psychoeducation in adolescents with anorexia nervosa. *Canadian Journal of Psychiatry, 45*(2), 173–178.

Goldstein, M. J., & Miklowitz, D. J. (1995). The effectiveness of psychoeducational family therapy in the treatment of schizophrenic disorders. In W. M. Pinsof & L. C. Wynne (Eds.), *Family therapy effectiveness: Current research and theory* (pp. 361–376). Washington, DC: American Association for Marriage and Family Therapy.

Goldstein, M., Rodnick, E., Evans, J., May, P., & Steinberg, M. (1978). Drug and family therapy in the aftercare treatment of acute schizophrenia. *Archives of General Psychiatry, 35*, 1169–1177.

Gonzalez, S., Steinglass, P., & Reiss, D. (1989). Putting the illness in its place: Discussion groups for families with chronic medical illnesses. *Family Process, 28*(1), 69–87.

Greenberg, J., Greenley, J., & Kim, H. (1995). The provision of mental health services to families of persons with serious mental illness. *Research in Community and Mental Health, 8*, 181–204.

**Guarnaccia, P., & Parra, P. (1996). Ethnicity, social status, and families' experiences of caring for a mentally ill family member. *Community Mental Health Journal, 32*, 243–260.

**Gunderson, J., Berkowitz, C., & Ruizsancho, A. (1997). Families of borderline patients: A psychoeducational approach. *Bulletin Of The Menninger Clinic, 61*(4), 446–457.

Harrington, R., Kerfoot, M., Dyer, E., McNiven, F., Gill, J., Harrington, V., et al. (1998). Randomized trial of a home-based family intervention for children who have deliberately poisoned themselves. *Journal of the American Academy of Child & Adolescent Psychiatry, 37*(5), 512–518.

Hogarty, G., Anderson, C., Reiss, D., Kornblith, S., Greenwald, D., Javna, C., et al. (1986). Family psychoeducation, social skills training, and maintenance chemotherapy in the aftercare treatment of schizophrenia. *Archives of General Psychiatry, 43*, 633–642.

Hogarty, G. E., Anderson, C. M., Reiss, D. J., Kornblith, S. J., Greenwald, D. P., Ulrich, R. F., et al. (1991). Family psychoeducation, social skills training, and maintenance chemotherapy in the aftercare treatment of schizophrenia, II: Two-year effects of a controlled study on relapse and adjustment. *Archives of General Psychiatry, 48*(4), 340–347.

Hogarty, G. E., Greenwald, D., Ulrich, R. F., Kornblith, S. J., DiBarry, A. L., Cooley, S., et al. (1997). Three-year trials of personal therapy among schizophrenic patients living with or independent of family, II: Effects on adjustment of patients. *American Journal of Psychiatry, 154*(11), 1514–1524.

Hogarty, G., & Ulrich, R. (1977). Temporal effects of drug and placebo in delaying relapse in schizophrenic outpatients. *Archives of General Psychiatry, 34*, 297–301.

**Hooley, J. M., Rosen, L. R., & Richters, J. E. (1995). Expressed emotion: Toward clarification of a critical construct. In G. A. Miller (Ed.), *The behavioral high-risk paradigm in psychopathology* (pp. 88–120). New York: Springer Verlag.

Jordan, C., Lewellen, A., & Vandiver, V. (1995). Psychoeducation for minority families: A social-work perspective. *International Journal of Mental Health, 23*(4), 27–43.

Kottgen, C., Sonnichsen, I., Mollenhauer, K., & Jurth, R. (1984). Group therapy with families of schizophrenic patients: Results of the Hamburg Camberwell Family Interview Study III. *International Journal of Family Psychiatry, 5*, 83–94.

Lam, D. H. (1991). Psychosocial family intervention in schizophrenia: A review of empirical studies. *Psychological Medicine, 21*(2), 423–441.

Laqueur, H. P., LaBurt, H. A., & Morong, E. (1964). Multiple family therapy: Further developments. *International Journal of Social Psychiatry, 10*(Congress Issue), 69–80.

Leff, J. (1994). Working with the families of schizophrenic patients. *British Journal of Psychiatry Supplement* (23), 71–76.

Leff, J., Berkowitz, R., Shavit, N., Strachan, A., Glass, I., & Vaughn, C. (1989). A trial of family therapy v. a relatives group for schizophrenia. *British Journal of Psychiatry, 154*, 58–66.

Leff, J., Berkowitz, R., Shavit, N., Strachan, A., Glass, I., & Vaughn, C. (1990). A trial of family therapy versus a relatives' group for schizophrenia: Two-year follow-up. *British Journal of Psychiatry, 157*, 571–577.

Leff, J., Kuipers, L., & Berkowitz, R. (1983). Intervention in families of schizophrenics and its effects on relapse rate. In W. R. McFarlane (Ed.), *Family therapy in schizophrenia* (pp. 173–187). New York: Guilford Press.

Leff, J., Kuipers, L., Berkowitz, R., Eberlein-Vries, R., & Sturgeon, D. (1982). A controlled trial of social intervention in the families of schizophrenic patients. *British Journal of Psychiatry, 141*, 121–134.

Leff, J., Kuipers, L., Berkowitz, R., & Sturgeon, D. (1985). A controlled trial of social intervention in the families of schizophrenic patients: Two year follow-up. *British Journal of Psychiatry, 146*, 594–600.

Leff, J., Vearnals, S., Brewin, C., Wolff, G., Alexander, B., Asen, E., et al. (2000). The London Depression Intervention Trial: Randomised controlled trial of antidepressants v. couple therapy in the treatment and maintenance of people with depression living with a partner: Clinical outcome and costs. *British Journal of Psychiatry, 177*(2), 95–100.

**Lefley, H. (2001). Impact of mental illness on families and carers. In G. Thornicroft & G. Szmukler (Eds.), *Textbook of community psychiatry.* London: Oxford University Press.

**Lehman, A. F., Steinwachs, D. M., Buchanan, R., Carpenter, W. T., Dixon, L. B., Fahey, M., et al. (1998). Translating research into practice: The Schizophrenia Patient Outcomes Research Team (PORT) treatment recommendations. *Schizophrenia Bulletin, 24*(1), 1–10.

Ling, S., Zhao, C., Yang, W., Wang, R., Jin, Z., Ma, T., et al. (1999). Efficacy of family intervention on schizophrenics in remission in community: Result of one year follow-up study. *Chinese Mental Health Journal, 13*(6), 325–327.

Linszen, D., Dingemans, P., Van der Does, J. W., Nugter, A., Scholte, P., Lenior, R., et al. (1996). Treatment, expressed emotion and relapse in recent onset schizophrenic disorders. *Psychological Medicine, 26*(2), 333–342.

Loveland-Cherry, C. J., Ross, L. T., & Kaufman, S. R. (1999). Effects of a home-based family intervention on adolescent alcohol use and misuse. *Journal of Studies on Alcohol, Supplement 13*(Mar), 94–102.

Marriott, A., Donaldson, C., Tarrier, N., & Burns, A. (2000). Effectiveness of cognitive-behavioural family intervention in reducing the burden of care in carers of patients with Alzheimer's disease. *British Journal of Psychiatry, 176,* 557–562.

Marsh, D. (1992). *Families and mental illness: New directions in professional practice.* New York: Praeger.

**Marsh, D. (2001). *A family-focused approach to serious mental illness: Empirically supported interventions.* Sarasota, FL: Professional Resource Press.

Marsh, D., & Johnson, D. (1997). The family experience of mental illness: Implications for intervention. *Professional Psychology: Research and Practice, 28*(7), 229–237.

McFarlane, W. R. (1994). Multiple-family groups and psychoeducation in the treatment of schizophrenia. *New Directions in Mental Health Services, 62,* 13–22.

**McFarlane, W. R. (Ed.). (2002). *Multifamily groups in the treatment of severe psychiatric disorders.* New York: Guilford Press.

McFarlane, W. R., & Deakins, S. M. (2002). Family-aided assertive community treatment. In W. R. McFarlane (Ed.), *Multifamily groups in the treatment of severe psychiatric disorders* (pp. 175–197). New York: Guilford Press.

McFarlane, W. R., Dunne, E., Lukens, E., Newmark, M., McLaughlin Toran, J., Deakins, S., et al. (1993). From research to clinical practice: Dissemination of New York State's family psychoeducation project. *Hospital and Community Psychiatry, 44*(3), 265–270.

McFarlane, W. R., Dushay, R. A., Deakins, S. M., Stastny, P., Lukens, E. P., Toran, J., et al. (2000). Employment outcomes in Family-aided Assertive Community Treatment. *American Journal of Orthopsychiatry, 70*(2), 203–214.

McFarlane, W. R., Dushay, R. A., Stastny, P., Deakins, S. M., & Link, B. (1996). A comparison of two levels of Family-aided Assertive Community Treatment. *Psychiatric Services, 47*(7), 744–750.

McFarlane, W. R., Link, B., Dushay, R., Marchal, J., & Crilly, J. (1995). Psychoeducational multiple family groups: Four-year relapse outcome in schizophrenia. *Family Process, 34*(2), 127–144.

McFarlane, W. R., & Lukens, E. P. (1998). Insight, families, and education: An exploration of the role of attribution in clinical outcome. In X. F. Amador & A. S. David (Eds.), *Insight and psychosis* (pp. 317–331). New York: Oxford University Press.

McFarlane, W. R., Lukens, E., Link, B., Dushay, R., Deakins, S. A., Newmark, M., et al. (1995). Multiple-family groups and psychoeducation in the treatment of schizophrenia. *Archives of General Psychiatry, 52*(8), 679–687.

McFarlane, W. R., McNary, S., Dixon, L., Hornby, H., & Cimett, E. (2001). Predictors of dissemination of family psychoeducation in community mental health centers in Maine and Illinois. *Psychiatric Services, 52*(7), 935–942.

**Miklowitz, D. J., & Goldstein, M. J. (1997). *Bipolar disorder: A family-focused treatment approach.* New York: Guilford Press.

Miklowitz, D. J., Simoneau, T. L., George, E. L., Richards, J. A., Kalbag, A., Sachs-Ericsson, N., et al. (2000). Family-focused treatment of bipolar disorder: 1-year effects of a psychoeducational program in conjunction with pharmacotherapy. *Biological Psychiatry, 48,* 582–592.

Minuchin, S. (1974). *Families and family therapy.* Cambridge, MA: Harvard University Press.

Moltz, D. (1993). Bipolar disorder and the family: An integrative model. *Family Process, 32,* 409–423.

**Moltz, D., & Newmark, M. (2002). Multifamily groups for bipolar illness. In W. R. McFarlane (Ed.), *Multifamily groups in the treatment of severe psychiatric disorders* (pp. 293–317). New York: Guilford Press.

Montero, I., Asencio, A., Hernandez, I., Masanet, M. S. J., Lacruz, M., Bellver, F., et al. (2001). Two strategies for family intervention in schizophrenia: A randomized trial in a Mediterranean environment. *Schizophrenia Bulletin, 27*(4), 661–670.

Montero, I., Gomez Beneyto, M., Ruiz, I., Puche, E., & Adam, A. (1992). The influence of family expressed emotion on the course of schizophrenia in a sample of Spanish patients: A two-year follow-up study. *British Journal of Psychiatry, 161,* 217–222.

Muela Martinez, J. A., & Godoy Garcia, J. F. (2001). Family intervention program for schizophrenia: Two-year follow-up of the Andalusia Study. *Apuntes de Psicologia, 19*(3), 421–430.

Mueser, K., & Fox, L. (2000). Family-friendly services: A modest proposal. *Psychiatric Services, 51,* 1452.

**Mueser, K., & Glynn, S. (1999). *Behavioral family therapy for psychiatric disorders.* Oakland, CA: New Harbinger.

Mueser, K., Webb, C., Pfeiffer, M., Gladis, M., & Levinson, D. (1996). Family burden of schizophrenia and bipolar disorder: Perceptions of relatives and professionals. *Psychiatric Services, 47*(5), 507–511.

Nicholson, J. M., & Sanders, M. R. (1999). Randomized controlled trial of behavioral family intervention for the treatment of child behavior problems in stepfamilies. *Journal of Divorce & Remarriage, 30*(3-4), 1–23.

Parikh, S., Kusumakar, V., Haslam, D., Matte, R., Sharma, V., & Yatham, L. (1997). Psychosocial interventions as an adjunct to pharmacotherapy in bipolar disorder. *Canadian Journal of Psychiatry, 42,* 74S–78S.

Pelchat, D., Bisson, J., Ricard, N., Perreault, M., & Bouchard, J. M. (1999). Longitudinal effects of an early family intervention programme on the adaptation of parents of children with a disability. *International Journal of Nursing Studies, 36*(6), 465–477.

Penn, D. L., & Mueser, K. T. (1996). Research update on the psychosocial treatment of schizophrenia. *American Journal of Psychiatry, 153,* 607–617.

Pickett-Schenk, S., Cook, J., & Laris, A. (2000). Journey of Hope program outcomes. *Community Mental Health Journal, 36,* 413–424.

Pitschel-Walz, G., Leucht, S., Bauml, J., Kissling, W., & Engel, R. R. (2001). The effect of family interventions in relapse and rehospitalization in schizophrenia: A meta-analysis. *Schizophrenia Bulletin, 27*(1), 73–92.

Randolph, E. T., Eth, S., Glynn, S. M., Paz, G. G., Leong, G. B., Shaner, A. L., et al. (1994). Behavioural family management in schizophrenia: Outcome of a clinic-based intervention. *British Journal of Psychiatry, 164*(4), 501–506.

Rund, B. R., Moe, L., Sollien, T., Fjell, A., Borchgrevink, T., Hallert, M., et al. (1994). The Psychosis Project: Outcome and cost-effectiveness of a psychoeducational treatment programme for schizophrenic adolescents. *Acta Psychiatrica Scandinavica, 89*(3), 211–218.

Russell, P. S. S., John, J. K. A., & Lakshmanan, J. L. (1999). Family intervention for intellectually disabled children: Randomised controlled trial. *British Journal of Psychiatry, 174,* 254–258.

Saldanha, D. (2002). Family intervention in the treatment of post-traumatic stress disorders. *Journal of Projective Psychology & Mental Health, 9*(1), 57–61.

Sanders, M. R., & McFarland, M. (2000). Treatment of depressed mothers with disruptive children: A controlled evaluation of cognitive behavioral family intervention. *Behavior Therapy, 31*(1), 89–112.

Schooler, N. R., Keith, S. J., Severe, J. B., Matthews, S. M., Bellack, A. S., Glick, I. D., et al. (1997). Relapse and rehospitalization during maintenance treatment of schizophrenia: The effects of dose reduction and family treatment. *Archives of General Psychiatry, 54*(5), 453–463.

Shi, Y., Zhao, B., Xu, D., & Sen, J. (2000). A comparative study of life quality in schizophrenic patients after family intervention. *Chinese Mental Health Journal, 14*(2), 135–137.

Simoneau, T., Miklowitz, D., Richards, J., Saleem, R., & George, L. (1999). Bipolar disorder and family communication: The effects of a psychoeducational treatment program. *Journal of Abnormal Psychology, 108,* 588–597.

Solomon, P. (1996). Moving from psychoeducation to family education for families of adults with serious mental illness. *Psychiatric Services, 47,* 1364–1370.

Solomon, P. (2000). Interventions for families of individuals with schizophrenia: Maximizing outcomes for their relatives. *Disease Management and Health Outcomes, 8*(4), 211–221.

Solomon, P., Draine, J., & Mannion, E. (1996). The impact of individualized consultation and group workshop family education interventions in ill relative outcomes. *Journal of Nervous and Mental Disease, 184*(4), 252–255.

Solomon, P., Draine, J., Mannion, E., & Meisel, M. (1996). Impact of brief family psychoeducation on self-efficacy. *Schizophrenia Bulletin, 22*(1), 41–50.

Solomon, P., Draine, J., Mannion, E., & Meisel, M. (1997). Effectiveness of two models of brief family education: Retention of gains by family members with serious mental illness. *American Journal of Orthopsychiatry, 67*(2), 177–186.

Steinglass, P. (1998). Multiple family discussion groups for patients with chronic medical illness. *Families, Systems & Health, 16,* 55–70.

**Tarrier, N. (1991). Some aspects of family interventions in schizophrenia. I: Adherence to intervention programmes. *British Journal of Psychiatry, 159,* 475–480.

Tarrier, N., Barrowclough, C., Vaughn, C., Bamrah, J., Porceddu, K., Watts, S., et al. (1989). The community management of schizophrenia. A two-year follow-up of a behavioral intervention with families. *British Journal of Psychiatry, 154,* 625–628.

Tarrier, N., Lowson, K., & Barrowclough, C. (1991). Some aspects of family interventions in schizophrenia II: Financial considerations. *British Journal of Psychiatry, 159,* 481–484.

Telles, C., Karno, M., Mintz, J., Paz, G., Arias, M., Tucker, D., et al. (1995). Immigrant families coping with schizophrenia: Behavioral family intervention v case management with a low-income Spanish-speaking population. *British Journal of Psychiatry, 167,* 473–479.

Tomaras, V., Mavreas, V., Economou, M., Ioannovich, E., Karydi, V., & Stefanis, C. (2000). The effect of family intervention on chronic schizophrenics under individual psychosocial treatment: A 3-year study. *Social Psychiatry & Psychiatric Epidemiology, 35*(11), 487–493.

Tompson, M. C., Rea, M. M., Goldstein, M. J., Miklowitz, D. J., & Weisman, A. G. (2000). Difficulty in implementing a family intervention for bipolar disorder: The predictive role of patient and family attributes. *Family Process, 39*(1), 105–120.

Van Noppen, B. (1999). Multi-family behavioral treatment (MFBT) for OCD. *Crisis Intervention And Time-Limited Treatment, 5,* 3–24.

Walker, D. W. (2000). The treatment of adult male child molesters through group family intervention. *Journal of Psychology & Human Sexuality, 11*(3), 65–73.

Wang, X., Ma, A., He, X., Sun, Z., Ding, Y., & Song, C. (1999). The effect of family intervention on the mental health of family members of patients with newly onset schizophrenia. *Chinese Mental Health Journal, 13*(2), 121–122.

**Weber, T. T., McDaniel, S. H., & Wynne, L. C. (1987). Helping more by helping less: Family therapy and systems consultation. *Psychotherapy, 24*(3S), 615–620.

Wiedemann, G., Hahlweg, K., Mueller, U., Feinstein, E., Hank, G., & Dose, M. (2001). Effectiveness of targeted intervention and maintenance pharmacotherapy in conjunction with family intervention in schizophrenia. *European Archives of Psychiatry & Clinical Neuroscience, 251*(2), 72–84.

**World Schizophrenia Fellowship. (1998). *Families as partners in care: A document developed to launch a strategy for the implementation of programs of family education, training, and support.* Toronto, Ontario, Canada: Author.

Wright, P., Takei, N., Rifkin, L., & Murray, R. M. (1995). Maternal influenza, obstetric complications, and schizophrenia. *American Journal of Psychiatry, 152*(12), 1714–1720.

Wynne, L. C. (1994). The rationale for consultation with the families of schizophrenic patients. *Acta Psychiatrica Scandinavica, Supplementum, 90*(384), 125–132.

Wynne, L. C., McDaniel, S. H., & Weber, T. T. (1988). Family therapy, family consultation, and systematic consultation. *Terapia Familiare, 27*, 43–57.

Xiang, M., Ran, M., & Li, S. (1994). A controlled evaluation of psychoeducational family intervention in a rural Chinese community. *British Journal of Psychiatry, 165*(4), 544–548.

Xiong, W., Phillips, M. R., Hu, X., Wang, R., Dai, Q., Kleinman, J., et al. (1994). Family-based intervention for schizophrenic patients in China: A randomised controlled trial. *British Journal of Psychiatry, 165*(2), 239–247.

Zhang, M., Wang, M., Li, J., & Phillips, M. R. (1994). Randomised-control trial of family intervention for 78 first-episode male schizophrenic patients: An 18-month study in Suzhou, Jiangsu. *British Journal of Psychiatry Supplement, 24*(Aug), 96–102.

Zhao, B., Shen, J., & Shi, Y. (1999). A comparative study on family intervention on schizophrenics in community. *Chinese Mental Health Journal, 13*, 323.

Zhao, B., Shen, J., Shi, Y., Xu, D., Wang, Z., & Ji, J. (2000). Family intervention of chronic schizophrenics in community: A follow-up study. *Chinese Mental Health Journal, 14*(4), 283–285.

Chapter 10   *Affective Disorders*

Steven Beach, Ph.D., Institute for Behavioral Research,
University of Georgia, Athens, Georgia

The unipolar depressive disorders are among the most prevalent of Axis I disorders in adulthood and they are especially common among those with marital and family problems. Therefore, persons with difficulties in both areas simultaneously are likely to be encountered by every couple and family therapist. Because marital and family interventions may help relieve the symptoms of depression and the interpersonal problems so commonly associated with depression, it is appropriate to examine the potential public policy implications of recent progress in this area. However, for the public to benefit maximally from wider availability of marital and family interventions for depression, it is critical that marital and family therapists develop sound clinical decision-making rules regarding which depressed persons are most likely to respond positively to marital and family therapy. The current review begins with a description of depression that recognizes its heterogeneity, its connection to marital and family problems, and its response to empirically supported marital and family therapy approaches. Public policy implications are underscored and guidelines for clinical decision making are suggested. I conclude with a brief discussion of potential future directions for research and a listing of Internet resources that may be useful to graduate students or others seeking information about funding for research or clinical tools.

In an earlier review of this topic, Prince and Jacobson (1995) concluded that, "marital therapy may be helpful when applied to outpatient depressed clients" (p. 388). The authors suggested that other forms of family therapy had been insufficiently evaluated to draw strong conclusions regarding their potential efficacy in the treatment of adult unipolar depression. Three additional studies of marital therapy for depression and two studies of parenting interventions for depression have appeared since that review. Accordingly, the database establishing that marital and parenting interventions may be potentially efficacious in the treatment of depression is stronger, albeit modestly so, than it was in 1995. As was true in 1995, other forms of family therapy have been insufficiently studied to draw conclusions regarding potential efficacy. At the same time, considerable progress has been made in providing a sound empirical foundation for public policy. This is due primarily to improved epidemiological evidence regarding the prevalence of marital discord among depressed persons and the temporal precedence of marital discord relative to the onset of depression. Accordingly, it is now possible to suggest that marital therapy and perhaps parent training are necessary and medically prudent in many cases of adult unipolar depression, and that these interventions should be more widely available than they are currently.

Introduction to the Psychopathology of Depression

What exactly is depression? Answering this deceptively simple question in detail could easily take up the entire chapter. On the other hand, providing no discussion of the psychopathology of depression leads to an overly simplistic view of depression that can hinder the work of researchers and practitioners alike. Below I provide a starting point for the discussion of marital and family therapy for depression in adults. (For additional detail the reader is referred to Gotlib & Hammen, 2002.)

Description

The symptoms of depression are relatively straightforward. In broad brush, they include depressed mood, a loss of interest or pleasure in activities, marked change in weight or appetite, insomnia or hypersomnia, psychomotor agitation or retardation, fatigue or loss of energy, difficulty concentrating, feelings of worthlessness or guilt, and thoughts of death/suicide. Someone with two to four of these symptoms for 2 years or more might receive a diagnosis of dysthymia. Someone with five or more of these symptoms for more than 2 weeks might receive a diagnosis of major depression, and someone with five or more symptoms for several days a month, every month for more than a year might receive a diagnosis of brief recurrent depression. The average length of a major depressive episode is about 6 months.

Major depression is often recurrent or chronic, but may also be limited to a single episode. However, current episodes of depression are much more likely to be recurrences than initial episodes (Coyne, Pepper, & Flynn, 1999) and because the average age at first episode has decreased dramatically over the past century (Weissman, Bruce, Leaf, Florio, & Holzer, 1991), current episodes are particularly likely to be recurrences when the patient is old enough to be part of a married couple. At the same time, even for those with recurrent depression, most of their lives will not be spent "in episode" (Judd et al., 1998). Accordingly, it is possible for the person to have marital and family problems that are not entirely overlapping with their depressive illness. As a result of these considerations, it has been suggested that depression should be thought of as a chronic, recurrent illness in most cases, and the implications of this shift in conceptualization for marital and family therapy have been discussed by Coyne and Benazon (2001).

Prevalence

Data from the National Comorbidity Survey provide a lifetime prevalence estimate for major depression of approximately 8.3% for cases involving five to six symptoms and 7.5% for severe cases involving seven to nine symptoms (Kessler, Zhao, Blazer, & Swartz, 1997). If less severe levels of depression are included, lifetime prevalence estimates increase to as high as 18% (Boyd & Weissman, 1981; Karno et al., 1987), with rates approximately twice as high for women as for men. Nor is depression confined to a single country or region. Each year, more than 100 million people worldwide develop clinically recognizable depression. Underscoring the need for sound clinical decision making, for a significant portion of these individuals, depression will result in a suicide, with some estimates suggesting that 15% of depressed individuals will eventually commit suicide (Hirschfeld & Goodwin, 1988).

Suicide. Suicide is the most salient complication of depression. It is not uncommon for therapists treating depressed individuals to confront substantial suicidal ideation and in some cases suicide attempts. Depressed individuals are at a 50-fold increased risk for completed suicide relative to the general population (Beutler, Clarkin, & Bongar, 2000). Because marital and family therapy provides a poor treatment fit when depressed individuals are actively suicidal (Beach, Sandeen, & O'Leary, 1990), it is appropriate to provide individually focused interventions such as cognitive therapy, interpersonal psychotherapy, or pharmacotherapy in such cases. Standing collaborations with other health care providers in the community can be useful in managing the complications associated with actively suicidal clients.

Patterns of comorbidity. Depression has high rates of comorbidity with other psychiatric disorders. With regard to other Axis I disorders, this comorbidity is created, in part, as an artifact of definitions: the presence of a mood episode is a prerequisite for schizoaffective disorder, and affective distress is part of the diagnostic criteria or in the clinical description of other disorders. Nonetheless, the data are noteworthy: comorbidity between panic disorder and major depression may be anywhere from 30% to 70% (Lesser, Rubin, Pecknold, & Rifkin, 1988), and rates of comorbidity with other anxiety disorders such as social phobia and generalized anxiety disorder are similarly high. Comorbidity between depression and substance use disorders is also common, with nearly half of alcohol/drug patients having a history of major depression (Miller, Klamen, Hoffmann, & Flaherty, 1996). As this very brief overview suggests, it may be relatively uncommon to find individuals who meet criteria for major depressive disorder without meeting criteria for any other lifetime diagnoses. This suggests that marital and family therapists working with depressed patients may often find that other diagnosable problems are present as well.

The Relationship Between Marital Distress and Depression

There is a well-replicated connection between marital distress and depression. In a quantitative and exhaustive review of the marital literature, Whisman (2001) found that, across 26 cross-sectional studies, marital quality was negatively associated with depressive symptomatology for both women ($r = -.42$) and men ($r = -.37$). Accordingly, there is a moderate relationship between global marital distress and depression and a significant, albeit small, gender difference in the magnitude of that relationship.

How Many Depressed Persons Are Maritally Discordant?

Whisman (2001) examined the level of marital adjustment in published studies that examined both diagnostic status and level of marital dissatisfaction, excluding those in which participants had to be both depressed and maritally distressed. Based on the resulting sample of 493 depressed patients from 14 studies, Whisman reported that the average marital adjustment score of persons diagnosed with depression was in the distressed range and approximately 1.75 standard deviations below the comparison sample with an average Dyadic Adjustment Scale (DAS) score of 93, suggesting that a need for relationship repair is associated with many cases of diagnosed depression. Thus, marital relationships are often (but not always) distressed among depressed men and women. (See also Whiffen & Johnson, 1998, for a review of the postpartum literature.)

However, marital adjustment scores provide only a cursory and impoverished assessment of marital problems, and one might wonder if a more detailed look would also suggest the presence of marital problems in need of marital therapy. Partially remedying this problem, Coyne, Thompson, and Palmer (2002) recently reported a study of 38 depressed outpatients and 35 depressed inpatients which they compared to a community sample. Replicating and extending the Whisman (2001) results, the authors found that approximately two-thirds of the outpatients and approximately half of the inpatients scored in the distressed range of the DAS. They also provided an excellent level of clinical detail regarding the types of complaints and patterns of affection characteristic of couples with a depressed wife. Especially telling, 42% of the depressed outpatients compared to 0% of the comparison sample reported that their spouse did not fulfill their emotional needs, and more than 60% of both husbands and wives in the depressed outpatient sample reported difficulty discussing problems compared to 24% and 37% of community wives and husbands, respectively (see also Zlotnick, Kohn, Keitner, & Della Grotta, 2000).

Potential vicious cycles. Illustrating the vicious cycle between depressive symptoms and marital difficulties, Davila, Bradbury, Cohan, and Tochluk (1997) found that wives with more symptoms of depression were more negative in their supportive behavior toward their husbands and in their expectations regarding partner support. These negative behaviors and expectations, in turn, were related to greater marital stress. Finally, closing the loop, level of marital stress predicted subsequent depressive symptoms (controlling for earlier symptoms). Likewise, in his review of self-propagating processes in depression, Joiner (2000) highlighted the propensity for depressed persons to seek negative feedback, to engage in excessive reassurance seeking, to avoid conflict and so withdraw, and to elicit changes in the partner's view of them. In each case, the behavior resulting from the individual's depression carries the potential to generate increased interpersonal stress or to shift the response of others in a negative direction. Consistent with a stress generation framework (Hammen, 1991), Joiner suggested that increased interpersonal negativity, in turn, helps maintain depressive symptoms.

Further illustrating the potential for stressful marital or family events to precipitate or exacerbate depressive symptoms, Cano and O'Leary (2000) found that humiliating events such as partner infidelity and threats of marital dissolution resulted in a sixfold increase in diagnosis of depression, and that this increased risk remained after controlling for family and personal history of depression. Further, Whisman and Bruce (1999) found that marital dissatisfaction increased risk of subsequent diagnosis of depression by 2.7-fold in a large, representative community sample, and again the increased risk remained significant after controlling for demographic variables and personal history of depression.

Other Family Sub-Systems: The Case of Parenting and Depression

It has long been noted clinically that depressed patients report considerable distress and difficulty in their parenting relationships (e.g., Weissman & Paykel, 1974) and some have attributed depressed mothers' level of dysphoria, at least in part, to her belief that she is an inadequate parent (Teti & Gelfand, 1991). This may, in part, reflect subtle difficulties in parenting associated with depression. For example, Lovejoy, Gracyk, O'Hare, and Neuman (2000) found evidence supporting Goodman and Brumley's (1990) hypothesis that depressed mothers would display more withdrawn behavior than nondepressed mothers. They also found support for Forehand, Lautenschlager, Faust, and Graziano's (1986) hypothesis that depressed mothers would display more negative parenting behavior, with a stronger effect for those in a current depressive episode than those with only a history of depression. Accordingly, although less developed than the marital literature, there is some evidence that a focus on parenting in depression may often be warranted for depressed persons.

Potential vicious cycles. In the area of parenting relationships, the reciprocal relationships between depression, parenting behavior, and parenting stress are also clear in broad brush (see Conger, Patterson, & Ge, 1995; Cummings & Davies, 1999). As a consequence, depressed parents perceive their children as having more problems, their children do have more problems on average, and relationships between depressed parents and their children are more distressed. Recent research suggests that strained parent-child relationships may also predict maintenance of depressive symptoms (Jones, Beach, & Forehand, 2001). It appears, therefore, that parenting behavior is another area in which stress-generation may connect depression and family relationships in a vicious cycle.

Is everyone at equal risk? Are all persons equally reactive or vulnerable to negative interpersonal events? A large body of literature suggests that this is not the case. Personality variables (Davila, 2001), interpersonal sensitivities (Joiner, 2000), individual differences in biological vulnerability (Gold, Goodwin, & Chrousos, 1988), various negative childhood experiences (Hammen, Henry, & Daley, 2000; Kessler & Magee, 1993), and other individual difference variables, have been linked to differential vulnerability to depression, differential vulnerability to stress, and differential vulnerability to recurrence. This literature suggests that everyone does not start with an equal chance of responding to negative interpersonal events with depression. In particular, it may be that some individuals are more sensitive to particular types of interpersonal problems and so may have a lower threshold for a depressive response (e.g., Hammen et al., 2000).

Is there a need to intervene? Even if intervention did not produce rapid reduction in depressive symptoms, marital and parenting problems appear to be areas in need of attention by many depressed persons and appear to be implicated in the maintenance of depressive episodes (Keitner, Miller, & Ryan, 1994). In fact, a growing body of literature suggests that failure to address marital and family issues in therapy for depression may interfere with the recovery process and increase the risk for relapse (cf. Hooley & Gotlib, 2000; Hooley & Teasdale, 1989). Accordingly, marital and parenting relationships may be particularly useful targets of intervention for depressed individuals.

Interventions For Marital Discord and For Parenting Difficulties

For both marital discord and for parenting difficulties there are well-specified approaches that are known to be efficacious (see chapter 1, Editor's comment for definitions of efficacious interventions). With regard to marital problems, several approaches to marital therapy have been found to be efficacious or possibly efficacious, including behavioral marital therapy, cognitive behavioral marital therapy, emotion-focused therapy, insight-oriented marital therapy, and strategic marital therapy (see Baucom, Shoam, Mueser, Daiuto, & Stickle, 1998; Johnson, this volume). Likewise, parent management training (Patterson, 1982; Patterson, Reid, & Dishion, 1992) is an efficacious intervention for a range of child behavior problems including conduct disorder (Kazdin, 1998), and has been elaborated and applied to a range of child behavior problems (McMahon, Forehand, Griest, & Wells, 1981; Sanders & Dadds, 1993; Taylor & Biglan, 1998). Accordingly, there is substantial reason to expect that depressed persons could be helped to enhance their functioning in these areas and so interrupt stress-generating processes.

Empirically Supported Approaches Work for Depressed Individuals
Several studies have examined the efficacy of marital therapy in reducing symptoms of depression and in enhancing marital satisfaction. Three trials compared behavioral marital therapy to individual therapy (Beach & O'Leary, 1992; Emanuels-Zuurveen & Emmelkamp, 1996; Jacobson, Dobson, Fruzzetti, Schmaling, & Salusky, 1991). Two clinical trials involved adaptation of individual therapies for depression to a couples format (Emanuals-Zuurveen & Emmelkamp, 1997; Foley, Rounsaville, Weissman, Sholomskas, & Chevron, 1989). There has been one trial of a cognitive couple therapy (Teichman, Bar-El, Shor, Sirota, & Elizur, 1995) and one trial comparing marital therapy to antidepressant medication (Leff et al., 2000), but these studies did not utilize empirically supported treatments for marital discord and did not examine change in marital satisfaction. Because of the importance of using empirically supported treatments as well as the value of assessing marital satisfaction, we examine first those studies that meet these criteria.

Three studies compared behavioral marital therapy to individual therapy with similar results. Jacobson et al. (1991) randomly assigned 60 married, depressed women to either behavioral marital therapy (BMT), individual cognitive therapy (CT), or a treatment combining BMT and CT. Couples were not selected for the presence of marital discord and so could be divided into those who were more and less maritally distressed. Beach and O'Leary (1992) randomly assigned 45 couples in which the wife was depressed to one of three conditions: (a) conjoint BMT, (b) individual CT, or (c) a 15-week waiting list condition. To be included in the study, both partners had to score in the discordant range of the DAS and report ongoing marital discord. Emanuels-Zuurveen and Emmelkamp (1996) assigned 27 depressed outpatients to either individual cognitive behavioral therapy or communication-focused marital therapy. The sample included both depressed husbands ($n = 13$) as well as depressed wives ($n = 14$). Consistent across the three studies, behavioral marital therapy and individual therapy yielded equivalent outcomes when the dependent variable was depressive symptoms, and a better outcome in marital therapy than in individual therapy when the dependent variable was marital functioning. In addition, in one of the studies, marital therapy was found to be significantly better than a waitlist control group (Beach & O'Leary, 1992).

Foley et al. (1989) tested an individual therapy for depression adapted for couples format. In their study, 18 depressed outpatients were randomly assigned to either individual interpersonal psychotherapy (IPT) or a newly developed, couple-format version of IPT. Consistent with the findings of the studies comparing behavioral marital therapy with an individual approach, Foley et al. found that participants in the two treatments improved equally on symptoms of depression. Both interventions also produced equal enhancement of general interpersonal functioning. However, participants receiving couple IPT reported marginally higher marital satisfaction scores on the Locke-Wallace Short Marital

Adjustment Test and scored significantly higher on one subscale of the DAS at session 16, indicating an advantage of a conjoint format with an explicit focus on communication relative to individually administered IPT.

Emanuels-Zuurveen and Emmelkamp (1997) involved spouses in the treatment of depression for persons not reporting marital distress. Spouse-aided cognitive therapy, as developed by Emanuels-Zuurveen and Emmelkamp, was similar to individual cognitive therapy, except that the spouse attended all sessions, working with the depressed individual in developing strategies to cope with the depression. The authors found that spouse-aided cognitive therapy was equally, but not more, effective than individual therapy in treating depression. Neither treatment had an effect on marital dissatisfaction.

Two of the studies reviewed above indicate that the effect of marital therapy on level of symptoms of depression is mediated by changes in marital adjustment. Beach and O'Leary (1992) found that posttherapy marital satisfaction fully accounted for the effect of marital therapy on depression. Likewise, Jacobson et al. (1991) found that changes in marital adjustment and depression covaried for depressed individuals who received marital therapy, but not for those who received cognitive therapy. Therefore, it appears that marital therapy influences depressive symptomatology either by enhancing marital satisfaction or else by producing changes in the marital environment associated with enhanced satisfaction. Cognitive therapy appears to work through a different mechanism of change (i.e., cognitive change, see Whisman, 1993).

Two additional studies have examined nonempirically supported marital therapies in the treatment of depression. In both cases the studies do not provide an assessment of change in level of marital satisfaction, and have significant methodological flaws. Nonetheless, they provide some incremental support for the potential value of marital therapy in the treatment of depression. Teichman et al. (1995) compared cognitive marital therapy (CMT) to cognitive therapy and a no-treatment control group in a sample of 45 married, depressed individuals. CMT was superior to cognitive therapy and no-treatment at posttherapy assessment. Leff et al. (2000) conducted a randomized control trial of antidepressants ($n = 37$) versus couples therapy ($n = 40$) in the treatment and maintenance of major depression. Depression improved as a function of therapy in both groups (but only on the Hamilton Rating Scale for Depression). At the same time, participants in the couples therapy condition demonstrated a significant advantage, both posttreatment and at a 2-year follow-up (but only on the Beck Depression Inventory).

Unless one treats different types of marital therapy as functionally equivalent, and uses a meta-analytic approach to combine samples (see chapter 12), there are not sufficient data to argue that marital therapy has been shown to be an efficacious treatment for depression. Nonetheless, cast within a stress-generation framework, the studies are sufficient to suggest several important conclusions. First, it is clear that efficacious forms for marital therapy can be safely and usefully applied to a depressed population. Furthermore, BMT emerges as a specific and efficacious treatment for marital discord, even when the marital discord is occurring in the context of depression. That is, BMT has been shown in three independent studies to produce significant change in marital distress in a discordant and depressed population, and in each case it has outperformed a control group and/or an alternative intervention.

Empirically Supported Therapies For Parent Training

As discussed above, parent training also appears promising as a point of intervention to interrupt the stress-generation process with some depressed patients. In an early suggestive attempt to examine the effect of parent training on depressive symptoms, Forehand, Wells, and Griest (1980) examined the effects of a parent training program in a sample of 15 clinic-referred children and their mothers. The program involved teaching parents to use social reinforcement and time-out. The clinic-referred families were compared to nonclinic-referred mother-child dyads (*n* = 15) pre- and posttreatment on measures of child adjustment, parent adjustment, home observation, and consumer satisfaction. Of relevance to our discussion of family therapies for depression, Forehand et al. reported that parents of clinic children were significantly more depressed than nonclinic mothers pretreatment, but not posttreatment (see also Dadds & McHugh, 1992; Webster-Stratton, 1994, for other demonstrations with depressive symptoms).

Researchers may have been hesitant to use parent training as an intervention for parents with a diagnosis of depression because depressed parents seem to do somewhat less well in standard forms of parent training than do other parents. For example, depressed mothers have greater difficulty learning parenting skills (e.g., Dumas, Gibson, & Albin, 1989) and are more prone to drop out of treatment prematurely (e.g., McMahon et al., 1981). Accordingly, one obstacle to the use of parent training may be providing it in a way that allows it to be successful with a depressed population.

In a recent demonstration of the way parent training could be modified to be more useful for depressed mothers, Sanders and McFarland (2000) compared two forms of behavioral family intervention to examine the effect of a parent training intervention (behavioral family intervention [BFI]) with that of a combination cognitive therapy/parent training intervention (cognitive behavioral family intervention [CBFI]). Forty-seven families in which the mother met diagnostic criteria for major depression and in which at least one child met diagnostic criteria for either conduct or oppositional-defiant disorder were randomly assigned to one of two conditions. Those assigned to the traditional BFI (*n* = 24) received instruction, role-playing, feedback, and coaching in the use of social-learning principles. Those assigned to the cognitively enhanced BFI condition (*n* = 23) received cognitive interventions integrated with interventions designed to increase personally reinforcing family activities, identify and interrupt dysfunctional child related cognitions and automatic thoughts, and increase relaxation.

In each case, therapy was provided individually once a week and was accompanied by two home visits each week. There were 12 sessions with either one or both parents present, with treatment completed over a 3- to 5-month time period. Of importance for the current review, both parenting interventions produced substantial reduction in depressive symptoms and negative cognitions, and there was no interaction of condition with time of assessment. There was also significant improvement in child behavior problems in both conditions. Significantly more mothers in the CBFI condition (72%) than in the BFI condition (35%) were nondepressed at follow-up, suggesting a superior effect for CBFI with regard to maternal depression at follow-up. Accordingly, it appears that a highly structured and comprehensive version of parent training can benefit parents who are depressed, but some direct attention to cognitive symptoms of depression may enhance longer-term effects on depression.

Another combination approach was attempted by Gelfand, Teti, Seiner, and Jameson (1996). They evaluated a multicomponent program in which registered nurses visited depressed mothers of infants at their homes to assess mothers' parenting skills, enhance mothers' self-confidence, and to reinforce mothers' existing parenting techniques. Depressed mothers ($n = 73$) were referred by their clinicians and carried a diagnosis of major depression. Nondepressed control mothers ($n = 38$) were recruited from the community and matched on social and demographic variables. Depressed mothers were either assigned to the intervention group ($n = 37$) or the usual mental health care group (i.e., ongoing treatment with referral source). The intervention group involved assessment of mothers' needs and the development of individualized programs including modeling warm interactions with the infants, offering mild suggestions, and building self-confidence by appropriately reinforcing parenting skills. Nurses visited mothers and infants 25 times in 3-week intervals over a period of 6 to 12 months, then phased out home visits over 4 final visits. Gelfand et al. reported that there were no significant differences on Beck Depression Inventory (BDI) scores between the depressed intervention ($M = 22.51$, $SD = 11.24$) and depressed control ($M = 22.06$, $SD = 10.36$) groups at the start of the study. However, the intervention group demonstrated significantly greater improvement in depressive symptoms (posttherapy $M = 13.86$, $SD = 9.51$) than those in usual care (posttherapy $M = 20.06$, $SD = 12.35$). Once again, this program suggests that parent training may be a useful point of intervention to break into a stress-generation process for some depressed individuals.

Unless one combines across parent training for parents of infants and parent training for parents of conduct disordered children aged 3–9, the available research is not sufficient to show that parent training, by itself, is an efficacious intervention for major depression among parents dealing with problematic children. However, the research does suggest that parent training, itself an efficacious form of therapy for child management problems (see chapter 4), can be provided to depressed persons in a safe and efficacious manner and may have beneficial effects both with regard to child outcomes as well as with regard to parental depression.

Breaking the Vicious Cycle With Marital and Parenting Interventions
    The research reviewed above suggests that marital therapy and parenting interventions have the potential to help reduce depressive symptoms and the interpersonal problems that often occur concurrently with depression. By alleviating the marital stress that may be maintaining the episode, the marital and family therapist can help alleviate both the symptoms of depression and the salient marital problems that may be so distressing for the depressed individual. Individual treatments for depression appear less able to provide relief from the symptoms of marital discord. Although the research is less well developed in the case of parent training as an intervention for the depressed, one might hypothesize similar patterns will emerge as additional work accumulates. If so, one would expect to find better response to parent training when the child's behavior problems are salient and seen as a serious problem (as in Sanders & McFarland, 2000), or alternatively when the child's problem behavior and the parent's inability to handle these problems is viewed as a major source of dysphoria and agitation. This suggests the value of parent training when the child carries a diagnosis such as conduct disorder or when the depressed adult is at a key transition that might render the parent relationship more salient, such as at the birth of a child. An advantage of parent training relative to marital therapy is that it may lend itself more easily to combination with cognitive therapy (e.g., Sanders & McFarland, 2000) because parent training is often conducted with only the depressed person in attendance. Parent training may also be easier for some depressed parents to accept than an offer of marital therapy. Accordingly, it may be a better point of entry into the stress-generation process for some depressed patients.

Effectiveness
    One potential barrier to the widespread adoption of marital and family therapy approaches in the treatment of depression is the suspicion that few people have a better outcome with marital and family therapy approaches than with individual approaches to treatment that are already widely available. It is therefore useful to examine this issue directly.
    Do any depressed patients show a uniquely beneficial response to marital and family therapies? Existing data and clinical experience suggest that many depressed outpatients have discordant marital relationships that are sufficiently distressed to warrant therapeutic intervention (Whisman, 2001; Coyne et al., 2002). Their complaints appear to be serious and pressing in many cases. In addition, O'Leary, Risso, and Beach (1990) found that for those depressed persons whose depressive episode followed a period of marital discord, marital therapy was uniquely beneficial compared to cognitive therapy. The effect was rather

striking. When discordant and depressed couples whose marital problems preceded their depression were given marital therapy, their marital satisfaction improved just as it did for others receiving marital therapy. In contrast, when the depressed wives in these couples received individual cognitive therapy, they showed deterioration in marital satisfaction over the course of therapy. Accordingly, there was an important and unique benefit to wives in this group of receiving marital therapy as the initial treatment for their depressive episode.

How many episodes of depression are preceded by marital discord? Whisman and Bruce (1999) examined the relationship between marital dissatisfaction at baseline and 12-month incidence of major depressive episode in the New Haven Epidemiological Catchment Area study among the 904 persons who did not meet criteria for a major depressive episode at baseline. Dissatisfied spouses were found to be nearly 3 times as likely as nondistressed spouses to develop an episode of depression during the year, the relationship remained significant after controlling for demographics and depression history, and the effect was not moderated by gender. For the total sample, 30% of new cases of depression during the year were *attributable* to baseline marital discord, suggesting the number of cases that could be prevented if marital discord could be prevented or alleviated prior to the onset of the depression. Further, between 30% and 45% of all new episodes were preceded by marital problems that were discernable in the absence of a depressive episode at baseline. This suggests a potentially large population of depressed persons who would find an initial focus on the marriage more beneficial than an initial focus on them individually.

Will partners participate? A second potential barrier to the use of marital and parenting interventions in the treatment of adult depression is the possibility that other family members will refuse to participate in the therapy. This might appear in randomized trials as refusal to be assigned to marital or parenting intervention, or as premature discontinuation of treatment. Although refusal of family members to participate need not preclude a systemic focus, it may limit the advantages of marital and parenting interventions relative to individual alternatives. Currently, however, there is equivocal evidence regarding the degree to which refusal to participate represents a threat to the effectiveness of marital therapy for depression. On the one hand, an effectiveness study of marital therapy for depression conducted 25 years ago in a primary care setting failed when it proved impossible to enlist enough husbands to participate (McLean & Miles, 1975). On the other hand, the Leff et al. (2000) study reviewed earlier found much greater acceptance of marital therapy than cognitive therapy, and their marital therapy condition produced a significantly lower dropout rate than did their medication condition. As these considerations suggest, an important focus of research on marital and parenting interventions for depressed persons will be to examine consumer response to referrals for such treatments. Research that closely monitors the issues that render referral for family treatment more and less acceptable to depressed persons and their families seems particularly timely (for a discussion of general issues and directions in the relationship between efficacy and effectiveness research, see Nathan, Stuart, & Dolan, 2000).

Clinical Decision Making

Given the current data we can begin to formulate initial guidelines about who should be treated from a systemic (marital or parenting) focus, and who may be better served by an individual focus (cognitive therapy, interpersonal therapy, or pharmacotherapy). Likewise, given the usual time frame for noticeable clinical response to most forms of intervention, it is possible to formulate guidelines for appropriate referral to another therapy should the initial response to treatment be inadequate (Beach et al., 1990; Ilardi & Craighead, 1994).

First, when depressed individuals report no or mild marital distress and little parenting difficulty, spouses or other family members often may be involved as helpful adjuncts to therapy (e.g., Emanuels-Zuurveen & Emmelkamp, 1997). The family psychoeducational model may be a useful framework in such cases (e.g., McFarlane, see chapter 9), and it is likely that the systemic element of treatment will be adjunctive to individual or pharmacological interventions, and may focus on strengthening support processes within the family (but see Clarkin et al., 1990, for a negative outcome with a psychoeducational framework). Conversely, when depressed individuals report substantial difficulties in marital and/or parenting relationships, and indicate that the current episode of depression followed the onset of the relationship problems, an initial approach that focuses on systemic problems (e.g., marital therapy or enhanced parent training) may produce positive outcomes and provide benefits that are greater than those obtained from an individual focus (e.g., Beach & O'Leary, 1992). When depressed individuals report substantial relationship problems, but these emerged only after the onset of the depressive episode, an initial focus on either the individual and his or her symptoms of depression, or an initial focus on the relational problems may be appropriate and useful. However, there is unlikely to be a unique benefit to an initial systemic focus relative to an individual focus (e.g., O'Leary et al., 1990).

An additional consideration in clinical decision making is suggested by Ilardi and Craighead's (1994) observation that individual cognitive therapy for depression yields substantial (but not full) treatment response within the first several weeks of treatment for those who are going to respond. A similar pattern has been noted for marital therapy for depression (Beach et al., 1990). This suggests that when clients do not show any change in depressive symptoms within the first 4 to 6 weeks of treatment, regardless of the initial approach being used, it may be appropriate to refer them for treatment using one of the other empirically supported treatments for depression.

Future Directions For Research and Therapy

There are many issues that deserve research attention and that will influence the use of marital and family therapies for depression. A solid foundation, like the one that is currently available in the area of marital discord and depression makes for more and better research opportunities. Below I highlight a few of the research themes that are emerging in this literature and that are likely to be a focus of some attention in the next several years.

Does Partner Satisfaction Matter?

The role of partner satisfaction in depression is of both theoretical and practical interest. If partner satisfaction is not consequential in predicting change in depressive symptoms, then it may make more sense to focus our therapeutic attention on the depressed individual. In this way we would sidestep the potential problem of partner recruitment. In addition, there are systemic approaches that can be utilized when only one member of the family is present, and other approaches that are being developed for marital work when a partner is absent (e.g., Halford, 1998).

Suggesting caution in the use of nonconjoint formats in marital therapy is the research with IPT reviewed above. The Foley et al. (1989) study suggested that IPT provided to an individual was not as effective at dealing with marital problems as was couple-IPT which included a focus on couple communication. Similarly suggesting caution is a recent study we conducted (Beach, Katz, Kim, & Brody, in press). We examined change in depressive symptoms among husbands and wives in established, intact relationships in 166 couples. Using structural equation modeling procedures we found support for the general marital discord model (Beach et al., 1990), with each partner's own marital satisfaction at Time 1 predicting their own later depression, even after including the effect of Time 1 depressive symptoms in the model. However, in addition, we found significant effects from each partner's satisfaction the other's later depressive symptoms.

These results suggest caution in moving to individual level interventions designed to enhance the marital satisfaction of depressed persons. If a partner's satisfaction cannot be enhanced without his or her presence in therapy, then effects on depression of an individual level approach to relationship enhancement may be diminished.

Why is partner satisfaction important? Why might partner satisfaction be important? One possibility is that satisfaction measures are more strongly influenced by negative partner behavior, particularly among distressed couples. The potentially important effect of deficits in positive, supportive behavior might therefore not be captured by self-reported marital satisfaction of the depressed person. An elaboration of this type of thinking can be found in work by Katz and Beach (1997) in which it was shown that having one's level of self-esteem verified by small positive supportive behaviors from the partner strengthened the effect of self-esteem on depressive symptoms. This type of research suggests the potential benefit of increasing positive interactions even among the nondistressed depressed. In particular, it suggests the potential benefit of efforts to increase positive interactions among depressed inpatients for whom positive interactions may have eroded considerably (Coyne et al., 2002). Again, caution is suggested however, by mixed results from family involvement in the treatment of unipolar depressed adult inpatients using a psychoeducational framework (e.g., Clarkin et al., 1990).

Attention to physical aggression. In recent research examining couple use of aggressive behavior in the context of conflict we found that couple aggression was strongly related to wife's depression at Time 1 and had a very strong lagged effect on wife's depression at Time 2—all net of effects attributable to own or partner marital satisfaction (Beach, Kim, Cercone-Keeney, & Brody, in press). Similar effects were not obtained for husbands. Research implications are twofold. First, it is clear that not all marital processes should be expected to show the same pattern of gender symmetry or asymmetry. Second, we may be able to account for significantly more variance in depressive outcomes if we include depressogenic marital processes that may not be captured well by measures of marital satisfaction. Clinical implications include another cautionary note for those attempting "unilateral" marital therapy for depression: it may be premature to encourage the widespread use of nondyadic approaches to marital therapy, as these may not be optimal for stemming the use of low-level physical aggression should this be present.

Conclusions

Marital therapy is probably appropriate for many but *not all* depressed persons who are married. Careful consideration should be given to differentiating between those who would benefit most from an individual approach, those who would benefit most from a systemic focus, and those for whom either approach would be equivalent. It appears that the potential population that might experience unique benefit from marital therapy for depression is large. If those who might benefit from a focus on increased positive interaction with their partner are included, the population may include most depressed persons. Unfortunately, there are no well-established methods of increasing positive interaction for such couples (but see Cordova & Gee, 2001). At the same time, there are reasons to be cautious about attempting marital therapy in those cases in which the partner is unavailable for conjoint therapy. There are a number of reasons to be concerned that marital therapy without the partner could be compromised in its effectiveness and that important marital processes such as low-level physical aggression might be overlooked. So, although there is much to be done in elaborating the points of contact between marital discord and depression, the promise of marital therapy for depression appears well founded.

There are also a number of new directions for research on the link between marital therapy and depression as well as parenting interventions for depression. In addition to expanded treatment outcome studies and investigations of clinical processes, it will also be important to focus on tests of basic theoretical propositions about the link between marital and family processes and depression. Of particular importance are tests of theory related to the role of partner satisfaction, partner effects on the impact of one's own low self-regard, and the role of positive interactions among nondistressed, depressed couples.

Coda

Another source of new insights about the link between family processes and depression may be the ongoing debate about the fundamental nature of depression. Recent research by Ruscio and Ruscio (2000) supported the view that depression may be distributed as a continuous, rather than as a dichotomous, variable. This implies that associations observed at any given level of symptomatology may have implications for other levels of symptomatology, whether in clinical or subclinical range. For example, the discovery of an association between major depression and couple distress might suggest that an association between dysphoria and couple distress exists also. However, it is important to note that the strength of the association between marital discord and depression may be greater for when the focus is on major depression rather than subclinical dysphoria (Whisman, 2001). In addition, recent research by Beach and Amir (in press) suggests that the story may be more complex than suggested by Ruscio and Ruscio and that some sets of depressive symptoms may act less like a continuum and more like a typology. Although the issue of continua versus taxonomies may seem unimportant for marital and family approaches, it will probably have important implications for future research in the area. In particular, much of what we think we know about the association between family problems and depression is based on measures of depression that conflate misery with somatic symptomatology. If these or other sets of symptoms should prove to function differently and are related differently to family processes, this could lead to a very different understanding of the way family processes come to be associated with depression. In turn, this may suggest novel approaches to treatment and prevention.

Suggested Sources For Grant Writing and Clinical Practice

Some places to look on the Internet for research-related resources include the following:

- Behavioral & Social Sciences Research Guide to Grants @ NIH
  obssr.od.nih.gov/publications/bssr-guide/sample.htm

■ Community of Science (customized searches of funding sources for individuals)
www.cos.com

■ Electronic Journal Services I
www.amedo.com

■ Electronic Journal Services II
www.freemedicaljournals.com

■ NIH Funding Information
grants.nih.gov/grants/index.cfm

Some places to look on the Internet for clinical resources related to depression include the following:

■ NIMH Depression
www.nimh.nih.gov/publicat/depression.cfm#ptdep3

■ Hamilton Rating Scale
healthnet.umassmed.edu/mhealth/HAMD.pdf

■ American Psychiatric Assocation—Post Partum Depression
www.psych.org/public_info/postpartumdepression111401.pdf

■ American Psychological Association—Depression
www.apa.org/psychnet/depression.html

References

References marked with a double asterisk are recommended for clinicians.

Baucom, D. H., Shoam, V., Mueser, K. T., Daiuto, A., & Stickle, T. R. (1998). Empirically supported couple and family interventions for marital distress and adult mental health problems. *Journal of Consulting and Clinical Psychology, 66,* 53–88.

Beach, S. R. H., & O'Leary, K. D. (1992). Treating depression in the context of marital discord: Outcome and predictors of response for marital therapy versus cognitive therapy. *Behavior Therapy, 23,* 507–528.

**Beach, S. R. H., Sandeen, E. E., & O'Leary, K. D. (1990). *Depression in marriage: A model for etiology and treatment.* New York: Guilford.

Beach, S. R. H., & Amir, N. (in press). Is depression taxonic, dimensional, or both? *Journal of Abnormal Psychology.*

Beach, S. R. H., Katz, J., Kim, S., & Brody, G. H. (in press). Prospective effects of marital satisfaction on depressive symptoms in established marriages: A dyadic model. *Journal of Social and Personal Relationships.*

Beach, S. R. H., Kim, S., Cercone-Keeney, J., & Brody, G. H. (in press). Physical aggression and depression: Gender asymmetry in effects? *Journal of Social and Personal Relationships.*

Boyd, J. H., & Weissman, M. M. (1981). Epidemiology of affective disorders. *Archives of General Psychiatry, 38,* 1039–1046.

Beutler, L. E., Clarkin, J. F., & Bongar, B. (2000). *Guidelines for the systematic treatment of the depressed patient.* New York: Oxford University Press.

Cano, A., & O'Leary, K. D. (2000). Infidelity and separations precipitate major depressive episodes and symptoms of nonspecific depression and anxiety. *Journal of Consulting and Clinical Psychology, 68,* 774–781.

Clarkin, J. F., Glick, I. D., Haas, G. L., Spencer, J. H., Lewis, A. B., Peyser, J., et al. (1990). A randomized clinical trial of inpatient family intervention, V: Results for affective disorders. *Journal of Affective Disorders, 18,* 17–28.

Conger, R., Patterson, G., & Ge, X. (1995). It takes two to replicate: A mediational model of the impact of parents' stress on adolescent adjustment. *Child Development, 66,* 80–97.

Cordova, J. V., & Gee, C. B. (2001). Couples therapy for depression: Using healthy relationships to treat depression. In Beach, S. R. H. (Ed.), *Marital and family processes in depression: A scientific foundation for clinical practice* (pp. 185–203). Washington, DC: American Psychological Association.

**Coyne, J. C., & Benazon, N. R. (2001). Coming to terms with the nature of depression in marital research and treatment. In S. R. H. Beach (Ed.), *Marital and family processes in depression* (pp. 25–43). Washington, DC: American Psychological Association.

Coyne, J. C., Pepper, C. M., & Flynn, H. (1999). Significance of prior episodes of depression in two patient populations. *Journal of Consulting and Clinical Psychology, 67,* 76–81.

Coyne, J. C., Thompson, R., & Palmer, S. C. (2002). Marital quality, coping with conflict, marital complaints, and affection in couples with a depressed wife. *Journal of Family Psychology, 16,* 26–37.

Cummings, E. M., & Davies, P. T. (1999). Depressed parents and family functioning: Interpersonal effects and children's functioning and development. In T. Joiner & J. C. Coyne (Eds.), *Recent advances in interpersonal approaches to depression* (pp. 299–327). Washington, DC: American Psychological Association.

Dadds, M. R., & McHugh, T. A. (1992). Social support and treatment outcome in behavioral family therapy for child conduct problems. *Journal of Consulting and Clinical Psychology, 60,* 252–259.

Davila, J. (2001). Paths to unhappiness: The overlapping courses of depression and romantic dysfunction. In S. Beach (Ed.), *Marital and family processes in depression* (pp. 71–87). Washington, DC: American Psychological Association Press.

Davila, J., Bradbury, T. N., Cohan, C. L., & Tochluk, S. (1997). Marital functioning and depressive symptoms: Evidence for a stress generation model. *Journal of Personality and Social Psychology, 73,* 849–861.

Dumas, J. E., Gibson, J. A., & Albin, J. B. (1989). Behavioral correlates of maternal depressive symptomatology in conduct-disorder children. *Journal of Consulting and Clinical Psychology, 57,* 516–521.

Emanuels-Zuurveen, L., & Emmelkamp, P. M. (1996). Individual behavioral-cognitive therapy vs. marital therapy for depression in maritally distressed couples. *British Journal of Psychiatry, 169,* 181–188.

Emanuels-Zuurveen, L., & Emmelkamp, P. M. (1997). Spouse-aided therapy with depressed patients. *Behavior Modification, 21,* 62–77.

Foley, S. H., Rounsaville, B. J., Weissman, M. M., Sholomskas, D., & Chevron, E. (1989). Individual versus conjoint interpersonal psychotherapy for depressed patients with marital disputes. *International Journal of Family Psychiatry, 10,* 29–42.

Forehand, R., Lautenschlager, G. J., Faust, J., & Graziano, W. G. (1986). Parent perceptions and parent-child interactions in clinic-referred children: A preliminary investigation of the effects of maternal depressive moods. *Behavior Research and Therapy, 24,* 73–75.

Forehand, R., Wells, K. C., & Griest, D. L. (1980). An examination of the social validity of a parent training program. *Behavior Therapy, 11,* 488–502.

Gelfand, D. M., Teti, D. M., Seiner, S. A., & Jameson, P. B. (1996). Helping mother fight depression: Evaluation of a home-based intervention for depressed mothers and their infants. *Journal of Clinical Child Psychology, 24,* 406–422.

Gold, P. W., Goodwin, F. K., & Chrousos, G. P. (1988). Clinical and biochemical manifestations of depression: Relation to the neurobiology of stress. *The New England Journal of Medicine, 319,* 348–419.

Goodman, S. H., & Brumley, H. E. (1990). Schizophrenic and depressed mothers: Relational deficits in parenting. *Developmental Psychology, 26,* 31–39.

**Gotlib, I. H., & Hammen, C. L. (2002). *Handbook of depression.* New York: Guilford Press.

Halford, W. K. (1998). The ongoing evolution of behavioral couples therapy: Retrospect and prospect. *Clinical Psychology Review, 18,* 613–634.

Hammen, C. (1991). *Depression runs in families: The social context of risk and resilience in children of depressed mothers.* New York: Springer-Verlag.

Hammen, C., Henry, R., & Daley, S. E. (2000). Depression and sensitization to stressors among young women as a function of childhood adversity. *Journal of Consulting and Clinical Psychology, 68,* 782–787.

Hirschfeld, R. M. A., & Goodwin, F. K. (1988). Mood disorders. In J. A. Talbott, R. E. Hales, & S. C. Yudofsky (Eds.), *Textbook of psychiatry* (pp. 403–441). Washington, DC: American Psychiatric Press.

Hooley, J. M., & Gotlib, I. H. (2000). A diathesis-stress conceptualization of expressed emotion and clinical outcome. *Applied and Preventive Psychology, 9,* 135–152.

Hooley, J. M. & Teasdale, J. D. (1989). Predictors of relapse in unipolar depressives: Expressed emotion, marital distress, and perceived criticism. *Journal of Abnormal Psychology, 98,* 229–235.

Ilardi, S. S., & Craighead, W. E. (1994). The role of nonspecific factors in cognitive behavioral therapy for depression. *Clinical Psychology: Science & Practice, 1,* 138–156.

Jacobson, N. S., Dobson, K., Fruzzetti, A. E., Schmaling, K. B., & Salusky, S. (1991). Marital therapy as a treatment for depression. *Journal of Consulting and Clinical Psychology, 59,* 547–557.

Joiner, T. E. (2000). Depression's vicious scree: Self-propagating and erosive processes in depression chronicity. *Clinical Psychology: Science and Practice, 7,* 203–218.

Jones, D. J., Beach, S. R. H., & Forehand, R. (2001). Stress generation in intact community families. *Journal of Social and Personal Relationships, 18,* 443–462.

Judd, L. L., Akiskal, H. S., Maser, J. D., Zeller, P. J., Endicott, J., Coryell, W., et al. (1998). A prospective 12-year study of subsyndromal and syndromal depressive symptoms in unipolar major depressive disorders. *Archives of General Psychiatry, 55,* 694–700.

Karno, M., Hough, R. L., Burnam, A., Escobar, J., Timbers, D. M., Santana, F., et al. (1987). Lifetime prevalence of specific psychiatric disorders among Mexican Americans in Los Angeles and non-Hispanic whites in Los Angeles. *Archives of General Psychiatry, 44,* 695–701.

Katz, J., & Beach, S. R. H., (1997). Self-verification and depression in romantic relationships. *Journal of Marriage and the Family, 59,* 903–914.

Kazdin, A. E. (1998). Psychosocial treatments for conduct disorder in children. In P. E. Nathan & J. M. Gorman (Eds.), *A guide to treatments that work* (pp. 65–89). Oxford, England: Oxford Press.

Keitner, G. I., Miller, I. W., & Ryan, C. E. (1994). Family functioning in severe depressive disorders. In L. Grunhaus & J. F. Greden (Eds.), *Severe depressive disorders. Progress in psychiatry* (No. 44, pp. 89–110). Washington, DC: American Psychiatric Association.

Kessler, R. C., & Magee, W. J. (1993). Childhood adversities and adult depression: Basic patterns of association in a US national survey. *Psychological Medicine, 23,* 679–690.

Kessler, R. C., Zhao, S., Blazer, D. G., & Swartz, M. (1997). Prevalen correlates, and course of minor depression and major depression in the National Comorbidity study. *Journal of Affective Disorders, 45,* 19–30.

Leff, J., Vearnals, S., Brewin, C. R., Wolff, G., Alexander, B., Asen, E., et al. (2000). The London Depression Intervention Trial. *British Journal of Psychiatry, 177,* 95–100.

Lesser, I. M., Rubin, R. T., Pecknold, J. C., & Rifkin, A. (1988). Secondary depression in panic disorder and agoraphobia: I. Frequency, severity, and response to treatment. *Archives of General Psychiatry, 45,* 437–443.

Lovejoy, M. C., Gracyk, P. A., O'Hare, E., & Neuman, G. (2000). Maternal depression and parenting behavior: A meta-analytic review. *Clinical Psychology Review, 20,* 561–592.

McLean, P. D., & Miles, J. E. (1975). Training family physicians in psychosocial care: An analysis of a program failure. *Journal of Medical Education, 50,* 900–902.

McMahon, R. J., Forehand, R., Griest, D. L., & Wells, K. C. (1981). Who drops out of therapy during parent training. *Behavioral Counseling Quarterly, 1,* 79–85.

Miller, N. S., Klamen, D., Hoffmann, N. G., & Flaherty, J. A. (1996). Prevalence of depression and alcohol and other drug dependence in addictions treatment populations. *Journal of Psychoactive Drugs, 28,* 111–124.

Nathan, P. E., Stuart, S. P., & Dolan, S. L. (2000). Research on psychotherapy efficacy and effectiveness: Between Scylla and Charybdis? *Psychological Bulletin, 126,* 964–981.

O'Leary, K. D., Risso, L., & Beach, S. R. H. (1990). Beliefs about the marital discord/depression link: Implications for outcome and treatment matching. *Behavior Therapy, 21,* 413–422.

Patterson, G. R. (1982). *Coercive family processes.* Eugene, OR: Castilia.

**Patterson, G. R., Reid, J. B., & Dishion, T. J. (1992). *Antisocial boys.* Eugene, OR: Castilia.

Prince, S. E., & Jacobson, N. S. (1995). A review and evaluation of marital and family therapies for affective disorders. *Journal of Marital and Family Therapy, 21,* 377–401.

Ruscio, J., & Ruscio, A. M. (2000). Informing the continuity controversy: A taxometric analysis of depression. *Journal of Abnormal Psychology, 109,* 473–487.

**Sanders, M. R., & Dadds, M. R. (1993). *Behavioral family intervention.* Needham Heights, MA: Allyn & Bacon.

Sanders, M. R., & McFarland, M. (2000). Treatment of depressed mothers with disruptive children: A controlled evaluation of cognitive behavioral family intervention. *Behavior Therapy, 31,* 89–112.

Taylor, T. K., & Biglan, A. (1998). Behavior family interventions for improving child-rearing: A review of the literature for clinicians and policy makers. *Clinical Child and Family Psychology Review, 1,* 41–60.

Teichman, Y., Bar-El, Z., Shor, H., Sirota, P., & Elizur, A. (1995). A comparison of two modalities of cognitive therapy (individual and marital) in treating depression. *Psychiatry, 58,* 136–148.

Teti, D. M., & Gelfand, D. M. (1991). Behavioral competence among mothers of infants in the first year: The mediational role of maternal self-efficacy. *Child Development, 62,* 918–929.

Webster-Stratton, C. (1994). Advancing videotape parent training: A comparison study. *Journal of Consulting and Clinical Psychology, 62,* 583–593.

Weissman, M. M., Bruce, M. L., Leaf, P. J., Florio, L. P., & Holzer, C., III (1991). Affective disorders. In L. N. Robbins & D. A. Reiger (Eds.), *Psychiatric disorders in America* (pp. 53–80). New York: Free Press.

Weissman, M. M., & Paykel, E. S. (1974). *The depressed woman: A study of social relationships.* Chicago: University of Chicago Press.

**Whiffen, V. E., & Johnson, S. M. (1998). An attachment theory framework for the treatment of childbearing depression. *Clinical Psychology: Science and Practice, 5,* 478–493.

Whisman, M. A. (1993). Mediators and moderators of change in cognitive therapy of depression. *Psychological Bulletin, 114,* 248–265.

Whisman, M. A. (2001). The association between depression and marital dissatisfaction. In S. R. H. Beach (Ed.), *Marital and family processes in depression: A scientific foundation for clinical practice*. Washington, DC: American Psychological Association.

Whisman, M. A., & Bruce, M. L. (1999). Marital distress and incidence of major depressive episode in a community sample. *Journal of Abnormal Psychology, 108,* 674–678.

Zlotnick, C., Kohn, R., Keitner, G., & Della Grotta, S. A. (2000). The relationship between quality of interpersonal relationships and major depressive disorder: Findings from the National Comorbidity Survey. *Journal of Affective Disorders, 59,* 205–215.

Chapter 11   *Physical Disorders*

Thomas L. Campbell, M.D., Departments of Family Medicine and Psychiatry, University of Rochester School of Medicine & Dentistry, Rochester, New York.

There is growing research on the role of the family in chronic physical illness and disabilities. At the same time, family therapists and family researchers have become increasingly interested in physical illness. Substantial evidence demonstrates that the chronic and serious physical illness has profound effects on other family members and on the family as a whole. In addition, there is a growing body of evidence demonstrating that families can have a beneficial or harmful effect on a family member's physical health (Campbell, 1986; Campbell & Patterson, 1995; Doherty & Campbell, 1988).

Can family interventions be beneficial in the prevention or treatment of physical disorders? This chapter will attempt to address this question. The focus will be on physical health and well-being as the outcomes of interest. There is substantial evidence that family interventions can improve family functioning and the emotional health of its members, regardless of whether one family member is physically ill. Whether family interventions can actually improve physical health is a more challenging question.

I will begin by briefly reviewing the evidence that families can influence physical health and will present some broad conclusions. Next, I will propose some pathways or mechanisms by which families can influence health and through which family interventions might be effective. A typology for organizing different types of family interventions will be described, followed by a discussion of different health outcomes that have been studied. I will then review the family intervention studies in four different areas: (a) family caregiving of elders, (b) childhood chronic illness, (c) spouse involvement in adult chronic illnesses, and (d) health promotion and disease prevention (health behaviors). I have focused mostly on randomized controlled trials and have described a few key ones. Finally, recommendations for future research and implications for family clinicians will be presented.

For several reasons, I have chosen to review all types of family interventions for physical disorders and not limit the review to marriage and family therapy. First, there are very few studies of family therapy for physical disorders, and a review of them would be very short. More importantly, studies of family interventions other than family therapy are very relevant to family therapists. They demonstrate the important role of the family in health care. Family therapists should be participating in the design and implementation of many of these interventions, even though they may not be considered traditional family therapy.

Family Interventions for Physical Disorders

Families and Health Research

A careful review of the research on families and health provides for the following conclusions.

Families have a powerful influence on health, equal to traditional medical risk factors. The strongest evidence for this statement comes from the social and family support literature. Numerous large epidemiologic studies have demonstrated that social support, particularly from the family, is health promoting (Berkman, 1995, 2000). In a 1988 *Science* journal article, sociologist James House (House, Landis, & Umberson, 1988) reviewed this research and concluded:

The evidence regarding social relationships and health increasingly approximates the evidence in the 1964 Surgeon General's report that established cigarette smoking as a cause or risk factor for mortality and morbidity from a range of disease. The age-adjusted relative risk ratios are stronger than the relative risks for all cause mortality reported for cigarette smoking. (p. 543)

Studies have shown that family support affects the outcome of many chronic medical illnesses. Berkman, Leo-Summers, and Horwitz (1992) found that after suffering a myocardial infarction, women who are isolated and have few or no family or social supports have 2 to 3 times the mortality rate compared to other women. Many stresses within the family, such as loss of a spouse and divorce, significantly impact morbidity and mortality.

Emotional support is the most important and influential type of support provided by families. Social and family support has been divided into different types of support: instrumental, informational, emotional, and a sense of belonging (Cohen & Syme, 1985). Instrumental support is the actual provision of services (e.g., driving the patient to the hospital) or caregiving (e.g., giving insulin injections) provided by family members. Informational support usually involves giving health-related information, such as advice on whether to seek medical care. Emotional support is providing a listening ear, empathy, and the sense that one is cared about and loved. A sense of belonging is the feeling that one is part of a family or other group that cares about its members. Although there is obviously overlap between these categories, research suggests that emotional support has the most important influence on health outcomes (Kiecolt-Glaser & Newton, 2001). This would suggest that it is not possible to replace family support with services that provide only instrumental and informational support.

For adults, marriage is the most influential family relationship on health. Marital relationships have been the most carefully studied family relationship and demonstrate the strongest influence on health. Even after controlling for other factors, marital status affects overall mortality, mortality from specific illnesses (e.g., cancer and coronary disease), and morbidity (Burman & Margolin, 1992; Kiecolt-Glaser & Newton, 2001). Married individuals are healthier than the widowed, who are in turn healthier than either divorced or never married individuals. Many large studies have shown that bereavement or death of a spouse increases mortality, especially for men (Martikainen & Valkonen, 1996; Osterweis, Solomon, & Green, 1984). Separation and divorce is also associated with increased mortality.

Several recent studies have demonstrated the impact of marital quality on morbidity and mortality from different chronic illnesses. Coyne et al. (2001) found that marital quality, measured by a composite of self-report and observation of marital interaction, was predictive of survival from congestive heart failure, after controlling for the initial severity of the heart failure. Marital quality was as strong a predictor of death as the severity of heart failure itself, and had a stronger effect for women than men. Dyadic negativity has been shown to worsen survival in women who have end stage renal disease and are on dialysis (Kimmel et al., 2000). Weihs, Enright, Simmens, and Reiss (2000) found that women with early breast cancer who do not confide in their spouses have higher recurrence rates than those who do have a confiding relationship. Marital stress has been shown to worsen coronary artery disease in women (Orth-Gomer et al., 2000). These findings suggest that loss of a spouse has the greatest health effects on men, but the impact of poor marital quality may be greater for women.

Negative, critical, or hostile family relationships have a stronger influence on health than positive or supportive relationships. In terms of health, "being nasty" is worse than simply not being nice. Research in the mental health field with schizophrenia and depression first demonstrated that family criticism was strongly predictive of relapse and poor outcome (Hooley, 1985; Hooley, Orley, & Teasdale, 1986; Kanter, Lamb, & Loeper, 1987). Similar results have been found with smoking cessation (Mermelstein, Lichtenstein, & McIntyre, 1983), weight management (Fischmann-Havstad & Marston, 1984), diabetes (Klausner, Koenigsberg, Skolnick, & Chung, 1995; Koenigsberg, Klausner, Pelino, & Rosnick, 1993), asthma, and migraine headaches. Physiological studies have shown that conflict and criticism between family members can have negative influences on blood pressure (Ewart, Taylor, Kraemer, & Agras, 1991) and diabetes control (Minuchin, Rosman, & Baker, 1978).

A recent comprehensive review of research on families and health identified key family protective and risk factors that have the strongest associations with health outcomes (Weihs, Fisher, & Baird, 2002). The protective family factors included family closeness or connectedness, caregiver coping skills, mutually supportive relationships, clear family organization, and direct communication about the illness. The strongest family risk factors were conflict or criticism, psychological trauma related to disease, external stressors, family isolation, disruption of developmental tasks by the disease, and rigidity or perfectionism. The authors argue that family interventions programs should target these protective and risk factors.

How Families Influence Health

While it is clearly demonstrated that family relationships have a powerful influence on health, the pathways or mechanisms by which this effect takes place is not as clear. It is well accepted that individuals with healthy family and social relationships are physically healthier, recover more quickly from physical illness, and live longer. The literature suggests at least three general pathways or mechanisms by which the family and other social relationships can influence health: (a) a direct biological pathway, (b) a health behavior pathway, and (c) a psychophysiological pathway. Each of these pathways will be briefly described.

Direct Biological Pathway

Other family members can directly influence an individual's health without the individual being aware of these influences through direct biological pathways. The most obvious example is the spread of infectious disease within families. Family members, living in the same household, are at increased risk of being infected with a wide range of airborne (e.g., tuberculosis, influenza, varicella) and bloodborne (e.g., hepatitis B) diseases from infected family members. Early epidemiological studies demonstrated that widowers were at a high risk of dying shortly after the death of their spouse, particularly from tuberculosis (Osterweis et al., 1984). Although it was hypothesized that the stress of bereavement may have lowered the surviving spouse's immunity and increased their susceptibility to tuberculosis, it is more likely that many individuals with tuberculosis spread their disease to their spouses before dying, putting their spouse at a higher risk of dying from the same disease.

Family members may also share the same toxic environments. In smoking households, all the children have higher rates of upper respiratory infections, ear infections, and asthma, and adults have higher rates of lung cancer. The family members of asbestos workers have been shown to be at higher risk of asbestos-related illnesses, such as cancer of the lining of the lung, due to exposure to asbestos fibers brought into the home.

Perhaps the most important direct family influence is through shared genes. The genetic revolution is demonstrating how much of our health and our behavior are influenced by our genetic makeup, and how clinically important the role of family history and genetics is in daily practice. The transmission of specific genetic diseases, such as hemophilia and Huntington's disease, and increased inherited risk of heart disease and cancer are important direct family influences.

Health Behavioral Pathway

The behaviors that influence our health are strongly influenced by our families. These behaviors include lifestyle behaviors (e.g., smoking, exercise, diet), health care behaviors (e.g., adherence to medical treatment), and family caregiving. All of these behaviors are usually developed, maintained, or changed within the family setting.

Family members tend to share the same lifestyle behaviors, including similar diets, amount of physical activity, and use of substances (e.g., tobacco, alcohol, and illicit drugs) (Doherty & Campbell, 1988). Parents' lifestyles influence what kind of behaviors a child or adolescent will adopt. For example, smoking is strongly influenced by family factors. Adolescents are much more likely to initiate smoking if either a parent or sibling smokes. Smokers tend to marry other smokers, smoke the same number of cigarettes as their partners, and attempt to quit at the same time (Venters, Jacobs, Luepker, Maiman, & Gillum, 1984). Smokers are much less likely to successfully quit smoking if their partner smokes or is critical of their attempts to quit (Coppotelli & Orleans, 1985). Nutrition is another obvious family activity. Family members usually consume similar amounts of calories, salt, cholesterol, and saturated fats (Doherty & Campbell, 1988).

Psychophysiological Pathway

Family relationships can influence physical health by changes in cognitions and emotions that result in physiological responses, which in turn can influence health outcomes. Much of the research on stress, including family stress, has focused on psychophysiological effects, especially neuroendocrine and psychoimmunological pathways. Of the top stressful life events on the Holmes and Rahe (1967) scale, 10 are family events. Children who experience high family stress have been shown to be at higher risk for infections and hospitalization (Beautrais, Fergusson, & Shannon, 1982). In their classical study of families with psychosomatic illness, Minuchin et al. (1975, 1978) found that certain patterns of family interaction were experienced as stressful to a diabetic child and resulted in rises in free fatty acids and eventually to diabetic ketoacidosis.

Recent research in psychoimmunology has shown how family interactions and events can influence the immune system. Bereavement is associated with a decrease in cellular immunity, which may explain some of the increased mortality after the death of a spouse (Bartrop, Luckhurst, Lazarus, Kiloh, & Penny, 1977; Schleifer, Keller, Camerino, Thornton, & Stein, 1983). Divorced or separated individuals have poorer immune responses than similar married persons (Kiecolt-Glaser et al., 1987). Among married women, marital dissatisfaction and conflict is correlated with both depression and decreased immunity (Schleifer, Keller, Bond, Cohen, & Stein, 1989).

Understanding these pathways or mechanisms is helpful in developing and testing family interventions and choosing appropriate mediating variables and outcome measures. Many interventions may target both the behavioral and psychophysiological pathways. For example, family interventions to improve the treatment of diabetes are likely to focus on mobilizing the family to help the patient comply with the complicated treatment regimen. The primary outcome variable would be glycosylated hemoglobin (or hemoglobin A1C), an excellent marker of blood sugar control. Intermediate or mediating variables would include adherence to diet, exercise, and medication. The intervention might also address family conflict, which may lead to emotional arousal, catecholamine release, and elevated blood sugars in the diabetic family members. Intermediate variables might therefore include family conflict and the patient's emotional health, especially anxiety and depression. Intervention studies that target both of these pathways and measure appropriate mediating variables will help us to better understand the processes by which families influence health.

Types of Family Interventions

Most of the family interventions in the literature can be loosely classified into one of three categories based upon the intensity of the family intervention and the level of knowledge and skill needed to provide the intervention. There is considerable overlap among these categories, but they can be helpful for organizing the literature and understanding what types of effects different types of interventions have across different studies. In some studies, the authors may call their interventions one term (such as family therapy), but the intervention more closely resembles another category (such as family psychoeducation). In addition, some studies do not provide enough information about the interventions to accurately assign them to one of these categories. In their review of family interventions, Weihs et al. (2002) used a similar classification scheme but with slightly different terms. These will be described with each type of intervention. Medical family therapy, a model of family therapy developed to help families with health problems (McDaniel, Hepworth, & Doherty, 1992), can include any or all of these types of interventions. The categories are:

1. *Family education and support.* These interventions are designed to educate family members about the target disease and how to manage the illness. They also may provide information, instrumental, and/or emotional support to individual families or groups of families who are coping with the same illness. In these programs, there is usually an assumption that the family is healthy and functional, and these programs rarely address family relationships. The program may be led by a professional, although rarely a family therapist, or nonprofessional such as a peer counselor who has coped with a similar illness in his or her own family. They do not provide systematic assessment of problem-solving and coping skills. Weihs et al. (2002) called this type of intervention family psychoeducation, a term that I reserve for the next category.

2. *Family psychoeducation.* Family psychoeducation provides more than education and support. These programs are usually focused on helping families cope more effectively with an illness or disorder and provide specific problem-solving skills. They address family relationships particularly as they are affected by the illness and in turn affect coping with

the illness. Family psychoeducation assumes that the family is healthy and that family problems result from ineffective coping. These interventions usually include specific guidelines for illness management, assistance with problem-solving skills, and expansion of the patient's and family's social network (McFarlane et al., 1995). Although family psychoeducation for mental disorders is often provided by family therapists who may consider psychoeducation to be a type of family therapy, most of the psychoeducational interventions reviewed here were not conducted by family therapists or labeled as family therapy or family psychoeducation. Few are systemic in the approach. Weihs et al. (2002) called this type of intervention, "Interventions that affect family relationships, quality and functioning" (p. 19).

3. *Family therapy.* Family therapy interventions are usually conducted by a family therapist using one of the family systems models or theories. In general, the focus is on the dysfunction within the family, rather than on the disease or illness. There is little or no education about the illness. The problem is considered to reside within the family. Therapy is provided to individual families for a limited number of sessions. In some interventions, the illness may be viewed as a result of the family dysfunction, as in Minuchin et al.'s (1978) classic work on psychosomatic families.

Outcomes of Family Interventions

Family intervention studies have used a wide variety of outcome measures to assess their efficacy. Many of the interventions for chronic diseases, such as diabetes, asthma, and hypertension have used physiologic measures of the disease process, such as glycosylated hemoglobin, pulmonary function testing, and blood pressure. In such diseases where there are such physiologic measures, they represent excellent measures for assessing the impact of the intervention on the physiology of the disease. For diseases in which such measures are not available, such as coronary heart or cerebrovascular disease, self-reports of symptoms or disability have been substituted. Measures of functional health status are reliable and valid self-report measures of overall health.

Many of these studies have also examined the impact of these interventions on health behaviors, such as smoking, exercise, and diet, or adherence to medical treatment. In studies of family involvement for health promotion, these behaviors are the primary outcomes of interest. The emotional health of the index patient and other family members are also important outcome measures for these interventions. Unfortunately, few of these interventions have examined family level outcomes, such as family functioning, marital satisfaction, or family/marital criticism or conflict. This is unfortunate, especially when the intervention does not improve the health outcome. In these cases, it is not possible to know whether the intervention did not change the target family factor (such as family criticism), or whether a change in family relationships did not result in any change in health outcomes (see discussion of smoking cessation in Health Promotion and Disease Prevention section). Finally, few studies have examined the cost and economic impact of family interventions. One notable exception is a recent study by Law and Crane (2000) which found that individuals in a health maintenance organization who received marital and family therapy had a 21% reduction in their use of health care services in the 6 months after receiving therapy.

Effectiveness of Family Interventions for Physical Disorders

Many types of family interventions have been developed and tested for a wide range of physical disorders. In this chapter, the interventions for physical disorders have been organized around the life cycle (elderly, adult illness, and pediatric disorders) with a separate section on health promotion and disease prevention.

Family Caregiving of Elders

In no other area of health has the family received as much attention as family caregiving of persons with chronic disabling conditions. With the aging of the population, the rising incidence of degenerative and disabling conditions in the elderly and fewer resources for professional caregiving, a growing percentage of older individuals must rely on family members for care. For example, it is estimated that over 40% of the elderly over the age of 85 have some form of dementia and one half of those individuals are cared for by family members in their own communities (Biegel, Sales, & Schulz, 1991).

Research has demonstrated that caregiving exerts a heavy toll on family members. Family caregivers have much higher morbidity and mortality than age matched controls. One study (Schulz & Beach, 1999) found that caregivers over 65 who were experiencing emotional strain were 63% more likely to die than age matched noncaregivers over a 4 year period. Caregivers suffer higher rates of multiple physical illnesses, depression, and anxiety. The incidence of depression among caregivers of persons with dementia has been estimated to be between 40% to 50% (Gallagher, Rose, Rivera, Lovett, & Thompson, 1989). They often restrict their social activities and reduce their time at work. The financial impact of caregiving on families can be enormous, both in terms of decreased wages of caregivers and the cost of providing equipment and services in the home for the patient.

Family caregivers are essential members of the health care team. They provide clinical observation, direct care, case management, and a range of other services. In chronic illnesses, such as Alzheimer's disease, these caregivers may devote years of their own lives to caring for a loved one. Unfortunately, our current health care system offers little in the way of institutional support for families who are burdened with caregiving. Managed care has shifted many of the burdens of caregiving from professionals in the hospital and other institutions to family members at home without providing adequate support. As hospital stays have shortened, elderly patients are being discharged home sicker and with more health care needs than in the past.

A number of effective interventions for the caregivers of patients with dementia have been developed and tested, including psychoeducational and family counseling interventions and family support/education groups. No controlled trials of family therapy for family caregivers could be found.

Family support groups for caregivers of patients with Alzheimer's disease have become quite common and are promoted by advocacy groups. These are usually open-ended groups that are professionally or peer-led and provide information and emotional support to families. Studies of these groups suggest that participants learn new information and report high levels of satisfaction, but the impact on the caregivers' emotional distress and sense of burden is inconsistent (Haley, Brown, & Levine, 1987; Kahan, Kemp, Staples, & Brummel-Smith, 1985; Orleans, George, Houpt, & Brodie, 1985).

Family psychoeducational programs provide more intensive skills training to help family caregivers manage many of the common problems presented by elders with dementia (Chiverton & Caine, 1989; Gallagher et al., 1989; Goodman & Pynoos, 1990; Toseland et al., 2001). These interventions usually include weekly group sessions led by a trained professional and typically last for 8 to 10 weeks. In randomized controlled trials, they have consistently reduced depressive symptoms, emotional distress, and the sense of burden of family caregivers.

An excellent example of an effective family psychoeducational intervention for family caregivers of Alzheimer's disease (AD) patients has been developed by Mittelman, Ferris, Shulman, Steinberg, and Levin (1996) and tested in a randomized controlled trial. These families attended individual and group instructional and problem-solving sessions where they learned how to manage many of the troublesome behaviors of patients with AD. They also attended an ongoing family support group and could access a crisis intervention service to help them with urgent problems. In Mittelman et al.'s study, the caregivers who received the intervention were less depressed and physically healthier than those who did not, and AD patients were able to remain at home for almost a year longer than those in the control group. The savings in nursing home costs were several times the cost of the interventions. Similar types of family support should be a part of the treatment of all patients and families with Alzheimer's disease and other dementias.

Sorensen, Pinquart, and Duberstein (2002) recently conducted a meta-analysis of 78 caregiver intervention studies representing six different types of interventions for different illnesses. They found a significant improvement (0.14–0.41 standard deviation units) across all six outcome variables (caregiver burden, depression, subjective well-being, perceived caregiver satisfaction, ability/knowledge, and patient symptoms). The effects were the smallest for caregivers of dementia patients and most consistent with the psychoeducational interventions. Caregiver ability/knowledge improved more than subjective burden and depression. Group interventions had smaller improvements than individual interventions.

These studies of family interventions for family caregivers suggest that providing education and support for family caregivers is necessary, but not sufficient to reduce their burden and improve their emotional health. Family caregivers need more intensive interventions that include skills training and assistance with problem solving. Similar results have been found in the few interventions for patients who have suffered a stroke and their families (Evans, Matlock, Bishop, Stranahan, & Pederson, 1988). Family psychoeducational programs for family caregivers are effective in improving both the physical and emotional health of the caregiver and can be cost-effective. These programs have many similarities with psychoeducational programs that have been developed and tested for schizophrenia, and can be used as models for family interventions for other physical disorders.

Pediatric Illnesses

It is self evident that family structure and function has a powerful influence on the course and outcome of most pediatric illnesses. For children, it is usually the parents who carry out most of the treatment of the illness. A robust body of research has documented many family variables that are associated with health outcomes for a broad range of chronic illnesses in children. For example, adequate control of diabetes and asthma is strongly correlated with healthy family functioning. Chronic family conflict, parental indifference, and low cohesion have all been associated with poor metabolic control in diabetes, while clear family organization and high parental self-esteem correlate with good control (Anderson & Kornblum, 1984; Gustafsson, Kjellman, & Cederblad, 1986). In a comprehensive literature review, Patterson (1991) identified nine aspects of family process which have been consistently associated with good outcomes in children with chronic illness and disabilities: (a) balancing the illness with other family needs, (b) maintaining clear boundaries, (c) developing communication competence, (d) attributing positive meaning to the situation, (e) maintaining family flexibility, (f) maintaining family cohesiveness, (g) engaging active coping efforts, (h) maintaining social supports, and (i) developing collaborative relationships with professionals. Many of these attributes have been targeted by family interventions for pediatric illnesses.

One of the earliest and best known family interventions in childhood chronic illness is the pioneering work of Salvador Minuchin. In a series of seminal studies, Minuchin et al. (1975, 1978) at the Philadelphia Child Guidance Clinic studied poorly controlled diabetic children and their families. These children had recurrent episodes of diabetic ketoacidosis, but when hospitalized, the diabetes was easily managed. It appeared that stress and emotional arousal within the family directly affected the child's blood sugar. In these families, Minuchin et al. discovered a specific pattern of interaction, characterized by enmeshment (high cohesion), overprotectiveness, rigidity, and conflict avoidance. They called these families "psychosomatic families."

To determine how these family patterns can affect diabetes, Minuchin et al. (1975) studied the physiologic responses of diabetic children to a stressful family interview. During the family interview, the children from psychosomatic families had a rapid rise in free fatty acids (FFA), a precursor to diabetic ketoacidosis, which persisted beyond the interview. The parents of these children exhibited an initial rise in FFA levels, which fell to normal when the diabetic child entered the room. Minuchin et al. hypothesized that in psychosomatic families, parental conflict is detoured or defused through the chronically ill child, and the resulting stress leads to exacerbation of the illness. Minuchin was the first investigator to demonstrate a link between family and physiologic processes.

Based upon this model, Minuchin et al. (1978) successfully treated psychosomatic families using structural family therapy to help disengage the diabetic child and establish more appropriate family boundaries. In 15 cases, the pattern of recurrent ketoacidosis ceased and insulin doses were reduced. The authors reported similar success with asthma and anorexia nervosa occurring in psychosomatic families. However, these early case reports lacked any standardized outcome measures or control groups. In addition, the psychosomatic family model has been criticized as blaming families for the child's illness (Coyne & Anderson, 1989). Wood et al. (1989) have proposed a more systemic and comprehensive biobehavioral model of childhood chronic illness.

Childhood asthma and diabetes have received the most attention of family researchers because they are common and serious pediatric illnesses that involve complicated treatment regimens and are thought to be exacerbated by emotional distress. Thus families may influence these disorders either by how well they are able to assist the child in adhering to the treatment or by modulating the level of family stress and the child's emotional distress. Both of these pathways are addressed in most family interventions for these disorders.

Asthma. Asthma has been strongly associated with psychosocial distress, depression, and disturbed family relationships (Liebman, Minuchin, & Baker, 1974). The only randomized controlled trials of family therapy for a childhood illness have been conducted for severe childhood asthma. Two studies involved a total of 55 children with moderately severe asthma and were based on structural family therapy models. Strengthening of boundaries between generations and addressing hidden conflicts were used to alter dysfunctional patterns of interaction. Both interventions improved asthma symptoms, clinical evaluation, and a number of measures of lung function (although they differed in the two studies). A recent Cochrane review (Panton & Barley, 2002) of these studies, considered by many to be the "gold standard" of evidence-based medicine, concluded that "There is some indication that family therapy may be a useful adjunct to medication for children with asthma" (p. 2).

Numerous family psychoeducational programs have been designed and tested for improving treatment of childhood asthma. In a review of this research,

Bernard-Bonnin, Stachenko, Bonin, Charette, and Rousseau (1995) identified 11 well designed randomized controlled trials of family psychoeducation for asthma. In their meta-analysis, the researchers found a significant improvement in several measures of asthma severity. Although the overall effect sizes were small (<.2), the results of these interventions were significantly better when limited to children with more severe asthma. This is an obvious issue that is worth highlighting across all disorders. Family interventions are more likely to improve health outcomes with more severe illness. Patients with mild disease are unlikely to need or benefit from family interventions.

Insulin-dependent diabetes mellitus. A wide range of family approaches has been systematically tested for childhood (Type 1—insulin-dependent) diabetes. Several studies have examined the impact of family education and support groups (Anderson, Wolf, Burkhart, Cornell, & Bacon, 1989; Dougherty, Schiffrin, White, Soderstrom, & Sufrategui, 1999; McNabb, Quinn, Murphy, Thorp, & Cook, 1994; Wing, Marcus, Epstein, & Jawad, 1991) on health outcomes. Fewer studies have tested more intensive psychoeducational programs that address collaborative problem solving and problematic family interactions (Galatzer, Amir, Gil, Karp, & Laron, 1982; Wing et al., 1991). In a review of the literature on family-based interventions for diabetes, Mendenhall (2002) identified 12 randomized clinical trials of family interventions for insulin-dependent diabetes mellitus (IDDM), 10 of which measured hemoglobin A1C (HBA1C), an excellent measure of chronic blood sugar control, as the primary outcome measure. Of these 10 studies, 7 demonstrated a significant improvement in HBA1C. In 2 studies, there was actual worsening of blood sugar control. Although one can conclude that these interventions were effective in improving diabetic control, it is not possible to determine which interventions were more effective. It is also important to note that these family interventions, some of which were fairly time intensive, were compared to usual care. How much of the improvements were specifically due to the family focus of the interventions cannot be determined.

These studies have also looked at the impact of the family interventions on other diabetes related outcomes, including the patient's emotional health and adherence to diabetic treatment programs. Most of these programs have increased overall self-care and specific aspects of diabetes care, such as adherence with diet, exercise, blood sugar testing, and insulin. They have also reduced patients' levels of distress and denial of the illness and increased self-esteem, perceived quality of life, and acceptance of the illness. It is not possible to determine which of these psychosocial improvements (diabetes-related behaviors or emotional health) contributed more to better blood sugar control. This is an important issue for future research.

Cystic fibrosis. Cystic fibrosis (CF) is a lethal genetic disorder in which children are missing a key enzyme in the lungs, resulting in progressive deterioration in lung function over several decades and eventual death. Complex treatment programs involving frequent chest physical therapy (cupping and drainage), aggressive treatment of infections with antibiotics, and use of synthetic enzymes have dramatically improved the survival of these children and young adults. Yet these treatments are very demanding upon families. Patterson, Budd, Goetz, and Warwick (1993) demonstrated that family variables predict the rate of decline of pulmonary function over a 10-year period. Bartholomew and Schneiderman (1982) developed separate psychoeducational groups for children and adolescents with CF and their parents. In a randomized controlled trial, they found that the children and adolescents in the families that received the intervention reported improved knowledge, self-efficacy, self-management of the illness, and improved overall health status. This study suggests that family psychoeducation may actually be able to extend the lives of those who suffer from this disorder.

Childhood cancer. In childhood cancer, a few studies have used family interventions to reduce the psychological morbidity associated with diagnosis and treatment. Two interventions designed to improve parental coping with the stress of the illness failed to show any significant decrease in parental distress (Hoekstra-Weebers, Heuvel, Jaspers, Kamps, & Klip, 1998; Jay & Elliott, 1990). Working with children with leukemia and their families, Kazak et al. (1996) were able to reduce the child's distress related to painful procedure using a cognitive-behavioral, family-oriented intervention. In another study, Kazak (1989) piloted a multifamily group intervention for survivors of childhood cancer to reduce the posttraumatic stress symptoms related to the diagnosis and treatment of the cancer. In a pre–post test design, they were able to show a decrease in posttraumatic stress and anxiety in the survivors and their family members.

Congenital heart disease. Two studies have examined the impact of family interventions to reduce the psychological morbidity associated with cardiac surgery for congenital heart disease (Campbell, Clark, & Kirkpatrick, 1986; Campbell, Kirkpatrick, Berry, & Lamberti, 1995). Both interventions provided separate informational and skills training separately to the child and one parent before cardiac surgery. The children in the intervention group were better adjusted at home and had higher functioning at school after the procedure. There were no differences in the parents' reports of anxiety, but the parents in the intervention group felt more competent in caring for their child.

These family interventions for childhood illnesses clearly demonstrate health benefits for asthma, diabetes, and cystic fibrosis, and show promise for reducing the psychosocial morbidity associated with cancer and cardiac surgery. The interventions need to be applied across a wider range of pediatric illnesses.

Adult Chronic Illness

Although there is a large body of research on the impact of marriage on chronic illness and overall health, there are relatively few family or marital intervention studies in adult physical illness. Most of the research in this area has focused on the role of the spouse as the primary caregiver. There are no randomized controlled trials for marital or family therapy for adult illnesses. Gonzalez,

Steinglass, and Reiss (1989) developed an innovative multifamily psychoeducational group intervention for families with chronic medical illnesses. Based upon their clinical work, they found that in many of these families the chronic illness tended to dominate family life and take over the family's identity. The goal of these groups is to help families balance the needs of the illness with the needs of the family by putting the illness in its appropriate place in family life. It is currently being studied as an intervention with a wide range of illnesses, including HIV/AIDS, adult cancer, and end stage renal disease.

Hypertension. Adherence with hypertension treatment remains a major public health problem. Less than one half of adults with elevated blood pressure are taking their medication as directed. Medication compliance has been shown to be significantly correlated with marital satisfaction in married hypertensive patients (Trevino, Young, Groff, & Jono, 1990). In experimental studies, blood pressure reactivity has been linked to marital interaction and conflict (Gottman, 1994). Ewart, Taylor, Kraemer, and Agras (1984) taught communication skills to 20 hypertensive patients and their spouses to help them reduce conflict and emotional and blood pressure reactivity during arguments. These couples showed less hostility, fewer combative behaviors, and a significant reduction in systolic blood pressure.

Two randomized controlled trials have examined the impact of a family intervention on adherence to hypertension treatment. Morisky et al. (1983) compared three psychoeducation interventions (brief individual counseling, counseling the spouse during a home visit, and patient support group) to improve blood pressure treatment in an inner city population. The family intervention was included after a patient survey indicated that 70% of the hypertensive patients at the clinic wished that their spouse or other family members knew more about their illness and were more involved. Educating and counseling the spouse improved treatment adherence and lowered both blood pressure and overall mortality. Overall the experimental groups had a 57% reduction in mortality, and the family intervention seemed to have the greatest effect. A similar study (Earp, Ory, & Strogatz, 1982) failed to demonstrate any benefits from involving a family member during a home visit, but the followup may not have been long enough to detect a difference.

Cardiac rehabilitation. Although there is evidence that families have a powerful influence on recovery and survival after a myocardial infarction, there are very few family interventions in cardiac rehabilitation. Spouses of heart attack patients have high levels of depression, anxiety, and guilt, and experience similar levels of overall distress as the patients (Bedsworth & Molen, 1982). Many male cardiac patients feel overprotected by their wives (Fiske, Coyne, & Smith, 1991). Emotional support provided by a family member (usually spouse) or confidant is a very strong predictor of survival after a myocardial infarction, stronger than any of the usually physiologic measures. For example, in the 3 months after a heart attack, elderly women who lack a confidant are 3 times more likely to die than women who have a confidant (Berkman et al., 1992).

Several studies have examined the impact of spouse involvement in cardiac rehabilitation on psychosocial outcomes. In one ingenious controlled study, wives of heart attack patients walked on the treadmill at the same workload as their husbands, 3 weeks after their husband's heart attack (Taylor, Bandura, Ewart, Miller, & DeBusk, 1985). These wives were much more confident and less anxious about their husbands' health and capability than wives in the control group who merely observed their husbands' tests. When these women actually experienced what their husbands were capable of doing, they were less overprotective, and the husbands had improved cardiac functioning 11 and 26 weeks after the heart attack. Of the three studies that included couple counseling as part of cardiac rehabilitation (Dracup, Meleis, Baker, & Edlefsen, 1984; Gilliss, Neuhaus, & Hauck, 1990; Thompson & Meddis, 1990), only one was able to show any improvement in the spouses' emotional health (Dracup et al., 1984). Patient outcomes were not examined.

Although observational research suggests that spouses play an important role in recovery from heart attacks, few couple or family interventions have been tested, and those that have report mixed results.

Non-insulin dependent diabetes. Non-insulin dependent diabetes (NIDDM or Type 2) afflicts over 15 million adults in the United States and is 10 times more common than insulin dependent diabetes, a disease of children and young adults. Most patients with NIDDM are overweight, and the major challenge for these patients is adherence with recommended diet, exercise, medication, and blood sugar monitoring. Only two studies have examined the impact of a couples intervention on diabetes outcomes. Gilden, Hendryx, Casia, and Singh (1989) included the wives of elderly diabetic patients in a 6-week diabetes education program. Patients with participating spouses showed greater improvement in knowledge, increase in family involvement, and more improvement in diabetic control than those without spouse involvement. Wing et al. (1991) enrolled obese diabetic patients and their obese spouses in a behavioral weight reduction program. Patients and their spouses were randomly assigned to an individual or couples program. At 1-year followup, there was no difference in overall weight loss in the two groups, but the women lost more weight in the couples groups and the men lost more weight when treated alone. There was no report of changes in blood sugar control. This study emphasizes the importance of examining gender effects in couples intervention. Marital interactions and interventions are likely to have very different effects on women than on men.

Health Promotion and Disease Prevention

It has been estimated that over one-third of all deaths in the United States can be directly attributable to unhealthy behaviors, particularly smoking, lack of exercise, poor nutrition, and alcohol abuse, and are potentially preventable. Much of morbidity or suffering from chronic illnesses, such as heart disease, cancer, diabetes, and stroke can also be attributed in part to these unhealthy behaviors.

These behaviors are usually developed, maintained, and changed within the context of the family. Health behaviors or risk factors tend to cluster within families, since family members tend to share similar diets, physical activities, and use or abuse of unhealthy substances, such as smoking. The World Health Organization (1976) has characterized the family as "the primary social agent in the promotion of health and well-being" (p. 17).

Cigarette smoking. Smoking remains the number one public health problem in the United States, directly causing over 350,000 deaths per year, mostly from heart disease and cancer. Smoking behaviors are strongly influenced by family members. Adolescents are 5 times more likely to start smoking if a parent or older sibling smokes (Bewley & Bland, 1977). Smokers tend to marry other smokers, to smoke the same number of cigarettes as their spouse, and to quit at the same time (Venters et al., 1984). Smokers who are married to non or ex-smokers are more likely to quit and remain abstinent. Support from the smoker's partner or spouse has been shown to be highly predictive of successful smoking cessation. Specific supportive behaviors such as providing encouragement and positive reinforcement predict successful quitting, while negative behaviors such as nagging or criticism predict failure to quit or relapse (Coppotelli & Orleans, 1985; Mermelstein, 1986). Recent guidelines from the Agency for Healthcare Quality and Research (AHRQ) for treating tobacco use and dependence recommend family and social support interventions as components of effective smoking cessation (Fiore, 2000).

Nine randomized controlled trials have studied the impact of partner support to assist with smoking cessation, involving over 1,700 subjects (Park, Schultz, Tudiver, Campbell, & Becker, 2002). Most of these interventions integrate a social support intervention with a traditional smoking cessation program. The partner, usually the spouse, participates in smoking cessation sessions, and the couples are given suggestions and feedback on helpful and unhelpful behaviors. The traditional smoking cessation programs usually include nicotine replacement, behavioral therapy, and relapse prevention.

The results of these studies have been mixed. A recent Cochrane review and meta-analysis (Park et al., 2002) found no overall impact of partner support on smoking cessation. In most of these studies, the amount of partner support reported by the smokers continued to predict successful smoking cessation, but few of the interventions had any impact on the level of partner support. These results suggest that partner support is important for smoking cessation, but that it is difficult to increase levels of support.

The inability of these interventions to improve partner support or smoking cessation may result from an overly simplistic and nonsystemic view of marriage. As marital therapists know, asking partners or spouses to be more supportive or less critical only occasionally has its desired effects. These behaviors are part of a complex marital relationship and are affected by the history and quality of the marital relationship. Unfortunately, none of these studies assessed the quality of the marriage. One might hypothesize that it is easier to increase supportive behaviors in couples that have higher levels of marital satisfaction. A more in-depth qualitative study of what happens to these couples when they participate in these smoking cessation programs would be very helpful to better understand the relationship between smoking behaviors and marital dynamics.

Weight reduction. Obesity is also a major public health problem and the focus of a recent Surgeon General's report. Over 30% of the population is considered obese (more than 20% over ideal body weight) and this contributes to numerous chronic illnesses, including diabetes, hypertension, coronary heart disease, and arthritis. Research has shown that overeating and obesity can play important homeostatic roles in families. The parents of obese children are less likely to encourage exercise and more likely to encourage their children to eat than other parents (Hanson, Klesges, Eck, & Cigrang, 1990; Waxman & Stunkard, 1980). The family has been shown to play an important role in both the development and the treatment of eating disorders such as anorexia nervosa and bulimia (Campbell & Patterson, 1995). Because eating disorders are generally considered mental rather than physical disorders, they are not reviewed in this chapter.

There are many similarities between the research on family interventions for smoking and obesity. Spousal support has been shown to predict successful weight loss (Streja, Boyko, & Rabkin, 1982), and criticism or high expressed emotion associated with little or no weight loss (Fischmann-Havstad & Marston, 1984). There are 10 randomized controlled trials of spouse or partner involvement in weight reduction programs (Black, Gleser, & Kooyers, 1990). The interventions are based upon individual cognitive behavioral approaches in which a spouse is viewed as reinforcing the desired behaviors. Spouses attend all the sessions and are instructed in basic behavior modification techniques, especially giving positive reinforcement and avoiding criticism.

Most weight reduction programs can demonstrate initial weight loss, but if followed for more than a year, the subjects return to their original weight. The results of the family interventions were mixed. In approximately one half of the studies, the intervention groups were able to maintain the weight loss for up to 3 years. A meta-analysis of these studies (Black et al., 1990) concluded that compared to individual interventions, couples interventions had a small, but significant, improvement in weight loss at the end of the program, which persisted for 2 to 3 months follow-up, but was no longer apparent at lengthier (1–3 years) follow-up.

Several findings from these interventions and observational studies are worth noting. Most of the studies that measured supportive behaviors were not able to demonstrate any increase in these behaviors. Subjects who reported higher satisfaction with their marriage or a more cohesive relationship lost more weight (Dubbert & Wilson, 1984). In another study, the greatest weight loss occurred in the group where the spouses were asked not to nag, criticize, or otherwise participate in their partner's efforts at weight reduction. These studies suggest that blocking partner criticism and addressing marital conflict and dissatisfaction may be more important than trying to increase supportive behaviors. Family interventions for childhood obesity have been more successful. Several studies have shown that parental involvement in weight reduction programs for children results in greater weight loss for both the child and the parent, with a high correlation between the parent's and child's weight loss (Epstein, Wing, Koeske, Andrasik, & Ossip, 1981). One program for obese adolescents found the best results when the adolescent and the parent received their training, thus respecting the adolescent's growing independence (Brownell, Kelman, & Stunkard, 1983). Parental involvement is clearly beneficial in the treatment of pediatric obesity. Spouse or partner involvement in adult obesity may be of value, but a better understanding of the marital dynamics of obesity is needed.

Nutrition and cardiovascular risk reduction. Diet is an obvious family activity. Families tend to share the same diets and consume similar amounts of salt, calories, cholesterol, and saturated fats (Nader et al., 1983). When one family member changes his or her diet, other family members tend to make similar changes (Sexton et al., 1987). Despite these findings, most nutrition and cardiac risk reduction programs are directed to individuals with no attention to the rest of the family. Several studies have demonstrated that a family intervention can change diet and promote a healthier lifestyle, but no one has compared a family to an individual intervention in this area.

The British Family Heart Study recruited over 12,000 middle aged couples from 26 general practices in England. Each couple received family-based counseling by a trained nurse about healthy lifestyles and cardiac risk reduction (Graham, Senior, Dukes, & Lazarus, 1993). At 1-year follow-up, the intervention group had reduced their smoking, blood pressure, and cholesterol level, and had a 16% reduction in their overall cardiac risk score. Smaller interventions studies have found similar results with small, but significant improvements in healthy behaviors (Knutsen & Knutsen, 1991; Perry et al., 1989).

Future Research and Direction

Research on family interventions for physical disorders is still in its infancy. We are just beginning to understand what family characteristics are important in physical health and how they influence health. This area of research is at the stage where research on families and schizophrenia was 30 years ago. However, this leaves lots of opportunities for new family researchers to become involved in this exciting area of research.

Most of the research on family interventions for physical disorders were not conducted by family researchers or based on family science. Medical and nursing researchers who believed, based upon their clinical observations, that families should be included in medical treatment were the principal investigators in most of these studies. Rarely is a particular family characteristic or variable targeted by the intervention, and pre- or postfamily assessment is usually absent. There are very few trials of family therapy for any physical disorders.

There is a tremendous need for family therapists and researchers to become involved in research on families and health and to help design and implement studies in this area. The following areas need to be addressed in the future:

1. More observational research is needed on families and health. We are just beginning to understand how families are influenced by health problems and vice-versa. As described earlier, a few family variables have been shown to be predictive of health outcomes, but the strength of this evidence is not strong. Recent research has focused on the role of family criticism, family conflict, and expressed emotion and its impact on physical health.

2. Both observational and intervention research needs to be based upon family theories and family science. Most of existing studies are atheoretical. Intervention strategies should be guided by theoretical models that hypothesize relationships between family and health variables, and then measure these family variables before and after the intervention. For example, studies of spouse involvement in smoking cessation and weight loss should measure marital satisfaction or quality as well as helpful and harmful behaviors before and after the interventions. Preintervention family assessment will also allow researchers to determine in which families the intervention is most effective.

3. All existing family intervention studies focus on a single disease. Some family interventions should be developed and targeted across several chronic diseases that have some commonalities. Interventions that have been shown to be effective for one disease (such as family psychoeducation for caregivers of AD patients) should be tested with other similar diseases (such as stroke or Parkinson's disease).

4. Intervention studies should measure multiple outcomes across several levels, including patient physical and emotional health, family members' physical and emotional health, family functioning, marital satisfaction or quality, and health care and overall costs. Many of the benefits of a family intervention may not be captured by traditional measures. For example, a family intervention may improve the health of other family members and reduce their use of health care services.

5. Family interventions should be adaptable to meet specific needs and characteristics of individual families. For example, families in which there is significant conflict, disengagement, or dissatisfaction will need a different and more intensive approach than more functional families.

6. More attention needs to be paid to the cost of family interventions and the potential financial benefits of the intervention for the patient and other family members.

7. Intervention studies need to describe the family interventions in more

detail so that they can be replicated, and to determine what the most effective ingredients of the intervention are. This will help researchers determine why one intervention is effective and another is not.

8. Family, and especially couple interventions need to pay close attention to gender effects. As noted earlier, marriage has very different effects on the physical health of men and women (Kiecolt-Glaser & Newton, 2001). Because marriage is often the primary source of social support for men, the presence or absence of a wife has the greatest impact on health, whereas women's health is most influenced by the quality of the relationship. Couple interventions are therefore likely to have very different effects on men and women's health. Only one intervention study has examined gender effects and found that women had better outcomes (weight loss) in couples treatment and men did better alone.

9. Family intervention studies need to include more diversity. Most current studies are conducted with white middle class families. Future studies should include different family types (e.g., single parent families, gay families) and families from different racial, ethnic, and socioeconomic backgrounds.

Implications for Marriage and Family Therapists

This body of research on families and health suggests that marriage and family therapists have an important, but unmet role in the treatment of physical illness. Family systems medicine is an interdisciplinary field that brings together physicians, family therapists, and other health professionals interested in how illness affects families, and how families affect illness and promote a biopsychosocial systems model of health care (Bloch, 1984). Family therapists should be a part of most health care teams, offering a family and systemic perspective that is so often missing. Much has been written about family therapists who work in primary care settings helping family physicians, pediatricians, and primary care internists care for patients and their families. There are also opportunities for working with medical specialties, especially rehabilitation medicine, reproductive health, oncology, cardiac rehabilitation, and geriatrics (Seaburn, Lorenz, Gunn, & Gawinski, 1996).

Medical family therapy (McDaniel et al., 1992) provides a framework and a set of practical skills for family therapists to work in medical settings. Its goal is to help families faced with health problems by enhancing agency, a sense of personal control and choice, and communion, a sense of interpersonal connection. It is beginning to be recognized as a specialty within family therapy with internships offered at some universities (Seaburn, Gawinski, Harp, & McDaniel, 1993). To work effectively in medical settings, family therapists need to overcome some of the barriers to collaboration, and develop skills for working with medical providers.

Family therapy training programs need to provide the knowledge and skills for all new family therapists to work in medical settings and with families with health problems. These programs should offer courses on medical family therapy, collaboration with medical providers, and psychopharmacology. Family therapy trainees should be provided with opportunities to work in medical settings under supervision during graduate school and internship.

Conclusions

This review of family interventions for physical disorders suggests that there are effective family interventions for some physical disorders and promising ones of others. For many chronic illnesses, no family interventions have been developed or tested. The most commonly studied and effective type of family intervention is family psychoeducation. It has wide appeal and applicability to numerous disorders. It appears to be more effective than programs that only provide family support or education. Families need more intensive assistance with specific problem solving and coping skills. Whether group family psychoeducation is more effective than individual family psychoeducation for physical disorders is not known and needs study. There are too few studies of family therapy for physical disorders to comment on its effectiveness, although family therapy is likely to be directed to a much more limited group of dysfunctional families.

The most effective family interventions have been in the treatment of family caregivers of dementia patients. Not only did these family interventions improve the physical and mental health of the caregivers, but were very cost effective. Mittelman et al.'s (1996) comprehensive intervention for family caregivers should be adapted to other chronic disorders. Family interventions for childhood disorders, especially diabetes and asthma, are effective in improving medical (e.g., HBA1C levels and pulmonary function), as well as psychosocial outcomes. Not surprisingly, family interventions are most effective at each end of the life cycle when much of the care is provided by family caregivers.

There is insufficient research on family interventions for adult illness to make any firm conclusions. Although enhancing family support for adherence to chronic medical treatments appears to have a powerful effect on health outcomes (Morisky et al., 1983), more research is needed to verify this. Studies of spouse involvement in cardiac rehabilitation have demonstrated little effect. Family involvement for health promotion and disease prevention programs offers great promise. Family-centered nutrition and cardiovascular risk reduction programs are effective in improving the health of multiple members, but have not been directly compared with individually oriented programs. Family based programs for obesity in children are clearly more effective than individual programs, but their effectiveness for adults is unclear. Partner or spouse involvement for smoking cessation has been shown to be ineffective.

Overall one can conclude that there is some evidence that family interventions can improve health outcomes in physical disorders. There is a need for more observational and intervention research on families and health, and family researchers and clinicians need to become more involved in this area of research. Only by better understanding how families can be used as a resource in medical care will our health care system become more family-oriented and higher quality.

References

References marked with a double asterisk are recommended for clinicians.

Anderson, B. J., Wolf, F. M., Burkhart, M. T., Cornell, R. G., & Bacon, G. E. (1989). Effects of peer-group intervention on metabolic control of adolescents with IDDM. Randomized outpatient study. *Diabetes Care, 12,* 179–183.

Anderson, B. J., & Kornblum, H. (1984). The family environment of children with a diabetic parent: Issues for research. *Family Systems Medicine 2*(1), 17–27.

Bartholomew, L., & Schneiderman, L. J. (1982). Attitudes of patients toward family care in a family practice group. *Journal of Family Practice, 15,* 477–481.

Bartrop, R. W., Luckhurst, E., Lazarus, L., Kiloh, L. G., & Penny, R. (1977). Depressed lymphocyte function after bereavement. *Lancet, 1,* 834–836.

Beautrais, A. L., Fergusson, D. M., & Shannon, F. T. (1982). Life events and childhood morbidity: A prospective study. *Pediatrics, 70,* 935–940.

Bedsworth, J. A., & Molen, M. T. (1982). Psychological stress in spouses of patients with myocardial infarction. *Heart & Lung, 11,* 450–456.

Berkman, L. F. (1995). The role of social relations in health promotion [Review]. *Psychosomatic Medicine, 57,* 245–254.

Berkman, L. F. (2000). Social support, social networks, social cohesion and health. *Social Work in Health Care, 31,* 3–14.

Berkman, L. F., Leo-Summers, L., & Horwitz, R. I. (1992). Emotional support and survival after myocardial infarction. A prospective, population-based study of the elderly. *Annals of Internal Medicine, 117,* 1003–1009.

Bernard-Bonnin, A. C., Stachenko, S., Bonin, D., Charette, C., & Rousseau, E. (1995). Self-management teaching programs and morbidity of pediatric asthma: A meta-analysis. *Journal of Allergy & Clinical Immunology, 95,* 34–41.

Bewley, B. R., & Bland, J. M. (1977). Academic performance and social factors related to cigarette smoking by schoolchildren. *British Journal of Preventive & Social Medicine, 31,* 18–24.

**Biegel, D. E., Sales, E., & Schulz, R. (1991). *Family caregiving in chronic illness: Alzheimer's disease, cancer, heart disease, mental illness, and stroke.* Newbury Park, CA: Sage.

Black, D. R., Gleser, L. J., & Kooyers, K. J. (1990). A meta-analytic evaluation of couples weight-loss programs. *Health Psychology, 9*(3), 300–347.

Bloch, D. A. (1984). The family as a psychosocial system. *Family Systems Medicine, 2,* 387–396.

Brownell, K. D., Kelman, J. H., & Stunkard, A. J. (1983). Treatment of obese children with and without their mothers: Changes in weight and blood pressure. *Pediatrics, 71,* 515–523.

Burman, B., & Margolin, G. (1992). Analysis of the association between marital relationships and health problems: An interactional perspective. *Psychological Bulletin, 112,* 39–63.

Campbell, L. A., Clark, M., & Kirkpatrick, S. E. (1986). Stress management for parents/children undergoing cardiac catheterization. *American Journal of Orthopsychiatry 56*(2), 234–243.

Campbell, L. A., Kirkpatrick, S. E., Berry, C. C., & Lamberti, J. J. (1995). Preparing children with congenital heart disease for cardiac surgery. *Journal of Pediatric Psychology, 20,* 313–328.

Campbell, T. L. (1986). The family's impact on health: A critical review and annotated bibliography. *Family Systems Medicine, 4,* 135–328.

Campbell, T. L., & Patterson, J. M. (1995). The effectiveness of family interventions in the treatment of physical illness. *Journal of Marital and Family Therapy, 21,* 545–583.

Chiverton, P., & Caine, E. D. (1989). Education to assist spouses in coping with Alzheimer's disease. A controlled trial. *Journal of the American Geriatrics Society, 37,* 593–598.

Cohen, S., & Syme, S. L. E. (1985). *Social support and health.* Orlando, FL: Academic Press.

Coppotelli, H. C., & Orleans, C. T. (1985). Partner support and other determinants of smoking cessation maintenance among women. *Journal of Consulting and Clinical Psychology 53*(4), 455–460.

**Coyne, J. C., & Anderson, B. J. (1989). The "psychosomatic family" reconsidered: II. Recalling a defective model and looking ahead. *Journal of Marital and Family Therapy, 15,* 139–148.

Coyne, J. C., Rohrbaugh, M. J., Shoham, V., Sonnega, J. S., Nicklas, J. M., & Cranford, J. A. (2001). Prognostic importance of marital quality for survival of congestive heart failure. *American Journal of Cardiology, 88,* 526–529.

**Doherty, W. A., & Campbell, T. L. (1988). *Families and health.* Beverly Hills, CA: Sage Press.

Dougherty, G., Schiffrin, A., White, D., Soderstrom, L., & Sufrategui, M. (1999). Home-based management can achieve intensification cost-effectively in type I diabetes. *Pediatrics, 103,* 122–128.

Dracup, K., Meleis, A., Baker, K., & Edlefsen, P. (1984). Family-focused cardiac rehabilitation. A role supplementation program for cardiac patients and spouses. *Nursing Clinics of North America, 19,* 113–124.

Dubbert, P. M., & Wilson, G. T. (1984). Goal-setting and spouse involvement in the treatment of obesity. *Behaviour Research & Therapy 22*(3), 227–242.

Earp, J. A., Ory, M. G., & Strogatz, D. S. (1982). The effects of family involvement and practitioner home visits on the control of hypertension. *American Journal of Public Health, 72,* 1146–1153.

Epstein, L. H., Wing, R. R., Koeske, R., Andrasik, F., & Ossip, D. J. (1981). Child and parent weight loss in family-based behavior modification programs. *Journal of Consulting and Clinical Psychology, 49,* 674–685.

Evans, R. L., Matlock, A. L., Bishop, D. S., Stranahan, S., & Pederson, C. (1988). Family intervention after stroke: Does counseling or education help? *Stroke, 19,* 1243–1249.

Ewart, C. K., Taylor, C. B., Kraemer, H. C., & Agras, W. S. (1984). Reducing blood pressure reactivity during interpersonal conflict: Effects of marital communication training. *Behavior Therapy 15*(5), 473–484.

Ewart, C. K., Taylor, C. B., Kraemer, H. C., & Agras, W. S. (1991). High blood pressure and marital discord: Not being nasty matters more than being nice. *Health Psychology, 10,* 155–163.

Fiore, M. C. (2000). A clinical practice guideline for treating tobacco use and dependence: A US Public Health Service report. *Journal of the American Medical Association, 283*(24), 3250–3254.

Fischmann-Havstad, L., & Marston, A. R. (1984). Weight loss maintenance as an aspect of family emotion and process. *British Journal of Clinical Psychology, 23*(4), 265–271.

Fiske, V., Coyne, J. C., & Smith, D. A. (1991). Couples coping with myocardial infarction: An empirical reconsideration of the role of overprotectiveness. *Journal of Family Psychology, 5*(1), 4–20.

Galatzer, A., Amir, S., Gil, R., Karp, M., & Laron, Z. (1982). Crisis intervention program in newly diagnosed diabetic children. *Diabetes Care, 5,* 414–419.

Gallagher, D., Rose, J., Rivera, P., Lovett, S., & Thompson, L. W. (1989). Prevalence of depression in family caregivers. *Gerontologist, 29,* 449–456.

Gilden, J. L., Hendryx, M., Casia, C., & Singh, S. P. (1989). The effectiveness of diabetes education programs for older patients and their spouses. *Journal of the American Geriatrics Society, 37,* 1023–1030.

Gilliss, C. L., Neuhaus, J. M., & Hauck, W. W. (1990). Improving family functioning after cardiac surgery: A randomized trial. *Heart & Lung, 19,* 648–654.

**Gonzalez, S., Steinglass, P., & Reiss, D. (1989). Putting the illness in its place: Discussion groups for families with chronic medical illnesses. *Family Process, 28,* 69–87.

Goodman, C. C., & Pynoos, J. (1990). A model telephone information and support program for caregivers of Alzheimer's patients. *Gerontologist, 30,* 399–404.

Gottman, J. M. (1994). *What predicts divorce? The relationship between marital processes and marital outcomes.* Hillsdale, NJ: Erlbaum.

Graham, H., Senior, R., Dukes, S., & Lazarus, M. (1993). The introduction of family therapy to British general practice. *Family Systems Medicine, 11*(4), 363–373.

Gustafsson, P. A., Kjellman, N. I., & Cederblad, M. (1986). Family therapy in the treatment of severe childhood asthma. *Journal of Psychosomatic Research, 30,* 369–374.

Haley, W. E., Brown, S. L., & Levine, E. G. (1987). Experimental evaluation of the effectiveness of group intervention for dementia caregivers. *Gerontologist, 27,* 376–382.

Hanson, C. L., Klesges, R. C., Eck, L. H., & Cigrang, J. A. (1990). Family relations, coping styles, stress, and cardiovascular disease risk factors among children and their parents. *Family Systems Medicine* 8(4), 387–400.

Hoekstra-Weebers, J. E., Heuvel, F., Jaspers, J. P., Kamps, W. A., & Klip, E. C. (1998). Brief report: An intervention program for parents of pediatric cancer patients: A randomized controlled trial. *Journal of Pediatric Psychology, 23,* 207–214.

Holmes, T. H., & Rahe, R. H. (1967). The Social Readjustment Rating Scale. *Journal of Psychosomatic Research, 11,* 213–218.

Hooley, J. M. (1985). Expressed emotion—a review of the critical literature. *Clinical Psychology Review, 5,* 119–139.

Hooley, J. M., Orley, J., & Teasdale, J. D. (1986). Levels of expressed emotion and relapse in depressed patients. *British Journal of Psychiatry, 148,* 642–647.

**House, J. S., Landis, K. R., & Umberson, D. (1988). Social relationships and health. *Science, 241,* 540–545.

Jay, S. M., & Elliott, C. H. (1990). A stress inoculation program for parents whose children are undergoing painful medical procedures. *Journal of Consulting and Clinical Psychology, 58,* 799–804.

Kahan, J., Kemp, B., Staples, F. R., & Brummel-Smith, K. (1985). Decreasing the burden in families caring for a relative with a dementing illness. A controlled study. *Journal of the American Geriatrics Society, 33,* 664–670.

Kanter, J., Lamb, H. R., & Loeper, C. (1987). Expressed emotion in families: A critical review. *Hospital & Community Psychiatry, 38,* 374–380.

**Kazak, A. E. (1989). Families of chronically ill children: A systems and social-ecological model of adaptation and challenge. *Journal of Consulting and Clinical Psychology, 57,* 25–30.

Kazak, A. E., Penati, B., Boyer, B. A., Himelstein, B., Brophy, P., Waibel, M. K., et al. (1996). A randomized controlled prospective outcome study of a psychological and pharmacological intervention protocol for procedural distress in pediatric leukemia. *Journal of Pediatric Psychology, 21,* 615–631.

Kiecolt-Glaser, J. K., Fisher, L. D., Ogrocki, P., Stout, J. C., Speicher, C. E., & Glaser, R. (1987). Marital quality, marital disruption, and immune function. *Psychosomatic Medicine, 49,* 13–34.

**Kiecolt-Glaser, J. K., & Newton, T. L. (2001). Marriage and health: His and hers. *Psychological Bulletin, 127,* 472–503.

Kimmel, P. L., Peterson, R. A., Weihs, K. L., Shidler, N., Simmens, S. J., Alleyne, S., et al. (2000). Dyadic relationship conflict, gender, and mortality in urban hemodialysis patients. *Journal of the American Society of Nephrology, 11,* 1518–1525.

Klausner, E. J., Koenigsberg, H. W., Skolnick, N., & Chung, H. (1995). Perceived familial criticism and glucose control in insulin-dependent diabetes mellitus. *International Journal of Mental Health, 24,* 64–75.

Knutsen, S. F., & Knutsen, R. (1991). The Tromso Survey: the Family Intervention study—the effect of intervention on some coronary risk factors and dietary habits, a 6-year follow-up. *Preventive Medicine, 20,* 197–212.

Koenigsberg, H. W., Klausner, E., Pelino, D., & Rosnick, P. (1993). Expressed emotion and glucose control in insulin-dependent diabetes mellitus. *American Journal of Psychiatry, 150,* 1114–1115.

**Law, D. D., & Crane, D. R. (2000). The influence of marital and family therapy on health care utilization in a health-maintenance organization. *Journal of Marital and Family Therapy 26*(3), 281–291.

Liebman, R., Minuchin, S., & Baker, L. (1974). The use of structural family therapy in the treatment of intractable asthma. *American Journal of Psychiatry, 131,* 535–540.

Marriott, A., Donaldson, C., Tarrier, N., & Burns, A. (2000). Effectiveness of cognitive-behavioural family intervention in reducing the burden of care in carers of patients with Alzheimer's disease. *British Journal of Psychiatry, 176,* 557–562.

Martikainen, P., & Valkonen, T. (1996). Mortality after death of spouse in relation to duration of bereavement in Finland. *Journal of Epidemiology & Community Health, 50,* 264–268.

**McDaniel, S. H., Hepworth, J., & Doherty, W. J. (1992). *Medical family therapy.* New York: Basic Books.

McFarlane, W. R., Lukens, E., Link, B., Dushay, R., Deakins, S. A., Newmark, M., et al. (1995). Multiple-family groups and psychoeducation in the treatment of schizophrenia. *Archives of General Psychiatry, 52,* 679–687.

McNabb, W. L., Quinn, M. T., Murphy, D. M., Thorp, F. K., & Cook, S. (1994). Increasing children's responsibility for diabetes self-care: The In Control study. *Diabetes Educator, 20,* 121–124.

Mendenhall, T. J. (2002). *Family-based intervention for persons with diabetes.* Unpublished doctoral dissertation, University of Minnesota, Department of Family Social Science.

Mermelstein, R. (1986). Social support and smoking cessation and maintenance. *Journal of Consulting and Clinical Psychology 54*(4), 442–453.

Mermelstein, R., Lichtenstein, E., & McIntyre, K. (1983). Partner support and relapse in smoking-cessation programs. *Journal of Consulting and Clinical Psychology 51*(3), 465–466.

Minuchin, S., Baker, L., Rosman, B. L., Liebman, R., Milman, L., & Todd, T. C. (1975). A conceptual model of psychosomatic illness in children. Family organization and family therapy. *Archives of General Psychiatry, 32,* 1031–1038.

Minuchin, S., Rosman, B. L., & Baker, L. (1978). *Psychosomatic families: Anorexia nervosa in context.* Cambridge, MA: Harvard University Press.

Mittelman, M. S., Ferris, S. H., Shulman, E., Steinberg, G., & Levin, B. (1996). A family intervention to delay nursing home placement of patients with Alzheimer disease. A randomized controlled trial [see comments]. *Journal of the American Medical Association, 276,* 1725–1731.

Morisky, D. E., Levine, D. M., Green, L. W., Shapiro, S., Russell, R. P., & Smith, C. R. (1983). Five-year blood pressure control and mortality following health education for hypertensive patients. *American Journal of Public Health, 73,* 153–162.

Nader, P. R., Baranowski, T., Vanderpool, N. A., Dunn, K., Dworkin, R., & Ray, L. (1983). The family health project: Cardiovascular risk reduction education for children and parents. *Journal of Developmental & Behavioral Pediatrics, 4,* 3–10.

Orleans, C. T., George, L. K., Houpt, J. L., & Brodie, H. K. (1985). How primary care physicians treat psychiatric disorders: A national survey of family practitioners. *American Journal of Psychiatry, 142,* 52–57.

Orth-Gomer, K., Wamala, S. P., Horsten, M., Schenck-Gustafsson, K., Schneiderman, N., & Mittleman, M. A. (2000). Marital stress worsens prognosis in women with coronary heart disease: The Stockholm Female Coronary Risk Study. *Journal of the American Medical Association, 284,* 3008–3014.

Osterweis, M., Solomon, F., & Green, M. (1984). *Bereavement: Reactions, consequences, and care.* Washington, DC: National Academy Press.

Panton, J., & Barley, E. A. (2002). Family therapy for asthma in children. *Cochrane Database of Systematic Reviews* (Issue 2) [Computer software]. The Cochrane Library.

Park, E. W., Schultz, J. K., Tudiver, F., Campbell, T., & Becker, L. (2002). Enhancing partner support to improve smoking cessation. *Cochrane Database of Systematic Reviews* (Issue 2) [Computer software]. The Cochrane Library.

**Patterson, J. M. (1991). Family resilience to the challenge of a child's disability. *Pediatric Annals, 20,* 491–499.

Patterson, J. M., Budd, J., Goetz, D., & Warwick, W. J. (1993). Family correlates of a 10-year pulmonary health trend in cystic fibrosis. *Pediatrics, 91,* 383–389.

Perry, C. L., Luepker, R. V., Murray, D. M., Hearn, M. D., Halper, A., Dudovitz, B., et al. (1989). Parent involvement with children's health promotion: A one-year follow-up of the Minnesota home team. *Health Education Quarterly, 16,* 171–180.

Schleifer, S. J., Keller, S. E., Bond, R. N., Cohen, J., & Stein, M. (1989). Major depressive disorder and immunity. Role of age, sex, severity, and hospitalization. *Archives of General Psychiatry, 46,* 81–87.

Schleifer, S., Keller, S., Camerino, M., Thornton, J., & Stein, M. (1983). Suppression of lymphocyte stimulation following bereavement. *Journal of the American Medical Association, 250,* 374–377.

Schulz, R., & Beach, S. R. (1999). Caregiving as a risk factor for mortality: The Caregiver Health Effects Study. *Journal of the American Medical Association, 282,* 2215–2219.

Seaburn, D., Gawinski, B., Harp, J., & McDaniel, S. (1993). Family systems therapy in a primary care medical setting: The Rochester experience. *Journal of Marital & Family Therapy, 19,* 177–190.

Seaburn, D. B., Lorenz, A. D., Gunn, W. B. J., & Gawinski, B. A. (1996). *Models of collaboration: A guide for mental health professionals working with health care practitioners.* New York: Basic Books.

Sexton, M., Bross, D., Hebel, J. R., Schumann, B. C., Gerace, T. A., Lasser, N., et al. (1987). Risk-factor changes in wives with husbands at high risk of coronary heart disease (CHD): The spin-off effect. *Journal of Behavioral Medicine, 10,* 251–261.

Sorensen, S., Pinquart, M., & Duberstein, P. (2002). How effective are interventions with caregivers? An updated meta-analysis. *Gerontologist, 43,* 356–372.

Streja, D. A., Boyko, E., & Rabkin, S. W. (1982). Predictors of outcome in a risk factor intervention trial using behavior modification. *Preventive Medicine, 11,* 291–303.

Taylor, C. B., Bandura, A., Ewart, C. K., Miller, N. H., & DeBusk, R. F. (1985). Exercise testing to enhance wives' confidence in their husbands' cardiac capability soon after clinically uncomplicated acute myocardial infarction. *American Journal of Cardiology, 55,* 635–638.

Thompson, D. R., & Meddis, R. (1990). Wives' responses to counselling early after myocardial infarction. *Journal of Psychosomatic Research, 34,* 249–258.

Toseland, R. W., Labrecque, M. S., Goebel, S. T., & Whitney, M. H. (1992). An evaluation of a group program for spouses of frail elderly veterans. *Gerontologist, 32,* 382–390.

Toseland, R. W., McCallion, P., Smith, T., Huck, S., Bourgeois, P., & Garstka, T. A. (2001). Health education groups for caregivers in an HMO. *Journal of Clinical Psychology, 57,* 551–570.

Trevino, D. B., Young, E. H., Groff, J., & Jono, R. T. (1990). The association between marital adjustment and compliance with antihypertension regimens. *Journal of the American Board of Family Practice, 3,* 17–25.

Venters, M. H., Jacobs, D. R., Jr., Luepker, R. V., Maiman, L. A., & Gillum, R. F. (1984). Spouse concordance of smoking patterns: The Minnesota Heart Survey. *American Journal of Epidemiology, 120,* 608–616.

Waxman, M., & Stunkard, A. J. (1980). Caloric intake and expenditure of obese boys. *Journal of Pediatrics, 96,* 187–193.

Weihs, K. L., Enright, T. M., Simmens, S. J., & Reiss, D. (2000). Negative affectivity, restriction of emotions, and site of metastases predict mortality in recurrent breast cancer. *Journal of Psychosomatic Research, 49,* 59–68.

**Weihs, K., Fisher, L., & Baird, M. A. (2002). Families, health and behavior. *Families, Systems & Health 20*(1), 7–46.

Wing, R. R., Marcus, M. D., Epstein, L. H., & Jawad, A. (1991). A "family-based" approach to the treatment of obese type II diabetic patients. *Journal of Consulting and Clinical Psychology, 59,* 156–162.

**Wood, B., Watkins, J. B., Boyle, J. T., Nogueira, J., Zimand, E., & Carroll, L. (1989). The "psychosomatic family" model: An empirical and theoretical analysis. *Family Process, 28,* 399–417.

World Health Organization. (1976). *Statistical indices of family health* (Rep. No. 589). New York: Author.

Chapter 12 *Meta-Analysis of MFT Interventions*

William R. Shadish, Ph.D., Department of Psychology,
The University of Memphis, Memphis Tennessee.

Scott A. Baldwin, B.S., Department of Psychology,
The University of Memphis, Memphis Tennessee.

M oses Herzog, the fictional academic whose moniker is the title for Saul Bellow's (1964) novel, once said "What this country needs is a good five-cent synthesis" (p. 207). Well, we are pleased to report that we are halfway toward that goal. In meta-analysis, we do indeed have a good methodology for the synthesis of scientific results. Unfortunately, as we will see later in this chapter, doing meta-analysis nowadays costs a lot more than just five cents.

The development and widespread use of meta-analysis is significant to both researcher and clinician in marriage and family interventions. Researchers benefit from a statistical tool that can be used to summarize the increasingly large research literature on such interventions, and which points to gaps in the literature that future research should address. Clinicians benefit in three ways: first in getting evidence they can show to third-party payers that the work they do is effective, second in having a practical way to inform themselves about the effectiveness and efficacy of marriage and family interventions, and third in a host of specific conclusions that may help them in choosing treatments proven to be effective for different problems. These uses resemble the movement in medicine and public health toward evidence-based medicine, a good model from which to view the meta-analytic literature.

This chapter has the following structure. First, we provide a brief history of meta-analysis, and summarize the key statistical feature of meta-analysis—the effect size. The latter material can be skipped by those with little interest in the methodology of meta-analysis. Second, we describe 20 meta-analyses that have already been done on the effects of both therapy and enrichment interventions with couples and families. In this second section, we summarize the overall results of these 20 meta-analyses, and then present more detailed discussions of the effects of different kinds of marriage and family interventions, the effects of marriage and family interventions compared to other kinds of intervention such as individual therapy, the clinical significance of these effects, the clinical representativeness of this research, and some intriguing findings about variables that may influence how effective marriage and family interventions may be. Also in this second section, we present the idea of Meta-Analytically Supported Treatments (MASTs); that is, treatments that have been shown to be effective in meta-analytic work. Third, we review methodological problems in this research, and offer a set of suggestions for improving future meta-analyses in this area.

Fourth, we present evidence about the costs of meta-analytic research, and review possible funding sources.

Meta-Analysis

A Brief History of Meta-Analysis

If you have been around long enough as a researcher, you have seen many innovations occur. Some of those innovations are passing fads, some are interim developments until something better comes along, and some become a minor but permanent feature of the scientific landscape. Occasionally, however, an innovation changes the very landscape of the field. Meta-analysis is the latter kind of innovation. Meta-analysis has become a nearly essential element in reviewing literatures on treatment effectiveness. By the 1990s, at least 1,000 meta-analyses had been done, and today the number is so large that there is no authoritative count.

Meta-analysis first came into the scientific community's spotlight with Smith and Glass's (1977) review of the effects of psychotherapy. Smith and Glass reported the results of a massive quantitative summary of 375 studies of psychotherapy effectiveness (later expanded to 475 studies; Smith, Glass, & Miller, 1980). The studies were conducted over many years, over different geographic areas with diverse clients, using different types of therapies and outcome measures. Over all this variability, clients receiving psychotherapy had better outcomes than control clients who received no treatment. Therapy outcomes were similar whether the therapies were behavioral or nonbehavioral, over varying levels of therapist experience, and over both brief and long-term therapy. With a few exceptions, the effects of therapy generalized over great heterogeneity in many moderators across these studies.

Today, 25 years later, we are aware of more than 140 meta-analyses in the field of psychotherapy alone.[1] The questions asked in these reviews range from very broad inquiries into the effects of psychotherapy in general (Smith & Glass, 1977), to very narrow examinations like Shoham-Salomon and Rosenthal's (1987) meta-analysis of the effects of including paradoxical interventions in psychotherapy. Among all the many psychotherapy meta-analyses, a number address aspects of marriage and family interventions, both with distressed and nondistressed populations. This latter set of meta-analyses is the topic of this chapter. Therefore, although this chapter is in some respects an update of the Shadish, Ragsdale, Glaser, and Montgomery (1995) article on marriage and family meta-analysis, it differs from that article in one important way. Shadish et al. (1995) described the results of a single meta-analysis, but the present chapter reviews results from many meta-analyses. In that sense, this chapter is not a meta-analysis, but a "meta-meta-analysis," attempting to provide both quantitative and qualitative summaries of what we have learned from the many meta-analyses reported herein.

What Is Meta-Analysis?

Meta-analysis is the use of quantitative techniques to summarize the results of scientific studies on the same question. This practice has a long history. In the early 18th century, the English mathematician Roger Cotes computed weighted averages of measurements made by different astronomers. In 1904, Sir Karl Pearson used quantitative methods to average results from six studies of the effects of a newly developed inoculation against typhoid (Shadish & Haddock, 1994; see also Cooper & Hedges, 1994; Dickerson, Higgins, & Meinert, 1990; and Hunter & Schmidt, 1990, for other historical examples). However, widespread adoption of such methods did not occur until Glass (1976) coined the term meta-analysis to describe quantitative techniques for cumulating results over studies.

Glass (1976) distinguished between primary, secondary, and meta-analysis, with these three phrases intended to differentiate between three different types of statistical analyses. According to Glass, primary analysis is "the original analysis of data in a research study" (p. 3). Secondary analysis is "the re-analysis of data for the purposes of answering the original research question with better statistical techniques, or answering new questions with old data" (p. 3). Meta-analysis is "the statistical analysis of a large collection of analysis results from individual studies for the purpose of integrating the findings" (p. 3).

The essential innovation in meta-analysis was the use of an effect size as a common metric over studies to measure how large is the effect of a treatment. A common metric is needed because different studies rarely use identical outcome measures, even if they address similar questions and invoke similar outcome constructs. Thus, one study of psychotherapy for depression might have used the Beck Depression Inventory while another used the Minnesota Multiphasic Personality Inventory (MMPI) Depression Scale. These measures have different metrics with different means and standard deviations, so averaging scores without converting them into a common metric would yield nonsensical results. Meta-analysis converts each study's outcomes to a common effect size metric, so that different outcomes have the same means and standard deviations and can be more readily averaged across studies.

Many different effect size measures are possible (Fleiss, 1994; Rosenthal, 1994). The two most appropriate effect size measures for meta-analyses of experiments are the standardized mean difference statistic (d) for continuous outcomes (Smith et al., 1980, Appendix 7; Shadish, Robinson, & Lu, 1999), and the odds ratio (o) for dichotomous outcomes (Haddock, Rindskopf, & Shadish, 1998). In the social sciences, d is the most common, and when both continuous measures (e.g., the Dyadic Adjustment Scale) and dichotomous measures (marriage or divorce at the end of therapy) were used as outcomes, the odds ratio is typically converted into d so that all results are in the same effect size metric. Cohen (1988) suggested that $d = .20$ is a small effect, $d = .50$ is a medium effect, and $d = .80$ is a large effect, norms that seem to match empirical observations of the prevalence of effects fairly well (Lipsey & Wilson, 1993).

A common concern of those who first encounter meta-analysis is the risks of combining diverse measures. After all, simply converting diverse measures into a common metric does not mean that it makes sense conceptually to combine them. To pick an extreme example, suppose an experiment measures family therapy outcome as the number of fights a couple has in a week and also as the child's grade point average. Does it make sense to combine these outcomes, especially if they are likely to be uncorrelated? This question is worth chapter length treatment itself, but here are some brief observations. First, it makes no difference whether the measures are correlated. Meta-analysis is not scale development in which items are expected to measure the same thing, and it is an empirical question whether the effects of therapy on both measures are similar despite their apparent conceptual differences. Second, meta-analysis has methods for testing whether it makes sense to combine effect sizes (e.g., heterogeneity tests), and recommended procedures for combining measures that violate these tests (e.g., random effects models). Third, the meta-analyst can always separate effect sizes into categories (e.g., self-report versus observational measures) to test whether results are significantly different over categories; if they are not different, combining them may still make sense. Fourth, it is nearly always possible to construct higher order constructs to account for diverse measures. Although the highest order constructs, such as "mental health" or even "family therapy outcome" may be quite broadly defined, they still unite the vast majority of measures included in outcome research. In the end, then, meta-analysts tend to treat this as an empirical question, combining results until critics can point to solid statistical or conceptual reasons why it should not be done.

Effectiveness/Efficacy for Marriage and Family Interventions: Meta-Analytic Findings

We searched for meta-analyses of the effects of marriage and family interventions through *PsychINFO* and *Dissertation Abstracts International,* by reviewing the reference sections of previous reviews on these topics, and by doing issue-by-issue hand searches of recent issues of journals that commonly publish such reviews (e.g., *Journal of Consulting and Clinical Psychology, Journal of Marital and Family Therapy*, and *Behavior Therapy*). Table 1 lists the $N = 20$ meta-analyses on the effects of marriage and family interventions that this search found. These meta-analyses are listed in the reference section with an asterisk (*) preceding them. These meta-analyses have been appearing about once a year for the last 15 years. Two meta-analyses are reported in both dissertation and publication form (Dunn, 1994; Dunn & Schwebel, 1995; Giblin, 1985, 1986; Giblin, Sprenkle, & Sheehan, 1985); we combine these two forms because both the dissertation and the publication presented the same information. One meta-analysis (Butler & Wampler, 1999) incorporates all the data from a previous meta-analysis by the same author (Wampler, 1982), so these two reports are counted as one

Table 1
Meta-Analyses of the Effects of Marriage and Family Interventions

Authors	Topic	Number of Studies
1. Butler & Wampler, 1999 (see also Wampler, 1982)	Couple Communication Enrichment	16
2. Cedar & Levant, 1990	Parent Effectiveness Training	26
3. Dunn & Schwebel, 1995 (see also Dunn, 1994)	Marital Therapy (Behavioral Marital Therapy, Cognitive Behavioral Marital Therapy, Insight Oriented Marital Therapy)	15
4. Dutcher, 2000	Marital Therapy (Behavioral Marital Therapy, Cognitive Behavioral Marital Therapy, Insight Oriented Marital Therapy)	17
5. Edwards & Steinglass, 1995	Family Therapy for Alcoholism	21
6. Giblin, 1985 (see also Giblin et al., 1985; Giblin 1986)	Premarital, Marital, and Family Enrichment	85
7. Hahlweg & Markman, 1988	Behavioral Marital Therapy, Behavioral Premarital Intervention	17 / 7
8. Hazelrigg et al., 1987	Family Therapy	20
9. Hight, 2000	Couple Enrichment	111
10. Johnson et al., 1999	Emotionally Focused Couples Therapy	4
11. Mari & Streiner, 1994	Family Therapy for Schizophrenia	6
12. Markus et al., 1990[a]	Family Therapy	19
13. Montgomery, 1991[b]	Family Therapy for Child Identified Problems	47
14. Pitschel-Walz et al., 2001	Family Therapy for Schizophrenia / Family Interventions vs. Other Interventions / Family Interventions vs. Usual Care	25
15. Plattor, 1991	Marital Therapy	25
16. Shadish et al., 1993 (see also Shadish, 1992)	Marital and Family Therapy / Treatment-Control Comparisons / Treatment-Treatment Comparisons	163
17. Stanton & Shadish, 1997	Family Therapy for Drug Abuse	15
18. Sweeney, 1991[b]	Marital and Family Therapy	163
19. Wilson, 1989[b]	Marital Therapy	62
20. Wilson, 1994	Marital and Family Therapy vs. Individual Therapy	44

[a] Some details of the methods used in this meta-analysis are only available in an unpublished foreign language manuscript that was unavailable to us (Markus, 1988).

[b] Montgomery (1991), Sweeney (1991), and Wilson (1989) report meta-analyses of a subset of the Shadish et al. (1993) meta-analysis.

meta-analysis. Three more meta-analyses (Montgomery, 1991; Sweeney, 1991; Wilson, 1989) examined subsets of studies in a larger meta-analysis (Shadish et al., 1993); we report these as four separate meta-analyses since they provide mostly different meta-analytic information.

Table 2 summarizes some general characteristics of these 20 meta-analyses. A number of features of these two tables are worth comment. First, meta-analyses are increasingly popular as graduate student theses and dissertations. More than a third of the meta-analyses we located were student theses and dissertations, most of which never made it into print (Dutcher, 2000; Hight, 2000; Montgomery, 1991; Plattor, 1991; Sweeney, 1991; Wilson, 1989, 1994). So if one wishes to locate all meta-analyses on a topic, clearly one must search for

Table 2 Characteristics of 20 Meta-Analyses of the Effects of Marriage and Family Interventions	
Characteristic	**Number of Meta-Analyses**
Publication Status of Meta-Analysis	
Published Journal Article	11
Unpublished Thesis or Dissertation	7
Both Published and Unpublished Forms	2
Therapy vs Enrichment[a]	
Therapy	17
Enrichment	4
Substantive Focus	
Both Marriage and Family	5
General Marriage and Family Therapy ($n = 3$)	
Marriage and Family Therapy for Drug Abuse ($n = 1$)	
Marriage and Family Enrichment ($n = 1$)	
Marriage Only	8
General Marriage Therapy ($n = 4$)	
Behavioral Marital Therapy ($n = 1$)	
Emotionally Focused Therapy ($n = 1$)	
Marriage Enrichment ($n = 2$)	
Family Only	8
General Family Therapy ($n = 2$)	
Family Therapy for Alcoholism ($n = 1$)	
Family Therapy for Child Presenting Problems ($n = 1$)	
Family Therapy for Schizophrenia ($n = 2$)	
Parent Effectiveness Training ($n = 1$)	
Family Enrichment ($n = 1$)	

[a] Hahlweg and Markman (1988) included both therapy and enrichment studies, and so is included in both categories.

unpublished work. Second, while most of the meta-analyses pertained to therapy for distressed couples, we located four meta-analyses about marital or family enrichment interventions (Butler & Wampler, 1999; Giblin, 1985; Hahlweg & Markman, 1988; Hight, 2000). The concepts of therapy and enrichment seem distinct, but in practice the two concepts sometimes overlap. One enrichment meta-analysis noted, for example, that "studies of clinic couples or families were included when the thrust was greater than symptom removal and processes of enrichment were employed" (Giblin et al., 1985, p. 259). Third, the 20 meta-analyses are spread evenly over both marriage and family therapy taken separately; and a number of more specific meta-analyses have examined the effects of marriage and family therapies on such problems as drug abuse, alcoholism, child problems, and schizophrenia. Fourth, most of the meta-analyses are fairly small, including less than 30 primary studies; but some are quite large, with the largest (Shadish et al., 1993) locating 163 randomized experiments on the topic. Clearly, then, the literature on marriage and family interventions is quite large, probably numbering several hundred experiments by now.

So what have we learned about the effects of marriage and family interventions from these meta-analyses? Frankly, it is very difficult to summarize all these varied meta-analytic results. Results are rarely comparable from meta-analysis to meta-analysis given variations in (a) the questions asked, (b) which primary studies are included and which are excluded, (c) how the same construct is differentially operationalized in different meta-analyses, (d) how effect sizes are computed, (e) how effect sizes are weighted prior to being combined, (f) the kinds of analyses that are then done, and (g) how all these results are reported. Nonetheless, despite all the many good reasons that argue against trying to summarize these very disparate results, we do exactly that in the sections that follow.

Marriage and Family Interventions Versus Controls
Figures 1 and 2 summarize results for those meta-analyses that compared marriage and family interventions to a no treatment or waitlist control. In both figures, error bars approximate 95% confidence intervals;[2] and drop bars indicate the difference between posttest and follow-up effect sizes, with drop bars in black indicating decreases at posttest and drop bars in white indicating increases at posttest (we could not estimate follow-up effects for some meta-analyses). For example, the Cedar and Levant (1990) meta-analysis is depicted first in Figure 1, on the left side of the figure. That meta-analysis reported a mean posttest effect size of $\bar{d} = .35$, marked by a diamond in Figure 1, and a followup effect size of $\bar{d} = .24$, marked by a square, with a black drop bar going from the diamond to the square to indicate the size of the decrease. Surrounding the posttest effect size of $\bar{d} = .35$ is the error bar for this effect (depicted as a vertical line that has horizontal lines at each end). The error bar marks the 95% confidence interval for the Cedar and Levant effect size. That interval is $.036 \leq \delta \leq .664$, meaning we are 95% confident that the true effect lies in that interval. Since the confidence inter-

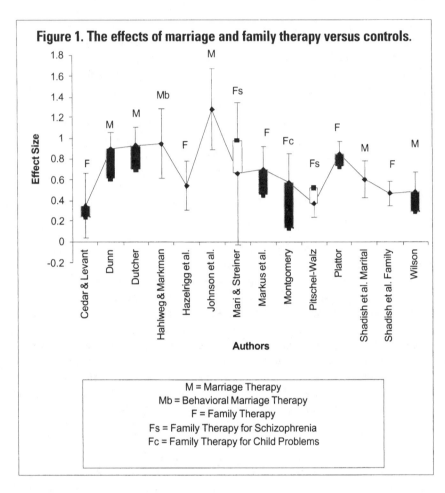

Figure 1. The effects of marriage and family therapy versus controls.

M = Marriage Therapy
Mb = Behavioral Marriage Therapy
F = Family Therapy
Fs = Family Therapy for Schizophrenia
Fc = Family Therapy for Child Problems

val does not include zero, the posttest effect size of $d = .35$ is significantly differ-ent from zero at the $\alpha = .05$ level.

Both figures suggest that marriage and family interventions are effective. Figure 1 shows the results for marriage and family therapy. Note several features of that figure. First, the 95% confidence intervals indicated by the error bars exclude $d = 0$ in all but one case (Mari & Streiner, 1994), suggesting that the effects of marriage and family therapy differ significantly from zero. Second, the drop bars show that effects at follow-up are generally smaller than those at posttest, though the difference between posttest and follow-up effects are rela-tively small. The simple average of the 12 meta-analyses yields $d = .65$ at posttest and $d = .52$ at follow-up. The only two drop bars that show an increase in effects from posttest to follow-up are for family therapy with schizophrenia. Third, note that the average effects for marriage therapy ($d = .84$) tend to be higher than the

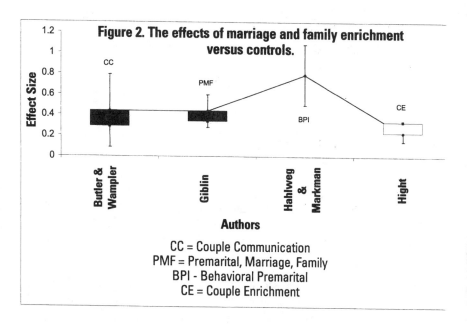

Figure 2. The effects of marriage and family enrichment versus controls.

CC = Couple Communication
PMF = Premarital, Marriage, Family
BPI - Behavioral Premarital
CE = Couple Enrichment

effects for family therapy ($d = .58$). This has been a very persistent finding in the meta-analytic literature, and some evidence suggest that this difference is due to the fact that family therapy is typically applied to less tractable problems than is marriage therapy. In those rare cases in which marriage therapy and family therapy were applied to similar problems, their effects were about the same (Shadish et al., 1993).

The results for marriage and family enrichment are similar (Figure 2), although the effects of these interventions are a bit smaller than for marriage and family therapy, with $d = .48$ at posttest and $d = .32$ at follow-up. Perhaps most noteworthy in Figure 2 is the high effect for behavioral premarital intervention, mirroring Figure 1's finding that the highest average effect size came from behavioral marriage therapy. This invokes, of course, the long-standing debate in psychotherapy meta-analysis about whether behavioral interventions tend to produce larger effects than do other interventions. We will return to this question at the end of this chapter. On the one hand, it is clear that much behavior therapy research is conducted with methods that tend to yield larger effects, especially the use of behavioral dependent measures that systematically yield larger effects. On the other hand, the finding of behavioral superiority has emerged with some consistency across many psychotherapy literatures, and it occasionally withstands efforts to adjust away that superiority with regression models that take such differential methods into account (e.g., Shadish, Matt, Navarro, & Phillips, 2000). So this finding is worth more study.

To put these effect sizes into better perspective, Table 3 shows how they

Table 3
The Effects of Various Social, Educational, and Medical Treatments

Topic	Effect Size *d*
Electroconvulsive Therapy for Depression	.80
Coronary Bypass Surgery for Angina	.80
Marriage and Family Therapy	.65
Marriage and Family Enrichment	.48
AZT for AIDS Mortality	.47
Dipyridamole Medication for Angina	.39
Neuroleptic Drugs for Dementia	.37
Anticoagulant Therapy for Thromboembolism	.30
Aortocoronary Bypass Surgery on Mortality	.15
Intravenous Streptokinase for Myocardial Infarction Mortality	.08

compare to effect sizes from meta-analyses of the effects of various other social, educational, and medical treatments (these examples are drawn from Lipsey & Wilson, 1993). Effect sizes in that table range from a high of $d = .80$ for the effects of electroconvulsive therapy for depression to a low of $d = .08$ for the effects of intravenous streptokinase to prevent mortality after a myocardial infarction. Of course, the interventions and outcomes in Table 3 are not strictly comparable to the family and marriage interventions and outcomes summarized in this chapter; but Table 3 does give a sense of the range of effect sizes found in a range of interventions, against which the effect sizes for marriage and family interventions fare reasonably well.

Direct Comparisons of Different Kinds of Family and Marriage Interventions
     Studies that directly compare two or more different kinds of marriage and family interventions provide particularly compelling evidence about the relative effectiveness of those therapies. Four meta-analyses did these kinds of comparisons, and on the whole, any such differences were small and usually nonsignificant. Butler and Wampler (1999) found that the Couple Communication program performed about the same as similar programs. Pitschel-Walz, Leucht, Bauml, Kissling, and Engel's (2001) review of family therapy for schizophrenia did find some differences among family therapies, including "studies testing brief interventions, which made in general a poorer showing, and studies testing the multifamily format, which seems to be more successful in the long-run than the single-family format" (p. 83). Shadish et al. (1993) found few differences among different theoretical orientations to marriage and family interventions, and those differences disappeared once other covariates were controlled. Wilson (1989) found no significant differences among different kinds of marriage therapies.

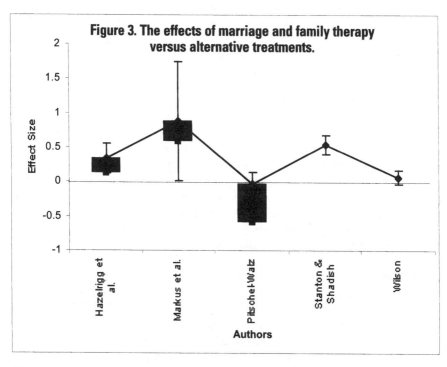

Figure 3. The effects of marriage and family therapy versus alternative treatments.

Family and Marriage Interventions Versus Alternative Treatments

How well do marriage and family interventions fare against alternative treatments? Figure 3, which includes both therapy and enrichment interventions, shows that at posttest they perform at least as well as, and sometimes better than, alternatives that include individual psychotherapy, placement in halfway houses, problem solving training, bibliotherapy, hospitalization, peer counseling, or group therapy. However, these effect sizes are quite small, tend to get even smaller at follow-up, and are usually nonsignificant.

Meta-Analytically Supported Treatments (MASTs)

In recent years, many therapists and researchers have discussed what has come to be known as empirically supported treatments (ESTs). These are clearly specified therapies (i.e., with a treatment manual or equivalent) that are efficacious in controlled research with a well-delineated population (Chambless & Hollon, 1998). The accumulated literature now includes many ESTs, and the associated research has contributed much to our understanding of effective treatments and good outcome research. In addition, ESTs are a valuable resource to the practitioner who has a client with a presenting problem, and is searching for a treatment that is shown to be effective in treating it. This specificity of ESTs is laudable, and to be encouraged.

However, ESTs have a number of problems. First is a problem of construct validity, that the label does not well represent what was actually done in ESTs. What makes ESTs uniquely identifiable is not being empirically supported—a trait they have in common with many therapies that are not ESTs—but rather having clearly specified manuals and clearly delineated populations. A label that more accurately reflects the operations unique to these treatments might be "effective, manualized, population-specific treatments" (EMPS). In addition, the EST label implies boundaries outside of which treatments are not empirically supported, even though meta-analytic reviews of psychotherapy suggest great empirical support for a huge array of therapies that are not on the official EST list.

A second problem is related to the first: that the EST literature misleadingly fosters the impression that other treatments have not been evaluated scientifically. For example, the EST Web site on borderline personality disorders includes a typical statement about ESTs: "While other psychotherapies may be helpful for treatment of borderline personality disorder, they have not been evaluated scientifically in the same way as the treatment listed here."[3] How many people, especially in the target audience of potential psychotherapists or their clients, will understand the subtle nuances of the last few words of that statement: "in the same way as the treatment listed here"? How many will presume that other treatments simply have not been evaluated scientifically in a credible way, despite the fact that 25 years of accumulated meta-analytic research shows that a huge number of psychotherapies have been scientifically evaluated as effective?

Third, an undue focus on ESTs obscures the fact that both practice and policy value effective treatments even if the studies do not utilize treatment manuals or the like. Examples include the Cochrane Collaboration's[4] meta-analytic summaries of the effects of medical and public health interventions, various summaries by the U.S. Department of Education that identify best practices in education, and the various Evidence-Based Practice Centers funded by the U.S. Government to do meta-analytic summaries of effective medical treatments. None of these require the treatment or population specificity of ESTs, yet all have had great impact on both policy and practice.

A fourth problem with the EST literature is statistical power. Any given study may fail to show statistically significant results by, for example, having too few participants or less reliable measures. Current incarnations of EST criteria require two studies of a proposed EST with statistically significant results. Many proposed ESTs fail this criterion not because they lack two studies, but because results were not statistically significant. Yet a meta-analytic summary of two studies may yield an effect size that is significantly different from zero even when each study by itself is nonsignificant. EST methodology could and should shift from an emphasis on significance testing to use of effect sizes and confidence intervals, a shift that would be consistent with other trends in statistics (Wilkinson & the Task Force on Statistical Inference, 1999).

To provide a complement to empirically supported treatments, therefore, we

propose the concept of *meta-analytically supported treatments*, or MASTs. MASTs have four characteristics: (a) effect sizes from more than one study of the treatment construct have been combined meta-analytically, (b) all of the studies contributing to that synthesis are randomized trials comparing the treatment to a control group, (c) the meta-analysis reported an effect size and significance test showing that the treatment produced pooled meta-analytic effects that are significantly larger than expected by chance, and (d) the meta-analysis used sound meta-analytic statistical methods such as aggregating effect sizes to the study level. Table 4 presents a preliminary list of the treatments that qualify as MASTs according to these criteria among the 20 meta-analyses of the effects of marriage and family interventions. The list contains 24 MASTs, including broad treatment constructs such as family therapy in general, and more narrow treatment constructs such as behavioral family therapy for child identified problems.

Not surprisingly, this list of MASTs and the list of ESTs that appears on the American Psychological Association Division 12 Web site[5] overlap in some cases, including family therapy for schizophrenia, family therapy for child conduct disorders, and behavioral marital therapy for marital distress. On the other hand, some MASTs are not on the EST list. For example, on the EST site for drug and alcohol abuse,[6] family therapy is not mentioned as an effective treatment; and the EST site for marital distress[7] omits systemic and eclectic marital therapies, both of which have clear empirical support in meta-analytic research.

We do not mean to minimize the importance of the two key operational differences between MASTs and ESTs; namely, that ESTs are described in written treatment manuals and use clients who have clearly delineated problems. These two differences allow therapists to make particular treatment recommendations to particular types of clients. On the other hand, such specificity can be misleading. Rosen and Davison (in press) pointed out that there are certain empirically supported principles, such as the use of exposure in the treatment of phobias, that are so well-established and superior to other treatment principles that to not use them might be unethical no matter whether they are represented on the list of ESTs. Meta-analysis would be an ideal methodology for demonstrating the effectiveness of such principles, because by its very nature meta-analysis reaches conclusions about principles that are presumed to be common to diverse treatment operations. Moreover, the specificity of ESTs tends to hide the empirical finding in meta-analysis that the effects of psychotherapy tend to generalize robustly across variations in presenting problem, over whether or not manuals are used, and indeed, over a very large number of other potential moderators.

We do not mean that practitioners can use any therapy with any problem. To the contrary, when ESTs or other demonstrably effective treatments or principles are available to treat a specific problem, there is much to be said for using them. But lacking such specific information, it is still sensible and ethical to refer clients to therapies that seem to work in general. After all, although the general prescription to do marital or family interventions is far less specific than an EST manual, it still points to a set of practices that are well differentiated from other interventions such as individual psychotherapy, consulting with clergy, or vacationing in the Florida Keys. The construct of marriage and family therapy also appeals to a set of practices in which clinicians have experience or training, or can locate further sources of training such as books and workshops.

In view of these points, practicing clinicians might use ESTs and MASTs in the following complementary way. When a practitioner has a client with a particular problem, they might choose an EST if one exists to treat that problem and if it seems contextually appropriate. If no EST for that problem has been approved, the clinician might review lists of MASTs for therapies that have been shown effective with that problem, or as a last resort, for MASTs that have general support even if not for that specific problem.

We suspect that meta-analytic searches for further ESTs and MASTs would prove fruitful in two respects. One is that meta-analysts could routinely code studies for EST characteristics but combine them meta-analytically rather than relying on the individual significance tests reported in single studies. This should increase the number of ESTs available to clinical practice. The second would be to search for treatments that are shown to affect the outcome at issue in a particular presenting problem. For example, a MAST might exist that reduces childhood depression, even though the clients in the studies might not meet the criteria for depression that ESTs require. If so, it would be reasonable to use that MAST for the depressed child in lieu of the absent EST.

Table 4 is just a first effort at identifying MASTs, and then just for family and marriage interventions. For example, we would like to recode the studies contributing to MASTs from scratch rather than relying on coding done by other researchers, to make sure the codes are accurate and the effect sizes were computed correctly. Even so, this list of MASTs makes the general point that marriage and family interventions are empirically supported treatments, even if they are not always on someone's list with that name.

Clinical Significance
A criticism of meta-analysis has been that effect sizes do not convey much information about clinical significance. A number of translations of effect size into other metrics have partially assessed this, such as comparing effect sizes to Cohen's norms of small, medium, or large effect sizes (Butler & Wampler, 1999; Markus, Lange, & Pettigrew, 1990), using Rosenthal and Rubin's (1982) binomial effect size display to convert effect sizes into a fourfold table that estimates the percent of successes and failures in both treatment and comparison groups (Pitschel-Walz et al., 2001), and conversions of effect sizes back into the metrics of original scales like the Beck Depression Inventory. However, three meta-analyses used more interesting methods to examine clinical significance.

One approach is illustrated by Edwards and Steinglass (1995), who examined the clinical significance of the effects of family therapy on alcoholism. Their

354 *Effectiveness Research in Marriage and Family Therapy*

approach took advantage of the fact that these studies report the same outcome measure: abstinence rates among alcoholics. Spontaneous abstinence rates are less than 5% among untreated alcoholics, so Edwards and Steinglass set 50% abstinence as a clinically significant effect for family therapy with alcoholics. By this criterion, 83% of the family or marriage therapy interventions yielded clinically significant results, compared to 50% of the nonfamily therapy treatment alternatives.

Hahlweg and Markman (1988) built on the fact that the Marital Adjustment Scale (MAS) or the Dyadic Adjustment Scale (DAS) are commonly used in many outcome studies of marital therapy. Scale norms suggest that a score of 100 on the MAS and a score of 97 on the DAS are considered indicative of good marital adjustment. Therefore, Hahlweg and Markman computed effect sizes by substituting those norms in the d statistic, so that a clinically significant effect size would then be $d > 0$. For nine studies that provided enough data to do this calculation, $d = 0.15$ ($SD = .41$). That is, the average treatment group mean achieved an MAS or DAS score that was higher than the norms for good marital adjustment, although clearly many clients were still distressed. If we translate this into percent success using Rosenthal and Rubin's (1982) binomial effect size display, we find that this translates into a clinically significant success rate of 54%.

Shadish et al. (1993) used a third method. Their database contained 19 studies that reported treatment and control group means on the MAS or the DAS at both pretest and posttest. They then computed the percent of studies that moved groups from pretest means below the norms for good marital adjustment to posttest means above those norms. Shadish et al. found that none of the control groups produced clinically significant results by this criterion, compared to 41% of the treatment groups. The latter figure is comparable to the 35.5% clinical significance rate reported by Jacobson et al. (1984) in their original study.

In all, then, marriage and family therapies produce clinically significant improvements in distressed clients, with success rates of 40 to 50%. Further, these three methodologies can be used in any literature in which the same outcome measure is used across many of the studies in the meta-analysis, and where that scale either has a cutoff for clinical significance or such a cutoff can be plausibly suggested. Further development of such methodologies would be a very welcomed advance in meta-analytic work.

Clinical Representativeness
Recent reviews of the psychotherapy outcome research literature show that most studies have been done in ways that do not well represent the conditions of actual clinic practice (e.g., Shadish et al., 2000; Weisz, Donenberg, Han, & Weiss, 1995; Weisz, Weiss, & Donenberg, 1992); for example, using clients referred through usual routes and experienced therapists in actual clinic settings. The issue is important because some meta-analyses in child psychotherapy suggest that such therapy is completely ineffective in clinically representative con-

ditions. Further, in part appealing to the efficacy-effectiveness distinction from public health, federal agencies have become more interested in funding research that is conducted under clinically representative conditions in order to understand whether therapy that is efficacious under ideal conditions is also effective under conditions of actual practice.

None of the marriage and family therapy meta-analyses have directly attended to this issue. Some have investigated individual moderators that would be part of clinical representativeness; for example, comparing therapy in university versus nonuniversity settings (Montgomery, 1991; Stanton & Shadish, 1997; Wilson, 1989), therapy that is manualized or not (Montgomery, 1991; Shadish et al., 1993; Stanton & Shadish, 1997; Wilson, 1989), referral source of clients (Hahlweg & Markman, 1988; Wilson, 1989), or using community-based therapists (Stanton & Shadish, 1997). But the question of whether marriage and family therapy works in clinically representativeness conditions can only be answered by finding studies that combine all these clinically representative characteristics in one study. Future marriage and family meta-analyses would be better if they incorporated codes about clinical representativeness from previous meta-analyses in other areas of psychotherapy (e.g., useful codes for this can be found in Shadish et al., 2000, Appendix 1).

Moderators of Treatment Effects

Historically, meta-analysis has tended to focus on main effects, on whether or not a treatment works. Meta-analysis has been less helpful in answering the famous question posited by Gordon Paul (1967): "What treatment, by whom, is most effective for this individual with that specific problem, and under which set of circumstances?" (p. 111). This is a hard enough question to answer in primary studies. Answering this question with meta-analysis requires examining moderators of treatment effects; that is, those variables that interact with treatment by varying the size or direction of that effect.

In general, meta-analysts have not studied moderators extensively. A graduate student in our laboratory at The University of Memphis has looked at this issue for 52 psychotherapy meta-analyses (Phillips, 1998; Phillips & Shadish, 2002). He found that the modal number of moderators examined in psychotherapy meta-analyses is one, and the median is five. For the 20 marriage and family meta-analyses that we reviewed in the present case, the situation is similar, with most meta-analyses examining fewer than five potential moderators of therapy effectiveness. It turns out to be surprisingly difficult to summarize those moderator effects because different meta-analyses use different labels for the same moderator construct, different constructs under the same label, different operationalizations of the same construct, and different ways of reporting all this. Even so, searches for such moderators are worth pursuing. Consider two examples.

First, a common finding is that the kind of measurement used in primary studies makes a large difference to effect size. For example, five meta-analyses found that behavioral measures produced larger effect sizes than other measures (Butler & Wampler, 1999; Giblin, 1985; Hahlweg & Markman, 1988; Hight, 2000; Shadish et al., 1993). Another five meta-analyses found that effect sizes were higher when outcome measures were specifically tied to what was done in therapy (Cedar & Levant, 1990; Hight, 2000; Montgomery, 1991; Shadish et al., 1993; Wilson, 1989). This measurement specificity effect has been found in psychotherapy meta-analyses in general (Matt, 1993).

Second, Sweeney (1991) focused entirely on interactions in her master's thesis on the effects of marriage and family therapies. Table 5 presents one of her results (Shadish & Sweeney, 1991) pertaining to the frequent finding that behavior therapies have higher effect sizes than nonbehavior therapies. The question is whether this finding reflects better patient outcomes, or whether it reflects artifactual confounds. Sweeney found that behavioral marriage and family therapy studies have unusually high effect sizes when they are conducted in university settings with measures that are reactive, specific, and manipulable, and have relatively few participants. Behavior therapies without these characteristics have effect sizes that are no better and no worse than nonbehavior therapies. That is, the larger effect sizes produced by behavior therapies may not reflect better patient outcomes, but rather may reflect artifactual differences in how studies are conducted.

Table 5
Variables That Moderated the Effects of Theoretical Orientation

Moderator	Behavioral *d*	Nonbehavioral *d*
Setting		
University	.73	.36
Nonuniversity	.35	.36
Measurement Reactivity		
High	.68	.58
Medium	.48	.39
Low	.07	.48
Measurement Specificity		
Treatment Specific	.72	.46
General Family/Marital Measure	.50	.44
General Measure	.13	.58
Measurement Manipulability		
Not Very	.15	.76
Moderately	.58	.55
Very	.55	.46
Number of Subjects		
Below Median	.77	.39
Above Median	.45	.48

Both of these examples suggest regularities that may underlie diverse meta-analytic results; however, regularities may not be salient because we have approached meta-analysis as a brute force empirical tool for finding out what works. We need better conceptual schemes and theory to clarify the conditions under which moderator effects occur. For example, the measurement specificity effect goes under many different names. One author calls it specificity, another calls it congruence, and yet another does not use any label at all. It takes experience with meta-analysis to see the common concept underneath the diverse labels. Too few researchers approach meta-analysis from this conceptual perspective.

Further, both these moderator findings have implications for how we should interpret the results of outcome research. For example, a common experience is to read a report of an experiment in which a treatment produces, say, a particularly large effect relative to other therapies. It is tempting to conclude that the *treatment* is more effective than other treatments. Yet that may be the wrong conclusion to draw. The large effect may simply reflect *how the outcome was measured.* If all therapies were measured with the same kinds of outcomes assessments, their results might be considerably more uniform—indeed, this is found to be the case routinely when such moderators are used in regression equations to adjust for apparent treatment orientation differences (e.g., Shadish et al., 1993). In this regard, it would greatly improve our capacity to interpret research if all studies were to adopt at least some uniform measures across experiments. For example, each marital study might include the MAS or DAS as a more general measure, and also a more specific measure tied closely to what was done in therapy.

Summary for Clinicians

This section has reviewed a great deal of material, so Table 6 summarizes some of the more important points for clinical practice.

Methodological Issues

This section has two purposes. The first is to highlight some of the key methodological issues in the conduct of meta-analysis that warrant improvement in future meta-analyses of marriage and family interventions. The second is to help clinicians know how to read and criticize the quality of the meta-analyses they may be reading. For those less interested in the details of these methodological issues, we summarize the key points in a table at the end of this section.

Study Design

Following the lead of Smith and Glass (1977), psychotherapy meta-analyses have typically included primary outcome studies with many different kinds of designs. The justification was that the question of whether or not design makes a difference to effect size should be an empirical question, and that mixing designs is not a problem if one can show that different designs yield similar results.

Table 6
Summary for Clinicians

1. Marriage and family interventions, both therapy and enrichment, are more effective than no treatment. Those effects tend to be maintained at followup.
2. Marriage therapy tends to have better outcomes than family therapy, but this seems to occur because family therapists often deal with more difficult problems (e.g., schizophrenia).
3. Different kinds of marriage and family interventions tend to produce similar results.
4. The effects of marriage and family interventions are comparable to or larger than those obtained by alternative interventions ranging from individual therapy to medical interventions.
5. Meta-analytically supported treatments (MASTs) exist that have strong empirical support. While marriage and family therapists should be encouraged to use those therapies called empirically supported treatments (ESTs) when ESTs are available, it makes excellent scientific and professional sense to use MASTs when ESTs are not available for a problem, as will often be the case.
6. Marriage and family therapies produce clinically significant results in 40%–50% of those treated.
7. The effects of marriage and family interventions in clinically representative conditions have not been studied much.
8. We do not know much about variables that moderate the effects of marriage and family interventions, although available evidence suggests that *how* the research is done has as strong an impact on outcome as *what kind* of treatments are used.

Among the 20 marriage and family meta-analyses reviewed here, only 9 limited their sample to randomized experiments (Johnson, Hunsley, Greenberg, & Schindler, 1999; Mari & Streiner, 1994; Montgomery, 1991; Pitschel-Walz et al., 2001; Plattor, 1991; Shadish et al., 1993; Stanton & Shadish, 1997; Sweeney, 1991; Wilson, 1989). The remaining 11 meta-analyses were split into two groups.

Six meta-analyses included both randomized and nonrandomized experiments (Cedar & Levant, 1990; Edwards & Steinglass, 1995; Hahlweg & Markman, 1988; Hazelrigg, Cooper, & Borduin, 1987; Hight, 2000; Wilson, 1994[8]); but only four of them tested for differences between the two methodologies (Giblin, 1985; Hazelrigg et al., 1987; Hight, 2000; Wilson, 1994). All four found meaningful differences; yet in three of these cases, the authors combined results despite those differences (Giblin, 1985; Hazelrigg et al., 1987; Hight, 2000). This practice is questionable. Given other evidence that psychotherapy quasi-experiments underestimate effects (Shadish & Ragsdale, 1996; Shadish et al., 2000), meta-analysts should test for design differences, and be very cautious about combining estimates from studies of different design if those estimates appear statistically or practically different.

Finally, five meta-analyses included not just randomized and nonrandomized experiments, but also pretest-posttest only designs with no independent control group (Butler & Wampler, 1999; Dunn, 1994[9]; Dutcher, 2000[10]; Giblin et al., 1985; Markus et al., 1990). Evidence suggests that the latter designs overestimate effect sizes substantially (e.g., Lipsey & Wilson, 1993). A technology for combining uncontrolled studies with results from controlled studies exists (Li & Begg, 1994), as does a technology for combining results from uncontrolled studies with each other (Shadish, Cook, & Campbell, 2002, p. 426, footnote 3). None of the present meta-analyses used those technologies. Consequently, these five meta-analyses may have substantially overestimated effects.

Study Quality Scales

Five meta-analyses (e.g., Butler & Wampler, 1999; Cedar & Levant, 1990; Hight, 2000; Mari & Streiner, 1994; Stanton & Shadish, 1997) used multi-item scales to see if methodological quality was related to effect size. Four of the five tested the relationship between quality and effect size. Three of the four found that effect sizes increased in studies with higher quality ratings (Butler & Wampler, 1999; Cedar & Levant, 1990; Hight, 2000), but the fourth found the opposite effect (Stanton & Shadish, 1997).

While it is worth exploring such scales, we have several reservations about the routine use of any scale that results in a single number to represent study quality. Scales that result in a single number representing design quality tend to combine multiple items into a total score that subsumes a very wide array of methodological variables related to quality. These can include design, sample size, measurement reliability, and representativeness of participants, to name just a few research characteristics. Clearly, these diverse items do not assess the same kind of "quality." Rather, some assess internal validity, some statistical conclusion validity, some construct validity, and some external validity. Thus, global quality assessments can assign identical total scores to studies with decidedly different validity characteristics. Lumping such diversity together may yield a total score of questionable utility or validity. Further, such scales are rarely if ever well developed psychometrically, with no evidence of factorial structure to justify scoring, or even evidence of simple internal consistency reliability. A recent empirical study found that the conclusion reached about study quality, and the conclusion reached by the review itself, can differ considerably depending on which quality scale is used (Jüni, Witschi, Bloch, & Egger, 1999). Global decisions about what makes a study good or bad are fraught with difficulty. Even the most sophisticated researchers can disagree about the dimensions that define quality and how these dimensions apply to each study.

In general, then, items measuring study quality should be scored individually rather than being summed into a total score. We also encourage further development of *multi-dimensional* quality scales as an important part of reviews.

However, researchers who develop such scales should (a) clarify the kind of quality they believe the scale and subscales assess; (b) provide psychometric data about the reliability, factors structure, and validity of the scales where multiple items scales are used; and (c) explore how conclusions about the relationship between quality and outcome would vary depending on whether the total score or the individual items were used.

Attrition

In randomized experiments, it is rare for outcome measurements to be obtained on all clients. Such attrition can seriously compromise the internal validity of inferences from randomized studies. Those few meta-analyses that looked at the question found that attrition was related to effect size (Cedar & Levant, 1990; Montgomery, 1991; Shadish et al., 1993; Wilson, 1994). In fact, one meta-analysis that looked at this question in detail found that family therapy was more successful at retaining clients than were other forms of therapy, especially at retaining more clients with the worst prognosis (Stanton & Shadish, 1997). This made family therapy outcomes look worse than comparison outcomes because comparison treatments were losing more of the bad prognosis clients.

In at least some cases, meta-analysts can estimate the effects of treatments taking attrition into account. For example, when authors of primary studies reported results on both treatment completers and an intent-to-treat analysis, Pitschel-Walz et al. (2001) always used the latter to get effect size estimates that took attrition into account. Taking this one step further, Mari and Streiner (1994) analyzed their data both as the authors reported it, and as an intent-to-treat analysis in which dropouts were treated as failures. They were able to do this because they limited their meta-analysis to relapse rates. Because relapse is dichotomous at the patient level, missing data can easily be rescored as a failure and the overall results recomputed. Mari and Streiner found that family therapy was effective when analyzed as the authors reported it, but not effective when dropouts were rescored as failures and included in the analysis.

Another meta-analysis (Stanton & Shadish, 1997) that included dichotomous outcomes in drug abuse also assumed that dropouts were failures, and estimated effects under that assumption. For continuous outcomes, Stanton and Shadish also wrote authors to obtain raw data, and then assumed that drug abusers who dropped out had the same drug use status as their pretest status. The pretest scores were then substituted for missing data. The meta-analysts then developed a general method for estimating the likely bounds of effects on dichotomous outcomes by making different assumptions about what happened to those who dropped out, including a user-friendly PC program for implementing those analyses (Shadish, Hu, Glaser, Kownacki, & Wong, 1998).[11] By implementing all of these methods, those authors found that the effects of family therapy with drug abusers were likely to be robust no matter what happened to those who dropped out of therapy. Given the prevalence of attrition, more attention to attrition analyses would greatly improve our confidence in meta-analytic results.

Publication Bias

Thirteen meta-analyses included both published and unpublished material (Butler & Wampler, 1999; Cedar & Levant, 1990; Dunn & Schwebel, 1995; Dutcher, 2000; Edwards & Steinglass, 1995; Giblin, 1985; Hight, 2000; Johnson et al., 1999; Plattor, 1991; Shadish et al., 1993; Stanton & Shadish, 1997; Wilson, 1989, 1994). Some other meta-analysts searched for unpublished material (e.g., Markus et al., 1990) but did not find any that met their selection criteria. The standard publication bias was found in the majority of meta-analyses that looked at the question (Cedar & Levant, 1990; Giblin, 1985; Hight, 2000; Montgomery, 1991; Shadish et al., 1993; Wilson, 1989); that is, published works have higher effects than unpublished works. Only Butler and Wampler (1999) found no difference between published and unpublished works. In general, therefore, those meta-analyses that excluded unpublished work may have overestimated the size of the effect (e.g., Hahlweg & Markman, 1988; Hazelrigg et al., 1987; Mari & Streiner, 1994). To ameliorate the latter problem, we recommend a search for unpublished dissertations in every meta-analysis. Many of them can be obtained at no charge using inter-library loan, and can help the researcher to assess whether publication bias is present.

Methods for Testing Posttest Versus Follow-up Effect Sizes

A number of meta-analyses reported separate posttest and follow-up effect sizes or tested for differences between them (e.g., Cedar & Levant, 1990; Hight, 2000; Mari & Streiner, 1994; Markus et al., 1990), and often observed a decrease in effects from posttest to follow-up. Very few of these meta-analyses, however, limited the test to studies that had both posttest and follow-up measures (Hight, 2000), and fewer still then used an appropriate multivariate procedure to perform that within-study test (Montgomery, 1991; Shadish et al., 1993; Stanton & Shadish, 1997; Wilson, 1989). Without this limitation, any observed differences between posttest and follow-up may be confounded with unknown between-study differences. The more appropriate analyses nearly always show no difference between posttest and follow-up, although the power of the test is compromised by the small number of primary studies with both posttest and follow-ups.

Effect Size Computation

The foundational statistic in a meta-analysis is the effect size. If it is estimated inaccurately, the accuracy of the meta-analysis is in doubt. Ironically, few of the meta-analyses reviewed in this chapter describe how effect size was computed, especially in cases where the usual means, standard deviations, and sample sizes were not available. For example, authors often say only that a criterion for including a primary study in the meta-analysis is that it provides sufficient information to enable effect size calculations (e.g., Giblin et al., 1985; Hahlweg & Markman, 1988; Hazelrigg et al., 1987; Hight, 2000; Markus et al., 1990). What this means, however, depends on how much the author knows about effect size calculations. Authors may exclude large numbers of pertinent studies for which good effect sizes could have been computed had the authors only known the appropriate method. Similarly, when the outcome is dichotomous, both d and r usually underestimate effects considerably, and a statistic like the odds ratio is often preferable (Haddock et al., 1998). Yet few authors state exactly how they treat dichotomous data. Finally, some authors use gain score means rather than posttest means in effect size calculations, either to adjust for selection bias at pretest or because that is all that the author of the primary study reported (e.g., Cedar & Levant, 1990; Giblin, 1985). However, using gain scores without adjusting for the pretest-posttest correlation results in an effect size that is not on the same metric as those computed only on posttest means, and that can be as much as 300% different from the posttest metric (Zhang, 1996). Effect sizes can be calculated in a very large number of ways, many computational errors can occur, and sophisticated judgments are often necessary to decide exactly which effect size index is best given available data. So researchers will benefit from computer programs that not only help clarify these issues but also automate the process to reduce error (e.g., Johnson, 1993; Shadish et al., 1999).

Miscellaneous Methodological and Statistical Issues

The 20 meta-analyses reviewed in this chapter performed unevenly on a host of methodological and statistical issues in meta-analytic work. First, one quarter of the meta-analyses treated effect sizes within studies as the unit of analysis, failing to aggregate those effect sizes to the study level (Butler & Wampler, 1999; Cedar & Levant, 1990; Edwards & Steinglass, 1995; Giblin, 1985; Plattor, 1991). This allows studies with more outcome measures to unduly influence meta-analytic results.[12] Second, a quarter of the meta-analyses did not report weighting effect sizes by a function of sample size (Butler & Wampler, 1999; Cedar & Levant, 1990; Edwards & Steinglass, 1995; Giblin, 1985; Hahlweg & Markman, 1988), a practice that is standard in meta-analysis. Third, only one meta-analysis used random rather than fixed effects models (Hight, 2000). The difference between fixed and random effects models is in the inferences they allow (Shadish et al., 2000). Fixed effects models infer confidence in conclusions that would be reached if the set of studies being meta-analyzed were to be repeated identically except with new participants. Random effects models infer confidence in conclusions that would be reached if these studies were repeated in ways that varied not just participants but also any other feature of the study such as the length of treatment, the kinds of outcomes measured, or the clinical representativeness of conditions. Since we are usually interested in generalizations of the latter kind, random effects models have become the accepted state-of-the-art for most meta-analyses. Fourth, when most meta-analyses tested for the effects of moderators,

---

Table 7
Recommendations for Doing Better Meta-Analyses

1. Test for differences between randomized and nonrandomized studies, and if they do differ, do not combine results in subsequent analyses.
2. Do not rely on scales that purport to measure study quality with a single number, but do include individual items that measure quality and test for their relationship to effect size.
3. Test for the effects of attrition on effect size, and if possible, explore the effects of different assumptions about attrition on the overall meta-analytic results.
4. Include both published and unpublished studies.
5. If the number of studies permits, test differences between posttest and follow-up effect sizes only from studies that include both time points.
6. Be careful to use the most up-to-date methods for computing effect sizes.
7. Aggregate effect sizes to the study level before computing average effects.
8. Weight effect sizes by a function of sample size when computing average effects.
9. Use random effects models in most cases to do the analyses.
10. If the number of studies permits, use regression to take into account redundancy among predictors of effect size.

---

they did so using univariate categorical tests. Only a few (e.g., Hight, 2000; Shadish et al., 1993) used regression equations to take into account redundancy among predictors. In part, this lacuna is due to the small number of studies in some meta-analyses, making regression statistically impractical. But in many other cases regression could and should have been done.

Methodological Recommendations
The criticisms in the previous sections suggest the kinds of practices that meta-analysts ought to be using in their work. To make these practices explicit, Table 7 lists a set of methodological recommendations for meta-analysts to follow.

The Costs of Meta-Analysis

Remember Moses Herzog's quote at the start of this chapter about the need for a good five-cent synthesis? What are the costs of meta-analysis? Olkin and Allen (1999) estimated that the number of hours it takes to produce a quality meta-analysis in medicine varies with the number of citations that the initial literature search discovers. In 37 meta-analyses that were conducted by a private company specializing in meta-analysis, the mean total number of hours was 1,139 (median = 1,110), with a wide range from 216 to 2,518 hours. They developed a prediction equation from this database of: Total time = $721 + 0.243x - 0.0000123x^2$, where x is the number of citations before applying exclusion criteria. Of course, this equation might not accurately predict the amount of time it would take to do a meta-analysis by someone who did not specialize in the task, or who did not have the same support systems that this private company might have had. Still, it is likely to provide a reasonable lower bound to the number of hours it might take to do a meta-analysis.

The costs of meta-analysis are substantially a function of these hours. Assuming, for example, that graduate student time is reimbursed at $10–20 per hour, costs might range from $2,000 for a very small meta-analysis to over $50,000 for a large one. If we use professionals who are paid more, costs will rise proportionately. To this we must add the material costs of obtaining and copying studies, printing coding manuals, buying computers and programs if needed, and paying administrative overhead. In response to an email to a meta-analytic listserve in which we asked about total costs estimates, we received two responses from researchers in organizations doing meta-analyses professionally, giving estimates of $115,000 in one case, and of $250,000 in the second. However, the author of the second email pointed out that one might distinguish between the costs of a full review that included a meta-analysis versus the costs of only adding meta-analytic methods to that review. After all, even a narrative review has to do many of the same tasks as a meta-analytic review, including searching for and obtaining studies, reading them, writing results, and paying administrative overhead. The author of the second email said that the incremental costs of adding meta-analytic methods to a narrative review was only about $15,000 or so.

Who reimburses these costs? We contacted the authors of most of the meta-analyses in this chapter to ask about funding sources. Only 4 of the 20 marriage and family therapy meta-analyses reported having grant funding (Hahlweg & Markman, 1988; Montgomery, 1991; Shadish et al., 1993; Wilson, 1989). In the latter three cases, the same grants supported the work, providing total costs of $144,000 from 1986–1990; and the principal investigator's Psychology Department provided considerable extra support in the form of copying, computer access, secretarial help, research assistant time, and the like. The grants came from the National Institutes of Mental Health and from the Russell Sage Foundation. The latter used to have a program on meta-analysis, but it no longer does. The remainder of the meta-analyses were either supported as part of the research mission of a university, or used student theses and dissertations as a vehicle for meta-analytic work. However, we know of meta-analyses in other areas that also were funded from federal sources, especially research labs that specialize in meta-analytic work; and informal conversations with representatives of many federal agencies suggest that they welcome meta-analytic proposals.

In summary, then, meta-analytic work is not cheap. In current dollars, the costs of a good synthesis are likely to range from $10,000 to $250,000. As Herzog said, we still need a good five-cent synthesis.

Conclusions

The present review differs from the one we did in 1995 (Shadish et al., 1995) in that the 1995 review reported detailed results from a single meta-analysis of the effects of marriage and family therapies, while the present study reviewed 20 meta-analyses. Nonetheless, the overall conclusions about the marriage and family research remain about the same. First, marriage and family interventions are clearly efficacious compared to no treatment. Second, those interventions are at least as efficacious as other modalities such as individual therapy, and perhaps more effective in at least some cases. Third, there is little evidence for differential efficacy among the various approaches to marriage and family interventions, particularly if mediating and moderating variables are controlled. Fourth, evidence that marriage and family interventions are effective in clinically representative conditions remains sparse, although there are some clear exceptions to that.

On the other hand, meta-analytic reviews of marriage and family therapy have provided some new and interesting directions. One is the increased evidence for the clinical significance of the effects of marriage and family interventions, shown across several quite different methodologies that all converge on about the same answer. Another is the increased attention to variables that moderate the effects of marriage and family interventions, although this area is woefully underdeveloped at a conceptual level. And finally, meta-analyses of marriage and family interventions are beginning to use more sophisticated meta-analytic methods, although again this progress has been uneven.

For those interested in pursuing meta-analytic work, Lipsey and Wilson (2000) provide a particularly useful introduction to practical meta-analysis. For those interested in seeing how meta-analysis can influence substantive debates about psychotherapy, we recommend Smith and Glass's (1977) original psychotherapy meta-analysis, Wampold's (2001) application of meta-analysis to the question of whether all psychotherapies have about the same effect, and Shadish et al.'s (2000) meta-analysis of whether psychotherapy works under clinically representative conditions.

In summary, then, the work we reviewed in this chapter shows that marriage and family therapy is now an empirically supported therapy in the plain English sense of the phrase—it clearly works, both in general and for a variety of specific problems. Yet there is much more that can be done, not just in the specific ways we have outlined in this chapter, but also by applying new methodologies to meta-analysis, ranging from response surface modeling where we predict results from ideal studies that do not even exist in our sample of studies (Rubin, 1990; Shadish et al., 2000), to mediational models that try to explain how treatments work (Becker, 1992; Shadish, 1996), to new computer programs that make doing all of this much easier (Borenstein & Rothstein, 1999; Shadish et al., 1999). We hope this chapter stimulates marriage and family researchers to continue producing and improving this kind of meta-analytic work.

References

References marked with an asterisk indicate meta-analyses included in this review.

Becker, B.J. (1992). Models of science achievement: Forces affecting male and female performance in school science. In T. D. Cook, H. M. Cooper, D. S. Cordray, H. Hartmann, L. V. Hedges, R. J. Light, T. A. Louis, & F. Mosteller (Eds.), *Meta-analysis for explanation: A casebook* (pp. 209–281). New York: Russell Sage Foundation.

Bellow, S. (1964). *Herzog.* New York: Viking Press.

Borenstein, M., & Rothstein, H. (1999). *Comprehensive meta-analysis.* Englewood, NJ: Biostat.

*Butler, M. H., & Wampler, K. S. (1999). A meta-analytic update of research on the couple communication program. *The American Journal of Family Therapy, 27,* 223–237.

*Cedar, B., & Levant, R. F. (1990). A meta-analysis of the effects of parent effectiveness training. *The American Journal of Family Therapy, 18,* 373–384.

Chambless, D. L., & Hollon, S. D. (1998). Defining empirically supported therapies. *Journal of Consulting and Clinical Psychology, 66,* 7–18.

Cohen, J. (1988). *Statistical power analysis for the behavioral sciences* (2nd ed.). Hillsdale, NJ: Erlbaum.

Cooper, H., & Hedges, L.V. (Eds.). (1994). *The handbook of research synthesis.* New York: Russell Sage Foundation.

Dickerson, K., Higgins, K., & Meinert, C. L. (1990). Identification of meta-analyses: The need for standard terminology. *Controlled Clinical Trials, 11,* 52–66.

*Dunn, R. L. (1994). A meta-analytic review of marital therapy outcome research: General and comparative analyses (Doctoral dissertation, The Ohio State University, 1993). *Dissertation Abstracts International, 54,* 5940B.

*Dunn, R. L., & Schwebel, A. I. (1995). Meta-analytic review of marital therapy outcome research. *Journal of Family Psychology, 9,* 58–68.

*Dutcher, T. D. (2000). A meta-analytic study of marital therapy modalities and clients' presenting problems (Doctoral dissertation, The Union Institute, 1999). *Dissertation Abstracts International, 60,* 5223B.

*Edwards, M. E., & Steinglass, P. (1995). Family therapy treatment outcomes for alcoholism. *Journal of Marital and Family Therapy, 21,* 475–509.

Fleiss, J. L. (1994). Measures of effect size for categorical data. In H. Cooper & L. V. Hedges (Eds.), *The handbook of research synthesis* (pp. 245–260). New York: Russell Sage Foundation.

*Giblin, P. (1985). A meta-analysis of premarital, marital and family enrichment research (Doctoral dissertation, Purdue University, 1982). *Dissertation Abstracts International, 46,* 470B.

*Giblin, P. (1986). Research and assessment in marriage and family enrichment: A meta-analysis study. *Journal of Psychotherapy and the Family, 2,* 79–96.

*Giblin, P., Sprenkle, D. H., & Sheehan, R. (1985). Enrichment outcome research: A meta-analysis of premarital, marital and family interventions. *Journal of Marital and Family Therapy, 11,* 257–271.

Glass, G. V. (1976). Primary, secondary, and meta-analysis. *Educational Researcher, 5,* 3–8.

Haddock, C. K., Rindskopf, D., & Shadish, W. R. (1998). Using odds ratios as effect sizes for meta-analysis of dichotomous data: A primer on methods and issues. *Psychological Methods, 3,* 339–353.

Haddock, C. K., Shadish, W. R., Klesges, R. C., & Stein, R. J. (1994). Treatments for childhood and adolescent obesity: A meta-analysis. *Annals of Behavioral Medicine, 16,* 235–244.

*Hahlweg, K., & Markman, H. J. (1988). Effectiveness of behavioral marital therapy: Empirical status of behavioral techniques in preventing and alleviating marital distress. *Journal of Consulting and Clinical Psychology, 56,* 440–447.

*Hazelrigg, M. D., Cooper, H. M., & Borduin, C. M. (1987). Evaluating the effectiveness of family therapies: An integrative review and analysis. *Psychological Bulletin, 101,* 428–442.

*Hight, T. L. (2000). Do the rich get richer? A meta-analysis of methodological and substantive moderators of couple enrichment (Doctoral dissertation, Virginia Commonwealth University, 2000). *Dissertation Abstracts International,* 61, 3278B.

Hunter, J. E., & Schmidt, F. L. (1990). *Methods of meta-analysis: Correcting error and bias in research findings.* Newbury Park, CA: Sage Publications.

Jacobson, N. S., Follette, W. C., Revenstorf, D., Baucom, D. H., Hahlweg, K., & Margolin, G. (1984). Variability in outcome and clinical significance of behavioral marital therapy: A reanalysis of outcome data. *Journal of Consulting and Clinical Psychology, 52,* 497–504.

Johnson, B. T. (1993). *D-Stat: Software for the meta-analytic review of research literatures* (version 1.1). Hillsdale, NJ: Erlbaum.

*Johnson, S. M., Hunsley, J., Greenberg, L., & Schindler, D. (1999). Emotional focused couples therapy: Status and challenges. *Clinical Psychology: Science and Practice, 6,* 67–79.

Jüni, P., Witschi, A., Bloch, R., & Egger, M. (1999). The hazards of scoring the quality of clinical trials for meta-analysis. *Journal of the American Medical Association, 282,* 1054–1060.

Li, Z., & Begg, C. B. (1994). Random effects models for combining results from controlled and uncontrolled studies in a meta-analysis. *Journal of the American Statistical Association, 89,* 1523–1527.

Lipsey, M. W., & Wilson, D. B. (1993). The efficacy of psychological, educational, and behavioral treatment: Confirmation from meta-analysis. *American Psychologist, 48,* 1181–1209.

Lipsey, M. W., & Wilson, D. B. (2000). *Practical Meta-Analysis.* Newbury Park, CA: Sage Publications.

*Mari, J. J., & Streiner, D. L. (1994). An overview of family interventions and relapse of schizophrenia: Meta-analysis of research findings. *Psychological Medicine, 24,* 565–578.

Markus, E. (1988). *Het effect van gezinstherapie: Een wantitatief literatuuroversicht.* Internal Report. University of Amsterdam, Department of Clinical Psychology.

*Markus, E., Lange, A., & Pettigrew, T. F. (1990). Effectiveness of family therapy: A meta-analysis. *Journal of Family Therapy, 12,* 205–221.

Matt, G. E. (1993). Comparing classes of psychotherapeutic interventions: A review and reanalyses of English- and German-language meta-analyses. *Journal of Cross-Cultural Psychology, 24,* 5–25.

*Montgomery, L. M. (1991). The effects of family therapy for treatment of child identified problems: A meta-analysis (Doctoral dissertation, Memphis State University, 1990). *Dissertations Abstracts International, 51,* 6115B.

Olkin, I., & Allen, I. E. (1999). Estimating the time for producing a meta-analysis from number of citations retrieved. *Journal of the American Medical Association, 282,* 634–635.

Paul, G. (1967). Strategy of outcome research in psychotherapy. *Journal of Consulting Psychology, 31,* 109–118.

Pearson, K. (1904). Report on certain enteric fever inoculation statistics. *British Medical Journal, 2,* 1243–1246.

Phillips, G. (1998). *Moderators of outcomes in psychotherapy meta-analyses.* Unpublished major area paper, The University of Memphis, Department of Psychology, Memphis, TN.

Phillips, G. A., & Shadish, W. R. (2002). *Moderators of outcomes in psychotherapy meta-analyses.* Manuscript in preparation.

*Pitschel-Walz, G., Leucht, S., Bauml, J., Kissling, W., & Engel, R. R. (2001). The effect of family interventions on relapse and rehospitalization in schizophrenia: A meta-analysis. *Schizophrenia Bulletin, 27,* 73–92.

*Plattor, J. R. (1991). Evaluating the effectiveness of marital therapies: A meta-analytic investigation (Doctoral dissertation, University of Miami, 1990). *Dissertation Abstracts International, 51,* 4605B.

Rosen, G. M., & Davison, G. C. (in press). Psychology should identify empirically supported principles of change (ESPs) and not credential trademarked therapies or other treatment packages. *Behavior Modification.*

Rosenthal, R. (1994). Parametric measures of effect size. In H. Cooper & L. V. Hedges (Eds.), *The hand-book of research synthesis* (pp. 231–244). New York: Russell Sage Foundation.

Rosenthal, R., & Rubin, D. B. (1982). A simple, general purpose display of magnitude of experimental effect. *Journal of Educational Psychology, 74,* 166–169.

Rubin, D. B. (1990). A new perspective. In K. W. Wachter & M. L. Straf (Eds.), *The future of meta-analysis* (pp. 155–165). New York: Russell Sage Foundation.

*Shadish, W. R. (1992). Do family and marital psychotherapies change what people do? A meta-analysis of behavioral outcomes. In T. D. Cook, H. M. Cooper, D. S. Cordray, H. Hartmann, L. V. Hedges, R. J. Light, T. A. Louis, & F. Mosteller (Eds.), *Meta-analysis for explanation: A casebook* (pp. 129–208). New York: Russell Sage Foundation.

Shadish, W. R. (1996). Meta-analysis and the exploration of causal mediating processes: A primer of examples, methods, and issues. *Psychological Methods, 1,* 47–65.

Shadish, W. R., Cook, T. D., & Campbell, D. T. (2002). *Experimental and quasi-experimental designs for generalized causal inference.* Boston: Houghton-Mifflin.

Shadish, W. R., & Haddock, C. K. (1994). Combining estimates of effect size. In H. M. Cooper & L. V. Hedges (Eds.), *The handbook of research synthesis* (pp. 261–281). New York: Russell Sage Foundation.

Shadish, W. R., Hu, X., Glaser, R. R., Kownacki, R. J., & Wong, T. (1998). A method for exploring the effects of attrition in randomized experiments with dichotomous outcomes. *Psychological Methods, 3,* 3–22.

Shadish, W. R., Matt, G. E., Navarro, A. M., & Phillips, G. (2000). The effects of psychological therapies under clinically representative conditions: A meta-analysis. *Psychological Bulletin, 126,* 512–529.

*Shadish, W. R., Montgomery, L. M., Wilson, P., Wilson, M. R., Bright, I., & Okwumabua, T. (1993). Effects of family and marital psychotherapies: A meta-analysis. *Journal of Consulting and Clinical Psychology, 61,* 992–1002.

Shadish, W. R., & Ragsdale, K. (1996). Random versus nonrandom assignment in psychotherapy experiments: Do you get the same answer? *Journal of Consulting and Clinical Psychology, 64,* 1290–1305.

Shadish, W. R., Ragsdale, K., Glaser, R. R., & Montgomery, L. M. (1995). The efficacy and effectiveness of marital and family therapy: A perspective from meta-analysis. *Journal of Marital and Family Therapy, 21,* 343–358.

Shadish, W. R., Robinson, L., & Lu, C. (1999). *ES: A computer program and manual for effect size calculation.* St. Paul, MN: Assessment Systems Corporation.

Shadish, W. R., & Sweeney, R. (1991). Mediators and moderators in meta-analysis: There's a reason we don't let dodo birds tell us which psychotherapies should have prizes. *Journal of Consulting and Clinical Psychology, 59,* 883–893.

Shoham-Salomon, V., & Rosenthal, R. (1987). Paradoxical interventions: A meta-analysis. *Journal of Consulting and Clinical Psychology, 55*(1), 22–28.

Smith, M. L., & Glass, G. V. (1977). Meta-analysis of psychotherapy outcome studies. *American Psychologist, 32,* 752–760.

Smith, M. L., Glass, G. V., & Miller, T. I. (1980). *The benefits of psychotherapy.* Baltimore: The Johns Hopkins University Press.

*Stanton, M. D., & Shadish, W. R. (1997). Outcome, attrition, and family-couples treatment for drug abuse: A meta-analysis and review of the controlled, comparative studies. *Psychological Bulletin, 122,* 170–191.

*Sweeney, R. (1991). *Interactions: A secondary analysis of marital/family therapy meta-analysis.* Unpublished master's thesis, University of Memphis, Memphis, Tennessee.

*Wampler, K. S. (1982). Bringing the review of literature into the age of quantification: Meta-analysis as a strategy for integrating research findings in family studies. *Journal of Marriage and the Family, 44*, 1009–1023.

Wampold, B. E. (2001). *The great psychotherapy debate: Models, methods, and findings.* Hillsdale, NJ: Erlbaum.

Weisz, J. R., Donenberg, G. R., Han, S. S., & Weiss, B. (1995). Bridging the gap between laboratory and clinic in child and adolescent psychotherapy. *Journal of Consulting and Clinical Psychology, 63*, 688–701.

Weisz, J. R., Weiss, B., & Donenberg, G. R. (1992). The lab versus the clinic: Effects of child and adolescent psychotherapy. *American Psychologist, 47*, 1578–1585.

Wilkinson, L. & the Task Force on Statistical Inference. (1999). Statistical methods in psychology journals: Guidelines and explanations. *American Psychologist, 54*, 594–604.

*Wilson, P. G. (1989). *The effects of marital therapy for the treatment of distressed couples: A quantitative analysis.* Unpublished master's thesis, University of Memphis, Memphis, Tennessee.

*Wilson, P. G. (1994). Marital/family versus individual therapy: A meta-analysis (Doctoral dissertation, Memphis State University, 1993). *Dissertation Abstracts International, 54*, 4414B.

Zhang, T. (1996). *The comparison between exact and inexact effect sizes computed by change score methods.* Unpublished master's thesis, University of Memphis, Department of Psychology, Memphis, Tennessee.

End Notes

1   See http://willshadish.psyc.memphis.edu/psychotherapy.htm

2   These error bars must be interpreted with great caution given that we had to estimate standard errors a variety of different ways when standard errors were not reported in the original meta-analysis, and that even when standard errors were included, they may have been computed in very different ways in different meta-analyses.

3   http://www.apa.org/divisions/div12/rev_est/bpd.shtml

4   http://www.cochrane.org/

5   http://www.apa.org/divisions/div12/rev_est/index.shtml

6   http://www.apa.org/divisions/div12/rev_est/drugs.shtml

7   http://www.apa.org/divisions/div12/rev_est/marital.shtml

8   Wilson (1994) initially examined differences between randomized and nonrandomized experiments, but excluded the latter when initial analyses suggested a trend ($p < .07$) toward overestimating effects in nonrandomized experiments.

9   Dunn (1994) notes that the sample included one study "in which the sample of couples served as their own controls" (p. 107).

10   Dutcher's (2000) sample of studies is nearly identical to Dunn's (1994) sample, and includes this same study without a control group.

11   The web site referenced in that article for obtaining that program is no longer available. However, researchers can obtain the program by clicking on ftp://141.225.10.58/aa.zip, which will download a zip file. Unzip the file, click on Setup.exe, and the program will be installed.

12   This statement applies to overall summaries of effects. When different kinds of effects are compared to each other, the most commonly recommended practice is that each study should contribute only one effect size to each cell of an analysis. If, for example, one is comparing self-report measures to observational measures, and a study has one measure of each kind, then the only cost of allowing that study to contribute one effect size to each cell is that the test of significance of the difference between the cells will be conservative (it will be harder to find a significant difference). Many researchers view that cost as acceptable. However, if that study had, say, two self-report measures and two observational measures, the meta-analyst should average the first two and average the second two before doing the test for differences between categories.